Houses of Glass

Second printing, 1991
First paperback edition, 1990

Originally published under the title *Das Glashaus. Ein Bautypus des 19. Jahrhunderts* by Prestel-Verlag, Munich. © 1981 by Prestel-Verlag. English translation © 1986 by The MIT Press.

This book was set in Baskerville by the MIT Press Computergraphics Department and printed and bound by Halliday Lithograph in the United States of America.

Library of Congress Cataloging-in-Publication Data

Kohlmaier, Georg.
  Houses of glass.

  Bibliography: p.
  Includes index.
  1. Glass construction. 2. Conservatories.
3. Greenhouses. I. Sartory, Barna von. II. Title.
NA4140.K5813 1986 721'.04496 85-15556
ISBN 0-262-11108-X (HB), 0-262-61070-1 (PB)

Houses of Glass

A Nineteenth-Century Building Type

Georg Kohlmaier
Barna von Sartory

translated by John C. Harvey

The MIT Press
Cambridge, Massachusetts
London, England

Contents

Acknowledgments vii

Introduction 1

1 **The Glasshouse as Mythos** 7
The Naturalness of the Artificial 7
The Stony Desert and the Green Oasis 8
The Illusion of Nature in the City 12

2 **The Idea of the Winter Garden** 25
An Indoor Garden under an Artificial Sky 25
The Contention between Gardener and Architect 26
Beginnings of a New Architectural Theory 27
The Private Winter Gardens 31
The Public Winter Gardens 37
The Botanical Collections 40

3 **The Glasshouse as Building Type** 43
Beginnings in Wood, Masonry, and Glass 43
Materials for a Green Trompe-l'oeil 44
The Development of the Iron-Frame Glasshouse 55
Summary Table 62

4 **Steam, Iron, and the Industrial Revolution** 67
Machine Tools and Power Sources 67
Railways 69
The "Age of Iron" 70
Engineering and the Building Industry 71
Works of Significant Designers of Glasshouses 74

5 **The Iron Skeleton** 77
Cast Iron 77
Wrought Iron 119

Appendixes
John Claudius Loudon (1783–1843) 139
"Sketches of Curvilinear Hothouses" (J. C. Loudon, London, 1818) 140
Iron as a Building Material 149

Catalog 151

Photographs, Engravings, and Plans 395

References for the Text 619
References for the Catalog 624
Bibliography 626
Sources of Illustrations 630
Indexes 636

Acknowledgments

This book owes its existence to the cooperation and the friendly advice of Julius Posener, Johann Friedrich Geist, Stefan Polonyi, Ernst Werner, and Stephan Waetzoldt. Julius Posener read the manuscript critically and encouraged us to publish unabridged the material on the analysis of load-bearing structures. Friedrich Geist discussed with us in detail the genesis of the glasshouse as a building type and gave us valuable stimulation. Stefan Polonyi and Ernst Werner, who share an enthusiasm for the history of iron-frame buildings, criticized chapter 5 from the viewpoint of logical aesthetics as well as from the viewpoint of statics and the science of space-frame construction. Exceptional too was the personal involvement which Stephan Waetzoldt, in the compass of the Fritz Thyssen Stiftung, had with the origin of this work. Furthermore, we are grateful to Brigitte Mudrak-Trost of Prestel-Verlag for her expert advice.

Houses of Glass

Introduction

With a smile the king drew aside the curtain. I was speech-less, for I saw an enormous garden, laid out in the Vene-tian manner, with palms, a lake, bridges, pavilions, and buildings like castles. "Come," said the king, and I followed him fascinated as Dante following Virgil into Paradise.

Maria de la Paz, description of the winter garden of King Ludwig II, 1883

The dream of a garden under glass became a reality in the nineteenth century. It was a dream of the entire natural environment of a tropical island enclosed in iron filigree and glass. The scientific control of natural processes—the basis of the new industry—was realized with the use of glass, iron, and steam in the cultivation of plants. Nature could be controlled, and not just for immediately useful purposes. Here the natural environment was regarded as a work of art. The glasshouse protected a flowering, fragrant, slowly growing picture—a transitory still life that placidly revealed the laws of life. Here was the anticipated reconciliation between man and nature. The utility-based nineteenth-century economy seemed to be abrogated. Inside the costly glass-and-iron structure was maintained an expensive, never-ending operation to keep the plants alive. Enormous sums of money were spent on producing a theater of nature. However, the glasshouse did fulfill a need, the breadth of which we can today only surmise. This need was intimately bound up with the social structure of the nineteenth century. Industrial growth was destroying nature, which was increasingly becoming a pawn, an item for exchange. Green became deficient in the city, and people had to go in search of it.

The magnificent displays of tropical plants brought with them the misgiving that colonialism and the organized exploitation of the world would set in motion the destruction of the existing state of affairs in distant lands. In order to preserve the vision of paradise, there was a need to conserve nature, at least symbolically, by putting it under glass. The nineteenth-century glasshouse was like a museum in which the masterpieces of nature were gathered together, listed in a catalog, and preserved for the future. However, the influence of the pictures was rather blunted in that the spectators considered them as items of popular science. The dismantling of nature took place behind the scenes, and the longed-for paradise retreated to even greater distances.

The double character of the hothouse made it the precursor of the great world exhibitions of the nineteenth century. Along a labyrinth of interwoven pathways, plants from all over the world were placed in the best lighting conditions, arranged according to land of origin, genus, and species. In the larger botanical gardens, the prices of the plants were indicated; the plants were cultivated for sale, and they migrated into private winter gardens and middle-class homes. Simultaneously, plant science was promoted in botanical institutions, in order that the economic potential of the newly discovered plants could be ascertained. In the public winter gardens, not only were individual plants presented but a complete show like a theatrical presentation was included in the entrance fee. Every camellia bloom that unfurled contributed to the prosperity of the pleasure establishment. The monumental winter gardens, which were run as commercial companies from the middle of the nineteenth century and in which thousands of people could assemble at the same time, proved that they could pay their way. In the international exhibitions, where the whole world displayed its commodities, the arrangement of the endless pathways was borrowed from the hothouse—the grouping of the displayed objects according to continents; the principle of diversity; the placing side by side of the smallest up to the largest, the most insignificant with the mightiest, the most common items with the rarest, all in accordance with the laws of aesthetics. Even the space and the construction of the hothouse were adapted to the purpose of displaying industrial products. Joseph Paxton's Crystal Palace—the venue of the first world exhibition, in 1851—was described as a giant greenhouse.

With the consciously pursued objective of bringing the public inside to view the plant kingdom, the winter garden was an early herald of the entertainment industry. The individual was seen as an anonymous buyer of a spectacle of nature and of organized amusement. The general desire for nature "at second hand" was the product of the city and the factory. Industry made haste to discover and make available the commercial aspects of the gratification of this need. Nature as a piece of work to be enjoyed, as a form of art, was at first restricted to the aristocracy and the upper middle class. The palm house and the intimate winter garden were private places in which the owner and his friends could become encircled and submerged in the stillness of the plant world. The public winter garden, in contrast, presented the aspect of a brightly colored jumble of visitors pressing fleetingly through a tropical flora for the sake of amusement.

Share capital made possible the popularizing of the enjoyment of nature in the city, taking advantage of the opportunity arising from the separation of free time from working time to offer something useful for sale. No longer the king, but the public now drew aside the curtain to the Garden of Semiramis. Under the glass canopy of the winter garden were concentrated all the amusements that had been strung separately along a street or a boulevard: a concert hall, a music hall, a theater, a café, an art collection, billiards rooms, a restaurant, and dance and banquet halls. Embracing all this was a panorama of fountains, waterfalls, and galleries with cascades of plants.

With the end of the century these buildings vanished from the mental horizon like a fata morgana, like a shimmering soap bubble that could not survive the forces of the times and burst into tiny pieces. The ventures of those times to overcome distance and set out on long journeys (in this instance, to bring back palm trees wrapped in wet cloth and to exhibit them in the glasshouse as a triumph over nature) seem today both naive and admirable.

This appears all the more peculiar in contrast with today's mass movement in the opposite direction. By means of organized mass tourism, people are now taken to see the actual scenes they desire. Nevertheless, they cannot attain their goal, because the unspoiled world, as formerly in the hothouse, confronts them only as a nature preserve—but this time in the authentic place. Television and films create a sense of proximity, which is in reality an unattached faraway world. The longed-for view of pure virgin nature, including one's own nature, retreats even farther from the field of view.

The mood that gave rise to the hothouses has passed away. The contemplation of orientalia no longer has its former fascination; we have become accustomed to other powerful attractions. The unique glass-and-iron shells that brought those feelings into existence are now like the fossils left behind by an extinct form of animal, partly damaged, partly overwintered in some forgotten place. However, the filigree constructions, the real part of the dream, stand before our eyes like a silhouette of the early industrial age and present their historical significance.

In present-day views of the history of building science, unanimity prevails that the ironwork construction of the nineteenth century reflects the industrial age in its most advanced form, both technically and aesthetically. The iron constructions, in comparison with traditional timber and stone buildings, were a qualitatively new step in construction and in the concept of space, and in that respect they became the basis for twentieth-century modern architecture.

This opinion depends on the recognition that progress in architecture is not only a matter of space and form but shows itself in the way the basic principles of construction embrace the level of development reached by productive forces and then make further advancement. Iron is a fully utilizable construction medium for buildings, compatible with productive forces and hence with capitalization. The manufacturing methods of the feudal period, which started the technology of iron extraction and smelting (particularly for the purposes of war), proved to be a hindrance to the production of iron for commerce in general and to the industrial organization of the same. Thus, iron entered relatively late into the construction of buildings. At the same time, however, a new method offered itself, the principle of which was derived from the industrially organized production processes. Iron made possible the mass production of building materials and hence led to the standardization of building components. The building process moved away from the building site to the factory. The building site became only the assembly area. Manual work could for the most part be replaced by machine processing. The mechanical properties of iron made it possible to span great widths with load-bearing members of only a small cross-section, an economy of constructional material that led to a reduction in the space taken up by the structural members. This resulted in the creation of interior space of a new order of magnitude in which the load-bearing structure occupied a vanishingly small proportion of the internal volume of the space enclosed. Wide and spacious halls, adaptable to changing purposes and functions, could be created.

The economic and technical factors that iron construction introduced into the building process simultaneously opened up new possibilities for the use of iron in mass production. No longer were individual components such as rafters, door jambs, doors, and flooring made on the site; now the building as a whole could be produced and offered for sale as a factory-made product. The economic basis of all this was no longer an individual person's capital but share capital subscribed by a large number of people.

For the purpose of building in iron it was logical to develop and standardize certain types of structural ironwork, and ultimately the types of whole buildings. The supply of prefabricated buildings, even multistory buildings, was the ultimate example of this concept. Buildings were being offered for sale in catalogs by the middle of the nineteenth century, and there was a wide range of choice. Iron construction in fact embodied the first stage of a far-reaching revolution in building technique. It opened up new architectural possibilities of function, form, and shape. The use of iron as a building material did not stop with its incidental use in traditional stone architecture. It was incorporated in buildings in which it was not just used incidentally but played a part in the whole structure: bridges, factories, warehouses, railway stations, arcades, department stores, covered markets, and various industrial and exhibition buildings.

These buildings rose along shopping streets and in the central business districts of cities. Their significance for production and trade, as well as their novel forms, made them a focal point of opinion and critical discussion. Particularly since 1900, the study of the history of building has selected these iron constructions as forerunners of modern functional architecture. From the middle of the nineteenth century, the teaching of building and construction work has occupied itself broadly and in detail with these structures.

Alongside the large iron structures there originated, almost unnoticed by architectural historians in the course of the Industrial Revolution, buildings that were constructed as completely transparent spaces filled with light. These were the hothouses erected for the cultivation and display of plants, especially those indigenous to tropical and subtropical climates. These glass-and-iron structures, located away from the city center in parks or botanical gardens, provided an enclosed climatic environment and hence made it possible to capture a strange and exotic world. Glasshouses developed into spacious winter gardens in which people could meet and enjoy themselves. So there arose, alongside palm, orchid, fern, and water-lily houses, the commercially operated winter gardens, floras, concert halls, theaters, and restaurants covered with glass-and-iron structures. In their most advanced state of development,

glasshouses reached the dimensions of exhibition buildings and, as temporary enclosed spaces, formed the prototypes of these. Paxton's Crystal Palace covered some of the trees in Hyde Park with a glass-and-iron structure of a type that had been tested for the greenhouses at Chatsworth.

In their most advanced form, hothouses are made of glass and iron from the apex right down to ground level. They were built almost exclusively of these two materials in the nineteenth century. On this account they are more closely associated with the development of advanced building technology than the usual types of building (except for iron bridges). The need for wide, brightly lit spaces into which the sun's rays could penetrate led to the development of filigree structures that in their ultimate form are unsurpassed in the history of structural ironwork.

Because the majority of glasshouses were conceived for the protection of plants rather than as permanent abodes for people, their structural forms and their spatial extent could evolve independent of the usual building precepts and aesthetic principles of the time. The goal of broad glass surfaces and curves could be pursued with single-minded dedication to the purpose of growing and exhibiting plants. The special place of hothouses (particularly in the second half of the nineteenth century) in the development of glass-and-iron structures, and especially in building technology, had its base therein to no small extent. The orientation toward the plant kingdom brought about not only the development of the transparent outer skin but also the solution of the problem of providing an artificial climate. In the twentieth century, this was to progress to the provision of natural conditions for the housing of people and for their working environments.

The partly tropical interior garden of the hothouses required complete imitation of the natural conditions of sunlight, temperature, shade, dew, rain, and air movement. Hence, the climatic control had to be adaptable to the widest range of individual requirements of the plants concerned and had to be directed particularly to maintaining the most sensitive aspects of their natural environments. Everything depended on the creation and the maintenance of an artificial warm and humid climate. The glasshouse, as a climate-enclosing shell that had to cover the scenery of a tropical garden, required for this purpose not only a wide structure of glass and filigree iron in a form that allowed the entry of the maximum amount of light but also (in comparison with other buildings) more advanced installations for heating, humidity control, and ventilation.

Because of the special technical and structural problems, these glass-and-iron structures belonged from the start primarily to the province of structural engineering, and not to architecture in the strict sense. The first experiments in the design and construction of these types of building, earlier than those connected with the roofing of railway stations, were made with greenhouses. The greenhouse experiments led to a series of technical innovations that affected productivity, building techniques, and the revolution of prefabricated buildings. Cast-iron and wrought-iron load-bearing structures were like signposts pointing the way to later engineering constructions that were to reduce the amount of mass to the minimum. The major technical problems of industrialized mass production and standardized building components and their assembly were thus solved earlier than they would otherwise have been. Problems of the sealing of large glazed areas and the heating and ventilation of large halls presented themselves in new forms and demanded technical solutions.

The experience gained in meeting these constructional demands by prefabrication methods encouraged the early designers to make use of these methods on a greater scale, especially in glass-and-iron buildings for exhibitions, railway stations, and glazed arcades. On the other hand, we find an influence of this large-scale construction on the development of the glasshouse in the late nineteenth century. The intricate network of the exchange of experimental construction experience and scientifically based building techniques is demonstrable not only in the historical development of glass-and-iron structures but also in the personal histories of individual designers. John Claudius Loudon, Richard Turner, Joseph Paxton, Charles Rohault de Fleury, August von Voit, Hector Horeau, and Alphonse Balat are the best known. There is a clear separation of the respective fields of work of the architect and the engineer in respect to the requirements of hothouse and exhibition buildings. Whereas architects applied themselves to monumental buildings and used the customary materials, dilettante builders took the opportunity offered in building commissions to design and build structures according to engineering principles.

The alignment of glasshouse building with the use of iron filigree structures and glass for the sole purpose of obtaining light from all sides brought about a turning point in architectural aesthetics. In the development of its artistic expression, the glasshouse had an advantage in that, while it was intended to have a monumental effect, it would not be untrue to

itself as a building intended for a definite purpose. Remote from the clutches of academic architects, engineering structures arose which by their shape could advertise their purpose. With the creation of the glasshouse there was the first historic appearance of a room completely flooded with light, "a spatial vacuum and yet a room," a negation of conventional stone architecture which in imitative representation of the load-bearing function of its hierarchically ordered members formed a massive barrier between exterior and interior. "No specially contrived effects of the expected light streaming through, no contrast between more concentrated and more diffused amounts of shadow and light, no embellishment— only uniform brightness."[1] The space is limited only by the framework of simple and uniform assembled structural members, which as a delicate, almost disembodied network opens onto an almost unending perspective.

The need for large continuous glass surfaces and curves, reaching down to the ground and held together only by a network of iron ribs and branches, encouraged the development of the glasshouse along the lines of the simplest geometrical shapes. Assembled from cubes, pyramids, cones, cylinders, hemispheres, and quadrants, the glasshouses in their simplicity and their aesthetic effect were a major phenomenon in the history of nineteenth-century building. Glass as a material in these shapes obtained a new aesthetic quality. In part reflective and in part completely transparent, it took away the material aspects of the building and gave it its much-admired lightness and elegance.

One can comprehend the conventional architectural style of historicism in the nineteenth century as an aesthetic antithesis to the prevailing constraints in the evolving industrial production. Its aesthetic content originated in the development of a self-supporting decorative space frame which disguised the essential construction rather than help to display it. By contrast, all the structural members of the glasshouse were visible. In addition to the plants, the elements of the structure were on display themselves and hence were to be perceived as part of the aesthetic effect. Structural form, spatial shape, and ornament were not separated and rendered independent. Their combined effect made it possible to understand the architectural structure at one glance. "There is nothing which cannot be comprehended down to the tiniest detail."[2] With its display of the structure as a self-evident manifestation of its inherent aesthetic aspects combined with a form built on the simplest possible lines, the nineteenth-century glasshouse appears today as a utopian anticipation of the avant-garde architecture of the early twentieth century.

In the subsequent compliance with commissions specifying the creation of the most brightly lit space possible, the glasshouse in the course of the nineteenth century came to be recognized as a building type in its own right. Not only was it a spatial and structural form with its own historical continuity, but it simultaneously provided the stimulus for the advance of iron construction generally. By providing a field for experiment with early prefabricated and standardized iron building elements, it prepared a way for a new architecture and a new aesthetic.

All the more astonishing is the fact that in the new literature about the glasshouse this relationship was indicated many times over but was not yet systematically investigated and described.[3] In contrast, important information about the construction of the early British hothouses is to be found in the contemporary accounts, particularly those by John Claudius Loudon (1817, 1818) and Charles McIntosh (1853). In 1842, M. Neumann described individual British, French, and Dutch greenhouse structures. The emphasis lay on their technical equipment, especially the heating and ventilation. The load-bearing structure was not considered. The same applies to the book by Carl David and Julius Bouché (1886), in which the advantages and disadvantages of the use of iron are discussed only in respect to its physical properties. The *Handbook of Architecture* (1893) gave the first review of the state of the art of greenhouse building, but without special treatment of structural details. Alfred Gotthold Meyer (1907), Hermann Jordan, and Eugen Michel (1913) considered the aesthetic aspects of the nineteenth-century iron buildings and were the first authors since the Industrial Revolution to turn their attention to the iron structures of greenhouses. With the aid of some specific examples, they described these as basic types of hall buildings. In the 1930s, Hans Pfann (1935) and Arnold Tschira (1939) occupied themselves with the theme of greenhouse construction, discussing almost exclusively the early history of iron greenhouse construction. George F. Chadwick (1961) made an important individual contribution to an understanding of all Paxton's work in his *Works of Sir Joseph Paxton*, in which the Chatsworth glasshouses are described in detail. Raymond McGrath and A. C. Frost published the results of their research into the interdependence of the glass industry and glasshouse construction in *Glass Architecture and Decoration* (1961). Finally, John Hix's important work *The Glass House* (1974) contains a history of hothouse and greenhouse gardening.

In none of these works on nineteenth-century greenhouse construction is there any clear mention of the importance of these buildings as engineering structures with specific spatial and load-bearing forms. One of the aims of the present work is to fill this gap. In this respect, A. G. Meyer (1907) proclaimed that "the greenhouse is the origin of all present day glass-and-iron architecture."[4]

Furthermore, an attempt has been made to discuss the social-utopian movement, which is linked with the development of an "artificial paradise." This refers to the argument that the general history of man can only be a part of natural history, that nature does not attain its true and essential forms until it becomes human through artificial intervention. At the same time, there arose a social order with its own laws of behavior in connection with the nineteenth-century glasshouse and its green contents. The technically and scientifically competent person was no longer to think of the world just in terms of exploitable raw materials, but as an individual body extending into the universe. Industrial development did not in fact have the power to bring about this utopia except by the alien form of manufactured goods.

1   The Glasshouse as Mythos

*Review and analyze all that is natural . . . you will find
nothing that is frightening. All that is beautiful and noble is
the result of reasoning and calculation.*

Charles Baudelaire, Curiosités esthétiques *(1859–60)*

The Naturalness of the Artificial

The nineteenth-century glasshouse was the reflection
of the city-dweller's new love affair with nature. The
domestication of the plants and animals of distant
lands under glass seemed to be the highest stage of
evolution. At the same time, the technical ability to
manipulate nature and man himself was revealed.
With the spread of botanical studies and classification of natural things as a Sunday hobby, the common man could feel that he had mastered nature. As
was characteristic of the time, the rational and pragmatic observation of nature was mixed with a senti-
mental feeling springing from self-pity that could no
longer look on nature without a sense of guilt. In the
purpose-oriented world of the middle class, nature
and man had their allotted roles. The plants in the
greenhouse, in spite of their artificiality, were representatives of the organic world that became ephemeral victims of inevitable death. In the majestic world
of the greenhouse, the plants lost the aspect of utility
and presented themselves to the eye as natural
beauty alone in elevated and at the same time
ephemeral shapes. A feeling of compassion arose out
of that. The plant world, for once divorced from any
kind of purpose, became the scene of an infinity of
appearing and disappearing, in front of which man
appeared as a nonentity. He had set foot in a foreign land and, in ecstasy, had seen the distant tropical forests of unknown continents. He had entered
into another age.

The greenhouse was a place of retreat from the
real world, but at the same time it was full of the
politics of the day. One can reconstruct a connection
between the growing social tensions in the expand-
ing city and the growth of the illusion of nature in
the form of greenhouses, parks, and green boulevards. It was not by chance that the first public winter garden (that in Regent's Park, London; 1846) and
the first recreational establishment to include plants

(the Jardin d'Hiver in Paris; 1848) came into being at
a time of sharpening conflict between class interests.
Similarly, in Germany "people's palaces" and numerous "floras" arose at the time of the Gotha Program and of socialist laws. The union of nature and
politics shows in the spread of "strategic greenery"
in the cities in the second half of the century, a process which was bound up with the efforts of
Georges-Eugène Haussmann and James Hobrecht,
on the one hand, and those of Countess Dohna-
Poninsky and Lord Rosebery on the other hand. The
introduction of greenery always had a moral and
ethical background in the "plight of the working
class" and its harmony with working conditions. In
this sense the illusion of nature in the city was always an illusion of society as well. The miniature
landscaped gardens Haussmann laid out as a "green
lung" in Paris fulfilled this function. "They were
planned for the stroller, for the worker on his evening out, for the Sunday tripper, who could imbibe
fresh air while walking through them, like a sovereign who sauntered meditatively through his estate."[5]

In the nineteenth-century city, nature could only
be enjoyed in its artificial form, as a product of man.
As such, nature was not natural. It had no character
until the eye of the city dweller gave it one. Oscar
Wilde's character Vivian gives expression to the late-
nineteenth-century concept of an artificial nature in
the following passage:

*But Nature is so uncomfortable. Grass is hard and lumpy
and damp, and full of dreadful black insects. Why, even
Morris's poorest workman could make you a more comfortable seat than the whole of Nature can. . . . I don't com-
plain. If Nature had been comfortable mankind would
never have invented architecture and I prefer houses to the
open air. In a house we all feel of the proper proportions.
Everything is subordinated to us, fashioned for our use and
our pleasure. Egotism itself, which is so necessary to a proper
sense of human dignity, is entirely the result of indoor life.
Out of doors one becomes abstract and impersonal. One's individuality absolutely leaves one, and then Nature is so in-*

different, so unappreciative. Whenever I am walking in the park, I always feel that I am no more than the cattle that browse on the slope, or the burdock that blooms in the ditch.[6]

In order to underpin theoretically his feelings of distance from nature, Wilde had Vivian reflect on the concepts of German idealistic philosophy, in which the existence of the outside world depends on the imagination of the individual: "For what is Nature? Nature is no great mother who has borne us. Things are because we see them, and what we see, and how we see it, depends on the Arts that have influenced us. . . . That white quivering sunlight that one sees now in France, with its strange blotches of mauve and its restless violet shadows, is her latest fantasy, and, on the whole, Nature reproduces it quite admirably. Where she used to give us Corots and Daubignys, she gives us now exquisite Monets and entrancing Pissarros." Certainly there would be, as Vivian surmised, few occasions when nature would become wholly modern. She mostly exhausts herself in mind-wearying repetitions. "Nobody of any culture, for instance, ever talks nowadays about the beauty of a sunset. Sunsets are quite old fashioned. They belong to the time when Turner was the last note in art. To admire them is a distinct sign of provincialism of temperament." The promenader comes to the conclusion that only art expresses itself, that visible nature is indeed a copy of art. "The only effects that she can show us are effects that we have already seen through poetry, or in paintings. This is the secret of Nature's charm, as well as the explanation of Nature's weakness."

The city-dweller in the industrial age could no longer experience nature in its elemental form, but could only experience it as altered by his own kind of existence. The dandy saw nature from the world of the salon, where art was the central point of the social world and where life was indeed thought of as a work of art. Nature was perceived as an end product—for the dandy a picture or a poem, for the bourgeois man a commodity. The aesthetics of nature originate from her separation from man, which emanates here from the processes of industrial production. The farmer too viewed nature in terms of end products, from the harvest on, but he was (while he still guided the plow himself) indeed a part of nature. The distance separating him from his element was due to the fact that he had never developed an aesthetic approach to his world. The sunset meant nothing to him; it even bored him. This scenario was just a part of his life, he did not view it as a picture. Therefore he was unable to distinguish it in terms of

greater or lesser excellence. On the other hand, industry had altered the city-dweller's sense of perception, in that what he looked on as raw material he allowed to become a second nature. A multitude of factors—the machinery of the working world—were involved in this conversion process. Wilde's proposal that nature equates herself to art is indicated in the process of industrial production, which was to turn into fact the nineteenth-century dream of supremacy over nature. Fauna and flora were to be assimilated in terms of maximum utility in the form of goods by means of cultivation. The city-dweller pondered retrospectively about nature in this form. Plants, like people, had to become adapted to urban conditions. The proof of that is seen in the planned use of greenery in the Haussmann era. "The newly introduced plants were the very diverse forms of winter-hardy sub-tropical species which Jean Alphand and his colleagues discovered and had brought to Europe. They were large, strong, and easily reared . . . and distinguished themselves by speedy adaptation and the great diversity of their leaf structure or . . . were easily grown from seed, and in good soil grew luxuriantly. It was characteristic of all of them that their enormous leaves and their size as a whole was viewed from greater distances, so that they did not vanish from sight when they were planted out in broad grassy areas"[7] The "group portraits" so much in favor around 1800—portraits of persons in a masterpiece of painting—were repeated in the greenhouse in the form of plant arrangements modeled after the oriental paintings of Eugène Delacroix, Alexandre Gabriel Decamps, and their contemporaries (fig. 1). The glasshouses were places for a spectacle of nature made possible by coal, steam, glass, and iron.

The Stony Desert and the Green Oasis

*Denn, Herr, die grossen Städte sind
verlorene und aufgelöste;
wie Flucht vor Flammen ist die grösste, —
und ist kein Trost, dass er sie tröste,
und ihre kleine Zeit verrinnt.*

*Da leben Menschen, leben schlecht und schwer,
in tiefen Zimmern, bange von Gebärde,
geängsteter denn eine Erstlingsherde;
und draussen wacht und atmet deine Erde,
sie aber sind und wissen es nicht mehr.*

—Rainer Maria Rilke, 1903

In the early days of industrialization, in the period from 1800 to 1848, there was an attempt to oppose the spread of tenement houses and land speculation

1
Eugène Delacroix, *Algerian Women in the Harem*. Louvre, Paris.

by the concept of a city permeated by greenery, which was to conform to the layout of a landscaped garden.

In the cities of the eighteenth century there were few green spaces available to the public. Battlements and fortification walls, although tactically out of date, sharply separated the countryside from the town, which was consciously organized as a political, economic, and cultural center of power. In this period of slow city growth, the introduction of green spaces within the city walls was considered unnecessary. Where present, they were restricted to avenues or esplanades, such as Unter den Linden in Berlin. Large gardens remained the preserve of the princes and the nobility, and often lay outside the built-up zone. With the faster growth of German cities and the strengthening of the political power of the middle class in the period of the War of Liberation, which expressed itself in the formation of a city militia and the representation of the people, there came a period in which these gardens were altered into public places. The English Garden in Munich was opened to the public in 1810. Then came the Tiergarten in Berlin, Herrenhausen Park in Hannover, the Herrengarten in Darmstadt, and others. The demolition of city walls began at the same time, inspired by the example of Paris under Napoleon I.

After that there were attempts to incorporate green areas in cities not just crudely, as occasion presented itself from time to time, but to raise them to a new concept. Examples of this are the city concepts of Romantic Classicism, which, formulated as an aesthetic program, stood in striking contrast to an evolutionary trend determined by utilization of the soil. This theme was pursued in the Berlin city plan. In 1797 Friedrich Gilly proposed, in his design for the Friedrich Memorial in the Leipziger Platz in Berlin, the concept of an ideal town resembling a garden interspersed with architectural objects. Friedrich Schinkel, in his architectural projects and in his paintings, also pursued the policy of breaking up areas of buildings with green spaces. In one of his paintings he transformed the Milan cathedral into a Trieste landscape. In his panorama Schinkel included buildings which acted as a backdrop, mixed with groups of trees. In this he satisfied the demand of Romanticism, which was endorsed by the landscape gardener Hermann Fürst Pückler-Muskau, using the concept of "architectural dispersion." Architects of that time traveled with a sketchbook in order to capture the union of buildings and landscapes and to be able to transfer this union to the city. Giedion said of Schinkel's sketchbooks that landscapers, not architects, would appear to have made the journeys.

Peter Joseph Lenné also pursued similar intentions in his concepts of city buildings. The dogma of separated buildings has its analogy in the requirement to isolate certain trees in order to let light into forests. In his 1840 memorandum "Decoration and Surrounding Highways for the City of Berlin," Lenné followed the idea of a comprehensive plan for city and landscape permeated with waterways and green spaces, ring boulevards, and splendid highways. Lenné also proposed concentric "circles of beauty" around Berlin and Potsdam. He wrote as follows about the plan for the surroundings to the Gärtnerhaus in Charlottenburg: "The impact of an Italian rusticity is to be enhanced by the use of Lombardy cultural elements which are located there. We see there groups of fruit trees where the trees are linked together with vine leaves and ground runners, then symmetrically laid out fields of tall maize, artichokes, cardoons, and even Italian sugar canes make up the picture of a picturesque luxuriance of southern vegetation and at the same time indicate an agricultural use of the soil."[8] Necessary lines of communication such as railways, roads, and canals were subordinated to this landscape aesthetic.

This pursuit of a nature idyll in the city was overtaken by industrial growth. Instead of the decentralization of the city advocated by Gilly, Schinkel, and Lenné, centralization in the form of industrial complexes and increased immigration of working people prevailed. It entered with elemental force and put an end to the dream of a harmoniously laid-out city. Within 80 years the population of Berlin increased from 180,000 to 1,800,000 and the number of persons per building from 30 to 72.[9] The city area was filled up with large blocks of flats, which replaced the existing green spaces. At the end of the century Berlin had the reputation of having outstripped every other European metropolis in terms of number of dwelling houses.

City planning was determined not by the eclectic principles of the "landscaper" in his pursuit of aesthetics but through the pragmatic approach of bureaucracy and technology. This was particularly true of Berlin and Paris, which were also the seats of centralized executive power. In Berlin, Stadtbaurat James Hobrecht and Polizeipräsident von Wurmb planned the highways, the buildings, and the natural decor, and therefore took upon themselves the determination of the core of the Berliner's life. More distinctly than in Paris, where in line with historical tradition a well-organized middle class and proletariat had emerged, city planning in Berlin during the

critical growth from 1853 on was subject to state supervision. In that connection, Werner Hegemann wrote:

At a time when Berlin had 450,000 inhabitants, its Polizeipräsident cast aside 20 years' worth of sensible suggestions by social planners and began to draw up the bold building plan (i.e., the street plan) that took over the immense green areas of the environs of Berlin and officially paved the way for the building of large blocks of flats. These high-density dwellings, with their . . . badly lit back yards, condemned four million Berliners to live in housing that neither the most stupid idiot nor the most diligent privy councillor or land speculator could have contrived more inappropriately.[10]

The Baupolizeiordnung of 1853 sanctioned the apartment blocks that had been developed step by step since 1800 as the foundation stone for the expansion of Berlin.

The green spaces banished from the city in the years of reckless financial speculation after 1870 became once more the motive for idealists to propose a new concept of city building. In place of the aesthetic aspect, the social impetus was now in the center of things. Green enclosures were now demanded as a necessity for the health, recreation, and morals of the working class. Arminius (Countess Dohna-Poninski), in her 1874 book *City Housing Problems*, wanted to see "recreation places in the open air for evening leisure and Sundays, especially for manual workers and the educated classes," in the form of parks in densely built-up areas. These spaces should form "a green belt round the city," and should be "capable of being reached by every inhabitant within half an hour."

These areas, making up the valuable green belt and maintained by the city authority, were only to contain buildings to one fifth of their areas; the remaining spaces were to be used by the owners and tenants for use as gardens, fields, meadows, woodlands, while simultaneously serving people of all social classes according to their various needs as open air recreation places, including allotments for kitchen gardening.[11]

. . . It is surely high time to consider the matter, that in our cities, where the inhabitants call themselves Christians, the alleys and gutters and narrow back yards are not suitable places for children to play, and that one must take pains to make suitable places available for them, and the necessary clubs, so that they do not stand around with nothing to do in the evenings of the best time of the year, and to see that the children do not crowd the yards and the streets in disorderly and unsupervised groups.[12]

Reinhard Baumeister wrote in 1876 about the "union between the inner life and nature" that was to be achieved through the provision of green spaces in the city. "The very favorable influence of such pleasure grounds in physiological respects has long been known, but even more important is the spiritual effect."[13]

The propositions for social reforms had just as little chance of having a measurable effect on city building as those of the Romantic Classicists. In general, short-sighted economies permitted major investments only when they were directly related to production, and this contributed to further increases in the density of the city. This also applies to the development of Paris.

The resuscitation of "circulation"—the fast, unimpeded flow of traffic and of speculative money as well—was passionately pursued by Haussmann. His program was not the containment of city growth but the widening of it under the supervision and control of the state. His purpose was not the decentralization of the city but further centralization at the cost of the depopulation of the countryside. The armistice period between the revolutions of 1848 and 1871 coincided with the period of his energetic intervention. The great Parisian traffic arteries originating around 1853 were not rendered unusable by the masses of vehicles and the overflow of pedestrians, but saturation was imminent.

In 1819, Chabrol, the Prefect of Paris, referred to the need to match the width of the Paris streets to the amount of carriage traffic. "One finds by experience the size of the road absolutely necessary for the road traffic in the principal quarters of Paris; it should be sufficiently wide so that when two carriages are parked on opposite sides of the road a third should be able to pass between them."[14] The road, in which two carriages seldom met from opposite directions, was chiefly to serve the parked vehicles. According to a statistic quoted by Edmond Texier in 1853, there passed along the Boulevard des Capucines within a period of 24 hours 9,070 horse-drawn carriages, 10,750 along the Boulevard des Italiens, 7,720 along the Boulevard Poissonière, and 9,609 along the Boulevard Saint-Denis. The circulation had increased greatly since the days of Chabrol, but the limits of congestion had not quite been reached.

In conjunction with the overpopulation of habitable areas, the overcrowding of the open public spaces and highways became a problem that could not be ignored. Between 1800 and 1853, the population of Paris had grown from 600,000 to over a million. Frégier,[15] the chief of the Bureau à la Préfecture de Police, gave a summary description of the especially decayed and miserable Quartiers Saint-Honoré, la Cité, Saint-Jacques, and Saint-Marcel: "Sometimes the back yard is only four feet square . . . and is full of ordure. Rooms open onto it. The overflowing lav-atories on the fifth floor let their fecal material fall onto the staircase, which is flooded with it down to street level." The wretched quarters described by Frégier were the scene of furious riots even before the general uprising of 1848.

The hurried work of restoration in the city of Paris promoted during the time of Napoleon III proved to be a good memorial to this administration. Baron Georges-Eugène Haussmann obtained the necessary means to build the colorful boulevards that had been part of the Paris city plan of 1853. Réau writes:

It was the traffic circulation of vehicles that Haussmann found particularly inadequate. There was also the strategic factor, the movement of soldiers, horsemen, and artillery. Let us return to the overpopulated and "dangerous" quarters noted by Frégier. They served as battlefields, not only because the population there was badly housed and in misery, but because it was easy for the rebels to keep the fight going there. To make a barricade in these straight roads it sufficed to turn round two vehicles and add some chairs and mattresses. The regular army has to advance unprotected without having the advantage of the long range of its weapons. It is not gratuitously that we attribute a strategic intention to Haussmann; this epithet often returns from his pen apropos his vistas.[16]

One can understand the satisfaction with which Haussmann wrote of having "erased the Rue Transnonain from the map of Paris."

The first green boulevards originated in the time of Louis XIV with the transformation of the old ring of fortifications around Paris. With the boulevards provided by Haussmann, green spaces also appeared in the center of the city. Haussmann used special extracting and planting machines by means of which it was possible to create almost overnight a dense avenue of trees, with their crowns touching each other and extending as imposing green horizontal lines into the distance. The grandiose effect of perspective that resulted was the essence of the Haussmann aesthetic. At the end of the boulevard, exactly in the vanishing point, Haussmann carefully located a *pointe de vue*, a hub of the radiating boulevards with an obelisk, an Arc de Triomphe, fountains, a monumental building to create the effect of distance, or the glass-and-iron front of a railway station. "I have never interrupted the line of any view . . . and with greater reason the line of a principal artery without giving my attention to the vista that one can add to it."[17] The boulevard network was tangential to or intersected the parks, which were laid out at wide intervals as further natural oases within the broad expanse of houses, so that the green avenues appeared as advance indications of them in the streets.

Haussmann was already well known before his appointment as Prefect of Paris as a lover of gardening.

The beautiful aspects of nature that decorated Paris could not, however, counteract the distress in the city and the revolutionary ferment. In the period between the two revolutions, Paris had grown from 1 million to 1³/₄ million inhabitants, and Haussmann's intervention quickly caused the price of bread and rents to rise to hitherto unknown heights. From the moral standpoint behind which his utilitarian attitude hid, Haussmann appeared as a representative of the nineteenth-century bourgeoisie. In his opinion the green spaces were contributors to health ("dispensateurs de salubrité") and to long life.[18] The revolution of 1871, which put an end to the empire and to the works of the prefects of Paris, proved that an attempt at the reorganization of a great city based on property speculation would not achieve the social reforms intended.

The Illusion of Nature in the City

If an invention promises happiness, then one dreads the thought of any improvement to it which is not guaranteed. One declines the prospect which could awaken the desire that has been put to sleep and fears that the glittering promises would even heighten the consciousness of the existing necessity. Thus will the poor man who suddenly acquires wealth through a legacy not want to believe the news at first; he will send away the bringer of the good news and reproach him for mocking at his poverty.
—Charles Fourier, 1808

The existence of the glasshouse is inconceivable without the reality of the cities created in the nineteenth century, with their colossal masses of masonry and their menacing human swarms. It is an expression of the opposition to the progressive isolation of industrially organized human beings from their contact with nature and of the unrenounced claim to recreate this union, even if only by way of illusion. In the secret world of the hothouse nature is on display, like an uncovered picture, as the illusion of a wide world, and simultaneously as a tangible earthly paradise brought nearer to hand. In the setting out of the display there is, however, a completely irrevocable separation from the object on which the gaze falls; nature is no longer available in its pure and guileless form but has a market value. She opens a window onto the tropics for an entrance fee. The more crowded the city, the greater was the desire for the delight of looking at nature in this way.

In the nineteenth century, the glasshouse was the most extreme contrast to the stone pavement of the city. Texier writes:

When one has traversed all the avenues of the landscaped garden, when one has seen all the animals in their very different forms and habits, when one has breathed the scent of the plants collected from all parts of the world, then one has to visit the glasshouses closed to the public, in which all the flowers and exotic plants are assembled. These glasshouses are open to a small number of privileged people; it is a real piece of good fortune to enter into these splendid edifices where the sense organs discover unknown stimuli. Nothing is more beautiful than the interior of these glass buildings. Emerging from the black avenues through fir trees spreading over the labyrinth of hills, one suddenly finds oneself in a hot damp climate in the midst of towering vegetation, which the tropical sun helps to project upward like green rockets rising from a pregnant soil. It is hard to define the impression created by the contrast. Having entered, one experiences a dazzling effect, which is repeated when one has taken another stroll outside. The River Seine, visible in the distance, is decked with these palms, these coconut trees, this banana plantation springing aloft in these glasshouses, and it takes an effort not to dream of the River Nile or the Ganges. The wealth of the vegetation which one has just admired, the animals one has examined, give one the idea of a new world which suddenly starts beyond one.[19]

In *Oliver Twist*, Dickens writes:

Although Oliver had enough to occupy his attention in keeping sight of his leader, he could not help bestowing a few hasty glances on either side of the way, as he passed along. A dirtier or more wretched place he had never seen. The street was very narrow and muddy, and the air was impregnated with filthy odours. There were a good many small shops; but the only stock in trade appeared to be heaps of children, who, even at that time of night, were crawling in and out at the doors, or screaming from the inside. The sole places that seemed to prosper amid the general blight of the place, were the public-houses; and in them, the lowest orders of Irish were wrangling with might and main. Covered ways and yards, which here and there diverged from the main street, disclosed little knots of houses, where drunken men and women were positively wallowing in filth; and from several of the doorways, great ill-looking fellows were cautiously emerging, bound, to all appearance, on no very well-disposed or harmless errands.[20]

The city is portrayed here as a part of nature, but at the same time as unnatural. As a flower of civilization and industrial progress, it is, as it were, a place where there is a process of organic decay; the victim is man, who does not appear to recognize it. At the end of this vision there is a megalopolis turned into a ruined landscape, like Gustave Doré's engraving of London in ruins (fig. 2).

2
Gustave Doré, *View
after Thousands of
Years (London De-
stroyed)*. Woodcut,
1872.

Another world revealed itself beneath the crystal roof of the hothouse. Peace and harmony seemed to reign here because nature herself appeared right and proper in that she was housed. The struggle for existence that raged outside was halted under the evergreen palms, which appeared to be involved only in the laws of organic growth. The glimpse of the city through the glass walls transformed it into an oriental fairy landscape—a fata morgana in the stony desert.

The existence of the nineteenth-century hothouse cannot be explained in terms of material factors alone. Incorporated within it are definite concepts of happiness. Its effect on its contemporaries consisted of contrast. The glasshouse filled with tropical plants was the dream of a happy unity of nature and man in the first part of the industrial age. Every epoch imagines its future as happy, as an intimate symbiosis of nature and man set in the present. There was a constant striving to give substance to the dream, to turn it into buildings. The glasshouse was the embodiment of the nineteenth-century dream. In the actual program of the exploitation of nature which had spread throughout the world, and which by the world dominance of capital was to have redeemed the middle class, a picture of paradise was outlined in which the destruction and alienation of nature had not come to pass and in which nature, with the help of technology, could become a comfortable home for man.

The paradise motif in the history of architecture has always been a favorite subject for the representation of illusions. Prospects of the landscape were on view through the windows, and painted scenes of nature on the walls provided pictures of it. The landscape invaded the home, where it was trapped in frescoes like a picture. With the introduction of the mirror in the Baroque period, the continuity of the walls was broken to form an illusion, and a direct connection with the outside world resulted. The cultivated landscape in front of the house became the symbol of control over nature.

In the nineteenth century, the window opened out onto nature. It became longer and even lost its identity in that the whole house became transformed into glass. Its outer boundaries were not clearly perceptible. Under the open sky were assembled the most fruitful trees of the tropics. With the growing control of nature, only hitherto unknown vegetation was able to transmit the concept of paradise; indigenous vegetation was regarded solely as the supplier of food for the city. Familiar rustic pictures were no longer useful as a contrast to the civilization that had

developed. The picture of the orient appeared in their place. This fascination increased greatly the early use of glass and iron to make glasshouses; these materials seemed uniquely suitable to achieve the nonmaterial effect necessary for producing that picture of utopia.

The Glasshouse as the Vanishing Point of the Social Utopia

To accept things as they are is no empirically exact formula, no positivism, but a formula for vulgarity, for cowardice, for misery. Understanding what has been means not what has happened, but what is continuing to happen. Utopia is the place in which the as yet unknown appears.
—*Ernst Bloch*

The glasshouse, with its greenery, was, as a symbol of the Garden of Eden on Earth, the convergence point of all nineteenth-century social utopias. While nature and hence history strove to procure their rights, the utopians perceived vistas of plants, glass, and iron—places of reconciliation without which they could not spread the word about the city proposed by them. Indeed, the industrial system involved in the development was always more or less recognized as the basis of life in the city and the country; at the same time it was clear to them that this system was supported by nature. Man was according to belief a work force yet more than merely a work force; he was a thinking, feeling, physical creature who in the stony expanse of the city had become almost entirely hired labor and who had cut himself off from his true nature. The purpose of this utopia was to give this nature back to him. The way to that should not be a return to nature but a step toward a humanized industrialization in which agriculture, nature, and society were to be provided for.

The dialectical starting point of this utopia consisted of reconciling man with nature not outside town and industry but in and through them. Of course, towns were no longer to turn into cities but into producing communities capable of supervision, communities in which people would still be in the position to constitute a lively social system contributing to their individual prosperity. At the focus of the proposals stood the deliberations about the organization of factory and agricultural work, in which people were to occupy themselves in forming a collective and the space necessary for it. The proposals materialized in garden cities, in which the green of the countryside combined with or even enclosed the factories. The place of communal life was a landscape converted into a park in the form of green highways and spaces which were partly roofed over by glass-

and-iron structures. The glasshouse, as a symbol of the new domestic comfort, was the idée fixe of the utopians.

In order to avoid the "evils of civilization," Charles Fourier proposed for his projects "phalanstery" production units, with a central administration and a planned economy, which were to accommodate about 2,000 people in a communal organization. These phalansteries were to be cities in miniature. They were to consist of a single axially laid-out built-up area about 1,800 feet long, divided into sectors by large green back gardens, with the countryside as a background. The center of the built-up area was to be a place for public gatherings, dining rooms, offices, clubs, and libraries. The factories were to be located on the level ground in the transept areas, and the domestic housing was to be beyond them. Pathways over roofs were to give access to the natural open-air environment, to a large central park, and to passages meeting in the yards and connecting all parts of the phalanstery. These passages were to serve as an artificial system for traffic and were to be laid out on a central plan, like all the buildings; they were to form a kind of winter garden. Inner galleries, which were to run along the first, second, and third stories, were to extend this pathway system.

In 1808, even before he had worked out the details of his phalanstery concept, Fourier had recommended his glass-covered passageways as the sign of the new logical society:

Palaces or chateaus must be interconnected by covered ways to protect people from the hardships of the weather, so that one is protected at assemblies, business meetings, or during recreation from the influence of the unpleasant times of the year, beneath which in "civilization" one has to suffer at every step. It must be possible to move from one building to another through heated or ventilated passages by day or by night, so that one does not run the risk, as in present day arrangements, of getting dirty or soaked, of catching a cold or pneumonia because of stepping out into the open air. . . . instead of having to traverse three or four roads as in civilization one strides through covered passageways between three or four adjacent buildings, avoiding heat and cold, wind and rain. These protective connecting routes are one of the thousand amenities kept in reserve for the new social order.[21]

Concerning the cooperative proposals made by Fourier, Elisabeth Lenk says: "Fourier believed that the first phalanstery would create an attractive force of such magnitude that within a few years there would certainly be worldwide spread of the principle of 'Passionate Series.' The social metamorphosis would only come to pass as the result of a single vigorous coup de main. Kings, clerics, savages, capitalists, and convicts will be harmoniously accommodated with all their various burdens into the new social order. Even the bloodthirsty Nero, the very best of all butchers, would have become a useful member of the 'harmony' without having had to change his nature."[22]

J. C. Loudon proposed in 1823 a utopia based on nature, not socially determined but worked out in surprising detail. In the form of a gigantic greenhouse covering whole tracts of land, it was to guarantee a supply of industrial material forever within a reliable environment of exotic diversity. In the background there is the notion of an intensive agricultural system, a vast market garden, incorporating a parklike landscape and a zoological and botanical garden. The intended accomplishment of the project by a large industrialized agricultural corporation shows that Loudon had in mind a steam-heated landscape, watered with artificial rain and covered by glass within the context of the town, into which domesticated nature could be brought. There was hardly any limit to the application of this type of light roof, Loudon wrote. Several acres—even a whole estate of moderate size—could be covered in this way if one used hollow cast-iron pillars for the supports. They could simultaneously serve to drain the rainwater from the roof. One could bring a shower of rain into the interior by using the Loddiges method, or one could use a roof which could be opened as required to allow the rain to enter. Any temperature required could be provided by steam heating pipes. Ventilation could also be provided. Such a roof could be built either as a plane ridged surface running from north to south, or as an octagonal or hexagonal tapering cone with a supporting framework for any angle, which would rise 100 to 150 feet from the ground. The largest oriental trees could grow under such a roof, and a flock of passing birds could settle in their branches. One could thus have a number of oriental birds and monkeys, and other animals too, in the hothouse. Furthermore, one could supply fresh-water ponds and salt-water lakes with water by machinery, and thus keep fish and polyps and other fresh-water or marine creatures.[23]

In 1841 Charles McIntosh attempted with the construction of a glass-covered garden in Dalkeith to demonstrate Loudon's vision. He kept up a corresponding interest at the same time in the railway station buildings of the time, particularly the North Midlands Trijunct Railway Station in Derby (fig. 3).

In 1838 Loudon proposed in his "Suburban Gardener" and "Villa Companion" to solve the problems of the town by siting the dwellings amid green spaces while retaining urban building forms. He proposed a house for two families situated in a kitchen garden within a housing estate for the middle class. The cubical house was to be surrounded by a glass-covered veranda to which small greenhouses were to be joined (fig. 4).

In 1817 the textile manufacturer Robert Owen, after the building of his model housing estate at New Lanark, submitted a plan to the government to establish an industrial estate of 1,200 inhabitants in dispersed dwellings with green spaces as an alternative to the industrial centers. The land surrounding the estate was to be cultivated. Owen's industrial estates, the starting point of the garden city concept, were real social utopias because they were organized not for pleasure and manufacturing (like Fourier's town) but strictly for industrial purposes. In order to alleviate the misery of the workers, Owen pursued the paternalism so much favored afterwards—the metamorphosis of the workers into property owners. This was to lead to countless other utopian proposals in which the collective happiness was to be expressed in the crystal glass of "people's palaces."

Pemberton's "Happy Colony" included a ring-shaped glasshouse as a meeting place for the urban community.[24] Loudon had already proposed in 1831 a large ring-shaped glasshouse to be filled with tropical plants in his plan for the Birmingham Botanical Gardens. It is not certain that Pemberton knew of this early concept of a vaulted winter garden built around a green interior. It is, however, certain that he had in front of him Paxton's Crystal Palace, which at that time was a new wonder of industrialized building techniques and which was to have a lasting effect on the proselytes of the garden city concept during the following decades.

Titus Salt, a textile manufacturer and a member of the Bradford City Council in 1851 (the year of the completion of the Crystal Palace), decided to move his factory into the country and to provide accommodations for his workers around it. Salt's town, built in the Neo-Renaissance style and named Saltaire, had 850 terrace houses and about 4,000 inhabitants. Two areas of allotment gardens attached to the town served for the self-sufficiency and recreation of the workers. The northerly garden area extended beyond the other side of the river into a wide landscaped park. The factory was sited to the northeast, at the junction between the estate and the park, so that there was hardly any smoke pollution because of the prevailing wind.

Salt succeeded in creating a workers' town that exhibited the socially useful elements of the town, in the form of terrace houses, open spaces, and public pleasure grounds, all transplanted to the countryside, and that simultaneously served as an antithesis to city slums. Connected with this was Salt's plan to buy the Crystal Palace from Paxton, dismantle it, and reassemble it at Saltaire as a factory building.[25] Inherent in this, more than 50 years before Henry Ford's concept of manufacturing, was the thought of releasing the worker from his gloomy confined existence and bringing him once again to the bright light of day. The noteworthy point here was that not only leisure but work as well was to be associated with the natural environment. This progressive idea, derived from the paternalistic notion that work should be humanized, demonstrates a concern for natural conditions in a period of blind exploitation of nature by most entrepreneurs.

It must be said in this connection that the so-called humanizing of work implied the maintenance of hired labor, although under improved conditions. In this light, the philanthropic interest taken in the morals and the preservation of paternalism by way of the "ethical uplift of the working class" was an insight into the fact that only by this was a revolutionary distribution of the industrial capitalist system to be prevented. "I will do all that I can in order to avoid such a great evil as polluted air and polluted water, and I hope to gather around me well fed, contented, and happy workers."[26]

Whereas the utopias emanating from Fourier had the countryside as the basis for the reconciliation with nature, several schemes from 1850 on aimed increasingly at the opposite: that the town should absorb some of the countryside and thus create a green environment for itself. Like a giant umbrella of glass and iron, there should be continuous halls, park landscapes, and boulevards where people could gather for social contact and pleasure. The concepts of the arcade and the winter garden merged into the idea of a continuous ring of glass which was to embrace the city center and beautify it. Just as commodities were to be displayed in the arcade, so was nature to be displayed in the winter garden.

The historical background of this megalomanic project was the state of industry existing about 1850, which made it possible to mass-produce the glass and iron components for these buildings at a low price. In this connection it was again the giant buildings constructed for the Jardin d'Hiver in Paris (1848) and Paxton's Crystal Palace (1851) that acted powerfully on utopian fantasies and brought them to fruition.

3
Charles McIntosh,
project for a glass-
covered landscape
with artificial climate
for the kitchen gar-
den of Dalkeith Pal-
ace, near Edinburgh,
1841.

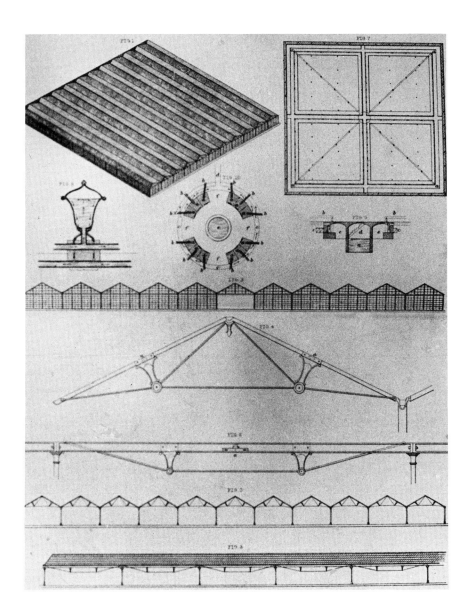

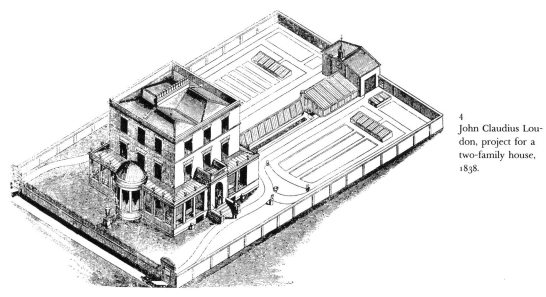

4
John Claudius Lou-
don, project for a
two-family house,
1838.

In 1848, after the banishment of the House of Orléans, there originated a plan (based on a report by
Gottfried Semper) to "cover the whole of the spacious gardens of the Palais National [in Paris] with
movable roofing, so that in summer the plants could
be put out in the open air, while in the winter they
could be covered."[27]

Several plans arose in London around the middle
of the century to extend the Crystal Palace into an
almost boundless form and make it into a significant
structural element of the city. In 1855 Paxton put before the Select Committee on Metropolitan Improvements a plan for a "Great Victorian Way," which
was to consist of a glass ring encircling the central
business district of London. The cross-section and
structure of this corresponded to the barrel-vaulted
main bay of the Exhibition Building. Covering an inner green boulevard, this ring of glass, together with
eight parallel railway tracks, was to connect the most
important stations, shops, business centers, and
parks. Even earlier, Frederick Gye and William Moseley (1855) had put forward plans of a similar order of
magnitude (inspired by Paxton) to the same committee. Gye, the director of the Royal Italian Opera in
Covent Garden, commissioned the building of the
Floral Hall (1855) by Sir E. M. Barry. This was a
glass-and-iron hall in Paxton's style. Gye also proposed a "glass street," the roof of which was to be
the width of King William Street and to have a
height of 70 feet. This arcade was to form a branching glass-covered promenade, with arches and rotundas, linking public buildings and extending into large
galleries and halls. Under the glass roof were to be
assembled reading rooms, exhibition halls, concert
halls, public assembly rooms, baths, cafés, business
premises, and a flower market.[28] Gye's plan, which
he had proposed in 1845, showed that large enclosed
spaces in the inner city, with artificial climate, had
occupied the thoughts of utopians before Paxton.
The concept of absolute control over nature was formulated here on a grand scale for the first time. The
naive assumption that with the help of technology
everything is possible was the parent of such a
utopia.

To this train of thought also belongs W. Moseley's
1855 plan for a "Crystal Way," which, like Gye's
plan, proposed a covered arterial route with several
levels for footpaths, railways, and vehicles. It was,
like Paxton's Great Victorian Way, to form a glass
ring within London.

These three proposals had in common the intention of organizing, or even preserving, the city,
which at that time was threatened with strangulation

by traffic chaos. The "circulation" of the city was to
be renewed and its "metabolism" improved by
means of glass arcades. These proposals were frustrated from the very start by a lack of capital. The
state was financing the conquest of distant colonies
and was not ready to bear the burden of such gigantic projects in urban reorganization, which were not
commercially viable. (Paxton's Great Victorian Way
had an estimated cost of 34 million pounds.)

Haussmann pointed the way to an "inner coloni-
zation" of cities, which at the same time opened up
a lucrative field for land speculation and trade capital; his green boulevards cut through the uncontrolled growth of Paris like a dissecting knife.

The wreck of these attempts made after the middle of the century to take away the dreariness of the
inner city with the help of the advanced technology
of the time and to satisfy the needs of the masses for
nature gave impetus to the idea of the garden city in
the following decades.

The intention in the founding of Saltaire was
clearly to preserve the elements of the city by transplanting a municipal working-class quarter to the
countryside. Here it was a matter more of resettling
a city production unit in the form of a factory, together with machinery, work force, and proprietors,
than of establishing a qualitatively changed way of
work and life. Saltaire was surrounded by unspoiled
country, but it was alien to the workers because factory work was a decisive factor. When a moment of
leisure occurred, nature kept the character of the
abstract.

Norman Shaw's founding in 1875 of Bedford Park,
a suburb of London, started the garden-city movement. Though this movement was associated with
paternalism, it was more radical in that it sought a
change in both the way of living and the way of
work. Sir Ebenezer Howard, a Parliament stenog-
rapher in London, was the most important champion
of this idea. Instead of industrial village, he wanted
to create self-managed collectives that would become
models for a general social renewal. "The garden
city itself should not be the result of migration
brought about by the good will of the factory proprietors to leave the misery of the city and capitalist
exploitation. It was to be a voluntary alliance of interests. It was to replace the city by the concept of a
new town to reverse the influx into the city and to
direct the tide of the people towards the idea of a
town in the countryside, ultimately leading to the rebuilding of the city itself. Howard did in fact see that
alongside a movement to the garden city it would
lead to a new way of life in towns throughout the

whole country; Megalopolis could not continue to exist. His goals lay far beyond what paternalism alone could achieve."[20]

Howard was no mere nature lover. Besides the disadvantages of the city, he clearly saw the inconvenience associated with life in the countryside: isolation caused by the wide open spaces, monotony caused by the absence of social institutions and facilities for recreation, more difficult and longer hours of work, and a troublesome way of life because of the absence of the traditional advantages which city-dwellers enjoyed, the lack of which prevented people from living in a healthy way and enjoying themselves "in bright sunshine and pure air." Therefore his goals were a greater level of reconciliation between town and country: the assimilation of nature into the existing technological system, appropriation of the land as municipal property, earnest cooperation through self-management, and direct exchange of the goods produced in the town and on the land while eliminating speculation and profiteering.

In 1898 Howard drafted the model of the "three magnets"—the Town, the Country, and the "Town-Country"—to promote his project. Each of the three sectors was described in terms of disadvantages of the first two compared with the advantages of the Town-Country. The Town-Country sector of Howard's tripartite diagram (fig. 5) contains only the advantages of the two other sectors, without their drawbacks, and for Howard this was the force that was to draw people together. "But," wrote Howard,

neither the Town magnet nor the Country magnet represents the full plan and purpose of nature. Human society and the beauty of nature are meant to be enjoyed together. The two magnets must be made one. As man and woman by their varied gifts and faculties supplement each other, so should town and country. The town is the symbol of society—of mutual help and friendly co-operation, . . . of science, art, culture, religion. And the country! All that we are and all that we have comes from it. . . . Our bodies are formed of it; to it they return. . . . Its forces propel all the wheels of industry. It is the source of all health, all knowledge. But its fullness of joy and wisdom has not revealed itself to man. Nor can it ever, so long as this unholy, unnatural separation of society and nature endures. Town and country must be married, and out of this joyous union will spring a new hope, a new life, a new civilization.[30]

Howard's circular garden city was to be located in the center of a 5,928-acre girdle devoted to agriculture. The city was to be traversed by six large radiating boulevards, dividing it into six equal parts, which were to be interconnected by five concentric

avenues (fig. 5). A main railway line and a circular railway round the city were to transport incoming goods from the outer ring of factories, warehouses, and markets to the dwellings, churches, and schools. Howard described the design as follows:

Running all round the Central Park (except where it is intersected by the boulevards) is a wide glass arcade called the "Crystal Palace," opening on to the park. This building is in wet weather one of the favourite resorts of the people, whilst the knowledge that its bright centre is ever close at hand tempts people into the Central Park, even in the most doubtful of weathers. Here manufactured goods are exposed for sale, and here most of that class of shopping which requires the joy of deliberation and selection is done. The space enclosed by the Crystal Palace is, however, a good deal larger than is required for these purposes, and a considerable part of it is used as a Winter Garden—the whole forming a permanent exhibition of a most attractive character, whilst its circular form brings it near to every dweller in the town—the furthest removed inhabitant being within 600 yards.[31]

The circular glasshouse in Howard's "Garden-City" was to be a great glass-and-iron structure, 3,720 feet from center to circumference, filled with plants and opening onto the park. This was the part of the town where nature was to be encountered and the aesthetic scene to be enjoyed for the general benefit of the crowd of strollers.

At the end of the century the social utopia of the middle class was the concept of a society freed from exploitation and reconciled with its condition—just as a greenhouse cancels the threatening aspects of the surroundings. That this utopia was not brought about was due to the fact that its authors misunderstood the laws of social development of their century. The mass production of goods, accelerated step by step with the help of industrial power, became the basis of all social relationships and the relationship with nature. The industrial development of the nineteenth century had achieved independence. It brought large-scale combination and centralization of the forces of production into towns and hence brought about further concentration of people and increased competition between them. Industry itself was, as it turned out, the only concrete utopia of the nineteenth century. This utopia demanded the absolute control of nature. In this context, Hegemann wrote: "Barracks and their backyard buildings had overrun the former gardens and the preserved remnants of the smaller cottages to such an extent that not even stubborn eccentrics who wished to hang on until death dwelt therein."[32]

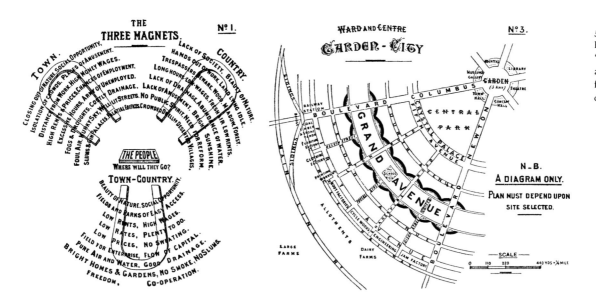

5
Ebenezer Howard,
"the three magnets"
and part of the plan
for an ideal garden
city, 1898.

The Glass Crystal

1. *Glück ohne Glas—*
   Wie dumm ist das

2. *Backstein vergeht,*
   Glasfarbe besteht.

3. *Das bunte Glas*
   Zerstört den Hass.

4. *Farbenglück nur*
   In der Glaskultur.

5. *Ohne einen Glaspalast*
   Ist das Leben eine Last.

6. *Im Glashaus brennt es nimmermehr:*
   Man braucht da keine Feuerwehr.

7. *Das Ungeziefer ist nicht fein;*
   Ins Glashaus kommt es niemals rein.

8. *Brennbare Materialia*
   Sind wirkliche Skandalia.

9. *Grösser als der Diamant*
   Ist die doppelte Glashauswand.

10. *Das Licht will durch das ganze All*
    Und ist lebendig im Kristall.

11. *Das Prisma ist doch gross;*
    Drum ist das Glas famos.

12. *Wer die Farbe flieht,*
    Nichts vom Weltall sieht.

13. *Das Glas bringt alles Helle,*
    Verbau es auf der Stelle.

14. *Das Glas bringt uns die neue Zeit;*
    Backsteinkultur tut uns nur leid.

—Paul Scheerbart, 1914

In the nineteenth century, the concept of the glass-house became joined to the idea of the earthly paradise. In essence this idea embodied the physical presence of nature, as encountered on an island. The requirement of tropical plants corresponded to the paradisiacal scene. The aspect of authenticity was carefully preserved thereby. The tropical world was transplanted and assembled in the manner of pictures. A landscape came into existence without the help of paint and canvas. Gauguin's dream world manifested itself under the glass bell jar.

At the start of the twentieth century the symbolic aspect of the glasshouse changed. World War I strengthened the desire for escapism, which had already taken root in the nineteenth century. The hope of peaceful commercial competition between the peoples of the world came to an abrupt end on the battlefields. Out of this disaster there spread in Germany two opposing trends, the perception of nature and urbanization, both of which were already in existence in the nineteenth century. In one trend there was a radicalized utopia of Expressionism, according to which the subjective discovery of happiness succeeded only in the emphatic embrace of the whole of nature or of the individual. In the other trend there appeared a tendency toward a reinforced pragmatism, which compelled the use of the new type of industry—mass production on conveyor belts and assembly lines. The belief in the omnipotence of technology again presented itself. Shiny machines were judged to be the force that would make the world free, without consideration of the nature of mankind. The magic spell, the New Objectivity, was known as Fordism. Both these trends found their expression in glass architecture, which arose from the idea of the glasshouse.

To the utopians of the "gläserne Kette" (glass or crystal chain)— the avant-garde of architectural Expressionism around 1920—the glasshouse symbolized not an earthly but a non-earthly Elysium. The utopianism of the nineteenth century, which involved the desire for a relationship with reality, was lost in abstraction. Not the plants and the people but the glass itself, as an expression of the "spiritual," was the content of the new proposals. The glass crystal became the highest symbol of purity and perfection in the hierarchy of natural forms. Glass appeared to these new utopians as the one material that was brought into view and yet also dematerialized by light. Glass found its true nature in the crystal, which on the one hand reflected light from its facets and on the other hand seemed to store up light. "No material prevails over other materials so much as does glass. Glass is a completely new, pure material in which matter is melted down and recast. Of all the materials we have it works in the most elementary way. It reflects the sky and the sun; it is like clear water; and it has a wealth of color, form, and character which is indeed inexhaustible and which can be a matter of indifference to no person."[33]

There was combined with the idea of the glasshouse as a crystalline object the elitist self-reliance of an artistic community defying the comfortable, narrow-minded bourgeoisie: "Just as all dwellings of man up till now were like soft buffers for his travels, attempts to rest comfortably and to let things take their course, so will glass architecture provide us with spacious accommodation which again and again will hinder us from lapsing into dullness, habit, and an easy-going disposition."[34] "The European is easy in the very place where he has no responsibility, but in the hard environment where he would have responsibility, under a jellylike interior he is blunt and brutal. Glass will change him. Glass is clear and angular, but in its hidden richness it is mild and soft."[35]

It is clear that the Crystal Chain is bound up with that tradition of the nineteenth century in which the glasshouse had developed as a building style and as an alternative way of living. J. C. Loudon, almost 100 years before, had described with similar emphasis and delight the aesthetic vision of his glass architecture and the progress inherent therein. Paul Scheerbart, the poet who wrote "The Glass Crystal," noted in 1914 while strolling in the glass landscape of the Berlin hothouses: "We already possess a glass architecture and it is in fact in the Botanical Gardens. The Botanical Gardens at Dahlem outside Berlin show that really imposing glass palaces are being made. Color of course is absent. In the evening sunlight the palm house and the cool house present such a mag-

nificent effect that one does indeed obtain a concept. . . ."[36] On another occasion he wrote: "The brick architecture of former times has often prevailed over the perpendicular. But to depart from the perpendicular in the walls seemed however impossible. It is quite different in glass architecture. The large palm house in the Berlin Botanical Gardens of that time no longer had perpendicular walls; their upward curvature started at a height of [10 feet]."[37]

The Crystal Chain burst open the boundaries of the classes of art and inserted architecture, sculpture, painting, and literature, linking them with each other into a medium for the representation of its vision. Although the idealism of these utopians did not progress as far as actual construction of buildings, there is a link with the New Objectivity. Bruno and Max Taut, Hans Scharoun, and other prominent members of the Crystal Chain were factory architects. Adolf Behne, an ideologist of the Crystal Chain, was at the same time the mouthpiece of the New Objectivity as the author of the book *Der Moderne Zweckbau* (Modern Purpose Building). The factors that united these movements of the 1920s were the rise of the massively built house, which served as a refuge for extinct life forms, and the movement toward glass as a building material through which the light of "modern civilization" could penetrate.

The "Troublesome Window"

The curtain has fallen . . . , a new dimension has opened up before us and the whole world has plunged into its space.
—Le Corbusier, 1922

True well-lit interiors into which light could penetrate without hindrance existed in the nineteenth century only in glasshouses. In the dwellings of the townspeople, twilight prevailed. This is true not only of the opaque brick masses of the tenement houses, whose windows received light only indirectly via wells, yards, basements, or dormer windows. In the houses of the upper middle class and the middle class, one could look out on the sun and greenery, but light entered through a narrow grid of windowpanes and just managed to filter through the carefully draped curtains before dissipating in the half-light within. On the floor lay Persian rugs, and there were dark, richly ornamented tapestries or papers on the walls. Massive wooden furniture appeared as dark silhouettes. Sofas, armchairs, and tables were covered with drapery. Clocks, mirrors, pictures, trophies, and weapons filled the room, as if intended to catch every beam of light that threatened to sneak into an empty corner. The sole representative of nature in this ensemble was the obligatory dwarf palm, which just managed to survive, miserable and stunted, in the half-light. People were similarly protected from light. In old photographs of boulevards hardly a single person is to be seen without a hat, or without hermetically sealed clothing.

The ambivalence toward light expressed itself most strikingly in the multiple curtaining of relatively large window openings, which can be interpreted as an echo of the middle-class separation between private and public life. Dolf Sternberger notes this relationship in "Störende Fenster" (troublesome windows),[38] in which he quotes the art historian Cornelius Gurlitt, a contemporary expert[39]:

Our usual large windows take the inner quiet from the room and put it back into too close contact with the outside world. . . . Every partly informed person is to some extent aware of how strong is the difference between the brightness of the incoming daylight and that of these strictly limited circumstances, and how much the color is damaged because of the onslaught of light. A gradation through ever thicker layers of curtaining of the covered glass surfaces up to the heavy opaque material will be best carried out in a way that one will be more clearly aware of the color of it.

However, even curtains appeared to the citizen of the late nineteenth century as insufficient and moreover paradoxical. After all, windows—an expensive part of a house—were in fact bought for their effect. "For what purpose does one purchase at great expense many large crystal clear window panes if one nullifies their effect by the narrow meshes of the lace curtain and by the mass of ornamentation?" Gurlitt said the following about bullseye glass, which made curtains superfluous: "The whole room appears dim and cozy. . . . We only feel at ease in it when we are alone, when we are without thoughts, or without the company of our friends. Whatever is going on outside lies far away. Not even the passing clouds are noticeable in the greenish medley of light."

A careful study of the effect of light and the comfort of the same has been passed on to us by the architect Richard Lucae.[40] In the same way as Gurlitt, but with the eye of the expert, he considers his view of the curtainless window and the effect of light in a "bare and cheerless" living room. He starts with a room which is provided on its long side with equally spaced window openings, and says: "The brightness of the day fills it . . . but the light runs about all over the room and illuminates the objects almost in an obtrusive way. No part has to endure deep shade, and whilst this nullifies any contrasts, it deprives itself of any poetic effect. These rooms always have the same conventional smile . . . but they do not inherently possess anything which is comfortable." The room becomes, according to Lucae, almost so prosaic

as to be uninhabitable if it comes to uniformly separated openings in the long wall for windows in a narrow space, or even at several places: "In such a room the sensation is completely absent which we want to have more than anything else in a living room, namely the feeling that we feel ourselves to be separated from the outside world, and linguistic usage calls such a room, very appropriately, a lantern."

It is an alarming thought that private life could stream outward into public and hence become desecrated. In the background of this dread undoubtedly stood the established conviction that the family environment was a place of safety to be protected at any price. At the same time, there were factors in the industrial age which worked toward the breakup of the family. The city appeared hostile to every first- or second-generation migrant from the countryside. The individual found himself inadequately adjusted to the diversity of attractions, and did not find himself at peace within it. The routine course and ritual of movement was possible only within the sphere of the home. Light-filled rooms with glass facades or roofs were acceptable only in public buildings, which formed places of congregation for transitory movement: stations, covered markets, exhibition halls, and hothouses.

Influences on the Twentieth Century

In the twentieth century the well-lit interior, which in the nineteenth century was reserved for plants, entered into the dwelling house with the coming of the New Objectivity. Brightness illuminating every corner became the essential substance of "free living."[41] The window was flung open; the house lost its solidity and its fortress character. The lace curtain as a filter of light vanished; clear mirror glass, as far as possible without any divisions, made the home an appendix of the outside world.

The architects and town planners set to work to meet the needs of a highly developed industrial world. Conveyor-belt operations, production lines, and automation provided a stream of goods. The conformity inherent in the industrial system pressed in that way to line up all human relationships into the mechanical division of labor and in the end to change humans into goods. This was resisted by the home environment, in which one could divest oneself of thoughts about the workaday world of industry and rebuild one's special individual character. Here one conducted oneself in a pre-industrial manner, while being in other respects a wholly modern man.

The revolutionary middle-class habits that were to have been dispersed with the appearance of changed building techniques became the order of the day. "The cogs of society," wrote Le Corbusier, "are seriously damaged, they vacillate between an advance of historic importance and its collapse. The various working classes of society . . . no longer have a suitable place of retreat today. Hence the key to the reproduction of today's destroyed balance is a building problem: architecture or revolution."[42]

Industry required a mobile work force, and the new view of the home was well suited to this need. "The house will no longer be this cumbersome object, which wants to defy the century. . . . It will no longer have an archaic character, with deep foundations rooted in the ground and erected with devotion, on which the cult of the family was supported for such a long time."[43] The dweller in the modern tenement building was to bring a minimum of personal possessions. Cupboards, shelves, wardrobes, and light fixtures were provided. All objects of daily use were to go into the cupboards provided. "Bare walls are wanted in the bedroom, in your large living room and dining room. . . . Teach your children that the home is only comfortable when it has light in abundance, and when the floor and the walls are uncluttered. Renounced are unnecessary furniture and oriental carpets. These are rented houses, which are rather smaller than those which your forefathers have been used to. Think of the economy in movement, arrangements and ideas."[44] Again and again there were references to the concept of unsettled man, whose possessions could fit in a rucksack.

Ocean travel had its influence: "Any serious-minded architect who observes an ocean vessel will recognize in it the liberation from centuries of accursed servitude. The house of the district magistrate is an expression of an obsolete world of small proportions. The ocean vessel is the first step toward the realization of a world that corresponds to the new spirit."[45] The house no longer needed to be anchored to the ground; the carpet of the lawn could extend under it like a green sea. Le Corbusier's Villa Savoie in Poissy (1928–1930) was a reflection of a ship he had converted to a hostel for the homeless of Paris. At the end of this line of development stood the mobile home, the aesthetics of which corresponded to the new form of manufactured goods. The possibility of producing houses in factories rather than at building sites paved the way, theoretically and aesthetically, for the New Objectivity.

As people adapted themselves to standardized goods, such as ready-made clothes, they were adapting not only to the products but also to the pro-ducer—the machine. In the exuberance of the machine cult of the New Objectivity there is the magic of this transformation to the principle of the new society. "Seize the opportunity, construct and compute the Globe!—the World, which is waiting for you. Simple and definite like the machine, clear and bold like the construction. The precision of its revolutions stimulates one, the harsh clanging sound of its action and the metallic luster of its material presents things in a new light."[46]

Le Corbusier preached the concept of the house as a "dwelling machine." According to his opinion, housing needs could be accurately determined and all movement within the home calculated. As in the factory, these factors could be optimized, thus avoiding any waste of space. A house could be made as precise and serviceable as a typewriter, a ship's cabin, or a motorcar.[47] "In every modern man there lives mechanics. The feeling for mechanics comes from our daily doing and striving. Our feelings for it are respect, thankfulness and esteem."[48]

The advocates of the "green city" concept proposed to replace the greenery displaced by buildings with green terraces, loggias, and roof landscapes. Their aim, without doubt, was to improve the living conditions of the city-dweller. The dwelling machine, with its minimized space and its industrialized manufacture, was to make possible low rents and, at the same time, a healthy life in the sunlight. A big step in that direction was the division of the town into work, recreation, and residential zones, connected by rapid means of transportation to the "green city." These proposals for a functional town found their final formulation in the CIAM "Charte d'Athènes," which determined city building decisively up to the present day.

This new organization of the town brought forth a new misery, but this time in well-illuminated houses. The utopia of the garden city movement from Fourier to Howard—namely the reunification of nature and society—was taken to absurd heights. Isolated and cut off from his historical background, the inhabitant regarded nature as strange because it was only there as a picture, a panorama.

The division of life in accordance with the "three routines" (work, recreation, and domestic life) gave rise to sharply demarcated forms of existence. Taylorism, which ruled the factories, split every job into specialized tasks, which found unity only via the conveyor belt. This "successful" production method was the basis for splitting existence into separate spheres.

Architects recognized the conformity of the New Objectivity and sought to use it in the execution of their work. However, even these progressive archi-

tects elevated this conformity to an ideology instead
of standing up to it critically. One can trace back to
this the transfer of mechanized motion into the
sphere of the home as well as the anonymous collec-
tivity of the city.

Le Corbusier preached the "three eights" system:
eight hours of work, eight of recreation, and eight of
rest. The home took on the duty to "renew the vigor
of muscle, mind, and body used up by hard work."[49]
To that end, sunlight, pure air, cleanliness, and
greenery were to be brought in front of the window.
The kitchen became a laboratory where cooking and
baking no longer served the joy of eating but the
pure necessity of nutrition. The bedroom of Erwin
Piscator, by Marcel Breuer (1927–28),[50] and the Frankfurt kitchen, by Ernst May (1929), serve only to concentrate the mind and make the body fit for the
day's business.

The window's changed function was now clear.
Gurlit and Lucae had been disturbed by the light entering the room, but now light was to enter with full
intensity. The window still formed a dematerialized
membrane between inside and outside, but now, in
the harsh light and the sparkling cleanliness, there
was no longer any retreat from the world of work.
The concept of the private man had been irreversi-
bly changed. The window extending along the whole
length of the dwelling would remind him of work
and make the outside world permanently present.
The "troublesome window" became ubiquitous. Thus
was completed the secularization of those social utopias that, with the glasshouse, sought to project a
reconciliation between nature and society.

The Idea of the Winter Garden

There is an inherent wonderful fascination in being able, in the middle of winter, to open the window of a salon and feel a balmy spring breeze instead of the raw December or January air. It may be raining outside, or the snow may be falling in soft flakes from a black sky, but one opens the glass doors and finds oneself in an earthly paradise that makes fun of the wintry showers.

Princess Mathilde de Bonaparte, 1869

An Indoor Garden under an Artificial Sky

The winter garden arose from the old and often-repeated dream of setting up a Garden of Eden by artificial methods. Whereas the hothouse had served primarily only for the preservation and rearing of plants, the winter garden was conceived for social purposes and pleasure and for private contemplation. It represented an indoor garden separated by glass from the outdoor garden and forming a culmination of it. To this aspect the winter garden owes its departure from its function purely as a plant house. It was subject to the rules of the gardener's art. The indoor garden was to correspond to the aspect of a quasi-natural landscape; however, the plants were to be exotic. It was also governed by construction methods and by spatial forms. The widths and heights of the usual plant houses were no longer sufficient to call forth the impression of a landscape.

The early winter gardens, originating in the Baroque era, were orangeries on country estates. Besides serving as showplaces, they were a necessary ingredient in the life style of the nobility. Often situated at the end of an axis and executed in a showy style as a contrast to the mansion, they not only caught the eye but also served as places for banquets, theatrical productions, and festivals. Among the most splendid orangeries of the eighteenth century are those at Versailles, St. Petersburg, and Vienna.

A contemporary account of the Vienna building (fig. 7a) gives an idea of the function of the orangery in the life of the aristocracy. The palace gardener Nicolaus Joseph Jacquin described it as follows:

a magnificent arched orangery which is perhaps the largest in all Europe because in a continuous span it is 600 feet long, 35 1/2 feet wide, and 25 feet high. It would be hard to find an equal. . . . Emperor Josef ordered banqueting tables to be set up in the orangery as he had seen in the St. Petersburg winter garden during his tour. Flowers of all sea-

sons exhaled their fragrance here even in the most severe winter, standing on a magnificent table, all round which stood orange and lemon trees beautifully illuminated, while behind the table there were a play and a ball in progress among this winter assembly room full of blooms. . . . During the Congress of Vienna the princely guests on the evening of October 11, 1814 dined at two tables with 62 place settings. One saw nothing but the flowering trees and plants, between them statues and fourfold waterfall streaming over rocks, lit by 3,136 lights.[51]

A further development of the winter garden was completed at the start of the nineteenth century when plant rooms were combined with living accommodations. Now the orangery, previously used only for festive occasions, became a part of the daily life of the nobility and the middle class.

The landscape gardener Friedrich Ludwig von Sckell outlined the new "English garden" principle as follows: "Our present-day garden, although it for the most part is an artistic creation, no longer equals that of the former artistic garden layouts, in which all forms had to be arranged according to the strict laws of regularity. It is nature that serves as the model for the newer garden. Its diverse and innumerable forms, which adorn the beautiful Earth, now decorate our gardens as well, but without requiring the slightest constraint of a timid forgery."[52]

The enthusiastic acceptance of the English garden, even before 1800, was at the same time a new trend in a changed society. The orangery and the trimmed box bushes were rejected as a sign of the absolute orderliness that Sckell criticized in 1825: "The tree must conceal its organic nature so that art in the general nature of its abstract form could demonstrate its authority. It must surrender its beautiful independent life for a dull symmetry and its lightly suspended growth for an appearance of solidity, which the eye demands of stone walls."[53]

In unison with the introduction of the "English garden" there developed a new concept of the dwelling house. The rigidly fixed prestige building was forsaken, and preference was given to convenience and comfort. In this initiation of middle-class standards and in the life of the aristocracy one can perceive the first stage of withdrawal into privacy. The aristocracy's new attitude to the home expressed itself architecturally in a transformation from subordination and Palladian-Classical symmetry to the less constrained arrangement of the "Gothic, Moorish, and Oriental" styles.

These diverse style forms were only the architectural cloak covering the changed contents of the building. In the late-eighteenth-century reorganization of the living accommodations according to an artistically conceived architecture fitting in with the garden and the landscape, the living rooms were laid out on flat ground and were closely linked to the winter garden. The garden and the sky continued outward, apparently without limits, through its glass walls. Nature came right into the house.

The Contention between Gardener and Architect

Out of the incorporation of a winter garden into the private home or castle there arose a conflict of aesthetics. This conflict was rooted in the unprecedented problem of combining masonry architecture with a transparent glass-and-iron building—as it were, with a non-architectural form. So long as the winter garden (like the orangery or the corridors leading to it) consisted of solid walls and roofs, no difficulty arose in achieving architectural unity. According to the prevalent architectural conservatism, a plant house made of glass and iron, as a purpose-built structure, belonged to the garden and not to the mansion proper. Above all, iron—the new industrial building material—was used by architects only hesitatingly, and then mostly in forms that, like the Gothic, could be derived from masonry architecture. Only such progressive architects as Humphrey Repton, John Nash, and Karl Friedrich Schinkel, who had already used cast iron in domestic architecture, took to such forms. Repton, known as the champion of the "English garden," planned with S. P. Cockerell in 1806 a palatial Moorish-Gothic "villa" that included a long winter garden. In this he incorporated Gothic pointed arch windows made of cast iron to match the style of the main building (fig. 674). In this and in similar examples from the period ca. 1800 it is clear that architects could not yet be convinced without a struggle to display iron in its functional form. In the building of the winter gardens, the contrast between form and function (which worked to the disadvantage of plant cultivation) became clear. It

is understandable that the style-conscious architects were less troubled by this contrast than the gardeners.

J. C. Loudon, who as a gardener became aware very early of the advantages of iron in glasshouse construction, incorporated in the building of winter gardens a plan that was not only constructive but also aesthetically new. In his writings of ca. 1800 there is formulated for the first time in the history of building the principle that glass-and-iron structures possessed just as much of an aesthetic claim to beauty as masonry architecture. He even went a step further: in a call to battle against stylistic architecture, he proclaimed that beauty and function are of necessity bound together and mutually dependent. He said that the structural imperfection of existing forcing houses had been known for a long time. Was any building more objectionable to look at than those glass roofs that gave the impression of lean-to sheds? Although they covered something that could be described as a showplace of the greatest luxuriousness, did their poor external shape make them suitable only for the kitchen garden? Or should they be attached to the house, or put in the most attractive part of the estate? Many attempts were made to conceal the lean-to appearance of the conservatories with stone walls. Loudon considered the structure of these buildings to be poor. The more noble these architectural forms appeared, the more the plants suffered from lack of light. The condition of the plants that passed the winter months in such conservatories proved this. Could it be right that the architecture of a building should conflict with its use? To say that buildings could not be beautiful unless the architecture exhibited the Greek or the Gothic order was a wrong idea of the age.

The horticultural societies of London and Edinburgh, whose members were men of rank and influence but scientific amateurs, were the leaders in these developments in horticulture. "It may readily be supposed that the subject of artificial climates, which by enabling the horticulturist to exhibit spring and summer in the midst of winter, and to bring to perfection the delicious fruits and splendid flowers of the torrid zone in a temperate or cold country, — which gives man so proud a command over Nature, and renders a skilful practitioner in such requisition among the opulent, — would receive an early attention from these societies."[54]

Beginnings of a New Architectural Theory

Loudon, following the principle that the beauty of a building arises from the simplest forms corresponding to the function, pioneered an uncompromising view of iron-and-glass architecture as structural engineering art. For him a winter garden had beauty only if it had a transparent glass skin that ensured the entry of as much sunlight as possible without casting shadows all over the interior, and the use of iron for the load-bearing skeleton, which made possible filigree constructions hitherto unobtainable, had its own inherent requirements.[55] The first winter gardens, constructed in the simplest geometrical forms, were assembled from iron sash bars. Joined to the massive house, they were consciously added to it as the contrast which was to be created from the union of nature, landscape, and living space. The element of surprise with which the owner of the house encountered the light-filled winter garden was also to be based on the overall architectural form. The effect of the contrast was considered thoroughly. The architectural unity of house and winter garden was to come about not by assimilation but by a consciously composed difference. Loudon's 1817 plan for his country house with attached winter garden in Bayswater (fig. 141) is an example of this attitude. The same intention is clear in the design for the villa at Sezincote (fig. 433), in which Loudon demonstrated that with glass-and-iron architecture a union of the oriental style and the winter garden was possible. Loudon's radical attitude toward the form of winter gardens was unique in his time; not until after the middle of the century was it taken up again, by August von Voit for the winter garden built for the kings of Bavaria Maximilian II and Ludwig II (1854, 1867–1869). This winter garden was built like a crown on top of the castle roof. The classical order of the masonry architecture was set off to a marked degree with a transparent structure to give a contrast. In place of statues and cornices, the iron framework could be seen against the sky (figs. 400–402, 652–655).

Opposing this modern attitude, most builders and architects followed the traditional paths of winter-garden design when introducing the use of iron and glass. They could not solve the contradiction of massive architecture adjoining the transparent, and therefore they advocated a separation of the winter garden from the house. Sckell, in his classic 1825 book *Beitrag zur bildenden Gartenkunst* (Contribution to the Development of the Art of Gardening), advised not only a proper distance from the house but even concealment: "Such . . . enclosures must stand by themselves, one must encounter them unexpectedly and be surprised by them; thus they must be concealed by shrubbery."[56]

Sckell ascribed no inherent architectural significance to glass-and-iron buildings, but tried to raise their value through classical formal language: "I have also . . . tried to give the hothouse an architectural value (because this is so seldom the case for buildings of this sort), and have embellished both end portals or entrances with the Doric order in accordance with the purest proportions and rules of architecture and provided them with facades."[57] (See figs. 391–393.) The strict system of Classicism was indeed adapted to the designs of the earliest plant houses. Facades with large window openings could be well integrated into the masonry members. The principle of repetition, with the continuing use of the same building components, as was necessary in the building of hothouses, could be used in full here.

Although iron and glass could be accorded acceptance within the classically oriented ideal, the appearance of iron was shunned by those who followed the trend toward extolling untouched nature. This was at the peak of Rousseauism, which recognized nature as the only ordering principle and considered each technical expedient an interference. This attitude led to attempts to give the iron used in the load-bearing structures of winter gardens a form and an ornamentation originating in the plant kingdom. For example, columns in hothouses were stylized as bamboo stems, capitals as palm fronds, and brackets as tendrils and branches (fig. 71).

This advance freed the iron structure from classical models and eased its development into the elegant and graceful filigree form. In the extreme application of naturalism, the requirement of the subordination of technology led to the concealment of the structure and finally to its renunciation. The desire for a complete picture of the natural form could be realized only if glass and iron were not visible. Neumann expressed the following opinion of the aesthetic principle inherent in the construction of such buildings:

What aim shall the builder of a large glasshouse have in mind when it comes to the arrangement of tropical plants? None other than the imitation of the rich disorder of a primeval forest in which he obliterates all traces of artificiality with a lively artistic sense and preferably tries to hide the evidence that one is moving below a glass roof. In fact why should one not replace the geometrically regular lattice or trellis work of the window pulley adjusters by as faithful as possible an imitation of the forms of the tree and its branches, and let the light enter directly through the uneven interstices just as through the canopy of a natural for-

6
M. Neumann, design
for a winter garden
as a nature scene,
1842.

est? Capricious lianes entwined between these artificial branches and twigs complete the artistic deception. Here they can cover the bare metal frame with their foliage, there they form graceful festoons hanging from the slender branches of large trees. In the midst of carefully chosen lighting a stream must meander, populated with tropical fish, now murmuring its way between rocks, now spreading out placid and still into a wide stream bordered with sand and pebbles. . . . Within such a glasshouse the inner world would reign supreme, the outside world would create almost no impression. Therefore one could keep it out of sight behind a thick belt of shrubs, but taking care to keep the shrubbery screen far enough away from the house that it does not prevent light from reaching it. The approach to this tropical forest would very suitably be a rocky and stony valley, decorated with yuccas and other plants which even when exposed to our climate take on a tropical appearance. Nearer the glasshouse itself the approach must change into a formal tunnel with the entrance door merging into the background. Beyond this the sudden transition from a confined and a comparatively dark space into a wide and very well lit glasshouse would generate a very pleasant sensation. Similarly, the exit door of the glasshouse must lead into a tunnel, which could perhaps emerge in the form of a natural cavern extending as far as the shrub screen, but not out into the open before reaching it.[58]

In respect to the aesthetic qualities inherent in the glass-and-iron structures of the winter garden, Paxton was quite uncompromising, like his contemporary Loudon. He was convinced of the great effect of his architecture, and he wanted to avoid any conflict between his large conservatories and his clients' residences. He therefore pleaded for an absolute separation of large winter gardens from the living accommodations, not in order to hide his engineer-

ing work but in order to preserve its purity of line: "If temples or other erection are visible from the house, it is indispensable that they should harmonize with it. But there is one edifice, totally opposite to a residence, which requires more complete and decided isolation, and must be situated in a spot where its own influence can be felt. . . . This is the Conservatory, which should not be near the mansion. . . . the outline of a conservatory is as remote as possible from that of a mansion, and the quantity of glass it contains renders it strikingly peculiar."[59] Paxton's Great Conservatory at Chatsworth, built on these principles for the Duke of Devonshire's palm collections, was erected out of sight of the house in a clearing in a wood. The heating equipment was placed underground, and the chimney was hidden by the trees. (See figs. 222, 527, 528, and 532.)

The aesthetic conflict the builders of the plant houses discovered in the combination of glass-and-iron architecture with stylistic building is characteristic of the whole of the nineteenth century. The building briefs for railway stations, exhibition halls, and floras brought new solutions with the synthesis of engineered buildings and historicizing form, which appeared after 1850. The fields of the architect and the engineer more often appeared to be unified in the person of the builder.

In the following quotation from Gottfried Semper the outward architectural form of the Jardin d'Hiver in Paris (figs. 417–421, 660–664) becomes the object of an aesthetic theory in which the possibility of using iron as a structural material in monumental building is critically examined. Thereby enters the stipulation—which even progressive architects like Semper had to follow—of an effectively weightless iron construction:

The Winter Garden in Paris, 1849: Winter gardens are ages old. The Romans had already used them to beautify their extravagantly laid out dwellings and villas, and may even have been more advanced in technical respects, particularly with regard to the efficiency of the heating equipment and effective use of the orientation, from all that we read about it and even see in a few Roman remains; we have once again recently taken this matter up and have almost had to start from ABC. Without doubt they were indeed much superior to us in the architectural and artistic understanding of this matter, which as we must admit until now has been solved by us in the crudest and most primitive way in a kind of naked railway style. It will be a long time until iron, and in general metal which has just taken its place as a building material, will be controlled in such a completely technical way that it ought to find recognition and appreciation as an artistic element together with stone, bricks, and timber in the art of making beautiful buildings.

To me, not a single example of an artistically sufficient iron construction of monumental importance has yet presented itself. Only in various practical applications, such as wide span roofs, particularly for railway stations, has it made a satisfying impression. Wherever it is otherwise used it reminds one, often very forcefully, of cold and drafty railway platforms, and makes any cheerful and festive state of mind impossible. The new Library of Sainte-Geneviève in Paris is a noteworthy example of the above, a building that presents many points of interest and is to be looked on as the most important work of the late Republican Period but in which the architect, Mr. Labrouste, saw fit to incorporate an unfortunately visible iron roof truss and even to coat it with dark green paint, so that the comfortable seclusion that is necessary for serious study is absent from the library room, which also serves as a reading room and hardly satisfies anyone at all.

Should the failure of this attempt to give the iron construction an expression as serious architecture actually originate from our experience in the use of this material? Possibly so! — However, this much is certain, that iron is the best of all hard and strong metals to use as a construction material, in slender bars and to some extent as cable, because of the small surface area it presents in these forms. This escapes the eye all the more the more consummate the construction is, and hence the art of building, which achieves its effect on the mind through the eyes, ought not to meddle with this almost invisible material when it is a matter of mass effects and not merely of simple accessory items. The beautiful and artistic display of metal in rods should be used as trellis work in fences, as a graceful network, but never as supporting members of large masses, as struts and pillars for the building structure itself, as a fundamental feature of the motif.

One could rebuke the Romans and Greeks for not understanding how to use metal in buildings to show off its inherent nature, and could quote as an example the bronze beams in the Pantheon, in which the metal is used in forms for which other materials, wood and in all cases marble, are natural. In this context I not only defend the architects of the Pantheon, I even assert that they had found the only correct solution that was available in bringing the properties of the material into unity with beauty. Who has the right to maintain that the use of iron in load-bearing members, supports and pillars, is accomplished most advantageously in the form of iron bars? On the contrary, does not calculation and experience show that hollow metal members according to their length axis direction have far greater strength than solid members to resist horizontal loads as well as vertical, when the cross-section area is the same? Is it not moreover known that metal is most often processed in the form of sheet and any structural defects are very easily recognized when it is in this form, whereas when the defects are inside a solid bar they cannot be detected? Why do we not copy the Romans and build sheet-metal roofs? To be sure, this was done for a long while, chiefly in Russia, where very strong sheet-metal beams were used as invisible supports for wide-span plaster ceilings and vaults. But so far as I know no one has taken up this construction method architectonically. I believe that this must happen if art is to obtain any sympathy for iron. Iron in the form of sheet will always retain a characteristic appearance, so that for example the suspended ceiling made of sheet-iron beams will generate a quite different style from the wooden ceiling.

Metal, in addition to the above-mentioned light and graceful trellis work, can be used exposed in the form of sheets for beautiful artistic buildings. In this form it was also used in bygone days as a very costly cladding for walls, and for those doors on which the greatest demands were made in respect to security, dignity, and beauty. One will forgive me for this digression, from which I will return to the main subject of this communication, the winter garden. The brief for a winter garden often calls for the exclusive use of iron in bar or cable form. The proof of this is so plainly evident that I do not need to bring it in here. What left me disappointed with my visit to the Paris winter garden was not in any way the overlight framework of the glass canopy. Were it at the same time solid (which is not sufficiently the case), then on the contrary I would have nothing else to take exception with but that the rather meager decorative work appears superfluous and that one has the feeling that this framework was a fundamental motif in the architectural parts of the design, and should even play a more important part in the facade of the building. I was displeased in that the whole layout consists of nothing more than an enormous glass case with no particular shape and an uninteresting ground plan, that artistic effect has too little part in this creation, and that the light, never wholly absent, resources of plant nature were never exploited for their effect but in a too refined and unnatural way. One could say: But it is a winter garden! We want to see not columns and arched arcades, not statues and paintings, but trees and plants. In addition there is no shortage of vestibules, paintings in them, recesses, caryatids and groups, fountains, etc. But that is the fault in it, that all this is present, and that it is not

7a
Banquet in the oran-
gery at Vienna-
Schönbrunn. Litho-
graph, 1839.

7b
Library and winter
garden. Copper en-
graving, 1816.

7c
Winter garden and
country mansion.
Copper engraving,
1825.

so good as if there were less of all these things. There is no combined effect of art with nature; no unity of the members. The enormous glass case with its quite unclear extent absorbs everything else and makes it appear like a stunted object, just as the first organisms that developed to a higher state made the rest appear only as trial outlines.

A garden necessarily needs a house to which it can belong; this house alone makes it into a true garden. Not until there is a house is it a true garden. Without the house and without the continuation of its architectural layout extending right into the spirit of the garden, the garden is not really a garden but a tame wilderness, in one word an absurdity. From the house as focal point art spread out like rays over nature, and conversely nature should have a powerful reverse effect on art. These primary stipulations of this necessary relationship within an architectural design are absent from the Paris winter garden. This facade is subject to the criticism that the entrance halls are so subordinated to the rest, so cheerless, so poorly fitted out and lit, that one makes haste through their gloomy spaces to reach the large glass-covered hall, the front part of which is given over to concerts and balls and in which the gardener develops his modern hothouse skills to the full. No foreground, no loggia with a shimmering chiaroscuro prepares the way for the transition to the warmth of the forcing house and the exotic plants. It alone is all in all. . . . Before the exile of the House of Orléans there was a scheme afoot to alter the whole wide area of the National Palace into a single grandiose winter garden with transportable roofing so that the plants could be out in the open air in summer and be covered in winter. This would have been a true winter garden in my understanding of the term. Only as a magnificent accessory to an even more important major work and all the ramifications from it has a winter garden significance and artistic effect.[60]

The Private Winter Gardens

The Winter Gardens of the Nobility

The spread of private winter gardens after 1800 was made possible by the introduction of tropical and subtropical plants and by the development of the technical means, especially heating, glass manufacture, and iron production. Aside from its inherent luxury, the winter garden was the recognized sign of an exalted position in society. Because the building, the upkeep, and the heating were very expensive, the possession of a private winter garden was a privilege that at first was restricted to the nobility.

To collect and display rare and exotic plants became during the course of the nineteenth century a passion similar to that associated with the possession of a picture gallery. Large collections, of palms especially, became renowned and were much coveted. The purchase of such collections was often the rea-

son for the building of a winter garden. The palm house on the Pfaueninsel in Berlin (1832) built by King Friedrich Wilhelm III owed its existence to the purchase of the palm collection from the Frenchman Foulchiron. This collection of botanical exotica was considered the best in Europe. Alexander von Humboldt, when he was beneath the Pfaueninsel palms, considered himself transported to the primeval forests of the River Orinoco.[61] The passion for collecting reached a peak in the Duke of Nassau's hothouses at Biebrich (1846), whose stock of trees formed the basis of the Frankfurt Flora.

Though the palm garden embodied the romantic yearning for distant, unspoiled places, the possession of one, along with the corresponding riches, often led to almost unlimited prodigality. King Leopold II of Belgium had a whole town of glass and iron, including a church, filled with palms and other tropical plants (figs. 209–214, 504–518). Behind the return to Romanticism was concealed the flight of the nobility from the reality of its loss of political power and of the final dissolution of long-established family estates. With the change from family-based enterprises to the anonymity of twentieth-century monopoly capital, the era of the private winter garden came to an end. Social recognition was withdrawn from extravagance, which came to be frowned on as an offense against the spirit and purpose of the use of capital.

The early private winter gardens were direct extensions of the living quarters. They were usually joined to the open rooms of the house—the salon, the library, or the billiards room. In a design by Humphrey Repton from around the end of the century, the glass door of the library opened into a winter garden (fig. 7b). The cast-iron-and-glass conservatory of The Grange at Hampshire (fig. 8), built by Sir Charles Cockerell in 1825 on the basis of a design by Inigo Jones, had a direct connection to the dining room and to the ladies' salon. In the winter garden built onto the palace of the Crown Prince Albrecht in Berlin by Schinkel (1832), the doors of the bedroom, the dressing room, and the prince's study opened onto a glasshouse filled with orange trees (fig. 151).

This relationship with the house was reversed when the winter garden came to be associated with the summer residence; the winter garden became a major part of the architectural whole.

An early example of this reversal is the Indian Villa, built in 1806 by Repton at Sezincote (fig. 674). In the Villa Berg of 1845 (fig. 443), the living quarters contracted to a gardener's house. The Villa Berg, located in the hills outside Stuttgart, included water-

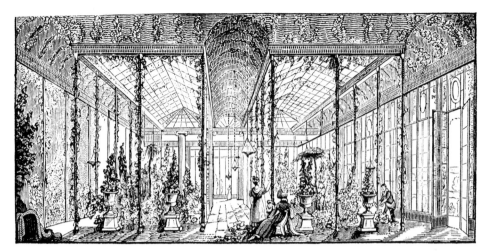

8
Charles Cockerell,
The Grange (Hampshire), 1825. Interior
view of the winter
garden. Woodcut.

falls, tropical birds, and statues. Nearby was the even more exotic "Moorish Villa" of the "Wilhelma," built in 1846 by Ludwig von Zanth (figs. 444–448, 689, 690). In a contemporary account this layout, with its mosquelike living quarters which opened at the side onto a long line of glasshouses, was associated with the fables of the Arabian Nights: "Open now are the magnificent greenhouses, whose high vaulted glass roofs made [the visitor] forget that he is not under the open sky. A southern flora unfolds with the most luxuriant profusion and an exciting display of color. . . . A corridor decorated with original arabesques led to a ballroom fitted out with extravagant ostentation, and to a room with glittering Turkish lances and shields, coats of armour, and Saracen sabres hanging on the walls."[62]

Technical developments of the 1830s allowed the nobility to build gigantic private winter gardens, some far larger than the railway stations of the time. "In England, this empire of immense power for which there are so to speak no obstacles, there is an abundance of glasshouses of the very greatest size. One can find all kinds of them there; several of them . . . have cost colossal sums of money and are objects of continuous high expenditure for the upkeep of plants which have come from all parts of the world."[63]

With its increasing size, the winter garden became a completely detached building. Many winter gardens were glazed from ground level right up to the apex. The most famous building of this kind was the Great Conservatory at Chatsworth, which Paxton built from 1836 to 1840 for the Duke of Devonshire (figs. 527, 528). With wondering admiration Neumann reported on the duke's passion for collecting:

On entering this conservatory the visitor is taken unawares by the glimpse of an immeasurable amount of exotic plants from all parts of the Earth. The scholarly and the amateur ask in astonishment about the tremendous fortune which must have been used in order to bring together here such a collection of vegetation of the most bold and rarest forms. Only the love of the equally charming and economically useful science of garden construction could have induced the Duke of Devonshire to build such a palace. The worthwhile use which he made of his wealth is disclosed at every step through his immeasurable park, which includes eighteen glasshouses in which the rarest plants of both the Americas and all regions of Asia thrive happily, and are separated only by a thin glass wall from the plants of our own climate.[64]

The total cost of the Great Conservatory was £33,000. (The cost of Paxton's Crystal Palace was £150,000. This sum was found to be too high for the British government to pay, and a joint stock company was launched to bear the cost.[65]) The vaulted roofs, consisting of countless glass panes in a ridge-and-furrow arrangement, were hailed as "cathedrals" of a new age.[66] The names of the plants filled a large catalog. Tropical birds and fish swam in ponds surrounded by extensive rock formations. When the queen visited Chatsworth, in 1843, the greenhouse was lit with 12,000 lamps. The royal party traveled through the building in open carriages. The winter garden lay in a wide expanse of parkland, in the center of which was a river channel near the house. On festive occasions a fountain built by Paxton was put into operation, which with the help of a steam engine reached a height of 88 meters. The fountain was first put into use for the visit of Czar Nicholas I in 1844.[67]

Not until 40 years later was the size of the Great Conservatory exceeded. Beginning in 1876, A. Balat, on the instructions of the King of Belgium, Leopold II, built in the middle of a glass landscape of connected glasshouses the large winter garden shown in figures 209–214, 504–506, and 509. This winter garden, adjoining which were theater halls, orangeries, banquet and assembly rooms, and a church, all made of glass and iron, became the center of royal life. However, the enormous cost of building this ideal town of glass and iron, and the annual upkeep cost of 600,000 francs, brought difficulties between the king and the parliament. While the king, almost obsessed by frenzied plant collecting and extravagant building ideas, prided himself on his "fairy world," new means had to be found to provide for its maintenance—for example, appropriation of the budget for the colonies. The last way out from the growing public criticism was the promise by the king to open his beloved world to the public as a "palace of the nation." The peak and the end of the development of the large private winter garden were reached at Laeken.

In the same period (1867–1869) and with similar late-Romantic intention, two winter gardens were built on the roof of the residence of King Ludwig II of Bavaria by August von Voit (figs. 652–655). Winfried Ranke gives a vivid account of one of these:

In the northwestern part of the Residenz, above the banquet hall, Ludwig II had a . . . winter garden erected from 1867 to 1869. The barrel-vaulted glass and iron roof had a much greater surface area than the existing one at the other end of the Residenz built by Maximilian II. The fitting-out was made more consistent with the exotic landscape. The scenery was again created by Effner, and represented a Kashmir valley. In the middle was a small lake, and on the west wall was a painted vista of the Himalaya Mountains. Apart from the original existing in the Residenz, King Ludwig II had perhaps received some ideas during a visit to the castle at Biebrich am Rhein in the summer of 1864. There the Duke of Nassau had a large winter garden and hothouse, the plant content of which was sold to the Frankfurt Palm Garden Company soon after Ludwig's visit. The royal head gardener Effner was dispatched to Muggendorf, Aschaffenburg, Lüttich, Brussels, Ghent, and Paris to choose plants for the new winter garden in order to set up a comparable display. In the previous year, Hofbauinspektor Mühlthaler had been to Ghent and Paris for the purpose of studying the heating equipment in the larger gardens and factories. From the photograph something is to be learned about the technical equipment, and the information that was obtained with much careful planning. The same thick lines running side by side are clearly evident in the water in front of the fisherman's hut. This is probably a device for producing wave motion on the artificial lake. The only entrance to the new winter garden was through the private apartments of Ludwig II. One could obtain entry only on the personal invitation or approval of the king, which indeed was not necessarily granted to all members of the royal family. Because the screening from public curiosity aroused the urge to see the exotic plants, it is no surprise that eminent men dressed themselves as gardener's assistants in order to look at the splendor of the winter garden forbidden to them. . . .

Schaufert is of the opinion that the arrangement of the details and the accessibility of the winter gardens of the Residenz rightly demonstrated the contrast between the characters of the father and the son. His account of Ludwig's artificial Far Eastern world runs thus: A painted landscape occupied the background of the space, representing a part of the Himalayas and giving an astonishing effect of perspective that lost none of its effect even when seen from close up. Giant palms and splendid tropical plants with their delicate feathery plumage or their broad leaves leaned over from all sides. A long trellised gangway through which the king stepped from his apartments directly into the garden was surrounded with superb climbing plants whose appearance was doubled by the use of mirrors. The right-hand path led to the king's favorite haunt, known as the grotto, which was part of a bold rising mass of rock. The winter garden itself was veiled in a dreamlike darkness; a small waterfall murmured through it in a melancholy way. The king would sit and dream here for hours on end. When the innumerable scattered bright lamps glowed in the flower beds and below shrubs and trees, hidden music sounded from behind the bushes, and the Swan Knight in the gilded boat passed him by in a half-dream, there was aroused in his mind the fantasy that more and ever more dangerously made him prisoner. From this grotto a small path led to the kiosk, quite a simple building, beyond which the path went via a tiny stone bridge to an attractive well, which was built like a fisherman's hut. Winding pathways encircled the lake and went through the grounds of a park-like layout and over a larger bridge back to the grotto entrance described above.

To the chosen few who could see the garden in its full splendor in 1883 belonged the Spanish Infanta Maria de la Paz and her young husband, Prince Ludwig Ferdinand of Bohemia. The young couple had been invited to dinner in the winter garden by the king, and the infanta described her impressions of the visit in a letter to her brother King Alphonso XII: "We went on a simple wooden bridge over a floodlit lake and saw between chestnut trees an Indian city in front of us. . . . We came to a blue silk tent covered with roses. In it was a chair supported by two carved elephants, and in front of it lay a lionskin. . . . The dinner had been laid out in an attached round pavilion behind a Moorish arch. The king showed me to the place of honor and gently rang a bell. Out of the hidden recess there immediately appeared a lackey, bowing deeply. This man was to be seen only when serving and removing the food, and when the king summoned him. From my seat I saw beyond the arch splendid plants lit by different-colored lights while invisible choirs sang softly. Suddenly a rainbow appeared. 'My God', I exclaimed involuntarily, 'this is indeed a dream. . . .'"

The following is a description from a popular magazine of the winter garden of Princess Mathilde de Bonaparte in Paris (fig. 9):

There is a wonderful attraction in being able to open the window and feel instead of the raw December or January air a mild balmy breath of spring. Out of doors it may be raining or snow flakes may be quietly falling from the sky, but one can indeed open the glass doors and find oneself in an earthly paradise that mocks the winter scene. One step leads us from Paris into a tropical garden. An enormous glasshouse that encloses Princess Mathilde's reception rooms like an external gallery brings about this miracle. The light buildings with their iron columns and transparent walls round off the main pavilion, which is laid out in an arc and extends on both sides along the wings, so that it is not possible to see both ends simultaneously and thus the extent of this transparent palace seems even greater. This light and attractive building has quite an individual character. It is not a hothouse in a simple meaning of the word, but much more is it a salon, or as one might say, a winter garden in which the richness of nature is found in lavish quantities combined with the splendor of luxury and art. Turkish, Persian, and Afghan carpets cover the whole floor, and delicate silk shoes never detect even the smallest grains of sand beneath their thin soles. One never sees soil in this garden except in places where giant plants climb out of their marble-surrounded borders and climb to reach the crystal roof, and seem to thrive as well as in natural soil. Here the palms extend their fantail foliage, here the Corypha palms allow light to shine through their broad green silk bands; there close by rises the bamboo, the ornament of a Japanese landscape, until its crown reaches the vault, while the tree ferns spread their decorative and sumptuous green all around. But we do not intend to turn this account into a botany course, nor do we wish to anticipate the rich fantasy of our readers.

Between these thick bushes a statue emerges here and there; here a Virgilian shepherd who is pulling a thorn from his foot, there a Florentine minstrel. Columns and pedestals carry candelabra and lamps; hanging from the ceiling are chandeliers entwined with lianes, their frosted glass looking like giant pearls. All conceivable forms of chairs offer themselves for rest and gossip: fauteuils, bergères, sofas, divans, poofs, tabourets, causeuses, dos-à-dos, and American berceuses of silk, velvet, Turkish leather, and embroidery, with the richest carving and gilding, all arranged in graceful arrangements. At the salon doors leading to the winter garden there are candelabra on pedestals with bases decorated with the letter M and the imperial crown. These candelabra carry lamps and double their light in the high mirror. But these are only weak strokes of the pen, written to describe this fairy tale. And this magnificent glasshouse is not merely a winter garden. It is at the same time a salon, a gallery, a cabinet for curiosities. Between the columns decorated with dragons which support the lamps there are placed against the walls beautiful pieces of furniture from China and Japan, tables made of rare woods, richly inlaid and decorated with the choicest works of art, and in particular the most splendid Venetian glasswork. . . .

If the glasshouse is a jewel by day, so much more is it by night, when the star-like lamps glitter between the green leaves; a truly magical aspect is then present. The French windows of the salon open, and on soft carpets rustle the trains of silk, velvet, lace, and gossamer, while gentlemen dressed in black and decorated with stars and orders look for a corner in which to chat. Small social circles gather in favorite places where they find their friends. Artist, poets,

9
Winter garden of Princess Mathilde de Bonaparte, Paris, ca. 1869. Wood engraving.

writers, and travelers coming at the very least from Timbuktu and Mesopotamia discuss art, try to uphold a paradox, tell of a discovery, or an anecdote, and describe a far-off land. Others look into stereoscopes, or observe from a distance the beautiful shoulders of the ladies, to which the lighting gives the luster of marble. One would imagine that the Decameron was transported from Florence to Paris. Suddenly there is a general hush; music has its say. One steps closer so as not to miss any of the concert. Leading performers consider themselves lucky to sing here, to play here. . . . Now and then, when the social gathering has reached its peak and the glitter and the diamonds are shining at their brightest, a more pallid bluish beam enters through the crystal roof of the glasshouse and spreads its gleaming drops on the broad leaves of the exotic plants—it is the Moon, which, uninvited but feeling at home in this forest, weaves its silvery threads into the Smyrna carpeting.[69]

The above accounts portray the winter garden as a place beyond the reach of ordinary mortals, an unreal world where amid rarities and rituals the nobility prepared to make its departure from the historical scene. As the nobility was relinquishing the acquisition of nature to the bourgeoisie (which, moreover, began to buy up the castles and mansions), it developed a sense of Romanticism for which the winter garden was the last refuge.

The Winter Gardens of the Upper Middle Class

With the accumulation of capital in the hands of the middle class in the form of machinery and factories, even before the middle of the nineteenth century, there was a financial basis for another social class to develop an expensive life style that would compete with the style of the nobility. In the forefront stood the major industrialists, who erected palatial residences with extensive parks and large winter gardens—often in close proximity to the nobles' estates. The major entrepreneurs of the time felt that they were the pioneers of industrial development, and they did not want to disown the source of their wealth—the factory. In fact, there was a desire to be able to see the factory through the windows of the residence. This proximity gave greenhouses a special attractiveness. A large winter garden could now be run economically in conjunction with the factory— the same steam that drove the machines in the factory could be piped to the winter garden for the maintenance of tropical plants. Examples of such greenhouses include the winter gardens of the Borsig industrial family in Berlin-Moabit, built in 1850 by Heinrich Strack (figs. 161, 162), the winter garden of the Ravenné family in Berlin (Hermann Ende and Wilhelm Böckmann, 1867), and the winter garden of the brewer J. Carl Jacobsen in Copenhagen (1876), designed by Jacobsen himself (fig. 306).

Theodore Fontane described a winter garden as an erotic place where the sultry atmosphere could liberate unexpected emotions in his 1882 novel *L'Adultera*. The palm house of this novel may have been inspired by the house of the Ravennés:

. . . they walked between long and low brick kilns, on the center path wide enough for only one person, to the place where this path led into the large palm house. A few steps further and they found themselves at the entrance to a tropical forest, while the vast glass buildings towered over them. Here stood the splendid examples of van der Straaten's collection: palms, dracaenas, tree ferns, and a winding staircase spiraled its way upward until it reached the dome and then went round this too, and further into one of the high galleries of the nave. En route no word was spoken. . . . Truly it was a fantastic foliage, formed of leafy crowns, almost closed over, and all over the girders and ribs of the vaults climbed orchids, filling the whole dome with their scent. One breathed blissfully but with difficulty in this dense foliage, and it was as if a hundred secrets spoke, and Melanie felt that this intoxicating scent was making her nervousness vanish. She recollected those external impressions, of natural things dependent on air and light, which require cool places in order to be fresh themselves. Crossing over a snowfield, in a frantic journey, and in biting east wind—there would her spirit be exalted and the bold courage of her soul return. But this soft relaxing air made her weak and relaxed, and the armor of her mind slackened, withdrew, and fell.[70]

The owners of such plant houses were considered plant lovers and great collectors. August Borsig prided himself on having one of the best plant collections in Europe in his glasshouse. J. Carl Jacobsen considered himself a patron of botanical gardens; the Large Palm House (1872–1874) and the Ny Carlsberg Glyptotek (1904) in Copenhagen were built with his cooperation. In America, General Paulding (a former mayor of New York) had a medium-size winter garden built on his estate Lyndhurst, near Tarrytown. This structure, which was bought with the estate by the railway magnate Jay Gould in 1880, had a glass tower and was connected to a row of company offices.

Besides these extensive winter gardens, numerous smaller plant houses were laid out in the cities by wealthy middle-class citizens. In the course of the nineteenth century the possession of one's own winter garden became widespread. Almost every story of a villa was provided with a veranda garden or a small conservatory. A competition announced at the 1872 Schinkel bicentenary called for the design of a villa for "a wealthy Berlin private person." The room specifications included "a small winter garden adjoining the lady's living rooms and having an entrance from them" and "a vaulted hall garden of

150 square meters which is to open eastward onto the curved terrace and westward . . . onto the Pfaueninsel."[71]

Two common elements in all these private winter gardens, whether belonging to the aristocracy or the middle class, were the peculiar shape and—corresponding to it—the private reception rooms. The patron's contemplation of the natural objects he had obtained was intimate, and he shared it only with friends.

The Public Winter Gardens

The building of this winter garden is a triumph of private industry.
—*Gottfried Semper, at the Jardin d'Hiver in Paris, 1849*

The luxury of southern vegetation, to which the nobility and the upper middle class had become accustomed, also held great attraction for city-dwellers in general. The early urban assembly places and centers of entertainment, especially dance halls, cafés, and restaurants, were the first reasons for the creation of public winter gardens. It was soon realized that the provision of glass-covered indoor gardens increased the attractiveness of the business.

These winter gardens for the citizenry were received with an enthusiasm that today is difficult to capture. The inhabitants of the cities felt a powerful urge to find a place in which they could gather freely and without restriction. The streets were exposed to the winter, and the covered streets—the arcades—were not heated, so people were not encouraged to linger and talk in cold weather. With the winter garden, rooms resembling open-air promenades allowed men and women to gather in the midst of a tropical plant display protected from unpleasant weather.

Loudon, who traveled all through Europe and visited the most famous gardens, gave an account of public life in a Berlin winter garden of 1840:

The air is heated by stoves, which are refueled from the rear. On the floor are orange trees, myrtles, and in containers are plants from New Holland. The bushes have stems mostly [3–5 feet] high, and around the stem is built a table, so that it seems as if the bush were growing out of the middle of the table. In addition there are everywhere plenty of movable tables and seats. In many of these gardens or orangeries there are also bands of musicians, sometimes also poetry is recited; on Sundays as occasion arises there are little plays. In the evenings the whole is brightly lit. In some of the winter gardens there are separate rooms with billiards tables for ladies who want to escape from the tobacco smoke; also rooms for card playing, and for small societies. If one visits these gardens in the early morning one finds there

gentlemen reading the newspapers, drinking chocolate, and discussing politics. After 3 o'clock one sees ladies and gentlemen and people of every sort sitting among the trees, conversing, smoking, with punch, grog, coffee, beer, or wine in front of them. . . . In the evening when the theatre is letting out there appear many well-dressed people of both sexes who visit these gardens before their journey home, to enjoy the beauty of the plant kingdom splendidly illuminated with artificial lighting and to talk a little about the play and the players. . . .[72]

The first large public winter garden originated between 1842 and 1846 in Regent's Park in London, founded by the Royal Botanic Society. The queen herself was the patron, and ladies of the wealthy classes were recruited as members. The three-story building, made entirely of glass and iron and illuminated by gaslight, served for evening occasions, large flower shows, social gatherings, and banquets. (See figs. 331–334 and 606.)

The Jardin d'Hiver (figs. 417–421, 660–664), opened in 1848 on the Champs-Elysées in Paris, was an important step in the development of such buildings. The innovations consisted of the increased overall dimensions and the multiplicity of the entertainments offered. The Jardin d'Hiver was a continuous glass hall that took in the ridges of the buildings on the Champs-Elysées, so that the boulevard continued under the glass roof.

Whereas the Regent's Park winter garden was reserved for an "educated" public, the Jardin d'Hiver was opened as an amusement establishment. On holidays, 7,000–8,000 people could be found there. This great number was a prerequisite for the economic operation of a business specializing in mass entertainment. The large amount of capital required for the building and the business could not be financed from private sources, but only via a joint stock company, as mentioned above.

The Floras

The Jardin d'Hiver became the prototype for a series of winter gardens that was created in Germany, especially from the 1860s. These "floras" enjoyed great popularity. They were funded by share capital, and like the Jardin d'Hiver they were a major technical advance. In contrast with the Parisian prototype, the glass vault of the plant hall was no longer directly connected to the restaurant and the assembly rooms. That arrangement had not taken account of the difference in climatic conditions between the rooms, and the damp tropical air had proved particularly damaging to adjoining assembly rooms. In the flora these were put in a separate multistory building and arranged so that they either faced the end of the plant hall or surrounded its sides. The large, glazed arched portals between the two parts of the building complex were eye-catching.

The multistory arrangement of the assembly rooms around a large glass hall had its counterpart in the railway station buildings of the second half of the century. The use of extensive and massive building units with historicizing forms of masonry architecture met the restorative trend of that time, which no longer made engineered glass-and-iron structures play a major part in creating the impression of space but concealed them behind "prestige architecture." Hence an important aspect of the existing winter gardens went missing. The direct connection between park and indoor garden was interrupted by massive stonework elements such as walls and battlements. The visitor entered via an imposing staircase; by following the axis of the building he then encountered, to his surprise, a mighty glass-and-iron hall filled with large palm trees.

The floras, which were built first in Cologne, then in Frankfurt, and finally in Berlin, were true amusement centers for the broad populace. The combination of recreation facilities made them popular for family excursions. However, the floras also offered, to those who were interested, the chance to increase their botanical knowledge. The promenade through the plants was simultaneously a "path of learning." The tropical forest of the flora was conceived not only as a "viridantia" (pleasure garden) but also as a "hortus" (botanical garden), and it provided for the visitor a universe of natural objects and sensual pleasures. In an 1869 description of the Frankfurt palm garden the naive enthusiasm that characterized the early days of the floras can indeed be detected:

The palm garden beneath the protective roof offers social events throughout the whole year. The far-off continents can be experienced in the hothouses. One sees the majesty of exotic growth and feels the sultry damp air of the primeval forest, the dry climate of the desert where cacti flourish; one smells the scent of the plants and the mould of the soil, and when one has got accustomed to the constant splashing of the water one can almost hear the vegetation breathing. An invisible breeze blows through the house under the glass roof, where the footsteps on the sandy paths and the low voices of the visitors combine with the intense stillness of the natural world. . . .[73]

Hotels and Spas

At the same time as the floras, in the middle of the nineteenth century, there originated the winter garden that also formed the central foyer of a luxury hotel. These indoor gardens were surrounded by restaurants and function rooms from which archways opened onto the garden.

Mostly situated close to the main railway stations, these halls attracted travelers from beyond the city. In the Berlin Central Hotel, built by Hermann von der Hude and Julius Hennicke in 1880–81, the winter garden and the surrounding rooms could accommodate 3,000 people.

Variations on this kind of winter garden formed the halls of some hospitals and spa buildings, as at the Leeds General Hospital (1868); the Kurtheater Göggingen, near Augsburg (Jean Keller, 1887); and the "Kuretablissement" of the orthopedist Friedrich von Hessing.

Art Collections, Aviaries, and Aquariums

Attempts to combine natural beauty with artificial beauty have been practiced from time immemorial in large garden layouts. In the winter gardens this unity was brought about in a concentrated way. Exotic plants were combined with objets d'art, and each reinforced the effect of the other. The visitor who lost himself in the contemplation of art and became exhausted could recuperate under the leafy canopy. Collection and recreation supplemented each other. Among the many winter gardens in which this unity was sought, the "Palace" of John Kibble in Glasgow (1872) is outstanding. White marble statues based on the ancient myths were displayed along gravel paths in the midst of tropical flora. The domed building (figs. 255–261, 557–563), originally lit by gas lamps, also served for concerts.

The continuation of this idea was the spatial union of museum and palm garden. The Ny Carlsberg Glyptotek in Copenhagen (figs. 307, 593–594), built by Vilhelm Dahlerup in 1904, is a late example. Beneath a central dome there was a palm garden with fountains, marble benches, and statues; the garden was surrounded by the art collection. The union of the two worlds was not as immediate as in the Kibble Palace, as the exhibition rooms were screened off by glass partitions for climatic reasons.

Another type of winter garden much in favor in the nineteenth century combined the plant and animal kingdoms. Even the early winter gardens contained butterflies, songbirds, and fish. The Glass Menagerie built by Henry Phillips in London (1830–31) and Paxton's Great Conservatory at Chatsworth held caged beasts and birds. The principle of providing the fauna with their natural surroundings, as in zoological gardens, was followed.

Aquariums and aviaries in winter gardens provided special points of interest. Arranged in accordance with the geography of the globe, fishes, reptiles, and birds were presented in habitats which included natural and painted scenery. The Unter den Linden aquarium in Berlin (figs. 169–174), painstakingly designed in 1869 with the collaboration of Edmund Brehm, took the visitor step by step from the world of birds to grottoes displaying amphibians and fishes.

People's Palaces of Glass and Iron

With the development of exhibition halls from 1850 on, winter gardens expanded to hitherto unknown dimensions. Even during the construction of his great exhibition building in Hyde Park, Paxton had the intention of changing it after the exhibition into a gigantic public winter garden. In his pamphlet "What Is to Become of the Crystal Palace?" (1851) he proposed that the structure be used to house an indoor landscape, which could be opened to Hyde Park in the summer by removing the lower part of the glass sides. "Here would be supplied the climate of southern Italy, where multitudes might ride, walk or recline amidst groves of fragrant trees, and here they might leisurely examine the worlds of Nature and Art, regardless of the biting east winds or the drifting snow. . . ."[74] Here was the outline of the plan to make the countryside available over the whole year in the middle of the city with the help of modern industrial methods. Fourier's utopia, with its glass-covered walks, now appeared to be technically feasible.

With the removal of the Crystal Palace to Sydenham in 1852–1854, Paxton put his proposal into effect. The center of the structure, including the sides of the nave and the transepts, became a winter garden. Plants, trees, and birds from all parts of the Earth were brought in, and to this panorama an art collection and a permanent display and market of manufactured goods were added. The whole was incorporated as a joint stock company, The Crystal Palace Company, which stated its intention in its prospectus, dated May 17, 1852: "Refined recreation, calculated to elevate the intellect, to instruct the mind and to improve the heart, will welcome the millions who have now no other incentives to pleasure but such as the gin-palace, the dancing saloon and the ale-house afford them."[75] The company nominated Paxton as director of the winter gardens, the park, and the hothouses. The Sydenham Crystal Palace, in its massive scale, constituted the first glass-covered urban "forum" combining trade, culture, and social contact.

The irresistible belief in progress, coupled with technical advances, led to proposals for public winter gardens of truly giant dimensions, even by present-day standards. As early as 1855, Paxton published a scheme for a "Great Victorian Way" (fig. 364), a glass-covered boulevard 9.6 miles long, 72 feet wide,

and 108 feet high. Covering the trees, it was to surround London like a ring and to serve as both a promenade and a route for vehicular traffic. In 1861 Paxton proposed for Saint-Cloud in Paris a domed Crystal Palace approximately 2,000 feet long and made entirely of glass and iron (fig. 367). The most realistic of all these projects was the Palace of the People designed for Muswell Hill in London by Owen Jones in 1859 (figs. 366, 633, 634). Jones, a colleague of Paxton in the building of the Crystal Palace, combined in this project all the features of the popular winter gardens. The Palace was to be funded by the share capital of a railway company. A million visitors per year were to be brought in by train. Joined to the winter garden, with its "hanging gardens," there was to be a 10,000-seat concert hall. Also adjoining the winter garden would be picture galleries, museums, entertainment centers, reading rooms, and other attractions, all arranged on multiple stories of glass and iron. The proposed "people's cathedral" was described in the *Illustrated London News* as follows: The railway passenger on arriving would be spared all the inconvenience and annoyance of the rising terrain, because he would only have to walk 6 yards from the station into the Palace. All visitors coming by carriage or on foot were to be protected from the weather. The Palace would be in use by day and night in winter and summer, because the concert hall would be easily accessible and brightly lit. Concerts and other events could be held here throughout the whole year. The extensive winter garden below the dome—joined to the concert hall—was to be a wonderful place for people to congregate, and it would also serve as the waiting room for the railway station. The Palace could provide other attractions: the park and the gardens, archery, cricket, the moving machines that were such a great attraction in Hyde Park in 1851, a fine arts section, a gallery of English history picture galleries, a natural history collection, lectures illustrated by experiments, first-class evening concerts, and promenades in the winter garden.[76]

Conceptually, the winter garden—originally conceived as a pleasure spot—became after the Industrial Revolution of the nineteenth century a social utopia where the working class was to discover its educational and recreational paradise. The winter garden in its highest expression was consequently a forerunner of the twentieth-century entertainment industry.

The decline of the large winter garden toward the end of the nineteenth century is partly to be ascribed to the means that made it possible: The railroads, which enabled the masses to visit winter gardens, also brought the rise of tourism. The southern landscape could be sold on the spot.

The Botanical Collections

The prerequisite for the development of technology and science in the industrial age was the practical exploitation of nature in such a way that natural processes could be understood and controlled and could be called upon whenever needed. The orientation of society toward nature can be read in the history of gardening. The garden was a realm in which control over nature could be exercised in frivolous, naive, and unmethodical ways. The botanical gardens of the period before the nineteenth century were scenes of a systematic comprehension of the plant kingdom, but the gardens of the nobility and the early middle class of the pre-industrial age showed a different attitude toward nature. The large Baroque garden and the "English garden" were clearly not intended for practical utility. The emphasis was on control over nature, and this was demonstrated in a symbolic way by the power and control over soil and human effort. One important aspect was the unproductive character of nature, which was emphasized by the trimmed hedges of the Baroque, the lawns and groves of the English garden, and the pasturing of wool-producing sheep.

As the nobility lost power, the Romantic trend increased the desire to return the garden to nature through non-interference and calculated wildness. This was the time of "architecture ensevélie," partly collapsed ruins, fish ponds with difficult access, pleasant river bends, and natural paths. The landscape garden goes back to the start of the eighteenth century and is associated with the name of William Kent.

In these manifestations of aristocratic and middle-class garden ideals there was careful control of the mise en scène of nature as a painting. One important aspect of the English garden was the reproduction of Italian paintings or Chinese gardens, pioneered in England by the architect William Chambers. "Soyez peintre!" was the call—set out plants, the building material of nature, according to the principles of the arts. However, nature, placed in a historical context, seemed "merely natural."

"The land of illusion is not only a fantastic microcosm. It is also the sum of experiences and the result of investigations into the most varied realms. . . . It is a plant garden and a zoological garden, a center of irrigation technology and a museum of mineral-

ogy. . . . an open-air museum is a monument to different people of all times. A natural history, a history of civilization, and a practical technology participate in the blossoming of these gardens and evolve into a new encyclopedia. This implies studies, research, discovery, and the search for documents and rare items. Botany and archaeology are developed on the same plan and in the same design."[77]

The gardens of middle-class people, which were mostly on a small scale at first, reflected the trend toward collecting, cataloging, and classifying. There was also, however, a practical side: How could knowledge of nature learned from gardening be put to practical purposes?

Voltaire's ideas about the garden are revealed in his letter of August 7, 1772, to William Chambers: "I have everything in my garden, parterres, little ponds, regular paths, very irregular bushes, . . . grapevines, pruned and wild fruit trees. . . ."[78]

The first botanical gardens were herb gardens, and most of those existing today got their start in this way or as kitchen gardens. The botanical garden goes back into antiquity (Theophrastos, 370 B.C.), but not until the fourteenth century did it reappear in greater numbers (Salerno, 1310; Venice, 1333). It spread in the sixteenth century with the founding of universities throughout Europe (Padua, 1533; Pisa, 1544; Bologna, 1568; Leyden, 1577; Paris, 1597). In Holland and Britain the cultivation of tropical plants from the West Indies was pursued with special vigor. The oldest botanical gardens in Britain are those at Hampton Court, Oxford, Kew, and Edinburgh. Some of the collectors began without primarily scientific aims;[79] their descriptions were not methodical and did not show the relationships among the plants.

The need to understand the outward forms of plants led at the end of the sixteenth century and in the seventeenth century to systematic investigations that bore out the intuition that in the plant kingdom there were interrelated groups (Otto Brunfels, Caspar Bauhin). Andrea Caesalpinus, in Italy in 1583, tried "by strict differentiation based on previously determined features" to classify plants *a priori* into definite groups, while German botanists set out to classify them on the basis of similarities rather than differences.[80] This disagreement between looking at nature in terms of dimly perceived kinships and in terms of *a priori* classifications determined the path of botanical research until 1736, when Carolus Linnaeus developed a "natural" system of classification that could not have been arrived at solely through the *a priori* approach. In Linnaeus's opinion, the laws could not yet be stated and there was a need for further research to determine the structure of the natural sys-

10
Tropical plants in
palm house at Kew.
Copper engraving,
1856.

tem. We must thank him and Bernard de Jussieu
(1759) for the first compilation of natural families on
the basis of general structural forms. (However, Linnaeus did not clearly recognize the features that
were to become the basis of classification, and he
advocated the fixity of species.[81]) The eighteenth-century theoretical botanists Antoine Laurent de Jussieu,
Auguste Pyrame de Candolle, Stephan Endlicher, and
John Lindley broke up the natural relationships
among plants and created new classes, which however were too narrowly defined. A great advance out
of this dilemma of systematization came with the
start of morphological investigations in zoology and
botany, which were pushed to the forefront in
France by Etienne Geoffroy Saint-Hilaire and Baron
Georges Curvier (1830) and in Germany by Johann
Wolfgang von Goethe and Alexander von Humboldt.

The progressive, modern view of nature in the
middle-class era expressed itself in Humboldt's new,
cosmology-oriented explanation of botany, which
was influenced heavily by German idealistic
philosophy:

*The systematically arranged lists of all organic forms, which
prior to this time were designated with the all-too-splendid
names of nature-systems, represent a wonderful linkage to
inherent relationships between similarity of form (structure),
to ways of looking at gradual development (evolution) in
leaf and calyx, in colorful flowers and fruits, but do not
represent a link to spatial or geographical grouping, i.e. to
zones of the Earth, to height above sea level, to temperature
effects which the whole surface of the planet exhibits. But*

*the highest aim of the physical description of the Earth
is . . . the recognition of unity in diversity, the investigation
of mutually reacting factors, and the inherent interrelation-
ships between earthly phenomena. Wherever individual peculiarity is mentioned, it is introduced only to bring the
laws of organic arrangement into harmony with that of geographical division.[82]*

When Darwin made it possible to interpret the origin of plant species as a historical process, botany
was joined with materialistic social theory.

In addition to its recreational aspect, the botanical
garden was the scene of the practical realization of
the above-discussed approach. By the start of the
eighteenth century, extensive parks had been created
out of the nuclei of medicinal gardens by William
Chambers at Kew (1760) and by Lancelot Brown at
Syon House (1767–1773). As an outcome of the systematization of nature through botanical research, the
many and varied plants were now displayed in a
way intended to suit both scientific and aesthetic
principles.

This interaction of theory and practice accompanied the growth of botanical collections from the
seventeenth century until modern times. The botanical institutions that had begun as medicinal gardens,
agricultural institutes, and colonial research establishments began to collaborate. In the Old Botanical
Garden in Berlin-Schöneberg, the Elector's "hop garden" was converted into a garden for vegetables and
"noble" fruit, then into an "apothecary garden" su-
pervised by the Academy of Sciences. Later, it served
as a "vegetable garden" for botany, theoretical physics, and medicine. In 1801 the garden was enlarged
for the cultivation of plants—especially dyestuff
plants, which were important in manufacturing. In
1809 the garden became affiliated with the university.
A geographical plant collection was added in 1879,
and a botanical center for the colonies in 1891.[83]

In this way botanical gardens grew very large,
thus giving work to a great number of plant specialists. In the end the high maintenance costs could
only be borne by the state. After about 1840 all the
large botanical gardens in Europe were under state
control. The collections that had been previously
spread across a whole country were gathered together into one place and made available to the general public.

During the seventeenth century, small collections
had been started up everywhere by lovers of the art
of gardening. In the "cabinet d'amateur" the layout
of a collection in conjunction with a modern concept
of the garden was a matter of painstaking deliberation. The reading of travelers' reports, philosophical
tracts, and literature on the art of gardening was the

prelude to the introduction of scientific research and to new experiments in the realm of botany. A voluminous correspondence evolved; plans and seeds were sent hither and thither. With the extension of the botanical system and the introduction of a great number of tropical plants, the more naive attempts at research and collection of scientific data and material were eliminated after 1800. Now gardens obtained their new plants through the spread of colonialism. Plants were cultivated in large greenhouses built especially for the purpose, and at the same time they were examined for potential economic use. The hothouses of the botanical gardens were improved to suit the aim of combining exhibition with systematic research.

Because the vitality of the plants in the greenhouses of these gardens was of primary importance, the structural and spatial form was more strongly oriented toward this purpose than in winter gardens. Nevertheless, the exhibition of nature was important too. Routes for visitors were devised with great care to facilitate viewing from the most favorable points and to guide the visitor step by step through the various species, families, and groups.

Because the various plants required special climatic conditions, different forms of halls developed—from the narrow hothouse to the spacious dome. The connection of these various compartments or houses to form a visual and architectural whole called forth a special form of enclosure that differed from the "cultivation house" and the winter garden in that the plants occupied the space and the people had to immerse themselves as in a forest, whereas in the winter garden the plants were crowded into restricted areas and the space was chiefly at the disposal of the viewers.

The form of the botanical greenhouse originated historically from the addition of individual greenhouses to a single building complex. As buildings constructed for particular plant species and their climates were assembled into a spatial unity, a symmetrical layout was established.

August von Voit, the architect and builder of the Glass Palace and the botanical glasshouse in Munich, described the principle of differential design for the display of plants as follows:

The primary requirement of the greenhouse . . . was that its volume, ground plan, cross-section, and external appearance be based on the appearance of the plants inside. This arranging was accomplished in various ways and was adapted to the size and the structure of the plants, and can therefore be bush-shaped, so that the tops of the plants form a globe;

11
Carl Ludwig Willdenow making a plant identification in the botanical gardens at Berlin-Schöneberg. Copper engraving by J. F. Leopold, 1810–11.

sloping on one side, so that the tops of the plants are aligned in a sloping plane;

sloping on two sides, so that the tops of the plants form two intersecting planes having equal slopes.

With these arrangements, the roof of the plant house obtains either a hemispherical shape, a lean-to shape, or a ridge shape, depending on whether proximity of the external surface of the glasshouse to the crowns of the trees is considered necessary for the growth of same. There is also a saving of space, so that no superfluous amounts of air have to be heated and the smallest possible glazed surface is obtained.[54]

Form and construction were not the only subjects of greenhouse research; there were equally great scientific and technical problems having to do with heating, ventilation, light and shade, and humidity. Behind the scenes, the glasshouse was a complex apparatus—the product of hundreds of experiments made by gardeners, botanists, other natural scientists, and engineers.

The botanical gardens have maintained their right to continued existence through their scientific and pedagogic value. Nineteenth-century examples survive in Belfast, Berlin, Brussels, Copenhagen, Dublin, Edinburgh, Florence, Leningrad, Lyon, Paris, Sheffield, and Vienna. The winter gardens, however, born out of an illusion of nature, were sacrificed to changing ideas and social conditions.

3   The Glasshouse as Building Type

Beginnings in Wood, Masonry, and Glass

The development of the greenhouse in central and northern Europe owed much to the predilection of the nobility and the wealthy bourgeoisie for the cultivation of Mediterranean, subtropical, and tropical plants, particularly citrus trees and palms. Orange houses that could be dismantled in summer and reassembled in winter[85] had been used in Germany since the middle of the sixteenth century. The trees (planted in the soil, not in pots) were covered by a kind of shed made of boards (fig. 92a). Here already is the basic concept of the winter garden as a space not only for plants but also for social enjoyment.

Builders soon sought to reduce the cost of assembly and disassembly by using fewer removable parts. The plants were surrounded by three permanent walls, and only the south wall and the roof were made movable (fig. 92c). Nevertheless, the structures remained technically imperfect. Gaps and joints had to be sealed after assembly, and satisfactory heating was not possible because the stove had to be portable.

The "permanent orangery" originated when the plants rather than their cover were made the movable element. In the Baroque garden, trees were planted in tubs or boxes.[86] The temporary orangery was replaced by the orangery proper: an elongated building with the south-facing front made of glass panes. The peak of the development of this type of orangery occurred between 1700 and 1730. Pains were taken to build the walls and the roof so that they would conserve heat, and iron stoves were installed.

The "glasshouse" came into prominence around 1700, alongside the masonry-walled orangery, and in the course of the eighteenth century it too evolved into an elongated building. In contrast to the orangery, the glasshouse was from the beginning a purpose-built structure; it was not subject to the demands of "high architecture."[87] Its supporting structure or space frame consisted chiefly of wooden planks. Its two initial forms were the glass-covered dung bed or small forcing house (fig. 12), used in Holland from 1700, and the "portable orangery."

Critical factors in the success of the glasshouse were the advances made in glass manufacturing and in heating. The botanical gardens in Pisa (1590), in Leyden (1599), and in Altdorf (1635) were not glasshouses in the present sense of the word; they were glazed only in small areas, and mostly with spun-disk panes. After 1700, glassmaking was improved and glass became cheaper. Besides glassblowing, the pouring process was known by then.[88] The basic glasshouse of about 1720 had walls at the sides and the back, while the south face and the lean-to or ridge roof were glazed. The heating—usually through ducts by stoves accessible from the outside—required further development; leaks could injure the plants, and much of the heat was lost. Not until the heating problem was solved could the structure be glazed completely. After 1750, with the establishment of the technological bases for more extensive glazing and better heating, glasshouses spread throughout Europe.

As the Baroque garden gave way to the English garden, exotic African and West Indian plants were introduced. The palm "became the love of a society weary of Europe."[89] The interest of the nobility and the upper middle class in tropical plants was widened further by the increase in botanical studies. Systematic research into the flora of the tropics began. Expeditions brought back shiploads of palms and ferns. The palm collection, once an expression of culture and wealth, became a part of the middle-class scene.

The hitherto low and narrow glasshouse now changed into a spacious conservatory. "The winter garden was now to be a landscape . . . and indeed a tropical one full of secrets. The winding path also made its debut in the plant house."[90] Shrubs and trees were assembled in groups, and grottoes, watercourses, and springs added to the illusion of nature.

The metamorphosis of the glasshouse into an indoor garden with a tropical climate was accompanied by a further increase in the size of the structure around 1880. "The care and upkeep of tropical plants and tree ferns, which was pursued with gusto since the beginning of the nineteenth century, immediately required halls of great spans and considerable heights in order to permit unhindered growth of the plants."[91] The new technological means which the Industrial Revolution made available enabled designers to transfer the spaciousness and the fullness of light of natural landscapes to greenhouses. In addition to the great improvement and cost reduction in glass manufacture and the replacement of stoves by central heating, these means included the use of iron as a building material in the place of wood and stone.

Materials

Iron

The transformation of the wooden space frame into an iron load-bearing structure was a logical one. The humid heat that was necessary to maintain tropical plants often destroyed wood in a short time; for example, the wooden palm houses in the Old Botanical Garden in Berlin had to be demolished after nine years because of rot.[92] Wooden structures were better suited to "coldhouses" and "temperate houses."

Iron was better suited than wood to the building of filigree structures that would let in large amounts of light. Iron also offered the possibility of building wide-span structures of this kind without having structural members projecting into the interior space. In contrast to wood construction, it was possible by using iron to make a glass dome supported entirely by curved sash bars, so that the sun's rays would always incident at some part of the glass surface. With the development of cast iron and rolling-mill techniques and the reduction in the cost of iron manufacture, these iron buildings became competitive in price with wood from the 1830s on—provided that one included the cost of care and maintenance—and could even be superior in this respect.

One disadvantage of iron glasshouses was the condensation caused by iron's high thermal conductivity. Attempts were made to avoid this disadvantage by cladding the sash bars with wood, providing drainage channels for the condensation, and double glaz-

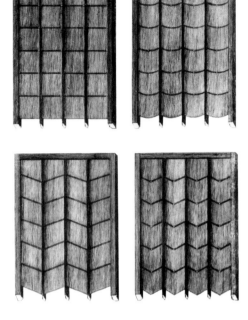

12
Early designs for forcing houses.

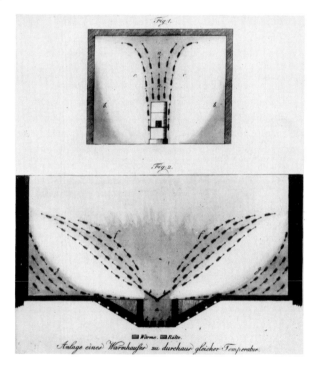

ing. The weighing of iron versus wooden sash bars and beams was pursued with passion in the technical world of glasshouse building until beyond the middle of the nineteenth century. Paxton and others were in favor of wood,[93] but Loudon forcefully emphasized the advantages of iron.[94] Iron soon came to be used almost exclusively in the major constructions.[95]

As Loudon noted in his *Encyclopaedia of Gardening*, eighteenth-century orangery construction paid too much attention to the architecture and too little to the plants. "Loudon was of the opinion that the form was only understandable if one realized the fact that these buildings had been built for promenading and banqueting."[96] The glasshouse, on the other hand, had to be in tune with plant cultivation, and hence was equivalent to a purpose-built construction for which not architectural prestige but the proper functioning of the artificial climate was the pressing need. Hence, the builders of the early greenhouses were not fettered by architectural concepts when they laid down the basic structural and spatial designs that became mandatory for glasshouse buildings during the course of the nineteenth century.

Glass

The physical history of architecture shows that throughout all centuries it conducted an untiring fight on the side of light versus the obstacle imposed by the law of gravity.
—Le Corbusier

In the Gothic style, glass attained importance as a space-enclosing material; however, it remained a relatively little-used material, seen mostly in churches. Not until the fifteenth and sixteenth centuries, in Holland, did the campaign begin to increase the window area in masonry walls. This movement is to be attributed mainly to the secular intentions of the increasingly wealthy middle class and the aristocracy in search of luxury. "More glass than wall" was the phrase that determined the designs of the external walls at Bramhall Hall and Hardwick Hall.

The development of iron structures in the nineteenth century, principally in glasshouse building, was closely linked to the industrialized methods of making glass. The concurrence of these two materials brought to the fore a new capacity for enclosing space, an architectural style that was both weightless and transparent. This style made great use of the inherent properties of glass and iron. The specifications for the beams and columns were met by iron in the form of standard structural elements. Between them there stretched a glazed area divided only by sash bars. Out of the early glasshouse constructions

there arose a glass-and-iron architecture which, at least at its outset, showed itself to be untrammeled by academic and stylistic assumptions. This development reached its peak in the Crystal Palace. Lothar Bucher's description, which he contributed at the opening ceremony of the Great Exhibition of the Industry of All Nations on May 1, 1851, conveys an impression of the gracefulness of the structure:

We see a delicate network of symmetrical lines but having no visible support created in order to obtain an aspect not related to the separation of the same from the eye, nor to the actual size of its meshes. The side walls are too far apart for them to be taken in at one glance, and instead of being confronted with a facing wall the eye projects on to an endless perspective which disappears into a blue haze. We do not know whether the fabric is suspended hundreds or thousands of feet above us, whether the roof is flat or built up from a number of small parallel roofs; for it casts no shadow at all, which would otherwise help the mind to comprehend the message from the optic nerve. If we let our gaze slowly descend again it meets the discontinuous blue-painted girders, first in the wide intervening spaces, now advancing even closer, then interrupted by a shining strip of light, finally merging into a distant background. Not until the sides give us our sense of direction, in which we seek out a single free-standing column, compare its height with a passing object and from it go on to follow a second and a third column, so slender as to be almost non-existent, are we able to make sense of it and satisfy the need the eye has for a reference point.[97]

The massive and the plastic styles were replaced by glass-and-iron architecture. Transparent glass, which emerged as an intermediary between the covered space and the sky, could embody the vision of an "architectura celesta" and the longing for a disembodied, "heavenly" architecture. German Expressionists propagated this "pure" architecture through the Crystal Chain correspondence. Paul Scheerbart emphasized the connection between glass and iron as follows: "Glass architecture is not to be considered separately from the Gothic.... as the Gothic cathedrals and castles came into being, a glass architecture was also wanted. It did not quite come into reality because the essential iron was not available. Not until this was so did the vision of glass become a reality."[98]

The oldest methods for making panes of glass were the cylinder and crown-glass processes. Before the birth of Christ the Romans made sheets of glass by a primitive pouring method. Not until 1000 A.D. were the two processes, which are probably of Syrian origin, introduced into Europe. They were used alongside each other up to the middle of the nineteenth century. A third process, which came into being in the seventeenth century, was used to meet the need for large glass sheets, particularly for mirrors.

The complicated process of manufacturing glass soon required the division of labor. However, the fact that at the start of the nineteenth century the secret of glass manufacturing was carefully guarded by family firms proved to be an obstacle to the transformation of glassmaking into a mass-production process; it led to a lack of skilled labor and hindered the establishment of new glassworks. In addition, high rates and taxes, including the window tax that was collected up to the middle of the nineteenth century, delayed the spread of glass as a building material.[99]

The price of glass, even in the time of industrialization, remained disproportionately high. Around 1600 a square foot of glass cost a farm laborer almost half a day's wages. A hundred years later, the relative price was still the same. In spite of technical improvements, the price of glass in Britain remained relatively high even until 1845. However, after this time it fell from 1s 2d per square foot to 2d.[100] This crucial price change was due to the rescinding of the high import duties. The consequence was the importation of large amounts of foreign glass, particularly from France, and the collapse of many small companies whose existence depended on protective tariffs. Now the way was open for the widespread use of window glass. Mass-production methods could now be used in glass manufacture.

The Cylinder Process

The first description of this process is found in "Schedula diversarium artium" (1000 A.D.), by Theophilus Presbyter.[101] Glass was blown into the shape of a cylinder and then cut and pressed onto a flat surface. The plastic glass was taken out of the melting pot with a blowpipe, blown into a hollow sphere, and worked into an elongated cylinder in a former. After further heating of the glass, the blowpipe was turned backward and forward in a trough in front of the kiln, and with repeated blowings, the cylinder was stretched out. Then the cylinder was cracked off at its ends and split longitudinally with a hot knife. It was then spread out on a rectangular table in a flattening kiln. The size of the sheet depended on the length of the cylinder, which was determined by the power of the glassblower's lungs.[102] The use of compressed air made it possible in the course of the nineteenth century to produce long cylinders and hence large flat glass sheets.

The Crown-Glass Process

In this process, much as in the method described above, a glass sphere was blown. However, it was then made into a circular sheet by rotation. An opening was made by cracking off the hollow sphere from the blowpipe. At the same time, it was attached by tongs to a punty on the opposite side. The sphere was opened out to a basin shape and then, by the centrifugal force of the rotating punty, was spun out to form a disk, which was divided into panes when it solidified. The thick center piece provided the so-called bullseye pane, and the rest of the disk was cut into flat window panes. This manufacturing process required the cooperative effort of ten specialists, and the quality of the product depended greatly on the dexterity of each of them.[103] The glass (also called mond glass) was distinguishable from cylinder glass by its purity and the brilliance of its surface. The sheets were flatter and thinner, though the relatively small size of the sheets was a disadvantage. This glass was used up to the middle of the nineteenth century.

The Mirror-Glass Process

The glass produced by the crown process and the cylinder process was indeed transparent and as a rule colorless, but it often had an uneven surface that distorted the objects seen through it. Unevenness caused only slight distortion in a window, but in a mirror it disfigured the image badly. To overcome this defect, various improvements in glass manufacture were tried until mirror quality was achieved. In 1688 the French glassmaker Louis Lucas de Nehou was able to make a glass sheet by a process of casting and rolling. Liquid glass was poured onto a flat metal plate and rolled into a plate with a metal roller. The raised edge of the metal sheet acted as a retaining barrier and determined the thickness of the glass. The glass plate was then ground and polished. Around 1700, sheets 47 by 79 inches were being produced in Lucas's factory. In 1750, dimensions of about 60 by 98 inches were reached, and around 1850, 138 by 179 inches.[104] The glass sheets so produced were mirror-finished and almost completely transparent. Although mirror glass had been made before the Industrial Revolution, on account of its expense it did not find its way into building as a structural material until much later. Even the glass for the Crystal Palace was produced by the cylinder process.[105]

Greenhouse Glazing

The extension of the transparent glazed surfaces of greenhouses was dependent on the glass industry. The major decrease in the cost of glass around the middle of the nineteenth century was decisive. Besides this, the gardeners had special needs in respect to the quality and the size of the panes.

Small glass panes, about 3 millimeters thick, were used in Loudon's earliest vaulted glasshouses. Their width was dependent on the spacing of the sash bars, which as a rule was between 7 and 10 inches, with the length about 6 inches. For improved discharge of water, they had a curved lower edge and were overlapped like roof tiles and puttied into the rebates of the iron sash bars. Their small length made them well suited to the construction of curved glass vaults.

A further improvement came with the use of curved glass sheets in the wing of the Belfast Palm House (1839–40) and in the Kew Palm House (1844–1848). These panes were 37 by 9 inches. The glass was tinted green by the addition of copper oxide in order to neutralize the heating effect. According to McIntosh, the original idea came from R. Hunt of the Museum of Organic Ecology.[106]

The desire to increase the transmitted light by reducing the number of sash bars led to the need for wider glass panes. Because glass in greenhouses constituted the major building material next to iron, and because improvements to the glass skin immediately made themselves noticeable in the concept of the building, the gardener's wish obviously gave a direct stimulus to the glass industry. During the building of the Great Conservatory at Chatsworth, between 1836 and 1840, Paxton met the problem of having to use greater lengths of glass for his ridge-and-furrow roof than were available. With the help of the greatest glass manufacturer in Britain, Robert Lucas Chance of Birmingham, he became acquainted with the improved cylinder process Chance had introduced in 1832. Chance (who was associated with the famous French glass manufacturer Georges Bontemps) had succeeded in blowing glass cylinders longer than was usual on the Continent, and thus was able to make longer glass panes. Instead of steel shears he used diamond tools to cut the glass to size. The glass cylinder was heated in a specially designed kiln and flattened on a bed of polished glass instead of on an iron plate strewn with sand.[107] When Paxton visited the factory, Chance was producing sheets 3 feet long by 10 inches wide. Paxton watched the process and stated his requirements. "Since they had so far advanced as to be able to produce sheets three feet long," he wrote, "I saw no reason why they could not accomplish another foot. . . ."[108] Chance managed to produce the required 4-foot-long sheet by careful blowing. This length then became the controlling spacing dimension of the Crystal Palace, which determined the detail of all three dimensions. In 1851, Chance, through improved mass production methods, supplied within a very short time almost 300,000 sheets—one-third of the total annual production of the British glass industry.

Glass and Illumination

The determination of the most suitable angle of incidence of light for a greenhouse—first experimentally and later theoretically—was a critical factor in the shape of the roof and hence in the shape of the space enclosed. The two most important roof shapes, the vaulted roof and the ridge-and-furrow roof, arose from these considerations. The way to the conclusive formulation of these two roof forms was found through countless experiments (particularly by gardeners), supported by scientific publications and discussions. In order to give a clear insight into the state of affairs in the first half of the nineteenth century, I quote from McIntosh's *Book of the Garden*:[109]

Hothouse-building. 1.—General Principles. . . . We need not refer to the original construction of hothouses, either in this country or on the Continent, further than to remark that they were by no means calculated for the preservation of tender exotic plants, and still less for the production of tropical fruits—as they were little other than large rooms, having windows in front, more in number and of larger size than those used in dwelling-houses. The first improvement on these was the adoption of what has been called the lean-to roof; this, till about the beginning of the present century, continued to be the form in general use, and for some purposes it will probably continue to be so. Various improvements, more especially as regards their internal arrangements, mode of heating, &c., were projected, and carried into beneficial effect by the garden architects of the day; amongst whom the late Thos. And. Knight held a conspicuous position. . . . Sir George M'Kenzie, a few years afterwards (1815) proposed what he thought to be the best form of roof for the admission of the greatest possible quantity of the sun's rays—namely, a hemispherical figure or globe; but as this figure seemed to be unattainable in practice, he then proposed to make the roof the segment of a circle. This may be said to have been the most scientific improvement suggested up to that period; and out of it arose the various modifications known as curvilinear roofs. . . .

The last and greatest improvement in hothouse roofs is certainly that of the ridge-and-furrow form, first suggested by the late Mr. Loudon about the year 1816, and afterwards so completely wrought out by Sir Joseph Paxton in the large house at Chatsworth, and elsewhere, and more recently by covering in nearly 29 acres for the Great Exhibition in Hyde Park, the most stupendous erection hitherto constructed of iron, timber, and glass, and exemplifying most clearly the possibility of extending the same kind of pillared covering over any space, however large. . . . From our own personal intimacy with the late Mr. Loudon, we know that the ridge-and-furrow principle of roofing was thought of

by him long before any exemplification of it had been attempted in Britain. To Sir Joseph Paxton, however, the
merit belongs of bringing this greatest of all improvements
into practical use; and even had the idea been entertained
by others, it is questionable if many would have had the
boldness or the means to have brought it to perfection.

Mr. Loudon's first idea of this mode of roofing suggested
itself to him after reading a paper by Sir George M'Kenzie,
published in 1815 in the "Transactions of the Horticultural
Society of London", "on the form which the glass of a forcing-house ought to have, in order to receive the greatest possible quantity of rays from the sun". . . .

The greatest advantage of a ridge-and-furrow roof is, that
any extent of area may be covered without internal walls.
Indeed, no walls whatever are required, as the sides and
ends may be glass close to the ground—the whole being supported on cast-iron tubular columns, with cast-iron valleys
or gutters. A good idea of the effect and practicability of roofing over a whole garden may be obtained by a careful ex-
amination of some of our most extensive railway stations—
that at Derby, for example, which we believe could be extended over a hundred acres if required. . . .

In the course of a lecture delivered by Sir Joseph Paxton
before the Society of Arts in London, he explains the principles of this improved roof as follows: "In the construction of
glass houses requiring much light, there always appeared to
me to be one important objection. In the plain lean-to or
shed roofs, the morning and evening sun—which is, on
many accounts, of the greatest importance to forcing fruits—
presented its direct rays at a low angle, and consequently
very obliquely, to the glass. As at those periods most of the
rays of light and heat were obstructed by the position of the
glass and the heavy rafters, so that a considerable portion of
time was lost both evening and morning, it consequently became evident that a system by which the glass would be
more at right angles to the morning and evening rays of the
sun would obviate the difficulty, and remove the obstruction
to the rays of light entering the house at an early and a
late hour of the day." This led him to the adoption of the
ridge-and-furrow principle for glass roofs, which places the
glass in such a position that the rays of light in the morn-
ings and evenings enter the house without obstruction, and
present themselves more perpendicularly to the glass at those
times when they are the least powerful; whereas at mid-day,
when they are most powerful, they present themselves more
obliquely to it. . . .

With ridge-and-furrow roofs there is no necessity for having glass houses on the lean-to principle—indeed, they
ought not to be so constructed: the valley and ridges should
run level from side to side; and except in cold and exposed
situations, where a back or northern wall may be rendered
necessary for shelter, it will be better for the plants, as well
as more elegant, if all the sides are of glass to within a foot
of the ground.

Sir Joseph Paxton recommends the pediments to rise perpendicular to the front upright sashes. We have placed all
ours at an angle of about 22°, the angles of the roof being
25°. This is, however, merely a matter of taste. A rather

massive wooden or cast-iron cornice should cover the front
wall-plate, which will give the appearance of finish to that
part of the elevation, and may be made to serve, at the
same time, for taking away the water that comes off the
roof. It is, however, better in most cases of this kind to make
the water pass down through the cast-iron columns which
support the front of the house, and which, with a view to
this, as well as for economy of metal, should be cast
hollow. . . .

In regard to the transparency of ridge-and-furrow roofs,
Mr Loudon remarks: "If we take the area of the bases of the
ridges as the total area of the roof, and then deduct from it
the space occupied by the bars forming the sides of the
ridges, and the ridge pieces and gutters," these roofs "will
not appear to admit the same proportion of light as a roof
in one plane; but the practical result will be different, in
consequence of the sun's rays being twice in the day perpendicular to one-half of the roof, the advantage of which to the
plants will far more than compensate for the obscuration
produced by the greater proportion of sash bars, which, operating chiefly at mid-day, and in very hot weather, is rather
an advantage than otherwise."

Regarding the angle of elevation. . . . This subject appears
to have attracted the attention of Boerhaave about the beginning of the last century, and was taken up by Linnaeus,
and still further pursued by Faccio, Adanson, Miller,
Speechly, and Williams of New York. The late T. A. Knight
published hints on this subject in the first volume of "The
Horticultural Society's Transactions;" and Sir George Mackenzie, in 1815, determined "that the form of glass roofs
best calculated for the admission of the sun's rays is a hemispherical figure;" and this Mr. Loudon at first considered as
"the ultimatum in regard to the principle and perfection of
form." The following quotation bears on this subject:— "The
theory of the transmission of light through transparent bodies
is derived from a well-known law in optics; and the influence of the sun's rays on any surface, both as respects light
and heat, is directly as the sine of the sun's altitude; or, in
other words, directly as it is perpendicular to that surface. If
the surface is transparent, the number of rays which pass
through the substance is governed by the same laws. Thus, if
one thousand rays fall perpendicularly upon a surface of the
best crown glass, the whole will pass through except about a
fortieth part, which the impurities of even the finest crystal,
according to Bouguer, will exclude; but if these rays fall at
an incidental angle of 75°, two hundred and ninety-nine
rays, according to the same author, will be reflected. . . .
The benefit derived from the sun's influence on the roofs of
hothouses depends, as far as respects form of surface, entirely
on this principle. Boerhaave applied it to houses for preserving plants through the winter, and, of course, required that
the glass surface should be perpendicular to the sun's rays at
the shortest day when most heat and light were required.
Miller applied it to plant stoves, and prefers two angles in
the roof—one as the upright glass, to meet the winter's sun
nearly at right angles, and the other as the sloping glass, to
meet it at an angle of 45° for summer use, and the better
to admit the sun's rays in spring and autumn. Williamson
prefers an angle of 45° in all houses, as do most garden-

ers . . . but Knight prefers, in forcing houses at least, such a slope of roof as shall be at right angles to the sun's rays, at whatever season it is intended to ripen the fruit. In one of the examples given, ("Horticultural Transactions", vol. i, p. 99) his object was to produce "a large and highly flavoured crop". . . . and he, accordingly, fixed upon such a slope of the roof as that the sun's rays might be perpendicular to it about the beginning of July, the period about which he wished the crop to ripen. The slope required to effect this purpose, in latitude 52°, he found to form an angle of 34° with the plane of the horizon. In the application of the same principle to the peach-house. . . . in order to ripen the fruit about midsummer, the roof was made to form an angle with the horizon of 28°. Both these houses, Knight informs us, produced "abundant crops perfectly ripened". . . .

The calculation of the inclination of angles, for the better determining the slope of hothouse roofs, is very differently practised on the Continent and with us. We calculate from the perpendicular lines of the quadrant, while they calculate from the base or horizontal line. A very excellent article on this subject will be found in "Paxton's Magazine of Botany". . . . Sir Joseph observes: "Both systems are equally good when understood; but an understanding is requisite, because an angle of 70°, which with us is well known to be a very flat roof, is with the French very steep; and the same slope as our 70°, on their system, is an angle of 20°". . . . After all that has been said on the angle of elevation, it is not at all strange that no particular angle should be fixed upon as the true one; because that which would be a very proper angle for a peach-house, for instance, at Torquay, would be a bad one at Thurso, the difference of latitude being considerable. . . . It therefore follows that the angle of elevation . . . must be made to correspond with the latitude the house is placed in, and also to suit the purpose for which that house is intended.

The Palm

Because the nineteenth-century greenhouse generally served for the cultivation and display of the flora of warm or tropical zones, it usually included tall, tree-like plants—particularly palms—which critically determined the form and the volume of the building.[110] The palm was universally designated in nineteenth-century botany, following Linnaeus, as the "prince of plants,"[111] because of its "noble and impressive shape," its fecundity, its usefulness for food and raw material, and its botanical peculiarity as a member of the monocotyledon family. This family comprises plants (such as grasses, lilies, orchids, and bananas) the germ of which has only one seed lobe (cotyledon), so that the bud originates from a crevice. Monocotyledons differ from other plants not only in external form but also in internal structure. As a rule, they send down no tap root but simple thread-like roots, and they have a single stem that does not branch out upward but carries a crown of leaves at the top. The stem is not divided into bark, wood, and pith core, but consists of a cellular structure in which the closed vascular tissues are irregularly oriented and not arranged in concentric rings. The leaves are mostly divided; i.e., they surround the stem and have simple parallel veins. Triplication is predominant in the flowers and parts of the fruit.[112] The stem is covered with scale-like remains of the leaf stalks instead of bark, and often with thorns and fibers or with circular scars. The leaves always grow outward from a single bud at the top of the stem or rootstock. They are arranged in pinnate fashion or fanning out with broad sheathlike bases at the stiff, channel-shaped leaf stalk. Their growth does not follow a spiral shape but unfurls as in grasses. The flowers are small, greenish, uniform, rarely androgynous, mostly polygamous. They form fleshy or dry stone fruits.[113] The simple structure and the fact that the metamorphosis of the leaves is present in all parts moved Goethe to assume that the palm was the "Urpflanze"—the ancestor of all plants. His visit to the botanical gardens in Padua, where he came upon a beautifully grown fan palm (*Bigonia radicans*), contributed to that belief.[114] The size of palms is extremely variable and ranges from dwarf size up to 100 feet high. They often tower over the surrounding vegetation. A well-known example of this is the coconut palm. "The straight high soaring stems, like firmly rammed-in masts, and the majestic crowns of leaves waving in the wind, give an imposing impression."[115] The fan often reaches 50 feet in length and 8 feet in breadth.

With few exceptions, palms are considered tropical plants. "The nearer to the Equator, the more the number of species and individuals increases, and conversely they decrease to the north and south. The 43° parallel[116] in Europe forms the northerly limit for palms, in Asia and America 34°; the southern limit in Africa is 36°. North of the Tropic of Capricorn 43 species of palm are known, south of Capricorn only 13. . . . Between the 10° north and south parallels more than 300 species are known. The greatest number of palms are found in the eastern hemisphere of the Earth in the Sunda Islands, in the western hemisphere in the river basins of the Orinoco and Amazon in South America. Considering its expanse, America is richest in palms of all parts of the Earth, for whereas the Old World—comprising Europe, Asia, Africa, and Antarctica, including the islands—has 307 species, the New World—that is, America alone—can boast of having 275 species."[117] The places in which palms grow are likewise varied. "Whereas a few in the hottest parts of the tropics are narrowly restricted to the coasts of the oceans and can hardly do without the influence of sea breezes, others prosper in the deepest interior up to 14,000 feet altitude on the summits of mountains, in the vicinity of perpetual snow. Some seek the humidity and deep shade of the tropical jungle; others live in arid deserts, exposed to the full heat of the sun's vertical rays. Some thrive most luxuriantly in swamps; others like very dry soil."[118]

The palms, which around 1872 were known to comprise approximately 600 species and which today are estimated to include over 1,000, are divided into two groups on the basis of the shape of the leaves: pinnate or fan. This division also corresponds approximately to a geographical distribution; the fan-shaped forms of palms are indigenous to the northern hemisphere and the pinnate forms to the southern. Naturally, the major interest from time immemorial was in those palms that were sources of food or raw materials for the indigenous inhabitants and for the colonial powers. These include particularly the date palm (*Phoenix*) of the Orient and North Africa, the sago palm (*Metroxylon*) of the East Indies and China, the oil palm (*Elaeis*) of Africa, Guinea, and South America, and the coconut palm (*Cocos nucifera*) of India and the South Seas.[119] These palms and others supplied through their fruits, leaf tips, and stems not only foodstuffs but also flour, fats, waxes, resins, and syrups (sago flour, palm oil, palm butter, coconut milk, palm wine, palm sugar, arak), as well as raw materials for clothing, building, and candle-making. These products were an important cause of the development of colonialization and the trade associated with it. Famous naturalists such as Humboldt, Darwin, and Gustav Wallis played a role here by combining their botanical interests with an interest in the possibility of practical uses for their discoveries. They had in mind not only the exploitation of nature but also the improvement of the living conditions of colonial peoples. This is clearly expressed in Wallis's 1876 report of his expedition to Brazil:

Totally in harmony with the tropical vegetation reaching its highest expression below the Equator stands the practical use which springs from economy and trade through the various plants. No province of the wide German Empire, comprising 150,000 square miles of geography, can boast of such fruitfulness and productivity as . . . the Hylaea in the Brazilian province of the River Amazon. There is only lacking the necessary urge to produce and use the blessings of nature. The well-to-do natives usually lacked the energy for enterprises, whilst the lower, labouring classes were usually too lazy, and for the worker from temperate zones the hot climate offers little enticement to emigrate. Nevertheless, the produce yielded by plants gained a slow but rising stimulus. When considering individual plants we shall and must di-

rect our attention to the palms, which dog our footsteps as such friendly companions by the wayside. To the first glance of the foreigner it is of course not evident that they have the capacity of outstanding usefulness in the country's economy. Nevertheless the gain is many-sided in the extreme in that these same plants provide wax, oil, butter, margarine, even drink and other foodstuffs, and again wood, bark, fibres, etc.[120]

A botanical report from the same decade on the oil palm has the same approach to the matter:

The technical use is now exceedingly varied, the need for it is greater and the importation increased, so that large companies, particularly British ones, have been formed to carry on the import and trade and to that end are using veritable fleets of ships. The pecuniary gain which is thereby obtained is however not the only consideration, but there is an even higher, a philanthropic aim, in which the production of palm oil in recent times has persuaded the heathen rulers of Guinea that there is more profit to be had out of this industry than from the trade in live ebony, negro slaves, which in spite of all prohibitions and preventive measures by civilized people have been carried away from those countries as objects for sale, even up to the most recent times.[121]

The economic use of the various species of palms by the colonial powers was an important reason for their inclusion in the botanical collections and winter gardens of the nineteenth century. The visitor often got the impression that his country had taken possession of whole continents full of these palms.

The more industrialization destroyed nature in the city environment, the greater was the longing for a natural life, which seemed to be possible only in distant lands. The travel fantasy of the middle class in the nineteenth century was linked with the palm. Another reason for the attraction of this plant was its connection with Eastern history and its association with the Holy Land. In addition, the palm was anthropomorphized. The very name, coined by the Romans, alludes to its similarity to the fingers of the hand (palma); likewise, the Aztecs called the palm macpalxochitlquahuitl—literally, "hand flower tree."[122] Its tripartite growth was compared to that of man. It was written that "the palm tree resembles man in many respects because of its straight, slender, upright shape, its beauty, and its separation into two sexes, male and female. If one cuts off its head it dies; if the brain suffers, then the whole tree suffers with it; its leaves if broken off will grow again as little as the arm of man will; its fibers and surface mesh cover it like the growth of hair covers man."[123]

Architectural interpretations of palm groves—rising, leafy vaults with steep basket-shaped arches—appeared in Egyptian and later in Moorish architecture. Although the inner relationship between palm symbols and architecture cannot be proved, it is evident that the nineteenth century was cognizant of it. Cast-iron columns used at the start of the nineteenth century imitated the palm-tree form. The Chinese teahouse built at Sanssouci by command of Frederick II in the eighteenth century had pillars shaped like palm trees. Nash's palm-tree pillars in the Brighton Pavilion (1815–16) are well known. In hothouse construction, several builders attempted to bring the architecture into harmony with the flora (figs. 70, 71, 73, 567, 615).

The palm also had religious aspects:

Worship of the palm dates from the primitive times of the oriental peoples and is on a par with sun worship. What was more natural than that uncultured men, as soon as they conceived the general idea of a god, discovered in two objects a godhead, in the sun as the source of all light and life, and in the palm as the feeder and preserver of man. This distinguished form of the palm, superior to all other plants, the noble bearing, the stern striving to reach the skies, the lightly built crowns waving with every current of air whose rustling noise led man to believe he was listening to an invisible being, its nourishing fruits, the materials for clothing and shelter—all these combined to create the sense of a higher being inherent in it, if not a godhead then surely the dwelling of the same.[124]

The date palm was especially important in this respect. Its branches and leaves, as can be learned from the Bible,[125] played a special part in the antiquity of the Middle East and in the Christian culture of the following age. The large palm groves which were later laid out in Europe, even in the nineteenth century, served primarily for religious purposes. For example, in 1872 the German *Magazin für Garten- und Blumenkunde* carried a note about the palm plantation in Elche. "This grove of palms obtains its major importance through the significant revenue it received from the sale of palm leaves, which are bought for use in the religious processions on Palm Sunday. Whole shiploads of artificially bleached palm fronds go from Alicante to France and Italy."[126]

Another basis for the origin of palm collections was the scientific interest in systematic botany as it developed. Palms, on account of their diverse forms and species, were always in the field of view of the most important botanists and made their mark through their simultaneous kinship with grasses and trees. Only fifteen species were known at the time of Linnaeus's death in 1778. Ruiz and Pavon discovered eight more; Humboldt and Aimé Bonpland described twenty new ones and mentioned others without being able to classify them. The fact that the

flowers were located in the high tops and therefore could only be obtained with difficulty added to the difficulty of botanical classification.[127]

The author of *Popular History of the Palms* (1856) called attention to the achievements of the botanists and nature researchers who had assembled the collections at Kew. He said that any visitor who knew anything of the history of botany would remember the names and exploits of Humboldt, Wallich, Bonpland, J. D. Hooker, Purdie, Wilson, Griffith, Linden, Hartweg, and others.[128]

The value that was placed on a beautiful palm collection is shown by the travels of the first palm to bear flowers in Europe, the Marie Thérèse Palm. In 1684 Prince William of Orange obtained the tree, at that time 30 years old, from India. In 1703 it came to Berlin, to the estate of King Frederick I of Prussia. In 1739 King Frederick William I presented it to Adrian van Steckhoven, who in 1773 passed it on to the Imperial Castle Gardens in Vienna, where in 1765 it began to flower and bear fruit.[129] Finally, it was placed in the Schönbrunn botanical garden in Vienna.

According to a report dated about 1800 there was in the Schönbrunn hothouse "a large quantity of beautiful and rare plants . . . from all five continents." This collection increased steadily during the following years through the work of the castle gardeners Nicolaus Joseph Jacquin and Franz Boos.[130]

At Herrenhausen, in Hannover, it was particularly Hermann Wendland who devoted himself to the study and culture of palms. In 1854 he published an "Index palmarum" in which he described 192 species. He was, as Guilmot wrote in 1880, "un spécialiste en fait des palmiers."[131] Around 1860 the "Berggarten" at Herrenhausen was the most comprehensive palm collection on the Continent. According to the *Encyclopädie der Gartenkunst*, the collection increased from 22 species in 1846 to 224 in 1854.

Private persons, particularly professional gardeners and representatives of the upper middle class, tried to compete with the great palm collections of the nobility and the state. The *Encyclopädie der Gartenkunst* named Berlin as a center, with the collections of the royal printer Decker (104 species), the judge Augustin (232 species), and the factory proprietor Borsig (69 species).

Whatever effect the palm collections may have had on the human imagination in that period, there was something extraordinary about the travels to distant lands. In the chapter of *Kosmos* about the "means of stimulating the study of nature," Humboldt describes this in a graphic way:

13
Three species of
palm, identified by
Gustav Wallis, Alex-
ander von Hum-
boldt, and Hermann
L. Wendland.

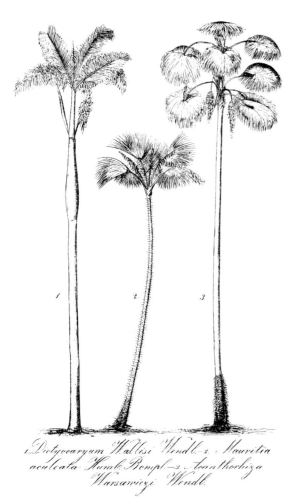

*1. Dictyocaryum Wallisi Wendl.—2. Mauritia
aculeata Humb. Bonpl.—3. Acanthorhiza
Warsewiczi Wendl.*

*The diversity of methods which painting has at its disposal
in order to arouse the fantasy and the most grandiose phenomena of sea and land and concentrate the same into a
small area is denied to our plantations and garden layouts;
but wherever in this the overall impression of the landscape
is reduced, there is compensation in particular through the
dominion which is everywhere exerted over the intellect. If
one looks down in the Loddiges' palm house or in the
Pfaueninsel at Potsdam from the high galleries in the bright
midday sun onto the profusion of reedlike and treelike
palms, one is for a moment completely deceived by the place
in which one finds oneself. One believes that one is looking
from the summit of a hill in a tropical environment onto a
small thicket of palms. One certainly does not have the vista
of deep heavenly blue, the impression of the greater intensity
of the light; nevertheless the imagination is even more active
here, the illusion greater than in the most skillful painting.
One associates every plant form with the wonders of a distant world; one becomes aware of the rustle of the fan-
shaped leaves; one sees their changing and vanishing illumination, when, gently moved by tiny air currents, the palm
tops touch each other. Such is the great attraction which
reality can ensure. . . .*[132]

The hothouse made it possible to copy the tropical
landscape to perfection, using the natural material—
plants—and letting the viewer forget the technical
apparatus.

The Artificial Climate

As long as greenhouses had small dimensions and
were (like the eighteenth-century orangeries) provided with a massive, heat-retaining north wall and a
solid roof, primitive stoves or smoke flues sufficed to
warm their interiors. After 1750, however, the increasing replacement of masonry walls by glass led
to the building of extended glass fronts, although the
north side and the roof were still solid with no windows. Any further development of greenhouses into
free-standing glasshouses with transparent roofs depended at that time on a solution of the heating
problem. The glazing created an enormous cooling
surface (heat loss with single glazing was about ten
times as great as that of a brick wall) and drastically
reduced the heat-storage capacity.

The development of hot-water and steam heating
at the start of the nineteenth century was the decisive step. These methods made possible free-standing
hothouses and winter gardens glazed on all sides.
The introduction of these heating methods coincided
with the spread of steam power for driving machinery and the increasing use of coal and coke for fuel.

Stoves (particularly tile-covered stoves) were the
usual method of heating in the early hothouses. Iron
stoves were soon abandoned on account of the too-
strong radiation of heat. The disadvantages of stove

heating included an uneven distribution of heat, greater fuel consumption in relation to the amount of air heated, and greater cost.[133]

Flue heating offered advantages over simple stove heating. It made possible the uniform and continuous heating of the space occupied by the plants. The flue installation consisted of clay or fire-clay ducts, of circular or square section, inserted into each other so that they were gas-tight and laid partly above and partly in the ground, covered with a grating. The flues had a gentle slope of 2.5–3 percent, which was sufficient to allow a draft up the chimney. Although flue heating was cheaper than stove heating, it also had great disadvantages. The slightest defect in the construction of the flues, or the wrong fuel, allowed smoke to escape among the plants, particularly in windy and rainy conditions. The plants were damaged badly by sulfur dioxide and soot; coke and the proper coal were the only satisfactory fuels.[134]

Hot-water heating, like steam heating, first came about in the early hothouses,[135] although the convective force of heated water was known 100 years earlier. The first use of water for heating a hothouse is attributed to Martin Triewald in Newcastle-upon-Tyne around 1716. Water was brought to the outside of the house for boiling and was fed through pipes below the plants. In 1777 the physicist Bonnemain informed the Academy of Sciences of the "principle of heating by water circulation." He had used this type of heating on a small scale in the breeding of chickens.[136] Water heating is based on the different densities of hot and cold water masses and the convective motion this causes, and is accomplished with a system of interconnected pipes in which water stands at equal levels in all branches.

The practical use of the convective force of hot water is associated with the discovery of human blood circulation. When the Marquis de Charbannes obtained a British patent for a highly developed hot-water heating system, in 1810, he knew of Bonnemain's work. At the same time, William Atkinson and Anthony Bacon were engaged in the improvement of hot-water heating, particularly the boiler. Whereas at first (for example, in Atkinson's system) only horizontal circulation was possible, the discovery of the siphon by Thomas Fowler led to the use of vertical circulation too. In 1825 the translation of Thomas Tredgold's *Principles of the Science of Heating and Ventilating Buildings*[137] appeared in Paris. Among the many hot-water heating systems that appeared in the 1830s, A. M. Perkins's high-pressure system was the most remarkable. Previously, water was not heated above the boiling point, but in Perkins's system it was. The boiler and the pipes had to be hermetically sealed and strong enough so they would not burst. Aside from the higher temperature, this system allowed faster circulation. Around the same time, Hood and Richardson published their treatise on the heating of buildings. In France, the technology of hot-water heating received greater attention about the middle of the century through the work of Grison, the head gardener at Versailles. In collaboration with the stove manufacturers Léon and René Duvoir he built heating systems which were also suited to domestic buildings.[138]

Neumann stated that "hot-water heating systems have undeniable advantages for the heating of greenhouses, and particularly all those places where it is a matter of maintaining a mild and very steady temperature. In addition, eight to ten hours after the heating has been turned off the temperature in the glasshouse does not fall to a dangerously low level. This type of heating is also suitable for those places where considerable quantities of warm air have to be produced." Neumann quoted as an example the Council of State building and the Treasury at the Quai d'Orsay. "The boiler of this heating system," he wrote, "is located in a cellar, but it sends through the pipes the water required for heating all the rooms on the first and second floors (45 feet high). These pipes run for a distance of more than 900 feet and heat all the rooms to 20°C within one hour. Therefore, every difficulty is overcome, and no one can say that the thermosiphon is not applicable to larger premises."[139]

The first initiatives toward steam heating came from Sir Hugh Platt in the times of Queen Elizabeth I, but not until 1788 was the idea reintroduced by Wakefield in Liverpool for hothouse heating. In the early method, a single pipe led from a boiler through the hothouse, and this pipe was always threatening to burst. In the most comprehensive account of the early use of steam, in 1792, Butler, the Earl of Derby's gardener, told of heating melon and pineapple houses with it. He used perforated pipes laid in a steam-permeable bed in which potted plants were placed. In 1807 the garden architect John Hay of Edinburgh carried out similar tests with pipes perforated along their whole length and laid in a bed of stone of 3 by 4 feet in cross-section. The stones were warmed up to steam temperature, and the heat stored in them was sufficient to heat a plant house for a full day in cold weather and for two to three days in mild weather. By about 1816, steam heating was far enough developed to be used to heat a spacious hothouse. It was already in use at this time in Loddiges Nursery at Hackney in London. Loudon, who built his first curvilinear hothouse here,

saw to it that in the pipes near the boiler the temperature was never less than 100°C, and that the
steam even approximately 650 meters away was
close to the same temperature. In 1821, Thomas
Knight used this nursery as an example of the advantages of steam heating in hothouses.[140] A hothouse at Sturge, near Bath, was heated successfully
by steam pipes surrounded with pipes containing
water. This system, which was based on the principle
of heat exchange between steam and water, allowed
the different advantages of hot water and steam to
be used.

Steam heating is based on the use of steam produced under pressure in boilers. Steam has a coeffi-
cient of expansion 1,700 times that of air. Therefore,
in a pressurized vessel there is pressure within the
steam itself and also pressure on the walls of the
vessel. The higher the steam pressure, the greater its
flow velocity in a closed system of pipes. At a pressure of 1 atmosphere, steam flows into a vacuum at
about 1,930 feet per second. If steam is conducted
through small-bore pipes, its pressure falls minimally
and it retains its flow velocity. Even these properties
came to be an important aspect of the use of steam
in hothouses. The fall in temperature in steam was
very slight even in large hothouse installations consisting of several separate units. A continuous heat
flow was maintained through the pipe walls. But the
extreme temperatures of steam heating brought difficulties for glasshouse management. The air dried out
quickly, and the high level of radiant heat damaged
the plants. Hybrid systems of steam heating let
steam directly into the plant houses from the pipes
from time to time, producing a dewlike precipitation.
On this subject Neumann writes:

*With all certainty to which experience leads, the high effi-
ciency of steam can be proved. Everyone who visited Taver-
nier's establishment in Paris was astonished by the change
that became noticeable after the introduction of steam, particularly in the orangeries. The vegetation is many times
more dense and reaches extraordinary proportions. The foliage is large and of a darker . . . green; the leaves of the orange trees, the fruits of which are called "apples of
paradise," reach a width of 5 1/2 inches on young bushes
which had been grafted two years earlier. The dew arising
from the steam dispersed the aphids that settled on the
young shoots of the orange trees. One should also note that
the large pavilions and greenhouses in the Jardin des
Plantes in Paris are heated with steam.*[141]

A comparison between stove heating and steam
heating at Loddiges Nursery showed the economic
advantages of the first steam-heating plant. A steam-
heating system 5,300 feet long was installed through
the many hothouses in which pineapples, camellias,

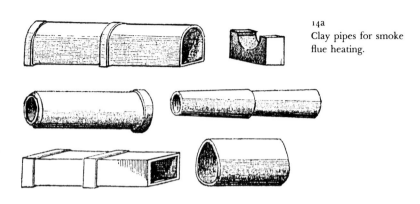

14a
Clay pipes for smoke
flue heating.

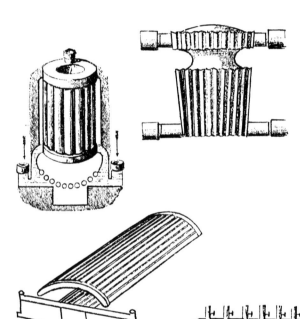

14b
English boilers for
hot-water heating.

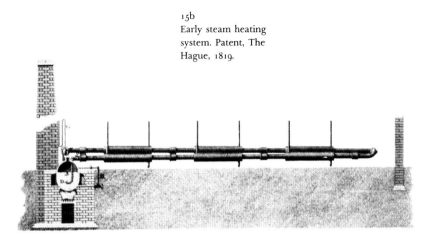

15b
Early steam heating
system. Patent, The
Hague, 1819.

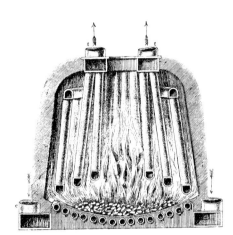

15a
Mass-produced
boiler for hot-water
heating.

palms, and other tropical plants were being cultivated. The previous stove installation, consisting of 38 stoves, needed 220 tons of coke. In contrast, during the severe winter of 1854–55 the steam-heating installation needed no more than 120 tons of coke.[142]

Even in the early days of hothouse construction there were deliberations about the maximum use of the natural heat of the sun. The designers of the hothouse buildings and orangeries of the eighteenth century sought by the use of parabolically curved rear walls to use the reflection of the sun's rays to heat and light the plant space. The thick brickwork of the north wall was intended to store heat. The all-round glazing of the hemisphere or cupola building, theoretically formulated by Thomas Knight (1811) and George Mackenzie (1815), was first put into practice in 1817 by Loudon. The use of hemispherical or parabolic surfaces was based on the knowledge that rays striking such a surface perpendicularly are reflected only to a very small degree.

Experiments made by James Anderson and J. C. Loudon at the start of the nineteenth century incorporated ideas about heating that were completely new at the time. In 1803 Anderson proposed a system of two superimposed glasshouses. The upper one would trap the sun's heat; the heat would then be transferred via ventilators to the lower one, which would have masonry walls. During the night, the heat would follow the reverse path and ameliorate the cold in the upper glasshouse. In 1805 Loudon described a similar system under the title "Several Improvements recently made in Hothouses." These proposals pointed the way to present-day attempts to use energy recovery in artificial climate technology.

A further development of eighteenth-century heating was hot-air heating, by which hot air was ducted through pipes instead of flue gases from a stove. The head gardener at Weimar Castle reported on a hot-air heating plant which was put into operation in 1825 in the hothouses of Count Magnis at Strassnitz. This plant was based on a system designed by Paul Traugott Meissner, a professor at the Polytechnic Institute in Vienna who in 1821 published an article titled "Heating with warm air."[143] Three stoves were used to heat hothouses with a total length of 197 feet. The system showed its advantages over flue heating. The first air-heating installation by Meissner was tested in a Vienna sugar refinery in 1820.[144]

In conclusion, it can be said that all heating methods used today have their origins in hothouse construction. Used with shading systems, ventilating devices, and artificial humidification, these heating systems produced an effectively constant climate throughout the year. To that extent, they were prototypes of present-day indoor climate-control systems.

The Development of the Iron-Frame Glasshouse

An understanding of the spatial and constructional types that evolved in glasshouse and hothouse building does call for some consideration of the requirements of specific types of plants and of the suitable degrees of heat and illumination. However, with only a few exceptions, the shapes of the buildings were not determined by their functional purpose. Like any other architectural creation, the hothouse had its shape determined by the conflict between form and function, and this also applies if one considers its function (plant culture) in the strict sense. Beyond mere utility, the inner purpose of architecture is, in the wider sense, the creation of enclosed space.

Space as the subject matter of architecture is a product of historical nature, and in that sense it is socially determined. Therefore it can never arise (ex ovo, as it were) strictly from the momentary purpose set forth. Spatial structures, like their constructional solutions, are considered in the design stage along with the historical material that can be drawn upon. For example, it is clearly demonstrable in greenhouse construction that the hall spaces, the dome shapes, and the construction methods are distinct from those of other hall-type buildings (such as churches, covered markets, factory workshops, and the later railway stations). The history of sense perception in architecture did not play an assertive role in the creation of space in greenhouses. The aesthetic treatment which this history had to consider became a deterministic purpose of the building. It was in this sense that Karl Kraus formulated the idea that architecture consists in raising the unnecessary to necessity.

Even considering these aspects, one can look on the hothouse buildings as early manifestations of functional building insofar as they followed unhindered the basic necessities for plants—maximum transparency and a suitable artificial climate—while at the same time they displayed the aspect of space and its construction.

Design Objectives

The spatial and construction aspects of greenhouse building were governed by the specific requirements of the plants, but at the same time also by the general environment by which they were surrounded. Besides the single purpose of cultivation, there was also the effort to exhibit, and from this arose the desire to provide a venue for social gatherings. The arrangement of the plants then had to take into account the movement of the people who gathered in the glasshouse, and this elevated the aesthetic demands. According to whether the needs of the plants or those of the people were to take precedence, three major types of glasshouse arose. In nineteenth-century terminology[145] these were classified as follows:

• Culture houses, in which ornamental and useful plants were grown and propagated and botanical experiments were carried out. (This category includes forcing houses, raising houses, propagating houses, and market gardens.)
• Conservatories, in which the most complete possible collections of plants were assembled and protected from the cold climate. These served the scientific purposes of botany as well as the purpose of exhibition. The distinctive and artistic arrangement of the plants imposed special requirements on the layout.

• Winter gardens, including extensions to country houses and castles and public entertainment establishments.

A special feature of the winter garden was its architectural ostentation, which on the one hand expressed a carefully thought-out design but on the other hand had an overloaded style. "These show houses, in which neither the rapid growth of plants nor a strict practice of scientific purposes is intended, are laid out in the most varied and uncontrolled ways according to the special requirements, in association with the surrounding spaces and building or distinguished by their individualistic architecture and artistic layout. Sometimes they are designed to lift the spirit of the person who views the greenery; sometimes there is the intention to interrupt a series of high-class residences and prestige buildings, changing the possible monotony by inserting a winter garden. In yet other cases there has been an intention to create a palm house to provide enjoyment at the sight of large and beautifully formed tropical plants and palms. Further, there is the creation of halls for displays of flowers to delight the eyes of city dwellers in need of spiritual uplift."[146]

The conservatories can be divided into three types: hothouses (calidaria), temperate houses (tepidaria), and coolhouses (frigidaria).[147] They were situated in accordance with a careful choice of position (airy, no sodden soil, protection from cold wind, and proper orientation to the direction of sunlight).

The minimum outside temperature for a hothouse ranged from 8°C to 18°C, and the best position was facing to the south or the southeast. A hothouse had to accommodate plants from the East and West Indies, Brazil, Africa, and tropical America. Because the plants could be put out in open air only during the warmest summer weather, there was a need for an artificial climate over almost the entire year. Dry hothouses usually occupied south-facing locations with a slight shift to the southeast, so that at 11 A.M. the sun's rays would strike the roof perpendicularly. Humid hothouses faced due south.

For a temperate house, the minimum temperature was 2°C–8°C. These houses were used to grow plants indigenous to the temperate or subtropical countries, such as North Africa, the Cape Colony (South Africa), New Holland (Australia), China, Japan, Chile, Peru, and the islands of the Atlantic.

For a coolhouse (greenhouse), the minimum temperature was 1°C–2°C and the best position was facing east, west, or even north. These houses were used to grow plants from the temperate regions of southern Europe, some parts of North Africa, southern North America, and the colder parts of China and Japan, and were required only to keep the plants free from frost in winter. Orangeries, which often doubled as greenhouses to accommodate plants during the winter period of cessation of growth, had to have a southerly aspect.

The more comprehensive the plant collections became, the more the conservatories were divided into separate types, with gradations in the size and shape of the plant hall and specific requirements for heating and illumination. Orchid houses had two or three divisions and a southerly aspect; cactus houses had low and high buildings and a southerly aspect; fern houses had water flowing over artificial rock outcrops; camellia houses were similar to coolhouses; victoria regia houses were generally low circular buildings with a heated pool of water in the center.

Space and Construction

The development of glass-and-iron buildings in the nineteenth century can be divided into four phases.

1800–1830 was the time of early industrialization and also marks the start of the use of iron as a building material. Cast iron was the form of iron predominantly used, and wrought iron was essentially produced only in the form of flat bars. Iron was employed according to the structural principles inherent in building in wood and stone: girders and arches. We can see here the early use of cast-iron load-bearing space frames.

1830–1850 was the time of the expansion of the Industrial Revolution. The introduction of rolled-iron I- and U-section bars, the development of early space frames, and the increase in the spans of railway stations and covered markets are characteristic of the period.

1850–1870 was the period of the introduction of industrialized mass production in most branches of manufacturing. Mass production from 1860 on led to the replacement of cast iron in space frames. The perfection and the widespread use of roof trusses, the perfection of cast-iron frames in exhibition buildings, and the improvement of wide-span halls were important.

1870–1890 saw further expansion of mass production of steel and refinement of the space-frame concept with the introduction of two- and three-hinge girders. Spans not hitherto attained were now possible in halls and bridges. Cast iron then vanished almost completely from use in roof trusses. In sharp contrast to the space frames now designed exactly in accordance with economic aspects, eclecticism broke into iron construction.

This division into periods can also be applied to the building of glasshouses between 1800 and 1900 and forms the basis of the following account.

1800–1830: Early Fantasies in Iron

The start was modest; the first iron greenhouses were small and were enclosed by simple, strictly geometric forms. Nevertheless, these were the first structures with frames made entirely of iron. The strength of these iron structures had to be found by experimental methods, as in bridge building. There arose in Britain at the start of the nineteeth century three basic types of space frames, with corresponding supporting structures.

• Greenhouses in the form of long buildings with lean-to or ridge-and-furrow roofs. The plane surface of the roof and the front simplified the glazing—particularly with double glazing, which was preferred in continental Europe. A common and characteristic feature of these buildings is the "open" framework formed by a combination of hollow-column supports and a ridge-and-furrow (Paxton gutter) roof. This type of construction allowed the roof area to be divided into a number of sections of basic structural elements so that the rain falling on the roof could easily drain away down the hollow columns. The earliest and simplest form of this type arose from the wooden-frame glasshouse with a ridge roof. This method was used in the "iron hothouse" at Hohenheim near Stuttgart, built in 1789, the first iron building. In 1803 a cast-iron three-bay hall-type building with a ridge-and-furrow roof was designed by Humphrey Repton for the Prince of Wales at Carlton House. In the following years there arose in Britain under Loudon's influence numerous simple greenhouses with these "folded" roofs. Fully developed types are the five-bay buildings built in 1823 and 1825 by the firm of Thomas Clark at Wollaton Hall and The Grange. Pairs of columns joined by sheet-metal vaults and Paxton gutters supported the glass ridge roof between them. The important outcome of the further development of this type is the complete ridge-and-furrow cover with gutters draining rainwater into hollow columns as the fundamental elements of the cast-iron space frame. Besides this form of construction we find the early use of cast-iron ribs for supporting the ridge roof and the beginning of the use of a load-bearing facade in the form of a cast-iron framework.

• Greenhouses with vaulted roofs. These glass-and-iron buildings with vaulted roofs, often consisting of curved wrought-iron glazing bars, are typically British and were only occasionally used in Europe. The vaulted greenhouse goes back to the theoretical proposals of Thomas A. Knight (1811) and George Mackenzie (1815), which were based on experiments to find the best illumination from the sun by using curved surfaces. The practical application of these trials came with Loudon's experimental buildings at Bayswater (1817) and Hackney (1820), for which rolled glazing bars were curved while they were still hot. The spans of these early flexible arch structures were remarkably great—approximately 33 feet. The characteristic feature of this type was the abolition of the distinction between roof and wall, beams and column supports by the use of a glass-and-iron curve right down to ground level.

• Greenhouses made of masonry, with the roof as in the preceding two types. This basic type was descended from the eighteenth-century orangery, but the massive walls were now broken up into narrow shafts separating windows, and the roof was completely glazed.

The large greenhouses were a further form of development, built around a central hall topped by a dome, transepts or wings, and end pavilions. An early example of this design, having a glass roof with wooden sash bars, is the greenhouse by Alessandro Galilei (1750), described by Richard Bradley.[148] The glasshouse at Sezincote, built by Repton and Cockerell (1806), is a variant on this theme, having an arcuate wing attached to the "villa" and terminated by a tower-shaped pavilion at the end. The Syon glasshouse, built by Charles Fowler, was an early culmination of this line of development. A high glass dome made of cast-iron ribs supported on iron columns dominated a structure consisting of a central hall, arc-shaped wings, and wing pavilions and enclosed by a dome and ridge roofs. A further example is the glasshouse in the Brussels Botanic Gardens built by Tieleman Franciscus Suys, which is reminiscent of a Baroque layout in its assembly of parts. In this type, the traditional prestige forms were incorporated as a counterpoise to the functionally designed iron structure. This contradiction in style and technique was taken up in the nineteenth century as a means of assimilating the iron structure into the local scenery.

1830–1850: A Period of Experiment

The second generation of iron greenhouses, built between 1830 and 1850, made use of the technical developments in iron construction to achieve the greater spans and heights that were demanded by the increasing scope of palm collecting and the efforts made to build glass halls and extensive indoor

gardens. The tropical landscape transplanted to the northern lands and made possible by an artificial climate was proof of the new technical possibilities of the industrial age. Glass-covered botanical gardens and winter gardens, such as the Jardin d'Hiver in Paris, were opened for the amusement of the public. Steam and hot-water heating and the significantly improved techniques of glass manufacture were important factors in the rise of these prototypes of the great exhibition buildings.

The ridge-and-furrow roof permitted an almost unlimited increase in the size of the halls in all directions of the space frame, in contrast to what was possible with the vaulted roof. There was hardly any limit to the application of this type of light roof. Several acres could be covered in this way if hollow cast-iron pillars were to be used for the supports. These pillars could simultaneously serve to drain the rainwater from the roof.[149] This thinking was applied to a variable prefabricated space frame with an optional number of stories and a range of spans by Paxton, who began his structural experiments with hall-type glasshouses at Chatsworth in 1832. With the construction of the victoria regia house at Chatsworth in 1849, Paxton perfected the combination of roof supports (valley beams), a ridge-and-furrow roof, a facade, and supporting columns by applying the box-frame principle. Thus, by incorporating the lessons learned from hothouse building in the first half of the century, he created the basis for the vast iron-skeleton buildings of the second half of the century: the exhibition halls, crystal palaces, and winter gardens.

The second line of development of the hall-type structure with a ridge or sawtooth roof was characterized by the use of curved cast-iron girders with their flanges converging toward the upper end and with ornamental reinforcement in the web between the flanges. This trend, which started at the beginning of the nineteenth century with Repton's glass hall, led to countless variations and ever-greater truss spans. Examples of this are Hector Horeau's winter garden in Lyon (1847, figs. 38, 372, 373) and his design for an "Exhibition Palace" in London (1850; fig. 39).

With the introduction of arched and parallel girders (figs. 55, 63, 111), an economical and technically advanced solution to the problem of the roof supports was found, and cast-iron ribs possessed no possibility of further development. In addition, the hanging truss (figs. 50, 107, 640, 683) and the marquee-type roof (figs. 412, 414) came into use. The Jardin des Plantes, by Charles Rohault de Fleury (1833), was the first large glasshouse on the Continent to

have a space frame made entirely of iron. Of historical and constructional interest in the Jardin des
Plantes was the multistory cast-iron facade, which
also served as the roof support (figs. 81, 658).

Out of the continued development of Loudon's
curvilinear roofs there arose circular and multibay
glass vaults of greater size. The interior supporting
structure consisted of a series of iron columns together with precast ribs having the circular or parabolic profile of the vault.

The first large circular building with a structure
built entirely of iron was the palm house at Bretton
Hall, built by Loudon in 1827. This bell-shaped glasshouse consisted of a dome placed above a ring of
columns with a low glass vault reaching down to
ground level and forming the base (figs. 200–203).
The superimposition of two glass vaults separated by
an interior cast-iron frame resulted in a rectangular
ground plan (possibly with semicircular ends) and a
basilicalike overall space form, with a main nave and
two aisles with apse-shaped ends. This space form—
according to H. Jordan a characteristic of greenhouse
design—reflected the desire to group the plants in
the form of a natural landscape, with the tall palms
occupying the middle space and the lower trees,
bushes, and ferns in the adjacent aisles.[150] With the
superimposition of the glass vaults, it was possible to
create a quasi-organic transition to the outside. A
special construction type also corresponded to this
space form: that of girders arranged like ribs.

This type first emerged in Loudon's 1823 project
for a country house with an attached winter garden.
The highly distinctive space form of this project was
descended from church architecture: a cruciform
plan with a nave and transept, surrounded by aisles,
and with a high glass dome above the crossing (fig.
7c). In practice, however, designers limited themselves around 1830 mostly to two superimposed tiers
of elongated hemivaults supported on the inside by a
line of cast-iron columns and on the outside by a
masonry base. Examples of this include the London
Coliseum (1830; fig. 330) and, stimulated by that, the
aisles in the glasshouse of the Jardin des Plantes
(1831; fig. 131).

Paxton's Great Conservatory at Chatsworth
(1836–1840), in which only the inner supporting structure was of iron (with wooden ribs), was the first
devlopment on a grand scale and in a technically sophisticated form of the basilicalike glasshouse with
nave and aisles. This building was vast for its time—
about 300 feet long and 130 feet wide, with a 66-
foot-high central vault having a clear span of 75 feet.
Its span exceeded those of the largest railway sta-

tions of the period. The transition from the ridge-
and-furrow roof with straight sash bars to the vault
is of technical interest here. Richard Turner used a
variant of this form in the Glasnevin glasshouse
(1840–1850; fig. 47). The zenith of this spatial and
constructional type was reached with the palm house
at Kew (1848), built entirely of glass and iron by
Richard Turner and Decimus Burton. Rolled-section I
beams were used here in a simple arch shape (figs.
46, 338–343, 613–619). The structure consisted of a
central nave (based on the Chatsworth prototype)
with surrounding aisles and two wings terminated by
hemidomes. This classical form later served as a favorite prototype and was repeated in countless
variations.

The gigantic glass-and-iron building of the Jardin
d'Hiver (1848) was a transitional form leading to the
exhibition building. Over 330 feet long, with a nave
and transept and encircling aisles, it had a cast-iron
space frame with a gallery and ribs extending down
to the ground with latticework stiffening (figs. 62,
417–421, 660–664).

Greenhouses made of masonry with iron roof
structures include the conservatory at Dalkeith Palace
(1830; fig. 37), the orangery at Kew (1836; figs. 36,
624), and the Enville Hall glasshouse (1850; fig. 246).
The combination of stone architecture with ironwork
in these prevented progressive structural designs
from appearing.

1850–1870: The Triumph of "Pure" Construction

The experimental phase of greenhouse building
came to an end around the middle of the nineteenth
century. By this time there was available a repertoire
of designs for spatial concepts and of corresponding
structural solutions. At the same time, enough structural preparatory work had been done to meet the
new demands for advanced designs for large exhibition buildings, winter gardens, and floras. In 1850,
Paxton was able to design the basic structural and
spatial concept of the Crystal Palace in a few
hours—during a committee meeting. This fund of
experience reflects a high state of detailed knowledge
about glass and iron and about the methods of mass
production.

The transfer of the fundamental structural and
spatial solutions of greenhouse building to the building of exhibition halls was helped by the similarity
of the building specifications, which even before 1850
led to numerous transitional forms. The basic requirements were large and dominating halls without
massive masonry walls or roofs, but having surrounding galleries; good illumination, achieved by

glazing the whole exterior skin; and a marqueelike temporary character to give variability and flexibility, all of which was to express itself structurally in light prefabricated parts that could be assembled and dismantled easily. There now appeared quite often glass-and-iron buildings in which the spatial and structural features of the glasshouse were combined with vaulted roofs, or with ridge-and-furrow roofs supported by a cast-iron space frame. The most important results of the phase from 1850 to 1870 were the spread of the multistory cast-iron space frame in greenhouse and exhibition buildings and the simultaneous success in the prefabrication of building components (which likewise were mostly made of cast iron).

In the construction of trusses, cast iron was progressively replaced by wrought iron. One exception was the cast-iron parallel-flange braced girder used as a standard element in Paxton-type space frames.

Cast-Iron Space-Frame Buildings (Hall Complexes)
This type was first seen in fully developed form in the Crystal Palace at London (figs. 84, 347–363, 626, 627, 648). (In the following account, only glass-and-iron buildings, which are spatially and structurally connected with the development of greenhouse buildings, are considered.) These buildings often had combinations of vaulted and ridge-and-furrow roofs and appeared in the form of a complex of halls. Examples are the Glass Palace in Munich, with its ridge-and-furrow roof (figs. 35, 395–399, 646, 647), and the winter garden in Dublin, with its barrel vault in the nave (figs. 239, 240).

Greenhouses with Lean-To or Ridge Roofs of Large Spans
Among the buildings with plane-surface roofs were elongated halls, partly of lattice-frame construction. In structural and spatial form (long halls with masonry sides), railway-station roofs appear more commonly as the prototype. Examples include the temperate house at Kew (figs. 54, 344, 345, 620–622) and the winter garden of Maximilian II (fig. 401).

Greenhouses with Vaulted Roofs Incorporating Basilica Designs

Long Halls The Kew palm house serves as an example of these. Other examples include the palm house in Edinburgh (figs. 48, 242–245, 543–548), where the glass vault covers a high "orangery" made of masonry; the extension to the glasshouse complex in the Jardin des Plantes (figs. 416, 657); and the crowning vault on the Schönbrunn glasshouse in Vienna by Franz von Sengenschmid (1882), which, strictly, belongs to the next period.

Buildings with a Dominant Central Structure Important here is the further development of the central building with glass-and-iron domes with basilica cross-section. The basic type created at Bretton Hall in 1827, having a dome space with a gallery below, was taken up again but with a greater span in the Kibble Palace (figs. 134, 257–261, 557–563). Here the structure was extended to extremes. In the center of the circular hall, supported on cast-iron columns, was a flat glass-and-iron dome supported only by slender wrought-iron sash bars and having a clear span of almost 66 feet and an overall diameter of 146 feet.

Flora Buildings: Long Halls with Vaulted Roofs, Combined with Multistory Masonry Walls
In the winter gardens that served as recreation centers, with concert halls, libraries, dance halls, and restaurants, the structure surrounding the glass-and-iron hall was often of masonry. Here there was no need to make the structure in the form of an iron skeleton. In their spatial and structural form these flora buildings resembled the standard main-line railway terminal. The roof was supported by arched wrought-iron lattice girders, which rested partly on masonry and partly on rows of cast-iron columns.

The flora type had already been formulated with the Jardin d'Hiver. The entrance section and the transept part were surrounded by masonry work. Here, as in the basement, there were rooms designated for general recreation purposes. The wrought-iron vault structure had an indecisive, experimental character.

The first flora in Germany, in Cologne, designed by H. Märtens and Georg Eberlein in 1864, was related in shape and structure to the Paris building, but lattice ribs were used (figs. 295–299, 585–588). After this came the Frankfurt flora (figs. 249–254, 554–556) by Friedrich Kayser, in which heavy-looking riveted box-section girders spanned the winter garden like the arches in a railway station, and the Berlin flora (figs. 163–168, 492, 492) by Hubert Stier, the first winter garden in which three-hinge arched ribs were used to support the roof. The Berlin flora, in which cast iron was completely ousted as a building material by wrought iron or steel in the form of riveted girders, marked the start of a new era of engineered steel buildings.

1870–1900: The Heyday of Iron Architecture

During this phase, as America was becoming known for her industrial potential, as railways were about to transform the world, and as preparations for war were soon to begin, iron found a ready market. Large amounts of capital were concentrated in the hands of a few tycoons who had survived the competition of previous periods, and the industrial upper middle class obtained unbridled power. The rationalism that enabled this class to reach its new position expressed itself most clearly in the new factory buildings. The verve of the pioneering period, which Paxton's buildings embodied in puritanically simple forms, continued in the giant frameworks of the factory complexes where goods were now mass-produced, and these goods were displayed en masse for the first time in the Crystal Palace. Paxton's continuous sawtooth-shape roofs now gave protection and light to pounding machines. Insofar as the modernity of glass-and-iron architecture had its origin in the logic of mass production, it was now unconditionally accepted in the factory building. Glass-and-iron architecture was valued by the new class for personal and public prestige.

However, while manufacturing establishments were designed in an uncompromising way, the previously sharply defined and clearly understood iron structures of exhibition buildings, winter gardens, arcades, and hothouses were now clothed with borrowed vestments and the false ostentation of historicism. Together with the leading social stratum, the middle class appeared to have lost the force of its self-confidence at the moment of its seizure of power. Only in its very own realm, in the production establishments, could it express itself and its age. Public buildings were no longer objects of its identity. The conflict between real political power and anxiety over wielding it publicly characterized the end of the century. In the world exhibitions that were now superseding each other, the "pure forms" of the machine now appeared side by side with overdone decoration. At the festival of manufactured goods that was being celebrated in these glass-and-iron buildings, the host withdrew discreetly. He did not want to be considered as more than the originator of such lavish display. The buildings were given to the public as a parting gift. In his retreat to prestige forms of the past, he was no longer inspired by the belief in progress. The more aggressive the ornamentation, the more it created the impression of riches for everyone. What was brought about in the factories—the destruction of man's feelings—was to be concealed here in the noble gesture of a feast for the eyes. Bertolt Brecht was of the opinion that if middle-class culture were one day to be overwhelmed and then exhumed, only the factory buildings would bear witness to its historic mission.

Most of the exhibition buildings, hothouses, and winter gardens erected during this period were characterized by contradiction. There were no longer new spatial forms, but the dimensions increased to keep up with the increasing numbers of curious visitors. The techniques were now mainly based on iron structures, which by the last decade of the nineteenth century consisted mostly of machine-welded steel. The girder, in its multiplicity of forms, often played the dominant role in building construction while forming the space frame. New structural concepts such as two- and three-hinge girders were put into use; these rose directly from ground level to create glass halls in the form of inverted boats. In addition, latticework domes arose which extended over the central space as space frames.

On the one hand, welded structures could now be made in rounded, organic shapes; on the other hand, standard rolled-steel section was made up into shapes resembling crude carpentry to build into plane roofs and facades. Thus we find plant houses with smooth glass fronts resembling factory buildings but having some architectural appeal because of their large overall dimensions and the symmetry, proportions, and rhythm of their building elements. To this category belong the glasshouses in Copenhagen (figs. 300–305, 589–592), Herrenhausen (figs. 275–278, 570, 571), Strasbourg (figs. 436–440), Tübingen (figs. 449, 450, 691, 692), and Innsbruck (figs. 282, 576, 577). These plant houses and winter gardens, characterized by objectivity and often by sternness, stand in contrast with those in which iron once more took a poetic form. It appears as if architects and engineers sought to rebel once more against the dictates of mass production and calculation. They indeed used standard steel section, but they changed its shape into concave and convex curves, producing striking shapes that suggested plant forms and thus anticipated Jugendstil. Among the buildings that followed these ideas were Balat's bell-shaped winter garden at Laeken (figs. 18, 122 , 209–214, 504–509) and Sengenschmid's palm house in Vienna–Schönbrunn (figs. 455–458, 694–697). Here, as in the vaulted palm house in Leningrad shown in figures 599 and 601, the Kew prototype lived on. In Alfred Koerner's hothouse at Berlin-Dahlem (figs. 115, 181–187, 483–485, 487–491), there was a synthesis of inherently objective construction and expressionism. This building, with its high vault and its slender three-hinge girders, proclaimed the utopia of glass architecture that the members of the Crystal Chain dreamed about but could approach only in a literary way—this was the building that inspired Paul Scheerbart.

Summary Table

1800–1830

Glasshouses with lean-to or ridge-and-furrow roofs

Iron Conservatory	Stuttgart-Hohenheim	unknown	1789	C.I.[151]
Conservatory of the Prince of Wales	London, Carlton House	H. Repton	1803	C.I.
Great Conservatory	Kassel, Wilhelmshöhe	J. C. Bromeis	1822	C.I.
Camellia house	Wollaton Hall (Nottingham)	T. Clark	1823	C.I.
Winter Garden	The Grange (Hampshire)	T. Clark	1825	C.I.

Glasshouses with vaulted roofs (Loudon type)

Experimental buildings	Bayswater, London	J. C. Loudon	1817	W.I.
Glasshouses	Hackney, London	J. C. Loudon	1820	W.I.
Palm house	Budleigh Salterton (Devon)	unknown	1843	W.I.
Palm house	Bretton Hall (Yorkshire)	J. C. Loudon	1827	W.I., C.I.

Glasshouses with masonry work and lean-to, ridge-and-furrow, or vaulted roofs

Conservatory	Sezincote (Gloucestershire)	H. Repton and S. P. Cockerell	1806	C.I.
Conservatory	London, Syon House	C. Fowler	1820–1827	C.I.
Conservatories	Brussels, Botanical Gardens	T. F. Suys	1826–1827	C.I.

1830–1850

Glasshouses with lean-to or ridge-and-furrow roofs

Conservatory (main pavilion)	Paris, Jardin des Plantes	C. Rohault	1833	C.I., W.I.
Conservatory	Capesthorne Hall	J. Paxton	1837	C.I., wood
Wilhelma	Stuttgart	L. von Zanth	1843	C.I.
Iron Conservatory	Nymphenburg	F. L. von Sckell	(1818) 1845	C.I.
Exhibition hall	Biebrich am Rhein	unknown	1846, 1861	C.I.
Winter garden	Hluboká nad Vltavou	F. Deer	1847	C.I., W.I.
Winter garden	Lyon	H. Horeau	1847	C.I., wood
Victoria regia house	Chatsworth (Derbyshire)	J. Paxton	1849	C.I., W.I., wood
Borsig winter garden	Berlin, Moabit	M. Strack	1850	C.I.

Glasshouses with vaulted roofs and basilica cross-sections

Anthaeum	Hove (Sussex)	M. Phillips	1832	C.I.
Coliseum	London	unknown	ca. 1833	W.I.
Conservatory (wings)	Paris, Jardin des Plantes	C. Rohault	1833	W.I.
Great Conservatory	Chatsworth (Derbyshire)	J. Paxton	1836–1840	C.I., wood
Conservatory	Chiswick, London	D. and E. Bailey	1840	C.I.
Winter garden	London, Regent's Park	R. Turner and D. Burton	1842–1846	C.I., W.I.
Conservatory	Killikee (Dublin)	R. Turner	1845	C.I., W.I.

Palm house	Belfast, Botanic Garden	R. Turner and C. Lanyon	1839–40, 1853	C.I. W.I.
Palm house	London, Kew Gardens	R. Turner and D. Burton	1844–1848	C.I., W.I.
Jardin d'Hiver	Paris, Champs-Elysées	H. Meynadier, M. Rigolet, Moehly	1846–1848	C.I.

Glasshouses with masonry work and lean-to, ridge-and-furrow, or vaulted roofs

Conservatory	Dalkeith Palace, near Edinburgh	W. Burne	ca. 1830	C.I.
Orangery	London, Kew Gardens	J. Wyatville	1836	C.I.
Conservatory	Enville Hall (Staffordshire)	Gray & Ormson Co.	ca. 1850	C.I., wood

1850–1870

Hall complexes with cast-iron space frames

Crystal Palace	London, Hyde Park	J. Paxton	1850–1851	C.I., W.I., wood
Crystal Palace	London, Sydenham	J. Paxton	1852–1854	C.I., W.I., wood
Crystal Palace	New York	G. J. B. Carstensen, C. Gildemeister	1852	C.I.
Glass Palace	Munich	A. von Voit	1853–54	C.I., W.I.
Palais de l'Industrie	Paris	C. F. Viel and A. Barrault	1855	C.I., W.I.
Great Palm House	Berlin, Botanical Garden	C. D. Bouché Herter & Nietz Co.	1857–1859	C.I., W.I.
Palm house	Munich, Botanical Garden	A. von Voit	1860–1865	C.I., W.I.
Conservatory	Breslau (Wroclaw)	unknown	1861	C.I., W.I.
Winter garden	Dublin	A. G. Jones, R. M. Ordish, Le Feuvre	1865	C.I., W.I.
Winter garden	Buxton, Pavilion Garden	E. Milner	1871	C.I., W.I.
Old Palm House	Bonn	Neumann	1875	C.I., W.I.

Glasshouses with lean-to or ridge roofs or greater spans

| Winter Garden of Maximilian II | Munich | A. von Voit | 1854 | W.I. |
| Temperate house | London, Kew Gardens | D. Burton | 1859–1863 | C.I., W.I. |

Glasshouses with vaulted roofs and basilica cross-sections

Palm house (extension)	Paris, Jardin des Plantes	C. Rohault	1854	C.I., W.I.
Floral Hall	London, Covent Garden	E. M. Barry	1857–58	C.I., W.I.
Palm house	Edinburgh, Royal Botanic Garden	R. Matthienson	1858	C.I., W.I.
Winter garden	Leeds, General Hospital		1868	C.I., W.I.
Winter garden	London, Royal Horticultural Society	J. A. Hughes, Fowke, A. Handyside & Co.	1860–61	C.I., W.I.

Kibble Palace	Glasgow, Queen's Park	J. Kibble	1872	W.I. (C.I.)

Multistory floras with masonry work

Flora	Cologne	H. Märtens, G. Eberlein	1864	C.I., W.I.
Flora	Frankfurt am Main	F. Kayser	1869–1871	W.I.
Flora	Berlin	H. Stier	1871–1873	W.I.
Alexandra Palace	London, Muswell Hill	J. Johnson	1872–1874	C.I., W.I.

1870–1900

Glasshouses with lean-to or ridge roofs

Aquarium	Berlin	W. Luer	1869	W.I.
Palm house	Copenhagen	T. Rothe, J. C. Jacobsen	1872–1874	W.I. (C.I.)
Great Conservatory	Strasbourg	H. Eggert	1877–1882	W.I.
Palm house	Herrenhausen	Auhagen	1879	W.I.
Conservatory	Tübingen	A. Koch	1885–86	W.I.
Palm house	Innsbruck	unknown	1905	W.I.
Subtropical house	Berlin-Dahlem	A. Koerner	1908–09	W.I.

Glasshouses with vaulted roofs

Winter garden of Ludwig II	Munich	A. von Voit	1867–1869	W.I.
Palm house	Florence	G. Roster	1874	C.I., W.I.
Winter garden	Laeken	A. Balat, H. Maquet	1875–76	W.I.
Central Hotel	Berlin	H. von der Hude, J. Hennicke	1880	W.I.
Palm house	Vienna, Schönbrunn	F. von Sengenschmid	1880–1882	W.I., C.I.
Winter garden	Glasgow	unknown	1880	W.I., C.I.
Palm house	Leningrad	unknown	1880–1890	W.I.
Palm house	Liverpool	Mackenzie and Moncur Co.	1896	W.I., C.I.
Ny Carlsberg Glyptotek	Copenhagen	V. Dahlerup	1904–1906	W.I., C.I.
Garden Hall	Paris	C. A. Gautier	1900	W.I.
Palm house	Berlin	A. Koerner	1905–1907	W.I.

16, 17
Cross-sections of interiors (scale 1:800). Figure 16 (left half of page) shows lean-to and ridge roofs: (1) Wollaton Hall, 1823; (2) Chatsworth, 1834; (3) Chatsworth, 1841; (4) Dalkeith Palace, 1841; (5) Nymphenburg, Munich, 1820; (6) Pfaueninsel, Berlin, 1829; (7) Jardin des Plantes, Paris, 1833; (8) Lyon, 1847; (9) Berlin-Schöneberg, 1857; (10) Kew, London, 1859; (11) Herrenhausen, 1879; (12) Glass Palace, Munich, 1853. Figure 17 (right half of page) shows vaulted roofs: (13) Langport, 1817; (14) Hackney, 1820; (15) Budleigh Salterton, 1843; (16, 17) Coliseum, London, 1833; (18) Bretton Hall, 1827; (19) Jardin des Plantes, Paris, 1833; (20) Lednice, 1843; (21) Kew, London, 1844; (22) Glasnevin, Dublin, 1850; (23) Jardin d'Hiver, Paris, 1846; (24) Glasgow, 1872; (25) Berlin-Charlottenburg, 1871; (26) Vienna-Schönbrunn, 1880; (27) Berlin-Dahlem, 1905; (28) Laeken, Brussels, 1875.

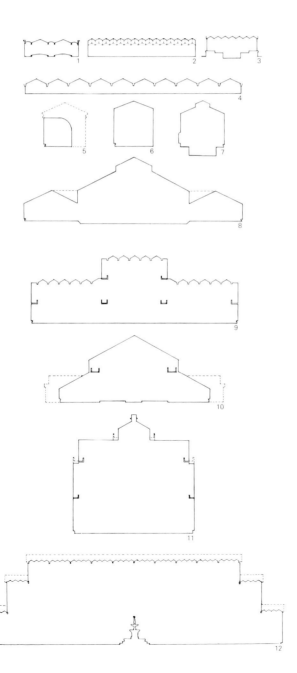

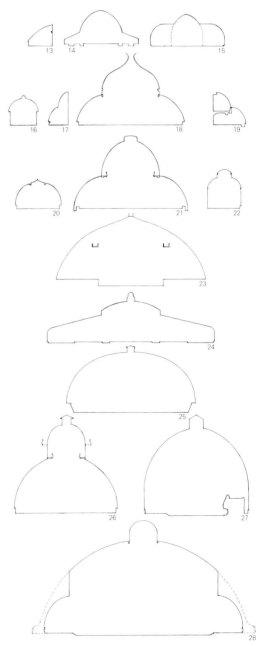

Steam, Iron, and the Industrial Revolution

Soon shall thy arm, UNCONQUER'D STEAM! afar
Drag the slow barge, or drive the rapid car;
Or on wide-waving wings expanded bear
The flying chariot through the fields of air.
—Fair crews triumphant leaning from above,
Shall wave their fluttering kerchiefs as they move;
Or warrior-bands alarm the gaping crowd,
And armies shrink beneath the shadowy cloud.

Erasmus Darwin, 1788

The Industrial Revolution was characterized by the transfer of manufacture to machine-powered mass production, in which the output of the individual worker was increased by dividing the job into separate operations, and by the change from manual labor to machine-operated tools. "The machine, which is the starting point of the Industrial Revolution, supersedes the workman, who handles a single tool, by a mechanism operating with a number of similar tools, and set in motion by a single motive power, whatever the form of that power may be."[152] For the definition of the concept, it was immaterial whether the machine was powered by a human operator or by natural forces: "When in 1735 John Wyatt brought out his spinning machine, and began the Industrial Revolution of the eighteenth century, not a word did he say about an ass driving it instead of man, and yet this part fell to the ass. He described it as a machine 'to spin without fingers.' "[153] However, the spread of the compass of machine-powered work and the development of machine tools required engine power.

The power was provided by James Watt's steam engine, which according to Watt's own words now appeared as "a general agent of major industry."[154] With its use, production became independent of natural forces (water power) and could be concentrated in towns, and the country way of life could be renounced. It could operate several machines at the same time, via transmission mechanisms. This first came about in the form of simultaneous operation of many similar machines, but later many different kinds of machines were combined to form a machine system.[155] "A real machinery system . . . does not take the place of these until the subject of labor goes through a connected series of detail processes that are carried out by a chain of machines of various kinds, the one supplementing the other."[156]

The division and organization of work constituted the germ of the Industrial Revolution from 1730 to 1860. Marx wrote: "Here we have, in the place of the isolated machine, a mechanical monster whose body fills whole factories and whose demon power, at first veiled under the slow and measured motions of his giant limbs, at length breaks out into the fast and furious whirl of his countless working organs."[157]

This system of machines, which evolved at the start of the nineteenth century in the textile industry, culminated after 1850 in the growth of heavy industry and then in the establishment of the railways as machines produced other machines. Thus manufacturing created its own technical basis and finally released itself from handwork and other manual production methods.

Machine Tools and Power Sources

The first machine tools appeared in the British textile industry: the spinning jenny (John Wyatt, 1735) and the power-driven loom (Edmund Arkwright, 1785). The Industrial Revolution was born in light industry, because the earliest accumulation of capital occurred in that industry but also because the capital investment required for the machines concerned was lower here than in heavy industry. Moreover, capital could circulate and bring profit faster.[158] Machine spinning led to a surplus of spun yarns and thus made the powered loom necessary. Together these machines caused the mechanical and chemical revolution in dyeing, bleaching, and printing. Now the inadequate means of transport proved to be a drag on large-scale industry and on the world market that was ready to receive its products.[159]

As tool and machine production expanded, the demand for iron and steel increased. The stagnation of charcoal-fueled iron production caused by the uncontrolled cutting of timber in Britain could be counteracted only by changing the smelting process to use coal or coke. With the blast furnace, invented by Abraham Darby II in 1735, no wrought iron could be produced but cast iron became economically available in larger amounts. (Charcoal was still necessary for the wrought-iron refining process.) The invention of crucible-cast steel by Benjamin Huntsman (1740) started the mass production of durable tools. With the increase in the number of blast furnaces after 1768, the coke-oven technology changed and the chemical processes became more controllable. The invention of the puddling process in 1784 made coal the predominant base of heavy industry.

With the use of the steam engine, blast furnaces became independent of water power and were moved near the iron-ore and coal deposits or into the towns. The need to transport raw materials and finished iron goods accelerated the building of canals and iron railways in the coal mines and in the industrial regions. The existence of the iron industry created the need for iron fire grates, coke-oven frameworks and cladding, railway lines, wheels, sleepers, bridges, lock gates, machines, cylinders, levers, flywheels, ships, and wagons.

There were limits, however:

Just as the individual machine retains a dwarfish character, so long as it is worked by the power of man alone, and just as no system of machinery could be properly developed before the steam-engine took the place of the earlier motive powers, animals, wind, and even water; so too, Modern Industry was crippled in its complete development, so long as its characteristic instrument of production, the machine, owed its existence to personal strength and personal skill, and depended on the muscular development, the keenness of sight, and the cunning of hand, with which the detail workmen in manufactures, and the manual labourers in handicrafts, wielded their dwarfish implements. Thus, apart from the dearness of the machines made in this way, a circumstance that is ever present to the mind of the capitalist, the expansion of industries carried on by means of machinery, and the invasion by machinery of fresh branches of production, were dependent on the growth of a class of workmen, who, owing to the almost artistic nature of their employment, could increase their numbers only gradually, and not by leaps and bounds. [160]

Not until the growth of the railway network was there internal pressure for the industrial organization of machine manufacture. [161] With the revolution in the transport sector, starting in the 1830s, it was possible to increase the rate of production. "But the huge masses of iron that had now to be forged, to be welded, to be cut, to be bored, and to be shaped, demanded, on their part, cyclopean machines, for the construction of which the methods of the manufacturing period were utterly inadequate." [162] Iron was the most important raw material. Cast iron was

dominant from 1750 to 1870, but from 1830 the importance of wrought iron increased steadily with the building of the railways. The Industrial Revolution in building had its origin in the iron foundries and the rolling mills and expressed itself basically in the removal of the building process from the building site to the factory.

The following is a summary of the development of machinery and means of transport.

Early steam engines and blast furnaces [163]

1698	First operational steam engine, by Thomas Savery, used for pumping water.
1706	Savery's machine used in coal mine at Broadwaters.
1712	Atmospheric steam engine invented by Thomas Newcombe. Attempts to alter the "fire engine" into a self-contained motor proved unavailing.
1767	Exhibition of 67 "fire engines" in Newcastle-upon-Tyne.
1769	Development of the steam engine capable of universal application by James Watt and Matthew Bolton. Conversion of the linear motion of the piston into a rotary motion by the double-acting steam engine.
1770	First steam-driven cylinder bellows made of cast iron by John Smeaton.

Mechanical working of iron

Rolling mills [164]

pre-1700	Early cutting and rolling mills for the manufacture of iron bars made of wrought iron.
1728	John Payne's patent for adjustable rollers.
1766	John Purnell's patent for round iron rollers.
1783	Adjustable rollers for manufacture of complex iron mouldings and for hardening.
1783–84	Cort's process. Use of rollers for forming and simultaneous pressing out of the dross made by the puddling process.
1820	Use of rollers for making iron section in the form of railway lines by John Birkinshaw.

Machine tools [165]

1774	Construction of the first drilling machine for metal by John Wilkinson. Accuracy of measurement $1/4$ inch.
ca. 1800	Invention of the iron planing machine by J. Element, the hydraulic press by Joseph Bramah, and lathe cutting by Henry Maudsley.

from 1784   Introduction of the steam hammer, which in the first half of the century was improved by James Nasmyth.

ca. 1850   Steam-driven machine tools—drilling machines, hydraulic presses, machine-turning lathes, planing machines, guillotines, and steam hammers—often used in combination within a single factory.

Railways[166]

1740   First trials of cast-iron rails by J. Wilkinson.

1767   Practical cast-iron railway by Richard Reynolds.

1770   Steam locomotive by N. J. Cugnot.

1776   Flanged rail by B. Cort.

1786   Cast-iron rails bridged between sleepers by William Jessop; after that the use of "fish-bellied" rails.

1804–1808   Trials by Richard Trevithick with steam locomotives for rail transport of iron ore.

1814   Construction of first generally usable steam locomotive by George Stephenson.

1825   First public railway line, between Stockton and Darlington, put into service.

ca. 1860   Success of railway traffic for international trade.

Railways

No invention has had such a great influence on the demand for iron as the railway.
—L. Beck, 1879[167]

The road network proved itself inadequate for bulk transport of heavy industrial goods because of tolls and the slowness of the transport companies.[168] Britain possessed a wealth of natural waterways, and around 1790 manufacturers and mine owners began to build canals and locks feverishly. This eased the congestion for a while. However, by the first decades of the nineteenth century this means of commerce also proved inadequate.[169] The disastrous obstruction in the waterways around 1820, intensified by the monopoly policy of the canal companies, had become a serious threat to British industry as a whole.

The way to the development of railways began with the transformation of the static steam engine into the self-propelled engine. One of the first attempts at this was the locomotive built by Cugnot in 1770. Other early attempts sought to build a machine that "actually had two feet, which after the manner of a horse it raised alternately from the ground."[170] Man had not yet understood that the locomotive and rails belonged to each other "like man and wife."[171]

Thus, the early success of steam-powered transport was on the water. Robert Fulton invented the steamship in 1807; the first steam-powered ship crossed the Atlantic in 1819.[172]

However, the guidance of vehicles by rails was already customary in the mines, where coal trucks ran on wooden tracks. The substitution of iron for wood was first made at Coalbrookdale, where Darby's foundry in 1767 had its internal transport system running on cast-iron rails with a U-shaped cross-section, developed by R. Reynolds. The external factor here was a general decline in the demand for cast-iron goods, so that the production of cast-iron rails became an important part of the trade of the British foundries.[173] Jessop's use of cast-iron rails in conjunction with flanged wheels to guide the car was a decisive improvement.[174] In a further development, rails were made with a T cross-section, and these were the prototype of the independent railway lines that became successful with the introduction of rolled wrought-iron rails by John Birkinshaw (ca. 1820). After that, the fragile cast-iron rails became obsolete. Building on the 1808–1814 experiments of R. Trevithick, and stimulated by the need for cheap transport of coal, G. Stephenson continued the development of the locomotive.[175]

In 1825 the Stockton–Darlington line, built in 1822 for the purpose of carrying coal, became the first public railway. This led to the overland transport industry, which from 1830 extended its network at a breathtaking rate, first in Britain and then in all industrial countries and their market outlets.[176]

The building of the railroads consumed great amounts of iron; it "not only demanded the creation of ironworks, but also opened up a new and larger market to them."[177] The foundation of competitive railway companies, which required investment capital, automatically followed the establishment of heavy industry. The enormous sums of money which were required for the building of the railroads made share capital necessary for the first time.[178] At the end of 1856 the capital invested in the Great Western Railway Company was £23,019,000. The building of the Paddington terminal in London alone cost £620,000.[179] By about 1860 the railway had created the world market by extending the trade network, and by its mass transport of people and goods it had brought about the further division of labor between town and countryside, agriculture and industry. The sudden growth of towns and the increasing agglomeration of people and capital in metropolitan areas were directly connected with the development of the railway network.

The spread of iron construction in architecture finds a parallel here. This is immediately apparent in bridge building: "All bridge construction before 1828–29 was like a prelude, and not until the railways were born did it press forward with strength."[180] The railway was also decisive in initiating the use of iron in the construction of factories, railway stations, covered markets, warehouses, and exhibition buildings. The concentration brought about by the railway was mirrored by the concentration of trade and business in giant buildings, such as the Crystal Palace at London and the Glass Palace at Munich. Indirectly, through the rapidly increasing use of wrought iron for the railways and through the consequent scarcity and increased price of this material, the iron foundries found an opportunity to introduce the lower-priced cast iron in greater quantities for building construction.[181]

The "Age of Iron"

Steam power put new life into the most important areas of trade and industry, and iron gained an unlimited dominance in the field of machines and building construction, which it owed especially to its powerful associates, steam and coal.
—G. Mertens[182]

Circa 1700

The techniques of iron production in Britain and on the Continent were developing very differently around 1700. Besides the traditional methods, which were lagging behind technologically, there already existed in Britain coke ovens and wrought-iron foundries.

The high temperatures needed for obtaining pig iron required a powerul continuous air blast, produced mechanically. This made the operation of blast furnaces dependent not only on the proximity of iron deposits to forests but also on the availability of water energy. Iron works, hammer forges, stamping mills, and cast-iron foundries moved from separate localities all over the country to sites by rivers. This furthered the division of labor and the specialization in the multitude of processes involved in the manufacture and shaping of iron products. The concentration of the mechanically operated devices and of the workers led to an early form of capital accumulation and hence to the raising of foundry work out of the realm of small business and the limitation of the guilds.

Cast iron was first obtained purely by chance in the form of liquid pig iron with the use of higher temperatures in the smelting process. With the rec-

ognition of its quality, it was systematically produced for the manufacture of goods in the fifteenth century. The basis of this was the refining process in finery hearths for pig iron (cast iron for cannon). Cast-iron goods, such as oven dishes and gratings, were generally produced by casting directly in the iron foundries.[183]

1700–1800

The progress in iron foundry techniques in the eighteenth century consisted essentially of the application of coal technology and the puddling process (a mechanized refining process). The development in iron casting, first in the shadow of pig-iron production, obtained its decisive impetus from the industrialization that came after 1750. Cast iron became an essential raw material for machines and for mass production in general. This material's ability to take up every shape with equal ease, and to be reproducible, went halfway toward meeting the requirement of mass production for standardized goods. This, along with the unusually low processing costs, made it possible for cast iron, toward the end of the century, to intervene in the building industry, which was hitherto reliant on timber and stone. It made its first appearance here in the form of mass-produced prefabricated building components. With the introduction of rolled iron section in 1820, wrought iron increased in importance as a building material.

Coalbrookdale was the place where Abraham Darby II discovered the coal-and-coke method of smelting iron ore. The fact that the wrought iron obtained by this means remained brittle favored the use of cast iron. By 1703, Abraham Darby I was making moulds of damp sand for casting iron, an important step in the direction of cast-iron work.

In this respect the discoveries of René-Antoine de Réaumur in the 1820s were also important. Réaumur, the first to consider iron founding from the scientific standpoint, developed small, mobile, and tilting smelting furnaces. A further step in the development of cast-iron techniques was Isaac Wilkinson's 1758 patent for casting tubular iron parts, the introduction of hot blast furnaces for large quantities of cast iron, and the invention of the cupola furnace by James Wilkinson in 1794. With the arrival of the cupola furnace, which was cheap to install and operate, iron casting became independent of the blast furnace. Cast-iron foundries now arose in British towns in the immediate vicinity of their markets.[184]

1800–1870

With the end of the eighteenth century a new period of iron production commenced with the industrialized production of wrought iron by the puddling process introduced in 1784. The steam engine supplied the large amount of power needed for the working of iron. It consequently served as a power source for the rolling process, which from the start constituted an integral part of the Cort process. With the revolutionizing of iron manufacture and working, Britain had by ca. 1800 become the greatest iron producer and hence the world's leading industrial nation. Her natural wealth of iron and coal could now be exploited in a systematic way. In the period 1800–1870, Britain's pig-iron production rose by a factor of 30. Around 1870 she was producing half of the world's output.

However, the large quantities of wrought iron required for the railways and for shipbuilding, factories, and machines could no longer be permanently supported by the established means of production in Britain. The puddling process (a great advance over the previous refining process) had to give way in the 1860s to the mass production of mild steel. The increasing needs of industry, particularly in the manufacture of machines, led to further improvements in the cast-iron process. This in turn had a marked effect on the advance of cast iron for components in bridges and in buildings generally. In Germany numerous books on artistic cast-iron work were published.

Theoretical and empirical observations spread and brought about the improvement of the smelting process in blast furnaces and foundries. The theory of the formation of dross (Jöns Jakob Berzelius) and the invention of air blast heating (James B. Neilson) formed the basis for rationalized blast-furnace works. The most important improvement in cast-iron techniques was the introduction of molding machines for the production of cast-iron parts (pipes, gear wheels, etc.), which were in great demand. Thus machines replaced manual work (1827: introduction of the pattern plate; 1845: pipe forming without a pattern by drilling in the casting sand; 1851: use of double-sided pattern plates; 1855: first lift molding machine at Paris World Exhibition; 1875: invention of double-sided pattern plate; 1885: introduction of metal drawing machines; 1890: first conveyor-belt production method).[185]

From 1856 the efforts to carry out mechanized puddling increased. In that year Sir Henry Bessemer registered a patent that was to revolutionize the future of iron production just as much as the puddling process did. It consisted of a new method of making steel, in which melted pig iron was converted into liquid steel or wrought iron by blowing air through it. In 1865 the Siemens-Martin process spread steel production. With these processes, iron production in

the hearth received a scientific basis and became a controllable chemical and mechanical conversion process. Production until then had depended on the skill of the operator, but now wrought iron of previously unattainable quality could be produced economically by industrial methods. This completed the Industrial Revolution in iron production, which during the same period expressed itself in the production of machines by other machines. These technical and metallurgical innovations favored the use of wrought iron and steel for building and at the same time prefaced the end of the "era of cast iron."[186]

Pig-iron production, 1800–1870 (millions of tons)[187,188]

	Britain	France	Germany	Rest of world
1800	0.190	0.060	0.040	—
1810	0.250	0.045	0.055	—
1820	0.370	0.140	0.090	—
1830	0.680	0.225	0.120	1.590
1840	1.400	0.405	0.190	2.770
1850	2.250	0.405	0.210	4.280
1860	3.890	0.900	0.550	7.360
1870	4.896	1.290	0.975	9.481

Engineering and the Building Industry

Purpose-built construction became a general requirement of industrial construction in the course of the nineteenth century. This state of affairs was at the same time an expression of the relationship between costs and profits. This logical trend was strengthened by the use of the new, fully mass-produced building material, iron, which replaced the traditional building materials, stone and timber.

Until the spread of rolled steel section in the second half of the nineteenth century, iron was an extremely expensive building material that had to be used economically. In addition, the new wide-span designs of bridges and halls favored the introduction of iron space frames. At the same time, higher rigidity and strength were required. Construction based on empirical experience could no longer be carried on in the old way with the new material. The introduction of iron had to be specially controlled. "The methods employed for this control, the scientific as well as the practical . . . evolved with and in iron buildings, and [were] therefore subject equally to the same controlling factors."[189] "They led to the extension of practice and empiricism through theory, the combination of separate bits of knowledge, into a system, a development of knowledge into a science in the form of a theory of statics and building science. Moreover, iron structures as space frames of individual members were a specially obvious incorporation of static forces operating in buildings, and consequently led to the use of that synthetic method by which problems in mechanics were transported out of the sphere of arithmetical operations and algebraic formulae into building science and were solved."[190]

At the start of the nineteenth century, the theoretical knowledge of statics and experimental building practice entered into a fruitful mutual relationship. This happy cooperation led to astounding developments in building, including the pioneering proposals for iron-and-glass buildings made by Loudon, Paxton, and their followers. Loudon's bold innovation, the entirely new "shell" form of Bayswater House and Bretton Hall, depended on a scientific concept from which he developed a detailed building procedure from the function of the building, and also on the practical experience he had acquired with the construction firm of W. and D. Bailey.

The basic principle of statics, expressed as the law of the equilibrium of forces, was already known in the time of Galileo Galilei, who researched the load-bearing behavior of collar beams and hence provided statements about the calculation of the bending behavior of stressed beams. This knowledge extended the application of Newton's Laws and of Simon Stevin's exposition of the triangle of forces. Important fundamental principles of elasticity were discovered by Robert Hooke, Edmé Mariotte, and Gottfried Wilhelm Leibniz, who researched buckling strength and the relationship between stress and strain and made a start at expressing these relationships in the form of physical laws. François Viéta introduced abstract quantities into the calculations, and Philippe de la Hire extended the work by introducing graphical methods. Building on the works of Johann Bernoulli and Leonhard Euler, Charles Augustin de Coulomb developed his theory of "internal forces" by determining the position of the axis of equilibrium (the neutral line) during the bending of a stressed beam, according to which the stress over the cross-section increases with the distance from the neutral line.[191]

Toward the end of the eighteenth century other theoretical laws were discovered for building structures, particularly bridges. "Nevertheless, practical experience still remained the reliable factor in the fields of architecture and civil engineering up till the end of the eighteenth century."[192]

The crucial change in the development and practice of the theory of statics came from France. This is all the more surprising in that Britain around 1800 was already absolutely dominant in the iron industry because of the invention of the puddling process, the

introduction of the steam engine, and the fact that all the fundamental inventions in the fields of mechanics and ironworking had originated there. The prominence of France in the formulation of theories was due to the central state control and the war economy. For the continued development of the military infrastructure, which was increasingly relevant to production, there was a need for work in the various branches of science, particularly mechanics. The higher technical institute of learning, the Ecole Nationale des Ports et Chaussées, was established as early as 1747. The state also founded a mining academy to promote the improvement of foundry practice. With the founding of the Ecole Nationale Supérieure des Mines in 1747 and the Ecole Polytechnique in 1794, instruction was given in mineralogy, mining, assaying, and foundry science in addition to mechanical sciences.[193] In Britain, on the other hand, the state took almost no interest in the matter of education; technical instruction was heartily ignored. Mechanics Institutes were founded in Birmingham in 1789 and in Glasgow in 1799; however, these provided only limited further education through evening classes.[194]

Toward the end of the eighteenth century there was a parting of the ways between architects and engineers. From this time on, engineers considered building science as "the natural sister of the mathematical sciences," whereas architects increasingly held building to be a matter of aesthetics and used mathematics simply for its laws of proportions.[195] The first large glasshouse structure, the cast-iron dome by François-Joseph Bélanger above the Halle aux Blés in Paris (1811), represents an attempt by the engineer Brunet to design the structure in a mathematical way.[196] A student of Soufflot, Jean-Baptiste Rondelet, published his "Traité théorique et pratique de l'art de bâtir," in which he gave a broad treatment of iron structures and developed a theory of vaults.[197] Statics computations became an important part of construction theory for the first time as the result of the work of Louis Navier. In his major work, "L'application de la mécanique à l'établissement des constructions et des machines" (1824), Navier attempted, after testing all the known theories of statics and dynamics by mathematical analysis, to formulate a scientific system with the intention of bringing theory up to the current level of practice. In his lectures at the Ecole des Ports et Chausées, condensed to the "Resumées" (1826), he aimed at the goal of "expounding the physical conditions operating in the constructions which engineers are in charge of and giving them the means of checking the strength of every member in the structure."[198] Although his theory was in practice concerned only with wood and iron bars (almost entirely with strutted roof trusses), Navier is considered today the founder of the section of mechanics subsequently known as building statics, which became a branch of science in its own right.[199] The knowledge of the material properties of iron was an indispensable requirement for the extension of the field of building statics. Qualitative improvements in the forging and working processes were subsequently made. Unbreakable and simultaneously economical structures were at last achievable under very high loads. Even in 1800, when Thomas Telford designed a cast-iron bridge to span the River Thames, no surveyor could be found who could test the breaking strength of cast iron.[200]

After 1820, when the rolling method of making rails was introduced, railway construction detached itself from building as "a branch of engineering."[201] With the development of railway engineering methods, the strength of iron had become one of the most important matters, particularly in the sphere of bridges and railway lines. "What requirements were to be fixed for the bearing strength of iron? Should cast iron or wrought iron have preference in bridges?"[202] The future of cast iron and wrought iron was decided by the consequent answers to these questions, in which practical experience played a part. The strength tests carried out between 1815 and 1830 were an important step. Building on the eighteenth-century experimental work on the mechanical structure and properties of cast iron by Réne-Antoine Réaumur and Emanuel Svedenborg, J. B. Rondelet in 1814–1817 provided new data by publishing the experimental results of Jacques-Germain Soufflot, A. Eytelweins (1803), and Thomas Young (1807). The last had introduced the concept of the modulus of elasticity. All these experiments related to the distinction between absolute and relative strengths (tensile, compressive, and shear strengths). The increase in the cohesive strength of iron under stress as far as rupture is associated with a change in state of the material, and there is a further increase provided that the stress does not exceed a certain limit. In practice the determination of elastic limits was even more important than that of absolute strength and stress, because it was essential for the determination of the safety of framework structures.[203]

Besides the experiments of the machine manufacturers Bramah and Banks and the bridge builders Rennie and Telford, investigations into the strength of wrought iron were made by Duleau (1820), Tredgold (1823), and Reynolds. These strength tests showed marked deviations in the results because of differences between the types of iron and the methods used. The absolute strength of pig iron was the most common test, but the ultimate strength of this was uncertain on account of its nonhomogeneous structure. The outcome of this series of tests was that the average absolute tensile strength of cast iron was significantly lower than that of wrought iron. On the other hand, in compression cast iron was stronger. Thus was extended on a scientific basis the intuitive and empirical knowledge of the builders of the early metal bridges and large buildings containing ironwork.[204] The methods of designing space frames were thereupon standardized. Hodgkinson and Leeds (1824) carried out experiments on new forms of girders in which attention was centered on the ratio between web depth and flange thickness.[205] Fairbairn, who investigated the problem of the cast-iron beam prestressed by a cable below it, demonstrated that the wrought-iron T beam was superior. Hodgkinson succeeded in finding empirical formulas for the determination of the cross-section of a solid or a hollow round column.[206] Further important developments in the theory of statics resulted from calculations related to the various members incorporated in braced beams.

Camille Polonceau and R. Wiegmann published works on the design of trusses in 1845, and in 1851 Karl Culmann published an extended theory of lattice girders in connection with his report on wooden lattice girders. Culmann based his work on bridges which had been built according to the methods of J. Stefan Long and J. L. Howe without knowledge of the behavior of their internal structures. The theoretical basis of braced girders, extended by the graphical methods of Culmann and Luigi Cremona, brought building science to a high level.[207] The effect of theory on the practice of iron construction, in association with the growing use of rolled-iron section (particularly the I beam), led to a growing trend toward cost-effective design of girders. Cast-iron roof trusses, which until the 1860s were often installed beside the first wrought-iron space frames, were now considered too heavy for further refinement.

"In point of fact, girder theory was first put into practice in connection with wrought-iron structures."[208] Such frameworks in their various forms were able to satisfy the requirements of theoretical statics far earlier than cast-iron ones, without making excessively high demands on the ideal of rationalized construction. The theories of bridge construction in the 1850s and the 1860s had a great influence on the future choice of material. Numerous failures of cast-iron bridges which appeared on analysis to have been caused by this material's poor impact strength and other strength limitations, led to a further reduction in the use of cast iron in construction work in favor of wrought iron.[209] Cast-iron girders, which were a controlling factor in iron construction in the first half of the century, were in essence erected in accordance with values found from practical experience. This applies also to wrought-iron girder structures. Even in 1845, the satisfactory girder cross-section used for the Britannia Bridge was designed empirically.[210] Even more remarkable is the development before 1850 of filigree ironwork, in which cast iron was used up to its limits of strength without any detailed calculations. The engineers followed the principles of economy and profitability in the same way as with wrought-iron constructions, besides considering elegance of line.

The filigree iron roof structures of the nineteenth-century winter gardens and hothouses have never been surpassed. The space frames of these buildings consisted of narrow curved sash bars and obtained most of their strength from the glass panes, which were held in place by putty. These were the first shell-type structures. Here, too, practice came before theory. Loudon obtained his knowledge from experiments. The first attempts to apply the theory of statics to the analysis of shells (curved roofs for locomotive sheds and gasometers) were carried out by J. W. Schwedler in 1863. In 1868, E. Winckler worked out the mechanical theory of two- and three-hinge arch girders. Therefore, not until about 1870 were all the structural forms of iron-and-glass buildings properly understood in terms of statics.

With the modern theory of statics there was an opportunity "by calculation to make the structure with cleaner lines and more elegant members, to balance out contrasts, to accentuate important structural members, and to distinguish accessories as important parts."[211] However, with the increasing theorizing about constructional improvement in the course of the nineteenth century, less use was made of this possibility.[212] Exceptions were the continuous transparent glass-and-iron hothouse buildings of the period 1800–1870. This building type became an important experimental field for designers in the development of iron space frames. The grounds for this statement are given in the following list of the special building commissions for totally glazed hall-type buildings. The fundamental experience gained here by experimental methods could also be applied to other building projects. The broad field of activity of the hothouse builders shows the close association between the design of hothouses and that of other large iron buildings—particularly the hall-type structures of railway stations, markets, arcades, winter

gardens, and exhibition buildings. Clearly visible in this is the trend toward separation of the activities of the architect and the engineer, which was later to become rigorous. It is also evident that amateurs had the opportunity to come forward as ironwork constructors, and that their numerous experiments made important contributions to the field of ironwork construction.

Works of Significant Designers of Glasshouses

John Claudius Loudon (1783–1843)

Large palm house built like glass dome, Bretton Hall, 1827

Designs of large, sometimes multistory winter gardens, proposals for application of their type of construction to schools and churches

Henry Phillips (1779–1840)

Aviary (also serving as hothouse), London, 1831

Anthaeum (winter garden), Hove, Sussex, 1832

Sir Joseph Paxton (1801–1865)

Numerous experimental designs for small hothouses, from 1833

Great Conservatory, Chatsworth, 1836–1840

Victoria regia house, Chatsworth, 1849

Crystal Palace, Hyde Park, London, 1850–51

Crystal Palace, Sydenham, London, 1852–1854

Designs for large exhibition buildings and winter gardens

Design for Great Victorian Way, 1855

Richard Turner

Wings of Belfast Palm House, 1839–40

Hothouses at Dublin and Killikee, 1842–1850

Vine house, Phoenix Park, Dublin, 1845–1850

Winter garden, Regent's Park, London, 1842–1846

Palm house, Kew Gardens, London (with Decimus Burton), 1844–1848

Roof of Broadstone Station, Dublin, 1847

Roof of Lime Street Station, Liverpool, 1850

Design for exhibition building in Hyde Park, London, 1850

Hector Horeau (1801–1872)

Design for Halles Centrales, Paris, 1845

Jardin d'Hiver, Lyon, 1847

Design for Chateau des Fleurs, 1847

Design for Jardin d'Hivers, Paris, 1846–1848

Design for exhibition building, Hyde Park, London, 1850

18
The Jardin d'Hiver
at Laeken, Brussels,
during construction,
December 1875.

Charles Rohault de Fleury (1801–1875)

Passage du Saumon, Paris, 1825 (with his father Hubert)

Glasshouse, Jardin des Plantes, Paris, 1833

Addition to glasshouse in Jardin des Plantes, Paris, 1854

Charles Fowler (1791–1867)

Glasshouse, Syon House, London, 1820–1827

New Market, Gravesend, Kent, 1818–1822

Hungerford Market, London, 1831–1833

Covent Garden Market, London, 1828–1830

August von Voit (1801–1870)

Glass Palace, Munich, 1853–54

Winter garden for Maximilian II, Munich, 1854

Great Palm House, Munich, 1860–1865

Winter garden for Ludwig II, Munich, 1867–1869

Rowland Mawson Ordish (1824–1886)

Winter Palace, Dublin, 1865

Winter Garden, Leeds, 1868

Royal Albert Bridge, Chelsea, London, 1872

5   The Iron Skeleton

The early nineteenth century was a period of morphological observations in the natural sciences. Cuvier, Goethe, and Humboldt interpreted living and extinct animal species according to their skeletons, and by this means they succeeded in reconstructing creatures they had not actually seen. The glasshouses, too, can be "reconstructed" through the study of their skeletons. It is not sufficient to rummage through archives, or even through existing buildings; no overall picture can be discerned in this way except with great difficulty. It seems necessary—as it were, by an architectural process—to start from the framework of the glass-and-iron building. Through a step-by-step description of the origin and the history of the parts of the dismembered skeleton, even a long-gone building can be understood. On the one hand, one can deduce the state of productive activity, which generally has an effect on building as well as on social life; on the other hand, one can decode how and at what stage the client and his building contractor as individuals used the existing elbow room. In a detailed record of typical forms of iron space frames one can consider the glasshouse's relationships with other buildings and with industry.

In the following account, cast-iron and wrought-iron space frames are considered separately in the interests of obtaining a better overall view. This conforms not only to the chronological course of building with iron but also to the fact that each of these materials evolved along its own typical construction lines in respect to form.

Cast Iron

Cast-iron load-bearing structures were characteristic of the early period of iron building, the first half of the nineteenth century. In this respect, manufacturing and construction techniques and economic and aesthetic factors were decisive.

The simplicity of the manufacturing process in comparison with that of wrought iron, and the easy shaping of cast-iron elements, soon led to a preference for cast iron in building. The refining and forging processes were not needed. The technology of forging wrought iron depended essentially on the state of development of the machinery involved, hammers and rollers. At the start of the nineteenth century, wrought iron was satisfactory only as a member under tension in load-bearing structures. Cast-iron structural members, by exploitation of the amorphousness of liquid iron, not only could be given any shape of section with great precision but could also be shaped according to the distribution of the stresses. Designing the individual parts to match the forces present gave rise to the early form of the composite space frame, in which the internal joints could be made not with nuts and bolts (as with wrought iron) but with a homogeneous mass of iron in a single casting. The size of the parts cast as single pieces was, however, subject to the technical limitations of the casting process; as a rule, the overall size was seldom more than 16 feet.[213]

The reproduction of cast-iron elements from patterns led from the beginning to the standardization of basic structural parts. Hence, cost-effective mass production was achieved earlier than with wrought iron. This enabled builders to bring development into line with the advance of industrial productivity. The Crystal Palace was the peak of this progress. Not until the advent of rolled iron section (I beams), in the 1850s, was cast iron ousted as a building material. Several forging and rolling operations were needed for the production of iron section in the 1820s. Not until the development of the railways did investments in capital-intensive heavy machinery such as rolling mills become profitable. As a result, from 1850 iron section could be made in greater variety and with higher quality, and because of its lower price could compete with cast iron. "Until the first half of the nineteenth century the production of wrought iron was so expensive that it was almost cast iron alone that could be considered for building purposes."[214] Even in 1858, the covered market in Lyon was made of individual cast-iron parts bolted together because this type of structure was cheaper than one made of wrought iron.[215]

Beyond these factors, which in the long run had their roots in the matter of profitability, there was a preference for cast iron in load-bearing structures because of the empirical methods of builders and architects. This became a controlling factor in building practice. The behavior of iron under load was still not determinable in the early period of iron construction work; the improvement of the load-bearing members was based entirely on values found by experience. Paxton used marching soldiers to test the breaking strength of the cast-iron braced girders for the Crystal Palace.[216]

Scientific knowledge about the load behavior of iron started with the wider use of wrought-iron section in supporting frameworks. The elastic properties of wrought iron were discovered in a series of experiments which formed the basis of the theory of elasticity and hence led to the laws of statics. The subsequent load tests carried out on rolled iron section in 1849 by C. F. Zorés paved the way to the scientific design of the cross-section shapes of beams. "The standard method of determining the strength of the structural members according to the breaking strength of the material used . . . was abandoned and the elastic limit of the material was taken as the standard for this purpose."[217]

As a consequence of the ignorance of the behavior of iron under load, most cast-iron structures were made stronger and more massive than was necessary, particularly those members that were under compression. Intuitively recognizing the low tensile strength of cast iron, the early users gave preference to curved shapes in their roof supports, in which most of the forces were compressive. In the same context, triangular ribs were used to great heights in roof trusses to support ridge roofs. As long as cast iron was significantly cheaper than wrought iron, the greater weight of cast-iron girders and columns, which was due to the greater thickness of the metal (at least 0.6 inch), played only a subordinate role. The use of cast iron proved especially advantageous in those places where its compression strength could be fully utilized. However, cast iron's resistance to corrosion and heat was also important. Most nineteenth-century builders also considered cast iron

more resistant to fire than wrought iron.[218] This, according to Wittek, was proved by the fire in the Munich Glass Palace.[219]

Faced with the difficult problem of making rigid load-bearing structures having multiple members without the theory of statics, builders readily resorted to forms that simultaneously served as ornamentation. The casting method provided sufficient freedom of choice for this, and cast-iron structures acquired shapes related to traditional architecture. Cast iron as a structural material facilitated "adaptation to antique designs" and "served for a long time as a surrogate for genuine constructions or had to adapt itself to classical models which had been developed out of wood and stone techniques."[220] This is attested to by numerous attempts to take the middle path between more functional construction and "art forms" in the development of cast-iron space frames. Like J. B. Rondelet before him, Richard Baumeister saw cast iron as a replacement for stonework: "The oldest cast-iron girder bridges . . . have high arched ribs made from many curved pieces, which in respect to statics obviously take the place of the voussoirs in stone arches."[221] Likewise, cast-iron columns, cornices, and brackets were examples of how this material could be substituted for stone: "It is now plain that one can also copy the free stylistic forms of stone. In fact this trend will be the best path for art. . . ."[222] In addition, the customary size and solidity of stone structural members, and the ornamentation and vaulting, could be captured in cast iron. The persistence of aesthetic tradition is especially evident in the development of cast-iron columns, which even in the era of scientifically designed girders were provided with capital and bases as in the classical orders.

The new technical possibilities of building in cast iron first became apparent on a large scale in the spanning of wider and higher halls. Limits to the spans inside which the strength of cast iron could be fully utilized were found, appearing even more distinctly than in the column supports already in use. The development of cast-iron spanning structures had its origins in the columns used in factory buildings. The greenhouse buildings of 1820–1870 were important structures in which occurred further rapid development of cast-iron girders and columns into integrated rigid space frames. The need for glass-and-iron halls with greater spans, considerable height, and maximum light penetration "gave the impetus to structural and technical measures that . . . led to major innovations which other branches of building science could hardly match."[223]

Space Frames

Beams

The first cast-iron beams, which came into use around 1800, had a variation in the depth or width of the cross-section (web), which was greater in the middle of the beam. This shows that the designers in the early stages of iron building were already following the engineering principles of the economic use of materials. (In a uniformly loaded beam that is not prestressed, the tension increases in the middle. With a uniform cross-section all along the beam, the strength is fully brought into use only in the middle of the span.)

A further step consisted of attempts to improve beams so that they would have uniform resistance to bending. Composite beams, for example with a prestressing cable below, were forerunners of the braced girder. The matching of a beam's shape to the forces within the beam also had an effect on the development of the cross-section. The forces acting in a beam divide themselves about the neutral axis into tension and compression. Equilibrium requires that the sum of all the forces occurring in the cross-section of a beam be zero. These forces increase linearly with the distance from the neutral axis; they are not uniformly spread over the cross-section. In iron construction work, where the economic need to save weight could be met by varying the cross-section of the beam, the dimensions of the flanges and the web were varied.[224]

This led to difficulties with wrought-iron beams. Before the method of rolling iron section (J. Birkinshaw's patent, 1820) was put into operation, rolled flat bars were often used in buildings. On account of their lack of lateral stiffness, they had only a limited use. (Such bars were used in the space frame of the "Paris Rose" around the turn of the century.[225]) On the other hand, cast-iron beams could be easily formed into any shape desired. A hindrance to their use, however, was the continuing lack of scientific knowledge of the behavior of cast iron under conditions of load. The shape given to the web and the flanges was intuitive, or based on varied experience. Cast iron differs greatly from wrought iron in its ability to resist tensile and compressive forces: For cast iron the ratio of tensile to compressive strength is approximately 1:3, whereas for wrought iron the two strengths are approximately equal.

This fact was at first not adequately understood by the designers of cast-iron beams. Even in 1825, Thomas Tredgold recommended upper and lower flanges of equal size. The error in this belief was not discovered until 1840, by Thomas Fairbairn.[226] In the 1820s, Fairbairn and James Lillie preferred beams with no upper flange and with a wide lower flange. Hodgkinson, in 1824, demonstrated the superiority of beams with a narrow flange above and a wide one below.[227] The satisfactory ratio of flange sizes according to Fairbairn was from 1:4 to 1:5.5. Thus, the maximum span attainable was 26 feet in a building and 40 feet in a bridge.

The first cast-iron beam introduced into space frames, often used with two supporting columns, was the rail used for railways or in mines. The flat rails nailed onto planks used by Reynolds (1767) developed into rails with a flange (Cort, 1776) and then into cast-iron rails with a bull's head profile on the upper surface (Jessop, 1786). The fish-bellied rail, produced until 1816, was not suited to the material properties of cast iron. The frequent fractures of such rails led to the invention of rolled section, which with the introduction of the Vignoles-type rail led to the shape of the rails used today (fig. 19).[218] For early use in buildings—for example, in a spinning mill built in 1801 in Manchester by Boulton and Watt (fig. 20)—cast-iron beams were produced with a section corresponding to the distribution of tensile and compressive stresses. There then arose the classical cross-section, with a large flange below and a small one (or, generally, none) above. The Watt beam of 1801 had a 13-foot span and was incorporated into a framework by large circular cast-iron collars in the cast-iron columns. This was a prototype for a series of 14-foot beams used for factory buildings in the following decades.[229]

Cast-iron beams were seldom used in greenhouse buildings. The reason for this lies not only in the aesthetic requirements of the visibility of the glass-and-iron construction, but also in the functional need to make beams in filigree form as much as possible in order to obtain optimum illumination. The beams were incorporated as members of the roof support structure or the facade, and mostly had the glazing fixed directly to the top of the flanges. The stress behavior was critical not only in determining the section, but also in determining the thickness of the joints, permitting the efficient shedding of rain and condensation water, and minimizing shadowing.

From the need to create a continuous smooth surface of glass there followed much effort to place the joints between the beams in order to reduce the cross-sections. This favored a hierarchical system of sash bars and ribs, with the whole structure reinforced with purlins. The beam shape of the sash bars is especially important on account of their special function as elements of the glazing. These cast-iron parts were often richly profiled, and their cross-sections had rebates instead of pronounced flanges (fig. 21a).

The desire to allow the greatest possible illumination, to seal the roof against rain, and to avoid drops of condensation led to a sash-bar cross-section that cannot be attributed to stress behavior alone. In cross-section, the cast-iron sash bars were mostly wedge-shaped, tapered toward the inside of the roof. Wooden sash bars, which were the prototypes of these, were still used in highly developed hothouse structures, including those of Paxton. Loudon used wrought-iron sash bars in his curvilinear roofs, and they then found wider use after the invention of the rolled sash-bar section in 1820. Cast-iron sash bars could certainly hold their own against the competition from rolled-iron ones for certain shapes. They were fitted on the inside of large windows or glazed spaces, even in the last quarter of the nineteenth century.

Cast-iron sash bars were more easily broken than wrought-iron ones and had lower resistance to impact and strong vibrations. However, they could be made in a greater range of shapes. Also, they were well suited for mass production; even around 1880 cast-iron window frames were much cheaper than wrought-iron ones. In addition, cast iron was more resistant to rust and fire.[230] The large number of types produced is evident in the Tanger Foundry's catalog, which in 1883 included over 3,000 window designs. The largest window cast in one piece listed in their catalog was 15 feet high and 6 1/2 feet wide.[231] Some of the earliest cast-iron window frames for a glasshouse still in existence are those of the Indian Villa at Sezincote (1806).

McIntosh's *Book of the Garden* mentioned the load-bearing sash bars in the hothouses at Dalkeith (1830) and at Woburn Abbey (1840),[232] which were made by box-casting. The sash bars of the glasshouse at Woburn Abbey, made by the Jones firm of Birmingham, served as supports for glazed wooden frames and had drainage gutters to take the condensation water.

In sash bars and frames there was a need to achieve very uniform thicknesses in the iron, in order to avoid the creation of uneven stresses as the iron cooled. Because of this, larger windows were assembled from two or three separate parts to prevent the bars from breaking, particularly at the joints. The casting of windows and frames was often done in open molds in hearth furnaces. The cross-section thus obtained had a scaly and porous surface and could be made in only the simplest forms. On the other hand, by the box-casting process, for which the mold consisted of two halves and was filled

when standing vertically, a uniform surface and a more delicate and artistic section could be achieved. Cast-iron lattice ribs were used in greenhouse buildings, particularly for the vertically glazed surfaces. Likewise, the miniature galleries in the roof structure were preferably made in the form of cast-iron postwork and window frames. The most complete example of a window area made with rich ornamentation is the vertical glass facade of the Wilhelma (fig. 682).

The "Paxton gutter" (figs. 22b, 25), supported by prestressed wooden beams of considerable span, was developed solely for use in glasshouses, to support continuous ridge-and-furrow glass roofs, or glass vaults, and at the same time to collect and discharge rainwater. Wrought-iron or cast-iron box-section or U-section beams were used in the 1850s to support ridge-and-furrow roofs in many hothouses, exhibition buildings, and railway stations (fig. 23). Fifteen years before the use of the Paxton gutter at Chatsworth, U-shaped cast-iron beams were used in the Camellia House at Wollaton Hall. The hollow cast-iron beams made by the firm of Thomas Clark at Birmingham had an external form resembling the masonry architecture of an architrave supported by columns. Their function was to support the weight of the roof by means of a row of hollow cast-iron columns and to discharge rainwater into them. The U section of the beam corresponded closely to the material properties of cast iron, insofar as the zone of tension on the lower surface was reinforced (fig. 22a). This gutter beam was a basic element in the space-frame structure of Clark's hothouses (figs. 467–470, 703–708), and R. Turner incorporated cast-iron gutter beams in his buildings as continuous eaves (fig. 47).

A further development of the simple beam, known from wooden building, involved prestressing a cable or bar below the beam in order to counteract the sag in the middle caused by loading (fig. 24). Cast-iron beams were reinforced from below by wrought-iron members in tension.[233] These were used in the first half of the nineteenth century, particularly in Britain by W. Fairbairn and in France by Charles F. Zorés. The noteworthy feature of this "hybrid structure" was the use of two different irons with different moduli of elasticity. Prestressed gutters, made entirely of iron after 1850, were commonly used in large hall-type buildings.[234]

For the greater spans used in bridges and roof trusses, the previously known method of changing the solid web into a framework of members not parallel to the upper and lower flanges was developed further. Georg Ludwig Friedrich Laves separated two

19
Cast-iron rails: (a) flat rail, 1767; (b) rail with outer flange, 1776; (c) I-section rail, 1786.

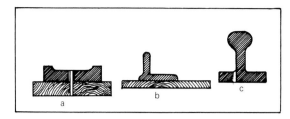

20
Sections of cast-iron beams and illustration of skeleton construction used in spinning mill at Manchester (Boulton and Watt, 1801).

21
(a) Cast-iron beam used by Ludwig von Zanth in Wilhelma at Stuttgart, 1842–1846; (b) wrought-iron beam used by Richard Turner and Decimus Burton in palm house at Kew, 1846–1848.

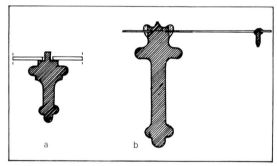

22
(a) Cast-iron gutter used by Thomas Clark in camellia house at Wollaton Hall, 1823; (b) patent drawing of wooden gutter by Joseph Paxton, 1850.

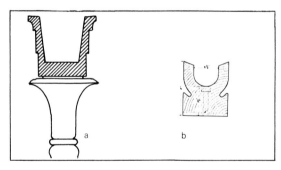

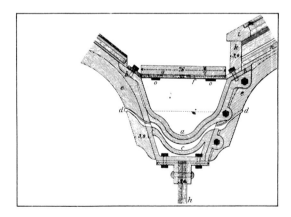

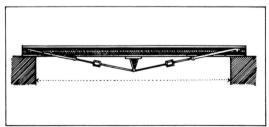

23
Cast-iron gutter used in Great Palm House, Berlin (Bouche, Herter, and Nietz, 1857–1859).

24
Undertrussed cast-iron beam.

wooden beams in the vertical plane to form fish-bellied beams (figs. 105, 274). Wrought-iron beams in this configuration were used in bridges.[235]

Whereas with such structures the flanges and the web could be put together as latticework and the assembly used as a beam, with massive cast-iron beams (omitting hybrid structures) the method used was to break up the web with ornamental openings. These composite beams had the disadvantage that the strengths of their individual structural members could be determined neither by calculation nor by experiment. Because of this, they were made too large and cumbersome-looking (until Loudon's experiments of 1817). Their advantage, however, was considerable weight reduction, and there was a simultaneous possibility of producing an aesthetically pleasing form. The importance of aesthetics in glass-house building can be seen in the shape of the cast-iron ribs in Burton's Temperate House at Kew (figs. 54, 344, 345, 620–622). Whereas the top parts of the main ribs of the wide glass roof were reinforced with a complex system of bars, the lateral parts of the beams were of cast iron with ring-shaped openings (fig. 26). Richly ornamented cast-iron beams were used to support the glazing in the topmost part of the facade of the Wilhelma (figs. 26b, 687, 688). Ribs with straight top flanges were used in the interior, and the spandrel was filled with rings. Inserted between rows of columns in the longitudinal direction of the hall, they carried the ridge-and-furrow roof; in the transverse direction they served as stiffening.

The solution of the problem of the simple cast-iron beam in "composite" beams of increasing spans led to a series of experiments in which the influence of bridge building can be detected, to the individually designed structures that determined the construction of glasshouses from 1820 to 1870, and eventually to the large exhibition halls of the 1860s and 1870s.

Ribs

The cast-iron bridge over the River Severn at Coalbrookdale (1775–1779) was a forerunner of the use of cast iron in roof supports.[236] The behavior of the cast iron under load in this first structure made entirely of iron became very well understood.

In the 236-foot-span bridge over the Wear at Sunderland (1793–1796), Payne, Burdon, and Wilson used girders assembled from cast-iron segments and perforated plates resembling voussoirs.[237] In consequence of the great loads and spans, these bridges were complex structures consisting of many individual members, whereas in the early cast-iron roof trusses, which at first mostly had short spans, there were attempts to use simple ribs cast in a small number of parts if not as a single piece.

The common elements in these trusses derived from ridge or sawtooth roofs are the straight adjoining upper flanges, the inserted arch of the lower flange, and the reinforcing rings and bars. In order to transmit the shear forces, beam types were also chosen in which the upper flange was turned vertically in the vicinity of the fixed support. When this method was used, not only were the trusses stiffened but they could be supported at the sides on masonry or between cast-iron columns. The earliest simple trusses were used in British factories and greenhouses. The roof truss of the spinning mill in Manchester built by Boulton and Watt was made from trusses about 26 feet long with massive brickwork buttresses (fig. 28).[238] In spite of the circular openings below the ridge, these trusses have a massiveness reminiscent of masonry bridges.

In the use of roof trusses as space frames for the glass roofs of greenhouses, there was a need to keep the structure as transparent as possible all the way around. For the glass-and-iron hall of Carlton House (1803)[239] Repton specified roof trusses supported on high cast-iron columns and made in a delicate filigree style (fig. 32). The solution of the triangle of forces followed in the Boulton and Watt beam was in fact negative and resulted in the form of circular openings; here Repton tried to make this positive by using a row of smaller rings.

In the ridge roof at Syon House (1820–1827), Charles Fowler used three forms of filigree trusses with no superfluous ornamentation. The simple execution of the narrow flanges, rings, and bars shows that the designer took to the new material with enthusiasm and saw beauty in its pure functional form. The approximately 23-foot-long trusses in the end pavilion were supported at the sides by masonry and carried a flattish sloped ridge roof. The cast-iron ridge member was bolted to the rafters. Noteworthy is the inclusion of a step in the top flange in order to receive the purlins (fig. 33). The ribs in the arc of the wings were smaller and had the shape of a flattish triangle with a gently curved lower flange. The supports of some rafters by columns placed in the center were not structurally obvious (fig. 34). The largest ribs, spanning approximately 30 feet and cast as one piece, were used in the wings of the dome-topped central structure. Cast more massively, they created in the perspective of the hall the impression of an iron vault which was in harmony with the masonry of the Renaissance architecture (fig. 35). The thick-

25
Joseph Paxton, undertrussed gutter, 1850 patent.

26
Cast-iron braced girders: (a) Decimus Burton, Temperate House, Kew, 1859–1863; (b) Ludwig von Zanth, Conservatory Wilhelma, Stuttgart, 1853–54.

27
Abraham Darby III and John Wilkinson, bridge over River Severn, Coalbrookdale, 1775–1779.

28
Matthew Boulton and James Watt, spinning mill, Manchester, 1801, section.

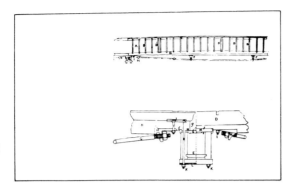

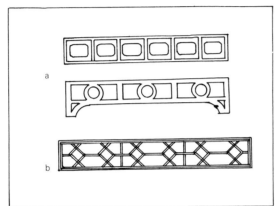

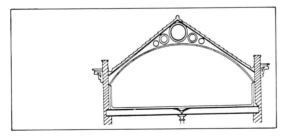

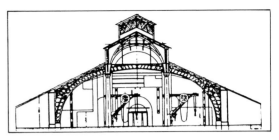

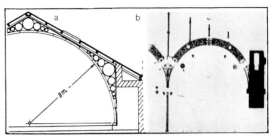

29
Carl Ludwig Althans, iron foundry, Sayn, 1824–1830, section.

30
Cast-iron roof trusses: (a) Karl von Etzel, Dianabad, Vienna, 1842; (b) Henri Labrouste, Bibliothèque Saint-Geneviève, Paris, 1844.

31
Desjardins, Market Hall, Lyon, 1858, interior.

ness of the flanges and web in the end pavilion and
in the wings was 0.6 inch—the minimum possible
with this casting technique.

The Architectural Conservatory, built by Sir Jeffry
Wyatville at Buckingham Palace in 1830 and removed
to Kew in 1836, had for its roof trusses 41-foot rafters whose tops had flanges running up to the gently
sloped glass ridge roof and whose bottom sides had
continuous flat curves. The rafters were supported
on masonry work and, at one-fourth of their spans
from the sides, by extremely slender cast-iron columns (fig. 36). Hence it was possible to keep the
depth of the web with its circular openings low, and
to achieve the filigree effect necessary in glasshouse
buildings.[240]

Less pleasing is the effect of the cast-iron ribs in
the circular glasshouse at Dalkeith Palace, built
around 1830 by William Burne (fig. 37). A high hollow circular column in the center, also serving as a
chimney for the boiler, functioned as an internal element for the radially placed 20-foot trusses supporting the conical glass roof. In the attempt to give the
interior supports for the arch the same height at
both ends, as in masonry work, the ribs were given
too much depth at the abutment with the center column. In relation to the span, the amount of ring and
bar components made the whole look bulky. The
economy otherwise followed in hothouse building
was abandoned in favor of a particular architectural
style. McIntosh remarked: "The roof is of wood, in
angular sashes, supported by unnecessarily heavy
girders, giving the interior a heavy and confused
appearance. . . ."[241]

Also worthy of note in this series of developments
are the roof trusses of the Sayn Foundry (fig. 29),
built by Carl Ludwig Althans between 1824 and 1830.
With its basilica style and its Gothic forms, it was
reminiscent of a church. An elliptical arch spanning
71 feet, assembled from bars whose form appears to
have been inspired by the Coalbrookdale Bridge,
supported the roof (with lantern and gantry) above
the foundry workshop with the help of hollow cast-
iron columns. The lantern top and the rows of columns formed a central nave, the ridge roof above
which was carried on filigree Gothic arches made of
cast iron. The large elliptical arch spanning the nave
was carried right down to the ground from the capitals of the columns and supported the lean-to roofs
of the 23-foot-wide aisles. Thus, the building was
supported at its sides as if by flying buttresses.[242] The
binder was made with a web thickness of 0.64 inch
and a maximum cast length of 26 feet without any
warping in the box mold.[234] With its T-shaped upper
and lower flanges and its radially fixed bars, it func-

32
Humphrey Repton,
design for conserva-
tory for Carlton
House, 1803.

33
Charles Fowler, Syon
House, London,
1820–1827, cast-iron
roof truss for corner
pavilion.

34
Fowler, Syon House,
London, roof truss
for wing.

35
Fowler, Syon House
London, roof truss.

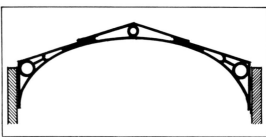

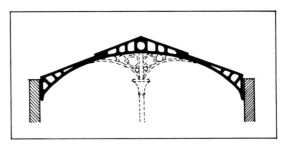

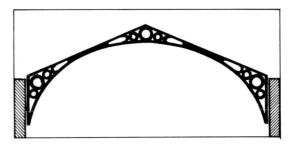

36
Jeffry Wyatville, Architectural Conservatory, Kew, 1836, section.

37
William Burne, Architectural Conservatory, Dalkeith Park, ca. 1830, section.

tioned as an arched braced girder, the outline of which was not distinctly seen through the ends of the strutting of the lean-to roof. This reveals the indecision of the designer in the choice of truss form: On the one hand, he terminated it in a type of rib with straight upper flange, as was common in a ridge roof; on the other hand, the tendency toward a vault form, taken down to ground level, is unmistakable. In their cross-section shape the trusses resemble those used later in the Great Conservatory at Chatsworth and at Kew.[244] The casting bay of the Sayn Foundry, with its mix of these two types of ribs, shows, as do the glasshouses built after 1830, two separate lines of development of wide-span roof trusses. One of these lines led to linear roofs, the other to curved, vaulted roofs.

Examples of the construction of wide-span roof trusses with linear tops are Horeau's winter garden at Lyon (fig. 38) and his design for the exhibition building in Hyde Park (fig. 39). The central hall of the octagonal winter garden at Lyon was spanned by four main trusses leading up to the lantern. In the downward direction, the lower flange of the roof, sloping almost to ground level, nestled against cast-iron columns. The trusses were reinforced with cast-iron ornamentation in the spandrels bolted at their vertical parts to the columns. A gallery at ground level increased the stability of this winter garden.[245] Horeau proposed to use a similar support structure

for the roof in his design for Hyde Park. The five-bay exhibition building was to be capped by a high center section of wide span with a ridge roof, which was to be intersected by a transept of the same height and shape. The aisles were covered by lean-to roofs which in two steps reached almost to ground level. As in the Jardin d'Hiver at Lyon, the roof trusses were supported on cast-iron columns. The lateral reinforcement had rafters and purlins of similar spans, corresponding to the longitudinal layout of the supports.[246]

A high point in this line of development of cast-iron roof trusses came with the beams spanning the central hall of the Glass Palace built in New York by G. J. B. Carstensen and Charles Gildemeister in 1852 (figs. 40, 68). With one main supporting structure designed in accordance with Paxton's principle of skeleton frames, its gently sloping latticework beams formed a semicircular arch. In view of the large spans, there was a surprising amount of ornamental filigree work, all in cast iron.

Other examples of such wide-span roof trusses in hothouses and exhibition buildings are found in the elongated hall of the Dianabad in Vienna (von Etzel, 1842), in the Sainte-Geneviève Library in Paris (Labrouste, 1844), and in the Market Hall in Lyon (Desjardins, 1858) (figs. 30, 31). The semicircular arched rib seen in the last two buildings shows the change of the roof truss to a rib with parallel curved upper and lower flanges, by which means the roof load was transmitted down via vertically placed columns.[247]

The purest and most highly developed cast-iron ribs were the circular (or sometimes elliptically curved) girders in which the curvature and profile were efficiently matched to the force distribution. These were first used in greenhouses, where from the start the efforts of the builders to achieve maximum illumination favored spherically curved glass surfaces, barrel or Gothic arches, cupola vaults, and so on. The advantage of these over lean-to roofs lay not only in lower sunlight reflection but also in the possibility of closely fitting the ribs to the curvature of the glass vault along its entire length. Thus, the connecting but disturbing link or spandrel between upper and lower flanges fell out of use. As long as the ribs had to withstand predominantly compressive forces, cast iron could be made up into this advantageous load-bearing form. An especially favored form had steeply parabolically curved ribs. However, in ribs of semicircular shape there were important outward forces. The obvious remedy for this was to counter the outward thrust, as in vault construction, by using wrought-iron ties, but designers tried to

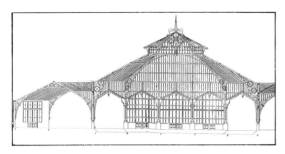

38
Hector Horeau, Jardin d'Hiver, Lyon, 1847, section.

39
Horeau, design for World Exhibition at Hyde Park, London, 1850.

Projet de M. Hector Horeau. — Coupe intérieure

40
G. B. Carstensen and Charles Gildemeister, Crystal Palace, New York, 1852, interior view of dome. Engraving.

avoid this remedy. Economy of construction led to the improvement of cast-iron filigree girders, which gave the necessary transparency through the sides of a space frame. The removal of the distinction between vertical facade and roof by changing it into a continuous curve was important. These curvilinear glass structures were a novelty in the history of architecture.

Pioneering construction experiments in the application of cast iron to building purposes were carried out in glasshouses by J. C. Loudon. As early as 1805, Sir George Mackenzie was designing spherically curved glass surfaces to trap the sun's rays and transmit them to the plants inside. Loudon took up this idea and put it into use in his buildings. From 1817 he used narrow wrought-iron sash bars curved by hot rolling as the basic load-bearing element in his curvilinear roofs. These load-bearing elements were fitted close together, at intervals of 7–8 inches, closely following the distribution of forces along the curvature so that almost no bending moment arose and only thrust forces had to be supported.

In the first glass-and-iron structures, glass panes were puttied in as stiffening for the surface of the vault. The disadvantage of this type of construction was that the span itself was limited because of natural mechanical principles. The iron members in the vertical plane formed a primary structure, like miniature ribs. So long as iron purlins, be it only in the form of sash bars, were omitted, there was no ranking of the space frame elements based on the different sizes of the members. This was essentially necessary with longer spans or openings in the roof skin for purposes of ventilation. In addition to his continuous shell structures, Loudon also occupied himself with designs of curvilinear roofs whose primary structure was made of wrought-iron sash bars fitted at a greater distance and carried on ribs stiffened by crossmembers. Sketches of such ribs with reinforcing bars are found in Loudon's "Remarks on the Construction of Hothouses"[248] (see figure 41 in this volume); their moldings followed the curved line of the glass vault, and experience with these is merged with knowledge of wrought-iron shell structures. Not only was Loudon, by intuition, already using the method of designing a space frame by making a framework of rigid triangles from bars and flanges; he was also taking account of the variation in the stress pattern by continuously narrowing the rib in the upward direction. If we imagine these ribs to be extended symmetrically and hinged above and below, then we have the prototype of the three-hinge girder.

Loudon himself probably experimented with these cast-iron ribs, though no existing or documented building proves this. However, buildings of the 1830s and the 1840s are known whose vaulted forms display Loudon's principles of the curvilinear roof, but with cast-iron ribs inserted as the main supporting structure. The Antheaum at Hove and the center pavilion of the hothouse in Dublin are examples of this.

The cast-iron space frame of the Chiswick conservatory was directly related to Loudon's designs. This structure was erected in 1840 by D. and E. Bailey, whose firm had collaborated with Loudon on a series of curvilinear hothouses from 1817 on. Curved ribs forming a wide pointed arch approximately 40 feet wide and 60 feet high, with lateral reinforcement and wrought-iron sash bars, made up the glass vault. The filigree cast-iron ribs, made of upper and lower flanges, reinforced by closely spaced radial bars, and tapering toward the ridge, rested on a masonry base (fig. 42). They were a refinement of Loudon's latticework ribs, and they pushed economy of design to further limits. There is in this hothouse the first example of a solidly engineered cast-iron barrel vault over a hall. The transparency of the structure brought much admiration.[249]

Two years earlier, in 1838, similar latticework ribs had been used in the 50-foot cast-iron roof trusses installed in Chartres Cathedral by Emile Martin to replace the chestnut trusses, which had burned. They were naturally still used in the form of wide pointed arches. This type of roof truss was in fact fixed in structural union with the radially placed struts supporting the purlins of the steep ridge roof (fig. 43).[250]

In 1844, H. Labrouste used cast-iron ribs in the roof trusses of the Sainte-Geneviève Library in Paris. These trusses were assembled from three prefabricated units to form a semicircle with parallel curved upper and lower flanges reinforced by rings. The joints to the three narrow cast-iron columns were made through the impost on the capital (fig. 30b).[251]

The wooden tie beams in the Great Conservatory at Chatsworth represent a building innovation in the application of not only cast-iron but also wrought-iron semicircular ribs, in arches and in frameworks. In this building the creation of space and the various forms of iron rib were further developed structurally. This free-standing building, 124 feet wide and 68 feet high, was created by the construction of two glass vaults, built in the ridge-and-furrow system, with a basilicalike cross-section. Rows of cast-iron columns joined by cast-iron girders carried the semicircular wooden ribs of the Paxton gutters to form a high nave with a span of 70 feet. The glass vaults of the aisles, reaching down to the low masonry base, abut-

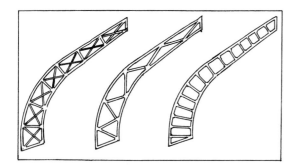

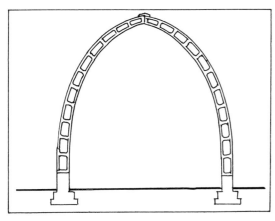

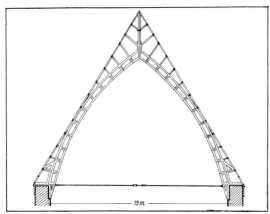

41
J. C. Loudon, braced
cast-iron roof
trusses, 1817.

42
D. and E. Bailey,
conservatory, Chis-
wick, London, 1840,
cast-iron roof truss.

43
Emile Martin, cast-
iron roof truss,
Chartres Cathedral,
1838, section.

ted from both sides onto the main iron frame at a height of 40 feet. The aisle had the same profile, but it had quadrant-shaped ribs. The ribs of the surrounding aisles also functioned as buttresses to support the lateral thrust of the main ribs of the nave. The semicircular and quadrant-shaped ribs did not match the distribution of the compression forces, as is the case with parabolic profiles. To obtain the necessary stiffness, the curved Paxton gutters were reinforced by iron ties placed underneath and anchored firmly into the foundations via iron anchors. By achieving a clear span of 70 feet across the nave, Paxton exceeded the dimensions reached in the largest railway-station bays of his time.[252]

The Great Conservatory gave rise to a series of vaulted glasshouses whose main supports, ribs, columns, and any reinforcing purlins were made of iron. In this connection the engineering structures of Richard Turner in Dublin as well as those of Paxton from 1850 on are of special importance.

In 1842 Turner designed a cast-iron main space frame for the Dublin glasshouse in which he modified the vaulting of the nave and the aisles by including vertical glass panes, thus departing from Paxton's basilica design. The flatly curved ribs of the nave and the sharply curved ones of the aisles made delicately filigree cast-iron spans which in their appearance anticipated curved rolled iron section. To obtain the lateral strength required to overcome the problem of the thrust of the vertical members caused by the great height of the structure relative to its width, Turner employed ornamental brackets. These were added as reinforcement at the supports of the vault at the upper ends of the columns and at the masonry foundation (fig. 47).[253] This reinforcing element could be omitted from the later design, in which Turner incorporated a wrought-iron roof with horizontal tie beams.

A high point in the construction of hothouses with filigree iron rib structures was reached in the Kew Gardens palm house in London, built by Turner and Decimus Burton between 1844 and 1848. In the Great Conservatory at Chatsworth, the nave and the adjacent aisles were covered by ribs spanning 42 and 21 feet, respectively. Turner and Burton modified Paxton's design to create a slight increase in the supporting area in the vertical area of the space frame which spans the nave (fig. 46). The ribs in the nave and aisles are I sections 12 inches and 9 inches in depth, respectively, and the maximum width at the top flange is 5 1/2 inches. The ribs so formed consist of 12-inch-long curved separate parts made of rolled

44
Joseph Paxton, Great Conservatory, Chatsworth, 1836–1840, section.

45
Paxton, Crystal Palace, Hyde Park, London, 1850–51, transept roof truss.

46
Richard Turner and Decimus Burton, palm house, Kew, 1844–1848, section.

47
Turner, tropical house, Glasnevin, near Dublin, 1842–1850, central pavilion. Design, 1842.

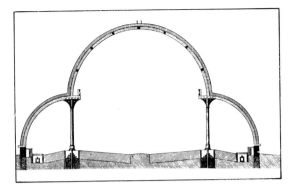

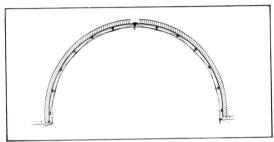

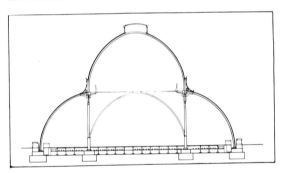

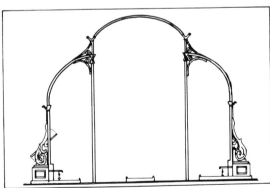

wrought iron, assembled into semicircular or quadrant-shaped arches (fig. 21b). According to McIntosh, Turner had originally planned to make the supporting ribs in this same profile but of cast iron.[254] This is confirmed not only by the division of the structure into prefabricated parts and the complex shape of the profile, but also by the overall appearance of the framework, with its powerful cast-iron brackets and the upward continuation of the columns (fig. 76).

The advance in rolling techniques and the use of curved iron section in shipbuilding at the end of the 1840s made possible the rolling of cast-iron beams to the required shape. It is generally believed that the first rolled I beam was introduced into building by Charles F. Zorés in 1849,[255] but the iron section arch at Kew Gardens, which must have been rolled before or during 1848, refutes this.

The glass vault of the hothouse in Edinburgh (1858) was in its external appearance almost a copy of Turner's palm house at Kew Gardens. The interior space frame consisted of columns, side arches, and brackets made of cast iron, but the ribs were of rolled iron. The remarkable feature of this hybrid construction was the almost exactly similar profile of the lateral arch girders in the lower flange of the rolled-section iron ribs. The cast-iron brackets extending from spandrels above the capitals of the columns merged into the ribs and were firmly bolted to them via wrought-iron gusset plates.

In 1850 Turner used 132-foot-wide prestressed arches made of rolled Vignoles-type rails for the upper flange of crescent-shaped tie beams supported by 9-inch cast-iron I-beam columns to span Lime Street Station in Liverpool.[256] The rolled-iron rib structure used in Turner's large palm house was an expression of the start of the change in building technology brought about by the introduction of rolled-iron I beams and a pioneering example for the future. At the same time, it was a milestone in the gradual withdrawal of cast iron from use in wide-span structures. With the general use of arched beams, cast iron was used as the main material only when, as in the Market Hall in Lyon (1858), its lower price gave it an advantage over wrought iron[257] or, as in the Leeds winter garden (1868) and the temperate house at Kew (1859–1863), the trend toward historicizing decorative forms and ornamentation brought it back into fashion. In the winter garden of the Leeds General Hospital, built by R. M. Ordish in 1868, cast iron was no longer used in its pure constructional form, but it was used as decoration in several ways (figs. 49, 314–316).[258]

The Ridge Roof with Tie

The iron ridge roof truss with a tie, the prototype of which was the prestressed beam, was a further step in solving the beam problem in a structure of triangular segments arranged side by side so that the load is supported at the joints between members and the bending forces in the form of compression or tension are distributed within appropriately sized members. In previous construction of wooden strutted roof trusses there were attempts to resist the horizontal forces by the use of beams and ties. The numerous "king and queen posts roofs" used in Britain from the 1820s were an early form of iron ridge roof. With these the principles of framework structures were still not known, but they did represent an advance in the technology of roof structures.

Simple ridge-with-tie roof structures were first made around 1820 from flat iron bars. In 1826, apropos of his journey through Britain, Schinkel drew in his sketchbook the iron-spanned rafter roofs of the Liverpool Market Hall and the gas works in Edinburgh. The roof of the Marché de la Madelaine in Paris (fig. 106), which appears to have been the prototype of these structures, was probably designed in 1824 by M. G. Veugny and built between 1835 and 1838. The lightness and gracefulness of its wrought-iron structural members were praised by contemporaries. Cast-iron ridge-roof constructions were rare, and without wrought iron for the tie rods they were inconceivable. After a study tour in Britain in 1836, Ludwig Ferdinand Hesse built the 56-foot roof trusses of the Schickler sugar factory in Berlin, incorporating cast-iron segments for stiffening.[259] The cast-iron girders of the 46-foot-wide market hall built on Réunion Island in 1836 were made of separate parts bolted together, and their joints were carefully detailed for the tie rod at the springing.[260]

Cast iron came into use to withstand compression in complex prestressed roof trusses with numerous members. Iron tie bars were more often incorporated in the construction of glasshouses with ridge roofs. They were distinguished by their filigree work, which compensated for the fact that they crossed the interior.

In 1846 L. von Zanth created a roof truss in the form of a simple classical ridge roof for the cast-iron Wilhelma glasshouse in Stuttgart, which is one of the few well-preserved cast-iron space frames of this kind in Germany. The glass ridge roofs of the wings are carried on triangular trusses spanning 22 feet. The struts form richly decorated cast-iron girders with a wedge-shaped, downward-narrowing cross-section, and the panes of glass between them are held in rebates (fig. 21a). Lightly propped at their ends by short vertical posts and resting on cast-iron brackets, they are held together by wrought-iron bars. A small vertical tie in the ridge gives additional stiffening. The strong impression of space in the long hall of this glasshouse is a direct result of the truss design.

The glasshouse in the Pavilion Gardens at Buxton, built by Paxton's assistant E. Milner in 1871, had richly decorated cast-iron ribs held together by additional wrought-iron ties (fig. 53).

Braced Roof Trusses

The revolution in building methods brought about by cast-iron structures received new and powerful impetus from the principles of statics, and in the second half of the nineteenth century this led to comprehensive changes in the techniques of building with iron. The mass production of steel, the introduction of rolled steel section, and the formulation of the theory of frameworks by Culmann in 1851 were decisive in this respect. The step-by-step replacement of cast-iron roof trusses by wrought-iron ones, which around 1870 led to an almost complete ousting of cast iron from this important branch of civil engineering, was an expression of this revolution. When cast-iron lattice girders came into use, in the 1850s, the prefabricated cast-iron skeleton building clearly represented the highest state of building technology.

The prestressed multipost ridge roof (also, erroneously, called "hanging work") evolved from the British roof trusses used in hall structures with ridge roofs and was not based on the statically appropriate and structurally rational arrangement of bars. "In the extended hanging work the purlins were placed indiscriminately outside the joints between members and stressed the upper flange into a curve."[261] Along the line of the flange in tension there was not only a reduction in the use of space but also a need for overlong compression members (struts). These disadvantages could be eliminated if the struts were to be positioned perpendicular to the rafters, the purlins perpendicular to the top flange (to take the load only at the joints in the framework), and the lower flange above the springing. This principle was the basis of the roof truss which Polonceau, Emy, and Wiegmann developed almost simultaneously toward the end of the nineteenth century. This type of construction, developed through bridge and railway station construction, was based on the knowledge that, through the formation of triangles by the strutting, a plane is created when loaded, and there is no distortion. This

48
R. Matthienson,
palm house, Edin-
burgh, 1858, section.

49
Rowland Mawson
Ordish and George
Gilbert Scott, winter
garden of General
Hospital, Leeds,
1868.

50
Ludwig von Zanth,
conservatory, Wil-
helma, Stuttgart,
1842–1846, section
through a wing.

51
Diagram of Polon-
ceau roof truss.

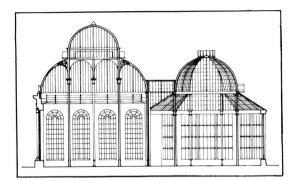

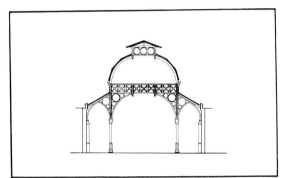

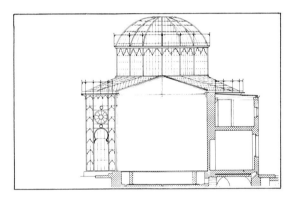

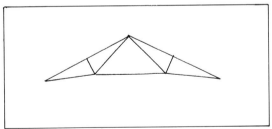

type of truss, developed from the beam with a prestressing cable below, has a characteristic framework
structure with the final arrangement of the strutting.
The individual bars have only to withstand the usual
tension and compression forces. There are no thrust
forces. Because the bars only have to take up the
equally distributed tension and compression across
the whole cross-section, they can be sized and
shaped for optimum performance relative to the material. With a small amount of material inserted, a
relatively wide span could be produced. These
trusses were accordingly predestined for structural
ironwork, in which economy of material had become
a major factor.[262]

In glasshouses constructed during the 1840s, the
1850s, and the 1860s one can find examples of the
pains taken by the builders to convert the design of
the triangular braced truss entirely into cast iron.
The use of such trusses in glazed ridge roofs created
an extremely cumbersome effect that almost destroyed the illusion of free space. Because tension in
stressed members was generally avoided (quite in
contrast with cast-iron structures), either posts and
diagonals reinforced by cast-iron ornamentation
were used or attempts were made to improve the
strength of the triangle-pattern trusses by introducing a curved profile for the bottom members.[263]

In 1861, as part of the hothouse joined to the castle of the Prince of Nassau in Biebrich, an exhibition
hall was built that contained cast-iron columns supporting a ridge roof with triangular-pattern trusses
made of the same material (fig. 52). The five-post
truss was fitted into the spandrel with cast-iron ornamentation. The two vertical struts left and right of
the center strut were made in the form of a hanging
king post below the lower member, joined by cast-
iron arches. These arches reached down at the side
as far as the columns and reinforced the whole
structure of the hall.[264]

Similar roof trusses, but with high arched bottom
profile, supported the wide center span of the Temperate House at Kew Gardens (fig. 54). The vertical
posts making up the sides and those in the ridge
area were reinforced by latticework in various sizes
and patterns. In the lateral spandrels, the latticework
had the form of cast-iron elliptical curves, which
were screwed to the top and bottom flanges.
Stamped plates were attached to them, which, like
the rings, were made double in the vicinity of the
closest approach of the top and bottom flanges of
the truss. In the center, the space between the
flanges was filled with latticework made of bars with
various slopes arranged diagonally like St. Andrew

crosses. The arch profile of the lower flange was made up of several individual members, of cast iron like the general infilling; the straight top flange was made of rolled iron section. The arches appear in perspective like a transparent latticework iron vault, and the forest of columns suggest a railway station more than a glasshouse. It is to be assumed that in the execution of this, in the details as in the whole, the determining factors were obscure constructions with few places in which the design logic could be seen as an aesthetic consideration of the effect of a cast-iron ornamentation inspired by the framework.[265]

The structural application of cast-iron frameworks to wide spans remained unsatisfactory, as the quoted examples show, and useless for further development. On the other hand, the cast-iron parallel-flange braced girders used in the Crystal Palace represented a significant advance in the history of iron construction.

Rectangular Braced Girders

The rectangular braced girder did not originate as part of the development sequence of iron roof trusses; rather, it was the direct result of bridge building. Made at first in wood (Long and Howe system) with diagonal bracing and iron tie rods,[266] it found early application in close-meshed iron frameworks for bridge building—an arrangement that resulted from ignorance about the mechanical behavior of iron frameworks. The first braced-girder bridge of this type was built over the Royal Canal in Dublin in 1845. The principle of the rectangular girder results from the solution of the problem by using straight parallel flanges and inserting a net of vertical and diagonal bars so that the height of this stiff frame is related to the span width and that optimum load behavior is achieved with the most economical use of strutting. Such girders were first made in the form of assembled flat bars, later in the form of rolled section.

The earliest proposals for cast-iron rectangular braced girders came from J. C. Loudon in his "Remarks on the Construction of Hothouses." He wrote: "As the weight of cast iron rafters, as hitherto adopted in hothouses, has been an objection to their use, I shall here give some forms which will render them nearly or entirely as light as wood. . . ."[267] The extremely fine filigree girders Loudon illustrated in several drawings were to be 20 feet long and about 1 foot high. The parallel upper and lower flanges were to be stiffened by eight braced sectors made up of diagonal and vertical members. The girders were to be cast in two or four separate parts and then bolted together. Additional vertical bars were to be cast and bolted on as additional reinforcement. This

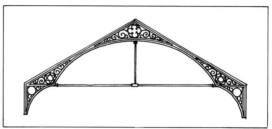

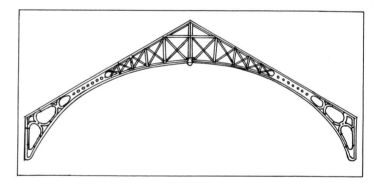

52
Exhibition hall, Biebrich, 1861.
Lithograph.

53
Edward Milner, conservatory, Pavilion Gardens, Buxton, 1871, roof truss in a wing.

54
Decimus Burton, temperate house, Kew, 1859–1863, nave roof truss.

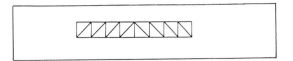

55
Diagram of a braced
girder used in the
Long and Howe
system.

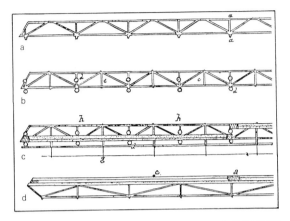

56
J. C. Loudon, cast-
iron braced girders,
1817: (a) basic design;
(b) with additional
vertical posts and
rollers; (c) with
wooden sashes for
sliding panes; (d) var-
iant of basic design
with greater width,
wooden sashes, and
sliding frames.

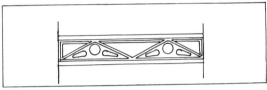

57
Joseh Paxton, Dav-
enport Conservatory,
Capesthorne Hall,
ca. 1837, cast-iron
braced girder.

58
Paxton, Crystal Pal-
ace, Hyde Park,
1850–51, braced gir-
ders: (a) 24-foot gir-
der (cast iron); (b) 48-
foot and 72-foot gir-
ders (hybrid con-
struction); (c) 72-foot
girder (hybrid
construction).

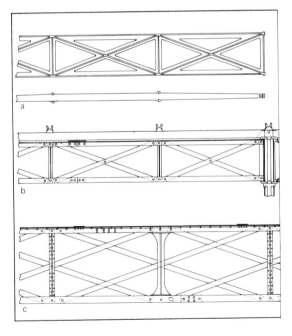

design fulfilled the double function of the girder: to
carry the weight of the roof and to serve as a roller
bearing for long sliding windows.[268] The girders developed empirically by Loudon, which were fitted at
a slope of 30° as rafters, were the first examples of
an accurately designed lattice based on the principles
of statics. Moreover, Loudon calculated the weight of
the girders and estimated the cost, including that of
assembly. One of Loudon's remarks shows how very
difficult it was at that time to obtain accurate statements about the mechanical strength of such a girder: "With regard to the strength of such a rafter, a
sufficient number of experiments have not yet been
made on cast iron to admit of a correct estimate."
Loudon was of the opinion that such a girder had to
be capable of bearing 100 times its own weight, or
double the weight of the glass roof.[269]

The cast-iron rectangular braced girder found its
perfected form in the Crystal Palace, which was designed by Joseph Paxton and developed in detail by
the construction firm of Fox and Henderson. It functioned not only as a rafter for the roof, but also as a
support for the gallery and a stiffening element. Incorporating specially designed connection pieces
(connecting in all four horizontal directions), and with
additional vertical hollow sections, it formed an integral load-bearing element of the space frame. As
early as 1837 Paxton had used cast-iron braced girders in the conservatory at Capesthorne Hall in
Cheshire to serve as lateral stiffening for the glued
wooden ribs in the high central nave (fig. 57). These
girders rested on cast-iron brackets and were bolted
to the purlins. The flanges and posts that formed the
perimeter of the girder were stiffened by diagonals
alone, without vertical members. Girders of this type
were the basic components of a rectangular braced
girder used by Paxton in four variations in the Crystal Palace.[270] These four types of girders are discussed in the following paragraphs.

24-Foot Cast-Iron Beam (fig. 58a) The standard 3-foot-
deep and 24-foot-long girder with standard end fixing was divided into three rectangular sections with
diagonals forming a flattish St. Andrew cross, terminated by vertical members. The dimensions of its
cross-section were based on the maximum load it
had to carry, according to whether it had to support
part of the roof or the floor of the gallery, which
weighed 9 and 15 tons respectively. Correspondingly,
the weight of the girder was either 1,080 or 1,340
pounds. In all, 2,400 such girders were used. Added
to that were 450 girders in the sections above the
gallery, which served only for stiffening. "Bending
moments caused by local loading did not occur be-

cause the roof load was only applied at three points, hence at the joints in the lattice."[271] Using the possibilities of the casting process, the girder was constructed so that it could optimally follow the stress distribution through its flanges. The flanges were wider in the middle of each section and narrowed toward the ends. The girders could be bolted together via a connecting collar on the column and held firm by small wrought-iron wedges (figs. 77, 84).

48-Foot Hybrid Beam (fig. 58b) This beam consisted of wood, wrought-iron, and cast-iron members bolted together, and served to span the 48-foot-wide halls of the aisles. Made to a standard depth of 3 feet, it had wooden struts, wrought-iron bar ties, and cast-iron vertical posts with a cruciform section.[272] As with the 24-foot beam, the internal joints were designed to be 8 feet apart. Angle-iron and flat bars formed the upper and lower flanges, and were butt jointed. The main wooden rain gutter and the Paxton gutter fitted transversely gave additional stiffening to the upper flange.[273]

72-Foot Girder (fig. 58b) This too was a hybrid construction. Stoutly built, it served to span the high central hall of the nave. According to a calculation by Ernst Werner, its tensile and compressive strengths "exceeded the present-day permitted stresses for the most commonly used steel, St. 37."[274]

72-Foot Girder (fig. 58c) At the intersection of the center bay with the barrel-vaulted transept, where the heavy load of the wooden ribs was taken up, there were rectangular braced girders 72 feet long and 6 feet deep, which, like bridge girders, consisted of narrow wrought-iron diagonals and cast-iron end posts. This type of girder was made in the form of double ties and diagonal struts and was riveted at the crossing points.[275]

The use of these types of girders demonstrates the influence of theoretical knowledge on the construction of the Crystal Palace. At the same time the limitations of the use of cast-iron braced girders are visible: They met the requirements for bridging smaller spans, but for wide spans wrought iron and wood were used instead.

The Glass Palace at Munich was built by August von Voit in 1853–54, largely on the prototype of the Crystal Palace. Voit, too, used rectangular girders as the elements of the space frame. The cast-iron roof and gallery girders, which had a span of 20 feet and a depth of 4 feet, were assembled from rectangular sections with vertical posts and diagonals (fig. 59a). The main trusses (fig. 59b), which had to span the 79-

foot hall of the nave, consisted of wood, cast iron, and wrought iron. The upper and lower flanges were made of wrought iron, in different ways. The upper flange comprised four angle-iron pieces which were riveted together by means of a horizontal fish plate. There was a gap of 1.4 inches between the corners, into which gusset plates were fitted. Flat iron bars formed the lower flange, which later had to be strengthened. "Upper and lower flanges were assembled from three pieces according to the length needed. The seventeen perpendicular members were of cast iron. Crosses were arranged in the sixteen rectangular sections, the main struts of which were of oak; the other struts were of wrought iron, and the two were bolted together in the middle."[276] The joint between the two types of girder at the cast-iron column was made via a hollow box section which, provided with a small projection, functioned as a bracket (fig. 85). The intersection angle of the strutting in both forms of girder was greater (45°) than in the Crystal Palace (30°), and the rectangular section was shorter. The sash bars and Paxton gutters of the ridge-and-furrow roofs consisted of wrought-iron section.

The rectangular girders used in these exhibition buildings proved themselves suited to hothouses. Small standardized cast-iron girders were used in 1857–1859 in the cast-iron palm house in the Old Botanical Garden in Berlin by Bouché, Herter, and Nietz. With a standard depth of 31 inches, they were cast in lengths of about 3 1/2, 8 1/2, 11 1/2, and 20 1/2 feet. They joined together pairs of cast-iron columns along the facade of the roof area to form the space frame, and they reinforced the 43-foot-long wrought-iron main transverse girders. The spaces within the cast-iron girders contained diagonal members (without vertical elements), and their intersection was set off ornamentally with a circle. It is noteworthy that the diagonal elements did not run exactly into the corners of the flanges, perhaps because the girders rested on a relatively wide abutment which projected from the octagonal connecting piece in the column (fig. 60). The wrought-iron braced girder, likewise made in standard depths, consisted of narrow diagonal flat bars and of flanges which were made up of two pieces of angle iron each. Cast-iron Paxton gutters (fig. 23) were bolted along the upper flange, and these held the supporting framework of the glass ridge-and-furrow roof. Only the sash-bar work of the glazing was made of wood.[277]

In the period 1850–1870, cast-iron rectangular braced girders came into general use in large cast-iron space frames. Examples include the girders in

59
August von Voit,
Glass Palace, Munich, 1853–54, braced
girders: (a) 20-foot
girder with conecting
piece (cast iron); (b)
79-foot girder (hybrid construction).

60
Bouché, Herter, and
Nietz, palm house,
Old Botanical Garden, Berlin-Schöneberg, 1857–1859,
braced girder.

61
Viel, Barrault, and
Bridel, Palace of Industry, World Exhibition, Paris, 1855,
braced girder.

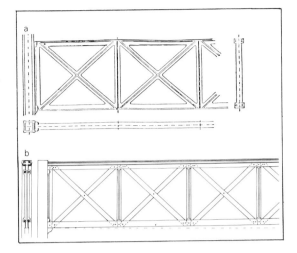

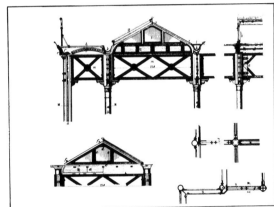

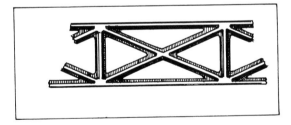

the Palais de l'Industrie (1855), the New York Crystal Palace (1852), and the Dublin Winter Garden (1865). (The last was, however, built without diagonals.)

Arched Braced Girders

Arched braced girders made completely of cast iron, proposed by Loudon in 1817 together with rectangular braced girders, are scarce in nineteenth-century glasshouse construction. Reasons for this may lie in the evolutionary sequence of arched girders for lean-to, ridge, and vaulted roofs as the framework replaced the interior cast-iron ring and bar work. As mentioned above, Burton attempted in 1863, in the Temperate House at Kew Gardens, to support the ridge roof of the center hall with 63-foot ribs, the cast-iron latticework of which created a cumbersome and structurally unsatisfactory effect. The logical change, from the viewpoint of statics, from the cast-iron arched braced girder to a girder consisting of triangular segments could not, as with the rectangular braced girder, be directly developed out of cast-iron structures. A major controlling factor here was the influence of bridge-building technology and the experience with wrought iron gained therefrom. As early as the 1840s there were forerunners of such frameworks in the American railway bridges built by Long and Howe.

The new wrought-iron structures, used for railway stations, exhibition buildings, and hothouses from about 1850, could not be designed by calculation until the 1860s, when J. W. Schwedler introduced two- and three-hinge arches.[278] Empirical methods of designing arched braced girders favored the semicircular form, which, although unsatisfactory from the viewpoint of statics, converted approximately one-fourth of the load into a lateral thrust. In order to avoid the disturbing visual effect of horizontal ties, there was an attempt to achieve the strengths necessary for wide-span structures by strengthening the ribs and the abutments.

A clumsy attempt to transfer the experience gained from the latticework structures of bridge building to roof trusses is shown by the cross-section of the Jardin d'Hiver, built on the Champs-Elysées in Paris by the engineer M. Rigolet in 1846–1848. Joseph Paxton visited this first large winter garden in its opening year, and it can be assumed that the impression he received was not without consequence for his design of the Crystal Palace.[279] The glass roof vault of the Jardin d'Hiver, over 130 feet wide and 66 feet high, was carried in a continuous wrought-iron arch, which was supported on rows of cast-iron columns. These columns formed a central nave reaching to the roof ridge and lower aisles. The sup-

port for the glass vault above the columns was provided by arches placed in the bays. The cast-iron
supporting structure, consisting of coupled pairs of
columns in the central hall, was continued in the
longitudinal direction by cast-iron elliptical arches,
which supported a cast-iron gallery.[280]

The 72-foot rib that Paxton used to span the main
hall of the Sydenham Crystal Palace (1852–1854) was
an important contribution to the development of the
"circular roof." The curved flanges, at a constant distance apart, were spaced by radial posts and crossed
diagonals. Every other radial post was joined onto
the purlins of the barrel-vaulted ridge-and-furrow
roof and was made of cast iron. The springing of the
8-foot-high ribs was of the same material.[281]

There was an interesting hybrid construction in
the archlike latticework rib of the Winter Garden in
Dublin, designed in 1865 by R. M. Ordish (a specialist in cast-iron engineering) and others. A spreading
framework abutment supported the lateral thrust of
the glass vault above the two-story cast-iron gallery,
which, following the Crystal Palace prototype, was
made of a prefabricated skeleton structure.[282]

The flora in Cologne, built by H. Märtens and
G. Eberlein, likewise had a barrel-vaulted main hall
made of wrought-iron lattice ribs, which rested on
projecting cast-iron brackets, and double columns at
the crossing and the ends. The lateral support was
created by the arcades of a two-story masonry
structure.[283]

Domes

Domes over circular or polygonal spaces appear in
early architectural briefs for iron structures. A high
dome had to withstand winds and had to have a
rigid, spacious framework of arches with few horizontal members. Stiffened arches formed the space
frame of the dome and took up the compressive
forces along their length. Horizontal rings were incorporated to withstand the tensile forces. In cross-
section the main girders, which also had to accommodate the glazing, were mostly in the characteristic
form of the cast-iron rib.

The first cast-iron-frame dome was constructed in
1811 for the Halle aux Blés in Paris by Bélanger and
Brunet. The rings and the ribs were made of cast-
iron parts bolted together. This dome was made as a
"jacket" construction, and no structural members
projected into the interior space.[284]

J. C. Loudon was the pathfinder for the early construction of iron hemidomes and complete hemispherical domes. Using the supporting frames he had
developed in 1817, Loudon built a series of hothouses with high glass domes. These domes, each

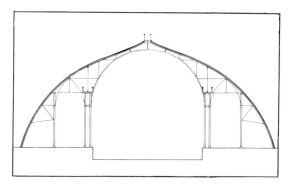

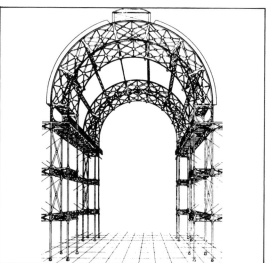

62
H. Meynadier de
Flamalens, Charpen-
tier, Rigolet, and
Moehly, Jardin
d'Hiver, Champs-
Elysées, Paris,
1846–1848, section.

63
Joseph Paxton, Crys-
tal Palace, Syden-
ham, 1852–1854, roof
trusses above nave.

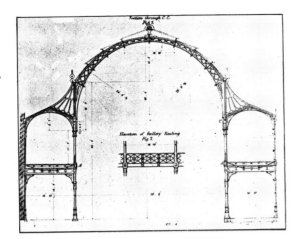

64
Alfred G. Jones,
R. M. Ordish, and
Le Feuvre, winter
garden, Dublin, 1865,
roof truss.

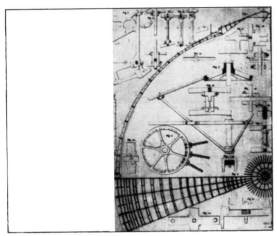

65
Bélanger and Brunet,
Halle aux Blés, Paris,
1811, section through
dome.

with an inner framework of cast-iron columns, extended down to ground level. The best-known of Loudon's domes are the two he built at Bretton Hall, Yorkshire, in 1827 and the one he designed for the Birmingham Botanical Gardens in 1831 (fig. 129).

The need in glass-and-iron domes for stability (which in glasshouses was supplied chiefly by a cast-iron ring or tambour), and the aesthetic and technical need to continue the arrangement of the tambour into the rising spans of the vault, led to the erection of a ranked series of space frames in addition to the use of Loudon's wrought-iron-type structure. Cast-iron ribs made up the main supporting structure, with wrought-iron sash bars inserted between them, all supported on horizontal rings. The characteristic structural shape of such domes is evident in the buildings designed by Fowler and Turner.

The domed space in Charles Fowler's Syon House glasshouse (1820–1827) served for the display of a palm collection. A ring of twelve cast-iron columns supported a parabolic vault above a ring girder resting on arches, which was propped on a cast-iron tambour. Twenty-four cast-iron ribs stiffened horizontally by four rings converged to the apex in a retaining ring. The curvilinear glass surfaces provided optimal illumination. This important dome structure, hardly mentioned in the literature, received much contemporary praise for its elegance and tastefulness.[286]

Another early cast-iron dome crowned the circular central pavilion of the Great Hothouse of Wilhelmshöhe, in Kassel, built in 1822 by Hofbaumeister J. C. Bromeis. Here the glass vault was carried by ribs and tie rings. Unfortunately there are no existing detailed drawings of the structure apart from a schematic ground plan and elevation.

A gigantic cast-iron dome structure (170 feet in diameter and 60 feet high) was projected at Hove in Sussex by H. P. Phillips in 1832. The glass palace, called the Anthaeum, was to have a winter garden as the focal point. Twenty elliptically curved cast-iron ribs (3 feet and 2 feet deep at the springing and the apex respectively) converged into a clamping ring. The ribs consisted of six prefabricated parts. Shortly before this wonder of building was completed, the diagonal reinforcement broke and the dome had to be pulled down.[287]

In the 1840s Richard Turner, described by McIntosh as a technically progressive builder of iron hothouses, published a series of projects for hothouses for "first class residences." The sometimes very different outline plans of these designs all called for curved glass surfaces in the form of elongated spaces and Gothic arches terminated by apse-shaped hemidomes or by raised full domes resting on a

cast-iron support. Cast-iron master ribs and
wrought-iron sash bars were to be used in the vault.
Turner's design for a circular hothouse with a central
dome and a lower vaulted gallery above cast-iron pilasters (figs. 66, 67) had a special beauty. Turner's
"Conservatory Project" for Colonel White at Killikee
near Dublin, with its domed tower projecting out of
the horizontal axis, was built around 1850.[288]

In 1853 Charles Lanyon, inspired by Turner,
erected a domed vault over the central part of Turner's Belfast hothouse. The 46-foot-high dome had a
ground plan formed by two semicircles separated by
short intervening straight lines. A lower gallery, also
vaulted, supporting the main vault on cast-iron columns, effected the junction with the two curvilinear
wings. Main and aisle vaults were supported by a
surrounding framework of greater diameter, into
which the main ribs were anchored after splaying
out. This gave a flowing line from the pinnacle down
to the base wall.[289]

After the building of the Crystal Palace, Joseph
Paxton proposed large iron dome structures resting
on skeletonlike cast-iron supports for winter gardens
and exhibition buildings. The three vast glass domes
called for in his 1861 design for the Exhibition Palace
at Saint-Cloud exemplify this.[290]

The New York Crystal Palace (figs. 40, 68), built on
the lines of Paxton's skeleton structure in 1852, was
given for its focal point a wide-span semicircular
dome with a cast-iron supporting frame in the form
of ribs, which were reinforced laterally by cast-iron
ornamentation. The springing was provided by an
encircling rim of rectangular braced girders, which
were supported by the ribs of the intersecting main
bay.[291] This last grandiose attempt to construct a
"weightless" wide-span space with the help of a fine
network of cast iron represents a gathering of all
that had been learned from the building of glasshouses.

Supporting Structures

Without doubt it was the iron space frame that
paved the way for the technical revolution in building, because in its field of application the limits of
stone and wood were immediately apparent. With
the use of cast iron, and later wrought iron, completely new possibilities arose to increase the efficiency and the economy of construction and to meet
the need for large spans. In parallel with the development of the space frame, iron replaced the usual
materials used in supporting structures. The use of
iron in supporting structures came to pass alongside
and partly independent of the development of the
iron space frame, but it was quickly seen that only
by the combination of these two innovations could

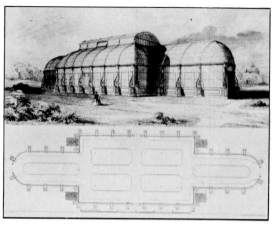

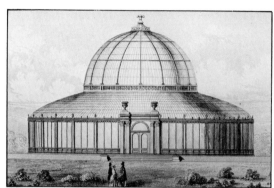

66
Richard Turner, con-
servatory for "First
Class Residence"
(project), ca.
1845–1850.

67
Turner, conservatory
for "First Class Resi-
dence" (project), ca.
1845–1850.

68
G. J. B. Carstensen
and Charles Gilde-
meister, Crystal Pal-
ace, New York, 1852.
Engraving.

all the possibilities and advantages of the new material be realized. Crucial for this step was the demand for exploitation of space through the use of glass and iron in the hothouse.

The hothouses were the first buildings with frames made wholly of iron. The most important result of this transformation, and the deciding factor in the design of spanning and supporting structures, was the use of standardized elements. Here cast iron played a decisive role.

Columns

The earliest iron columns were made of cast iron, which was capable by itself of supporting large compressive forces. Hollow cast-iron columns, with their favorable load-bearing behavior, their suitability for mass production, their ease of assembly, and their low manufacturing cost, determined to an increasing extent in the course of the Industrial Revolution the supporting structures of buildings. Though their use decreased around 1900 in favor of rolled iron section, it is justifiable to speak of the "run of victories"[292] of cast-iron columns in the nineteenth century. They proved thoroughly competitive in the times of technically fully developed wrought-iron structures. Even in the 1890s, Johann Bauschinger established cast iron's general usefulness and its superiority over wrought iron in the event of fire.[293] In its widespread use, as for example in the factory and railway buildings being put up everywhere, it served the immediate advance of industrialization.

Cast-iron columns were used even before 1800.[294] The need to create spacious interiors without recourse to massive structural elements led to the use of iron columns in British factories, especially cotton mills. In their 1801 building in Manchester, Boulton and Watt used hollow round columns, which were advantageous from the viewpoint of statics. Study of Barré's tables (1870) concerning the strength of cast-iron columns shows that the higher strength of solid columns must be obtained with a smaller amount of material. Hollow columns were cast upright as a rule, so the core had to be a rigid mass. Around 1700, a forerunner of this process was used in the making of cast-iron pipes (fig. 69). On technical manufacturing and assembly grounds, the process was changed for the making of columns so that the base, the shaft, and the capital were cast separately, and the bearing surfaces were machined flat for better distribution of pressure.

The material property of cast iron that allows it to take up any shape with great accuracy offered the opportunity to make columns resemble classical styles. This circumstance, at the same time, made it

more difficult to find a form in keeping with the iron. No only were cast-iron columns given the ornamentation of stone columns, but an attempt was also made to increase their volume beyond the needs demanded by statics in order to create the impression of mass and solidity. A. G. Meyer commented critically on this in connection wih the building of the New Museum in Berlin (1841–1845):

The desire to create larger spaces with the greatest amount of transparency led the designer to introduce cast-iron columns. . . . In contrast to the above-mentioned purpose there is the load-bearing core surrounded by a cast-iron sheath of considerably greater circumference, and this from its Attic base via its fluted shaft to the Corinthian capital has a form completely analogous to the stone column. Certainly the strengthening of the natural slenderness of the ironwork eased the minds of the people of that time in terms of aesthetics, but for us . . . there remains a disquieting feeling about the false thickness of the columns, that the iron and its bearing strength are not correctly matched.[295]

In hothouse building, where the designers were absolved from the constraint of stylized architectural forms, the cast-iron column could be made from the start in accordance with its load function. The occasional aesthetic concessions were small and unimportant. The continuing goal of a substantial decrease in the weight of the structure in the interest of maximum transparency led to the development of extraordinarily slim cast-iron columns, completely freed from antique styles, that could demonstrate by their forms the structural possibilities of the new material.

The same trend toward engineering economy can be seen in the supporting structures of the hothouses. Figure 74 compares some cast columns offered for sale in the catalog around 1875 with a hothouse column.

A special feature of the hollow cast-iron columns used in hothouse construction is their functional integration into the space frame while simultaneously serving as drainpipes for the rainwater collected by the Paxton gutters above. Another characteristic feature is the plant symbolism often seen in leaf-shaped capitals, columns resembling bamboo and palm stems, scrolls, and flowerlike brackets. The addition of vegetative forms was not merely for ornamental purposes, but was often a device for merging the column into a structural element of the roof span. The iron brackets in Turner's hothouses in Belfast, Dublin, and Kew Gardens are examples of this.

The first hollow cast-iron columns used in a greenhouse, made in 1803 for Carlton House in London by Humphrey Repton, were designed to support a ridge-and-furrow roof. John Nash's columns in the

Royal Pavilion at Brighton (1815–16) had capitals in the form of palm leaves.[296] From 1817 on, J. C. Loudon installed totally undecorated cast-iron filigree columns to support his vaulted wrought-iron roofs. The Camellia House (1820) in Hackney, London, is an example of this. In the glass dome at Bretton Hall, Loudon used sixteen slender iron columns in a ring. Charles Fowler's large cast-iron columns for the conservatory of Syon House in London (1820–1827), which carried high glass domes resting on cast-iron arches, likewise illustrate the renunciation of traditional column forms. Without taper, and cast with smooth circular outlines, they terminated in goblet-shaped capitals. Metal disks incorporated in the shafts served as tensioning elements for vertical wires that held the climbing plants.

The builders' attempts to make the columns in hothouses slender led to columns whose form was based on their main function, without any symbolic interpretation. Examples of this are the central columns of the glasshouse in the Jardin des Plantes (Charles Rohault, 1833), which had a cruciform elaboration of the cross-section, and the smooth, slender double columns in the Jardin d'Hiver, which no longer displayed any classical elements.

The most important contribution of the cast-iron glasshouses in the period 1820–1860 to the development of iron columns was the use of standard columns. Early applications of standardization in glasshouse building were made by the firm of T. Clark at Wollaton Hall in Nottingham (1823) and at The Grange in Hampshire (1825), where the columns conducted rainwater from the gutters to an underground cistern from which it was pumped back to water the plants. McIntosh, who described the construction in detail, proposed the use of similar columns to circulate heating water.[297]

The development of a coupling spandrel to make junctions in all directions was necessary for the further application of cast-iron space frames to prefabricated construction. The preliminary stage in the making of joints in space frames can be seen in the development of the "assembled" column in hothouse building, and a preliminary stage of the assembled column involved columns that were bolted to the ribs via specially cast brackets and upright posts that permitted various joints between cast-iron ribs. In the last case there arose the beginnings of a multistory structure via the introduction of small encircling galleries which were supported by these brackets or arched girders. Examples of the development of a special part for joining cast-iron arches are the cast-iron brackets of the Wilhelma in Stuttgart (1842–1846) and the palm house in Belfast (1853). In

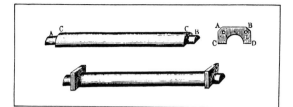

69
Deparcieux model forms, Versailles and Marly, cast-iron pipes with flanges, end of seventeenth century.

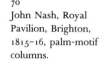

70
John Nash, Royal Pavilion, Brighton, 1815–16, palm-motif columns.

71
Columns with plant motifs: (a) winter garden, Liechtenstein Castle, 1843; (b) winter garden, Grimston Park, Yorkshire, 1830–1840; (c) Richard Turner, palm house, Botanic Garden, Belfast, 1839–40, wing.

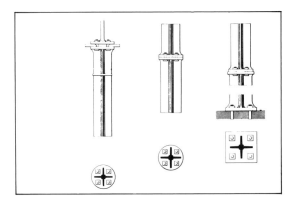

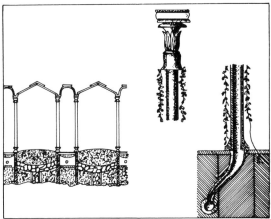

74
Hollow cast-iron columns: (a) from catalog of Coalbrookdale Company, 1875; (b) in Bicton Gardens palm house, Budleigh Salterton, ca. 1843.

72
Charles Rohault de Fleury, conservatory, Jardin des Plantes, Paris, 1833, columns with cruciform section.

73
Thomas Clark, camellia house, Wollaton Hall, 1823, hollow cast-iron columns with gutters and rainwater drainage.

the glasshouse at Syon House (1820–1827) the post even had the form of a trapeziform spandrel. In both these cases the joint to the lateral reinforcement arches was effected in one plane only and led to the development of a gallery.

The first joints in three planes (six directions) were those used in a gallery in Paxton's largest hothouse, the basilica-style palm house at Chatsworth, Derbyshire (1836–1840). The glass vaults of the nave and the aisle were clear indications of a multistory structure in the spanning frame. The smooth, hollow columns, free of any decoration, tapered from a bottom diameter of 10 inches to a top diameter of 8 inches and terminated in a cup-shaped thickening. After the prototypes of the palm houses (e.g., the Thomas Clark designs), the columns served as drainage channels for rainwater. A square hollow cast section placed above the round columns (or perhaps cast with it) functioned as a coupling piece between the wooden arches and the girders and the lateral reinforcing arch, together with the brackets for the gallery. Whereas the cast-iron parts were bolted together with fish plates located on the capital, the wooden parts were bolted to shoes integral with the casting. The cast-iron gutters were offset from the axis of the columns on account of the central position of the ribs.[298]

In 1848, Turner and Burton effected a technically elegant and aesthetically beautiful solution to the problem of the joint between columns and ribs in the large palm house at Kew. By the use of arched iron girders in a cross-section design similar to that of the main hall at Chatsworth, the structural form of the supporting structure was simplified. Round columns approximately 26 feet high terminated in a circular connecting piece, so that a joint could be made on three principal planes. The joint to the ribs and to the transverse girders was made by stout, arched cast-iron brackets bolted by fish plates to the post. In their projecting, ascending form, with rosettes as cover plates for the bolted joints, they looked like opened flowers. An arched bracket projected out into the hall to support the surrounding gallery. Although the transfer was not effected entirely via the brackets, this joint can be considered an early stage in the development of the three-dimensional joints used in later iron structures.[299]

To understand the development of easily assembled space frames that could be built up in the vertical direction by adding on members via connecting pieces and in the horizontal plane via complicated joints to the ribs and diagonals, it is necessary to recapitulate the experience hitherto gained in solving this difficult problem, particularly as concerns hot-

houses. This important engineering achievement was due to Paxton's success in the construction of the Crystal Palace. Here was effected the transformation of the simple hollow cast-iron column into one assembled from several parts and joined by a special connecting piece to a multistory structure of bolted-together horizontal beams and vertical ribs.

The Load-Bearing Facade

A special line of development of assembled supporting structures involves the load-bearing framework, which until 1870 appeared as a supporting member in glasshouse structures while holding the glazing of the facade. Load-bearing frames probably came to be used on the exterior of glasshouses through their use with display windows, where the important matter was to solve the problem of the massive aspect of heavily loaded columns appearing between cast-iron frames. E. Brandt described an "interrupted cast-iron wall," with wide head and base plates, used for gallery construction around 1870,[300] and in 1895 C. Scharowsky described square-section hollow cast-iron columns joined together by a beam with circular openings in the web.[301]

In the above-mentioned cases, it was essentially a matter of making stout floor joists. In hothouse construction, on the other hand, filigree-form load-bearing frameworks were used from the start. They formed the lightweight space frames for glazed areas. In the small-span glasshouses of the first quarter of the nineteenth century, the only vertical support members were the window sash bars, which were structural members of the facade and which supported the roof. Examples are seen in the many small forcing houses with lean-to roofs and in Loudon's curvilinear vault (1817). With increasing spans and the need to support the glass roof on rafters, sash bars with stouter sections at a constant distance apart came into use. Hence, the obvious thing to do was to retain the continuous framework of sash bars and to combine every other one into a rigid frame in order to increase the strength of the vertical glass surfaces. This led to the development of the filigree load-bearing framework.

Richard Turner developed the cast-iron load-bearing framework as a feature of the facade. It was a characteristic structural member in his many buildings, and it contributed significantly to their strength. In 1842 Turner used glazed cast-iron frames to support the roof vault of the Palm Hall at Glasnevin near Dublin and also incorporated them in the corners. At the eaves they supported the surrounding cast-iron guttering. Turner used a similar element in the Winter Garden in Regent's Park, London, and in

75
Josph Paxton, Great Conservatory, Chatsworth, 1836–1840, detail of column with bracket and top fittings.

76
Richard Turner and Decimus Burton, palm house, Kew, 1844–1848, detail of column with connecting piece and brackets.

77
Joseph Paxton, Crystal Palace, Hyde Park, 1850–51, detail of connection collar.

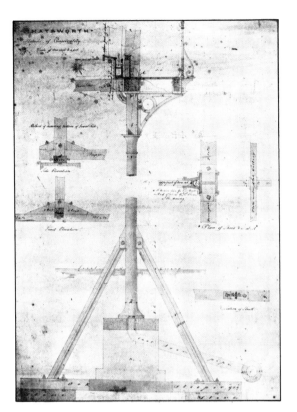

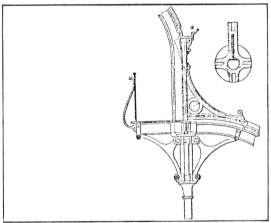

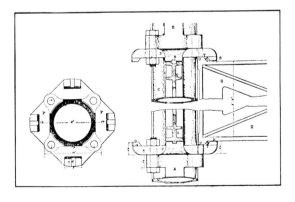

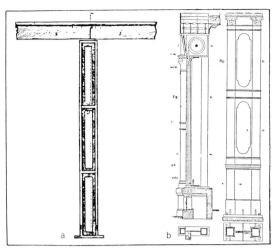

78
Cast-iron stanchions: (a) E. Brandt, 1870; (b) C. Scharowsky, 1895.

79
Richard Turner, conservatory, Glasnevin, central pavilion, 1842–1850, cast-iron stanchions.

his 1845–1850 design for a circular hothouse (fig. 67).
In all these buildings the load-bearing facade, which
would otherwise have had only sash bars, featured
filigree cast-iron posts and ornaments filled in with
red and blue glass.[302] In 1842 L. von Zanth used a
similar structural element in Moorish style in the
cast-iron facade of the Wilhelma. The load-bearing
framework incorporated into the cast-iron facade
was extended to the whole of the space frame. This
type of construction was the basis of the early prefabricated iron load-bearing facade. Even in the
1920s cast-iron space frames were commonly used
supporting structures in the vertical glass surface of
the encircling tambour and propped vaults, or in the
low fronts along the base area. Frames consisting of
horizontal or vertical rectangles were reinforced by
vertical posts and were sometimes made in considerable sizes (floor levels), cast in one piece. Examples of
this are constructions with curvilinear roofs, such as
the tambour of Syon House in London (1820–1827),
the palm house in Belfast (1839–40) and Bicton Gardens at Budleigh Salterton, Devon (1843).

A masterpiece of the cast-iron technique is von
Zanth's use of standardized load-bearing members in
the facade of the Wilhelma (fig. 680), where cast-iron
pilasters joined with finely ornamented arches and
girders to form a supporting structure for the cast-
iron spans of the glass hall.

From the viewpoint of the history of construction,
the cast-iron load-bearing framework is of the greatest interest as a standardized prefabricated part in
the construction of multistory designs. Here it is likewise a matter of the integration of assembled columns into an iron skeleton. Structural cast-iron
facades appeared in the late 1840s on factories and
glasshouses (particularly in New York, Boston, and
St. Louis), and they often determined the character
of a whole street. The New York factory of James
Bogardus (1848–49; fig. 82) may be considered a prototype of cast-iron prefabricated multistory buildings.[303] However, as was completely unnoticed then,
glasshouses of high quality had been built according
to this principle as much as fifteen years earlier.

Charles Rohault had built two 50-foot-high glass
pavilions with ridge roofs in 1833 in the Jardin des
Plantes in Paris.[304] The load-bearing frameworks built
into the glass facades consisted of prefabricated pilasters and girders made with openings to the inside.
The two-story supporting members, with a gallery at
half the total height, were made of six vertical parts
bolted together so that a connecting piece and a
bracket formed a lateral joint to the girders and to
the cornice. This made around the three main sides
of the glasshouse a rigid iron skeleton in the plane of

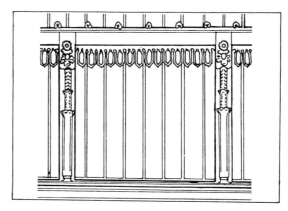

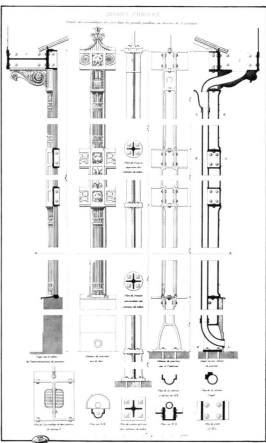

80
Turner, palm house,
Botanic Garden, Bel-
fast, 1839–40, cast-
iron load-bearing
framework of wing.

81
Charles Rohault de
Fleury, conservatory,
Jardin des Plantes,
Paris, 1833, cast-iron
framework and col-
umns assembled
from prefabricated
parts.

82
James Bogardus, Bo-
gardus factory, New
York, 1848–49, cast-
iron prefabricated
building. Engraving.

the facade, the space between which was glazed and which shared the weight of the vaulted wrought-iron roof structure. Two rows of cast-iron columns of uniform cross-section, similarly bolted together, were situated in the middle third of the hall and completed the iron load-bearing structure. Because the joints of the prefabricated parts of the load-bearing framework were made in the plane of the facade alone, there was no three-dimensional joint or coupling piece. Paxton visited this glasshouse and received ideas which he could later use in the building of the Crystal Palace.[305]

The Cast-Iron Space Frame

The cast-iron space frame follows as a structural principle the construction of a rigid supporting system of columns and girders which have joints designed so that additions can be made both horizontally and vertically, thus forming a multistory frame. This was first accomplished on the grand scale in the construction of the Crystal Palace, which brought widespread recognition not only of the use of cast iron but also of the idea of completely prefabricated buildings.

As noted above, the basic principles of cast-iron glasshouse construction were already in existence during the first half of the century. In the area of spanning structures, the standard-size rectangular girder proved to be the ideal load-bearing element for prefabricated multistory buildings. In the area of supporting structures, a development occurred that led via the need for integration with rib systems to the "assembled column" with integral brackets. In spite of the advanced structural designs that existed, not until 1850 was there any development of a connecting piece that could join prefabricated parts in six directions (i.e., in three planes). The reason for this lay partly in the building specifications; in a glasshouse the division into stories with horizontally stacked girders manifested itself only in narrow surrounding galleries. The building specifications for large exhibition buildings gave new impetus to the building of cast-iron hothouses.[306]

As has already been stated, the iron space frame made its appearance around 1800 in the building of cotton mills. The basic type consisted of a multistory iron frame made of columns placed one above the other with internal undivided spaces and massive surrounding walls. In keeping with the spans of the cast-iron girders used at the time, the rows of columns were placed at 14-foot intervals.[307] The first building of this kind (1892–93), a warehouse in Milford by William Strutt with two internal rows of cast-iron columns placed one above the other, had

wooden beams for the ties, which carried the brickwork vault. The birth of the iron space frame was completed with the flax-spinning mill built in 1796–97 at Shrewsbury by Charles Bage, which had iron girders joining three rows of columns. The character of a type of British factory building that developed over the next 50 years finally manifested itself in the seven-story cotton mill built at Salford, near Manchester, by Boulton and Watt in 1799–1801 (fig. 83).[308] Cast-iron columns passed through rings in the beams, one directly above the one below. The cast-iron beams were covered with brickwork vaults. The development of an iron space frame of columns joined together gave an impetus to the production of cast-iron girders. The cross-sections served as patterns for the later development of the shape of the girder to match the strength of the material.

In the overall sequence of the development of British cotton mills there was still no appearance of special coupling joints between columns and girders. The whole framework obtained its strength not from its iron members but only from masonry walls and massive floors. The iron building frame was developed further in various American factory and office buildings erected between 1850 and 1880 which showed the perfection of the iron frame in their load-bearing cast-iron facades. The facade, which had first proved its validity in the hothouses of the Jardin des Plantes, was no longer a surface with openings made in it but was now a glazed load-bearing frame.

However, with both the British and the American buildings created between 1850 and 1880 (a time which people liked to call the "cast-iron age"[309]), it was a matter of intersections of columns and girders, and the cast-iron ridge members above the columns. There were no structures in which a connecting piece joined the iron girders and hence made an important contribution to the strength of the whole framework. The Singer Building in New York (ca. 1855), for example, had capping vaults to reinforce the structure.[310]

In hothouses and exhibition buildings—where the visibility of the structurally important joints had to be considered from the start and where separated massive elements, but never massive floors, could be incorporated—engineers were compelled to find simple solutions to the problem of force-transmitting joints in the iron framework.

In 1831, in his second design for a large glasshouse dome for the Birmingham Botanical Gardens, J. C. Loudon designed a three-story cast-iron space frame with an internal framework to be built by his wrought-iron-shell method. There were to be three circles of cast-iron double columns in an interior space 200 feet in diameter and 100 feet high. The pairs of columns placed at distances of 60 feet were to be joined one above another and tied radially by iron arched girders, as well as along the distance from ring to ring by narrow braced girders which contributed to the lateral strength. The supporting structure was to be matched to the rising curve of the dome, and below the conical glass apex it was to reach up to the level of the third story, continuously to a height of about 80 feet. In the center of the dome there was to be a circular space about 40 feet in diameter, formed out of a ring of cast-iron columns placed close together, which was to form a high-rising rigid iron cylinder with an ascending spiral-shaped stairway with similar braced girders as breastwork. From the spiral stairway there was to be access to the radial galleries at three levels and thence to the concentric passages. This filigree structure of columns and girders was to support the sash bars of the glass dome, which, extending down to ground level and in conformity with the internal floor system, was to be divided into ring-shaped shells one above the other. The vertical framework was to form "assembled columns" in the form of slender cast-iron shafts provided with capitals. From the existing section and perspective sketches by Loudon (fig. 129) it is evident that this was one of the earliest attempts to design a skeleton construction based only on the strength of the ironwork. The main elements of the Paxton-style space-frame building—the hollow vertical columns bolted together, the cast-iron braced girders, and the ridge-and-furrow roof—had already been propagated for hothouse building by Loudon two or three decades before the building of the Crystal Palace.[311]

The specification of the giant glass-and-iron building for the 1851 World Exhibition called for a 700,000-square-foot hall, as undivided as possible, to be built in a very short time. (The announcement of the international competition for the design was made on February 21, 1850; the exhibition was to open May 1, 1851.) It was to be low in cost and capable of being dismantled and erected elsewhere for further use. In the checking of the competition designs by the Building Commission, and in the consideration of them individually on June 22, 1850, it emerged that the specification could be met only through a thorough exploitation of the possibilities offered by industrialized building. In this situation, Paxton's concept of a cast-iron space frame made of prefabricated standardized parts seemed to be the salvation of the project.[312] The realization of this revolutionary concept for iron construction proved that at that time cast iron could best be exploited by the

forces of production if the economic and technical specifications of the building brief were met in an optimum way. If up to 1850 the principle of prefabrication and standardization of cast-iron parts for assembly into space frames appeared as an additional stipulation, then it proved its worth for the first time as a philosophy of construction in the building of the Crystal Palace. This demonstrates not only the form of every point of detail in the space frame, but just as much the adaptation of production techniques and works organization to mass-produced building. One can compare this with Charles Dickens's report in "Household Words."[313]

Paxton's Crystal Palace corresponds to the classical formulation of iron space frames,[314] and also to that of pure prefabricated building. About 1,000 assembled stanchions formed the core of the space frame, consisting of 3,300 round hollow columns and about as many connecting pieces for joining together the rectangular braced girders to make roofs and galleries. All the hollow columns were made in standard lengths (about 19 feet for the ground floor, about 17 feet for the first and second floors), with an external diameter of 8 inches. The problem of having to use components too strong for their respective purposes was overcome by varying the thicknesses of the column walls (from 1.1 inch down to 0.05 inch) for the various loads. This was also done with the other cast-iron parts in the space frame. In the process of box casting, which was the basis of the manufacturing of hollow columns, it was easy to change the wall thickness of the casting by simply changing the clay core, without interrupting production. The tops and bottoms of the columns were provided with flanges, which were cast integrally with the rest and which were easily joined to the connecting pieces by four strong bolts. These joints were covered with cast-iron coverings of small capitals and bases after the assembly of the space frame.

The ground-floor columns had screw-on feet of various thicknesses, and these rested on base plates in the concrete sockets of the foundation. Their different heights allowed the whole building to be level while resting on the sloping ground in Hyde Park, so that no excavation was needed. Integral cast tubular struts led the rainwater via the hollow columns down into the drainage system.

The technical revolution in space-frame construction was embodied in the connecting piece, a 41-inch-high three-dimensional joint with clawlike grips that was used to couple hollow columns one above the other and to join standard rectangular girders in all four horizontal directions (fig. 77). Noselike projections from the connecting piece corresponded with

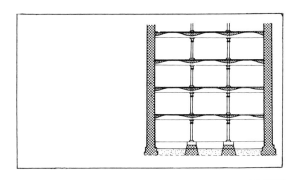

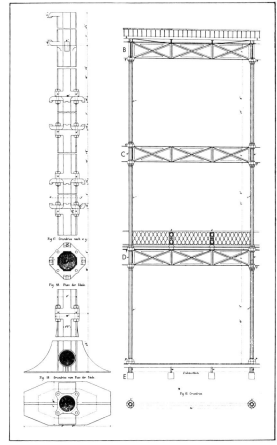

83
Matthew Boulton
and James Watt,
spinning mill,
Manchester, 1801,
cast-iron space
frame.

84
Joseph Paxton, Crys-
tal Palace, Hyde
Park, 1850–51, cast-
iron space frame and
detail of supporting
column.

notches on the girders. Secure fixing was effected by iron wedges in the vertical direction and by copper wedges in the horizontal. The 24-foot girders were also joined to the columns by two bolts. Not only did these matching joints in the connecting pieces stiffen the whole space frame, but by bringing the girder close to the axis of the vertical supports the load was also transferred without bending occur-ring.[315] The bolted joints with the columns also served simultaneously as a means of fastening and as attachment points for the diagonal tensioning wires. With the use of these precisely made structural members, the cast-iron space frame of the Crystal Palace was assembled in the following order: base plate, ground-floor column, connecting piece, first-floor column, connecting piece, second-floor column, and top connecting piece. About 3,500 tons of cast iron, 550 tons of wrought iron, and 500 tons of glass were used in the building of the Crystal Palace.

The filigree effect of the framework structure of the Crystal Palace was, as mentioned above, derived from pre-1850 hothouse building.[316] The concept of the glasshouse was not only the origin but also the substance of Paxton's design; the transept of the building was to cover some large trees in Hyde Park, and in addition Paxton wanted to reuse the building as a gigantic hothouse after the end of the World Exhibition.[317] In the transfer of the Crystal Palace to Sydenham (1852–1854) and in his project for the Great Victorian Way (1855), Paxton planned to cover extensive park landscapes with glass.[318]

In the cast-iron space frames of the next two dec-ades, in which Paxton's design was taken up with enthusiasm and developed further, there was contin-ued use of the typical construction principles of glasshouse building. This is shown in the following examples.

In the Munich Glass Palace (1853–54), August von Voit applied Paxton's construction principle in a modified form. Cast-iron columns joined by connect-ing pieces rose from a 20-by-20-foot base and had three stories attached, which were made of the above-described cast-iron rectangular braced girders or as hybrid constructions. The columns had an oc-tagonal hollow interior with four semicircular les-enes. They rested on brick foundations and served for the removal of rainwater from the roof. The builders (the Cramer-Klett Company, later MAN) ob-tained optimal transfer of load by making a special machine for turning the columns.[319] The external outline of the column was concealed, with the box section placed over it. Small corbels provided the springing for the cast-iron braced girders at the level of their bottom flanges. The end post of the girder

had two flanges, by means of which it was bolted
horizontally above and below to the connecting
piece. In addition the columns were provided with
cast-iron capitals and bases. An attempt to convert
this exhibition building into a hothouse came to
nothing because its demensions were too great.[320] Instead, Voit built between 1860 and 1865 a cast-iron
palm house nearby in the Old Botanical Garden. In
this palm house the principle of space-frame construction was modified for the building of the dome-
capped central hall. The facade of round columns
and horizontal girders, about 46 feet high and divided into four stories, was built as a load-bearing
structure and stood in front of the continuous vertical glazing. Compound columns fitted together in the
interior of the hall extended the supporting structure. A wrought-iron frame of braced ribs supported
the glass dome. A cast-iron bracket for every story
formed the springing and was bolted to the postwork of the facade. At the roof ridge and above the
main portal the building was decorated with ornamentation and groups of figures made of cast iron.
This skeletal facade assembled from many prefabricated parts is by virtue of its delicately executed
work a witness to the high state of cast-iron and
prefabrication techniques.[321]

Paxton's principle of space-frame construction was
applied directly in the cast-iron Great Palm House
built by Bouché, Herter, and Nietz in 1857–1859 in
the Old Botanical Garden in Berlin. There were 108
tubular cast-iron columns in pairs forming the supporting structure of the 57-foot-high glass building,
and with the eight interior columns they supported
the rectangular braced girders and the ridge-and-furrow roof. The shafts of the high central part of the
palm hall were made of four standard-length columns bolted together with attached octagonal connecting pieces. The connecting pieces were cast with
integral brackets to provide the abutments for the
girders. The joints between the two were made with
bolts. By using pushed-on octagonal connecting
pieces it was possible to make joints for girders at
any desired level. The columns in the line of the facade had integral cast-iron flanges for attachment to
the glazing framework. They rested on a cast-iron
wall plate, which was firmly connected to the column via a socket and was anchored to the masonry
plinth at the base. (A similar joint was already in use
in 1853 for the detached columns at the Borsig
works.[322]) The engineered design developed specifi-
cally for this hothouse lacks the classical simplicity of
its prototype, the Crystal Palace; nonetheless, it was
used in a surprising number of early German iron-
space-frame buildings.[323]

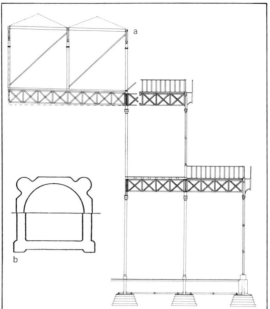

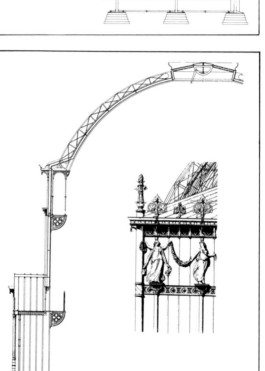

85
August von Voit,
Glass Palace, Mun-
ich, 1853–54. (a) Sec-
tion through nave;
(b) cross-section
through column and
connecting collar.

86
Voit, Great Palm
House, Old Botanical
Garden, Munich,
1860–1865, cast-iron
space frame with
dome.

87
Bouché, Herter, and
Nietz, Great Palm
House, Old Botanical
Garden, Berlin-
Schöneberg,
1857–1859, longitudi-
nal section of cast-
iron space frame.

88
Bouché, Herter, and
Nietz, Great Palm
House, Old Botanical
Garden, Berlin-
Schöneberg, details
of supporting
members.

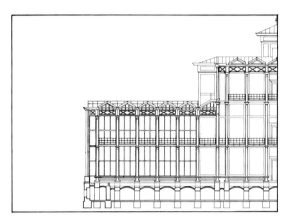

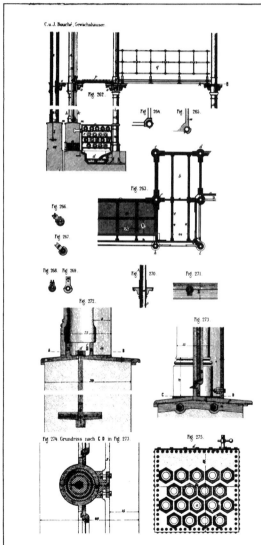

Variations of the Paxton principle of space-frame construction were used in the hothouses in the Breslau Botanical Gardens (1861), the glasshouses in the Pavilion Gardens at Buxton (1871), and the Old Palm House in Bonn (ca. 1875). In all these examples the multistory space-frame principle was expressed in the supporting elements in the facade.

In the classically built Breslau hothouse, at the positions of the round columns, were pilasters with square cross-sections and connecting pieces for joining the girders of the ridge-and-furrow roof. The glasshouse in the Buxton Pavilion Gardens was built by E. Milner, a colleague of Paxton. The framework of the facade was a quote from the Crystal Palace. The columns placed one over another to make two stories were separated by glass windows with semicircular arches on top and carried a canopy roof structure made of wrought iron.[324] The Old Palm House in Bonn, built with a raised center part and two lower transepts, had the same design for its two- and three-story space frame, so that double columns were used at the corners. This large hothouse was one of the last of the cast-iron space-frame constructions.

In Britain the example of the Crystal Palace led to a euphoric acceptance of such structures by the following generation of engineers and architects. The fall in the price of glass in the 1860s also contributed to the acceptance of glass-and-iron buildings.

Between 1857 and 1859 the classically educated architect Edward M. Barry built the Floral Hall in London, the cast-iron facade of which was assembled from pilaster-type frames with semicircular arch windows between and with richly decorated architraves. The load-bearing frames were infilled with colored glass after the manner of Richard Turner's buildings. Above this framework stood a barrel vault made of wrought-iron lattice ribs, which was a copy of the transept of the Crystal Palace and which, like that transept, terminated in a large semicircular rosette made of cast iron. The nave was internally strengthened with cast-iron columns and was not divided into stories.[325]

In 1859 the architect Owen Jones, who had advised Paxton on the matter of decoration for the Crystal Palace, designed the projected Palace of the People at Muswell Hill in London. This glass palace was to have been erected over a railway station and was to have a giant dome-shaped palm hall as its focal point. Its spatial concept was based on a yearly flow of a million visitors. The framework, of cast-iron columns and cross-members, illustrated a number of new forms based on the box building principle. A long nave covered with a glass ridge roof above the three stories was to be flanked by eight square five-story glass towers. Apselike glazed extensions were to terminate the structure, which was to be partly covered with a ridge-and-furrow roof.[326]

The Winter Palace built in Dublin for the 1865 International Exhibition had a three-story cast-iron space frame. A gallery structure built around a barrel-vaulted center bay with latticework ribs and supported on cast-iron columns made a strong frame for the springing of the roof support structure. The connecting pieces used in this space frame to provide joints in three directions to the ribs had small bolted-on brackets at the first-floor level to carry the girders of the gallery. In the production of an arched rib for the ridge roof of the gallery, the builders seem to have been seeking compatibility with the traditional architectural mode. The roof ribs were bolted directly to the connecting pieces in the second story and served as abutments for the cast-iron "flying buttresses" of the roof structure. High columns reaching as far as the start of the main wrought-iron girders provided the springing for these through inward-projecting brackets and thus transmitted the lateral thrust to the buttresses. Along the axis of the hall these columns were braced with arched girders and thus formed glazed clerestories for the three upper floors. The overall skeleton was erected without reinforcement by diagonal ties, which had proved inconvenient in the Crystal Palace. R. M. Ordish, the resident engineer at the site, had been employed as a specialist in cast-iron prefabricated structures in the building of the Leeds winter garden and the Royal Albert Bridge over the Thames.[327]

The Crystal Palace in New York (1852) and the Palais de l'Industrie in Paris (1855) were further applications of the Paxton system.[328]

After the heyday of the unadorned space frame, there arose a trend toward hiding the cast-iron framework behind ornamentation and masonry. This is illustrated by the Alexandra Palace at Muswell Hill (1872–1874) and by the large floras built in Cologne (1864) and Leipzig (1882).

Prefabricated Construction

The prefabricated cast-iron building, which appeared in broad applications in the United States and Britain around 1850, was the product of an advanced state of industrial production and of the concentration of capital in the hands of major companies. The manufacturers of such buildings were not satisfied with the production and sale of individual building components; they offered whole buildings, sometimes with interior equipment. Such a building could be com-

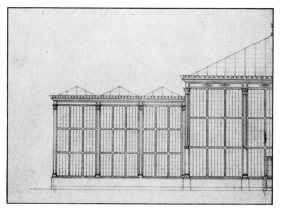

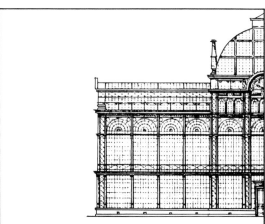

89
Conservatory, Botanical Garden, Breslau, 1861, facade.

90
Neumann, Old Palm House, Bonn, ca. 1880, facade.

91
Owen Jones, Palace of the People, Muswell Hill, London (project), 1859. Woodcut.

petitive only when produced in large quantities. This meant that every individual part of the building had to be mass produced and hence completely standardized. Buildings could be prefabricated for storage and offered for sale by catalog in various designs.

The hothouse was the earliest building type used for such experiments in prefabrication. The need to provide a constant climate for plants in summer and winter had already led before the era of glass-and-iron buildings to the development of hothouses which were built of small elements and could be easily assembled and dismantled. In 1620 Salomon de Caus published a design for a mobile orangery for the Elector Palatine in Heidelberg (fig. 92a). "It covers 30 small and 400 medium-size trees, and is made of wood, and is assembled every year at Michaelmas. The orange trees are kept warm throughout the winter by four stoves so that in periods of severe frost one can stroll in this orangery without noticing the cold. . . . The postwork is removed around Easter in order to leave the trees uncovered throughout the whole summer."[329] The "removable orangery" at Belvedere in Vienna shows the further development of the mobile hothouse (fig. 92b). In the orangery in the Ducal Park at Meiningen, built around 1800, large building components of wood and glass came into use, which in winter formed the roof and south front and in summer revealed an open grotto made of masonry. The slightly backward-sloping glass facade, with wooden frames and a line of columns placed inside, carried a lean-to roof (fig. 92c).[330]

With the technical possibility of replacing wood by iron, and the increasing demand for plant houses, the opportunity arose to apply mass production of building components to hothouse construction, which until then was based on the principle of annual assembly and dismantling. Thus, the next step was that of buildings which, independent of the location of their erection, could be mass-produced in the form of standard components. The first known building made with an iron frame is the hothouse at Hohenheim, near Stuttgart, built around 1789 in combination with some Romantic ruin architecture. Like the cast-iron bridge over the River Severn (built, by chance, at the same time), it represents a turning point in the history of building. Here iron as a building material was first used exclusively in a load-bearing structure, and thus the way was open for industrialized prefabrication.[331]

In the next 40 years, attempts to construct buildings with frames made entirely of iron remained exceptional, apart from hothouses. They appear more as historic curiosities than as advances in building techniques, and most were part of the quest for sim-

ple replacement of wood and stone by cast iron. The intrinsic economic and technical advantages of the new material remained unexploited. The Gothic "Kreuzberg Memorial," built in 1818 by Schinkel, was a masonry building translated into cast iron. The architect of the Winter Garden and Castle of Count Schwarzenberg in Hluboká nad Vltavou (1840–1847) followed the same intention in reproducing Gothic masonry architecture for cast-iron components of facades. The desire to maintain the true plastic effect of the model was the reason for the use of such covering structures, which often needed internal reinforcing frameworks. In 1832 the architect François Thiollet published an English method proposing the use of hollow cast-iron boxes filled with concrete and dovetailed together.[332]

The development of the prefabricated iron building in the period 1820–1840 continued in British hothouse building. The wrought-iron glasshouses with curvilinear roofs were the first steps in that direction. There followed the pioneering experiments of Thomas Knight to discover the most satisfactory angle of incidence of light and the best artificial climate (1808), and those of G. Mackenzie concerning the construction of spherically curved glass-and-iron buildings aligned like an observatory and following the path of the sun (1815).[333] Then, in 1817, J. C. Loudon, in his "Remarks on Hothouses," made proposals for curvilinear glasshouses, for the construction of which he took up the proposals of his predecessors and pursued them further. Enthusiastically publicizing iron as the ideal material for his purpose, he invented as early as 1816 a wrought-iron sash bar which was to serve as a single structural element and which could be shaped while hot to match any desired curve. Loudon was the first to solve the problem of a building made only of glass and iron in the form of a generally useful shell structure. As early as his 1817 paper in which he compared the relative costs of wood and iron, Loudon saw the commercial potential of his invention. He advertised in a catalog a series of basic types, which were to be produced with the help of the firm of W. and D. Bailey. Loudon built Bayswater House (fig. 141) to test the actual possibilities of his construction for covered markets, schools, theaters, and even churches.[334] The alliance of Loudon with the Bailey firm led to the construction of a series of large buildings, including the pine and vine house at Langport in Somerset (1817), Loddiges Nursery at Hackney (1818), and the hothouse at Bretton Hall, Yorkshire (1827), which in their elegance and lightness of construction were unsurpassed in later times.

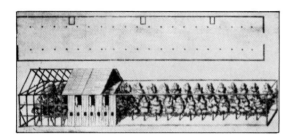

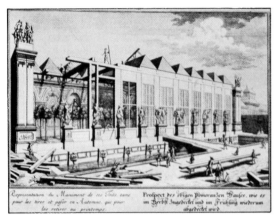

92a
Temporary wood-
and-glass orangery,
"Elector Palatin,"
Heidelberg, 1620.
Engraving by Salo-
mon de Caus.

92b
Temporary wood-
and-glass orangery,
Lower Belvedere, Vi-
enna. Engraving,
ca. 1730.

92c
Temporary wood-
and-glass orangery,
Ducal Park, Meinin-
gen. Engraving,
ca. 1800.

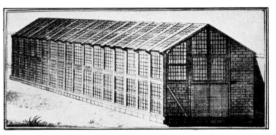

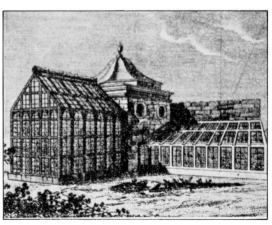

93
Early glasshouse,
Schwöbber, ca. 1714.
Copper engraving.

94
First iron-frame
house, Stuttgart-
Hohenheim, 1789.
Copper engraving.

In fact Loudon's buildings were the first technically mature and commercially exploitable iron-frame houses. There were, however, limits to their size—and thus to their applications—because the construction was based on the use of curved wrought-iron sash bars. Cast iron was preferable to wrought iron for these purposes until well beyond the middle of the century because of its inherent suitability to mass production and its lower cost. This explains the fact that the iron-frame building, now for the first time capable of being made from prefabricated standardized parts, found its form in cast iron.

The Camellia House at Wollaton Hall in Nottingham (1823) and the Winter Garden at The Grange in Hampshire (1825), both erected by the hothouse firm of Thomas Clark of Birmingham, are the earliest examples built according to these principles. The basic concept of this type of construction is the use of rows of columns along narrow paths, dividing the area into separate parts. The rows of columns support cast-iron gutters and sheet-metal barrel vaults above the paths. These structural elements form a space frame when assembled, into which the glazing is inserted above the plant beds. The hollow interior columns conduct rainwater from the gutters down into underground cisterns. The firm of Thomas Clark, which built these hothouses, had set up business in the autumn of 1818 on Lionel Street in Birmingham. The firm's name was originally Jones and Clark. "The firm's first order book from 1818, which is still intact, shows on the first page two lean-to forcing houses, one for the Duke of Newcastle, at Clumber Park, Nottinghamshire. The subsequent order books are filled with sales to nobility, including in 1844 the glass sashes for Queen Victoria's Frogmore, the glass forcing houses near Windsor. The first order for abroad was in 1839 'for two ranges of hot water apparatus for heating a pine house for His Majesty the King of Württemberg, Stuttgart.' Before the publication of their *Book of Designs of Horticulture* (1875), an elaborate conservatory had been manufactured and shipped to Buenos Aires. This order marked the beginning of their export business, which was to expand to prefabricated buildings and windows for Japan, New Zealand, Australia, Africa, Holland, and America. By this time the firm's name was Henry Hope, with the letterhead 'later Clark and Hope, formerly Clark.' Hope's metal windows are still known throughout the world."[335]

A decade after the building of the Camellia House at Wollaton Hall, in 1834, Joseph Paxton wrote an article in the *Magazine of Botany* about a glasshouse with a ridge-and-furrow roof built of prefabricated components. "This was a glasshouse 97 ft. 6 in. long and 26 ft. from the back wall (of brick) to the front, the height of the rear being 13 ft. 6 in. at the valley and 15 ft. at the ridge and 8 ft. 6 in. in the valley and 10 ft. to ridge at the front. The sloping roof was of ridge and furrow pattern, without rafters and with extremely thin sash bars of wood, supported by 3 in. diameter cast iron columns 6 ft. 6 in. apart along the front of the house and an internal row along the centre. The front columns were hollow and discharged the rainwater from the roof to a gravelled path outside, so that no external gutters or downpipes were needed. There were no doors, the vertical lights forming the sides sliding in grooves so that access could be effected at any point desired."[336]

The drawings Paxton published in connection with this are unusual in their presentation. According to the details in the building commission, Paxton specified the elementary building components individually: cast-iron columns forming the frame with separate footings and wooden base plates, a standard facade element filling the space between the pair of columns, and a view of the folded roof elements with gutters, all of which with the pairs of columns formed the basic unit. This mode of presentation, adequate for the contents, was a novelty in the design of buildings. It declared itself no longer an objective-oriented design in which catalog-listed add-on components could be assembled into various kinds of buildings. In fact, the important parts of the supporting framework, the gutters and sash bars of the roof, were even made of wood. However, the method used by Paxton here to differentiate the main building elements (such as columns, girders, and roof skin) according to their various functions opened the way to their standardization, and therefore to the feasibility of making them by mass production. The winter garden built about 1840 at Deepdene Castle at Swinton Park, Yorkshire, is one example of the application of the Paxton construction principle.[337]

For the 1834 glasshouse Paxton had to solve three major problems. The first problem had to do with the development of optimal light transmission through the glass skin, which had to be economical as well as stable and durable. Paxton had already found the solution in the 1831–32 rebuilding of the Old Orangery at Chatsworth in the form of the ridge-and-furrow pleated roof. The second problem was the development of a beam with the maximum span for the smallest cross-section, a beam that also would withstand exposure to the elements and would carry off rainwater. This beam, made in the well-known form of the Paxton gutter, was introduced for the first time in 1834. It rested directly on the iron columns, with a slope. In the next stage of development, with the increasing need for greater spans, the roof structure and the main supports were separated and placed on two different planes. In 1849, in the victoria regia house at Chatsworth, Paxton used prestressed gutter beams as secondary beams, which were gently sloped to carried rainwater to the main gutter beams.[338] This construction principle of hierarchically ranked elements, which was facilitated by prefabrication, was put into use on a large scale in the building of the Crystal Palace. The third problem was to develop a hollow cast-iron column of small cross-section and high strength that could easily be attached to girders in all directions. Paxton solved these requirements by following the principle he had established in 1834. He applied this to the Crystal Palace in technically superior ways with the help of the connecting piece shown in figure 77.

A prefabricated-building industry came into existence in the 1840s. From 1839 to 1841 a prefabricated cast-iron building housing a steam-powered mill was exhibited in Constantinople.[339] Hundreds of prefabricated houses, some of them completely mobile, were supplied to the United States.[340] In 1851 there were many iron dance halls in Britain, and in Germany a removable marquee was being used for festivals.[341] Bogardus's cast-iron factory building in New York (fig. 82) was erected in 1848–49; this, along with the early attempts of Daniel Badger, anticipated a series of iron factory buildings with fronts and load-bearing frames made of cast iron. In the 1850s there arose in lower Manhattan whole streets of ready-made multistory buildings with cast-iron frames. From 1850, prefabricated iron hothouses in a variety of forms and sizes were offered by catalog to the growing upper middle class in England.

As rolled wrought iron was replacing cast iron in bridges and buildings, the foundries discovered another field of production in the manufacture of ready-made pavilions, conservatories, palm houses, and garden houses. "It was a new and considerable development of the architectural use of this material."[342] A typical hothouse of this period was built near London for Sir Henry Bessemer, the inventor of the steelmaking process named after him, by Messrs. Banks and Berry. It had a cruciform ground plan and a central dome, and was made completely of cast iron except for the sash bars and the rafters of the dome.[343] The economic success of prefabricated houses of this type is shown by the large number of garden buildings offered for sale at the Great Paris Industrial Exhibition of 1855. On display were a se-

95
Joseph Paxton, greenhouse, Chatsworth, 1834.

96
Paxton, Chatsworth greenhouse, 1834, details of basic elements of column, facade, and roof.

97
Winter garden of Deepdene Castle, ca. 1840.

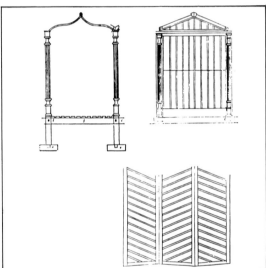

98
Paxton, plan view,
section, and details
of ridge-and-furrow
roof system, 1850.

99
Paxton, victoria regia
house, Chatsworth,
1849.

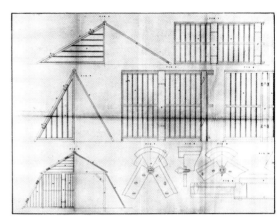

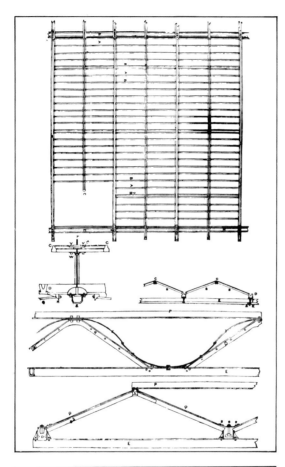

100
Paxton, temporary
hothouse, 1858

101
E.T. Bellhouse &
Co., prefabricated
iron dance hall at
Balmoral Castle.

102
Advertisement for
prefabricated cast-
iron hothouse, 1868.

ries of prefabricated greenhouses, one- and three-compartment hothouses, houses combined with aquariums, and an extensive "warm house." They were built in simple basic geometrical shapes so that the ends always formed a semicircular apse. At the Vienna World Exhibition of 1873 a large ready-made palm house of glass and cast iron (fig. 104) was shown. In a central pavilion on a square base with semicircular apses on two sides it had a vaulted glass roof made of wrought-iron sash bars, which rested on the supporting structure of the cast-iron facade. With the development of a load-bearing facade, no interior columns were needed.

Of the late use of cast iron to decorate prefabricated buildings, it has been written that "the simplicity of the work of Paxton and Decimus Burton was unfortunately forgotten, and engineers and architects frequently produced designs that were really conceived for carved marble or terra cotta, although they were executed in cast iron."[344]

In 1880 Messrs. Messenger & Co. of Loughborough published a catalog of "Artistic Conservatories" which offered glasshouses in a variety of choices, built according to a patent system.[345] The catalog included conservatories small and large, built into masonry or detached, two-story conservatories, winter gardens, glass verandas, and hothouses combined with aviaries and aquariums. In the text there was less emphasis on construction than on style. The construction system was based on cast-iron columns and facade elements which were firmly anchored into the foundations and which formed the support for an easily erected roof.

A technically improved type of prefabricated glasshouse, developed with much perseverance and representing a high point in catalog-offered buildings, is illustrated by the palm house built in Florence in 1874. An example of its versatile framework, mostly made of cast iron in the "Gothic style," was on view to the public in the gardens of the Royal Horticultural Society as early as 1860 (figs. 369, 370). Also on display was a ready-made open pavilion that was destined to be the prototype for buildings in India (fig. 371). Ornamentation and embellishments from the arsenal of historicism appeared with these iron buildings as a concession to the tastes of the period. Meanwhile, the principle of prefabricated building extended itself as a technically progressive factor in the construction industry and became an authentic part of the repertoire of a new generation of engineers.

103
Messenger & Co., depiction of interior of prefabricated cast-iron conservatory, 1880.

104
Prefabricated cast-iron palm house, World Exhibition, Vienna, 1873.

Summary: The Birth of the Prefabricated Building and the Iron Space Frame

Cast iron dominated the early period of iron construction work. As the inner skeleton of the building—as the supporting structure—this material was able to hold its position against the competition from wrought iron until the 1870s. Its most important characteristic was its suitability to mass production, which led to the standardization of basic building components. This progressed so far that much of the building work could be transferred from the site to the factory. Beyond this general principle, which implied a revolution in building, cast iron generated forms of supporting structures without which modern building techniques could not have been conceived. All these general and specific forms of industrialized construction were initiated and brought to fruition in the iron-frame hothouse.

The requirements of a modern building, which not only exhausted the existing forces of productivity but also gave impetus to them, were being developed step by step from 1800 on. The four basic elements were first worked out individually by empirical means and then improved; they were then brought together to form a structural whole that appeared to have been conceived as a single entity.

These four elements were the following:

• hollow columns, which could be placed one above another to form an open framework,
• a pleated roof, adapted to the arrangement of the columns and capable of being extended in any direction to cover a large area,
• a load-bearing cast-iron facade, and
• prefabrication.

The integration of these four main elements took place in three stages, which were in progress simultaneously:

• the formulation of the most important building elements—columns, girders, and roof skin—into typical designs for mass production and assembly (1800–1830),
• the combination of these elements into a space-frame system, and
• the transfer of these construction forms to large hall structures, and its reciprocal effect on the development of space frames for hothouses (1850–1870).

The empirical experience gained in the building of cast-iron hothouses was of fundamental significance, and it was transferred by the builders to halls, railway stations, markets, arcades, floras, and exhibition buildings. The close connection between hothouse specifications and those for large hall buildings was shown by the work of Loudon, Paxton, Phillips, Turner, Fowler, Horeau, Rohault, Voit, and Ordish.

On account of the lesser loads and the transparency required, the hollow cast-iron columns of the halls were made in filigree form as much as possible, often with ornamentation simulating plant forms; nevertheless, their structural function in the building was always maintained. An important additional function of the space frame was the removal of water from the roof. Like the girders and the ribs, the columns were prefabricated. Experiments with multistory space frames were undertaken, and as a result one can observe numerous transitional forms in the development of the connecting piece joining columns and ribs. The path of this development went via the "composite column," which can best be seen in the large glass buildings with vaulted roofs.

The most important result of this line of development was the creation of the ridge-and-furrow roof and the framework structure corresponding to it: hollow cast-iron columns forming an open structure, with gutter beams and a "folded" roof. The roof surface was divided into small sections of channels and ridges, so that the rainwater falling on it could easily flow away. McIntosh wrote in this connection that "the last and greatest improvement in hothouse roofs is certainly that of the ridge-and-furrow form, first suggested by the late Mr. Loudon about the year 1816, and afterwards so completely wrought out by Sir Joseph Paxton in the large house at Chatsworth . . . and exemplifying most clearly the possibility of extending the same kind of pillared covering over any space, however large."[346]

Straight beams came into use as gutter beams at Wollaton Hall (1823) and The Grange (1825), serving simultaneously to remove rainwater via hollow columns and to support the roof. Solid cast-iron beams having Watt's section, which were used in factory buildings from 1801, were ruled out on account of their clumsiness.

The first space-frame system was that of the project for the glass hall of Carlton House, in which beams in conjunction with ribs serve as supports for the ridge roof.

The space-frame system with the ridge-and-furrow roof, which Paxton developed in numerous experiments at Chatsworth from 1834, had been developed to such an extent in the middle of the nineteenth century that the basic elements for the cast-iron skeleton were at hand, ready-made for prefabricated building methods. Paxton used prestressed wooden gutter beams to support a glass roof, and these were laid on hollow cast-iron columns. By means of prestressing from below, the beams were given sufficient inclination for rainwater to drain away, and they could also be used in greater spans. The gutter beams used in Paxton's patent hothouse (1834) to carry the folded roof rested directly on the columns in the line of the facade. In the victoria regia house Paxton improved the roof frame by the use of gutter beams as cross-members, which, acting as main beams, rested on another set of gutter beams. This hierarchical arrangement not only permitted an economical development of the structural elements according to their structural function, but also increased the distances between columns and made them independent of the small distance between the furrows of the roof. Thus Paxton could transfer the roof support structure of the victoria regia house to the Crystal Palace.

A characteristic structural element in hothouse building was the use of facades as load-bearing frameworks, as at Syon House and at Wollaton Hall. The load was carried directly in the plane of the glass, which comprised a framework of columns with glass infilling. Turner used this method in almost all his buildings from 1842. With the pavilion of the hothouse in the Jardin des Plantes in Paris (1833), Rohault created the first load-bearing cast-iron facade made of many prefabricated parts in a two-story structure. The use of the cast-iron facade in factory buildings was initiated by Bogardus in New York in 1848–49.

Prefabricated, mass-produced glass-and-iron buildings were a further outcome of the development of cast-iron load-bearing frameworks in glasshouse building. These prefabricated systems, freely offered for sale and independent of the site, first appeared as English hothouses. The basis for this lay in the development of the space frame and in the construction method of the hothouse. The limits inherent in glass and iron and the simple basic shapes of plant houses were also important, but market forces were crucial. Before the middle of the century, the possession of a hothouse or a small winter garden was still the sign of wealth and social privilege.

The development of factory-made buildings began with the type of hothouse that had hollow cast-iron columns and a ridge-and-furrow roof, and then continued with the development of the type of space frame that simultaneously formed the major axis and the basic elements of the cast-iron skeleton. The earliest proposals in this direction were made in a pamphlet, dated 1817, in which J. C. Loudon advanced the idea of mass-produced curvilinear glasshouses and the use of cast iron for them. A practical model was supplied by the Clark firm in 1823 and 1825.

After that, Paxton's trials were crucial; they began with relatively modest hothouses such as the "patent" house at Chatsworth (1834) and progressed through the victoria regia house (1849) to the roof system of 1850 and the 1858 project for a mobile house.

The scope of mass production increased after 1850. Ready-made hothouses were offered for sale in catalogs and by the 1870s firms were making concessions to "stylistic forms." These buildings had been limited in scope up to 1850, but between 1850 and 1870 larger hall-type buildings of glass and iron began to be offered.

The multistory cast-iron building originated in the building of British factories, such as the Milford warehouse of 1792, and the basic cast-iron skeleton in its complete form in Paxton's Crystal Palace of 1850–51. The development of a self-supporting cast-iron frame with a connecting piece for joining columns and girders in three directions was the jumping-off point for solving the problem of building prefabricated filigree structures without recourse to masonry walls and floors. The development of gallery structures in the large plant halls led in stages to the development of assembled columns to make multistory frames by using single joints to the connecting girders and roof supports. The way pursued to that end, after the early attempts at open space frames at Wollaton Hall (1823) and The Grange (1825), resulted in the hothouses in the Jardin des Plantes (1833) and the palm houses at Chatsworth (1836–1840) and Kew (1844–1848) and in the Jardin d'Hiver (1848).

Great spans could only be covered by arched structures. However, a further structural element was needed in the strong self-supporting cast-iron space frame, and this had to be designed for the exhibition building where there were high multistory hall structures with wide and heavily loaded surrounding galleries. This was the rib system usable as beams in any desired direction in the pleated roof and the gallery, as well as for a reinforcing element in the three planes of the upper stories. The typical form of such a rib system for cast-iron space frames after 1850 came into use for the first time in the Crystal Palace in the form of the rectangular braced girder. For this purpose the Long and Howe system of bridge building with braced girders was applied to buildings. We find the beginnings in the development of the cast-iron rectangular braced girder in Loudon's early projects (1817 and 1831, in the Birmingham winter garden project) and in Paxton's early work (1837). The principle of the braced girder was then applied in the building of the Crystal Palace (1850–51) in a qualitatively different way. There were cast-iron girders as a standard element of the space frame, and ribs of greater spans for covering the central nave and to support the barrel vault of the transept, made in a hybrid construction of wood, cast iron, and wrought iron. The crucial element in this structural concept was the design of a standardized connecting piece to make the joints between the span structure and the vertical supporting members. Thus the principle of prefabrication of standard elements, which had been pursued in hothouse construction up to 1850, came to fruition.

The cast-iron space frame of the Crystal Palace represented the highest state of the art of industrialized construction of that period. The subsequent cast-iron space frames used for exhibition and hothouse buildings, with their fundamentally new solutions to design problems in space-frame engineering, proved this. Cast iron was the qualitative and quantitative controlling factor for space frames until 1870.

Wrought Iron

The Girder

Wrought-iron structures were not produced to any great extent until the end of the 1840s, although it was possible to produce the material for them by mass production in the form of rolled section. The impetus to apply wrought iron came from the need for railway lines. Even as late as 1858, for the building of the Market Hall at Lyon, a cast-iron structure was cheaper than one of wrought iron. In the greatest construction works around the middle of the century, such as the Crystal Palace, the ratio of cast iron to wrought iron used was 6.5:1 (approximately 3,500 tons to 550 tons).[347]

That wrought iron could succeed as a building material was determined by its elastic properties compared with cast iron, by its ability to withstand tension effectively as well as compression. In the middle of the nineteenth century several cast-iron buildings collapsed without warning: the bridge over the River Dee at Chester (1847) and the Joiner Street Bridge in London (1850), for example. A further advantage of wrought iron was that the beam lengths were not limited by internally generated stresses, as they were with cast iron. With the development of the riveted joint, wrought-iron parts could be firmly joined together, whereas cast-iron elements could only be joined by bolts and wedges. Also, a wrought-iron beam could have one-third the weight of a cast-iron beam of the same tensile strength.[348]

With the need for greater spans in railway construction, for which wooden structures were not suitable, wrought-iron structures came into widespread use for the first time after 1840. When assembled girders, rolled bar section, and tie members were incorporated, spans were achieved which could not have been attained in any other way.

Rolled Section

The first wrought-iron-frame houses were built by J. C. Loudon from 1818. They consisted of curvilinear sash bars for glazing, made of rolled wrought iron. The iron section used for sash bars is the earliest known evidence of the use of rolled iron in buildings. By the end of the eighteenth century it had become possible to roll flat and round bars. They were, however, of only limited use in building, on account of their low strength, most of all when used as ties. Around 1817 the ironwright firm of W. and D. Bailey of Holborn, London, in collaboration with Loudon, succeeded in rolling iron section for window frames and sash bars.

L. Beck has ascertained the yearly amount of steel section manufactured with the help of a travel report "concerning a scientific and metallurgical journey made to England in 1823, which had been undertaken by the structural enginner Defrénoy on instruction from the Ministry, which appeared in collected form under the title 'Voyage métallurgique en Angleterre', with seventeen illustrations."[349] An extract from this report runs: "Rolled steel section was only used a little. Defrénoy and Elie de Beaumont mention in passing rolled section angle iron, which they had seen during their travels, and included a faulty drawing."[350] This report refers to 1823 as the year in which the rolling of angle iron was described for the first time. In the context of research into the Loudon-type shell structure, it can be demonstrated that much earlier there was production of complex rolled-iron section for the building industry.

Loudon wrote in his "Sketches of Curvilinear Hothouses" (1818) that he had already invented and written about rolled-iron sash bars in 1817. From then on it was possible to manufacture such sash bars as articles of trade. First specified for curvilinear hothouses, they could be bent to any desired radius of curvature. Loudon wrote that they were made to any desired size, and in fact were supported without using any rafters, but only by the position and curvature of the sashes, often by increasing their dimension.[351] The sash bars had a cruciform cross-section with a rebate for holding the glass panes. The section could be made double or as a half-section (fig. 132a).[352] In order to simplify the rolling, the sash bar was preferably put together from three flat iron strips, and these were then welded together in the rolling mill.

In Britain in the 1820s the profile and the overall section were being executed in smaller dimensions particularly suitable for sash bars. The first to appear on the British market was rolled angle section; later, around 1830, T section appeared. Angle and T-section iron were being rolled in Germany from 1831 and 1839 respectively. These sections continued to be used for roof and bridge building for almost 20 years.[353]

Wrought-iron section, which at the end of the eighteenth century was made from rolled flat bar, was not suitable for beams on account of its low strength. Not until the rolling of wrought-iron beams could a replacement for cast-iron beams be found. Early forms of rolled-iron section were developed by Henry Cort (1783) and by J. Parnell (1787).[354] Large rolled sections were not produced economically until the need for rails increased. J. Birkinshaw obtained a patent in 1820 for the rolling of iron railway rails.[355] The T section replaced the wedge-shaped section. In 1830 the American L. Stevens added a flange below to form an I section. In this form the rails used by the railway companies quickly came down to satisfactory prices, and the sections were also used in buildings; for example, G. L. F. Laves proposed in his 1850 design for the London World Exhibition competition to use rails for the main girders.

The rolled T section still did not provide the optimal cross-section for beams. The optimal shape—the I beam—was found by means of the theory of statics and tests. The tensile and compressive forces in the outer zones of the beam could be countered and withstood satisfactorily by using equal-size flanges joined together by a web. "The introduction of the I beam was an important event in the history of building techniques, because with it some completely new forms of contruction emerged, and most important the principles of building took another direction. The iron period in building truly began with this material."[356]

Even at the start of the nineteenth century, L. M. H. Navier had recommended I beams as sections of least cross-sectional area for the greatest strength. In 1847 M. Deleuze used a cruciform-section beam for a slaughterhouse in Paris, but its strength was unsatisfactory. In collaboration with Charles F. Zorés he developed an inverted T section, but no rolling mill could be found to produce it and it had to be manufactured from flat bar and L section. In 1848 Zorés tested a beam of this type made by M. Chibon; it showed warping on the upper flange. Zorés therefore proposed to strengthen the upper flange. In 1849 he succeeded in rolling such a beam for the first time.[357] This beam, 5.6 inches deep and having a span of almost 18 feet, served as a roof support.[358] The I beam appears to have already been used in Britain by this time. W. Fairbairn reported on an experiment carried out in 1845,[359] and in 1845 an I beam was rolled to specifications by Eugène Flachat. Turner used curved I beams in the Kew hothouse (1848) and in the Lime Street Station (1851). In 1850–51 Zorés made the upper flange thicker than the lower one,[360] and in 1852 he succeeded in rolling U-section iron. He advertised the first range of sections, which was a first step toward the standardization of sections. In 1862, 3-foot-deep beams were assembled from several parts. In 1867, at the World Exhibition in Paris, a 3.3-foot-deep and 330-foot-long uniform rolled wrought-iron beam was introduced. In Germany, I beams were rolled for the first time in 1857. By riveting angle and sheet iron together it was possible to produce very deep girders. The best examples of such sheet-metal beams can be seen in Robert Stevenson's Britannia Bridge (1847–48).

The Rafter Roof with Ties

The rafter roof with ties was derived from methods of building with wood that had been in use since antiquity. Its structural principle consisted of the separation of tensile and compressive forces. The use of a system of rigid triangles, the transformation of the bending moments into tension and compression which could then be distributed among individual members of the structure, and the selection of the most suitable material meant that the optimal cross-section for the beams could be chosen. This roof-support structure was therefore an important advance in the development of the space frame.

In contrast with cast iron, for which the maximum stress in the middle of the beam could be countered by making the web deeper there, with wrought-iron load-bearing beams there was the possibility of using "composite girders" of "uniform strength." Proceeding from wooden beams, this entailed in its simplest form the prestressing of the girder by a tension bar underneath, arching the beam up slightly (hogging). One form of this prestressed beam (made, in fact, of wood) was the "Laves beam," developed by G. L. F. Laves in 1839, which was used in the hothouse at Herrenhausen (fig. 105). The beam was split into an upper and a lower part, which were kept separated by posts. The strength was considerably increased by this method. Paxton too used prestressed gutter beams in the construction of the Crystal Palace. Such prestressed beams made entirely of wrought iron are scarce, but the framework suggested the next obvious step forward. The innovators of framework structures, K. Culmann and R. Wiegmann, started from the structural concept of the prestressed beam.[361]

Early forms of the wrought-iron "prestressed rafter roof" which are to be regarded as the forerunners of braced roof trusses were to be found in the 1820s in Britain and France. (See, for example, figure 106.) A simple rafter roof made of wrought iron came into use around 1840 in the "Iron Hothouse" at Nymphenburg, Munich (fig. 107). An extended four-post roof truss was constructed in 1845 by the architect Christian Leins to cover the main staircase well of the Villa Berg in Stuttgart (fig. 108) is an example of the scarce prestressed canopy roof. The roof had diagonal master rafters above a square ground plan. Two masonry walls in the room carried a central ring of purlins made from small rectangular braced girders. The four hip rafters made of T-section iron met in the apex of the roof and were held together below by ties. The lantern roof was located in the upper ring of purlins, and had perpendicular glass walls.[362] Rohault's canopy roof for the hothouse in the Jardin des Plantes was one of the early space frames made of wrought iron. The principle of the construction consisted, as in the Villa Berg, of a combination of ties and braced beams which ran the length of the hall as continuous purlins to the abutment of the lantern roof.

The Suspended Roof

In order to increase the strength of the wide-span girders, suspended structures were introduced very early into bridge building. The first known suspended roof appeared in an 1825 theater design by Heinrich Hübsch.[363] The roof over the "Panorama" in the Champs-Elysees in Paris, built by Jakob Ignaz Hittorf in 1838–39, was another important suspended structure. McIntosh, who in his *Book of the Garden* (1853) was the first to propose the use of the suspended roof for hothouses, referred in his design to the prototype of suspension bridges. The cast-iron columns along the facade in this design projected like pylons above the ridge roof. The gutter beam placed between them in the depth of the room, made of wrought-iron sheet and angle iron, was suspended from two cables between the columns and carried the ridge-and-furrow roof. By locating the joints of the cables in the box profile of the gutter

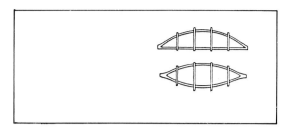

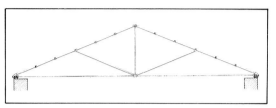

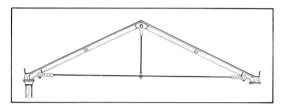

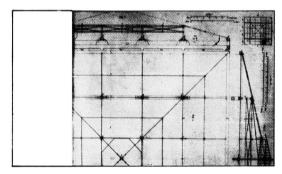

105
Georg Ludwig Friedrich Laves, beams, Herrenhausen, 1839.

106
M. G. Veugny, wrought-iron truss, Marche de la Madelaine, Paris; designed 1824, built 1835–1838.

107
Friedrich Ludwig von Sckell, wrought-iron roof truss, iron-frame conservatory, Nymphenburg, Munich, 1807.

108
Christian Leins, wrought-iron polygonal roof, Villa Berg, Stuttgart, 1842.

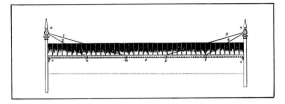

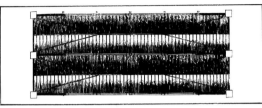

109
Charles McIntosh,
side view of sus-
pended roof (design),
ca. 1841.

110
McIntosh, view of
suspended roof
(design), ca. 1841.

beam, McIntosh ensured that the roof skin was not pierced by the tension members. All the structural parts were thus outside the enclosing glass walls and the roof. Thus he obtained a "columnless" space free from supporting members, having a greater span and a variable lateral extent. The structural aspect of the proposed principle was the use of slender columns, with no abutments under tensile stress to confuse the structure.[364] Probably on this basis, McIntosh proposed a variation in which columns carried tensioning rods connected to the beams. In contrast to the previous proposal, the columns were aligned not with the girders but with the ridge of the roof, so that the prestressing was applied diagonally across the roof.[365]

The Braced Girder

The braced girder originated from the further development of the "prestressed rafter roof," from the earlier wooden structures, and via scientific experiments on the load-bearing behavior of combinations of triangles. Not until after 1851 was the response of beams to loads accurately measured, by K. Culmann.[366] In 1830 Stefan Long developed a rectangular braced girder made of wood. From 1839, together with J. L. Howe, he built braced arched ribs for railway bridges and stations, also of wood. For general building purposes up to about the turn of the century the braced girder was mostly of a hybrid construction of cast and wrought iron, often including wood as well. The braced girder made completely of wrought iron was not made until after 1850, when perfected rolling techniques were available.

The Rib

Whereas cast-iron ribs evolved predominantly by analogy with masonry building and the associated technology of vaults, wrought-iron ribs were modeled on early wooden structures. Even in the sixteenth century, the architect P. Delorme had proposed the use of curved planks as rafters.

Curved iron rafters provided clear interior spaces in railway-station concourses, covered markets, exhibition buildings, and hothouses. Beyond their aesthetic beauty, which showed itself in the development of barrel vaults, they had the advantage of a favorable stress distribution; the ribs followed the force distribution and were predominantly in a state of compression alone.

Turner was one of the first to use rolled-iron I beams in curved shapes for roof ribs. Experience gained in glasshouse construction made it possible for Turner to use rolled Vignoles-type I-section rails for the upper flange of a sickle-shaped girder in the Lime Street Station in Liverpool. The I section consisted of two blunt butt-jointed pieces bolted together by double fish plates. Six struts projected from this upper flange and, strapped together by diagonal bars, were joined at their lower ends to the continuous lower flange. These main ribs rested on a cast-iron wall plate supported by cast-iron columns.[366]

The Braced Rib

The need of longer and higher halls for greater spans led at the end of the 1840s to attempts to replace the simple, sometimes prestressed rib with braced ribs. Cast-iron ribs, which with their reinforcing rings represent an early form of iron framework, were limited in their spans and as a result could not satisfy the requirements of clear spanning over large halls. Experience with Polonceau ribs, "king and queen post" roofs, and rectangular braced girders encouraged builders to transform the same rib forms into wrought-iron frameworks. The curved upper and lower flanges of the rolled-section ribs were reinforced with triangles built of struts and diagonals. The more rigid frame that resulted, which was continuous and did not have the annoying tie members, made high hall buildings possible. An early form of such braced ribs, made of wood, was first used in American bridge building by Long and Howe (for example, in the 1848 Cascades Bridge for the Erie Railway).

Wrought-iron braced ribs were rarely used in the 1840s, but in the 1850s they were commonly used as structural members in railway stations, exhibition buildings, and winter gardens. "In fact the important ironwork arch structures in building did not arise until the introduction of the three-hinge arch in the 1860s."[367] The way to this widespread use was paved by a number of experiments with iron-frame buildings that led to precise knowledge of the behavior of ribs under load. The wrought-iron braced ribs Rigolet introduced in 1848 in the building of the Jardin d'Hiver in Paris are notable. Taking up the principles of cast-iron structures together with those of wrought-iron frameworks, Rigolet invented a rib form in which the upper and lower flanges almost converged at the apex of the arch but diverged widely toward the springing. Whereas the bell-shaped upper flange from the apex to the ground level ran in a single arch and supported the weight of the glass roof, the semicircular lower flange rested on a row of double cast-iron columns joined together by braced iron girders. The space between the upper and lower flanges was filled in with bar

struts and diagonals down to the spaces of the two adjoining aisles. Transverse purlins were placed in the intersections to reinforce the ribs. Diagonal ribs at the intersections of the transept and the nave met at the apex, and each of them was supported at its bottom end by four cast-iron columns. One can consider the rib basically as a single braced member running down to the ground via the internal columns. This structure, designed by intuition through the combination of different space-frame systems, was admired by the contemporary world for its lightness and elegance.[368]

Further progress in the application of the braced rib to buildings was based on bridge designs, such as the Long and Howe girder, and led to the construction of circular roofs. The semicircular ribs with constant web depth were a transformation of the rectangular braced girder to an arch profile. These may be regarded as the earliest generally useful braced ribs with arch profiles. They first came into use with the reassembling of the Crystal Palace at Sydenham. In the Great Conservatory at Chatsworth, Paxton had introduced ribs made of planks glued together as supports for the glass vaults of the nave and aisles (fig. 44). In the building of the Crystal Palace, Paxton applied this type of construction to the covering of the transept, in which diagonal wrought-iron tie bars served for the infilling (fig. 45). At Sydenham, Paxton replaced the wooden plank ribs with iron roof ribs having two circular concentric flanges, between which were posts and diagonals. The ribs rested on a row of double cast-iron columns. A similar type of rib was used at the Paris Exhibition of 1855, where the glass roof of the central hall was supported by ribs made of flanges and angle iron.[369]

A further development of the semicircular braced rib was carried out between 1867 and 1869 by Voit in the building of the winter garden of Ludwig II at Munich. The ribs were anchored into the flat roof of the existing building, and to withstand the increasing stress they were made thicker at the springing than at the apex. The glass was fastened to the inside surface of the lower flange so that the supporting structure was only visible through the glass. The upper and lower flanges of the ribs were made of U section riveted together. Similar filigree-work braced ribs narrowing toward the apex acted as supports for the glass roof of the central pavilion of the palm house in the Botanical Garden in Munich, built by Voit in 1865. Resting on cast-iron corbels and supported by double columns, the hinged braced ribs at the springing were an early form of wrought-iron two-hinge arch.

The nave and transept of the flora building in Cologne (H. Märtens and G. Eberlein, 1864) were covered by glass barrel vaults carried by braced ribs that narrowed toward the apex, like those of previous buildings by Voit. Supported by cast-iron brackets underpinned by double columns, they were built like two-hinge arches. The crossing formed by the nave and transept barrel vaults was covered by diagonal braced ribs, as in the Jardin d'Hiver.[370]

A notable hybrid cast- and wrought-iron construction was used in the Winter Palace in Dublin (1865). The large central hall was spanned by braced ribs having web dimensions related to the stress distribution. An elevated abutment formed the springing. It was thus possible to transfer the lateral and vertical thrusts to the cast-iron gallery structure of the ribs. The flanges of the wrought-iron ribs consisted of angle iron riveted together at the intersections of diagonals. The ribs of the arch were reinforced by nine rolled-section purlins, which in turn supported a predella-shaped glass roof.[371]

The wrought-iron structure of the Great Palm House at Vienna-Schönbrunn (F. von Sengenschmid, 1880–1882) consisted of arched braced girders, which in the pavilions were supported on box girders by cast-iron columns. Such braced girders likewise formed the lower termination, and they were firmly anchored into the foundations by specially made footings. The load of the double-glazed roof was taken up by the lower flanges of the ribs. The whole framework was visible from the outside, and its flowing lines were reminiscent of a ship. Thus, seven years before the building of the Eiffel Tower—considered a monument to iron engineering—there was already in existence at Schönbrunn an iron-frame hothouse of aesthetically pleasing construction.[372]

The Exhibition Hall for Garden Science, built in 1900 in Paris by C. A. Gautier, was a typical example of the development of braced-rib space frames. The central hall was spanned by braced girders made of rolled steel which, also forming frameworks in the vertical plane, extended to ground level. Here, however, the space frame was hidden behind screwed-on ornamentation.[373]

The Three-Hinge Arch

The three-hinge arch was first used in J. W. Schwedler's engine shed for the Bochum steam hammer (1865). The space frame did not yet have the form of an arch but was built on a similar principle. The Unterspree Bridge in Berlin, built in the same year, served as the model. There followed in 1866 the hall of the Ostbahnhof (East Railway Station) in Berlin,

also built by Schwedler on the same principle. In 1868 E. Winkler was the first to work out successfully the mathematical principle of the three-hinge arch in relation to the two-hinge arch and the rigid arch.[374] The architect H. Stier and the engineer O. Greiner built the flora in Berlin-Charlottenburg (fig. 114) incorporating this technical innovation. The arch was constructed on the mathematical principles of statics applied to the line of columns, and had a parabolic shape, with the braced rib narrowing upward to the apex. The apex hinge was a flap, and the bottom hinge was a pinned shoe.[375] The concourse of the Ostbahnhof can be considered a forerunner of this type of structure. In the following decades, particularly in the period 1875–1900, the large railway stations of the European capitals often had space frames with three-hinge arches.

A well-constructed later example is the palm house in Berlin-Dahlem, built by the architect A. Koerner in 1905–1907. Its space frame, outwardly visible on all sides, represented an aesthetic manifestation of steel architecture. The high braced girders narrowed downward into a tapering steel shaft in which the hinge was located. This development, which conformed to the principles of statics, was a reversal of the concept of conventional ribs, which become wider toward the base. In order to show off the principle, the architect (as Peter Behrens was to do in the Berlin-Moabit turbine hall of 1909) raised the hinge point to a plinth at eye level, as a demonstration of modern building science.

The Great Palm House in Berlin (fig. 115), one of the last large filigree-work buildings constructed, was intended to fulfill not only aesthetic but also functional requirements.[376] In the following period, with the drop in the cost of iron and the simultaneous rise in wages, riveting was replaced by welding and wage-intensive filigree work in beams was replaced by coarsely profiled box girders or steel section supplied to the building trade.

The Space Frame

Continued work on the framework principle was based on combining single-plane girders and three-dimensional structures into a rigid major supporting element. The first structures of this kind were bridge piers. These were three-dimensional frameworks, and their improved riveted joints contributed significantly to their spread. The first important bridge of this kind was the Douro Bridge at Porto, Portugal, built by Gustave Eiffel in 1877–78. Eiffel is seen as the protagonist of such space frames, and the Eiffel Tower in Paris (1889) represents a peak of this line of development.

111
August von Voit, wrought-iron roof truss, winter garden of Ludwig II, Residenz, Munich, 1869–70.

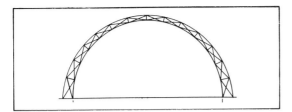

112
Franz von Sengenschmid, wrought-iron roof truss, palm house, Vienna-Schönbrunn, 1882.

113
Charles Albert Gautier, wrought-iron two-hinge braced arch, garden hall, World Exhibition, Paris, 1900.

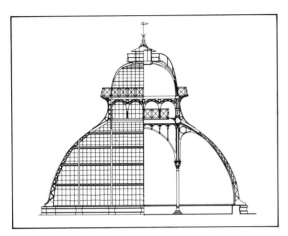

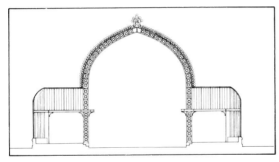

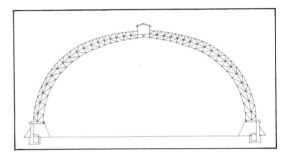

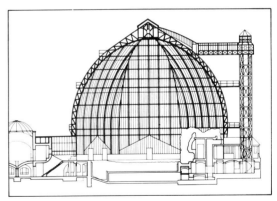

114
Hubert Stier, Johannes Otzen, and H. and O. Greiner, wrought-iron three-hinge braced arch, flora, winter garden, Berlin, 1873.

115
Alfred Koerner, wrought-iron three-hinge braced arch, Great Palm House, botanical garden, Berlin-Dahlem, 1905–1907.

Three-dimensional frameworks seldom came into use for domestic and office buildings, but after 1880 they were more often seen in factories. In glasshouse buildings this new construction method was taken up early in the three-hinge braced ribs of the Berlin Flora (1873), which consisted of two connected braced girders in the horizontal plane. In 1879 the architect Auhagen combined braced ribs, joists, and rafters made of riveted frameworks in the palm house at Herrenhausen, which can be considered a forerunner of later factories built on this principle. This glass-and-iron building was supported on latticework columns located along the facade and in the interior, which were reinforced in three planes by crossmembers. It can be regarded as an early manifestation of steel space-frame construction.[377]

The Dome

The term *dome structure* refers to a vaulted roof over a circular or polygonal base. Among the large dome structures of the nineteenth century were exhibition buildings and other buildings intended for the assembly or the movement of large numbers of people: arcades, exhibition buildings, winter gardens, and hothouses. Domes found use in locomotive sheds and gasometers.

The earliest designs for wrought-iron-frame domes and hemidomes were created by J. D. Loudon and G. Mackenzie between 1817 and 1820 (figs. 117, 124, 126). The first major wrought-iron dome to be built was that over the east choir of the Mainz Cathedral (fig. 118), built by Georg Moller in 1828. It was made of flat wrought-iron section, and every third ring was strengthened by reinforcements projecting into the triangular space. The dome above the dining hall of the Wiesbaden Castle (1839) was held together by a kind of sickle-shaped rib with vertical posts (fig. 119). These two buildings established the two basic types of dome: the mantle dome (in which the forces generated by bending moments were taken up in horizontal members in the form of rings, and in which space was created by the combination of vertical ribs and horizontal rings) and the type in which the ties were passed through the interior of the dome.

For hothouses and winter gardens there arose a unique type of dome: a glass dome extending down to ground level, terminated by an apselike quarterdome. An early but technically advanced example of this was the palm house at Kew (1844–1848). Its transepts terminated in quarter-domes supported by six ribs of wrought-iron section. Tubular spacers were inserted between the ribs, and in the interior were horizontal tension and compression bars (fig. 46).[378]

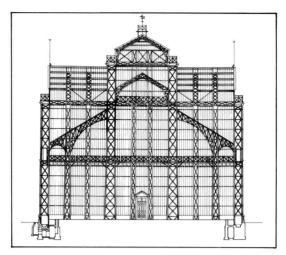

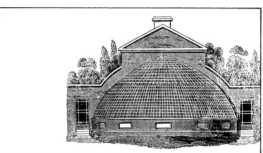

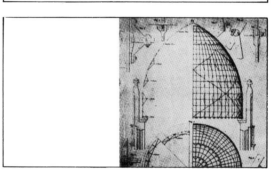

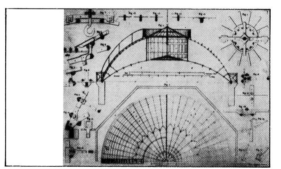

116
Auhagen, section of space frame, palm house, Herrenhausen, 1879.

117
George McKenzie, design for conservatory dome, 1815.

118
Georg Moller, dome of Mainz Cathedral, 1828.

119
Görz, "covering" dome of Wiesbaden Castle, 1839.

An early example of domes made of braced arched ribs is offered by the apselike ends of the transept and nave of the Jardin d'Hiver (1846–1848). The ribs, anchored in masonry at the base, formed hemidomes as shown in figure 62.

An especially filigreed dome was that of the central pavilion of the palm house in Belfast. On a base of two semicircles separated by straight lines was a helmetlike glass vault, supported by thin ribs held together by horizontal half-rings. In spite of these reinforcing rings it was still necessary to fit lateral ties on account of the intervening straight section.

The 1859 project for a "Palace of the People," by Owen Jones, called for a giant dome extending down to ground level and covering a winter garden.[379] Ribs of lattice work were to be joined together by purlins to make a space frame. This iron vault was to be stiffened by diagonals in the plane of the supporting structure, similar to those used in Schwedler's constructions from 1863.

Numerous victoria regia houses built after the 1860s had a circular or polygonal base and were covered with flattened domes. One example of this was the victoria regia house (1882) in the Old Botanical Garden in Berlin-Schöneberg (fig. 121). Around a central pond, a low masonry wall served as a base for a flattened glass-and-iron dome, which was terminated by a ventilating lantern. The curved main ribs were made of rolled section.

One of the largest domes was that of the Laeken winter garden, near Brussels, built in 1875–76 by A. Balat. The structure consisted of 36 braced ribs, rising from a low stonework base and supported by 36 stone columns and a ring-shaped architrave. The ribs were located on the inside in the upper part of the dome and on the outside in the lower part, giving a lively contrast between a continuous glass surface above and a framework-dominated surface below. The impression created by the dominant ribs on the outside is an early example of an architecture in which the function of the space frame was emphasized. This was furthered by the wrought-iron ornamentation of the bases of the columns, the archways above the stonework supports, and the large crown-shaped lantern. The ribs of the bell-shaped dome were braced and tapered upward, widening out to 1 foot at the springing. The ribwork was supported above the architectural ring by an iron framework, with a transition produced by an ornamental structure of smaller arches and infillings. This arrangement created two different interior space forms simultaneously: a central dome space and a low encircling gallery. The ribs were held together at the apex by a prominent cylinder of iron circles in the

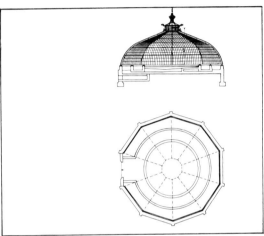

120
Owen Jones, design for dome with lattice trusses, Palace of the People, Muswell Hill, 1859 (project).

121
Schulze, dome of victoria regia house, Old Botanical Garden, Berlin-Schöneberg, 1882.

plane of the tops of the ribs, forming the lantern ring, which in turn was capped by a small dome. The ribs were reinforced horizontally by braced girders.[380]

A later example of filigree work in domes like that at Laeken, where there was a division into main vault and a vaulted gallery above, is the palm house at Sefton Park in Liverpool (1896). A glass dome was erected on an octagonal base, and the curved, lightly stilted braced ribs of the gallery and the dome were supported on the side by cast-iron columns connected by brackets to a crossmember, which was also braced (fig. 324).[381]

Most domes of the sort described here obtained their shape and strength from a hierarchically assembled structure of curved latticework master ribs and purlins in a ring. This structure was designed in accordance with the laws of statics. Because the spatial combination of the supporting members inside the dome could not be grasped as such, it was handled like a conventional post-and-beam construction. This led to an overdimensioning of the iron dome and a simultaneous disregard for the specific load-bearing functions of its parts. In the 1860s the work of J. W. Schwedler led to a turning point in the design calculations of the three-dimensional space frame: "One will reach a correct conclusion about the dome if one considers it as a thin elastic surface of double curvature, instead of starting out by considering an elastic bar. There is obviously a connection between the continuous surface and the construction made of separate members joined together, and in fact a connection of that kind in which the individual structural members of an articulated system must essentially follow in the same directions which in the continuous surface are followed by the major elastic forces." Schwedler demonstrated that, for equilibrium to exist, "the equilibrium of this surface (surface of rotation) must be in agreement with the equilibrium of a thin shell of the same shape (dome) assuming that the stresses are evenly distributed according to the thickness, or in addition if the bending moment of any strip of the dome surface can be omitted from consideration compared with the major forces."[382] In describing the dome structure over the tank of Imperial Continental Gas AG in Berlin (1861), Schwedler said: "The whole structure obtained its high degree of rigidity from the purlins and the one-inch-thick boards nailed on as cladding; hence the diagonals are important only before the structure has been given a cover."[383]

Although at that time homogeneous shells could not be made on account of defects in building materials, Schwedler had set up the theory for their

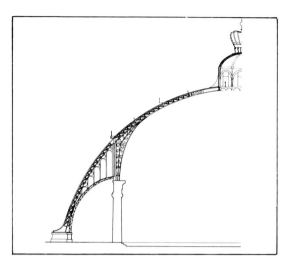

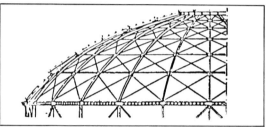

122
Alphonse Balat and Henri Maquet, braced roof truss, winter garden, Laeken, 1863.

123
Johann Wilhelm Schwedler, dome as space frame, locomotive shed, St. Johann, 1863.

Building[385]	Year	Span (meters)	Thickness (meters)	Thickness:Span
St. Peter's, Rome	1590	40	8	1:13
Frauenkirche, Dresden	1722	24	1.25	1:19
Halle aux Blés, Paris	1811	38.86	0.70	1:55
Palm house, Budleigh Salterton	1843	9.60	0.05	1:192
Kibble Palace, Glasgow	1872	19	0.07	1:270
Gasometer roof in Fichtestrasse, Berlin	1876	55	0.15	1:360
Zeiss Planetarium, Jena	1923	40	0.06	1:666
Covered market, Basel	1925	60	0.085	1:700
Exhibition building, Paris	1956	205	0.13	1:1,570

Note: The diameter-to-thickness ratio of a chicken's egg is 100:1.

mathematical design. The rigidity of the structure was provided by the wooden cladding of the dome, and the whole calculation was worked out as for a continuous shell. Hecker added to the theory of these structures in his paper "Frameworks in Space": "To resist shear the structure is reinforced by the inner ring and through the joints in the other rings riveted in the same way, but most of all by the wooden cladding, as was already noted by Schwedler earlier. It would be a useful exercise to make further experiments to determine to what extent the dome-shaped shell is suitable for supporting loads. . . . one has to admire the bold and, as experience has shown, practical views of Schwedler, who has hit the mark regarding the defects in the theoretical calculations of that time."[384]

Until the introduction of steel-reinforced concrete, the shells could only be made of bars. During assembly they did not give a continuous surface, but when the structure was completed and the wooden cladding added the whole could be considered a continuous surface. Further development led to shells made in the form of one-layer domes—for example, those designed by Buckminster Fuller, or the framework surfaces made of bars which Frei Otto designed for the Mannheim Garden Exhibition.

Digression: The Shell

The following digression brings in a more comprehensive description of this form of space frame. This is necessary because in iron hothouse construction, unnoticed by the experts, a technical innovation came about.

In the effort to develop easy and therefore economical methods of construction, the shell-shaped roof became very important in the history of space frames. The principle of the shell is based on the fact that the forces existing, in contrast with those in girders, ties, or glass panes, are not in the plane of the individual load-bearing members but are distributed all over the surface. Ribs, purlins, and diagonals combined in the usual way are subject to bending when they form a vaulted roof. This type of load distribution leads to great deformation and requires considerable expenditures for material. On the other hand, in shells designed in a more favorable manner, only tension, compression, and shear forces occur, and there is a very economical use of iron.

Though they are not accounted for in the historical records of the development of iron space frames, from 1817 on there were glasshouse structures (by J. C. Loudon and his successors) in which curved iron bars were used. These are to be considered the earliest shell-type roofs according to present-day views. Although not designed on a basis of theoretical statics, they owed their existence to a series of experiments by which their mathematically satisfactory shapes had been discovered. These shell-like roofs were brought into existence for the sake of transparency, and this stimulated their continued development. The table above, which begins with masonry domes, shows the progress in span in relation to skin thickness that was achieved in shell structures with the use of iron and glass, and later with shell and concrete. As this table shows, Loudon's curvilinear roofs were an important step in the development of the space frame.

Frans Dischinger defined *shell* in his 1928 publication "Schalen and Rippenkuppeln" (shells and ribbed domes).[386] One understands by the word *shell* a structure, formed by single- or double-curved surfaces, in which the skin thickness is small in comparison with the diameter. In these structures, tension, compression, and shear forces tangential to the curvature of the shell give rise to a state of membrane stress. Accordingly, shell structures must as a rule be made of materials which can resist the tensile and compressive stresses. From this aspect, thick-skinned masonry structures cannot be regarded as shell structures. Masonry vaults cannot withstand any tensile forces, which break up the homogeneous stress distribution into segments and lead to a behavior under stress in which each segment behaves like a curved beam. However, there are special cases of flat frameworks in which only compressive stresses occur. For these shells, a material that can simultaneously take up compressive and tensile stresses is no longer required. Thus we can differentiate between a continuous shell made of a homogeneous material and a discontinuous one made of different materials assembled together.

The curvilinear hothouses under consideration here are discontinuous shell structures made of wrought iron and glass, in which iron sash bars arranged like arches constitute the primary load-bearing structure and the lateral strength is provided by the glazing (which serves as a secondary structure).

Loudon's vaulted structures formed rotational shells. If a small segment is cut from a hemisphere of such a shell, which is composed of a large number of small segments, then the upper part starts to sink while the lower part bulges outward. The spatial stress behavior of the shell immediately becomes apparent: the downward-moving upper segments wedge themselves against one another, but the lower part must collapse by moving outward. Compression is generated in the upper part of the spherical calotte, tension in the lower part. The compressive stresses act tangent to the meridian, the tensile stresses in horizontal rings. The change of force from compression to tension occurs at the transition point, which for a hemisphere is located at 51.8°, i.e. approximately in the upper third of the vault. The state of membrane stress is undisturbed only while a continuous support at the base exists. With discontinuous point supports, such as columns, there appear bending moments.

In a flat calotte that lies above the transition point, or in a dome shaped according to the lines of columns, there occur not only longitudinal forces but also latitudinal forces as pure compressive stress. Dif-

ficulties arise in the perimeter zone, in which the forces in the vertical plane must be diverted. The simultaneous occurrence of compressive and tensile forces can lead to deformation of the rim of the shell. To avoid this, Dischinger proposed a steep transition curve to the calotte. With this arrangement, the transition point lies within the shell, as with a flat calotte. The stresses in the ring change over from compression to tension in the narrow marginal zone. This development was already in use in 1867, in the first version of the Kibble Palace.

As mentioned above, the curvilinear roofs of Loudon's hothouses were among the earliest wrought-iron roof structures. We find here the first known examples of the use of rolled section to make space frames. The basic elements of the glass-and-iron roofs were curvilinear sash bars about 2 inches deep, usually rolled as cruciform section so as to receive the panes of glass in the rebates (figs. 132, 133). Placed about 8 inches apart, they made up, together with the glass panes, a vault that could support its own weight without needing horizontal ties. Loudon described the use of such roofs in his "Designs for Curvilinear Hothouses" (1818).[387]

The designs included in Loudon's text and the later manifestations of this style have roof frames in which a zone of distortion was formed. These were designed either by intuition or by experiment. The small bending moments made horizontal tie members unnecessary in many cases. Loudon's use of glass as a structural member to stabilize the roof in the horizontal direction was very bold.

In his "Remarks on the Construction of Hothouses" (1817), Loudon described a circular-base hothouse which approached a parabolic shape in the vertical profile and which had only vertical rib sash bars. At the same time, he illustrated a bell-shaped glasshouse with vertical supports and sash bars and horizontal rings (figs. 124–126). Two years earlier, G. Mackenzie had proposed in a report to the London Horticultural Society a glasshouse with a spherical structure abutted onto a masonry wall (fig. 117). Around 1820 Loudon designed a temperate house for Loddiges Nursery, in Hackney (figs. 262–267) that leaned against a masonry wall and had a flat half-barrel vault which terminated at both ends in segments of spheres. In 1827 Loudon built at Bretton Hall, Yorkshire, a glass-and-iron structure with a ring of sixteen cast-iron columns carrying a bell-shaped vault, upon which was placed a ring-shaped cylindrical shell which, starting from the capitals of the columns, extended down to the ground (figs. 200–203). In his detailed description of the Bretton Hall building in the *Encyclopaedia of Cottage, Farm, and Villa Ar-*

124
J. C. Loudon, design
for hemispherical
dome of conserva-
tory, 1817.

125
Loudon, ground plan
of hemispherical
dome of conserva-
tory, 1817.

126
Loudon, design for
bell-shaped dome of
conservatory, 1817.

127
Loudon, design for
conservatory exten-
sion, Indian Villa,
Sezincote, 1817.

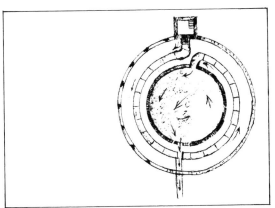

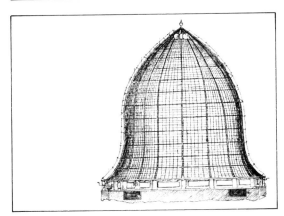

chitecture (1833),[388] Loudon asserted that the wrought-iron space frame of the sash bars did not constitute a rigid structure until the glass had been added. Not until after the slightly curved panes were fitted did the shell-like strength come into existence. The glass took over the job in the plane of distortion—along the ring—of transmitting and resisting the compressive forces.

In 1831 Loudon extended his series of designs of large curvilinear hothouses by conceiving two hothouses, gigantic for those times, for the Birmingham Horticultural Society's botanical gardens in the countryside near Edgbaston (figs. 190, 497).[389] Their dimensions and their technically advanced designs anticipated the greenhouses at Chatsworth and at Kew. In the first design Loudon proposed a circular glass vault built over a central tower, which served as a central heating unit. The supporting structure consisted of a ring of cast-iron double columns. Joined above by iron arches, they formed a rigid iron frame which terminated in a ring shape and constituted the supporting core of the structure. The inner and outer semi-barrels of the large glass vaults were supported on this framework (fig. 128). At the base they rested on the cast-iron frameworks of the vertical sliding windows. The design of a rigid frame made of pairs of columns around an internal path determined the springing for the glass roof, and such designs were also used at Wollaton Hall (1823) and Lednice (1843). In Loudon's second design for the Birmingham Horticultural Society (fig. 129), the external form of the glass vault was a conical dome narrowing to a point. The internal space frame consisted of a cast-iron skeleton structure of three stories. This comprised three rings of double columns, which were matched to the increasing height of the dome and placed one above the other to form the stories. The columns were joined by crossmembers, which followed the horizontal and vertical planes. In the middle, a cyclindrical space extended up to the apex of the dome. A spiral staircase provided access to the three stories. The interior of the glass vault was divided by four horizontal rings and rested on a cast-iron frame. The four horizontal rings of the dome were supported, as in the first design, by a vertical cast-iron framework and by ring-shaped lateral girders. Curved wrought-iron sash bars carried the glazing, and the central space was covered by a flattish dome. By skillful combination of a cast-iron internal supporting frame and horizontally divided roof segments, Loudon succeeded in covering a vast space with a filigree structure of small spans. This design, like the preceding one, proves that Loudon designed his roofs according to the principle of the shell and believed himself capable of erecting large public buildings as well as small greenhouses.[390]

Around the same time (1830–31), a large glass dome above a circular base was built in the Loudon style by Henry Phillips in the Surrey Zoological Gardens near London (fig. 130).[391] This dome covered a menagerie and an aviary as well as a tropical plant display. It was supported on the inside by a ring of cast-iron columns and at the perimeter by a low masonry wall. It may be assumed that the roof (up to the internal ring-shaped horizontal ties) was built without purlins and rafters and consisted only of curved sash bars. In its day, this building was the largest conservatory in Britain besides the similar structure by Loudon at Bretton Hall.

Loudon developed his curvilinear structures in collaboration with the London firm of W. and D. Bailey. This firm also built numerous curvilinear greenhouses without Loudon's collaboration, but it did continue to apply his principle to them. One early example was the Pantheon Bazaar (1834), designed by Sydney Smirke. This elongated building was roofed by a barrel vault of glass and iron with light pointed arches. It was made without interior columns, entirely supported by sash bars and glass above a cast-iron frame of vertical ventilating windows. The glass barrel vault was intersected in the middle by a short transept, which covered the two side entrances.[392]

In 1840 D. and E. Bailey, the successors to W. and D. Bailey, built the transept of a glasshouse for the Royal Horticultural Society in Chiswick. Departing from Loudon's principles, they incorporated cast-iron ribs as the main arch girders for the roof vault.

A perfect example of Loudon's framework structure, still in existence, is the palm house in Bicton Gardens at Budleigh Salterton in Devon. The date of construction and the builder's name are not known, but the year of construction was probably about 1843. According to Hix, the building was erected by D. and E. Bailey. The main vault is erected on a rectangular base with an attached semicircle. Two side vaults, adjoining to the right and the left, enclose a rectangle. A masonry wall supports the structure at one side. The main supporting structure consists of a cast-iron framework on the perimeter of the ground plan, on which the curved sash bars of the vault rest. This gives a shape approaching a rectangular hyperbola arch; that is, the profile is linear at the tops and bottoms and circular in the middle, giving a bulged-out appearance. The sash bars are stiffened by the glazing and have a cruciform cross-section; they are

the only support for the main dome except for a wrought-iron of curved bar in the plane of the outermost intersection of the main and side domes. Because the small quarter-domes open onto the main dome, they are supported together with the latter by a small cross-member of the same cross-section and by their cast-iron columns. The low ring stresses are sustained by the resistance to bending of the sash bars. Thus, no appreciable tensile stresses occur in the dome, and the designer was able to dispense with horizontal rings. The ridge of the main vault is terminated by a rigid girder in the rearward masonry wall. When one considers the exposed position of this greenhouse, in an elevated position on a little hill near the coast, its 140 years of existence prove the inherent strength of this filigree structure.

The vault of the pavilion of the greenhouse in Sheffield Botanical Gardens, built in 1836 by B. B. Taylor, is an elegant structure of sash bars, glass, and cast-iron columns. The sash bars between the columns are reinforced by very thin purlins running around the vault in five rings, one above the other. In addition, tie bars extending across the interior space between opposite columns hold the vault together. Because Taylor exceeded the maximum span of about 30 feet set by Loudon and did not support the roof laterally with masonry in a rear wall, he was compelled on the grounds of safety to incorporate ties.

There are on the Continent two roofs in the Loudon style worth mentioning: the transept of the glasshouse in the Jardin des Plantes in Paris (Rohault, 1833) and the winter garden of Liechtenstein Castle in Lednice (Devien, 1843). The transept of the Paris glasshouse consists of two stepped rows of semi-barrel vaults in a stepped arrangement. The Lednice winter garden, with its pairs of cast-iron columns, is reminiscent of Loudon's Birmingham building. The semi-barrel-vault-shaped glass roof rests on a masonry base and is supported by trusses. The architect, Davien (without doubt an Englishman), knew Loudon's buildings and imitated them here.

From the 1840s to the end of the century, Turner created several greenhouses and winter gardens that advanced Loudon's shell principle. In the transept of the palm house in Belfast (1839–1841), a curving sash-bar roof was erected on a vertical cast-iron framework, sloping gently upward. At the rear it rested on a masonry base. On the inside, in the middle of the vault, the sash bars were strengthened by a row of columns and a cast-iron horizontal beam; this was retrograde in comparison with Loudon's design, but it was necessary because the sash bars were long and straight and therefore subject to bending.

128
Loudon, design for
ring-shaped conserv-
atory, Botanical and
Horticultural Gar-
den, Birmingham,
1831.

129
Loudon, design for
domed conservatory
with internal cast-
iron space frame,
Botanical and Horti-
cultural Garden, Bir-
mingham, 1831.

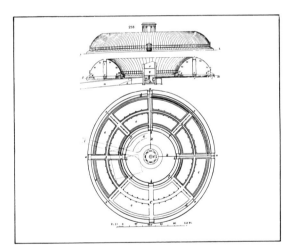

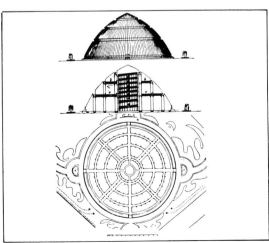

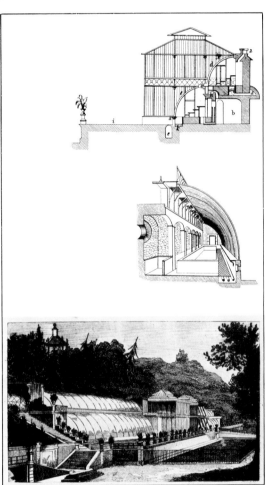

130
Henry Phillips, Glass
Menagerie, Surrey
Zoological Garden,
London, 1831.

131
Charles Rohault de
Fleury, conservatory,
Jardin des Plantes,
Paris, 1833.

Turner followed a similar procedure in the construction of the transept of the Dublin glasshouse (1842–1850), in which a glass-and-iron barrel vault was supported by two interior rows of columns. Also noteworthy was the construction between 1842 and 1846 of the winter garden in Regent's Park, London, also by Turner. The hall of this building consisted of four rows of vaulted glass roofs, which intersected in the middle and at the sides by glazed lateral barrel vaults. The lean-to roofs were carried on rows of cast-iron columns and beams. Although there were sliding windows in the ridge area, the roof was supported by uniform sash bars of constant cross-section.

The Kibble Palace in Glasgow Botanical Gardens, built in 1872 and still in a good state of preservation, was a late manifestation of glass-and-iron shell construction and a peak of nineteenth-century iron construction. Its basic space frame originated in 1867 on the estate of John Kibble. It was dismantled in 1872, loaded onto a ship, and erected again in extended form in Glasgow. The central space, covered by a depressed dome, has two interior rings of cast-iron columns, which support via an I-section girder a roof made only of sash bars and glass. The sash bars, made of flat bars screwed to angle iron, spring from the cast-iron framework at the perimeter; they change from a curved to a linear profile, giving a conical surface. A vertical framework made of window sashes forms a low tambour for a flattish dome. The sash bars are held together at the apex of the dome by a small lantern ring. Because they follow the ring of columns, they are not subject to bending and therefore require no horizontal ties to take up outward stresses. One can detect today a rotational distortion of the sash bars. Under the load of the roof, they have departed from the direct radial direction to the center of the dome and are now deflected from the meridional plane. However, the distortion is slight; the edges of the glass panes have only been pressed up against the edges of the rebate in the iron section. A condition of equilibrium was reached by this distortion of shape. The tensile stresses in the sharp bend at the outer perimeter of the hall are resisted by ties in the form of round iron bars.

The Sash Bar

Wrought-iron sash bars could not compete with wooden and cast-iron ones until rolling mills were developed. As mentioned above, Loudon was a pioneer in the development and use of iron sash bars, which he made in such a way that they could also be an integral part of the space frame in the form of shells for curvilinear roofs. These curved sash bars

had a cruciform section so that on one side there was a rebate for the glass pane and on the other side there was the depth which created the necessary stiffness.

Loudon described the development of sash bars in his "Remarks on the Construction of Hothouses" (1817). The starting point was the flat wrought-iron bar, to which various galvanized iron parts were attached by screws to hold the glass and to remove condensation on the inside. The next logical step was to make this composite section by rolling instead of building it up from individual parts. The first kinds of section which Loudon proposed in May 1816 at the Horticultural Society were whole and half sections with a rebate (fig. 132a).[393] With the section of greater depth he achieved not only increased strength in the sash bars but also a reduction in the overall amount of material used, and hence a reduction in the loss of internal illumination compared with sash bars having wide rebates. These sash bars could be bent to the desired curvature while hot or cold, and immediately after shaping they were given an anti-corrosion coating or were galvanized.[394]

For gently sloping roofs, such as ridge-and-furrow roofs, Loudon proposed a combination of a rolled sash bar with a galvanized sheet-metal gutter fastened underneath to carry off the condensation. A further development introduced by Loudon consisted of preventing leaks in the glazing by incorporating in the section profile of the rolled sash bars small water channels or gutters (fig. 139, part 28). Later examples of this device may be seen in the *Handbook of Architecture* (1894).[395] Besides those made as a single piece, other sash bars were also constructed from L section and flat bar. One example of these is the curved sash bar used in the Kibble Palace in Glasgow, where flat steel bar was attached to an L section to provide the rebate (fig. 134b).

Sash bars for windows were the earliest of all rolled sections. In Britain they were made even before rails for railways.[396] Their manufacture in the form of angle section and L section was in progress as far back as the 1820s in Britain and France. Three main types of rolled-iron sash bar can be distinguished. With *L-section* sash bars, the glass panes were placed on the horizontal flange. The depth of the rebate was determined by the thickness of the glass. Because the panes overlapped one another, the depth had to be at least twice the thickness of the glass plus that of the putty bed. With long roofs, expansion joints were a preferred means of taking up thermal expansion. *Cruciform-section* sash bars were a further development of Loudon's type. For the same amount of material, they were stronger than L-

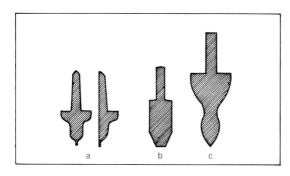

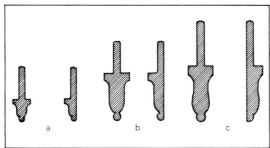

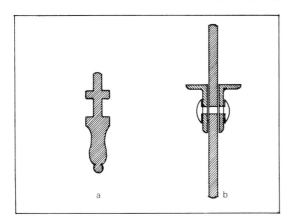

132
Wrought-iron sash
bars designed by
(a) J. C. Loudon
(1817), (b,c) Charles
McIntosh (1853).

133
Wrought-iron sash
bars designed by
Rohault (1837).

134
Wrought-iron sash
bars designed by
(a) Ludwig Persius
(1838), (b) John Kibble
(1865, 1872).

section bars. This was the basic sash bar used in green-houses. When purlins were used to support these sash bars, a technically more difficult joint was required. The difficulty of achieving a perfect seal with exposed putty led to the provision of means to remove water via channels in the rebate. Condensation was removed by additional channels at the bottom edges of the bars. The aim was not merely to control runoff, but also to increase the strength of the sash bar while saving material at the same time. These *gutter sashes*, which were developed for use in glass-houses, may be considered the forerunners of the curtain-wall sash bars of the twentieth century.

Iron sash bars were generally susceptible to the formation of condensation on the inside because of their high thermal conductivity. Much condensation occurs in hothouses on account of the humidity necessary for the cultivation of the tropical plants. Because cold drops of condensation falling on plants caused damage to them, in the last quarter of the nineteenth century iron sash bars covered with wood were used instead of the gutter types, which were effective only when the condensation could be led away unimpeded by lateral joints. The Copenhagen and Berlin-Dahlem greenhouses are examples of this. For the present study, however, cruciform-section iron sash bars are significant in the context of the shell structures used. The iron sash bars which Loudon proposed in 1816 at the Horticultural Society (fig. 132a)[398] were used in the first shell structure built by Loudon in Bayswater.

In 1833 Charles Rohault, the builder of the glass-houses in the Jardin des Plantes, made a study tour of England. His detailed report, illustrated with drawings, was published in 1837 in the *Allgemeine Bauzeitung*. Rohault provided descriptions and 1:1 scale drawings of the sash bars used in shell structures. The designs he described were those used at Hackney and those used in a glasshouse with "curved glass roof" built by the firm of W. and D. Bailey, who were Loudon's partners. This report contains accurate information about the sash bars used by Loudon and the usual iron section used at the time. The "curved rebated rafters" were made by rolling. The iron arches rested on cast-iron plate below, and at the top against the masonry wall, without any intermediate support. Rohault wrote: "The small size of the rebate used here catches the eye. This does in fact cause some difficulty in fixing the panes, but there is the advantage over the larger rebate which casts unnecessarily wide shadows. All the iron components are very malleable. They can be worked cold and bent with hammers, and in this work the smiths have a special dexterity. The bar would be able to support the weight of a man, should he try it, without buckling. When one wants to join it to the next bar one files down the part forming the cornice of the section, lays it above the cross-member, and obtains a joint by means of two wedges to hold it."[399] (See figure 133.)

McIntosh's *Book of the Garden* contains two full-size diagrams of rolled-wrought-iron sash bars (fig. 132). He notes that these sections were used more often than others, were made by machines (i.e., they were rolled) and were cheaper and stronger in relation to their dimensions than cast-iron sash bars. They were, however, susceptible to rust, and they had to be painted immediately after manufacture.[400] Elsewhere in the same book were sketches of the sash bars Loudon had used at Bretton Hall. "These sash bars," wrote McIntosh, "were nearly two inches deep, and half an inch thick in the thickest part, and weighed only about one pound per lineal foot."[401]

With this information, the amount of glass and iron used in the shell structures can be estimated. The smaller sash bars used in Loudon's buildings for spans of about 6–9 meters (20–30 feet) weighed about 1.1 kilogram per running meter, on the basis of figure 132a. For a sash-bar spacing of 17 centimeters (6.8 inches), the roof frame without the glass weighed 6.5 kilograms per square meter. According to McIntosh's statements about Bretton Hall, a 1-meter length of sash bar weighed 1.66 kg. For 17-cm sash-bar spacing, that gives a space-frame weight of 9.8 kg per m² for a clear span of 17 m. These figures prove the economic advantage of iron and explain the lightness and elegance of the early shell structures.

Summary: The Wrought-Iron-Shell Glasshouse as a New Form of Space Frame

In the early days of the use of iron for building it was J. C. Loudon who, as the inspired and wholly committed champion of the new material, sought to use it in the building of greenhouses. Loudon's theoretical investigations to find the optimal roofing method for greenhouses started out from the need to make the maximum use of the sun's rays in winter. He observed the sun's irradiation on the glass panes and the reflection from them for various angles of incidence. Loudon published the results of his work in 1817 as "Remarks on the Construction of Hothouses." He found the ideal form for the covering of a hothouse to be a dome or a folded or pleated roof. With such roofs, the sun's daily radiation falls perpendicularly on the glass panes for a relatively long time and the reflection of the rays is kept to a minimum. At the same time, George Mac-

kenzie came to similar conclusions: "Sir George Mackenzie believed that in the determination of the best forms of glass surfaces for forcing houses it was best to start from the assumption that those surfaces were to be preferred which while the sun was shining caused the rays to fall perpendicularly somewhere on the glass daily throughout the whole year. He then noted that this can be realized if the glass roof has the shape of half a semicircle pointing toward the sun in such a way that it corresponds to the greatest section possible of the circle which the sun follows during its daily course. Because it is hardly practical to give each pane the shape of a small section of a spherical surface, we must be satisfied with a polyhedral glass surface as the form that most nearly approximates the spherical shape."[402] Rohault, the builder of the glasshouse in the Jardin des Plantes, wrote: "The main advantage of the use of curved iron rebated ribs for glasshouses [is] . . . high uniformity in the incidence of the sun's rays."[403]

Further consequences of Loudon's investigations were the discoveries that, if possible, no part of the roof structure should project into the enclosed space, and that the surface area of the frame and sash-bar work should be minimized in order to maximize the glass surface and thus let in more sunlight. The optimal roof form was, accordingly, a shell structure with maximum glass content. The perception that these requirements could be met was the reason that Loudon had such enthusiasm for iron and described its properties with such passion. (See Loudon's "Sketches of Curvilinear Hothouses," pp. 230 ff.)

Loudon's principle gave rise to the curvilinear roof, a whole new form of space frame. Discontinuous shell structures consisting of iron bars and glass were produced for the first time, and their development from 1817 to 1872 resulted in an individual building type. Maximum transparency and lightness were achieved in immaterial-appearing structures with spherical surfaces that sparkled in the sunlight and seemed to be like thin, weightless membranes drawing the outside world in.

How right it is to regard the shells made of sash bars and glass as discontinuous is shown by the example of the Kibble Palace. The central dome, resting on twelve columns, is formed by sash bars set along meridional lines. These sash bars converge into a ring in the center of the dome. As figure 560 shows, the structure has rotated about the vertical axis to such an extent that the panes that were not completely rigid have rotated but have had the necessary strength to withstand further rotation. The S-shaped distortion of the sash bars caused by the rotation can be seen clearly. The glazing had the function of transmitting the shear stresses. Loudon described the structural importance of the glazing in another discontinuous shell as follows: "As the iron frame was erected before it was glazed the slightest wind could set the dome into motion from ground to apex. . . . as soon as the glass was fitted it stood completely firm and rigid."[404]

It was daring indeed to produce a structure in which glass took on an essential strengthening function. This unique innovation in architecture, practiced only in shell structures built in the Loudon style, yielded a transparency never before obtained.

The second field in which Loudon's experiments led to a pioneering achievement was the development of rolled iron section. From the start, Loudon used rolled-iron bars in the construction of his shell buildings. Each of more than twenty window-frame shapes and styles could be manufactured in two pieces by a simple change in the machine.[405] Before this time, rolled section had not been available for building. Its use in Bayswater House demonstrated the possibility of industrialized building methods for the first time.

Third, iron's durability and economy were demonstrated. Iron ribs lasted longer than wooden ones, and there was less glass breakage. Iron sashes were more rigid than wooden ones, and thus they were not subject to the same failure process.[406] The Kibble Palace is still in excellent condition, and the glasshouse at Hluboká nad Vltavou is still in full working order.

Finally, Loudon, through publications and through actual buildings, made new aesthetic claims for his glass-and-iron architecture. Though he described himself as a "philosophical garden artist," and though he was neither an architect nor an engineer, Loudon gave great impetus to the development of structural ironwork. His glasshouses occupy an important place in the history of nineteenth-century building.

Appendixes

John Claudius Loudon (1783–1843)

Loudon was born on April 8, 1783, at Cambuslang in Lanarkshire, Scotland. He grew up in Edinburgh, and occupied himself from very early on with plants and gardening. In 1803 he went to London, where he immediately obtained commissions as a landscape gardener because of his excellent training in botany, chemistry, and agriculture. In the same year (1803) he published his article "Observations on the Layout of Public Places in London" in *The Literary Journal*. In this he attacked the planning of the time. In place of the dark yews and firs that grew in London's squares he proposed to plant sycamores and almond trees—not only for their beauty but also to reduce the dust of the city. These proposals were taken up, and even today these deciduous trees are found in all London's squares.

In his first book, *Observations on the Shaping and Management of Useful and Ornamental Plants*, Loudon described in detail the beauty and necessity of woods. *A Short Treatise on the Several Improvements Recently Made in Hothouses* appeared in 1805. In 1806 he published his comprehensive *Treatise on Forming, Improving and Managing Country Residences*, which was illustrated with copper engravings of landscape scenes. Two pamphlets on agricultural practice (1807 and 1809) were followed in 1812 by *Hints on the Formation of Gardens and Pleasure Grounds* and *Observations on Laying Out Farms, in the Scotch Style, Adapted to England*.

In 1813 Loudon made a journey through Sweden, Germany, Poland, Russia, and Austria, during which he inspected large castles, estates, gardens, and parks. After he had thoroughly studied the glazing of forcing houses, there appeared *Remarks on the Construction of Hothouses* (1817) and *Sketches of Curvilinear Hothouses* (1818), in which he presented his ideas about the space-frame patterns he had studied. Also in 1818 he published *A Comparative View of the Usual and the Curvilinear Process of the Roofing of Hothouses*. In 1819 he made a further journey through France, Italy, and Belgium. Immediately after his return he started work on the *Encyclopaedia of Gardening*, the first edition of which appeared in 1822. In 1823 he wrote about the cultivation of pineapples and published anonymously *The Greenhouse Companion*, a book of which he had written at least part.

In 1825 the *Encyclopaedia of Agriculture* appeared, and in 1826 Loudon founded *The Gardener's Magazine*, which at first was wholly devoted to the making of gardens and which Loudon edited until his death. In 1828 Loudon began to publish *The Magazine of Natural History*, which was not so successful as *The Gardener's Magazine* but which was very popular and often imitated. In 1829 he proposed in *The Gardener's Magazine* the creation of 1 1/2-mile-wide "breathing spaces" around London. In another article he advocated the use of sewage as a fertilizer. In the same year, he published his *Encyclopaedia of Plants*. He published the sumptuous *Illustrations of Landscape Gardening and Garden Architecture* in 1830. The success he had with his *Encyclopaedia of Cottage, Farm, and Villa Architecture* encouraged him to publish a monthly series, the *Arboretum Britannicum*. From 1834 to 1838 Loudon edited *The Architecture Magazine*, the first periodical devoted exclusively to architecture, and in 1838 he began to edit the *Magazine of Natural History*.

In 1836 he started work on a further journal, *Suburban Gardener*, so that he was simultaneously editing five separate monthly periodicals. There followed in 1839 the second supplement to *Hortus Britannicus*, in 1840 the supplement to the *Encyclopaedia of Plants* and *The Derby Arboretum*, in December 1841 the first of ten monthly issues of the *Encyclopaedia of Trees and Shrubs* (a summary of the *Hortus Lignosus Londinensis*) and in 1842 the first supplement to the *Encyclopaedia of Cottage, Farm, and Villa Architecture* and the *Suburban Garden Artist*.

In 1843 Loudon published *On the Layout, Planting, and Management of Churchyards*. He was unable to finish *Advice for Young Gardeners, Foresters, Stewards, and Farmers* because of illness and financial troubles, but his wife completed it with the help of Sir Joseph Paxton, Dr. Jamieson, and his secretary Wooster.

In addition to his wide-ranging activity as a publisher and as a garden architect, Loudon was known for his influence on conventional architecture and on furniture (which originated with his 1833 *Encyclopaedia of Cottage, Farm, and Villa Architecture*). However, the architectural importance of his glass-and-iron buildings did not find adequate appreciation, though his obituary notice in *The Builder* did say that he had had a profound effect on the taste of the period and that his major work (the *Encyclopaedia*) was valuable to architects and to furniture manufacturers.[107]

After the importance of the iron structures of the nineteenth century was recognized, Loudon was seen as one of the most important instigators of the early development of steel buildings. As a theorist and experimenter with the new building material, he came to be regarded as an equal to Paxton. His research was seen to have laid the foundation for the large-scale development of the Paxton style of architecture.

Sketches of Curvilinear Hothouses
[J. C. Loudon, London, 1818]

Publisher's note: At the time of translation, the original document was not available to the translator or the publisher. The following is an abbreviated translation, in reported-speech form, of Jutta von Sartory's German rendering of the original.

This publication describes proposals for the design of hothouses and their various possible uses in the garden and in general architecture. The designs are based on the recently invented rolled-iron glazing bars.

Defects in the construction, the beauty, and the transparency of hothouses had been known for a long time. The defects in construction were noticed by men of taste, the defects in transparency by forward-thinking garden architects. It was hardly possible for buildings to be more repulsive to the eye than those with suspended sawtooth glass roofs, according to Loudon. Although they covered showplaces of the greatest luxury, their external ugliness made them suitable only for kitchen gardens. It would be more appropriate to attach these buildings to the residence, or at least to put them in the more elegant part of the estate. Numerous attempts had been made to do this. To make them more tolerable

135
John Claudius Loudon (1783–1843).

136
Sir Joseph Paxton
(1803–1865).

when this was done, the lean-to appearance of the hothouse was disguised by stone columns, window-sills, and other decorative features. Loudon believed the construction of such buildings to be based on faulty design, characterized by architectural mould-ing, and thought that the plants suffered from lack of light, which was cut off by the masonry. Plants that had been wintered in such winter gardens showed the effects of lack of light. Loudon ques-tioned the effectiveness of a building whose architec-ture was opposed to its use.

One could start from the premise that in that en-lightened and liberal age buildings could still be beautiful without exhibiting the orders of Greek and Gothic architecture. Mr. Alison remarked that the grandeur of forms arose wholly from the associations which people combined with them. Was it not possi-ble for glass roofs to have a more lofty and appro-priate nature than being merely lean-tos or glass-covered arcades? Imagine instead of a row of glazed lean-tos a row of separate glass bodies (figure 138, sketches 18 and 19), almost totally transparent. Inside them would be a friendly climate, and the plants would receive the sun's rays unimpeded all through the day. The construction would combine maximum strength with durability. What impression would be created? Instead of the usual winter garden built di-rectly onto a residence, the reader was asked to imagine a lightly vaulted, completely transparent roof (figure 137, sketch 10). Combined with that there could be high circular towers, spherical projections matching the size and the style of the houses. There might be glass oriental cupolas or other beautiful forms, all transparent and durable. These new shapes and this almost complete transparency could only be an improvement, satisfying both the man of taste and the garden architect. The invention de-scribed in this account gave scope for the greatest possible beauty and variety of shape, great transpar-ency, and a strength that could at the time be ex-ceeded only by the strongest British metals. The invention would fulfill its purpose.

Concerning hothouses as a group, since their in-vention approximately 120 years before this date no improvement whatever had been made to their ex-ternal form. Mr. Knight had noted that, although de-signed for the same purpose, hardly two had the same shape. Usefulness was regarded as more im-portant than beauty, and no great advance in utility was aimed for. Mr. Knight had stated that the shape which allows the greatest amount of light to pass through the narrowest piece of glass and gives the most uniform warmth with the least amount of heat-ing fuel must generally be the best. If this statement

were true, then it would be very easy to prove that few of the hothouses of that period had been built properly.

The experience of 15 years as a garden architect and visits to all the important hothouses in Great Britain and on the Continent put the author of these "Instructions" in the position of being able to pro-pose improvements to hothouses taking note of the writings of Sir Joseph Banks, Mr. Williams, Sir George Mackenzie, and others who were writing about this topic. These improvements corresponded to all the ideas about beauty, diversity, or elegance of shape, and satisfied the most extravagant expecta-tions about stability and transparency to light. The essential basis of these improvements was the use of rolled-iron glazing bar sections of great strength and elegance, which could be curved in any direction with no loss of strength and even with an increase in strength. These bars had been described for the first time in 1817 in "Remarks on the Construction of Hothouses" shortly after they had been invented. Loudon intended in his 1818 publication to advertise the various applications of these bars and to make them more familiar to the public. Loudon's account, based on a general summary of the state of hot-houses in Britain and on the Continent, noted that there would shortly be an agreement made in Lon-don so that every worthwhile improvement would be made available as an article of trade. The manufac-ture of the recently invented glazing bars, under Loudon's control, would be undertaken by the firm of W. and D. Bailey of 272 High Holborn, London.

The essential advantages of a massive wrought-iron section or round bar over wood and all the other materials previously used were as follows:

1. They could be bent in any direction without loss of strength. Thus they made possible the construc-tion of hotbeds or forcing houses of every imagina-ble variety and beauty of form.

2. They could be made in any desired size, and needed no rafters. Their strength depended on the position of the curvature, and in some cases it could be increased by increasing the dimensions (figure 137, sketch 10; figure 139, sketch 20).

3. They made greater transparency possible. The best wooden forcing houses, such as those which had just been erected by Mr. Aiton in the Royal Kitchen Garden in Kensington, excluded one-third of the light; the best metal frames and iron rafters one-fourth to one-sixth. The new hothouses did not ex-clude more than one-tenth.

4. They had longer life and there was less glass breakage. Iron-section glazing bars assembled from two parts, even when provided with water excluders,

corroded because of dampness, and this broke the panes. The new sections were in one piece and were therefore not subject to the same destructive process. 5. They were cheaper than copper or any other iron or other metal section. In some cases they were even cheaper than wood, and in general the price did not exceed that of wooden rafters and glazing bars.

Independent of the curved designs put forward in this account, which realized the full extent of the advantages of these sections, there were others for use with every type of hothouse, hotbed, or germinating space. They could be constructed as shown in sketch 21 of figure 139 or mounted in a wooden frame, which was cheaper than any other material of similar durability. They were suitable for the most varied glass domes, movable glasshouses, and skylights, for which they had the necessary strength. They could also be used for the windows of shops, department stores, depots, barracks, hospitals, churches, theaters, houses, servants' quarters, and farm and domestic buildings. In general, they were desirable in any building in which strength, lightness in appearance, durability, and protection against fire and burglary were wanted. On the other hand, they were not recommended for the living rooms of elegant villas, where complex shapes (particularly scrolls, friezes, and cornices) were desired. Complex forms could not be produced with the simple machines used for the manufacture of these economical sections.

There were other areas of application: as rafters for sheet iron or copper roofs for houses, very large buildings, or verandas. One type of section (figure 139, sketch 25) could, when made in longitudinal halves, be used advantageously for some types of frames, or for door and window shutters in which the panels were infilled with sheet iron and inserted in rebates. This created the possibility of making rooms or whole buildings fireproof, burglar-proof, and generally durable.

Further details of the advantages of rolled-iron glazing bars for hothouses were given in Mr. Knight's and Sir George Mackenzie's "Horticultural Transactions for 1817 and 1818," and in the article "Horticulture" which was published in 1817 in the Edinburgh Encyclopaedia.

Five of the ten different kinds of glazing-bar section illustrated are shown in sketches 23–27 of figure 139. The differences between these and the rest are chiefly in shape and size of the moulding. Each bar could be produced in two halves by a minor change in the setting of the machine, by which means over twenty different kinds were produced. They could be zinc-plated to protect them from rust for many years.

Description of the sketches

Figure 137, sketches 1–3:
Pointed hemisphere, designed for a small detached hothouse in a flower garden. Covered inside with grapevines, it can serve the dual purpose of a summer house and a vinery. Near to or connecting with a salon, it is intended for use as a winter garden for flowering plants.

Figure 137, sketches 4–6:
Oval house adaptable internally for a wide range of special purposes. Iron roof on backward-sloping part. Doors are indicated by letter *a*.

Figure 138, sketches 7–9:
Spherical form, equipped internally as a hothouse for pineapples. Compared with the roof width, it has a greater bedding area than is usual. Letter *a* indicates one of two pillars supporting an attached arch to carry the weight of the upper part of the rear wall.

Figure 137, sketches 10, 11:
Dome-conservatory with rafters, beams, or ties. If the aisles are not needed, the row of pillars can be replaced by a row of glazing bars. Some decorated iron bars are then incorporated as buttresses in place of the aisles to support the weight of the central roof. Rosettes or marigold windows, fastened to pivots, serve as air intakes.

Figure 138, sketches 12–15:
Peach or cherry house in which the glazing bars lie on iron ribs and are rotatable, forming a hinge. They are operated by a chain, so that all those in a row can could be simultaneously raised to any desired angle not exceeding the vertical to suit the position of the sun during the day, or the season of the year, and to permit the entry of rain. Letters *b* indicate transverse partitions supporting the sloping rear wall.

Figure 138, sketches 16, 17:
Hothouse for vines, with roof attached at the apex and built on the sawtooth or double-meridian principle. Individual houses are joined in series and placed beside a wall which forms the lobbies with backward-sloping roofs—an arrangement very useful in winter to prevent a sudden entry of cold air, and to provide ventilation in summer.

Figure 138, sketches 18, 19:
Overall view of curvilinear hothouses attached to garden walls. Letter *a* indicates door or vestibule, *b* indicates a forcing house, *c* a pineapple house, *d* a peach or cherry house built on the principle shown in sketch 12. This was the only design at that time in which trees or plants could receive the advantages of fresh air combined with those of a hothouse. No

other hothouse could admit rain or the direct rays of the sun at any point. *e* indicates double meridian roofs, as in sketch 17. *f* indicates the section of an almost spherical body.

In all these cases the ventilation is by openings close to the ground in the front and at the ends, and close to the top of the rear wall, or by movable panes (as shown in sketches 39 and 40) in the lower and upper parts of the glass roofs. Steam-pipe or flue heating is to be used. Steam is considered to be much the best. Mr. Kewley's "artificial garden" is recommended. Bells indicate the temperature, which is regulated by moving the ventilators, raking the fire, etc. This sophisticated machine is intended to give protection against extremes of weather and, as a whole, to be independent of the attention of the gardener. The drawings do not show the wire trellises, water pipes, and all the other secondary interior devices used in hothouses. A distinct improvement is achieved by not having brick or stone front and end walls. The roof rests on cast-iron ribs (sketch 29). Internal projections from these ribs carry the heating or steam pipes; on the outside there is a box holding a linen curtain. An internal gutter for the condensation and an external one for the rainwater run below the horizontal bar joining the ribs and carry the weight of the roof glazing. The advantages of the very light external curtain are described by Dr. Wells in his "Essay on Dew," chapter VI, and Mr. Leslie in "Experiments on Concentric Cases."

Figure 139, sketch 20:
This shows a roof, 50 feet high and 50 feet wide, which is intended to be either covered with glass for a winter garden or covered with thin iron sheet for churches, schools, theaters, assembly and training halls, markets, etc. Only one type of glazing-bar section is used (sketch 23), not straight as at *a* in sketch 20, but with a curved profile. When glazed and reinforced with horizontal bars inserted into the angle of the curved line (*d,d* in figure 21), this is able to carry its own weight like a massive iron arch. The glass has a shape curved in every direction. Besides the advantages for light penetration, this is much less susceptible to breaking in the event of a hailstorm than a glass roof made of flat panes (the moment of force is proportional to the sine of the angle of slope).

For even greater strength the pitch shown as *b,b* would need to be increased to any angle less than 45°, as in *c,c*. For a roof or house of average dimensions, say 20 feet × 20 feet, the profile is made in one plane as in *a,a*, reinforced by triangular cross bars as in *g,g*, joined together by a dovetail joint at

the channel or projection outside the roof, with the round bar *f* running through the cornice to the inside. None of them impede the rain on the outside or the condensation on the inside. For an iron-sheet roof, the sheet edges are turned into the rebates and covered with a revited-on strip as in *d,d*. It is claimed that roofs of this kind, painted with Le Souf's anti-corrosion paint and protected from electrolytic action at the base, will last for centuries. The iron and copper roofs of Moscow and the iron- and zinc-plated iron sheets of Warsaw, constructed on a relatively unscientific basis, are quoted as proof of the principle, which also creates an elegant effect. Doors covered with iron sheets in accordance with the above descriptions are produced for domestic houses.

Figure 139, sketches 31–33:
These show double-meridian glazed units for covering hotbeds used for special purposes. The section (sketch 28) used in the unit in sketch 31 is excellent for gardeners wanting to raise early gherkins because the condensation cannot drip onto the plants but is drained away by the channels.

Figure 139, sketch 30:
A movable glass cover for the protection of orange bushes in winter and for a general heat conserver in summer. *a,b,c,d* show the ends of a rectangular roof of the center and the aisles. Below them are shown the triangular ends used when the whole is placed against a wall, with a small door (*e,f,g,h*) in each of the outer parts. The framework is made of the section shown in sketch 24 and round bars as in sketch 24.

Figure 139, sketches 31, 35, and 36:
Glass bells and often movable glasshouses for plants and shrubs. Prototype buildings erected in Bayswater as proof of what has been described.

Figure 140, sketches 37, 38:
Perspective view of a group of hothouses representing the diversity of the roof types built in accordance with the above designs and using the section described. Included is a hothouse comprising all types of wood, metal, and patent sections as used by the various builders of glasshouses in Britain.
a) A group of formerly used window frames, comprising 13 different kinds of and 7 different types of glazing.
b) The section (sketch 23) in its simplest form, with glass guttering that stops exactly one-eleventh of the light from passing through the roof.
c) Tall pyramidal-shape house with convex sides, primarily suited for winter gardens and hothouses.
d) Use of the section for vertical internal partitions and to form the ends.

e) Curved roof consisting of movable window frames, as in sketch 12.

f) Sawtooth roof, as in sketches 17 and 20.

g) Single-curve roof following the direction of the ribs, as in sketch 10.

h) Double-curve roof sloping laterally and longitudinally. This part of the roof shows the potential of the section for a hothouse on a building site sloping in the longitudinal direction, and on a level site. This was not previously considered possible, and could lead to very important results where gardens slope very steeply to the east or west, or when a residence is to be joined by a glazed area to a farm building, a garden, or other adjacent parts which are much above or below its own level.

i) Sloping quarter-dome or quarter-sphere, as in sketch 5.

k) Box containing an external curtain for a part of a roof 5 feet wide, which extends over the roof ridge from base to the other.

l) Plan of a zigzag wall, needing fewer bricks than a 9-inch wall and stronger than a 14-inch wall. The covering of the battlements could be sometimes made of cast iron in a distinctive and elegant design.

m) Iron roof and iron-clad doors to the steam boiler house and cylinder of Mr. Hawley's equipment for heating, control, and ventilation of all groups except a.

n) Anteroom heating, which heats a. The ventilation there is as shown in the figure.

o) A small, cheap, satisfactory, and durable roof made of treated paper nailed to thin boards and covered with a mixture of plaster and concrete. This type of roof had been in use for 50 years in Britain and France for churches, farm buildings, and some factories.

p) Paths below the bottom part of the roof, lying 2 feet below ground level.

q) Pineapple or plant bed heated by a steam chamber below it.

r) Entrances.

s) Nearby is a gherkin bed covered with window elements, as in sketches 31–33, with a fourth frame, the whole having seven types of glazing. Four removable covers made of section as in sketch 27 leaning against the ends of the bed.

t) The Bayswater stream.

Figure 140, sketches 39, 40:
Tin-plated glazed ventilators for the apex or the almost flat areas of glass roofs, as at *x* in sketches 37 and 38.

Figure 140, sketch 41:
The same for perpendicular windows or for steep slopes.

Figure 140, sketch 42:
This shows the way to link an indefinite number of very varied ventilators together and how they can be simultaneously closed by hand or by a cord to Mr. Kewley's equipment. There are advantages to be gained from this kind of ventilation, but the details had to be omitted.

The section, in whatever form it is manufactured, occupies less than half the space required by woodwork and therefore is better for the removal of water than wood.

In this publication Loudon invited commissions for hothouses and other garden constructions. Orders for skylights, windows, iron roofs, iron doors, fireproof buildings, and so on were to be sent to him or to the firm of W. and D. Bailey. No charge was generally made for designs or inspections of the building site when an order resulted, but travel costs were always charged. If no contract resulted, the usual architect's fee of 5 guineas per day would be the maximum charge.

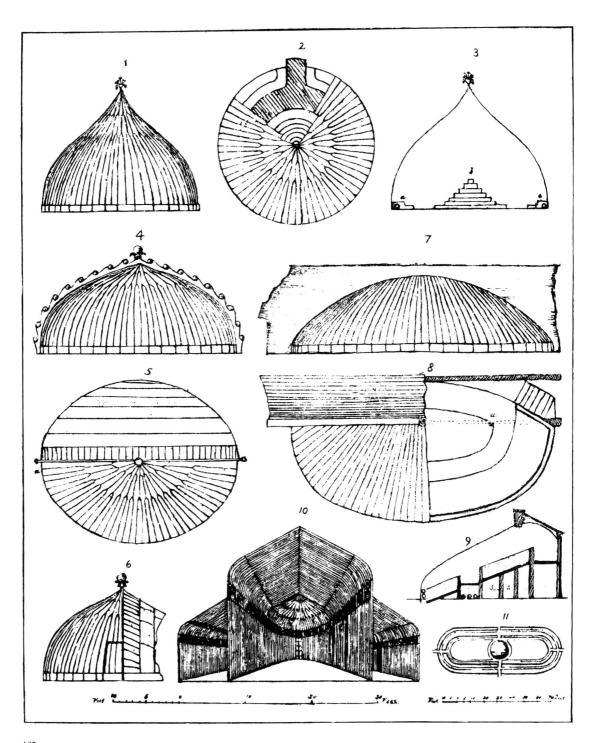

¹37
Roof forms for
conservatories.

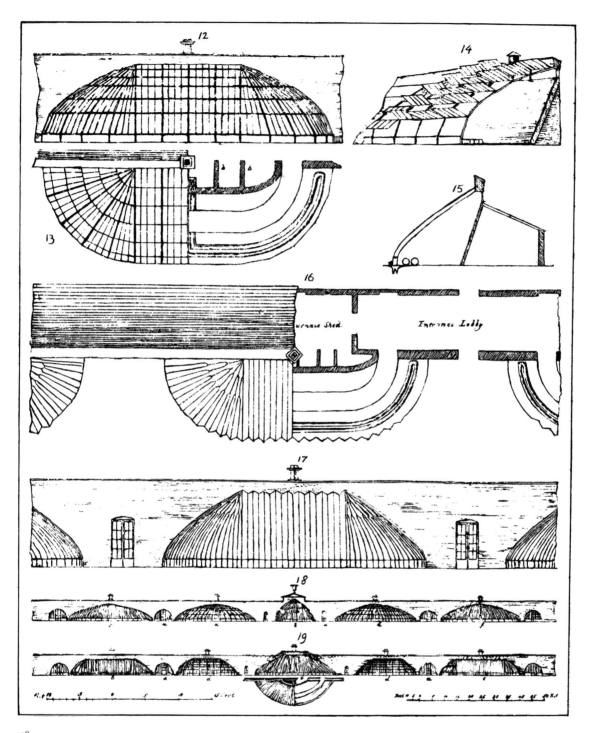

138
Roof forms for
conservatories.

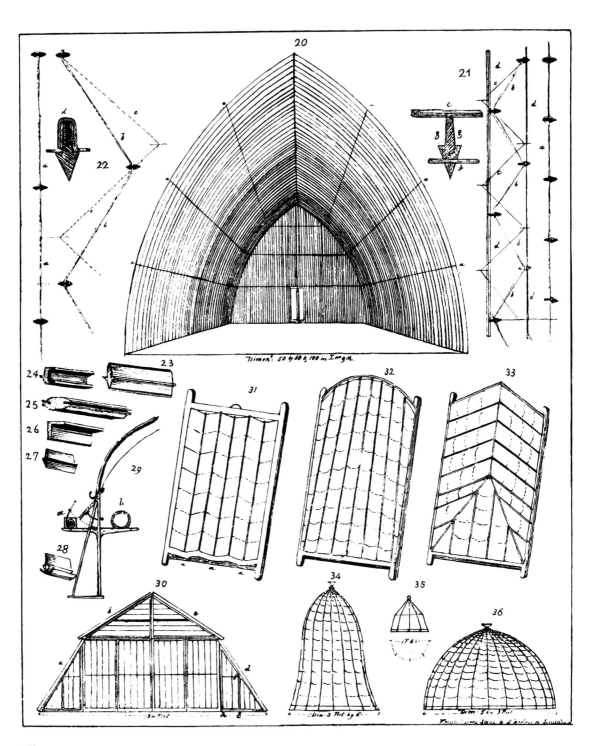

Details of conservatory roofs.

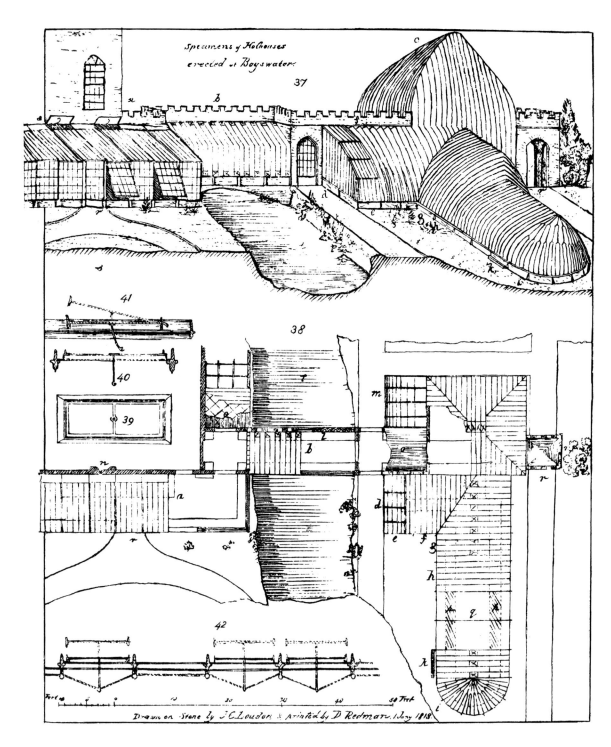

Specimens of Hothouses
erected at Bayswater

Drawn on Stone by J C Loudon & printed by D Redman 1 July 1818

140
Loudon, experimental glasshouses, Bayswater House,
1817–18.

Iron as a Building Material

Iron is classified in accordance with the scheme established at the end of the nineteenth century into pig (cast) iron and malleable iron (wrought iron, steel). "The nomenclature indicates the characteristic differences. Malleable iron is supple, particularly when hot . . . and can be drawn out so that it can be easily made into all kinds of shapes by mechanical means; pig iron is a raw material which has incorporated into its composition several of the components of its ore and thus has lost so much of its malleability that it can only be shaped by molding when in the molten state.[408]

The various properties of the two kinds of iron are due primarily to variations in the carbon content. The carbon content is responsible for the individual criteria for distinguishing the two major kinds of iron and the types originating from them:

Pig iron, in present-day practice the starting material not only for cast iron but also for steel, contains more than 1.7 percent carbon, is brittle, and cannot be worked mechanically.

By *cast iron* is meant the application of the carbon-containing pig iron by pouring it into a mold, whether it is by "direct casting" from the blast furnace or by "indirect casting" (i.e. the production of pig iron for storage until a later second melting and subsequent casting). "The melting point of pig iron lies between 1,050 and 1,200°C, lower than that of wrought iron, from 2,000 to 2,250°C."[409]

Steel contains less than 1.8 percent carbon and can be worked by rolling, pressing, and forging when hot but also when cold. It can be hardened by sudden cooling. Depending on the kind of processing, one distinguishes between *best iron* and *mild steel*. Whereas with the former the melting point is not exceeded and the steel is obtained in a pasty state, the latter is produced in the liquid state.

According to the classification that was customary in the nineteenth century, one understands by the term *wrought iron* all those kinds of iron obtained by removing carbon from pig iron to obtain a mechanically workable metal. This was accomplished either by the puddling process in a pasty state (best iron) or by the Bessemer, the Thomas, or the Siemens-Martin process (mild steel). The iron thus produced has a lower carbon content than steel (0.1–0.7 percent) and is therefore softer and more easily worked.

The specific properties of *cast iron*, its forms (gray and white), and its alloys are described in detail in the literature.[410] Here we will mention only its outstanding ability to be cast, its excellent behavior when poured into molds, its good resistance to corrosion, and its strength. Cast iron distinguishes itself by its high compressive strength, in which it can compete with wrought iron. A special characteristic, and one that is crucial for its use in construction, is its relatively low tensile strength. Whereas the compressive and tensile strengths of wrought iron are in the ratio 1:1, for common cast iron the ratio is approximately 3:1.

In the search for an unequivocal terminology for the typical forms of glasshouse structures of the nineteenth century, some unclear and ambiguous notions have been put forth. As an example it is sufficient to quote the concept of "suspended work," which, taken over from bridge building and applied to roof structures, often proved unsuitable. For some supporting structure forms, therefore, we have partly chosen the old nomenclature:

Spans are structures spanning the spaces between columns.

Prestressed rafter roofs signifies on the one hand beams prestressed on the underside by rods or cables and on the other hand braced trusses for ridge roofs, which are held together by horizontal tie members between the springing and sometimes by an additional vertical (king-post) member from the ridge. This type of structure is often referred to in the old literature as "suspended work," a concept which we, with some reservations, have taken over when appropriate.

Supporting structures are perpendicular or inclined structural members that serve chiefly to withstand compressive stresses.

Supporting frameworks describes a typical vertical framework structure which is often used instead of a single pillar support if a gap must be kept free.

Catalog

Introduction

Most of the glasshouses of the nineteenth century, whether hothouses or exhibition halls, were conceived outside the architectural styles that were usually specified in building commissions. Originating mostly in connection with large gardens, glasshouses did not conflict with stylistic architecture. They could be adapted all the more easily to their purposes, and in consequence they brought forward a new aesthetic based on pure structure. Free from the constraints of cities, they offered the joy of experimentation. Engineers and gardeners who were dilettantes at building could grasp the technical possibilities in unconventional ways.

Whereas stylistic architecture recapitulated history, the builders of the glasshouses had to conceive designs for contents that were ephemeral—plants or exhibitions. The trend toward the temporary was inherent in the plant houses and the exhibition buildings, and it expressed itself in the construction. Not suitable for industry and serving only for exhibitions or recreation, many of the glasshouses were left to decay, unappreciated, in less than a decade.

Of the buildings included in this catalog, fewer than half are still in existence and many of these are threatened with demolition. In this respect, the catalog is not only an inventory of the historically important glasshouses but also a chronicle of senseless destruction. One other intention is to advance a point of view about the architectural quality of these glasshouses by comparing them, and hence to create an awareness that will contribute to their preservation.

The catalog centers on plant houses that influenced glasshouse construction in important ways. Other forms, such as simple forcing houses, winter gardens, floras, and exhibition buildings, are also included. Certain exhibition buildings were included because of their direct connection with plant houses, whether through their use as winter gardens or through their similarity of construction.

The catalog is arranged in the alphabetical order of the cities and parks in which the glasshouses were, or still are, located. [*Publisher's note:* The desire to keep the numbering of the illustrations the same in the German and English editions required that the alphabetical order in the English edition follow the German spellings of place names in the original edition. Thus, Cologne appears where it would appear if spelled *Köln*, Copenhagen where it would if spelled *Kopenhagen*, and Vienna where it would if spelled *Wien*. The exact ordering of the catalog can be seen in the table that follows this introduction.]

The site plans, most of which have been reproduced on a scale of 1:5,000 or 1:10,000, give a general impression of the surroundings. The glasshouses themselves are made more distinct in the plans by hatching. The more important glasshouses have been reproduced in plan, elevation, and section so far as the particulars have been available. Therefore, existing plans have been redrawn with uniform density of hatching and reproduced on a 1:400 scale. The large exhibition buildings are an exception; because of their size they have been illustrated on a scale of 1:1,000. The redrawing has been necessary because the details were difficult to decipher and were given in different scales and in various forms of representation. The uniform reproduction makes the buildings comparable with each other in respect to size and three-dimensional structure. Some glasshouses, particularly those built by anonymous engineers, had to be measured and drawn from individual structural assumptions for lack of specific information. Accuracy in the dimensions was the aim, but because of photographic processes and the conversion of old scales some unimportant errors may have been made. Plans and sketches that express the architectural intention with special clarity have been reproduced in their original form, partly as supplements to the schematic diagrams. Again, the engravings and lithographs reveal, in addition to the architectural form of the buildings, the way they were seen by contemporaries. The sources of the materials used for the diagrams are indicated in the comments. The photographs, contemporary engravings, and plans that follow the catalog represent a comprehensive collection and are intended to clarify the development of glasshouse types.

Contents of Catalog

Bayswater	Bayswater House	Experimental glasshouses
Belfast	Botanic Garden	Palm house
Berlin	Pfaueninsel	Palm house
Berlin-Glienicke		Orangery, forcing house
Berlin	Wilhelmstrasse	Winter garden of "Palais Prinz Albrecht"
Berlin-Schöneberg	Royal Botanical Garden	Hothouses, palm house, Great Palm House, victoria regia house
Berlin-Moabit	Villa Borsig	Winter garden, forcing house
Berlin-Charlottenburg		Flora, banquet hall, palm house
Berlin	Schadowstrasse	Aquarium
Berlin	Central Hotel	Winter garden
Berlin-Dahlem	New Botanical Garden	Great Palm House, victoria regia house, subtropical house
Biebrich	Castle gardens	Hothouse of Prince Adolf von Nassau
Birmingham	Botanical Gardens	Hothouses
Bonn		Old Palm House
Bournemouth		Winter garden
Breslau	Botanical Garden	Conservatory
Bretton Hall, Yorkshire		Palm house
Brussels	Botanical Gardens	Tropical house
Brussels (Bouchot)	Jardin Botanique	Victoria regia house
Brussels (Laeken)	Royal Park	Winter garden, Serre Chapelle, Serre du Congo, Serre aux Palmiers
Budleigh Salterton, Devon	Bicton Gardens	Palm house
Buxton	Pavilion Gardens	Hothouse
Capesthorne Hall, Cheshire		Davenport Conservatory
Chatsworth, Derbyshire	Duke of Devonshire's estate	Hothouses, Great Conservatory, victoria regia house
Chiswick	Chiswick Gardens	Conservatory
Dresden	Pillnitz Castle Park	Palm house
Dublin	National Botanical Garden	Tropical house, New Palm House
Dublin	1865 Exhibition	Winter Palace
Edinburgh	Royal Botanical Garden	New Palm House
Enville Hall, Staffordshire		Conservatory
Florence	Orto Botanico	Palm house
Frankfurt am Main	Palm Garden	Flora
Glasgow	Botanical Gardens	Kibble Palace (Crystal Palace)
Glasgow Green	People's Palace	Winter garden
Göttingen	University Botanical Garden	Small conservatory
Grimston Park, Yorkshire		Winter garden

Hackney	Loddiges Nursery	Camellia and palm house
Hackney		Glasshouse with hemidome
Herrenhausen	Park Herrenhausen	Palm houses
Hluboká nad Vltavou (Frauenberg)	Schwarzenberg Castle	Winter garden
Hove, Sussex	Anthaeum	Winter Garden
Innsbruck	Botanical Garden	Palm house
Karlsruhe	Residenz	Conservatories
Kassel	Wilhelmshöhe	Great Conservatory
Killikee		Colonel White's conservatory
Cologne	Botanical Garden	Flora
Copenhagen	Botanical Garden	Palm house
Copenhagen	Villa Jacobsen, Carlsberg Brewery	Winter garden
Copenhagen	Ny Carlsberg Glyptotek	Winter garden
Cracow		Palm house
Langport, Somerset		Forcing house
Lednice (Eisgrub)	Liechtenstein Castle	Winter garden
Leeds	General Hospital	Winter garden
Leipzig		Crystal Palace
Leningrad (St. Petersburg)		Palm houses
Lille		Palais Rameau
Lisbon, Belém	Palais Burnay	Conservatory
Liverpool	Sefton Park	Palm house
London	Syon House	Great Conservatory
London		Pantheon Bazaar
London	Surrey Zoological Garden	Glass Menagerie
London	Regent's Park	Warm house, temperate house, winter garden of Royal Botanical Society
London	Royal Botanical Gardens	Conservatories, Architectural Conservatory, palm house, temperate house, victoria regia house
London	World Exhibition, 1851	Crystal Palace
London	Sydenham	Crystal Palace
London		Great Victorian Way (project)
London	Covent Garden	Floral Hall
London	Muswell Hill	Palace of the People (project)
London	Muswell Hill	Alexandra Palace
London	Brompton	Winter garden, kiosk
Lyndhurst		Conservatory
Lyon		Jardin d'Hiver
Lyon	Parc de la Tête d'Or	Great Conservatory
Madrid	Parque del Retiro	Palacio de Cristal

Magdeburg	Friedrich-Wilhelms-Garten	Palm house
Malmaison		Parc de la Malmaison
Meiningen	Ducal Park	Orangery
Munich	Royal Gardens	Conservatories
Munich	Old Botanical Garden	Conservatory, Glass Palace
Munich	Residenz	Winter gardens
Munich	Old Botanical Garden	Great Palm House
Paris	Jardin des Plantes	Conservatories
Paris	Champs-Elysées	Jardin d'Hiver
Paris	1855 World Exhibition	Hall
Paris	1900 World Exhibition	Garden Hall
Pau	Jardin Public	Winter garden
Pavia	Orto Botanico	Conservatory
Philadelphia	World Exhibition, 1896	Horticultural Hall
San Francisco		Conservatory
Sezincote	Indian Villa	Conservatory
Sheffield	Botanical Gardens	Glass Pavilion
Strasbourg	New Botanical Garden	Great Conservatory
Stuttgart-Hohenheim	Hohenheim Park	Iron Conservatory
Stuttgart-Berg	Villa Berg	Conservatory
Stuttgart		Wilhelma, conservatories
Stuttgart		Conservatories
Toronto	Allan Gardens	Conservatories
Tübingen	Old Botanical Garden	Great Conservatory
Warsaw	Lazienski Park	Orangery
Warsaw		Palm house
Vienna-Hietzing	Duke of Brunswick's gardens	Conservatory
Vienna-Penzing	Mayer Gardens	Forcing houses
Vienna-Schönbrunn	Schönbrunn Park	Conservatories, Great Palm House, Sundial House
Vienna	Burggarten	Old Winter Garden, New Winter Garden
Wollaton Hall, Nottinghamshire		Camellia house

Descriptions

Bayswater, near London

Bayswater House
Experimental Greenhouses (fig. 141)
architect: John Claudius Loudon
built ca. 1817–18
demolished

Loudon built these greenhouses on his estate, Bayswater House, in order to test his theory of curvilinear structures. Stimulated by Sir George Mackenzie's basic proposals of 1815 for a hemispherical glass-and-iron greenhouse, Loudon brought wrought iron to public notice in 1817 in his "Remarks on the Construction of Hothouses" and in 1818 in his "Sketches of Curvilinear Hothouses," in which he described wrought-iron sash bars as filigree space frames.

One of Loudon's theoretical aims was economy of construction; iron was expensive. He also wanted to maximize the transmission of light by using slender structural elements. The shape of the spherical or barrel-shaped curved roofs had the effect of causing the light rays to strike the glass surface perpendicularly as much as possible, depending on the position of the sun, so that only an insignificant amount of light was reflected. The light-transmission factor likewise led to the idea of placing the framework in the plane of the glass surface, thereby reducing the shadow cast by parts projecting into the interior.

In his sketches dated 1818, Loudon called on the experience he had gained from his Bayswater experiments. The glasshouses attached to his house were the first curvilinear iron structures built. As forerunners of all later glass-and-iron buildings of this type, these experimental buildings already had all the features of shell-like structures. The weight of the roof was supported by completely uniform structural members—the wrought-iron sash bars.

Loudon had settled in Bayswater, one mile west of London, in 1815. Alongside a masonry wall attached to the house and crowned with battlements he built greenhouses of various sizes and shapes, joined together and passing over a small bridge. As figure 141 suggests, it was Loudon's intention to test a variety of possible glasshouse designs and to pick out the most difficult structural details, such as the intersection of doubly curved surfaces or turning points in the ridge line of the vaults. Loudon used thirteen different types of beams and covered them with seven kinds of glazing. At the same time, he tested the possibilities of ventilation by sliding or skylight windows and the problems connected with the sealing and shadowing effects of glass surfaces.

It is assumed that Loudon erected his glasshouses in Bayswater with the help of his later partners, the structural ironwork firm of W. and D. Bailey of Holborn, London. Because this firm eventually collaborated with Loudon in the building of covered markets, schools, theaters, and churches, the Bayswater glasshouses can be considered prototypes for development work that Loudon already had in mind.

The Bayswater sketches also demonstrate Loudon's advanced ideas in the field of architectural aesthetics. Here, and later at Sezincote, he consciously restricted his engineering structures to simple geometric shapes.

References: Gloag 1970, pp. 45, 46; Loudon 1817, 1818.

141

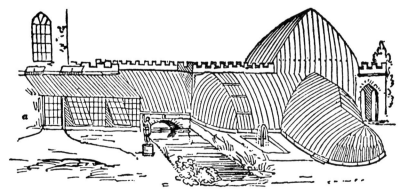

Belfast

Botanic Garden
Palm House (figs. 142–147, 471–477)

length: 175 feet
width of dome: 67 feet
height: 46 feet
architects: Charles Lanyon, Richard Turner
*builders: Hammersmith, Dublin; Richard Turner (wing);
Thomas Young, Edinburgh (dome)*
built 1839–40, 1853

Although it was not, this palm house gives the impression that it was built in a single operation. With the participation of Richard Turner of Dublin, the glass vault was erected in accordance with Loudon's principles. The helmetlike central dome, with its curvilinear wings, approached the ideal of glasshouse design that was being publicized at the time by McIntosh and Turner.[1]

The flowing transition between straight and curved glass surfaces, in combination with a ground plan in the shape of an elongated oval, created a domelike space that in its three-dimensional aspect had no counterpart at the time. The effect of the dome is heightened by the inclusion of a gallery, with semicircular elements projecting upward in a ring around the top of the dome. The whole outline of the building is decided by the simple rhythm of these elements. It appears as if the builders recognized and consciously decided upon such difficult matters as how to handle the intersection between the wings and the dome in a state of enthusiasm about the possibilities inherent in iron constructions. The overall shape, in which the plant element is brought into prominence through the flowing transitions between the surfaces, is underlined by the development of the detail of the load-bearing elements and by the ornamentation. The capitals and the girders do not have classical prototypes but are freely formed as wrought-iron garlands. It is probable that the dome was designed and built under the influence of Turner's palm house in Kew Gardens, although Turner was no longer directly involved in this undertaking.

The foundation stone of the palm house was laid in June 1839 by the Marquess of Donegal. In the following year the two wings, each 66 feet long, 20 feet high, and 20 feet wide, were completed at a cost of £1,400. The cast-iron parts and the structure were manufactured by Turner at his Hammersmith Works in Dublin. The original design put forward in 1843

by Charles Lanyon (later the director of the company) included a low central dome on a square base with a vertical front and two terminal domes at the ends of the wings (fig. 143). Lanyon's final (1853) design for the Palm House was significantly different from his original one. Instead of low square rooms with plane fronts which rose only a little above the wings, he placed a 46-foot-high elliptical dome with a minor axis of 46 feet and a major axis of 67 feet. This dome spanned the space between the two wings, and its front extended beyond the vanishing line of the wings (fig. 144).

Although the dome is different from that of the large palm house in Kew Gardens, completed by Turner in 1848, it is more like the Kew Gardens dome than Lanyon's original design. It is probable that Lanyon was influenced by the palm houses that Turner had built. The dome of the Belfast palm house was not built by Turner's company but by that of Thomas Young in Edinburgh. The hothouse was originally heated by two brickwork flues. Hotwater heating equipment and a "Cockey's Patent Boiler" were installed in 1862. New boilers were installed in 1871 and 1881. Before the central dome was built, the west wing served as a temperate house and the east wing as a hothouse. When the dome was built, tall palms could be put on display.

The palm house was built in three sections. The wings, built first, are 66 feet long and are like elongated glass corridors backed by a traditional-style masonry wall on the north. Simple cast-iron window frames form a low vertical wall on the south, resting on a sandstone base. Sash bars run up from this frame, curved at first, then straightening, to lean against the base of the dome. The sash bars are also supported in the middle by a purlin carried on filigree columns 2 inches in diameter (fig. 476). The structure, which shows the Loudon influence, does not however have the maturity of Loudon's buildings. It reveals a hierarchy in sash-bar size across various sections.

The central structure, added to the existing wings later, was made without seams. With its towering dome and bold forward projection, it is the dominant part of the building (figs. 145–147). The dome has a base formed by two semicircles corresponding to the widths of the wings, separated by a rectangular area. The wings lead around the dome and form a lower gallery. The frameworks made from individual members are also used as vertical walls and thus exhibit architectural competence. The curved sash bars terminate on this gallery, converging against an

142
Site plan, ca. 1851.

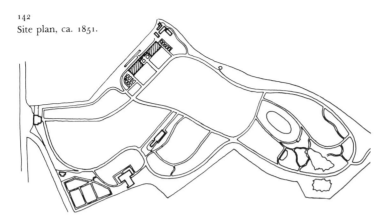

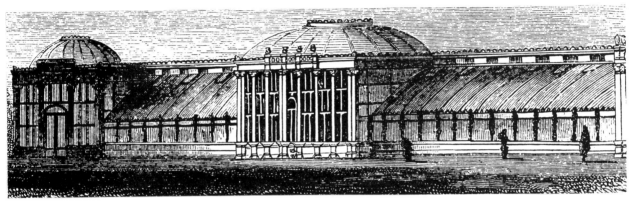

143
Design, 1843.
Woodcut.

interior horizontal iron ring supported on fourteen columns. A tambour above this cast-iron ring, similar to that around the lower framework, carries the dome proper. This has a pointed apex supporting a barrel vault which is terminated with two quarter-calottes. The whole vault is held together by ties in a lantern ring. As in the wings, but more pronounced, the sash bars here are arranged in order of magnitude according to their load-bearing function. Every eighth sash bar in the gallery, and every sixth in the dome, is reinforced (figs. 471–474). This construction method, with the radially narrowing areas of glass, gives the outside of the building the elegant appearance of plantlike shapes flowing together. The sash-bar arrangement made possible the development of a rosette which marks the apex of each quarter-dome. The structural principle works here, as in all important works of architecture, simultaneously as an ornamental principle. The sash bars form a web which by its graphic effect limits the space and creates an artificial sky (fig. 471). The glass-and-iron roof of the palm house is made of manually worked wrought iron, like earlier constructions.

Built before the large exhibition buildings, this palm house represents an intermediate stage in Loudon's space frames and hierarchic frameworks. At the same time, this building pointed the way to the great iron constructions of later decades in which the flowing formal language of the structure was derived from the relationship between the static forces and also emerged as an aesthetic principle.

The palm house is extant but very dilapidated.

Source: library of Belfast Botanic Garden.

References: McCracken 1971; McIntosh 1853; *The Gardener's Chronicle*, August 1874, June 1875, January 1898, December 1904.

144
Overall view of Belfast Botanic Garden, ca. 1853. Woodcut.

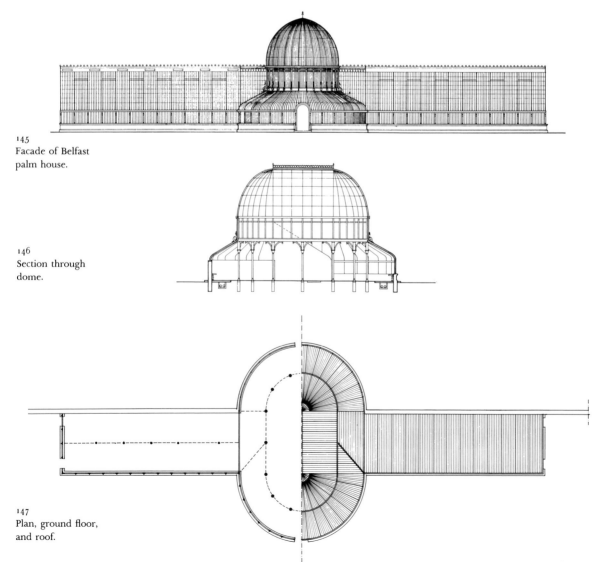

145
Facade of Belfast palm house.

146
Section through dome.

147
Plan, ground floor, and roof.

Berlin

Pfaueninsel
Palm House (figs. 149, 150, 478, 479)

length: 109 feet
width: 46 feet
height: 46 feet
architect: Albert Dietrich Schadow (assisted by Karl Friedrich Schinkel)
built 1829–1831
burned down in 1880

The palm house on the Pfaueninsel, a wood-and-iron building, was one of the first large hothouses in Germany. It combined a building style that had originated with the orangeries and the large, simple shapes and surfaces of Classicism. The delicately formed glass front, in the shape of antique orders, was assembled from a linear framework of narrow columns. The garden artist Friedrich Ludwig von Sckell had worked on this architectural expression of form during the building of the hothouse in the Old Botanical Garden in Munich in 1820. The palm house by Johann Conrad Bromeis in Kassel (1822) is also in this tradition.

Schinkel, who had an important part in the building of this palm house, preferred to use large glass surfaces supported only by the framework of sash bars and columns. His designs for a warehouse in Unter den Linden and his theater at the Gendarmenmarkt are examples of this.

The oriental forms used in the Pfaueninsel palm house were played against the rigorous objectivity of the building. A tower structure topped by an onion-shaped cupola and an internally located pagoda were evidence of an exotic world which expressed itself in oriental ornamentation as well as through the palm trees themselves. The capitals and bases of the columns blended in with the plant kingdom. The use of oriental forms in hothouse buildings is of English origin, as the buildings of John Nash and Humphrey Repton show.

The palm house on the Pfaueninsel was a prototype for future hothouses in Germany. Georg Ludwig Friedrich Laves adopted in his palm house at Herrenhausen (1846–1849) not only the spatial form but also the structure of the facade. The framework front of the large cubic glass-and-iron building in the Old Botanical Garden in Berlin (1859; fig. 480) was in this style.

The Pfaueninsel is an island on the Havel at the southern end of the Wannsee. In 1793, Friedrich Wilhelm II chose this place to lay out a park based on the English style. In 1822 it was turned into a zoolog-

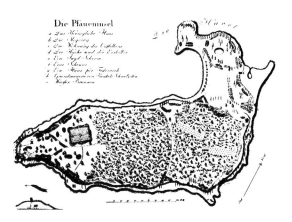

148
Site plan. Copper engraving by L. Humbert, 1810.

ical garden on the advice of the zoologist Martin Hinrich Carl Lichtenstein. The zoo was surrounded by a romantic landscaped garden in the 1820s. In the effort to create a rural scene, romantic buildings (a ruined castle, a mausoleum, a farmhouse, a gentleman's residence, etc.) were built, partly after sketches by Schinkel. Layouts of this kind, which after the French Revolution sprang up all over Europe, were a kind of refuge of the nobility from the harsh reality of politics.

When the plant lover Foulchiron found himself compelled to sell his large palm collection, which was considered to be one of the best in Europe, the director of the Berlin Botanical Gardens advised the king of the unique opportunity to acquire it. The giant trees were bought up, and the building of the palm house started immediately.

The crown prince suggested that a marble pagoda which an English general had brought back with him from Bengal be set up in the park. On Schinkel's advice, the design and execution of the project was handed over to Albert Dietrich Schadow. The original intention was to site the pagoda separately, but in the later design it was incorporated in the palm house.

According to Pett (1966), "No European garden of that time had such large specimens on display, and in general the importance of this collection lay much less in the number of species than in the size of the specimens present."[2] Alexander von Humboldt expressed the opinion that he felt himself to be transported back into the primeval forests of the Orinoco whenever he was in the Pfaueninsel palm house. The painting by Karl Blechen (fig. 478) shows the grandiose effect that arose from the unity of architectural and plant forms.

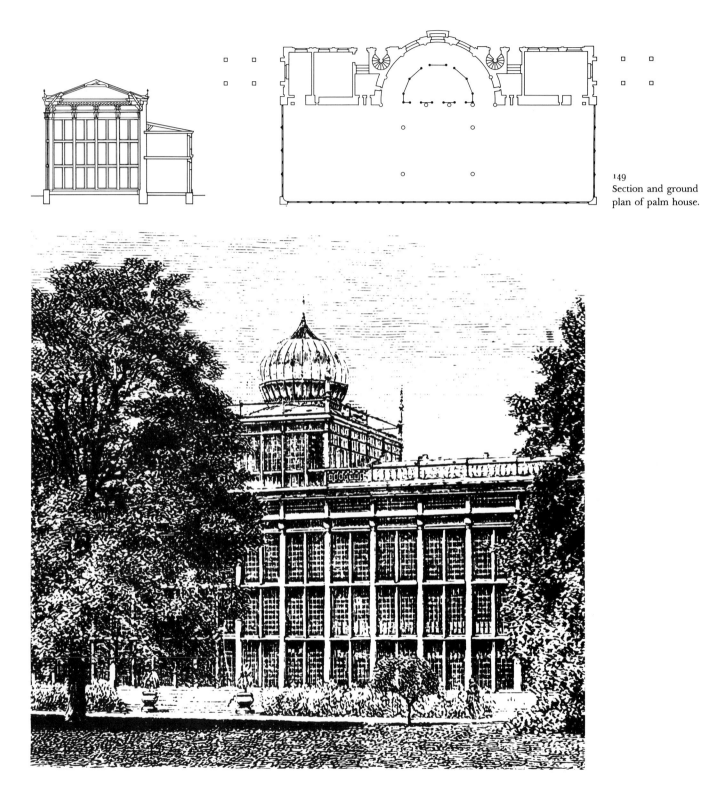

149
Section and ground
plan of palm house.

150
Front of palm house.
Drawing from pho-
tograph by Hans
Junecke.

The plant house had a rectangular base and a lean-to roof at a gentle angle. Three sides were formed by large continuous glass surfaces; the rear side was masonry, with a semicircular niche and two lower lateral extensions. A towerlike glazed structure capped by an onion-shaped cupola was put on the main central part. The large semicircular niche accommodated the pagoda and formed a kind of gallery.

The building was 109 feet long, 46 feet wide, and 35 feet high up to the lower edge of the ridge of the lower roof. There were 4,290 square feet of glass in the main building. The masonry on the north wall and the corner pillars stabilized the framework of the facade, which was built of wooden columns reaching up to the height of the eaves. They were reinforced by connecting ribs. The masonry walls and the wooden columns supported the roof trusses, the central part of which was in turn supported by four cast-iron columns and by horizontal braced girders. The roof trusses were inside the skin in both wings of the main building and were provided with large window areas between the rafters. The columns that closed off the apse were made of cast iron and supported the middle and upper floors by filigree iron arches. The columns and the masonry pillars were decorated with capitals, both inside and outside the building. Above the roof cornice, richly decorated cast-iron latticework surrounded the building.

Source: Staatliche Schlösser und Gärten Verwaltung, Schloss Charlottenburg, Berlin.

References: Poensgen 1950; Pett 1966; Breuer 1923; Hinz 1937, pp. 44–46.

Berlin-Glienicke

Orangery and Forcing House

architect: Ludwig Persius (assisted by Karl Friedrich Schinkel)
built 1839
destroyed in 1914; now being rebuilt

A domed glass-and-iron forcing house combined with an orangery was an important feature of Glienicke Park, which was created by the combined efforts of Peter Joseph Lenne, Prince Hermann Pückler-Muskau, Friedrich Wilhelm IV, Schinkel, and others during the first half of the nineteenth century. In contrast with the park's romantic buildings, the forcing house and orangery was most modern. In shape and construction it had an affinity with the newest and most technically advanced of British hothouse buildings of the period: Loudon's vaulted glasshouses.

The forcing house and orangery were incorporated relatively late into the park. The first event here was the 1814 acquisition of the Klein-Glienicke estate by Prince Karl August of Hardenberg, who two years later gave the garden designer Lenné the commission to make a park in the vicinity of the castle. With the purchase of the estate by Prince Carl of Prussia in 1824, Schinkel was entrusted with the structural repair and Lenné with the job of changing the whole estate into a continuous landscaped park. Prince Hermann introduced his ideas into the design via Lenné, and Carl's brother Friedrich Wilhelm IV added to Schinkel's work some of his own designs. A series of design sketches by Friedrich Wilhelm IV and Schinkel were concerned with the plan of the orangery, the architecture of which was to be in harmony with the main front of the castle. With these sketches in mind, Schinkel's student Ludwig Persius designed the orangery in the form of an elongated masonry building with a ridge roof. The southeast wall of this was interrupted by five-sided glazed bow windows between the columns. The arcades corresponded with the coachyard adjoining the castle. Transverse to the orangery, at the southwest end, there was a low forcing house with a curvilinear glass-and-iron roof, terminated by small towers at both ends and backed by a masonry wall. The wrought-iron space frame of the forcing house, with closely spaced narrow sash bars similar to those used by Loudon (fig. 132a) but with a double rebate, was designed for double glazing (fig. 134a). The cross-section of the forcing house was a flat parabola to allow maximum illumination, with the base of the framework resting on a masonry foundation at the front and at the rear on cast-iron brackets projecting from the masonry. The building was destroyed at the start of World War I. Reconstruction in the original design was started in connection with the comprehensive rebuilding of Glienicke Park on the occasion of the bicentenary of Schinkel's birth in 1981.

References: Sievers 1955, vol. 3; *Zehlendorfer Chronik*, second enlarged edition (1979).

Berlin

Wilhelmstrasse
Winter Garden of "Palais Prinz Albrecht"
(figs. 151, 151a)
length: 116 feet
width: 18 feet
architect: Karl Friedrich Schinkel
built 1832
demolished 1873

This "winter garden," also called an orangery, was
built on the ground floor on the south front of the
Palace. Situated on a terrace in front of the building,
it opened inward via a straight stairway to the private apartments of the prince and the princess.

Two rows of slender columns held up wooden
beams running along the length of the building and
supporting a lean-to roof, the lower side of which
was attached to the postwork of a continuous front
window. The "winter garden" was terminated on the
west side by a glass semicircular apse which, placed
on a higher level, formed a terrace reached by steps
leading directly from the garden.

Reference: Sievers 1954, vol. 2, pp. 167–171.

Berlin-Schöneberg

Royal Botanical Garden, Potsdamer Strasse

Hothouse (figs. 480, 481)
The Royal Botanical Garden in Potsdamer Strasse
was laid out in 1679 to replace the former Palatine
Hop Garden. Kind Friedrich I altered the layout to
create pleasure gardens with forcing houses and an
orangery. Friedrich Wilhelm I turned it into an
"apothecary garden" and placed it under the supervision of the Sozietät der Wissenschaften. Under
Friedrich II, the "herb garden" served the common
purposes of botany, experimental physics, and medicine, but it deteriorated during the Seven Years' War
as the result of financial troubles. Later it was again
extended and reequipped, but it fell into decay
through mismanagement. A reorganization plan approved in 1801 provided for the extension of the Botanical Garden for the cultivation of useful plants for
factories and manufacturers—particularly herbs for
dyestuffs. Carl Ludwig Willdenow put the plan into
effect and was able during the war against Napoleon
to make progress with the garden and keep it in
good order. With Willdenow in charge, a turning

151
Interior view of win-
ter garden of "Palais
Prinz Albrecht."
Engraving.

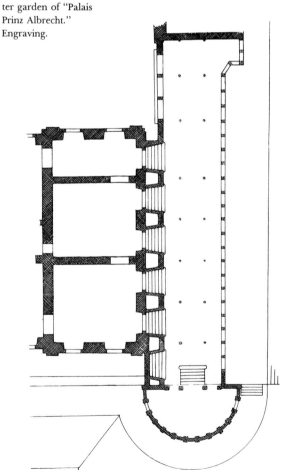

151a
Ground plan of win-
ter garden of "Palais
Prinz Albrecht."

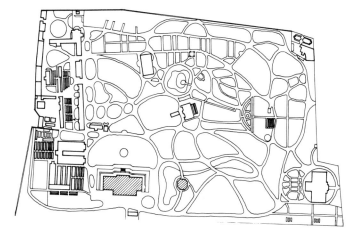

152
Site plan of Royal
Botanical Garden,
Berlin-Schöneberg,
1896.

point in the garden's further development was reached. He saw to it that the 1,200 plant types already in the garden were increased to 7,700.

In 1809 the administration of the garden was incorporated with the newly founded University of Berlin. From then on, the garden developed continuously. In 1855 the area of the garden was significantly increased on the west side in order to install there a large palm house and a comprehensive arboretum. In 1879 a plant-geography unit was added. A botanical center for the colonies was incorporated into the garden in 1891.[3]

By 1897 the garden had become ringed with blocks of flats and was too small, so it was removed to the Dahlem district in the southwest corner of Fichtenberg bei Steglitz. The Royal Botanical Garden, bounded by the Potsdamer Strasse, the Elsholzstrasse, the Grünerwaldstrasse, and the Pallasstrasse, had by 1896 numerous hothouses in which 10,000 plant species and 40,000 specimens were cultivated. With a total of 19,000 plant species, the Berlin Botanical Garden was surpassed only by those at St. Petersburg and Kew. The hothouses were established one by one to meet increasing needs. Noteworthy are the buildings erected to Schinkel's designs: the palm house (1821), the orchid house (1863), the fern house (1874), and particularly the Great Palm House (1857–1859) and the victoria regia house (1882).[4]

The building operations in the Botanical Garden were planned and managed for 30 years, from 1843 to 1873, by Carl David Bouché. Before his appointment as Inspector of the Botanical Garden in 1843, Bouché was an assistant in the garden and then the head gardener on the Pfaueninsel. In the palm house built by Schinkel and Schadow he gained his basic experience in the breeding and cultivation of tropical and subtropical plants and their dependence on the construction, lighting, heating, and ventilation of the

plant house. As Inspector of the Botanical Garden he found—as Paxton had at Chatsworth—a field of activity for the development of hothouses. In a series of experiments, in which he took into account the experience of British hothouse construction, he attempted to find the ideal constructional and spatial form for iron-frame hothouses. His special interests, besides wrought-iron braced girders, were cast iron and the possibility of erecting completely prefabricated buildings. He compiled the knowledge he obtained in the practice of gardening into a fundamental theoretical work, *Bau und Einrichtung der Gewachshäuser* (building and equipping of hothouses), in which he also put forward numerous projects and model designs in addition to plans and detailed drawings of the Great Palm House (1857–1859) and the victoria regia house (1863). This book, published posthumously in 1886 by his son Julius Bouché, Inspector of Gardens in the Botanical Garden of Bonn, was, with Neumann's *Glasshouses* (1842), one of the most important standard works on the problems of the nineteenth-century hothouses.

Source: library of Botanical Garden, Berlin-Dahlem.

References: Zentralblatt der Bauverwaltung, 1882, 2, p. 133; *Architektenverein zu Berlin*, 1877, pp. 165 ff.; 1896, vol. 2, pp. 252 ff.; Ring 1884, vol. 2; Bouché 1886, pp. 15, 120, plates XXII–XXIV; *Jahrbuch des Kgl. Botanischen Gartens Berlin*, 1895, vol. 1, pp. 34 ff.; Timler and Zepernick 1978, pp. 3–41.

Palm House (fig. 153)
architect: Karl Friedrich Schinkel
built 1821

Schinkel built the first palm house of the Royal Botanical Garden in the form of a truncated cone, the top of which was covered by a nearly flat glass roof. The supporting framework of wooden planks formed the space frame together with the glass below it. The two entrances and the two chimneys of the heating plant were placed symmetrically along the axis. The low cruciform base was of masonry. The total height of this palm house was 33 feet, and the diameter was 43 feet. The simple geometric form echoed the architecture of the French Revolution, such as the drastically simplistic cenotaphs and memorials by Etienne-Louis Boullée, Claude Nicolas Ledoux, and Jean-Jacques Lequeu.

The conical shape guaranteed the plants uniform illumination from all sides, and the total glass surface had a more favorable ratio to the internal area than with rectangular buildings.

Ten years later, Loudon designed hothouses for the Birmingham Botanical Gardens that resembled this one in their three-dimensional geometry.

153
Woodcut of palm
house, Berlin-
Schöneberg.

The rectangular pattern of the external space frame was, in spite of its circular shape, an anticipation of the facade structures of the palm house built later on the Pfaueninsel (fig. 150).

As a result of dampness in its timbers, this palm house was replaced after only 9 years.[5]

Great Palm House (figs. 154–156, 159)
length: 178 feet
width: 57 feet
height: 57 feet
architect: Carl David Bouché
builder: Gustav Herter and Nietz
built 1857–1859
total cost: 405,000 marks
demolished in 1907

The Great Palm House consisted of a glass-and-iron main building for the plants and a masonry annex at the rear containing a staircase, a workshop, and residential quarters. The main front faced east. The ground plan of the main building formed a long rectangle with a central section projecting to the east. The space form was determined by pure cubic forms. Square wings, markedly lower, adjoined the cube-shaped central part. The pure cubic building elements stood out clearly because the outer parts of the building, the perpendicular glass surfaces and the simple glass lean-to roof, were all built without orna-

mentation. With its simple combination of glass squares, this palm house was a notable example of early-nineteenth-century objectivity.

The palm house stood on a terrace-shaped earth embankment that raised it above its surroundings. A wide, axially placed exterior staircase led to the main entrance.

The 57-foot-high central structure stood on a square base with 57-foot sides and with two wings 33 feet high, 60 feet long, and 57 feet wide. The covered surface area of the glasshouse was 10,186 square feet. A double row of tubular cast-iron columns 6 inches in diameter, placed 4 feet apart along the external walls, formed the core of the space frame, which was reinforced by galleries which surrounded and divided the interior.

Cast-iron and wrought-iron braced girders 2½ feet deep supported the roof, dividing it into a series of separate ridge roofs surrounded by a gallery. Wrought-iron braced girders (48 feet long in the central section and 43 feet long in the wings) spanned the glass hall, and 8½-foot cast-iron braced girders formed the spans. The tubular columns stood on and were bolted into a low masonry plinth which surrounded the glass-and-iron roof.

The outer row of columns was glazed on the outside by stout windows with ventilating panes sliding in the sashes, and on the inside by windows in wooden sashes. The strong roof glazing consisted of

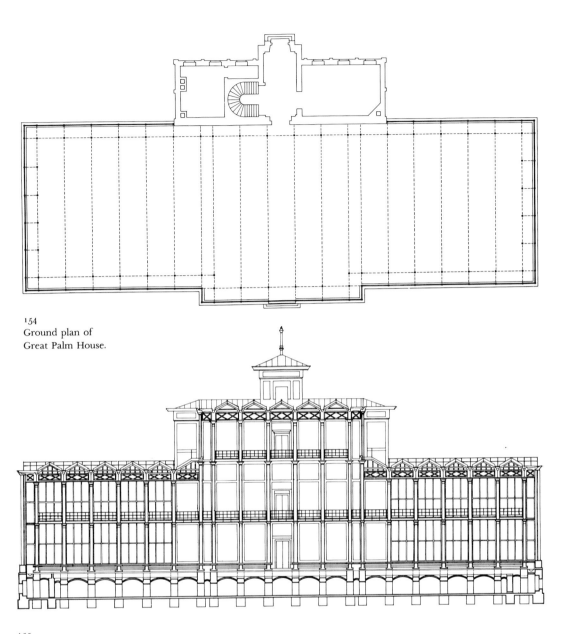

154
Ground plan of
Great Palm House.

155
Section.

156
Structural details of
roof.

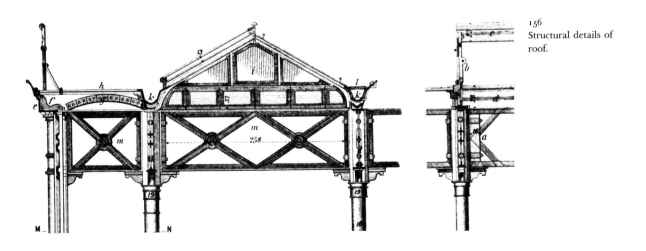

half-inch-thick plate glass reinforced with wire. Rain-water from the roof was collected in double cast-iron gutters lying in the long braced girders, and was led down the inside of the hollow columns into drains in the ground, and from there into storage tanks in the cellar. From here the water was drawn to spray the plants. The cellar, which was covered with a brick-work vault and surrounded by a wide banked terrace, contained the water-heating and steam plant.

The cast-iron parts of the space frame were standardized on the model of Paxton's Crystal Palace. The supports consisted of individual columns bolted together and separated by connecting pieces for the joints to the braced girders. Bolted-on cast-iron brackets served as abutments for galleries and joists. The master girders that carried the lean-to roof were made of iron section and flat rolled steel bars riveted together. The girders along the outside were also made of cast iron (fig. 156).

The Great Palm House was demolished in 1907 during the dissolution of the Old Botanical Garden. A few of the cast-iron columns were used again in a pergola in the utility yard of the New Botanical Garden at Dahlem, and are to be found there today. Figures 480 and 481 show the Great Palm House shortly before its demolition.

The heating system of the Great Palm House was the product of long years of trials and experiments by C. J. Bouché. There was a double installation. On the one hand, the palm house was heated directly by hot water provided by two boilers. The eighteen copper tubes of this system, each 4 inches in diameter, were placed in the floor of the glasshouse and behind the masonry base; from here fresh air warmed by the hot-water system could be brought in via channels which could be shut if necessary. On the other hand, there was steam heating. Two boilers working at a pressure of 5 atmospheres heated the floor of the palm house, which was covered with a 2-foot layer of soil. By opening the vents located in the top of the vault, it was possible to deliver a part of the heat stored in the cellar directly to the atmosphere of the palm house and during the winter it was filled with warm air in this way twice a day. In the morning the temperature was raised to 12°C by the water heating, and on the release of steam to 15–17°C. This maximum temperature was retained until 3 P.M. but in very cold weather it sank to 12°C at 7 P.M. When the temperature dropped to 10°C, the hot-water heating, which was in operation for an average of only 8 hours daily, was turned on again. According to Bouché: "At the start it appeared to be a very risky venture to build a large glass-iron house of that kind in such a northerly latitude as Berlin,

but in fact the installations have proved so satisfactory that even in the most severe cold there has been no difficulty in maintaining the temperature required during the day and at night, and in fact without excessive use of fuel—a demonstration therefore that even in northerly climates the iron structure can be considered advantageous for hothouses."[6]

Victoria Regia House (figs. 157, 158, 160)

external diameter: 50 1/2 feet
height: 17 feet
architect: Schulze
built 1882
demolished 1907

This victoria regia house was built by Bauinspektor Schulze to replace the first such house, built in 1852 with the collaboration of C. D. Bouché, which had fallen into decay. The site chosen, which lay to the south of the Great Palm House, was slightly raised and was partly surrounded by water. It took its shape from the type of victoria regia house common throughout Europe. The central structure was in the form of a flattish dome, and the circular pool for the plants was in the center. The basic form, a regular decagon, was covered by a dome-shaped glass-and-iron structure, which had its foundations in a 3-foot-high masonry wall. An iron retaining beam was fitted to take up the lateral thrust of the structure. The ribs in the dome were made of 6-inch-deep rolled iron I beams, which formed a parabola that changed over to a linear profile toward the top. The ribs were held together at the top by a U-section ten-sided ring. The lantern was built on top of that. The

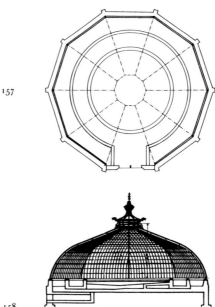

157

158

159
Great Palm House,
Berlin-Schöneberg.

160
Victoria regia house,
Berlin-Schöneberg.
Engraving.

ribs were reinforced horizontally by a system of purlins made of 4-inch-wide iron bar. The framework of
curved parallel iron glazing bars placed on this load-
bearing structure held overlapping panes of Rhenish
"doppelglas," 12 inches wide and mostly 16–20
inches long.

The building had an excavated pond of water for
the victoria regia in its center, and a ring-shaped
pool around the outside for small tropical water
plants. Copper pipes were laid around the wall of
the pond to heat the water. There were louvers in
the lantern and ten ventilating slots above the base
wall. Figure 160 illustrates the spatial effect of this
compact structure made of thousands of glass panes.
The cost was 18,200 marks, of which the iron frame
accounted for 4,200 marks. The work was carried out
by the firm of Schlieder & Schmidt, of Leipzig.

Berlin-Moabit

Villa Borsig
Winter Garden and Forcing House

length: 115 1/2 feet
width: 33 feet
architect: Heinrich Strack
built 1850
demolished 1911

August Borsig's winter garden, situated in a narrow
space between his residence and his factory, is an
expression of the social image the industrial magnate
presented to the public in the nineteenth century.
Borsig, one of the most successful early industrialists
in Germany and the founder of locomotive production on the Continent, had built for himself in Alt-
Moabit in 1848 the first factory combined with a
mansion in Berlin. "August Borsig, born in 1804 in
Breslau, learned the carpenter's trade there from
1820 to 1823, then went to Berlin and from 1823 to
1825 was at the Royal Industrial Institute founded by
Beuth. After that he entered into practical developments in machinery building, which by now had
taken up the whole interest of the young carpenter,
in the Egel iron foundry at the Oranienburg Gate.
He obtained promotion there and by 1827 was entrusted with a permanent position as a factor. In
1837 he likewise opened at the Oranienburg Gate a
machinery building plant with fifty workers. He very
soon started up there the rapidly developing construction of locomotives. In 1847 he founded as a
second undertaking his own ironworks at Moabit,
which were opened in 1848."[7]

On land previously occupied by a gunpowder mill,
on the bank of the River Spree, Borsig had built a
new factory and a grandiose villa residence by the
architect Heinrich Strack (1805–1880). A park laid out
by Peter Joseph Lenné separated the factory from
the villa. Joined to the left-hand corner pavilion of
the villa (which comprised the salon and the living
rooms), and directly accessible via a staircase, was
the cast-iron-and-glass winter garden as a colonnaded hall, which at its side was joined to a cast-
iron-frame forcing house (fig. 161).

At the start of the twentieth century, the location
of the factory in the middle of the city, which in the
meanwhile had enveloped it, proved untenable. With
the relocation of the factory on the outskirts of Berlin, the mansion was given up.[8]

The hothouses of Villa Borsig, which were highly
regarded in their time, were built with cast-iron
frame parts made in the Borsig factory. Whereas the
winter garden was built as a masonry colonnaded
hall with skylights and large window openings in ac-
cord with the Renaissance style of the residence, the
forcing house and the large palm house were made
of iron and glass. The forcing house had a long glass
front which opened onto the garden. This front comprised slender cast-iron columns at uniform intervals
and had a richly decorated cast-iron frieze with figured reliefs in the form of genies. The glass lean-to
roof was constructed on the British ridge-and-furrow
principle. The palm house was located in the park,
detached from the house. With its high cubic shape
and glass lean-to ends, it is reminiscent of the Great
Palm House in the Old Botanical Garden in Berlin.
All the buildings were provided with hot condensed
steam from the steam engines in the factory. "The
warm water was disposed of into two ponds in the
garden and this made it possible to plant out of
doors the magnificent tropical water plants like Nelumbium (lotus), Nymphae, Limnocharis, Papyrus, etc.
in the open ground of these small flooded areas, and
they flourished in an undescribable way, which they
were unable to do any more luxuriantly in their na-
tive lands. They formed scenes which no European
gardens had hitherto exhibited."[9] The plants for the
palm house were procured from the most varied
gardens in Europe. An expedition by H. Harsten to
Colombia offered the opportunity to obtain scarce
tree ferns. In 1852 a special glasshouse was built to
house the victoria regia.

Neumeyer comments: "The botanical interests and
the hobbies of the manufacturer and his rich collection of exotic fauna were noticed with appreciation
by the Berlin public. The dream of the countryside
becomes tangible to the occupier of such an estab-

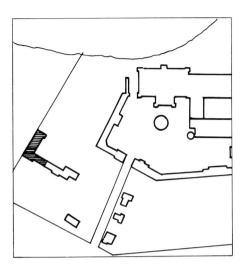

161
Site plan, ca. 1896.

162
Borsig factory with
villa, winter garden,
and forcing houses.
Engraving, ca. 1883.

lishment; public recognition and indirectly therefore publicity for the name of Borsig beyond the world of industrial production confirmed his status. The manufacturer appeared as a guardian and lord of nature simultaneously: as a guardian in that he took it into his care; as lord of nature in respect of his background of production methods which first of all made it possible to dispose of his power over nature by transplanting hitherto unknown and exotic plants from the tropics and the rest of the world. That this 'hobby' of Borsig was more than just that is proved by the fact that his hothouses were open to the public on regular occasions. The gardens were part of a process which would be described today as 'public relations.' "[10]

References: Neumeyer 1973, pp. 15–19; Martius 1965, pp. 262 ff.; *Die Gartenflora*, 1894, 43, pp. 4–12.

Berlin-Charlottenburg

Flora (figs. 163–168, 492, 493)
overall length: 396 feet
overall width: 270 feet
architects: Hubert Stier, Johannes Otzen
engineers: H. and O. Greiner
built 1871–1873
demolished 1902

The Berlin flora, which consisted of a public recreation center and a palm house, was the third establishment of its kind in German. Earlier floras had been established in Cologne (1864) and Frankfurt (1869). Of these three, the Berlin flora was not only the most ornamental and costly but also the largest in terms of internal space. Its assembly rooms had no equal in the whole of Germany. Brought into existence via a joint stock company, it was a typical product of the "Gründerjahre," the years of reckless financial speculation that followed the Franco-German War of 1871. Not until the expansion of capital and employment in Berlin in the 1870s did the social basis for such buildings as the Flora exist. Palm houses became a matter for joint stock companies, and as part of the entertainment industry became involved in producing a profitable return on the capital invested.

   The building site (fig. 163) was the former Eckhardtstein Park, close to the Charlottenburg castle gardens. The flora arose on the eastern corner of the site, because here a raised piece of ground could be used for "an imposing position for the building" and "gave the opportunity for the construction of ter-

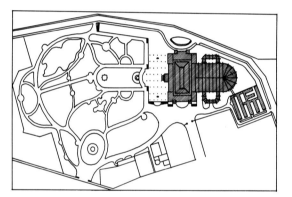

163
Site plan.

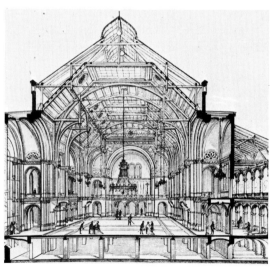

164
Perspective section through festival hall.

races."[11] Moreover, there was here a firm building foundation just below the surface. The main front of the building faced east.

As with the floras in Cologne and Frankfurt, there was an attempt here to combine a palm house, an extensive promenade-and-concert garden, and banquet rooms. But whereas in the Cologne flora the palm house also served as a banquet room, following the example of the Frankfurt Flora, here the banquet room and the palm house were "two distinct buildings connected only by doors and transparent glass walls, each treated according to the practical and technical aspects appropriate to it."[12] The building was divided into two parts by building it with two axes at right angles to each other and differentiating the two parts more distinctly than in the Cologne example.

Banquet Hall

A large hall formed the heart of the banquet building. Designated for concerts, it was also suited for festive gatherings of every kind. The interior space was one of the longest, not only in Berlin, but among halls generally at that time. The 9-foot-wide galleries that adjoined the banquet hall proper opened toward the banquet hall through archways, the dimensions of which thereby increased the actual dimensions between the outer walls to 98 feet in width and 174 feet in length.

The relationship between the palm house and the long hall was crucial for the architectural development of the latter. This led to the idea of dividing up the space of the hall by using a glass partition of the greatest possible dimensions. It was made 25 feet wide and 46 feet high. In addition, the floor of the hall was raised as much as possible above that of the palm house, so that it formed an 8-foot-high terrace in front of the room from which wide staircases led down on both sides to the palm house. The layout of the large opening gave the architecture of the hall the motif of an arcade setting of three equal-size archways. This arrangement simplified the positioning of the private boxes that were built into a second story, above the gallery. There was further seating space between the large archways, and between the columns there were individual boxes with specially constructed balconies in front. There were also two large archways situated on both sides of the hall. From one of these the musicians' gallery was built out into the hall; on the opposite side was a box for the imperial family. Beside the long wall facing the park was an open hall 135 feet long and 18 feet

wide. This hall, which obtained light from the palm house and looked out toward the gardens, was also provided with a skylight (fig. 493).

Concerning the aesthetic form, the architect Stier noted:

For the aesthetic appearance of the building that primary intention has been decisive which I previously applied to other commissions, but particularly my designs for the German Parliament building. Thus I have endeavored to follow modern architecture, namely not to build on the basis of a single style of my own choice taken from the series of the historical developments of the art, but on the basis of this overall development as a unity, of all matters of those two lines of style, which each for itself and each in its type in the history of building to the present, reached the most individualistic and highest development—the Gothic and the Renaissance. In this work also there is a combination between the Gothic principle for the structural base and the proportions and the decoration of the Renaissance. At the start of this design work the help of such a talented representative of the Hannover Gothic School as Herr Otzen was needed in these efforts. I am very grateful for help with aesthetic aspects, particularly from the Berlin School and its Renaissance specialists. The combination of Gothic and Renaissance should also be recognizable in the basic layout of this hall, which combines a ceiling like that of Gothic town halls with masonry work similar to that in the Rhenish thermal bath establishments. The new building follows quite closely, at least in its dimensions, the sizes of the prototypes quoted. The exterior of the building is made in brickwork following the monument principle of the Middle Ages, . . . and its detailing is in keeping with the nature of the material used, unimpeded as far as possible, i.e. by avoidance of the large architectural elements which can only be copied by using sandstone blocks. The character of the building portrayed here has permitted the lively use of colorful tile patterns and the polychromatic treatment of all individual parts suitable for the purpose. A light yellow tile provides the basic tone for the masonry, the colored patterning is kept to a dull red.[13]

Palm House

Stier described the palm house (figs. 165, 166, 168, 492) as follows:

The palm house is a building which primarily allows enough space for the display of a tropical scene of plants and landscape, a requirement for form and construction which determined from the start the essential parts. A wide open space had to be created without breaking it up in any way with columns or abutments, and having its surrounding walls constructed so that light and sunshine could enter from all sides with the least possible hindrance. This had to be an iron-and-glass structure of the simplest and most natural form in order to meet these stipulations. A width of 37.6 m between the columns was in fact attained without any special difficulty. The length of the building was partly governed by the terrain, and after that by the chosen distances

165
Ground plan of
flora.

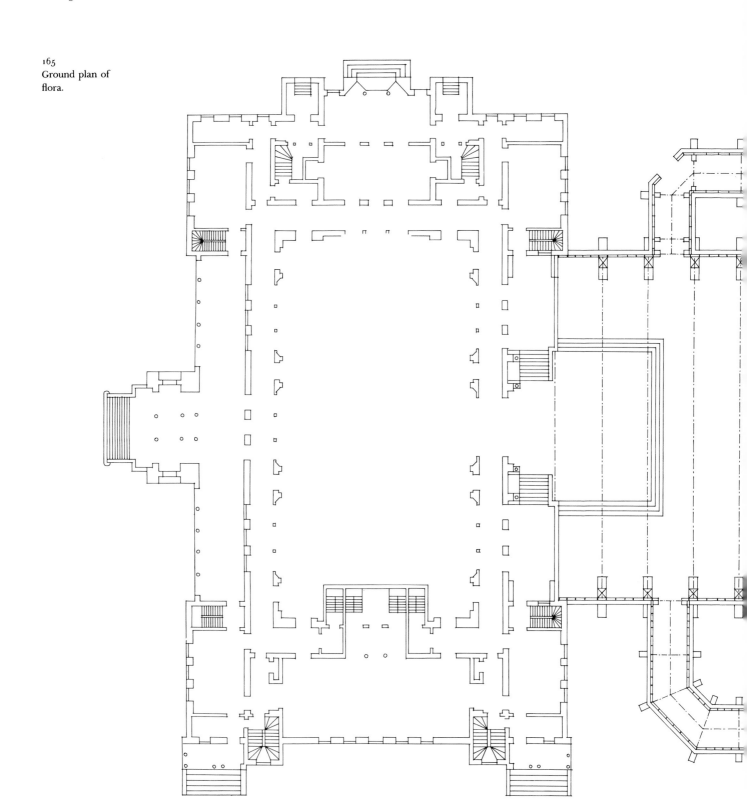

166
Section through
palm house.

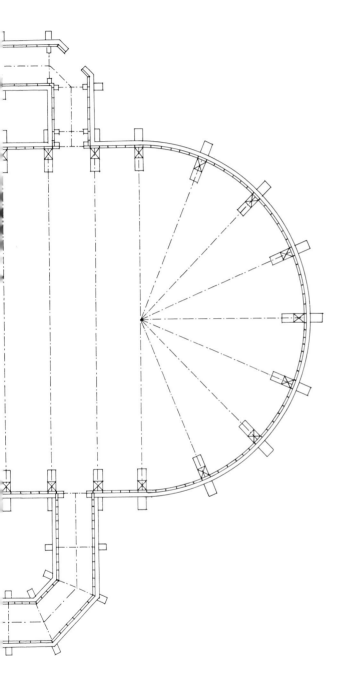

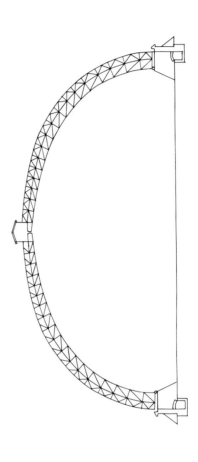

167
Interior view of
palm house, 1871 de-
sign. Woodcut.

between the columns and the ribs. The distance between
ribs was chosen as 5.64 m; nine rib assemblies are arranged
to make a total length of 50.7 m. On the east side there is
a terminating hemidome, so that the total length of the
building comes to 69.5 m. The building specification called
for an attempt to produce an aesthetic effect by the choice
and the detailing of the ironwork. The size of the building
and its high basic cost did not lend themselves to any richly
decorative embellishment. Whether that could have been
carried out successfully remains doubtful, because any decoration of that type would never have been able to compete
with the plant decoration, and would always have been detrimental [to]the latter, or even damaging. The aesthetic aspect had accordingly to limit itself to simple and distinct
arrangements of the structure itself, and to make a satisfactory space based on the same. The engineers W. and O.
Greiner, who originated the design, detailing, and costing of
the building, have taken this factor into account.

As a basis for the assessment of the weight of the cross-
members and ribs the builders had available for study the
bills of quantities for the materials used in the prototype chosen, the Berlin railway station, which was built some time
before the start of this work, and which was only slightly
smaller. The stipulation that the open space should not be
impaired in any way by tie beams led to the use of the
hinged girder roof with the ends of the girders having their
abutments on solid masonry columns. Aesthetic reasons were
the controlling factors in the choice of the profile of the ribs.
These start with a parabolic curve which changes over to a
linear sector at the upper end. All the longitudinal joints

were located above the ribs so that the shape of the latter
could stand out quite clearly and unimpaired; the same
considerations moreover were applied in the mounting of the
double-glazed skin in such a way that the outer glass layer
rests on the upper flanges of the girders, while the inner
glass layer is suspended from the lower flanges. Diagonal
joints have been avoided throughout, so that the interior
space essentially forms a barrel vault carried only by the
symmetrically repeated main ribs. There were also aesthetic
grounds in particular which instigated the closing of the
ends of the building with hemidomes, although this involved
considerable difficulty and greater cost. The iron frame does
not rest immediately on the ground. The abutments of the
ribs are fixed to the columns 2.5 m high between which
there is a masonry wall of the same height surrounding the
whole building. The inner edge of this terminates on the
outer glass skin so that the width of the space between these
walls increases to 41 m. The bottom part of the glasshouse
obtains a certain distinctiveness of outline, which was desirable as a solid background for the plant decoration. At one-
third of the height a projecting gallery runs round the whole
of the interior, two gangways are attached to the outside,
and there is a lantern built into the apex of the roof for
ventilation. . . .[14]

The joint between the two halves of the ribs is made by
two plates bolted to the top flanges of the ribs; it prevents
lateral displacement and allows only a rolling movement of
the ends of the girders against each other. The hinges at the
abutments likewise prevent sliding movement. The necessary

longitudinal stiffness of the building is obtained through the structure of the hemidome, which consists of nine half-ribs. Only the main ribs are hinged to each other; the others are joined firmly together by braced girders. . . .[15]

The erection of the iron space frame, which was made by the Vulkan Company, was as follows. Each rib was supplied by the factory in two prefabricated parts, which were joined together on the site. The two half-ribs were first raised into position by a block and tackle mounted on scaffolding. Then the lower end was lifted onto the masonry abutment and the hinge pin inserted, then fastened to the scaffolding at the top, until the other half-rib was lifted up in the same way and the two could be joined together by the plates. At the top hinge small mobile trolleys were used for fitting the crossbeams into place, and for the glazing. The trolleys were moved from rib to rib.[16]

Double glazing was used. The two glass surfaces were 16 inches apart. The glass panes were 25 inches wide and 20–31 inches long; the length was determined by the distance between adjacent kinks in the curved profile of the ribs. A horizontal piece of angle iron was attached to each kink. The distance from one piece of angle iron to the next was covered with two panes of glass, the lower of which was fixed to the angle iron by means of two glazing clips made of folded brass strip while the upper pane lapped the lower and was fastened to it by the same kind of glazing clip. The panes of the outer roof skin were held in the rebates by putty and prevented from coming loose by zinc retainers. Interconnected gutters were provided on the sash bars of the inner glazed surface for the removal of condensation.

The uniform humid warm climate which was essential for vigorous growth of the vegetation was produced by a low-pressure hot-water system. The heating was designed for an average temperature in the glasshouse of about 17°C, assuming an external temperature as low as −20°C. The heating equipment in the large palm house in Kew Gardens in London served as a model. The heating equipment came from Ormson, a specialist manufacturer of heating systems for hothouses.[17]

Historical Details

After the founding of the Flora Company in 1871, Otzen was commissioned to do the design work. At the beginning of the construction of the building, while the design work was still in progress, Stier took over the technical and art work after Otzen had withdrawn from his part in the undertaking. Concerning rumors of an argument, Stier referred to his own participation as follows: "The sketches of Mr. Otzen comprised all essential fundamentals of the general layout. Further, they already contained detailed information on the layout of the ground plan and of the external masonry work of the banqueting hall structure, of which many items have likewise been retained. The whole of the interior architecture, however, the whole structure, like the aesthetic detailing, remains my exclusive preserve. Even the motifs taken over from the first sketches because they were recognized as right have been completely worked through by me."[18] A comparison of the interior palm garden as conceived by Otzen (fig. 167) with that actually built by Stier shows in fact not only an altered spatial design but also a different structural design.

Toward the end of the nineteenth century, the surroundings of the Flora became a desirable area for rented accommodations. In 1902 the Flora fell victim to land speculation. The Flora-Terrain-Gesellschaft, an undertaking organized by Johann Wihelm Carstenn, divided the site into separate parcels of land.

Contemporary Comment

The Flora was to be "a winter garden provided with all the attractions of art and nature, with large palm houses in the vicinity of the building from where one can make an excursion on fine winter days and can stroll below palm trees and bananas without worrying about December storms." The article quoted continues as follows: "Because the Flora has been built in a large park long known to all Berliners on account of the grandeur of its old trees (in the Baronry of Eckardtstein at Charlottenburg), and there is the intention to rearrange the latter with the help of a recognized master of all kinds of landscape gardening to lead the way and to stage large open-air concerts for the visitor, the Flora is hence to exercise an important force of attraction in summer because if there is an outbreak of bad weather one can always find protection from storm and rain in the halls filled with foliage and blooms. One gladly exchanges a spell in a Central European park with one in the magnificence of the form and color of the tropical world, spending hours in it, particularly if it is raining outside. The flower displays promise to be a specially powerful attraction because till now Berlin has had none of these in suitable places. Whereas in the smaller halls it was only possible to wonder at the beauty of individual plants, here it will be possible to display a garden within the primeval forest and create a feeling of surprise in the visitor. His sense of feeling for artistically laid-out scenes of plant life will be satisfied no less than the botanist's and gardener's thirst for knowledge.

168
Structural details of
palm house.

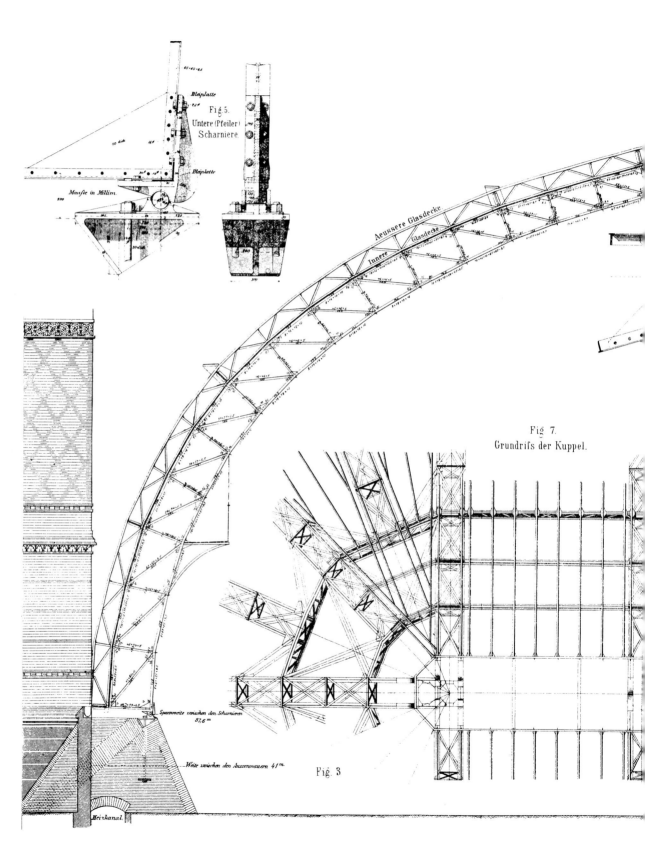

Fig.5.
Untere (Pfeiler)
Scharniere.

Bleiplatte

Bleiplatte

Maasse in Millim.

Aeussere Glasdecke

Innere Glasdecke

Fig. 7.
Grundrifs der Kuppel.

Spannweite zwischen den Scharnieren.
37,6 m.

Weite zwischen den Aussenmauern 41 m.

Fig. 3

Heizkanal.

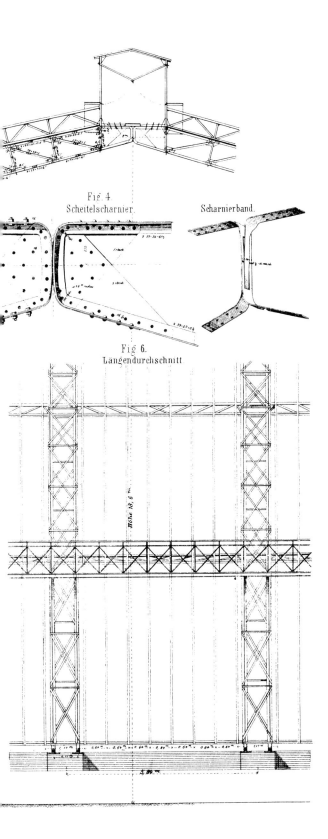

Fig. 4
Scheitelscharnier.

Scharnierband.

Fig 6.
Längendurchschnitt

"The Flora company has grand ideas in mind. If it is to bring this concept to a successful outcome it will at first need great financial resources, and then dependable and skilled leadership. We hear that the resources have been provided, and that there will be no lack of management; there are people in charge of the undertaking who will guarantee its success: the Prince of Puttbus, and the Polizeipräsident of Berlin, Mr. von Wurmb. The foundations of the plant palace have come into being under the lead of Otzen, already well known for his Hamburg buildings, and the whole establishment is expected to be completed within fifteen months at the most. Thus it is to be expected that the Berlin Flora will present to the public palm houses on a par with the Crystal palace of the London Horticultural Society, and the Cologne and Frankfurt Floras, which are the most imposing in this form of architecture. The patron of the festivals to be arranged in the Flora will be able to indulge himself in the illusion of being in those famous gardens of the ancient Orient, and to walk through the city of the seven hills, which, however grand and sumptuous they might have been, must have missed the completeness of the exhibited species and the tasteful organization, as opposed to those horticultural museums developed with all the aids of our time. In addition to the rapid means of transport, the sense of landscape beauty and degree of botanical knowledge of our time, there are to be listed iron and glass, which allow us, in our latitudes which are hostile to the plant life of the south, to achieve more than the civilizations of antiquity."[19]

Source: Staatliche Schlösser und Gärten Verwaltung, Schloss Charlottenburg, Berlin.

References: *DBZ*, 1873, no. 32, pp. 121–122; no. 40, pp. 149–151, 164–166; no. 44, pp. 163–166; no. 46, pp. 171–172; no. 68, pp. 258–259, 269–270; *Architekturverein zu Berlin*, 1877, pp. 167–169, 344–345; *Über Land und Meer*, 1871, 13, vol. 26, no. 48, pp. 8, 14; Rave 1961, pp. 561–562.

Berlin

Schadowstrasse
Aquarium (figs. 169–174)

length: 257 feet
width: 112 feet
height: 59 feet
architect: W. Luer, with Alfred Brehm
built 1869
demolished in 1930s

Aquariums were often built as parts of the nineteenth-century glasshouses, and some that were built separately are analogous to the glasshouses in respect to space and structure. Like a hothouse, an aquarium—with the help of glass and iron—encapsulates a landscape which is to be discovered by the observer, scene by scene, along a route determined by the architectural layout.

According to a contemporary account:

The site chosen for the premises in Schadowstrasse presented a major difficulty because of the fact that there was no side lighting available, even by installing a steep glass roof. Only overhead lighting was possible. The premises were built in two stories, and given the constraints of the location the procurement of the necessary light involved great difficulties. The upper floor included a terrarium for animals which live above the Earth's surface, while the lower floor housed an aquarium to accommodate aquatic animals. To enter the premises from Unter den Linden one climbs a wide stairway to the ticket office, then on up to the terrarium on the upper floor. Here one at first passes through a room containing enclosures for reptiles, amphibians, etc. from the tropics on either side of the spectator. At the end of this room one comes upon a grotto, which extends through both floors and which has depicted on its walls the geological strata of the Earth as a vertical section through the Earth up to and including the Alluvium. In the upper floor one can see trees and bushes occupied by birds, while in the lower story the floor space is occupied by a tank which obtains its water from a waterfall and which contains salamanders and the antediluvian animals. . . . From here one strolls round a large octagonal room which contains birds and which is separated from the tank below by a strong glass ceiling. The whole space represents in miniature a terrain from mountains to meadow and even down into the swamps. The distribution of the animals follows a geographical arrangement, tropical regions, northern parts of Asia, Africa, Australia, Europe. From here one arrives in a vaulted room which displays river animals, water trickles down the rock formation walls, plants decorate it, and birds which like to live by water make up the living contents. In this ramble one has approached closer and closer to the northern regions, the vegetation decreases step by step and one enters the bottom of the staircase which leads to the lower floor where bare rocks are on display. There is a broad granite stairway, of which three steps at a time are hewn out of a single large block, and on descending it one sees small pools at the side, in which there is on view an artificial fish culture, starting from the egg and then on to the growing fish. Having arrived at the foot of the stairs one finds oneself "below the surface of the sea," and one makes the return journey from north to south. One first comes to tanks with marine creatures from the North Sea, then to a larger tank with creatures from the eastern seas. The latter tank holds as much water as that in the Hamburg Aquarium and the largest one in the Paris Exhibition. The octagonal center room which one now enters is divided by a row of columns so that a double route is offered, and a seat allows one to look back at the room one has just left. The large central tank, which one can walk around, contains creatures from the Atlantic Ocean. In this sector of the journey one is led past a grotto illuminated from below, which contains three-foot long marine turtles, and its walls appear as sloping layers of slate. Further away there are tanks with smaller creatures, and finally there is a pool as if in a basalt cave. Then a few steps lead one to the previously described geological grotto, after which one passes by a large pool which displays the inhabitants of the Mediterranean Sea. When in the large central room, one has ascended to a raised floor which is five feet higher up and reached from the above-described room via the last stairway. Between the latter and the central room there is a double row of columns, and between them the terrain is deepened again so that a small stream can traverse it. The rainwater collected from the two main roofs is fed down through gutters and from there drips from stalactites in the roof of a cavern through which the stream flows. The perspective of the whole is terminated by a high vaulted space, which in one-sixth of the actual size represents an imitation of the famous "Blue Grotto" of Capri.

From here one passes under the main stairway, which leads to the upper floor, on to the exit, a glass door which opens into the restaurant occupying the whole parterre space. A small flight of steps leads down to a level four feet below that of Schadowstrasse, and there is also a second door which invites one to make a visit to the second restaurant located in the basement. The "Scylla and Charybdis" successfully negotiated, one emerges into Schadowstrasse. Throughout the whole establishment a continuous circulation of visitors is achieved, so that on the busiest of days one may not fear any blockages. There is a steam boiler and an engine room in the basement, which has a glass roof. A hand pump below the basalt cave provides for the supply of the water tanks in case the mechanized pump should need repair work. The whole of the central space of the establishment has a basement below it which contains in large cisterns the water, which is cut off from light and air 24 hours a day and stored until it is needed. So far as concerns the arrangement, there is a prerequisite that the "special peculiarities" of the inhabitants must be catered to. But here the inhabitants are the animals, because the visiting people are to be regarded as passing guests. Thus the central room of the terrarium, which is inhabited by birds, is given an architecturally stylized leafy canopy; the trees on the eight

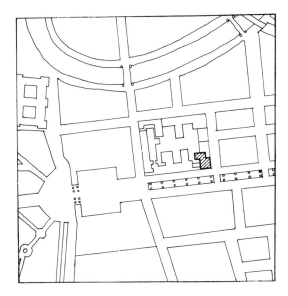

169
Site plan.

170
Voliere. Engraving.

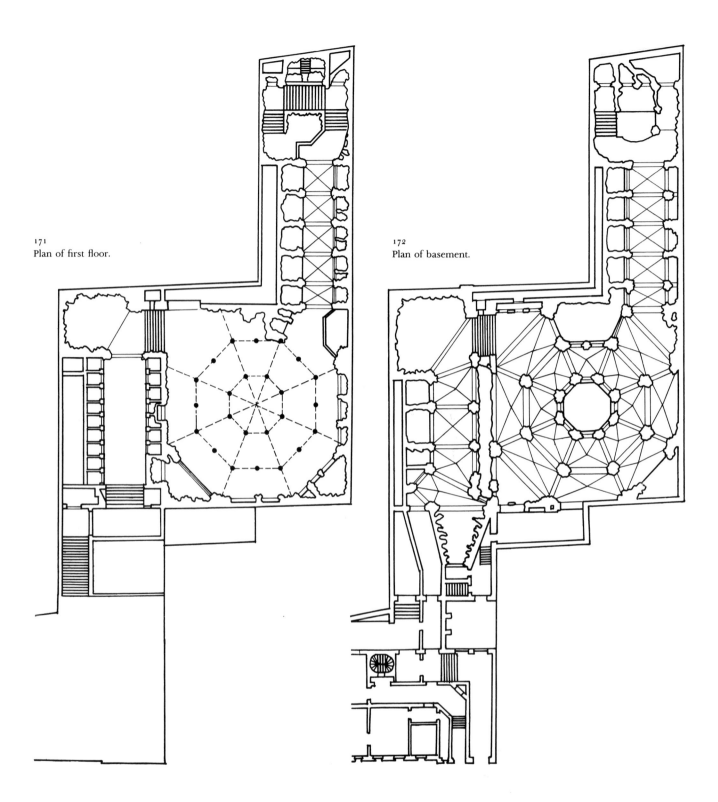

171
Plan of first floor.

172
Plan of basement.

173
Section.

174
"Stroll under the
Meeresspiegel."
Engraving.

corners of the octagon are really iron columns which also
support the iron roof. The branches are in fact wrought-iron
spandrels and curved girders painted green to give the
impression of a leafy canopy. The spectators stand in the
dark and see the brilliantly illuminated objects on display.
A part of the ceiling is provided with horizontally movable
ventilators in order to provide the necessary air and light to
the interior foliage. The animals on the lower floor like clear
water and a stony, rocky environment, so all the columns
and the vault are made of natural stone, but the larger
surfaces on account of the cost have been made of brick,
with a cladding of natural stone. In short, in all of the con-
structions, which were often very difficult to design, the
principle of working together with natural forms applies.[20]

The grotto that forms the central part of the two-
story building passes upward from a 66-foot-square
base via an octagonal opening to the second floor.
The columns are grouped around this opening, and
they support the upper floor and the roof. On the
lower floor they are made to look like stalactites.
They are made of rough stonework and form arches
reaching up to the ceiling. The aquarium, which

forms the central part of this area of the grotto, is
placed beneath the light coming from the opening in
the ceiling. The square central space of the upper
floor forms the terrarium, covered by a double ceiling which is supported by the iron columns arranged
in a double octagon. The ceiling structure consists of
Polonceau girders in the central part with prestressed
rafters around the outside, which are arranged so
that the outer glass roof forms an octagonal pyramid. The interior glass ceiling extends horizontally
and forms a dome above the central space. It is carried on wrought-iron filigree arches. A kind of leafy
canopy is formed above the iron columns and arches
through which the daylight filters

References: *ZfBW*, 1869, 19, parts 4–10, pp. 432–435; *Architekten-*
verein zu Berlin, 1877, p. 173; 1869, pp. 246–248; *DBZ*, 1869, 3,
no. 20, pp. 229–233; Ring 1883, vol. 1, pp. 106 ff.

Berlin

Central Hotel
Winter Garden (figs. 175–180, 494)

length: 247 feet
width: 75 feet
height: 58 feet
architects: Hermann von der Hude and Julius Hennicke
built 1880–81
demolished

The Central Hotel is representative of a new type of hotel, which was conceived not only to provide overnight accommodation but also as a place for entertainment and a regional meeting point for the upper class. A very large banquet hall formed the focal point of the establishment. This led to the acceptance of the winter garden type of structure, the integration of which with catering and leisure facilities had already been accomplished in the Flora.

"There was an intention to create a large concert and restaurant locale, satisfactorily heated, and open on every day of the year, like a garden decked out with greenery, well lit and ventilated, built to the style of the Parisian 'café-concerts.' Here visitors could enjoy musical or theatrical productions without being dependent on the uncertain weather...."[21] In the Central Hotel this specification was carried out in an exemplary fashion.

"The available site of 9,210 m² area within a block of buildings made the maximum use of the space necessary on account of the high cost of building land. The layout of the winter garden is adapted to the constraints of the site, and surrounded by buildings on all four sides it obtains its light through the ceiling. The enclosing structures around the winter garden made necessary a narrow spatial connection with the adjoining rooms, which were interconnected one to the other and with the winter garden.

"Berlin had at that time in addition to the Kroll Rooms and the Berlin Flora no specially designed banquet center that could cater to up to 1,000 guests. This need was met in the quietest part of the city by the winter garden room."[22]

The hall of the winter garden had the shape of a rectangle 247 feet long and 75 feet wide. Its surface area of 18,700 square feet was covered with a glass roof 58 feet high at the ridge. This hall was connected by cloakrooms and the north entrance to Dorotheenstrasse on the south and via the restaurant rooms to Georgenstrasse. The concert and theater stages occupied the center of the long west side, while on the east side (Friedrichstrasse) there was a terrace leading via staircases to the assembly rooms

(fig. 177). The walls and terraces were decorated with various types of temperate plants; the remaining space was left vacant apart from two groups of palms which stood on marble bases containing aquariums. A pool with fish and water plants was built integral with the terrace. The floor of the winter garden was concreted over and strewn with quartz chippings in order to create a gardenlike effect between the groups of palms.

The roof of the winter garden was spanned without horizontal tie members by an iron structure consisting of curved braced ribs with purlins. The braced girders, set 10 feet apart axially, had the profile of a parabola at the bottom, changing to a straight line toward the top. The glass roof had the shape of an elongated arched ridge roof. The arched girders abutted onto wrought-iron brackets projecting 10 feet outward. The brackets were anchored into the masonry on three sides of the winter garden, and on the long western side 5-foot-wide outward-facing masonry pillars with 36-foot-high masonry work provided counterbalance and anchorage to withstand the thrust of the brackets. The wall areas of the winter garden were integrated with the brackets via a system of half columns and masonry pillars with round-arched recesses. Above that rose in stilted arches the rising shoulders of the frame associated with the brackets. The space so formed had a cross-section reminiscent of a basilica with low aisles at the side. By this means a room was created without interior columns. The amazing effect of space thus produced was only obtained by exploiting to the limits the stressing of the bracket structure. In terms of statics, the construction principle was like a system of arched ribs with three degrees of freedom, similar to the ribs of the winter garden in Munich. Early models of these braced ribs were found in the Floras in Cologne (1865), Frankfurt (1869–70), and Berlin (1873). This type of construction was used in greater spans in railway stations, for example in the Lehrter railway station in Berlin (figs. 178, 179).

A contemporary report noted that "the 2-m-long and 0.72-m-wide double glazing panes are bedded in putty with 5-cm laps on I-section wrought-iron purlins and the zinc-painted sash bars placed between them. The question concerning the need to cover a hall of this type with single or double glazing when it was to be used for housing tropical plants as well as for social purposes presented the opportunity for contrary viewpoints to be examined. Single glazing was chosen in the end. The correctness of this judgment was later confirmed in that after four months' use, which included a very severe January with high

175
Site plan.

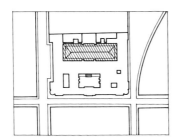

176
View from Doro-
theen- and Fried-
richstrasse.
Engraving.

snowfall, neither dripping of condensation nor cooling at the roof had any detrimental effect on the
palms."[23]

The supply of fresh air and the removal of stale
air was to some extent effected by air ducts in the
shoulders, which discharged into the open air via the
roof of the winter garden. The adjoining assembly
rooms were connected to this ventilation system. A
powerful convection current arose in the evening,
helped by the gas lighting, and made its exit through
the five lanterns built into the roof ridge. The winter
garden had steam heating, for which the pipes were
led through conduits along the length of the room.
The radiators in these conduits had 7,700 square feet
of heating surface. The warm air emerged from the
conduits through cast-iron gratings in the floor.

References: ZfBW, 1881, 21, 1–3, pp. 175–188; atlas sheets
38–42; Ring 1884, vol. 2, pp. 124–125.

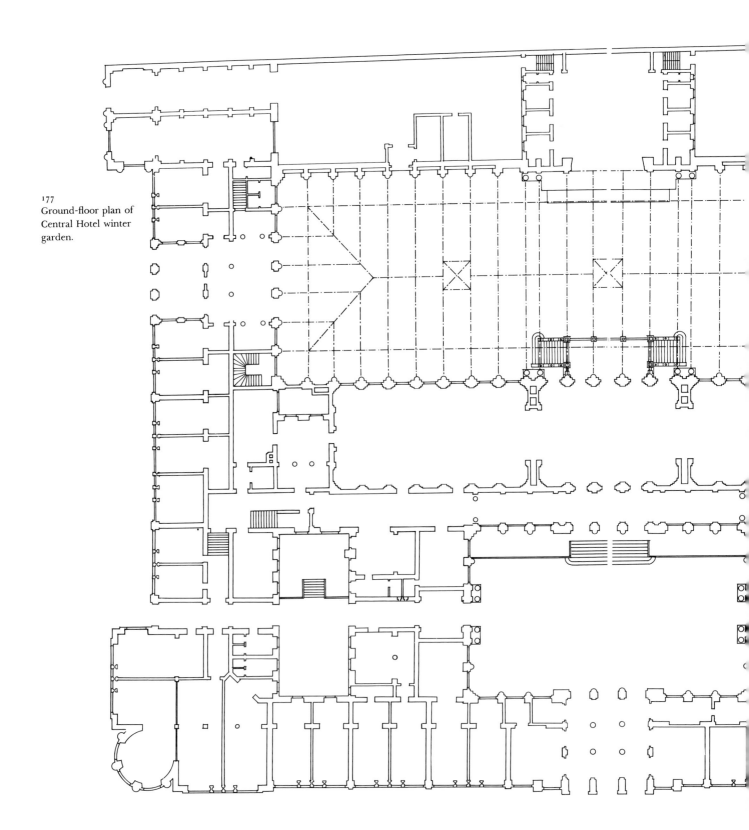

177
Ground-floor plan of
Central Hotel winter
garden.

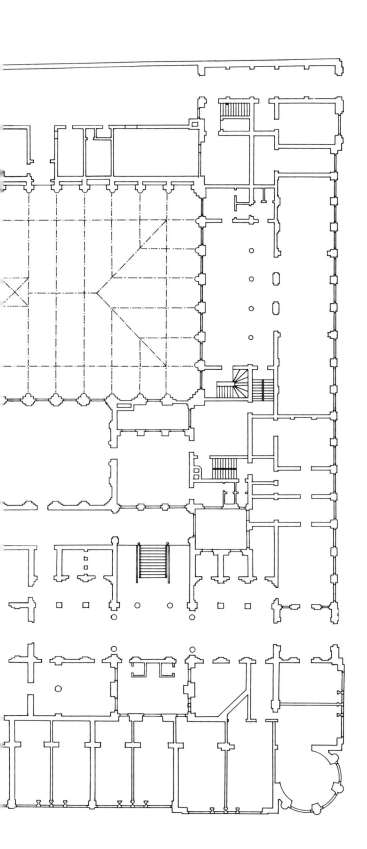

178
Section.

179
Structural detail of
roof rib springing.

180
View inside Central
Hotel winter garden.
Engraving, ca. 1880.

Berlin-Dahlem

New Botanical Garden

The reason for the establishment of the New Botanical Garden was the growth of Berlin after the speculative period, with its inevitable consequences of scarcity of building land. Air pollution caused by industrialization was also a factor. The Old Botanical Garden was broken up in 1897, and a parcel of land in the southern part of Berlin (Dahlem) which was already owned by the state was made into the New Botanical Garden. Two hothouses were built in the northeast corner of the garden on a raised site.

The display houses were not detached, as in the Old Botanical Garden, but were built joined together in a single building complex. The site plan (fig. 181) makes the general layout clear. There is a symmetrical arrangement around an inner courtyard, with the Great Palm House and the victoria regia House as central features. The Subtropical House, although not directly connected with this group of buildings, forms a structural unity with it. It has a commanding position, and because of its size it can be seen from a distance.

Great Palm House
length: 198 feet (with wings, 505 feet)
width: 96 feet (with wings, 261 feet)
height: 76 feet
architect: Alfred Koerner
builder: Heinrich Müller-Breslau
built 1905–1907
damaged in 1943; rebuilt in 1960s

The glass-and-iron Great Palm House by Alfred Koerner is one of the most important buildings of its kind. Here the nineteenth-century developments in vaulted hall buildings found their culmination and their conclusion. The structural designer and builder was the famous Heinrich Müller-Breslau. The three-hinge construction of the vaults and the size of the enclosed space caused astonishment at the time. However, contemporary architectural critics (with the exception of Paul Scheerbart) made no mention of this imposing building, even though widespread discussion was kindled two years later by Peter Behrens's use of braced girders, which in terms of statics were three-hinge arches, in the AEG turbine hall.

Like Koerner with the Palm House, Behrens had returned to the foot of the roof truss as a significant structural element. Behrens's rusticated concrete corner pylons were intended to invest the AEG building with a "Cyclopean force." He tried expressly to rep-

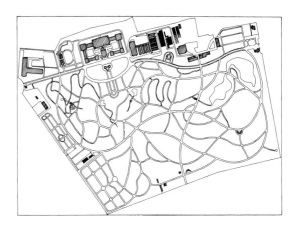

181
Site plan.

resent the "might of industry" in this element of the building. This purpose was also served by the cornice projecting from the long side of the hall. The imposing effect came from the use of a facade, so that only the columns of the load-bearing structure revealed their function. In this firmly maintained contrast between structural work and architectural effect the contemporary critics saw a revival of the "new art of industrial construction." But ten years later, after the construction of new factory halls that displayed the structural engineering principle for all to see, Behrens discovered a new interpretation. Behrens accented the row of roof ribs by creating the impression through the bases that the ribs were supporting the weight of the roof. He combined the feeling of tension one receives from the hall with the stiffness of a temple tympanum interrupted at several points. This was noted in 1919 by Erich Mendelsohn. Later, Ludwig Hilbesheimer in *Grosstadt Architektur* (1927) and Adolf Behne in *Der moderne Zweckbau* (1926) expressed similar thoughts. Their point of departure was the principle of the New Objectivity. But it was just this principle—not theoretically formulated, but practically executed—that had determined the construction of the Great Palm House at Dahlem. The complete absence of attributes of monumental architecture (such as plinths, pilasters, and cornices), and the correspondence between form and contents, between space and function, gave the building a uniform, self-evident, naturally effective shape. That the critics of 1909 found no starting point therein for appropriate comments is due not only to the missing connotation of the plant house but also to the fact that they were ideologically restricted to the viewpoints of traditional architecture. The Great Palm House, on the basis of its bold construction, was one of the "most modern" buildings of its time.

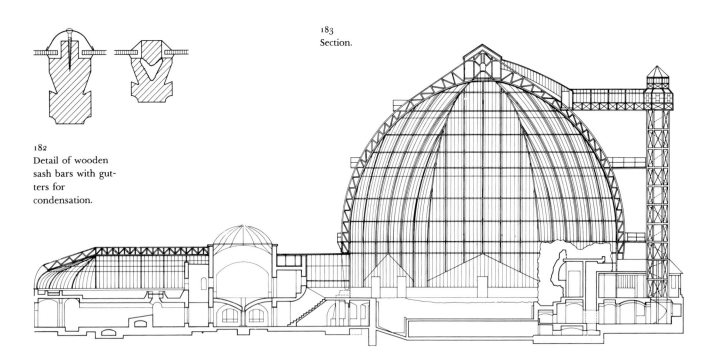

182
Detail of wooden
sash bars with gut-
ters for
condensation.

183
Section.

The space frame is made of braced arched girders joined together on the principle of three-hinge arches. They form a large hall, which is terminated at the ends by two half-octagonal domes. The glass skin is fixed to the inside of the frame, for functional reasons, and the framework is clearly visible.

We have here an example of the deliberate use of structural elements that characterizes important works by structural engineers. The execution of the bases of the girders has a demonstrative aspect. The hinges are set on a granite foundation; the stresses are distributed by the convergence of the girders via the ornamental work of narrow perpendicular steel bars. The relationship to the well-known structural details of Behrens's AEG turbine hall is unmistakable (figs. 486, 487). The external steel frame has forerunners in the palm houses at Vienna-Schönbrunn (1880), the Frankfurt Flora (1869), and the Laeken Winter Garden (1875–76).

John Hix in his book *The Glass House* has described the Great Palm House as a work of German Expressionism, in which the development of the ribs in the form of compressed pointed arches and the faceted type of interrupted vaulting of the glass skin may have been the motive. In fact Paul Scheerbart, the author of *Glasarchitektur* and co-founder of *Frühlicht*, obtained the direct stimulus from this for his "architettura celesta."

Alfred Koerner, the architect of all the Dahlem hothouses, describes the construction of the Great Palm House as follows:

The advantages which the lightweight means of building offer for the layout of new buildings, but particularly for their operation and maintenance, caused the Ministry to authorize A. Koerner, in association with the Director of the Garden, Dr. Engler, to inspect hothouse designs in Holland, Belgium, and later in Russia too. The outcome of the visit to Holland and Belgium was a preference for the lightweight building method, but the state gardeners were not convinced that the same would be applicable in our climate of longer and more severe winters. Not until the same observations were made in Russia, particularly in the Imperial Gardens in St. Petersburg, and in the market gardens there, was the feasibility realized of managing with single glazing alone to protect the contents from severe winter weather. The greatest nuisance of the old construction method was that the iron sash bars, which had been used for a long time, and the iron space frame, were located between the warm humid air of the interior and the cold air outside. This caused very cold drops of condensation to form on the inside surface of the ironwork and they caused damage when they fell on the plants. This inconvenience was only partly alleviated by the superimposed second glass skin, which in addition had the very great disadvantage of reducing the light transmitted. In the new method of construction the sash bars were not made of iron but of wood, a poor conductor of heat and a material on which the usual drops of condensation did not appear. The second protective glass skin became superfluous; the sunlight could enter unhindered, and even on cloudy days it could have been effective in photosynthesis. The wooden glazing bars require support from below, for which various methods have been devised. For the new buildings of the propagating house at Dahlem a space frame has been made of iron girders as slender as possible and casting the minimum amount of shadow. This consisted of U-section ribs and I beams for purlins, which supported the wooden sash bars of the glass roof. Because these iron parts are fitted only to the interior of the heated room and nowhere come into contact with the cold outside air, there is absolutely no troublesome condensation effect on the outside.[25]

American pitch pine was chosen for the sash bars because it is particularly resistant to rot.

The design of the large display houses paid particular attention to the conditions in the warm houses. Because the gardeners did not want the plant collection disturbed, the supporting framework was installed external to the glass, open to the sky, and the wood-and-glass roof structure was suspended from it. Thus a continuously open interior space was created, untrammeled by columns and tie bars. The glass roof for the Great Palm House, like those for the smaller houses, was made in 6 1/2-foot-wide sections consisting of five glass panes with sash bars 7 1/2 feet long and attached at these distances to the iron framework. The ribs were made of curved I beam type N.P. 18, reinforced with short braced purlins placed three sash-bar lengths apart. These ribs transferred the load to gallery purlins placed 23 feet apart, which consisted of two braced girders. The horizontal braced girders supported the surrounding gallery. The second braced girder in the sloping glass roof and parallel to it was joined to the first by a rigid bracket to make a firm prism, the third side of which remained open. Thus the rolled-up shading blind could be installed below the gallery. The gallery purlins transferred the weight of the roof to the master ribs, set 20 feet apart, which as simple braced girders joined to make a three-hinge arch resting on a basalt foundation wall. Six master ribs carried the roof of the long building, which was terminated on both sides by a hemi-octagonal dome 40 feet wide at the base. Two half-ribs located next to the longitudinal axis protected the building from the wind along that direction. The iron structure was built, as figure 185 shows, with a distinctly flowing line, without diagonal bracing. The ribs and the purlins were simple braced girders that cast no shadows and met the eye of the visitor on the inside only as a fine network. The glass ceiling reinforced this impression, softening the contours of the structure. The supporting iron parts remained in the open air and did not extend into the heated space. The rule that a hothouse should have only one "air mass," never two layers at different temperatures, was followed with great care here.

The Great Palm House was partly destroyed by bombs in 1943. Between 1963 and 1968 it was fitted out with vacuum-formed acrylic panels and provided with a new hot-air plant. The original character was mutilated through the use of large plastic sheets, and with the removal of the filigree sash-bar work the dome lost its scale. The loss of architectural effect can be seen by comparing figures 483 and 484.

Victoria Regia House

length: 51 feet
width: 46 feet
architect: Alfred Koerner
built 1905–1907
damaged in 1943; rebuilt in 1958

The victoria regia house, with its bell-like glass vault, is a miniature counterpart to the Great Palm House. The lower story, made of brick and stone cladding, forms an opening to the whole complex in such a way that a centrally located aquarium is surrounded by passages, which in the next section lead into a vaulted hall. From here a short staircase leads into the Great Palm House and into the upper story of the victoria regia house. The pond in the center is covered by a glass-and-iron structure similar to that of the large house. The glazing is attached to the underside of the steel frame.

Subtropical House (figs. 186, 187, 488–491)

length: ca. 145 feet
width: ca. 66 feet
height: 52 feet
area: 9,658 square feet
architect: Alfred Koerner
built 1909
damaged in 1943; rebuilt completely in 1958

The subtropical house resembles a three-story basilica with an apse and two towers at the front, all transformed into glass and iron. Koerner wrote that "the cross-section was the outcome of the requirement to provide separate locations for both low and tall plants, so that they were all as close as possible to the light, and the lower plants were not shaded by the taller plants."[26] The architectural execution of the building has a high quality not only in respect to structure but also in respect to decoration and detail. The building was designed on simple geometrical lines, and the interplay of glass and iron is enhanced by the crystal ornaments on the towers and the roof. The ironwork arch linking the two stair towers at the front entrance is without doubt an allusion to the castle ruin on the Pfaueninsel.

Not only the ornamental treatment of the catwalk space but also the riveted joints and the window fittings are in the best tradition of Jugendstil, which preferred to bring structural elements to the fore and play down the aesthetic aspect.

184
Great Palm House
complex with victo-
ria regia house and
wings, plan of
ground floor.

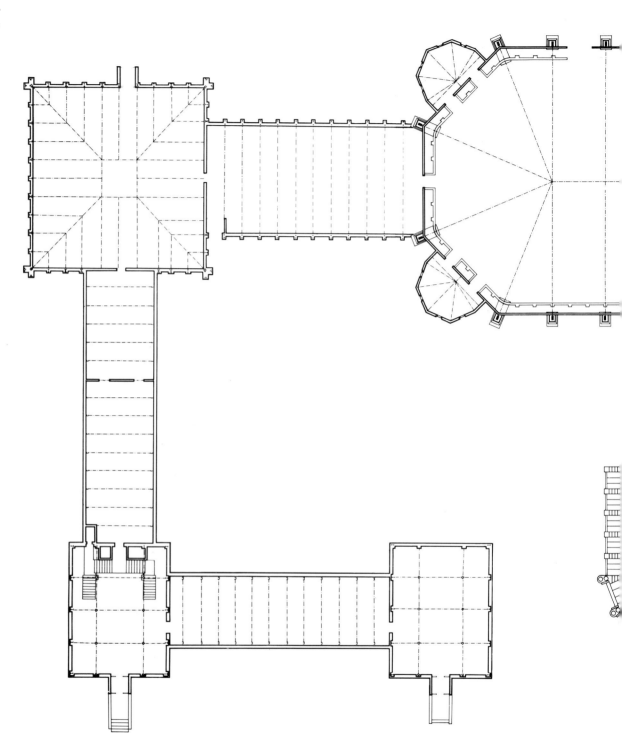

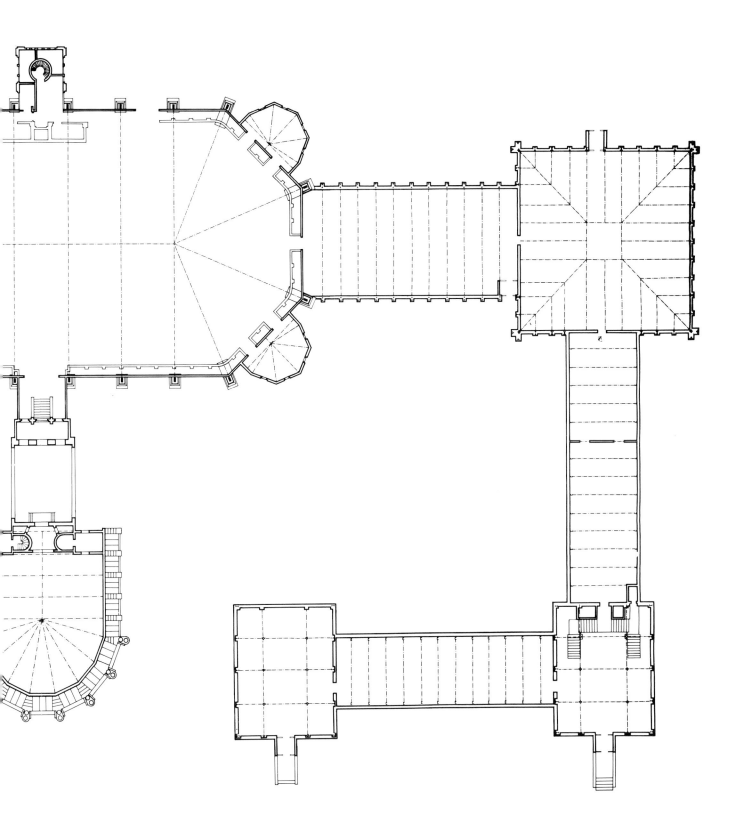

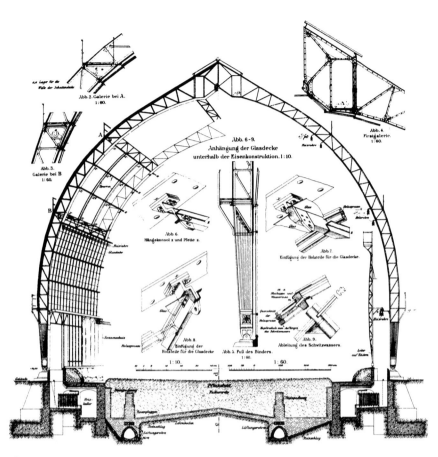

185
Structural details of
Great Palm House.

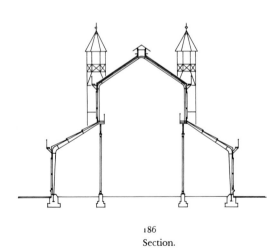

186
Section.

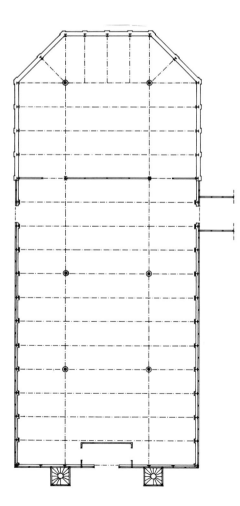

187
Ground-floor plan.

The steel structure of the nave consists of rigid framework roof trusses resting on a continuous run of braced girders, which are in turn supported below by cast-iron columns. There are similar ribs supporting the aisles. The trusses are made of sheet steel riveted to form I beams and are tapered to match the load values. The trusses are held together laterally by I-section purlins. In contrast to the Great Palm House, the glazing here is fitted externally. The reason for this is that the danger of formation of condensation is not present with the expected average temperature of 5 to 6°C. Moreover, with thicker glass on the roof, all the side walls are provided with windows which can be left open during the summer months. In an attempt to develop the large casement windows, the architect strengthened the filigree wooden framework with quadrant-shaped hinges and stressed diagonal members. The addition of these members provided structural continuity.

Source: library, Botanical Garden, Berlin-Dahlem.

References: ZfBW, 1909, 59, parts 4–6, pp. 202–222, atlas sheets 25–30; Koerner 1910; *Zentralblatt der Bauverwaltung*, 1897, no. 21, pp. 231–233; Deutsche Bauzeitung (publ.): *Baukunde des Architekten*, 1902, vol. II, pp. 362–365; Timler and Zepernick 1978, pp. 42–93; *Architektenverein zu Berlin*, 1972, part XI, pp. 124–132.

Biebrich

Castle Gardens
Hothouses of Prince Adolf von Nassau (figs. 188, 189, 495, 496)
length: 330 feet
width: 165 feet
area: 49,500 square feet
architect: unknown
built 1846 (New Exhibition Hall 1861)
removed to Frankfurt in 1869; demolished in 1906

The cast-iron-frame hothouses built for Prince Adolf von Nassau in Biebrich (near Wiesbaden) were some of the earliest hothouses designed in the grand style. In their time they were counted as the greatest hothouse establishment in Germany. The layout took for its architectural style the principles of traditional palace architecture, but with masonry elements replaced by glass surfaces. Beneath this glass shell, as in the nineteenth-century exhibition buildings, was a room arrangement that encouraged visitors to circulate from hall to hall.

The layout consisted of a central building with a high glass dome placed on a tambour with adjacent wings set at 90° and ending in square corner pavilions. Display houses were sited between the wings in

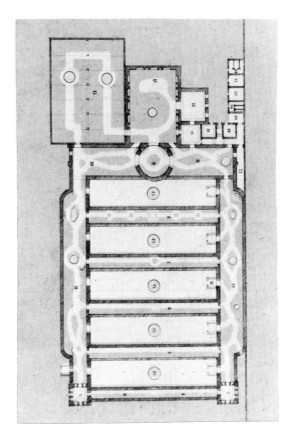

188
Ground-floor plan of
Biebrich hothouses.
Lithograph, 1861.

a terraced layout. Exhibition halls were attached at the rear of the middle pavilion, some of them having entrances which took the visitor unawares.

One can presume that the architect of this establishment obtained various ideas from British hothouse building and applied them here. The development and arrangement of a glass dome set between wings is reminiscent of Syon House in London (1820–1827). The use of curvilinear glass roofs demonstrates a knowledge of the works of John Claudius Loudon and Richard Turner. The Moorish ornamentation, which at that time was being used by Ludwig von Zanth, Karl Friedrich Schinkel, and other architects, indicates a possible influence from Humphrey Repton and John Nash. This ornamentation appears particularly on the corner pavilions and the two-story exhibition halls.

The hothouses proper were approximately 100 feet long and had a total depth of about 230 feet. Adjoining them was a 66-by-99-foot exhibition hall and a "conifer house" approximately half as large. The central curvilinear hothouses between the wings were glass corridors 10 feet wide and 100 feet long. They

189
Overall view. Litho-
graph, 1854.

opened onto uncovered enclosed gardens 33 by 99 feet in size. The crowning feature of the whole layout was a round palm house with a high filigreework glass dome. The hothouses served simultaneously for cultivation and exhibition. In one corner pavilion was the entrance; in the other was the office of the director. North of the circular dome in the central axis was a conifer house which was architecturally set off with pilasters. Adjacent to it on the west side was the exhibition hall, built later.

Thus, in its ground plan this complex of hothouses appears to have been built very coherently and to be representative of the circumstances of the times. Study of the lithographs (figs 495, 496) leads one to conclude that at the start of the 1860s a new and larger exhibition hall replaced the original one, which lasted until about 1854. As can be seen in figure 496, there was a basilica-style hall with cast-iron columns. The triangular roof trusses were made on the pattern of a strutted frame. From the existing particulars one cannot determine whether these cast-iron trusses were cast as a single piece or were assembled from separate parts. The closed roof surfaces and the absence of side walls suggest that these halls, like their predecessors, were used only for plant and flower displays.

After the enforced dissolution of the royal household of the Prince of Nassau in 1866 as the result of the ending of the independent status of the Rhineland by Prussia, the plant houses and all their plant contents were sold to the city of Frankfurt am Main. Partly rebuilt in the gardens of the Flora, they were demolished in 1906.

Comment from 1861

"Once again the munificence of His Highness the Prince of Nassau, as if under the rule of the true Maecenas in the floral kingdom, has opened to the public, not used to such highly poetic delights in our matter-of-fact age, which is called upon from the stream of movement with the times, to carry poetry to the grave, not only his winter garden, but by the construction of a gigantic and magnificent exhibition hall and even more by truly princely subsidies has spurred on the specialists to help crown the work with the products of their art. . . . Local knowledge has been indispensable in the orientation of the layout and so it presents to you an area of 51,000 square feet, which even with the greatest variety of breaks in a perspective more than 300 feet long still forms a harmonized whole, a glasshouse complex which by its large decorative features transports us into a park of idealistic form, yet with all its changes of the familiar spots, the fairy-like cascades, the eye-catching seas of flowers, dark glades, spouting fountains, paths with creepers, palms representing tropical vegetation, leaves behind an impression that can hardly be obliterated."[27]

Source: Bildarchiv der Landeshauptstadt Wiesbaden.

References: *Deutsches Magazin für Garten- und Blumenkunde*, April 1861, 14, pp. 84–91; Schoser 1971, pp. 1–4.

Birmingham

Botanical Gardens
Hothouses (figs. 190, 191, 498)

The Birmingham Botanical and Horticultural Society, founded in 1829, acquired a large garden from Lord Calthorpe. In 1831, J. C. Loudon proposed (among other designs) a conical glass dome over 200 feet in diameter and 100 feet high. This proposal was rejected on account of the high cost, and instead the design for a dome-vaulted hothouse with side wings was taken up and brought into being.[28] On an engraving dated 1851, apropos of an exhibition in the Botanical Gardens, a circular hothouse with a tambour-capped glass dome is illustrated (fig. 191). The dome structure, consisting of a fine pattern of vertical sash bars resting on a cylinder, reminds one of Loudon's curvilinear hothouse. One may presume that this hothouse came into existence with Loudon's collaboration.

In 1852 Joseph Paxton presented the Society with a new water lily just introduced into Britain, and a special hothouse was built for it. In 1869 a new palm house was built to the design of F. B. Osborn on a 50-foot-square base, with a plane lean-to roof and square lanterns. Four round cast-iron columns with machined spiral fluting and small Corinthian capitals supported the roof. The space frame was reinforced with diagonal iron rods between the columns, which ran together and met at the top of the columns, held by a ring like the one used by Paxton in 1851 in the London Crystal Palace. The joists of the lanterns were also strengthened by the use of iron struts on the inside. This small hothouse (fig. 498) is still in existence today.

References: Loudon 1832, pp. 407–432; 1835, pp. 336–339.

190
John Claudius Loudon, projects for vaulted winter garden, 1831: (a, b) first project; (c, d) second project.

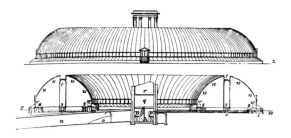

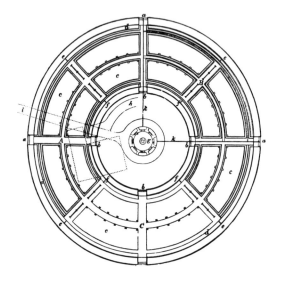

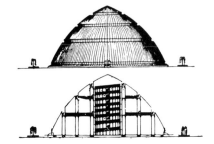

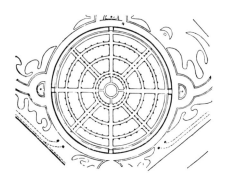

191
Domed greenhouse at Birmingham, 1832. Woodcut, 1851.

Bonn

Old Palm House
length: 112 feet
height: 43 feet (wings), 61 feet (center)
architect: M. Neumann
built ca. 1875
demolished

The Old Palm House in Bonn was a large glass-and-iron structure consisting of a high middle section capped by a glass dome, and having wings. A lean-to roof was later attached to it. The glass facade was assembled from cast-iron columns superimposed on each other and joined together by richly decorative ironwork. The columns and the architrave formed a two-story framework, the spaces in which were filled by large glass windows with closely spaced sash bars below the eaves and terminating upwards in round arches. No relevant documents exist, apart from an old view of the facade, and so no statements about the internal structure can be made.

Noteworthy is the structural arrangement of the externally fitted space frame at the corners, in the wings, and in the middle section, where greater loads were supported. The columns were reinforced by an architrave at the junction between the vertical pairs of columns. These columns may possibly have been supplemented by a further pair of columns placed on the inside—a principle which was applied in the larger palm house at Herrenhausen (1879).

The architectural appearance of the building was conservative. The starting point of the proportions and the arrangement of the facade was the historicism of stone architecture, which was dominant at that time. (See figure 90.)

Reference: Durm et al. 1893.

Bournemouth

Winter Garden (figs. 192–196)
length: 228 feet
width: 106 feet
height: 59 feet
architect: Fletcher Lowndes & Co.
built 1875–76
demolished

This winter garden, built by a private company for £12,000, was never profitable as a winter garden. In 1893 the central space was converted into a concert hall, and from then on only the wings served as a winter garden. Thus, the building fulfilled a function like that of the floras in Germany: It was a venue for entertainments and festivals in a romantic milieu of plants.

The weight of the dome was carried on four cast-iron columns joined together by braced girders. The bottom of the glass vault was supported on a row of narrow columns, which at the same time enclosed the windows that surrounded the building. Adjoining this central part of the building on both sides were low wings, also with vaulted glass roofs. The whole structure stood on a stone plinth. As with the exhibition buildings of its time, the decor was no longer traceable back to the structure itself, as it had been in Paxton's designs. Rather, the idea was to decorate a technically thoroughly developed glass-and-iron shell afterwards. The supporting members, some of which were made of rolled iron section (braced girders), lacked the lightness and elegance of their predecessors.

Source: archives of Bournemouth Central Library.

Reference: *Gardener's Chronicle*, 20.1.1877, vol. 37.

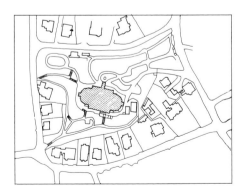

192
Site plan, 1930.

193
Overall view of
Bournemouth winter
garden. Engraving,
1875.

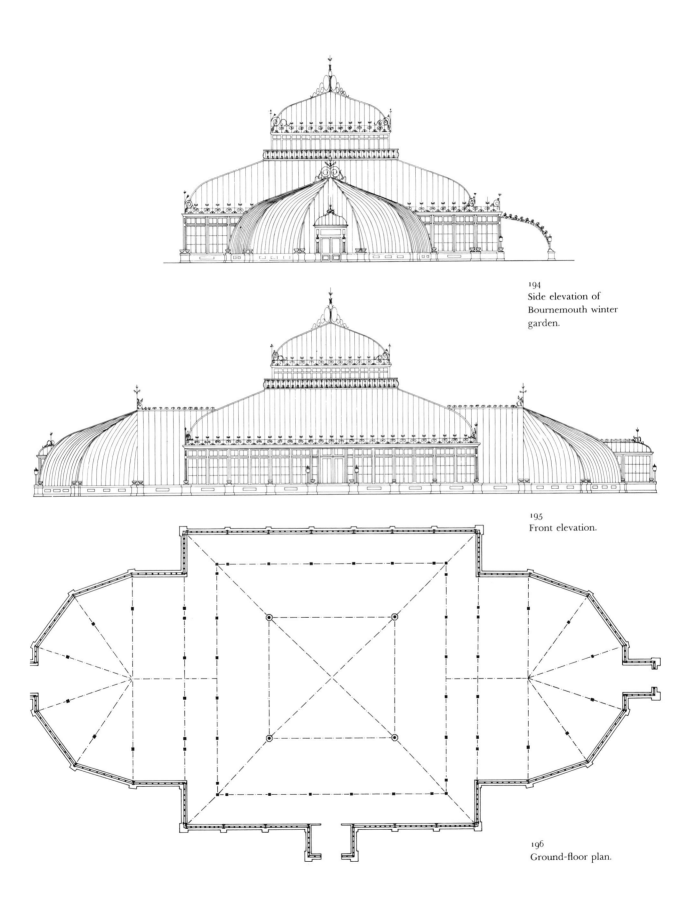

194
Side elevation of
Bournemouth winter
garden.

195
Front elevation.

196
Ground-floor plan.

197
Site plan, 1870.

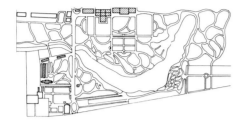

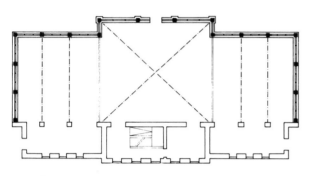

198
Ground-floor plan.

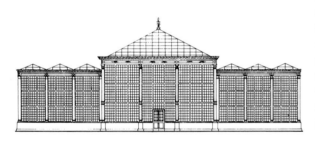

199
South (top) and east
fronts.

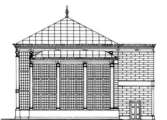

Breslau

Botanical Garden
Conservatory (figs. 197–199, 499–501)
length: 102 feet
width: 53 feet
height: 36 feet
architect: unknown
built 1861
demolished except for one wing

Built on the edge of the Botanical Garden, this conservatory belongs to the evolutionary series of classical buildings. Spatial form, proportions, and ornamentation were borrowed from classical stone architecture. The front of the structure consisted of glazing on a rectangular network of sash bars and cast-iron columns. The visible supporting framework, with the extensive glass surfaces between its members, made up the cubic forms of a well-proportioned building. In its overall appearance, in which structure and form were immediately self-evident, the conservatory had a kinship with early forerunners of post-1900 objective architecture.

The base plan of the glass hall, comprising three squares with a prominent central section, was surrounded on three sides by a plinth on which stood cast-iron columns shaped like narrow pilasters. These columns supported a pyramidal roof in the middle, and on the wings there were small ridge-and-furrow roofs at a lower level, with hipped ends. These roofs were supported at the rear by masonry work. The ridged side roofs were structurally related to Paxton's ridge-and-furrow roof.

Bretton Hall, Yorkshire

Palm House (figs. 200–203)
diameter: 100 feet
height: 60 feet
architect: J. C. Loudon
built 1827
demolished 1832

The Bretton Hall palm house, built by Loudon for Mrs. Beaumont, was the largest glass building of its time in England. Charles McIntosh, the connoisseur of European gardens, described it as the wonder of the age. The central structure, erected on a circular base, was covered by a bell-shaped glass-and-iron dome. François-Joseph Bélanger had built a glass-and-iron dome resting on a ring of masonry for the Halle aux Blés in Paris in 1807–1811, but a continu-

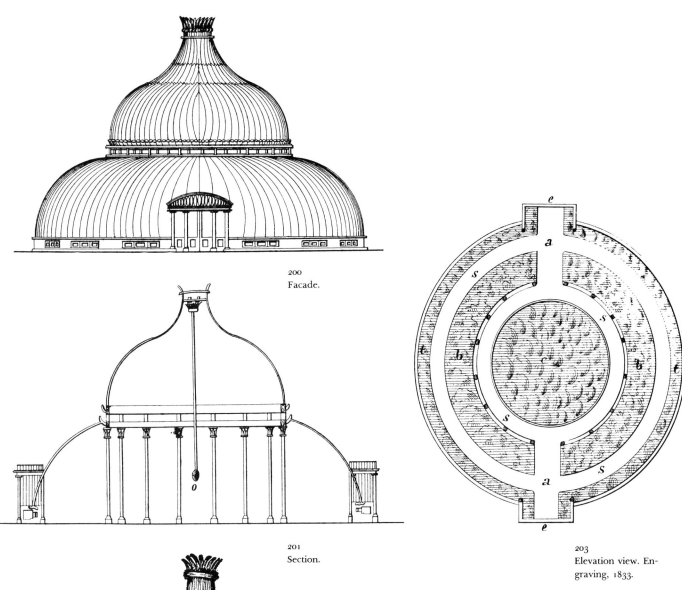

200
Facade.

201
Section.

202
Ground-floor plan.

203
Elevation view. Engraving, 1833.

ous shell with an external shape like a bell from ground level to apex was the next step in the exploitation of iron.

In its cross-sectional form the Bretton Hall palm house can be seen as a forerunner of the hothouses built by Paxton at Chatsworth (1836–1840) and by Turner and Burton in Kew Gardens (1844–1848). The motif of a vaulted hothouse in the shape of a bell was taken up in the large winter garden at Laeken by Balat.

The internal space frame of the building consisted of a ring of sixteen hollow cast-iron columns with capitals shaped like plants. On these rested a cast-iron framework in the form of a ring for the upper part of the glass vault. This also formed the abutment for the lower half-barrel vault, which formed a kind of ambulatory around the inner circle of columns. Reaching right down to the ground, it was supported above a span of 22 feet on a stone base. The space frame of the glass dome consisted only of slender wrought-iron sash bars with a cross-shaped section, which followed the profile as arches. Horizontal tie rings were absent. The carefully fitted and puttied panes participated actively as part of the load-bearing structure, as originally reported by Loudon. In terms of statics, a dome constructed in this way can be considered a shell structure, having a volume generated by rotation of an ogee. The boldness of this structural concept can be seen in the fact that the ratio of the greatest span (56 feet) to the thickness of the iron sash bars (2 inches) is 1:336. A chicken's egg has a ratio of 1:100 in this respect.

The upper part of the dome of the palm house had particular structural and aesthetic individuality. From the inside concave curve of the bottom half-barrel vault, the dome changed over to a convex profile, which terminated in a circular ventilation opening at the apex. It was decorated with a garland of cast-iron feathers, like a wigwam. Here Loudon consciously referred back to the symbolism of the tent in order to accentuate the transitory character of his building.

The bell shape (Loudon himself called his building a "campanulated house"[29]) corresponded to the spatial arrangements of the plants—tall palms in the middle, shorter plants in the surrounding gallery. The ironwork was made by W. and D. Bailey of Holborn, who had been associated with Loudon since 1817. The ribs of the dome weighed only a pound per foot run.[30] From these statements it can be calculated that, with an estimated sash-bar spacing of about 8 inches, approximately 1½ pounds of iron per square foot of roof surface was needed. The total building cost came to £10,000. The building was heated by steam through a ring of pipe under the soil in the gallery. Ventilation was by louvers in the stone base, by movable windows in the abutments, and by openings in the ridge of the roof.[31]

References: McIntosh 1853, vol. 1, pp. 129, 363, 364; Loudon 1833, p. 24; Neumann 1862, p. 171 ff.

Brussels

Botanical Gardens
Tropical House (figs. 204–208, 502, 503)
length: 455 feet
width: 100 feet (dome)
height: 66 feet (dome)
built 1826–27

The large tropical house in the Botanical Gardens in Brussels is one of the oldest of the existing large hothouses. As a public building it was without equal. In the formal language of the classical palace architecture, and with its austere axial structure, cupola-shaped central part with subordinate wings, corner pavilions, and terrace-like parterres, this building is to be considered as a model for later hothouse buildings in which iron and glass were used instead of massive building materials.

Before the French Revolution, Belgium possessed only one botanical garden, at the University of Louvain, which was dissolved in 1788 and amalgamated with the University of Brussels. The first botanical garden in the present-day center of the city remained in existence only temporarily. When in 1826 the fortification works were demolished in the reorganization of the capital, the botanical garden was also demolished to make way for an industrial exhibition building. In order to preserve the valuable stock of plants, a private venture was started by five rich middle-class citizens. They formed a registered company, the first joint stock company in Belgium, which linked their interest in the plants to a building project. The shareholders commented upon their initiative as follows: "The great enterprises and marvels which amaze us owe their existence to the spirit of association and participation of the most flourishing nations."[32]

The company's first step was the purchase of a suitable site. The garden design was produced by the garden architect Petersheim as a combination of French, Italian, and English styles. Who the architect of the hothouse actually was is a matter of controversy. The preliminary design came from the well-known architect Tieleman Franciscus Suys, but it proved to be too expensive to carry out. Preference

204
Site plan, 1885.

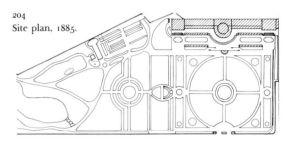

205
Lithograph by Jobard, 1827.

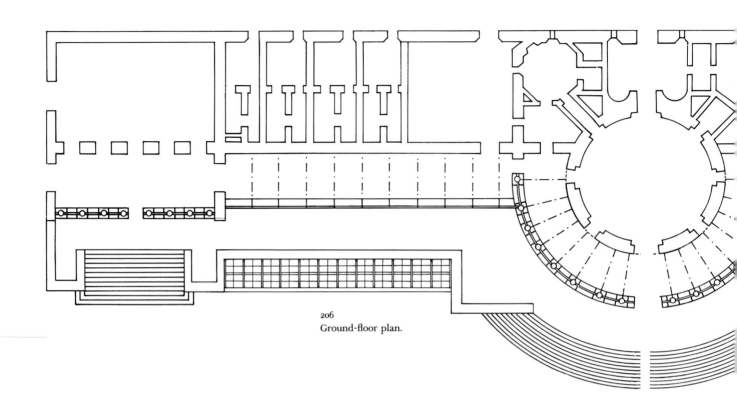

206
Ground-floor plan.

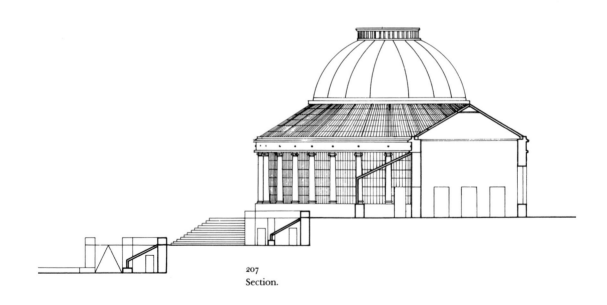

207
Section.

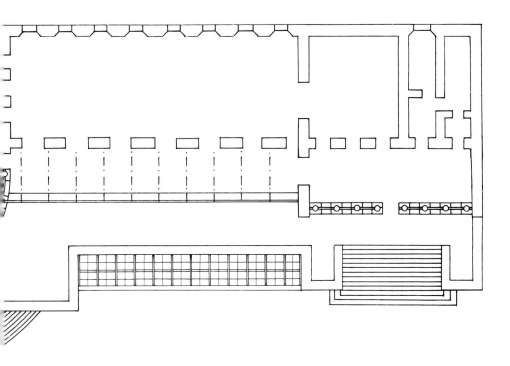

208
During construction.
Lithograph by Lavis
de Vitzthumb, 1827.

was shown for a design by Gineste, a theater architect. All the evidence indicates that Meeus-Wouters, who was commissioned to carry out the work, was concerned not only with the detailing, the choice of material, and the supervision of the work, but also to a great extent with the design philosophy.[33] In 1829 the building work was inaugurated with a banquet, a public holiday, and fireworks.

According to the opinion of the time, the gardens and the building were interpreted as a creation of "fort belle allure." The people of Brussels called the building their Acropolis. Victor Hugo proclaimed it one of the wonders of the world.

The members of the board of directors who were appointed by the city linked the Botanical Gardens with the fulfillment of cultural interests in the service of the public, whereas the supporters of the other trend were chiefly concerned with getting the maximum return on the capital invested. The latter group prevailed, and a total commercialization of the Botanical Gardens came about. A pavilion for the sale of popular plants was built, and price stickers went on all the plants. The company was said to have "transformed the glasshouses into kinds of market stalls."[34] Under these circumstances the Botanical Gardens and their associated buildings went into a decline. With the building of the Gare du Nord in 1841 in the vicinity of the Botanical Gardens, an opportunity presented itself to the commercially oriented group to divide up the site and exploit it by land speculation. The threatening dissolution was prevented by the promise of municipal assistance, and the company came under state control. The continuing conflict was resolved in 1870 when the city acquired the Botanical Gardens. The company was liquidated and the Botanical Gardens were rescued.

A glazed peristyle fitted out with Ionic columns, in the middle of the large tropical house, carries a gently sloping glass roof. There is a rotunda ("Palais de Flore") with a dome overhead. At the ends of the building, glass-covered orangeries stand between columns and an architrave. The central section is joined to the orangeries by two 112-foot-long hothouses, which on the main frontage have a lean-to roof and are glazed all over. Behind the rotunda there are adjoining rooms for administration and for the gardeners. The rooms situated below the terrace are used as workshops for the hothouses.

Sources: archives of City of Brussels; library of National Botanical Gardens of Belgium.

References: Balis 1970, pp. 11–15; Neumann 1862.

Brussels

Bouchot
Jardin Botanique
Victoria Regia House (fig. 513)
diameter: 46 feet
height (inside): 13 feet
architect: Alphonse Balat
built 1859

The architect Alphonse Balat, well known for the building of the large hothouse complex at Laeken, designed this hothouse, which was built first in the Zoological Gardens, then in the Brussels Botanical Gardens, and finally at Bouchot, about 6 miles north of the center of Brussels. Balat solved the problem of connecting the bell-shaped dome to pointed arch structures by extending the internal space of the dome by eight recesses which terminated vertically. The dome is supported by eight ribs rising from the corners of the octagon and joined together at the apex by a lantern ring. Ornamental use was made of the braced girders and the wrought-iron ribs. Curved iron sash bars, which intersect the barrel-shaped glass shell of the recesses, support the glass roof as well as the ribs. With this intersection of three-dimensional forms Balat achieved a variety of lightweight spatial forms.

The building is extant.

Sources: archives of City of Brussels; library of National Botanical Gardens of Belgium.

Brussels

Laeken
Royal Park
Winter Garden and Conservatories

The technical possibility of creating large transparent buildings with artificial landscapes was used extensively in the Royal Park at Laeken during the last third of the nineteenth century. Thirty-six separate buildings, including winter gardens, hothouses, and orangeries, were constructed here and were linked by glass corridors into a continuous glass complex and connected to the royal castle—an idealistic town of megalomanic dimensions, comparable to the architectural designs of the Revolutionary period (Boullée, Ledoux). The winter gardens and the glass corridors formed an interconnected indoor space nearly a mile in length and covered an area of almost 5 acres.

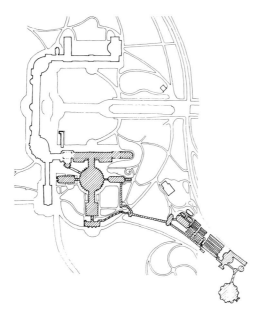

Buildings of this order of magnitude designated for use by the public had indeed been designed, but none had actually been built before. The execution of these ideas did not arise from the public purposes of an urban community but, in an irony of history, from orders given by the sovereign, and for his own purposes. The King of Belgium Leopold II (1865–1909) was the initiator and in part the designer of the layout at Laeken. Increased state revenue formed the economic and the ideological basis for the acquisition by conquest of colonies, particularly in Africa. These acquisitions were represented by collections of tropical plants in the glasshouses at Laeken. However, such an undertaking by a king in the era of the middle classes was questioned. A long, drawn-out conflict with financial authorities arose on account of the expense of the Laeken project. Meanwhile, Leopold's passion for flowers and exotic plants increased steadily. "The flowers were poetry to him and were for him a revenge against the exigencies of reality."[35] Leopold commissioned the French landscape gardener Laine to transform the purchased piece of land into an English park with splendid views and a multitude of artificial lakes. But the focal point of the establishment was to be the glass-and-iron hothouses, which were to enclose a tropical landscape of hitherto unattained size and abundance of flora. With the rebuilding of the old orangery (originally built by the Dutch) there began a chain of hothouse building which continued without a break for 25 years. The king appointed Balat, who also carried out the reconstruction of the castle, as the chief architect. His most notable buildings are the riding school (1873), the great rotunda (1876), the addition to the orangery (1883), the palm house (1885), the Diana Glasshouse (1886), and the Serre du Congo. "The collection of orange trees at Laeken," wrote Leopold in 1908, "is together with the camellia collection the most beautiful on the continent. The orange trees of Laeken are infinitely more beautiful than those of Versailles and those in the Tuileries. The collection of camellias is absolutely unique."[36]

However, Leopold's battle with the financial authorities compelled him to compromise. Around 1900 he allowed the hothouse buildings to come under state control through an endowment. At the same time, the hothouses were opened to the public for a few days in the year. But the upkeep and operation of the hothouse area entailed heavy costs, and it was proposed that the costs be partly covered by the budget for the colonies. The king's continued building activity, which seemed to follow the most aggressive ideas, brought bitter opposition from the public. One particularly controversial plan involved the installation of an underground railway. The pressure of public opinion caused the king to emphasize toward the end of his reign that Laeken should take on a public function as the "Palace of the Nation."

The layout at Laeken is notable not only on account of the extraordinary order of magnitude of the whole design but also on account of the architectural and structural quality of its individual buildings, such as the Winter Garden with its wings, the Serre du Congo, the Serre aux Palmiers, and the Serre Chapelle. The bell-shaped glass rotunda of the winter garden, the arched ribs of which were consciously made to play a part in the hierarchy of spatial forms, is one of the most splendid structures of its kind.

Winter Garden (figs. 210–214, 504–509, 514)
diameter: 185 feet
height: ca. 100 feet
architects: Alphonse Balat, Henri Maquet
built 1875–76

Balat's winter garden (Jardin d'Hiver) at Laeken is one of the largest glass-and-iron structures built in the nineteenth century. A ring of 36 white marble Doric columns support 36 ornamental curved lattice girders, which, joined to the lantern-topped dome, break up the outline of the glass skin in a downward direction and give it an external structure. There is a place for tall palms in the central space formed by the columns. A 26-foot-wide corridor outside the ring of columns is joined to two elongated wings situated on one axis and covered with glass barrel vaults. One of the wings leads to the Serre du Congo, the other to the old orangery. The royal pal-

210
Facade.

211
Section and view of
interior structure.

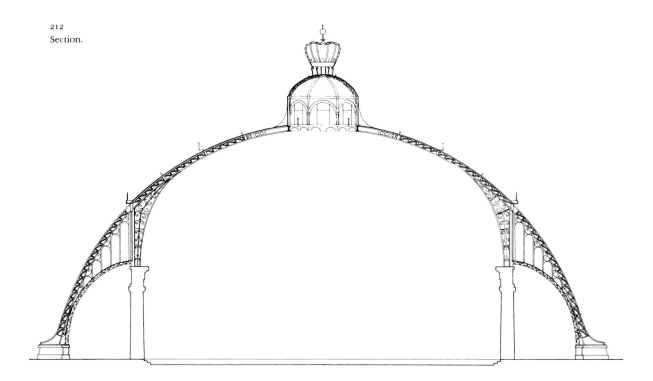

ace joins onto the orangery, which is provided with a glass theater. This complex of rooms, the focal point of which is the winter garden, was designated for festive occasions and is linked by glass corridors to a further ensemble of hothouses.

Alfred Meyer describes the spatial and structural aspects of the Laeken winter garden in his 1907 book *Eisenbauten, ihre Geschichte und Ästhetik* (iron buildings, their history and aesthetics):

In monumental and stone architecture [the bell] has only found a use until now as a depressed dome above a high masonry base, and then relatively seldom, because the major trend in dome construction is toward the steep upward-pointing curve. The concept of shaping a dome structure to rise directly from the ground like a flat hill was of course never taken up until the development of iron space-frame structures. A hothouse again provided the occasion, this time the work of a Belgian architect Balat, who merely had to put into effect the idea of his royal client. Leopold II, in pursuance of his large decorated buildings of the 1870s of the older orangery halls of his castle at Laeken, 4 km north of Brussels, wanted to add on a centerpiece winter garden. The palms demanded a high central space. It was suggested that it be given a lower surrounding corridor. This basilica type of design for hothouses was well established and had already been used by Paxton at Chatsworth. But there, and also elsewhere, this was the case mostly with elongated buildings; at Laeken as a centralized building. This is important here for the historical aspects of style, like the combination of a hemisphere and a rectangular aisle which one is accustomed to seeing in the ambulatory of medieval churches, but the doubling of the whole into a centralized

building space was very rare. But the most important individuality remains in the iron framework of the whole of the illuminated space and the execution of the curvature, which can be very easily compared to a flattish bell, or a shell. There are 36 powerful stone Doric columns on a masonry plinth with correspondingly stout stone entablatures surrounding the large circular space with a diameter of 41.25 m. Its height has been matched to the almost 8 m wide adjoining ambulatory, which has a quadrant-shaped cross-section. It too rests on a masonry base, but consists only of iron and glass. In keeping with the main basilica theme there is a low clerestory, which can be considered as a tambour in relation to the main dome above it, around the inside circle of the ambulatory and above the circle of columns. The main dome itself has only a flatly curved outline, and it supports at a height of 25.64 m above ground level a 12-sided 8 m wide lantern with a model of the royal crown on top. The whole of this part too consists only of iron and glass.

The new attractiveness of this spatial form has its origin, apart from its transparent clarity in every sense of the term, in the dominating appearance of the curved glass surfaces, and in its finely proportioned curvature. But it has been substantially heightened, not only on the inside but outside, through the lines of the space frame used in the construction of this glass body. There are 36 braced girders on the inside rising from the same number of columns; richly decorated iron ribs which rise from immediately below the round arched arcades of the clerestory and arranged in groups of three to twelve radially by abutting against the 12-sided unusual lantern with a surrounding ring of semicircles. Thus the whole interior of the building is very richly variegated because of the effective contrast between the straight lines and the multiplicity of curves in this crowning struc-

213
Ground-floor plan.

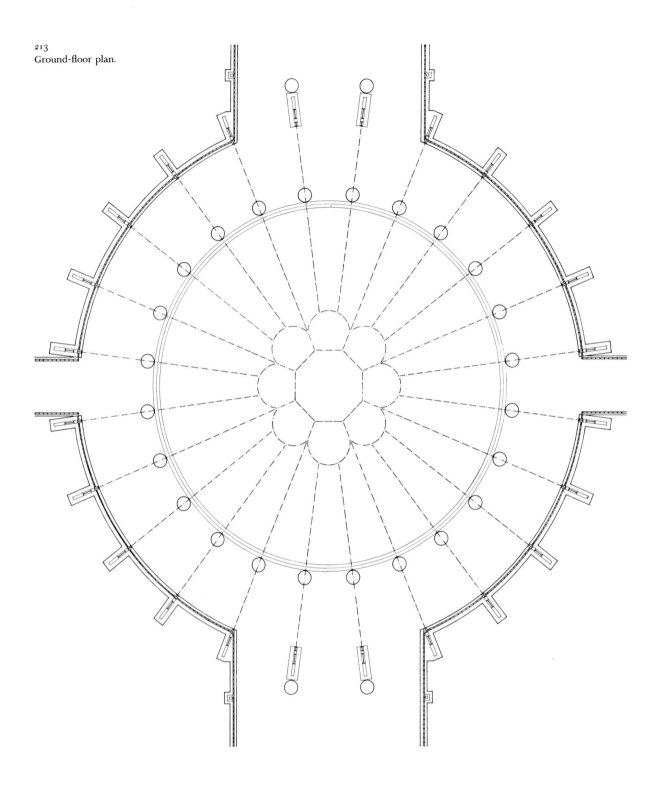

214
Overall view
ca. 1876. Engraving.

ture with its separate parts, in which all the ribs hasten to meet each other like converging rays. But even more effective is the message conveyed by the lines in the outer framework. The 36 ribs there rise from the masonry plinth at the base up to the lantern as unbroken curved ribs. Their external outline shows an uncommonly fine depressed curve which cuts into a stone base below and runs upward with just as elegant indentation into the base of the lantern with an equally elegant embayment. Its inside, lower, outline follows the quadrant vault of the low ambulatory. The intervening wedge-shaped space created between the lower and upper ribs is infilled with Gothic style arcades. Even disregarding the great charms of the different lines of the arches and the curved surfaces themselves, the overall appearance of this dome structure retains its notable individuality. However, one is through the Gothic arrangement of the ribs accustomed to seeing similar strutted ribs, but these adapt themselves easily to be in harmony with the more or less harsh flat surfaces of the roofs. At Laeken, however, they nestle tightly against the curved surfaces of the glass roof with the same degree of curvature, and the external dominating outline of the braced ribs is common to the aisles and to the nave over considerable distances. It therefore brings together into an artistic unity an austere as well as a pleasing spatial form. In the series of buildings this royal hothouse at Laeken has a significance similar to that of Gautier's Paris hothouse in the evolution of elongated halls, but it is much larger, and above all it is a pure iron and glass building in which all the ornamentation is most expertly executed in iron."[37]

The central heating plant was built next to the winter garden, with a chimney capped with a minaret. Three miles of pipe, covered with cast-iron gratings, are housed in channels in the ambulatory of the circular building and exposed in the wings along the walls. Double glazing is used. In the upper part of the dome it is fixed to the outside; in the lower part it is on the inside, so that the space frame can be seen from the outside. This arrangement brings about a sense of excitement when one sees the proportions between the continuous glass skin of the upper part and the glass surface broken into segments by the ribs of the lower part of the dome.

The building is extant and well maintained.

Serre Chapelle

overall diameter: 73 feet
diameter of dome: 99 feet
architects: Alphonse Balat and Leopold II
built ca. 1886

A small glass-covered corridor called the Chemin du Paradis joined the palm house to the Serre Chapelle, which also served as a tropical house. The Serre Chapelle, built at the highest point of the Royal Park, is a church made entirely of glass and iron and decorated with exotic plants. According to Borncrêpe, "this hothouse church is the personal work of Leopold II. In the course of his many travels the late King visited several important horticultural institutions, among them the celebrated tropical houses in the Royal Gardens at Kew, and the Palm Garden in Frankfurt. When he conceived the idea of building the Chapel he talked freely to the architect Balat and, with a pencil in his hand and apologizing for not knowing the details of the design, sketched the main outlines of his idea. Balat was to put this concept into being. Obedient to His Majesty the pencil sketched, this time in outline, modifying this, deleting that, adding one detail, reinforcing another. Then the architect resumed his work. No less than six or seven designs were referred to the great builder, and each one had several alterations made, until finally the design decided upon corresponded entirely to the desired concept."[38]

The chapel is a compact circular building surrounded by a low corridor to which is joined a set of radiating small chapels to form a chevet consisting of ten apses. The 82 1/2-foot-high dome is supported by iron ribs which rise from a ring of twin columns made of granite. The ribs are reinforced at the bottom ends by round iron arches placed between them. The ridge roof of the ambulatory is attached to this structure. The interior has been rebuilt; otherwise the building has not been altered.

Serre du Congo

base area: 99 × 99 feet
height: 66 feet
architect: Alphonse Balat
built 1886

The Serre du Congo and the hothouse of the Escalier Blanc are parts of a scheme in which glass buildings, descending in steps to the gardens, are placed alongside the dominating winter garden. The central dome of the rotunda is once again taken up in the Serre du Congo, which, with its five little towers, serves as a counterbalance to the large bell. The Serre du Congo, which in silhouette is reminiscent of Byzantine church architecture, is extant and well maintained.

Serre aux Palmiers (fig. 512)

length: 148 1/2 feet
width: 99 feet
height: 49 1/2 feet
architect: Alphonse Balat
built 1885

This palm house, simple in overall shape and devoid of decoration, is a remarkable example of early objective architecture, on a par with the best examples of early factory buildings. The flattish dome above a compressed ellipse, with adjoining vaulted wings, reminds one of Baroque architecture. However, the matter-of-fact way in which the problem of enclosing space is solved by using glass and iron allows one to forget this leaning toward tradition. The interior on the other side of the glass skin can be perceived from the outside, and this lends the structure its modernity.

The development of the elongated dome had its origins in the fact that palms find ideal environmental conditions below a glass canopy. The large opening in the center of the front, need for the movement of large palm trees, is an integral part of the projecting glass wall.

This tropical house is one of the most important of Balat's Laeken buildings because, without any accessories, it expresses itself as a pure form of purpose building. It is extant and well maintained.

Sources: archives of City of Brussels; Royal Albert Library, Cabinet des Estampes.

References: Deutsche Bauzeitung (publ.), *Baukunde des Architekten*, 1902, vol. 2, pp. 361, 437, 438; Meyer 1907; Borncrêpe 1920, pp. 177 ff.

Budleigh Salterton, Devon

Bicton Gardens
Palm House (figs. 215–218, 519–525)

length: 69 feet
width: 32 feet
height: 27 feet
architect: unknown; possibly D. and E. Bailey
built ca. 1843

The small, steeply vaulted, delicate Bicton Gardens palm house is the only existing early English hothouse built in Loudon's style. The buildings of similar structural principles mentioned in the literature, like Sir George Mackenzie's "warm roof" (fig. 117), the Bayswater glasshouses (fig. 141), Mrs. Beaumont's

215
Site plan.

Conservatory at Bretton Hall (figs. 200–203), and the Pantheon Bazaar conservatory in London (fig. 327) were all demolished in the nineteenth century. No other building in existence today shows the filigree work of iron sash bars supporting a glass dome with such technical daring.

This building provides powerful evidence of the pioneering attitude of British engineers. At the same time, it is important as a representative of Loudon's structural types and as a manifestation of the modern art of building as seen in the early industrial period. Because the space frame and the external glass skin are in a single plane and the use of master ribs has been avoided, the pure geometrical forms—inside as well as outside—are clearly noticeable. The combination of a high vaulted glass dome with two lower lateral domes which intersect with it and penetrate it in three dimensions gives rise to an architecture which is logically developed from the ironwork. This building rises elegantly from the ground to the apex and is made entirely of glass and iron, in striking contrast to the conventional architecture of its time.

Bicton Gardens, situated on high ground between Exmouth and Sidmouth, approximately a mile from the village of East Budleigh, was built in an extensive Baroque park which merged into an English landscaped garden. On the crest were built charming hothouses and orangeries with a broad view of the nearby sea from their terraces. Bicton Gardens was originally, from 1500, part of the estate of the Rolle family. In 1750 an Italian garden was laid out here by Baron Rolle of Stevenstone, the design of which was ostensibly conceived by André Le Nôtre, the creator of the gardens at Versailles. The focal point of the layout is a rectangular pool with a fountain

and statues. A temple-like orangery and five hothouses built along a high brick wall form the top boundary of the gently sloping Baroque garden (fig. 215).[39] The palm house, set a little distance apart from the Baroque garden and joined to it by a short pathway, was probably built around 1843. The architects of this curvilinear glass object were probably D. and E. Bailey, who built numerous glasshouses around 1820 using Loudon's space-frame system. Details of the ironwork of the vault remind one of these buildings—for example, the camellia house for Loddiges at Hackney (figs. 262–267). Pevsner supports the theory that the palm house was built around 1825, but Hix favors a later date, after 1843. The fact that Loudon visited Bicton Gardens in 1843 but did not mention the palm house in his *Gardener's Magazine* and the similarity of the ventilation arrangement to that of the curvilinear house at Chiswick (built in 1840 by W. and D. Bailey) lend support to Hix's opinion.[40]

The 27-foot-high main vault of the palm house is built on a 30 × 15-foot rectangular base, and the attached semicircle has a radius of 15 feet. Side vaults, 20 feet high, adjoin symmetrically left and right. An 8-foot-high cast-iron framework runs along the base, which itself is made of narrow pilasters, decorated with rosettes, and curved architraves. Above this rises the graceful sweep of the glass vault. The palm house is bounded at the rear by a brick wall, which is joined to the vault along its length (figs. 216–218). All three glass vaults are made of very thin T-section sash bars, which follow the line of the profile. Placed approximately 7 inches apart at the bottom of the surrounding ribs of the space frame, they run upward into the apex of the vault, merging so that their number is reduced, as in rosettes. The adjoining front and side vaults are made of parallel sash bars. The ridge of the main vault is capped by a narrow iron cover plate with louvers for ventilation. The only additional support from below for this glass skin consists of curved metal bar rafters which follow the inside profile of the roof of the main vault and the wings. Horizontal retaining rings around the insides of the wings, also made of curved bars, are supported at the intersection of the vaults and on the inside of the side vaults by iron columns only 2 inches in diameter. The additional reinforcement, which was incorporated with an obvious playfulness, was needed because the forces transmitted down the line of the glass skin through the sash bars could no longer be withstood by the bars themselves, as is the case with closed vaults. These iron bars tend to vanish from sight when seen against the light coming from the sky, and appear as little more than a net-

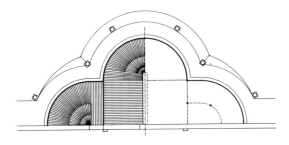

216
Ground-floor plan
and view of roof.

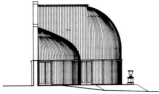

217
Side facade.

218
Section.

work of pencil lines. This is an unsurpassed example of the fine filigree work that characterizes all hot-houses built in Loudon's style. It is the product of an engineering achievement the basis of which had not yet been worked out by means of mathematical analysis. Loudon wrote about this kind of structure in 1818, and in the Bicton Gardens palm house we find confirmation of what he predicted.[41]

References: Hix 1974, pp. 24–27; Loudon 1818; James 1973, pp. 3–9.

Buxton

Pavilion Gardens
Hothouse (figs. 219, 220, 526)
architect: Edward Milner
built 1871

These elongated glass-and-iron buildings enclose a large octagonal concert hall with a dome roof, a theater, a restaurant, a café, and a hothouse, all connected by glass corridors. The complex is still in existence today, after being rebuilt, and is fulfilling its original function. All the buildings were designed by Edward Milner, the assistant with whom Paxton had collaborated on the Great Conservatory at Chatsworth.

The complex of pavilions and corridors incorporated some of the elements of the Crystal Palace in its structure. Figure 220 illustrates the use of round cast-iron columns for the corridors, joined together by horizontal cast-iron frames with inscribed semi-circular window arches. In the cubic-styled hothouse, which served as the palm court, the columns are raised to about twice the length of those outside and they end in richly decorated capitals supported by a pyramidal glass roof. The horizontal bracing of the corridors continues through the middle of the facade and reinforces the slender columns. These support a strongly profiled architrave which projects above the tops of the columns. The glass canopy forming the roof is supported in the corners by four diagonal iron girders braced by round-section steel bars above the hall. The hothouse facade has the simple geometrical form of well-proportioned and segmental cubic shapes and is covered by a pyramid, but has been robbed of its decorative elements. The adjoining cast-iron-frame corridors have been replaced partly by wooden structures and partly by a solid roof. The round arches of the windows and the projecting glass roof above the entrance have been removed. The horizontal strip has been faced with

219
Site plan, 1974.

220
Woodcut of
conservatory.

sheet metal. As a result of this interference with the original design, the building can be recognized only by its basic shape.

Source: Department of Technical Services, Town Hall, Buxton.

Reference: Chadwick 1966, p. 146.

Capesthorne Hall, Cheshire

Davenport Conservatory (fig. 221)

length: 151 feet
width: 40 feet
height: 25 feet
architect: Joseph Paxton
built ca. 1837

At about the same time (1836–1840) the Great Conservatory at Chatsworth was built, Joseph Paxton also built an extensive hothouse at Capesthorne Hall, Cheshire, for Edward Davies Davenport, who was a friend of the Duke of Devonshire, Paxton's employer and patron. Capesthorne was extended by Edward Blore in 1837. The conservatory, erected below the new buildings, was a three-bay basilica-style building. Its first illustration is in a view of the house dated 1843. It is probable that the design of the hothouse was completed before Paxton went on his travels in October 1838. In contrast to the Great Conservatory, this building was not in the curvilinear style, although the rafter frame of the nave was made of laminated wood. The roof was of normal lean-to ridge-and-furrow construction, like the roofs of the wings. The vertical glass front appears to have been a plane structure with cast-iron columns. The

221
Interior view. Water-color by James John-son, ca. 1843.

hothouse was accessible from the library and was joined to a chapel. It had a special forcing-house section for tropical plants. The conservatory survived the fire at Capesthorne in 1861, but like its large predecessor it was demolished around 1920.

The noteworthy point about the Capesthorne conservatory is that it was a hothouse covered with plane surfaces with a ridge-and-furrow roof and a perpendicular front, which Paxton later brought to maturity in the Crystal Palace. The design problem of the best column-and-beam arrangement for a gently sloping ridge roof was not solved here; Paxton did not accomplish this until a decade later in the building of the victoria regia house at Chatsworth.

Reference: Chadwick 1961, pp. 98–99.

Chatsworth, Derbyshire

Duke of Devonshire's Estate

Hothouses (figs. 527–535)

Chatsworth, the scene of Joseph Paxton's first work, was the summer residence of the Duke of Devonshire, one of the richest of England's peers. It is situated in the county of Derbyshire in a broad valley through which the River Derwent flows. The position of the park is determined by the hilly nature of the landscape and its continually varying scenery. According to an 1881 account, "the landscape gardener could not wish for better for his purposes. Indeed one may make the statement that nature herself has provided here almost all the stimulus for the creation of an imposing garden and park on the grand scale. Sir Joseph Paxton, the real creator of the present day park and gardens at Chatsworth, found here on the scale provided by nature a very advantageous field for his artistic capabilities. We must not forget either that the execution of his designs was in part due to the favourable climatic conditions in England generally, and in particular the quite unusual financial resources compared with our standards on the Continent which were available."[42]

Paxton came to Chatsworth in 1826 as a trained gardener. Working scientifically from the start, he was concerned with the design and development of glasshouses as part of his gardening work. The series of glasshouses he built here began in 1828 with small forcing houses. In 1832 he covered in the old orangery with a wooden structure. With the palm house (1833) he experimented with a roof and supporting system which he would later perfect in the Great Conservatory.

222
Site plan.

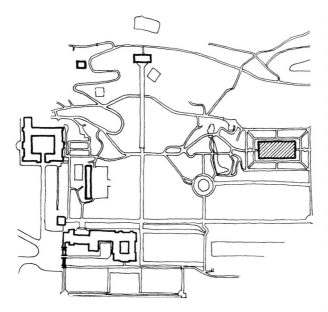

Toward the end of the 1830s, on the recommendation of the Duke, Paxton simultaneously built hothouses in other places besides Chatsworth—among them the large conservatory at Capesthorne. In 1848 he covered the "Conservative Wall" with glass. In 1849 he built the victoria regia house, a building in which he brought his roof and roof-support system to a final state of perfection. Although all these glasshouses built by Paxton at Chatsworth were made partly of wood, they were in their structural and manufacturing techniques the models for the large glass-and-iron structures of the succeeding period. Paxton consistently tried to apply the technical possibilities of advanced industry to his hothouses. By differentiating the important structural elements (beams, columns, roof skin) according to their individual functions, he succeeded in inventing building parts which were standardized and assembled in separate operations, so that it was no longer a matter of making buildings piecemeal and individually. This provided the basis for the installation of machinery for the mass production of the components. Thus Paxton succeeded in transferring an important part of the building process from the site to the factory, and in this way he brought about the prerequisite for the industrialization of the construction industry. Paxton's Crystal Palace, the greatest exhibition building of the nineteenth century, was made possible by these means. George F. Chadwick's book gives the most comprehensive and painstaking description of Paxton's work at Chatsworth.

The chief problem that had to be solved in Paxton's time was the development of a glass roof that would have highest strength, durability, and (not least) light transmission. Furthermore, there was a need to develop a space frame of the maximum span for the minimum cross-section—a space frame that would be structurally separate from the plane of the glass skin and at the same time capable of removing rainwater. Finally, there was the development of a column with the minimum diameter to support the roof and transmit its compressive force foundations. These three basic building components of the hothouse structure were made by mass-production means. In spite of the fact that glass had already been used for a considerable time for hothouses in botanical gardens and orangeries, there was until the early nineteenth century little attempt to rationalize the design principles of such structures. The main knowledge of the subject which had filtered through was that of the dependence of the optimum transmission of the sun's rays on the slope of the glass surface. In this connection, Sir George Mackenzie in 1815 for the first time proposed a hemispherical shape for hothouses. In 1816, J. C. Loudon developed proposals resulting from these considerations into curvilinear glass domes, simultaneously with proposals for a pleated glass roof. This system is now known as the ridge-and-furrow roof. Loudon even proposed the principle of the pleated roof in combination with the curvilinear roof—a very daring structure which, until its realization, made necessary a series of experiments in hothouse building. Loudon himself did not have the chance to carry out these experiments on the grand scale in order to prove his theory. It remained to Paxton to investigate this highly important development on a large scale and to raise it to the standard of industrialized production. Loudon had advocated the use of iron in hothouses, but Paxton at first preferred to use the hybrid wood-and-iron structure. This combined utility, durability, and ease of supply, and it was very suitable on economic grounds. According to Paxton's own report (ca. 1831–32), he went on to translate the principle of the ridge-and-furrow roof from theory into practice:

For several years we used all the ingenuity we possessed in endeavouring to make flat wooden roofs as light as possible, on account of their cheapness, and we certainly did succeed in making them much lighter than we remember to have seen them in any other place; but as we never mean from this time either to erect flat roofs ourselves, or recommend them to be erected by others, it will not be either interesting or useful to detail our numerous experiments.

About three years ago it occurred to us that wooden roofs would admit much more light, if the sashes were fixed in angles. We tried a small range of houses on this principle, with the sash bars fixed lengthways, the usual way, and raf-

ters to bear up the lights. These houses were very light, and the plan appeared to possess several advantages—1st., more morning and evening sun were received, and at an earlier hour than a flat roof house; and 2ndly., the violence of the mid-day sun was mitigated by the disposition of the angled lights receiving the sun's rays in an oblique direction. Subsequent experience has led us to make several more alterations, such as doing away with rafters altogether, changing the longitudinal position of the sash bars, &c. . . .[44]

With the observation about "fixing in angles" Paxton meant the pleated glass roof, which in future was to be the major principle behind all his glasshouses. In 1832 Paxton used for the new ridge-and-furrow system for the first time in the rebuilding of the old 1697 orangery into a "warm house." In 1834 he described his by now fully developed system in the *Magazine of Botany*, referring to an actual example (fig. 223):

This was a greenhouse 97 ft. 6 in. long and 26 ft. from the back wall (of brick) to the front, the height of the rear being 13 ft. 6 in. at the valley and 15 ft. at the ridge and 8 ft. 6 in. in the valley and 10 ft. to ridge at the front. The sloping roof was of ridge and furrow pattern, without rafters and with extremely thin sash bars of wood, supported by 3 in. diameter cast iron columns 6 ft. 6 in. apart along the front of the house and an internal row along the centre. The front columns were hollow and discharged the rainwater from the roof to a gravelled path outside, so that no external gutters or down-pipes were needed. There were no doors, the vertical lights forming the sides sliding in grooves so that access could be effected at any point as desired. The floor was slatted so that dust could be swept through, and the house was heated by flues from four fires.[45]

Thus, Paxton had in a relatively short time invented and refined the vocabulary of these structures, which were to see service for the next 30 years. His attention was applied to buildings of varied form and size, but during that time he used the same basic components. The main innovation was to be consummated in the construction of the girders. In 1852 Paxton described this to the Royal Commission. As Chadwick reports, "He had perfected the covering, and the structure supporting it could be greatly varied to suit changing conditions and changing uses."[46]

Paxton's relationship with industrialized prefabrication is shown clearly in the design of the roof of the Great Conservatory at Chatsworth. The large numbers of identical pieces of iron section needed for the sashes could be produced in an economical way only by machines. Paxton developed a woodworking machine driven by a 3-horsepower steam engine. With a combination of saws and a router he was able to make the required section. In 1838 he had developed this into an efficient machine that required only

three operations to produce each sash bar: A coarse saw cut up the boards into sections, which were cut and shaped on one side and then on the other side. For the development of this machine, Paxton was awarded the Silver Medal of the Royal Society of Arts in 1840. For the Great Conservatory, 40 miles of sash bars were made with this machine, which meant a saving of about £1,200 in labor costs.

For such a large greenhouse as the Great Conservatory, further development work was necessary to make the glass cover suitable for the span. Paxton combined the pleated roof principle with curvilinear roof shapes as well as lean-to roofs. In 1836 he tested such a curvilinear cover on a 60-by-26-foot forcing house. The roof had the shape of an ellipse. This glasshouse sheltered the victoria regia plant until the building of a special house for it 13 years later. The supporting ribs of this building were boards joined together like lamellae to form a girder, which was then cut to the desired curvature. (Loudon's *Encyclopaedia* carried a report on a further design with a curvilinear roof by Paxton for the Loddiges brothers at Hackney in London.) When Paxton started the Great Conservatory, in 1836, the roof system was so well developed that it could be mass produced on a large scale.

Simultaneous with the solution of the basic problem of the roof elements, Paxton turned his attention to the problem of the supporting structure—in particular the removal of the rainwater. The famous Paxton gutter was made so that it collected the rainwater and led it away into hollow cast-iron columns.

223
Prefabricated conservatory, 1834.

In 1836, when he had already done the preparatory work for the Great Conservatory, Paxton experimented with the Small Forcing House, using the above-mentioned curvilinear roof and using curved gutters for the first time.

Wood was the material Paxton preferred to use for the members of the ridge-and-furrow roof and for the gutter beams, all of which were directly exposed to the weather. He used iron for the members that were protected from the direct effects of the weather and that had to perform functions for which wood did not have enough strength: hollow columns, tie rods, bolts, joints in girders carrying heavy loads, braced girders for the large spans of flat roofs, and prefabricated facades. Some authors have implied that Paxton's buildings were wholly made of iron, but the existing buildings and plans refute this. His own statements prove that he preferred wood in certain places:

My opinion is, after great experience—and I have gone into that question without the smallest prejudice in favour of wood—my belief is that (unless it is made of copper or brass) wood will last longer than iron in such a place. Wherever my experience goes, that is the result, and I have tried the roofs in every possible way.

If I had tomorrow morning to put up a roof, and you gave me the money to spend it for doing it in metal, I have no doubt I could put it up so much cheaper in wood, that the interest of the money I should have over would put a perpetual roof on for everlasting.

Paxton based his argument on the economy of the wooden roof together with its durability:

If you have wooden bars and iron gutters you will have the greatest difficulty in the world in making them act together. The two do not act together. Metal expands and contracts and is subject to certain influences; wood is a non-conductor and is not affected in that way. My plan is to spread the whole of the covering upon the iron and fasten it to it. I should never bring any iron to exposure to the atmosphere. I think if you had at all an inclination to put up iron gutters, you should have our gutters at Chatsworth, which have been up twenty years. See how well they stand, where the water is carried off from the wood, because I maintain that the great principle to keep wood from rotting is to keep it exposed to the atmosphere. Wherever you keep wood covered up it will not last very long; for instance, if you lead these gutters they would not stand; they would rot three times as fast. You have only to take care that the water is quickly delivered from it, and to keep it well painted, and there is no end almost to the time that good wood would last.[47]

Great Conservatory (figs. 224–226, 527, 528, 530–532)

length: 279 feet
width: 124 feet
height: 68 feet
architect: Joseph Paxton
built 1836–1840
demolished ca. 1920

A remark made by the Duke of Wellington about his visit to Chatsworth in 1893 shows what an impression the Great Conservatory made on contemporaries: "I have travelled Europe through and through, and witnessed many scenes of surpassing grandeur on many occasions, but never did I see so magnificent a coup d'oeil as that extended before me."[48] The appearance of the building was in fact revolutionary. The completely detached building, 66 feet high, descended on all sides from the ridge down to the ground in two glass vaults. The glass vaults were made on the ridge-and-furrow principle and segmented at the same time. Through the curvature of the ridges and furrows, made wholly of glass and running from top to bottom, the conservatory obtained the character of a giant crystalline mountain in which the surroundings were reflected as well as the sky. The interrupted crystal surfaces of the outer shell created a form with a quality of glazing that was not attained again. In spite of its imposing size, the building had an ethereal appearance hitherto unknown in the history of architecture. The interior space formed by the glass vaults, with their lines of cast-iron columns, was compared to a cathedral.[49]

As with all buildings that openly convey the aspect of the modern to the observer, the aesthetic appearance is only a reflection of the whole logical structure created from the building brief, which not only contains technical possibilities but also presses for further progress. If we compare the Great Conservatory with the largest hall buildings of its time, the railway-station concourses, then its importance becomes clear. The architects and the engineers of that time were competing with each other to reach the greatest spans. The first Lime Street Station in Liverpool (1836) had a conventional wooden framework with a span of 55 feet; the first Euston Station in London (1835–1839) had iron beams spanning 139 feet; Derby (1839–1841) had iron beams spanning 112 feet, and the first Temple Meads Station in Bristol (1839–40) had a wooden hammer beam roof with a clear span of 72 1/2 feet. Thus, it is clear that Paxton could compete with the most experienced engineers of the time by using a clear span of 71 feet.

The location of the Great Conservatory, far from
the house in a clearing in the woods, shows that in
those days people were conscious of the entirely new
designs and wanted to avoid having a conflict with
the traditional architectural styles. Paxton wrote in
this context about the function of a hothouse as follows: "If temples or other erection are visible from
the house, it is indispensable that they should harmonize with it. But there is one edifice totally opposite to a residence which requires more complete
and decided isolation, and must be situated in a spot
where its own influence can be felt. This is the Conservatory, which should not be near the mansion. . . . the outline of a conservatory is as remote as
possible from that of a mansion, and the quantity of
glass it contains renders it strikingly peculiar."[50]

By careful study of the account books for the
building of the Great Conservatory, Chadwick has
been able to reconstruct the progress of the building
method. The amounts spent were £1,416 in 1836,
£5,221 in 1837, £5,231 in 1838, £6,458 in 1839, £11,673
in 1840, and £3,100 in 1841. The total cost was
£33,099 10s 11d. "The first item of the account is a
payment of £38 15s. 0d. to John Marples, foreman
carpenter, on January 12th 1836, 'for making the
Model.' The making of a model, of course, presup-
poses that the conservatory had already been designed, and the model may have been intended to
show to the Duke; alternatively, it is possible that the
purpose of the model was to try out different constructional systems in miniature."[51] Further entries in
the accounts for the same year were for traveling ex-
penses to London, Hull, and Hove. In Hove, Paxton
visited Henry Phillips's glass Anthaeum, which later
collapsed. These journeys showed that Paxton was
looking for information in all directions before he
began his great design. He also went to see Robert
Lucas Chance, the Birmingham glass manufacturer,
probably at an early stage in the design of the
glasshouse.

After the building was settled in terms of structure
and proportions it became necessary to specify the
size of the space frame of the whole structure, which
was determined by the maximum length of the glass
panes in production at that time. In using the ridge-
and-furrow system, Paxton wanted to increase the
span of each sash bar and to avoid lapping the glass.
Chance tried to mass produce glass panes 3 feet long
and 10 inches wide by improving on a process introduced from France into Britain in 1832. During a
visit Paxton learned more about the new process of
manufacturing glass panes and urged that it was capable of producing 4-foot panes.[52] Paxton was right:

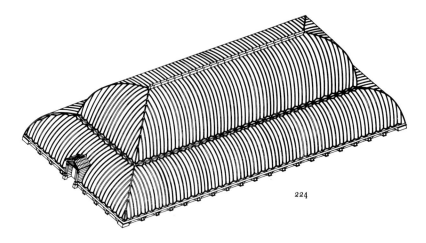

224

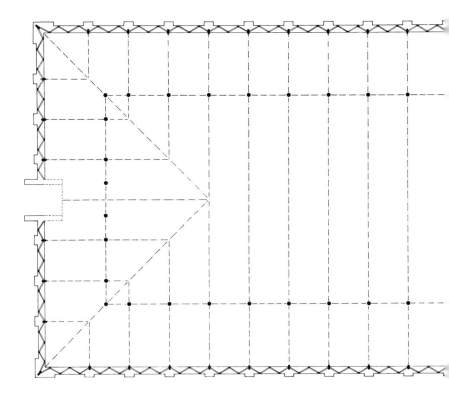

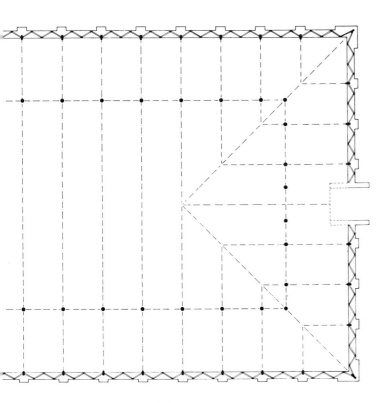

225
Ground-floor plan,
tentative
reconstruction.

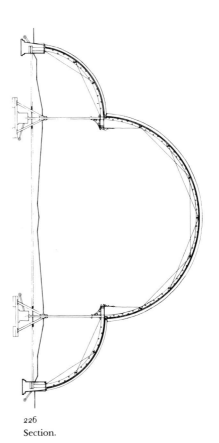

226
Section.

Chance found it possible with skilled blowing to make sheets 4 feet long, and Paxton got all the glass he needed.

Chadwick has described the method of building as follows:

The first operation on the site was that of leveling and excavation for the foundations and for the heating chamber beneath the structure, and for the access tunnel beneath the cascade, for it was a matter of principle with Paxton that the service aspects of the building should be entirely invisible and the conservatory present the same aspect to the gardens on all four sides; even the boiler flue was taken, underground, up the hillside for some distance into the woods to an isolated chimney-stack for this reason, a procedure which would result also in increased draught for the furnaces; both flue and stack still survive.

A basement wall, 2 ft. 6 in. high, of local gritstone, was built to provide anchorage for the main ribs of the side "aisles"; this "running sub-basement" was arched, the arches containing iron valves for the ventilation of the conservatory. Iron pillars, in two parallel rows 70 ft. apart, eighteen in each row, were then erected to support a horizontal rectangular frame of iron beams. This frame supported the upper ends of the segmental ribs of the lower aisles and the lower ends of the ribs of the main span: the lower ribs spanning 28 ft. 6 in. horizontally and 40 feet vertically; each rib supported two panels of the ridge and furrow roofing, one to either side. These ribs of the main span were of wood, as was the whole of the roof except for the iron columns and boxframe which supported it. The ribs were made up of separate timber laminations bent on a template and nailed and bolted together. . . .

The wooden ribs took up the compression forces and bending moments generated by the thrust of the vault. In the drawing of the structure there are tensioning cables on the underside of the ribs, which were located in the middle of the arch and formed a second plane to take up the tension forces in the way that the lower flange of an I beam works. The drawing does not show whether the prestressing was brought about in the manner of a three-dimensional framework, diagonally by several bars in the form of a net, or whether the prestressing had only one bar. The wooden supporting rafters were modeled on the Paxton gutter. The gutters for rainwater were integral with the supporting structure. Thus, the rainwater was deflected from the vertical line of descent to the horizontal guttering. The terminating points of the reinforcing members of the nave were on the cast-iron gallery which surrounded the nave on all four sides and which was joined to the columns by cast-iron spandrels. This gallery above the columns formed with the cast-iron arches which supported it a horizontal reinforcement in the plane of the junction between the nave and the aisles. In addition

there were purlins running between the ribs for longitudinal reinforcement. In order to increase the spacing between the ribs and therefore to achieve greater transparency of the glass vault, Paxton included pairs of ridged roof panes as the basic unit; at one end they were supported directly by the ribs and at the other end by the purlins. Paxton solved the difficult problem of the junction between the vaults of the nave and the aisles by the use of a rectangular gutter beam which had the depth of the ridge-and-furrow work and which collected water along the length of the gallery and led it into the hollow columns. Reinforcement of the cast-iron columns by hip rafters from the foundation contributed to the overall rigidity.

The hothouse was heated by eight boilers via 7 miles of 4-inch iron pipes, which were laid in heating corridors deep enough for someone to walk upright along them. The fuel, stored below ground level, was supplied to the boilers by a small tramway. The ventilation was provided by iron valves in the basement wall and by openings at the gallery level and at the ridge of the roof.

The entries in the accounts for 1839, totaling £11,673, show the great cost of the glazing relative to the rest of the building work. In view of the enormous glass surface, cost-effective methods of glassmaking and of glazing had to be achieved. To this end Paxton straightaway used the method of mass producing glass panes that he himself had optimized. This avoided the waste of cutting the sheets. The concept of the ridge-and-furrow applied to the vault included the possibility of using flat glass sheets in spite of the curvature of the roof. (At the time it was probably not possible to cover the curved surfaces with curved glass panes, as would be done later at Kew Gardens.) The glazing process too required a mass-production method in order to save labor and time. The device constructed for this purpose was probably the prototype of the glazing trolley used later for the large exhibition buildings. Unfortunately there are no documents about it in existence. Probably a system of counterweights or movable pulley blocks was necessary to move the trolley over the curved ribs. The whole of the trolley may have run on the ribs. Dr. Granville commented:

Of this huge mountain of glass the largest portion was already glazed, and seemed to me to promise the grandest effect when the whole shall be completed. Nor was the ingenious contrivance (equally the invention of Mr. Paxton's own mind) for glazing the flanks and loftiest slopes of this Hill, as well as for covering its ribs with paint, less entitled to admiration. Its merits are simplicity and complete success.

*I must leave my readers to guess how a dozen or two paint-
ers and glaziers may be enabled to crawl spider-like, freely
and nimbly, over a surface of such fragile materials, without
either bending a single one of the slender ribs, or fracturing
a pane of glass. The whole construction, in fact, reflects
great credit on the ingenuity of the architect.*[54]

A list of the contents of the Great Conservatory at
Chatsworth would fill a whole catalog. There were
tropical birds, gold and silver fishes in ponds, and
extensive amounts of crystalline and other rocks.
When Queen Victoria visited Chatsworth in December 1843 the hothouse was lit by 12,000 lamps. The
royal party traveled in open carriages through the
inside of the Great Conservatory. Heinrich Fintelmann, the Inspector of Gardens at Potsdam, who
visited the Great Conservatory in 1882, wrote:

*The whole glass roof is built on the ridge-and-furrow princi-
ple, which gives the advantage that the rays of the midday
sun can never fall perpendicularly on the glass panes, so it
is not necessary to shade the plants at this time. If one takes
into consideration the relative size of this giant hothouse,
there is a colossal saving of time and broken glass sheets! For
our continental winter conditions the use of this method of
glazing for similar-size plant houses would definitely have
the disadvantage of collecting great masses of snow and ice,
because of which conditions the strength of the glazed surfaces would be subjected to a not always favorable test. Glasshouses built in this way ought to have, in addition to other
protective measures, arrangements to guard against the force
of severe storms, like a sheltered position within dense plantations of trees, protection from hills, or from other buildings.
Sir Joseph Paxton, as is well known, had the building of
this hothouse to thank for his selection to supervise the construction of the large exhibition building of 1851 in London. For the satisfactory completion of this exhibition
building the title of baronet was conferred on Paxton. The
interior of the Chatsworth hothouse is accessible by a wide
drive which at the middle leads round a prominent round
feature. This is a forest of the Muses in the very essence of
the phrase.*[55]

The enormous extent of the building and its architectural quality caused doubts to arise in the professional world that Paxton, a gardener, could be the
sole designer. The sixth Duke of Devonshire, who in
his *Handbook* described the estate, spoke of "this
extraordinary monument of Paxton's talent and skill
in the execution of which he was cordially met and
assisted by Mr. Decimus Burton." This statement can
lead to various interpretations, among them that
Burton, the later architect of the Kew Gardens hothouses, made a significant contribution to the "architectural appearance."[56] However, the architectural
appearance of the Great Conservatory as described
goes back to the intrinsic logic of the structure con-
tradicts this belief. This could have been achieved

only through the development of numerous glasshouses. Burton at this time could not call upon any
personal experience of hothouse building; furthermore, all his later experiments in this field were
made in collaboration with the builder Richard
Turner of Dublin, and these have no close structural
affinity with Paxton's buildings—which demonstrably
include many glasshouses.

The Great Conservatory, a singularity in the history of building, lasted for 80 years. It was dyna-
mited in 1920 on account of its high cost of
maintenance. The five attempts needed to demolish
it testify to the strength of the structure.

Victoria Regia House (figs. 227–232, 529)
length: 62 feet
width: 54 feet
height: 18 feet
architect: Joseph Paxton
built 1849
demolished

The victoria regia house at Chatsworth, built one
year before the Crystal Palace, is of particular importance in the development of Paxton's glass buildings.
With the completion of this building Paxton had created the basic elements that made it possible for him
to undertake work on large exhibition buildings.
From the large hothouses he took over the basic
structure of the vault over the nave as a structural
element for the transept of the Crystal Palace. From
the victoria regia house he borrowed (in modified
form) the roof structure and the cast-iron facade as a
basic element of the external skin. Paxton gathered
together the knowledge he had gained with the victoria regia house in his 1850 patent for a new type of
roof. This was all the more important for Paxton because the design for the Crystal Palace was already
in progress and he felt that he had to protect his invention by patenting it.

When Paxton acquired the victoria regia plant, in
1849, he put it into an existing greenhouse, the glasshouse with the curvilinear roof previously mentioned. However, the rapid growth of the plant made
a new house necessary. He designed a glasshouse on
an almost square masonry foundation in the middle
of which was a circular pool 40 feet in diameter. The
space was enclosed by a ridge-and-furrow roof, and
the sides were facades divided by cast-iron columns.
The building's appearance showed it to be a purpose-
built structure, the architectural richness of which
consisted of the simple repetition of the separate elements forming the roof and the walls.

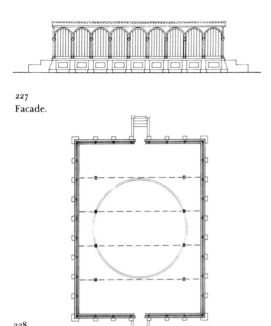

227
Facade.

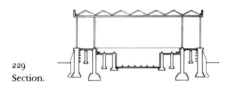

228
Ground plan.

229
Section.

As can be seen from the shape and development of the structural members of this glasshouse, it was Paxton's aim to make a building that would exploit to the full its load-bearing capacity, partly for the sake of economy but particularly to achieve maximum transparency in the roof. The maximum load-bearing capacity was obtained on a basis of experience and experiment, and not by preliminary mathematical calculations based on the theory of statics, in which a safety factor is always included. The ridge-and-furrow roof and the then well known Paxton gutter were supported by master joists assembled at right angles to the lines of the ridges and furrows. Until then, Paxton gutters had been used as the main horizontal load-bearing members. In this design Paxton developed a hierarchy in the members of the space frame by arranging the horizontal elements perpendicular to each other in two planes. The four 54-foot master joists, which extended over the pool in 34-foot clear spans, were wrought-iron beams 5 inches deep, reinforced by 1-inch-diameter round steel bars. They were supported on eight hollow cast-iron columns $3\frac{1}{2}$ inches in diameter. The Paxton gutters, spanning $11\frac{1}{2}$ feet, lay across these master joists and carried the ridge-and-furrow roof. The facade along the masonry base consisted of a series of cast-iron columns 6 feet apart, joined by round cast-iron arches. They carried a fascia which covered the ends of the roof. The glass facade behind the columns consisted of separate 5-by-10-inch panes of glass in wooden sashes. The whole structure stood on a 37-inch-deep base, in which the pool was inserted.

G. F. Chadwick's account emphasizes the technical standard of this hothouse:

A consideration of the lily house would be incomplete without a further reference to its inhabitants and the ways in which their comfort and well-being were secured. Apart from the main tank there were eight smaller tanks in the angles of the house which held other aquatics: Nymphaea, Nelumbium and Pontederia. The main tank had a central deeper part, 16 ft. in diameter, which contained the soil for the Victoria; embedded in the soil were 4 in. diameter iron heating pipes, whilst 2 in. diameter lead pipes were placed in the shallow part of the tank. The house as a whole was heated by a system of 4 in. iron pipes running round inside the basement walls. Thirty openings between the piers of the basement wall allowed for low-level ventilation, and opening lights in the roof "made to open by simple machinery" gave additional ventilation when required. Four small water-wheels were provided in Victoria's tank to give gentle motion to the water and a cold water supply was placed above each so that the water temperature could be modified as required (average tank temperature 83°–85°F, house

230
Section with view of
interior.

231

*80–90°F). It is interesting to note that Paxton had foreseen
the potentialities of electric light—this nearly twenty years
before the invention of the dynamo—but had been unable
to use it to help Victoria's growth due to its expense; how he
would have generated it is not clear, but he was certainly
interested in, and experimenting with, electro-magnetic phenomena at various times.*[57]

The 1850 patent mentioned above, published in
The Civil Engineer and Architect's Journal, has for the
proposed design a structure similar to that of the
roof of the victoria regia house (fig. 232). The essential difference is that the secondary joists (the Paxton
gutters) were undertrussed with round steel section
and not the master joists. This allowed the clear
span of the secondary joists to be increased. As in
the supporting structure, the rainwater drainage was
effected in two stages. The Paxton gutters collected
the water and led it to the master joists, which were
likewise made of channel section. From there the
water ran down into the hollow cast-iron columns.
By the reinforcement of his gutters Paxton obtained,
in addition to greater strength, a slope in two directions. The patent was awarded to Paxton on January
22, 1851. "Paxton describes his invention as relating

to 'improvements in the construction of the description of roofs known as ridge and valley roofs, part of
which improvements are also applicable to other descriptions of roofs.' . . . Two sheets of drawings were
attached to the specification, showing typical constructional details of Paxton's roofs."[58] From the illustrations of the roof system it is clear that Paxton
had in mind mass production and wide application
of this roof system. It was not intended for hothouses alone, but also for a variety of buildings. At
the time when he was building the victoria regia
house, he was also experimenting with glass roofs
for dwelling houses. He also investigated the possibilities of the application of his glass roof to railway
stations and assembly halls.

References: Chadwick 1961, pp. 73–103; *Die Gartenzeitung*,
1882, vol. 1; Fintelmann 1892, pp. 31–83; Schild 1967, p. 36;
Loudon 1839, vol. 15, p. 450; *The Gardener's Chronicle*,
31.8.1850, vol. 10, no. 35, pp. 548, 549; Neumann 1862, pp.
174 ff., 274 ff.

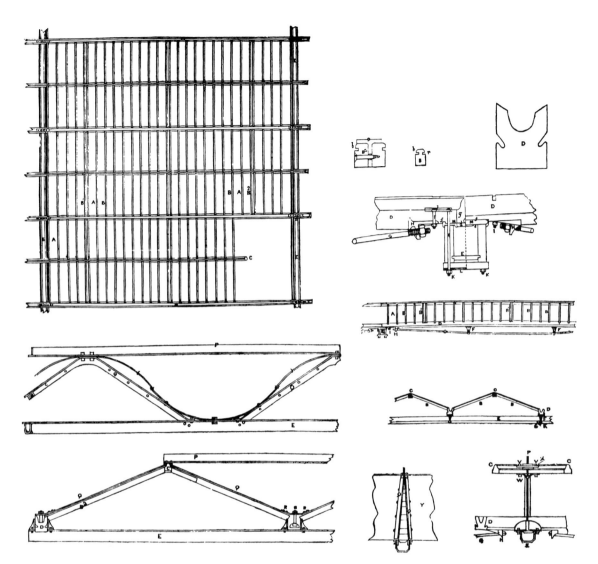

232
Paxton's patent roof
system, 1850, details
of supporting
structure.

233
General view. Engraving, ca. 1840.

234
Interior view. Engraving, ca. 1840.

Chiswick, London

Chiswick Gardens Conservatory (figs. 233, 234)

length: 185 feet
width: 30 feet
architects: D. and E. Bailey
built 1840
demolished

The Chiswick Gardens Conservatory was the completed part of what was to have been a grandiose layout with a central dome 121 feet in diameter and four adjoining wings. The conservatory actually built was one of these wings. The work was carried out by the firm of D. and E. Bailey in partnership with Loudon, and the buildings consisted of a steeply rising glass barrel vault. The height of this vault led, in contrast to the usual practice of this company, to the use of cast-iron filigree work in the form of braced arched ribs reinforced by purlins and forming the main space frame. The sash bars of the curvilinear roof were laid over that. Contemporaries compared the undecorated structure to "some gigantic glass bubble which looked as if a strong wind might burst or sweep away altogether."[59]

The building was for the Royal Horticultural Society in London, which had previously leased a building behind the Duke of Devonshire's Chiswick House in 1821. A national school for horticultural science was founded here in 1824. Joseph Paxton started his career here. The President of the Royal Horticultural Society—William Cavendish, Duke of Devonshire—was interested in the building of hothouses, and he soon commissioned Paxton to build the Great Conservatory at Chatsworth. He was also the initiator of the building of the Chiswick Conservatory.

References: McGrath and Frost 1961, pp. 118, 119; Hix 1974, pp. 115–117.

Dresden

Pillnitz Castle Park Palm House

width: ca. 40 feet
height: ca. 40 feet
architect: unknown
built ca. 1856

The Palm House near Dresden is a notable example of early functional architecture, with the simplicity of its spatial form and the elegance of its delicately made ironwork. The high central space, alloted to palms, is formed by extremely slender cast-iron columns set out as a hexagon and covered by a gently sloped hexagonal pyramidal roof. Low cube-shaped wings adjoin it, with lean-to roofs joining onto the gutter level of the central part. The wings are backed by a masonry wall. An archway provides access to a long, low glass corridor with a simple ridge roof. The round iron decorative columns are placed in the plane of the large glass surfaces and stand on a low carved stone base. They are reinforced horizontally by beams which run around the hexagonal cylinder of the central space at gutter height. Beams projecting from the ridges of the wings join the columns together in the gutter angle of the central space. The roof above this structure has its apex embellished with a palmette.

The building is extant.

Source: Amt für Denkmalpflege, Dresden.

Dublin, Glasnevin

National Botanic Garden

Tropical House (figs. 236–238, 536–540)

length: 333 feet
width: 33 feet
height: 40 feet
architects: Richard Turner, William Clancy
built 1842–1850

This extensive glasshouse is due chiefly to the work of Richard Turner, who extended Loudon's space frame into a coherent structure with an organic effect that can be detected all over the building. The interior columns lose the classical form and merge into arching branches made of thin steel. These columns, which resemble plants, support a vault made only of sash bars and glass panes. The establishment consists of three pavilions connected by passages. It seems as if Turner deliberately preferred one of the most difficult of architectural problems, namely the intersection of curved glass surfaces. In contrast with the winter garden in Regent's Park, Turner inserted cubic elements into the lines of intersection. This contrast of plane and curved glass surfaces, which governs the whole layout, gives it a special aesthetic charm. Turner's incorporation of double cast-iron columns into the facade increased the lightness of the glass wall of the central pavilion and at the same time gave it a prestigious appearance without introducing any clumsiness. The central pavilion is the only example of this invention still in existence.

The builder of the Great Conservatory, built to the pavilion system in 1842, was essentially R. Turner. The first contract for one of the wings was concluded with William Clancy, but the brief for the second wing and the central dome went to Turner. He fulfilled it in 1850. Turner came from Dublin. His name appears for the first time in a Dublin directory dated May 1, 1813, in which he is mentioned as businessman in St. Stephen's Green. In 1818 his name appears as Richard Turner & Co., and later he is mentioned as an "ironmonger." In 1836 he enlarged his company and moved to Shelburne Street in Dublin as the "Hammersmith Works." This company, which not only fabricated iron structures but also designed them, became a leading technical company in British hothouse construction in the middle of the nineteenth century. The two wings of the Belfast palm house are the first known examples of work by this firm. Then came the buildings at Regent's Park (1846), Kew Gardens (1844–1848), and Killikee (1845–1850). Turner also built structures for railway stations, such as the roof of Broadstone Station in Dublin (1847) and part of the roof of Lime Street Station in Liverpool (1850). Together with his brother, Thomas, an architect, he submitted a design for the Crystal Palace; however, it was rejected on account of its high cost.[60]

The basic spatial concept of the Glasnevin tropical house is a pavilion system 333 feet in length, which consists of a raised central structure on a rectangular base and a glass roof sloping down on all sides with symmetrical wings adjoining. Six cast-iron columns with Corinthian capitals are set in two rows in the interior of the central building and support an upright standing lantern, above which is a vaulted glass roof. From the lantern outward there is a sloping curved glass roof to the top of the facade framework and rearward to the masonry work of the north side. In the facade there are the glazed double columns mentioned above, which are joined onto the main frontage by steel straps to the inner columns and masonry work. Arches of round steel section between the inner columns and the facade form a kind of arcade. The glass vaults formed by the closely spaced sash bars of the wings are supported on a row of columns, which are joined together by rafters branching out from them and outward to the sash bars.

The building is extant and well maintained.

Reference: McCracken 1971.

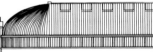

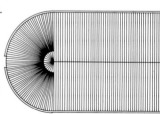

235
Site plan, 1975.

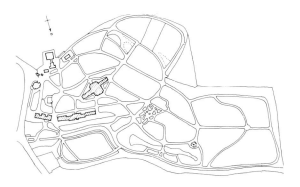

236
Section through cen-
tral pavilion, 1850.

237
South front.

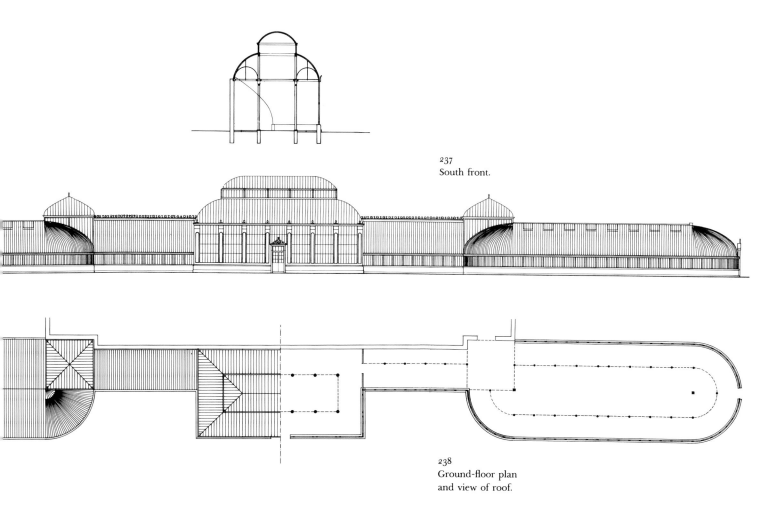

238
Ground-floor plan
and view of roof.

New Palm House (figs. 541, 542)

length: 99 feet

width: 79 feet

height: 66 feet

architect: Paisley

builders: Boyd & Co.

built 1884

This large glasshouse has a rectangular base which is terminated at one end by an apse formed by hipped corners. Cast-iron columns support a high central building, which, standing in a kind of miniature gallery, is covered with a vaulted glass roof. Adjoining this building is a surrounding corridor, above which the upper roof form is repeated. The outer walls are made with wooden posts. On the north side the glasshouse is protected by a solid masonry wall. The aesthetic character of the architecture is determined by two glass vaults at different levels, which break at the ends of the apse and rise in an elegant line.

The building is extant and well maintained.

Reference: The Gardener's Chronicle, 18.10.1882, vol. 42, p. 488.

Dublin

1865 Exhibition
Winter Palace (figs. 239, 240)

length: 356 feet

width: 84 feet

height (interior): 60 feet

architects: Alfred G. Jones, Rowland Mawson Ordish, Le Feuvre

built 1865

demolished

The Dublin Winter Palace, built for the 1865 International Exhibition of Arts and Industry, was a large glass-and-iron building which was bounded along its length by a massive buttressing structure. It had a basilicalike form. The high nave was roofed by a glass barrel vault, which was supported at its sides by the lower aisles. Cast-iron members looking like flying buttresses supported the base of the roof, having a concave curvature and running into the convex roof to make a flowing joint between the aisles and the roof.

The Winter Palace was conceived as a landscape-covering winter garden with two concert halls, a reading room, practice rooms for the orchestra, dining and refreshment rooms, and an extensive art gallery. The winter garden, over 330 feet long and about 80 feet wide, was surrounded by a gallery which extended outward into a terrace. From here the visitor had a good view of the park, which like the winter garden served for public recreation.

The three-story space frame consisted of a two-story cast-iron surrounding gallery built of rows of columns and joists which supported the gallery and its lean-to roof. This gallery, surrounding the whole winter garden, served as an abutment for the barrel vault over the nave. The ribs of the vault were semicircular braced girders, made of wrought iron, which narrowed upward, following the distribution of the stresses. Located at the column separation of 17 feet, they were braced by posts and diagonals. The abutment, which consisted of cast-iron struts, also served to counter the lateral thrust of the gallery. Thus the architect avoided the use of troublesome ties running across the interior space. The abutment frameworks were visible externally and extended away from the clerestory on which the glass roof rested. The framework of the surrounding gallery was built of prefabricated cast-iron elements in the form of columns, connecting pieces, and brackets on which the cast-iron beams were laid in the longitudinal and lateral directions. Iron ribs cast entire with inscribed arches formed the frame of the lean-to roof of the gallery (fig. 239).[62] The ventilation of this large building was done mechanically by a shaft running along the roof, which could open the overlapping glass windows of the vault by means of cables. This method was tested to solve the problem of the overheating of glass-covered halls during the summer. (Paxton attempted to solve the same problem by the use of linen shades.) The structure of the extremely light and bright hall of the Dublin Winter Palace had a forerunner in the Industrial Palace of the Paris World Exhibition, built ten years earlier.

References: Walmisley 1950, p. 21; Gloag and Bridgwater 1948, p. 254; *Illustrated London News*, 18.3.1865, 24, vol. 46, no. 1306, pp. 258, 262.

239
Section.

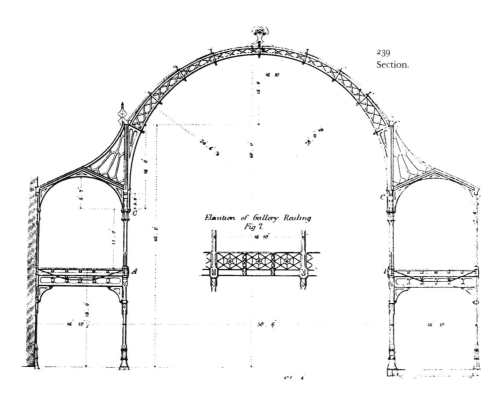

Elevation of Gallery Railing
Fig 7

240
Woodcut, ca. 1865.

Edinburgh

Royal Botanic Garden
Palm Houses (figs. 241–245, 543–548)

Old Palm House
diameter: 59 feet
height: 46 feet
architect: unknown
built 1834, rebuilt 1860

New Palm House
length: 99 feet
width: 56 feet
height: 69 feet
architect: R. Matthienson
built 1858

In the Edinburgh Palm House, the most northerly hothouse in Britain, the stone architecture of the orangeries was combined in a very effective way with a transparent glass vault. An arcade wall in the classical style is topped with a wide architrave, on which rests the glass-and-iron roof. Like the solid masonry work, the roof structure is an invocation of historical examples. The final stage of orangery development is taken up by the solid masonry work, in which the solution of the wall problem by the use of window openings was pushed to the limit. The application of that method gave the appearance of a temple built of columns and an architrave. In the roof structure the architect followed one of the most advanced engineering structures of that time, the palm house in Kew Gardens (1848). At Edinburgh, a structure almost exactly like the central pavilion of the Kew Gardens palm house was placed on the masonry base. The result of this leaning toward various building and structural elements is a hothouse of remarkable architectural quality, the effect of which is due to the contrast between solid masonry and filigree ironwork.

The combination of a historicizing form with an iron frame, roof, or dome was a frequent problem of prestige architecture in the nineteenth century. In hothouses this problem was taken up and solved earlier than in (for example) railway stations. Examples may be seen at Syon House, the Brussels Winter Garden (1828), the "Palm Temple" in Kew Gardens (1836), the Old Palm House in Kassel (1822), and the palm house in the Vienna Hofburg (1823). The palm house in Edinburgh, with its high glass vault, represents a peak in this development sequence.

Like many other botanical gardens, the Edinburgh garden had its origin in the medicinal gardens of earlier centuries. The Old Palm House was built in

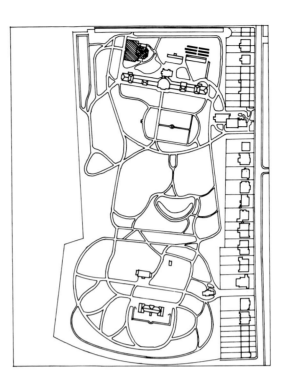

241
Site plan, 1890.

1834 in the form of a palm house on a rectangular base, with a wooden-frame lean-to roof. It cost £1,500 to build. In 1855 this house was found to be too small; many palms had already pushed their crowns through the glass roof. Because of this state of affairs Professor Balfour, Regius Keeper, persuaded Parliament to grant of £6,000 for the erection of a new building. This was built on the west side of the older one and was opened in 1858. After the removal of the palms, the timber of the old building was found to be in such a poor state that a new roof was needed. In 1860 an iron roof was erected in the shape of a dome. A glass screen separated the two parts of the building; one part contained palms and trees of hot climates, and the other was for those of temperate climates.[63]

The octagonal Old Palm House and the New Palm House both have sandstone walls with large window openings. The wooden rafters of the Old Palm House rest on the surrounding architrave and are reinforced by an inner ring of eight columns. The adjoining new building on the west side has a base in the shape of a rectangular 99 feet long and 56 feet wide. The surrounding walls, which are interrupted by large window openings with circular arches and pilasters in the Tuscan style, reach a height of 35 feet. The glass-and-iron roof vault rests on the external stone wall. The roof forms an elegantly shaped dome built in two tiers, each 17 1/2 feet high. The lower part of the vault spans the outer walls at half the roof height, where it has its springing on four-

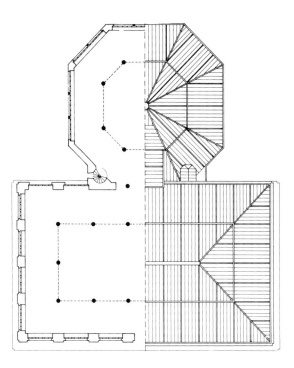

242
Ground-floor plan
and view of roof.

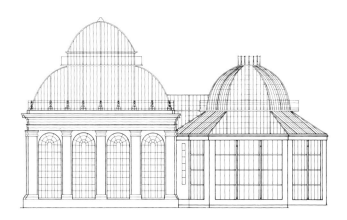

243
Side elevation.

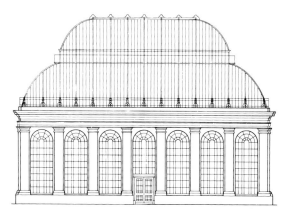

244
Front elevation.

teen extraordinarily slender cast-iron columns. The columns have richly decorated cast-iron arches above, making a horizontal base on which rests the upper part of the vault, with a low vertical ventilating gallery separating the two vaults. The roof converges into a pointed apex at a height of 69 feet. The solid masonry work and the glass-and-iron structure placed on it have the same height. The two glass shells, vaulted on all sides, form in cross-section a basilicalike space of a comletely new type. While the walls present to the eye stability and make a solid boundary to the enclosed space, the slender iron columns and the space frame of the roof create an impression of a glasshouse standing by itself high above a tall base. The palm house in Kew Gardens served as a model for the central part of this building; not only the shape of the enclosed space but also the marrying of rafters and sash bars was taken from it. (Compare figures 543 and 613.) The Old Palm House, which was given a glass-and-iron roof in 1860, made with the new building a spatial unit. The line of the junction measures 121 feet. The form of the lean-to roof was retained up to the inner ring of columns. Above this was placed an octagonal dome, the apex of which was 46 feet high. In combination with these rebuilding measures, the pilasters of the walls were removed and replaced by cast-iron columns and bases. This created a large glass surface of considerable height with iron columns, reminiscent of the multistory glass fronts of early warehouses.

Arched trusses made of I section 6 1/2 feet apart form the frame of the glass vault; every other truss occupies the position of one of the columns. The trusses located on columns are reinforced at the joints by vertical stanchions with cast-iron ornamental spandrels. Curved sash bars 16 inches apart run from one abutment to the opposite one without purlins for reinforcement. The glazing is single and consists of curved glass panes 16 by 26 inches. This arrangement gives the roof its special transparency. The technical problem of the springing of this large glass-and-iron arched structure—the interrupted walls can withstand only limited amounts of lateral thrust—was solved by incorporating a horizontal cast-iron retaining frame at the level of the architrave, so the growth of the palms is not impeded by troublesome tie rods in the interior.

Both buildings are extant and well maintained.

Source: library and archives, Edinburgh Royal Botanic Garden.

References: *ZfBW*, 1887, vol. 37, parts 1–3, pp. 74, 75; *The Gardener's Chronicle*, 23.5.1874, vol. 34, no. 21, p. 662.

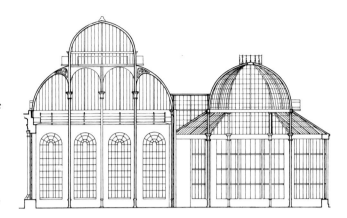

245
Section through old and new palm houses at Edinburgh.

Enville Hall, Staffordshire

Conservatory (fig. 246)
length: 151 feet
width: 70 1/2 feet
height: ca. 66 feet
architects: Grey and Ormson
built 1850
demolished

In 1850 there arose at Enville Hall a conservatory, built for the Earl of Stafford and Warrington, which had the stylistic vestments of historicism. The prototype for it was no longer the space typology developed in hothouse construction, but the English stately home in Saracenic or Gothic style, with its many towers, pinnacles, and pointed arches. The base and body of the conservatory determined the position of the alcove-shaped towers with sharply pointed concave pyramidal tops and the two octagonal-based onion-shaped domes. The facade of continuous windows terminated upward in a line of flatly curved arches. The large number of contrasting elements gave the building an extremely exciting silhouette, without architecturally uniting into a whole.

The facade fronts were joined together in Gothicizing tracery, the skeleton of which had an affinity with stone architecture but in reality consisted of cast iron and wood. All the openings in this ornamental "embroidery" were glazed. Iron structures supported the roofs. The domes were glazed, and were supported internally by cast-iron columns.[64]

References: McIntosh 1853, vol. 1, p. 171; *The Gardener's Chronicle*, 1855, vol. 15, no. 48, pp. 790, 791.

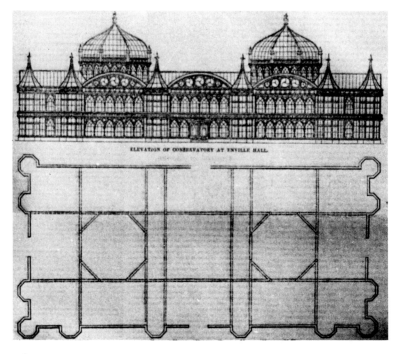

246
Facade and ground
plan of Enville Hall
conservatory.

Florence

Orto Botanico, Via Micheli
Palm House (figs. 247, 248, 549–553)
length; 125 feet
width: 61 feet
height: ca. 60 feet
architect (according to English patent system): Giacomo Roster
built 1874

The palm house in Florence, with its basilicalike form, is one of the most elegant glass-and-iron structures of the late nineteenth century, largely because of its simple and clear spatial form. The pointed, arch-shaped central glass vault on a rectangular base, curving down on all sides, rests by means of a cast-iron retaining frame on a row of cast-iron columns. A lower vaulted gallery surrounding this high central space has a glass roof carried by a vertical framework. Gracefully executed portals on the front and the sides give the building a structural coherence, the aesthetic effect of which is enhanced by the blending of intersecting glass vaults. The satisfactory structural development of the chosen spatial form also plays an essential part in determining the overall appearance of this building. The sash bars, the braced girders, and the columns are reduced to a minimum cross-section corresponding to the force. Other than here, such transparency was reached only in the heyday of the experimental hothouse in Britain.

The effect of this building in terms of space and structure is no longer based on an individual concept of the architect, but on a thoroughly formulated type of hothouse and exhibition building. We have already seen this type of building in 1860 in the form of a prefabricated system sold by catalog as "Conservatories in the Garden of the Royal Horticultural Society, London" (fig. 370). The motive for the building of this glasshouse was an international garden exhibition of the Royal Tuscan Company for Horticulture in May 1854, similar to that in London in 1874. There can therefore be no wonder that direct links in form and technical execution existed between the two buildings. The supporting members were given dimensions based on mathematical calculations, and the joining points were made so that addition of further parts was possible. Through the multiplicity of the structural parts, each developed for its own purpose, there arose an architecture whose expression was not restricted by prefabrication.

The glazed barrel vault of the nave, supported on 24 cast-iron columns, is supported vertically by delicate riveted braced girders in the form of a de-

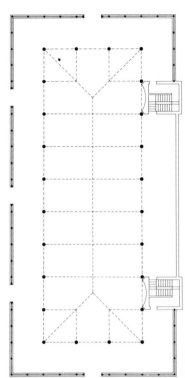

247
Ground-floor plan of
Florence palm house.

pressed pointed arch. The horizontal thrust forces
are counteracted by tension cables. The horizontal
reinforcement is provided by filigree braced girders
riveted to the vertical members. The forces in the
vertical ribs are led via vertical members which yoke
together the windows of the gallery down to the
round cast-iron columns. The capitals above the columns are strengthened by rolled-iron section. A surrounding balcony projects inward, while outward
there is a glass vault of the surrounding corridor.
This has no secondary reinforcing joists, but supports
itself through the sash-bar structure, which rests on a
vertical window framework structure with cast-iron
filigree columns. This vault too is spread outward to
the columns. The whole space frame is made of
rolled-iron and cast-iron elements, which are joined
together by rivets or bolts. This allowed complete
prefabrication, so that the parts could be put together at the building site. The glazing is in the form
of glass panes lapping like roof tiles. A lantern provided ventilation along the edge of the main vault.

The building is extant and well maintained.

Reference: *The Gardener's Chronicle*, 23.5.1874, vol. 34, no. 21.

Frankfurt am Main

Palm Garden
Flora (figs. 249–254, 554–556)

The flora in the palm garden of the city of Frankfurt
am Main (1871) set the standard for the shape of this
type of building in the speculative years of the nineteenth century. As for the Cologne flora (1864), there
was here an intention to combine assembly rooms
with a plant display as an architectural unit for the
purposes of making a profit out of the investment.
In Cologne this brief was carried out in such a way
that the centrally sited palm hall was surrounded by
a ring of assembly rooms made of solid masonry.
But this design hindered the growth of the plants,
which could receive light almost only from the
vaulted roof above, and at the same time interfered
with the efficient use of the assembly rooms, which
would have been better laid out in the center. Spatial
unity was achieved in the Frankfurt flora by designing the layout of the assembly rooms and the plant
display house so that each had its own distinctly
bounded space, and all rooms were interconnected.
The Berlin flora (1871) had in its spatial aspect an affinity with this kind of design. The basic internal arrangement was similar to that at Cologne.

The palm house of the Frankfurt flora is a remarkable feat of structural engineering, executed in the
manner of railway-station concourses, with wide-

span glass-and-iron structures, but no decorative work. Riveted iron ribs and girders were used, as in railway stations. The building form of the railway-station concourse was applied not only structurally but also as an appropriate space frame for the flora building, while being redesigned in detail for its changed purpose. As in the large urban railway stations, the main glass-and-iron hall is surrounded and enclosed by a pincerlike solid body executed in a historicizing architectural style. The New Exhibition Hall, erected in the vicinity of the flora in the same park in 1906, has characteristics related to exhibition buildings in the way that many glass-and-iron halls of varied heights and cross-sections are integrated into a compact building structure having a compartmented interior space which architecturally determines the movement of the visitors.

The flora in the Palm Garden in Frankfurt am Main owes its existence to the rise of the Prussian hegemony in Germany through the war of 1866. The Rhineland became part of Prussia. The winter garden of Prince Adolf von Nassau at Biebrich was the basis and reason for the founding and stocking of the plant collections in the Palm Garden; they were sold to the Palm Garden Company after the dissolution of the Prince's estate. When it became known that the prince had it in mind to sell these plant houses and their contents, the citizens of Frankfurt were stimulated to acquire this establishment, to transfer it to their city, and to incorporate it into the commercially operated Palm Garden. To this end they formed a joint stock company on the initiative of the gardener Heinrich Siesmayer. The operating costs were to be covered by the visitors' subscriptions and the sale of day tickets. The acquisition was completed in 1868, and in August 1869 the transfer of the hothouses and plants to Frankfurt began.

The company chose for the site a piece of land on the Bockenheimer Strasse in Frankfurt's West End, which was partly in municipal and partly in private

and institutional ownership and which was particularly advantageous for the construction of a garden establishment because the abundance of water "led to the expectation that effective landscaping with a water element for boat trips [could] be easily carried out."[65] This area of about 13 1/2 acres was leased to the Palm Garden Company by the city for a period of 99 years at a low rent. After this period the establishment was to become the property of the city without payment. In 1869, under the supervision of the architect Friedrich Kayser, the building of the Great Palm House was started; at the same time the hothouses brought over from Biebrich were erected.

That the Flora building was taken to with enthusiasm by the public is clearly evident from the number of visitors during the first 14 days after the opening: 60,000. The Flora had a double function to fulfill; on the one hand it had a plant exhibition house and botanical garden, and on the other hand it offered amusement and recreation facilities. Great importance was attached not only to traditional plant arrangements but also to the "phenomena of the present day in so far as they concerned new introductions and improvements to existing plants." "People were encouraged to collect once more within the compass of general cultivation throughout the year the less well known, the forgotten or lost plant types, and to bring them into more vigorous circulation. . . . By good concerts—there were two concerts daily by the resident orchestra of forty musicians, and in winter there were symphony concerts too— horticultural offerings were efficiently backed up by the restaurant service and were also supported in this direction by the maintenance and the entertainment account."[66] The Flora became the major scene of numerous festivals, balls, and other gatherings. The promoters were delighted by the enthusiastic praise from the public, and by the middle of the 1870s the need for expansion made itself felt. In 1908 there was an addition of 44 1/2 acres. A serious fire in 1878 reduced the assembly building to ashes and damaged the stock of plants. The assembly building was rebuilt in 1879 by the architect Theodor Schmidt and was again opened to the public. In 1920 the assembly building was again rebuilt, by the architect Ernst May in the style of the New Objectivity. The whole of the Garden came into the ownership of the City of Frankfurt in 1931.[67]

The whole establishment was so conceived that the assembly building and the Palm Garden were spatially one unit, but at the same time their various purposes were developed and perfected in accordance with different structural principles related to the

249
Site plan, 1908.

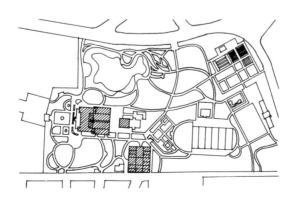

specialized building components. The assembly building forms the main feature, as the solid glass-and-iron structure at the head of the palm house. Built in the Neo-Renaissance style, it creates a prestige effect with its loggias and the layout of columns in the front. The large banquet hall opens, via a two-story gallery supported on columns, onto the palm house. The two parts of the interior, separated only by a screen of mirror glass, form a visual unit. The impression on the visitor made by the interior space on the occasion of the opening ceremony was described as follows:

We are standing on the terrace. With one glance we perceive a dream come true; we are overcome and deeply moved. How often have we listened to the poetic narrator, when he spoke of the splendor of the tropical vegetation, the groves of palms from foreign perpetually milder climates, and thus aroused our yearnings? These pictures have imprinted themselves indelibly on our fantasies—and here we wander in reality amongst all the magnificence of the tropics. Who could resist getting into a festive mood? The splashing of the waterfall that gushes opposite the terrace against the background of the gardens, foaming over artistically placed rocks down into the pools, draws our attention to itself before the other scenes. This is what spreads such refreshing coolness throughout the whole building, which so pleasantly surrounds us. What an abundance of the noblest gigantic leaf forms is gathered on both sides of this unique building! How beautifully do the broad fronds of the fan palms contrast with the upward thrust of the narrow vertical shafts of the Dracaena australis and the delicate pinnate foliage of exotic ferns! Araucaria and other noble coniferous trees soar high above the compact masses of the plants below and by their strange symmetrical growth remind us of a prehistoric plant picture. Tall marble vases full of luxuriant leaf plants and lianas decorate the corners. Flower beds make a fine show of dazzling colors on the lawns extending into the distant background. This profusion has an almost bewildering effect; every turn in the path presents new scenes. We must again mention the Palm House, which is a masterpiece of its kind and makes an important contribution in that the enjoyment of its interior scene is not impaired in any way. No supporting structures or suspended members or girders limit the view. The whole of the 50,000-square-foot surface is covered by a single boldly curved glass roof.[68]

The palm hall, with its 99-foot span of riveted iron ribs, reminds one of the large railway-station concourses of similar structural form. The lines of the rather flat elliptical arches forming the vault come down to meet the eye. At the same time it makes abundantly clear the advance which the art of engineering design had achieved in overcoming the difficulties inherent in large spans. The early railway-station halls in Britain were already covered by wrought-iron roof trusses. One of the first constructions of this type was Paddington Station in London

(1848). This had a three-bay layout without tie-bar members. The side bays transmitted the thrust down to masonry abutments. This structure served as a model for hall-type buildings until the middle of the nineteenth century. In order to avoid troublesome tie-bar members and at the same time to reduce the lateral thrust caused by the force of the wind, the ribs of the Flora were made of one-piece I-section beams bent to elliptical curves, which, placed above perpendicular connecting pieces, could transmit the forces directly down to the foundations. This method of railway-station construction enjoyed great popularity before the introduction of the three-hinge arch (cf. the Berlin Flora). Later, in the 1880s, these arches were made without the vertical connecting pieces as two- and three-hinge arches for large railway station halls.

The ribs of the Flora, arranged in a row at distances of 19 feet in the hall, are reinforced at the weakest point (above the transition point from the elliptical arch to the vertical) by a gusset made of riveted wrought-iron bars. Several purlins provide longitudinal stiffening for the ribs. It was possible to dispense with a gallery at the ridge of the hall. On the narrow sides, the hall is enclosed at one end by the solid masonry of the restaurant section and at the other end by a vertical glass wall. The glass hall was surrounded by a flower gallery, which was replaced by a new arrangement in the nineteenth century. The iron structure is made in such a way that the main effect is created only by the spatial form, without any ornamental accessories. "The Frankfurt Palm Garden shows that its curves can make an imposing effect with no decoration of the girders made entirely out of sheet iron, in which only the rivets enliven the broad iron surfaces. There is a greater aesthetic charm as the direct result of the thousands of these tiny parts all working together to mitigate the effect of powerful uninterrupted masses of iron and the overpowering gigantic widths of the spans."[69]

It is surprising that the builders of the extremely high and large glass vault chose not to use double glazing, which was usually used in earlier hothouses. The Flora was provided with single glazing. The ring formed by the flower galleries to a height of 22 feet protected it on three sides, but difficulties arose in the course of the operation of the Palm Garden because of the single glazing. In the severe winter of 1870–71 the temperature often fell to just above freezing, and this low air temperature in combination with the unheated soil damaged the plant population considerably.[70]

A Perkins high-pressure water heating system was installed for heating. The pipes had a total length of over 10,800 feet, and the heating was by three stoves. The side galleries were heated by the waste steam from an engine used in the waterworks in the garden. In 1893 a central low-pressure hot-water system was added to the old heating plant.[71]

Dolf Sternberger wrote the following in 1969 concerning the Frankfurt Palm Garden:

In the Palm Garden the plants are displayed in the same way as are the animals in the Zoological Garden at the opposite end of the present day inner city area. The impact of the visual message is much more powerfully impressive than that in the pleasure gardens of the gentry and in country estates. At the present day moreover an important stimulus is generated by the special exhibitions, which benefit countless occupiers of private gardens and plant breeding centers. In this sense this garden forms an individual focal point, and a generally effective means of "culture" in the dictionary sense of the word, for culture really means nursing. However, the incomparable magic of the Palm Garden stands apart from all its usefulness and diversions. It lies in that phantasmagoria of the captured Orient, which was incorporated in the Great Palm House from the very start of the creation of the establishment. One only has to step out of the rooms and corridors of the assembly building into the green twilight where the finely fan-shaped and giant-leaved, the high-reaching and wide-sweeping plants, the exotic luxuriant images crowd in from all sides as in an artificial primeval forest, and plunge with body and mind into the sultry atmosphere of the forcing house with faraway daylight trickling down diluted from the glassy heights, to be completely swallowed up by the mosses on the ground. There is no song of birds, no chattering and chirping to be heard; even human voices are muted, and only a solitary drop falls ghostlike—was it here or was it there? Somewhere from a secret hiding place a tiny spring ripples. Ribbed lobes of dark green silky surfaces hang in the path, and reveal their mysteries. The growth itself appears omnipresent and presses down on us from all sides. It is demanded of us as well that the majestic silence be allowed to absorb our whole existence, and make all trace of us disappear.

The steady increase in the plant contents and the growing numbers of visitors moved the Flora Company to break up the fine old cast-iron hothouses that had come from Biebrich and to replace them with a new building to meet the current requirements. "The intention was to create an establishment which should offer the best result obtainable, not only in respect of monumental effect and bold outlines in its appearance, but also in respect of internal arrangements and fitting out."[72] To that was added the need, as in most botanical gardens, to include a victorian regia house. In 1906, under the supervision of H. Richter, with the help of Thomas Martin and August Siebert, a start was made on the new build-

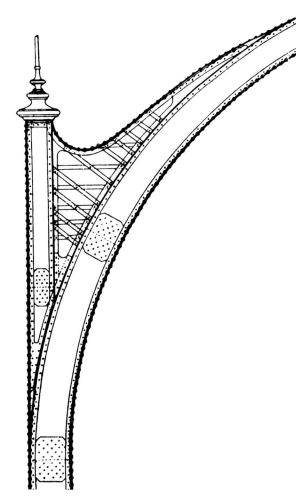

250
Detail of riveted roof truss in palm house.

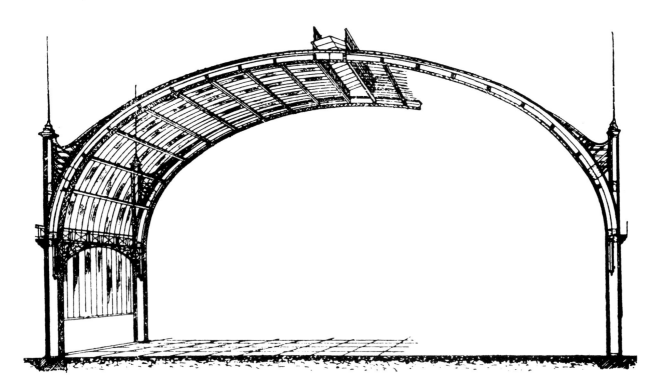

251
Section through
palm house showing
details of structure.

ings, after study tours had been made in 1904 to learn about the current state of the art of hothouse construction. The Philipp Holzmann Company was commissioned to carry out the masonry work. The large central hall with its dome was made by the Frankfurt company Rohnstadt and Zweigle.

An elongated central hall forms the background of the building, which is 200 feet long, 43 feet wide, and 26 feet high. There is a 49-foot-high dome structure in the center, standing on a square base. Perpendicular to the axis of the central hall are smaller display houses with simple ridge roofs set out (six on the left and five on the right). The victoria regia house is an exception, having greater dimensions and an arched roof. By the linking together of these eleven smaller display houses through the central hall there arose an overall layout with a rectangular ground plan, which made it possible to bring about a continuous circulation of visitors similar to that in a big exhibition building. The domed central hall is of particular architectural and structural interest. Ogee arch-shaped braced ribs made of standard steel section spanning 43 feet stand on masonry walls at the sides, which are interrupted by round arched openings. The ribs are continuous down to the ground and are anchored in the masonry. The laterally placed display houses are connected to the central hall by these openings. The central dome is likewise made of arched braced ribs, which spring from the masonry base and terminate upward in a lantern on the ridge. The diagonally placed hip rafters form part of the main space frame. The sashes are made of wood in order to avoid condensation. The iron ribs have different thicknesses according to the sizes of the houses. They are joined together by iron purlins. A thick iron wall plate runs along the whole length of the structure. The steel structure of the victoria regia house was made with special care. The ogee-shaped ridge roof reaching down to the ground is supported on two internal rows of columns. The longitudinal and transverse ribs which rest on these columns are curved and narrow upward according to the strength required, and are braced by riveted bars and joined to the columns. The lower flanges of the ribs are in the form of an ornamental development of the supports as regards capital, shaft, and base to make an integrated component of the same. The structural detailing of the central hall was intended to help avoid the appearance of an empty hall. The circular arched openings in the side walls and the projecting stone entrance portal on the west side indicate application of the principles of Art Nouveau. The victoria regia house shows the same stylistic expression.[73]

References: Festzeitschrift für 11. Deutsches Turnerfest, Frankfurt a. M., 1908, pp. 96–99, 121–122; Die Gartenkunst, 1906, vol. 8, pp. 137, 138; Schoser 1969; Möller's Deutsche Gärtnerzeitung, 2.6.1906, vol. 21, no. 22, pp. 258–270, 352–354, 591–594; Über Land und Meer, 1870, 12, vol. 24, no. 41, pp. 6–12; Frankfurt und seine Bauten, 1866; Die Gartenflora Regels, 1872, vol. 21, pp. 115–117.

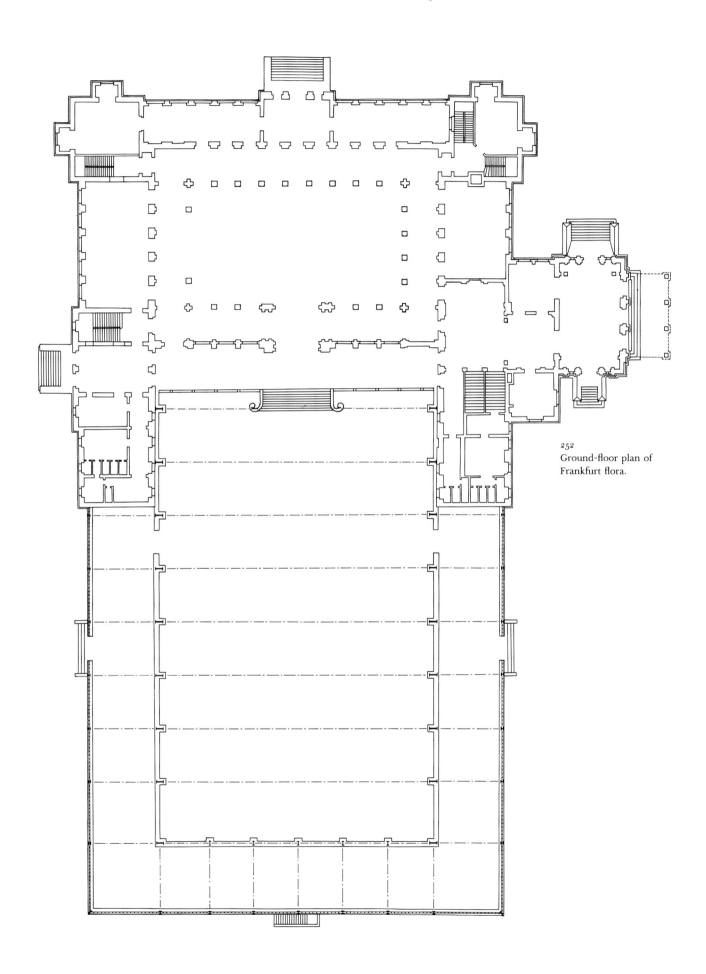

252
Ground-floor plan of
Frankfurt flora.

253
Section through
palm house.

254
Lithograph (ca. 1880)
showing front of
Frankfurt flora.

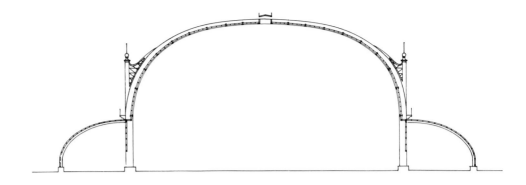

Glasgow

Botanic Gardens
Kibble Palace (Crystal Palace) (figs. 255, 257–261, 557–563)

length: 150 feet (entrance front)
height: 36 feet (with lantern, 43 feet)
diameter of central dome: 146 feet
architect and engineer: John Kibble
builder: James Boyd
built 1872

The Kibble Palace is, in its technical execution and its spatial quality, the late peak in the development of glass-and-iron filigree work. The idea of the crystal palace, the enclosure of space by a transparent shell, is embodied here with a radicalism that has no equal. Not only were the existing technical possibilities completely exhausted, but a new standard of industrialized building construction was set.

The Kibble Palace, with its flat central dome, cruciform vaulted glass corridors, and small cupola, was erected as an exhibition building. There was also a prior intention to convert it into a winter garden, and this was later put into effect. The object of the large exhibition building—to cover large spaces and form an indoor landscape—was realized through the use of mass-produced space-frame elements that could be incorporated in any number desired. The need for such a structure to be adaptable to a rapid change of objective by alteration in the size and shape of the spaces, or even in the extreme case to be dismantled and assembled elsewhere, determined the structural development of the framework down to the smallest detail. Thus, the building elements were produced in a hierarchy based on their strength requirements, and the multiplicity of their shapes was limited by their functions. This procedure led to a diminution of the cross-sections of the individual members of the structure. Hence, a bright and airy space was created in which the ironwork of the structure no longer appeared as massive. It was with these aspects in mind that Paxton and Kibble conceived their crystal palaces.

Kibble succeeded in reaching his objectives of transparency by the use and further development of the Loudon type of filigree work and the curvilinear technique. Of the larger Loudon-type glasshouses, there are to our knowledge three in Britain besides the Glasgow building, and one on the Continent, still in their original form. In the Kibble Palace, the filigree construction in which the iron frames of the windows form the space frame has been pushed to the limit in respect of the span distance. A network

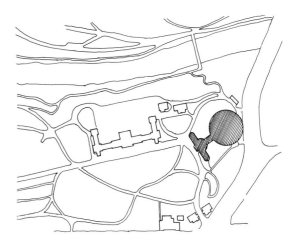

255
Site plan, 1970.

256
Caricature of John Kibble, *The Baillie*, 1873.

of thin glass sections, thickening toward the center, forms a gigantic dome space and also acts as the space frame. The forces are distributed throughout the curved surfaces of the glass. The celebration in 1972 of the centenary of the completion of this building testified to the technical perfection and durability of this structure.

The Kibble Palace had its origin in a conservatory which Kibble built in 1865 on the property of his Coulport House on the banks of Loch Long. The hothouse was dismantled in 1873 and was reassembled, with its structural members extended, in the Glasgow Botanic Gardens. The original building, which was considerably smaller than the one in Glasgow, like it consisted of two domes of different sizes, with two short glass corridors as wings attached to the smaller one. It is described as follows in a contemporary report:

It is constructed of iron and glass, the roof being supported by fluted columns and a framework of the most elegant description. On each side of the entrance hall there is a chamber or gallery, one of which is filled with rare plants, while the other resembles a solemn temple in its configuration. This apartment is one of the greatest sights within the conservatory. It is arched from side to side, and over all the framework, including the columns, walls and roof, living mosses and lichens in not less than a hundred varieties are growing green and smooth as a Brussels carpet. A circular basin of pure water occupies the centre of the apartment, and the whole effect is at once striking as well as pleasant to the eye. Returning to the entrance hall, we proceed onward and reach a circular area surmounted by a glass dome. Here also we have a second fountain, in the centre of which stands a gigantic Dracaena about 20 ft. high, which blossomed last year for the first time. All around the walls, in painted iron pots and boxes, may be seen hundreds of rare plants, including about a dozen varieties of the South American Araucaria. We also observed orange and citron trees hanging with fruit in various stages of growth, not forgetting a couple of golden citrons upwards of twelve inches in circumference each. Leaving this apartment we enter the great circular area, which most fitly completes the picture. The over arching glass dome is supported by 12 columns, and rests on a circular basement of fretwork finished in the Moorish style, and the whole interior is done up in white and gold. Here we have a third circular fountain, in the centre of which is a romantic looking island studded with rocks and models of the most famous ruins in Greece and Rome. Two or three model ships are riding quietly at anchor in the island-harbours, and a tug steamer, about 15" in length, with machinery and everything complete, may be seen hauling a vessel round the circle or into port as the case may be. Around the walls are fifty life size statues after the greatest masters, such as Laocoon, Apollo, Belvedere, Diana, Perseus with the head of Medusa, the Venus de Medici, the Greek Slave, Gibson's tinted Venus; Thorwald-sen's Eve, Canova's Three Graces, Andromeda, etc., etc., standing life size or in gigantic proportions amid shrubs and flowers from every part of the globe.[74]

In 1872, seven years after the erection of his private conservatory, Kibble proposed to the Glasgow Corporation to use the glass-and-iron structure in enlarged form as the basis for a crystal palace that would accommodate 5,000 people under each of its two domes. Having a good sense of business, he stipulated that the profits from the operation of the building should come to him for a period of 20 years. Kibble undertook to dismantle his building, to transport it from Coulport to Glasgow, and to erect it in the Botanic Gardens, where it was to be enlarged at his expense. After 20 years the ownership was to be transferred to the Glasgow Corporation and the citizens of Glasgow in perpetuity. During those 20 years Kibble had the right to arrange concerts and other entertainments and to charge entrance fees for them. The Coulport conservatory was dismantled in May 1872 and loaded onto a raft, which a tug towed up the River Kelvin to Glasgow. As he had promised to the corporation, Kibble increased the diameter of the main dome to 146 feet, lengthened the connecting corridor to 36 feet, and extended the two wings into an impressive-looking front of 150 feet.

"The Art Palace is erected at the east end of the gardens near the principal entrance. The foundations are of stone, the structure itself of glass and iron and the internal supports consisting of graceful iron pillars. Entering by the main door which faces west we find ourselves in the small Dome which has an area of 60 sq. ft. and a height of about 34 ft. In the centre is a pond 27 ft. in circumference rising from which is an ornamental stand, containing pyramidal rows of flowers and miniature fountains. To the left is a transept 50 ft. long by 28 ft. wide, which has been arranged as a moss house. Although only half finished as yet, it presents a singularly fresh and pretty picture of a mossy cell. . . .The corresponding transept on the left of the small dome is being prepared for the reception of models of ancient ruins and famous buildings, such as the Parthenon, the Temple of Jupiter, the Colosseum of Rome etc. At present one cannot well judge of what it will ultimately become, but the plan is one which promises highly artistic results. Passing through the corridor which leads from the small Dome, and, noticing by the way the pictorial effect which is obtained by a series of advertising transparencies fitted up in the roof, we enter the main Dome, a magnificent circular expanse, flooded with light, and, by its harmonious arrangement of flowers and tree ferns and statuary,

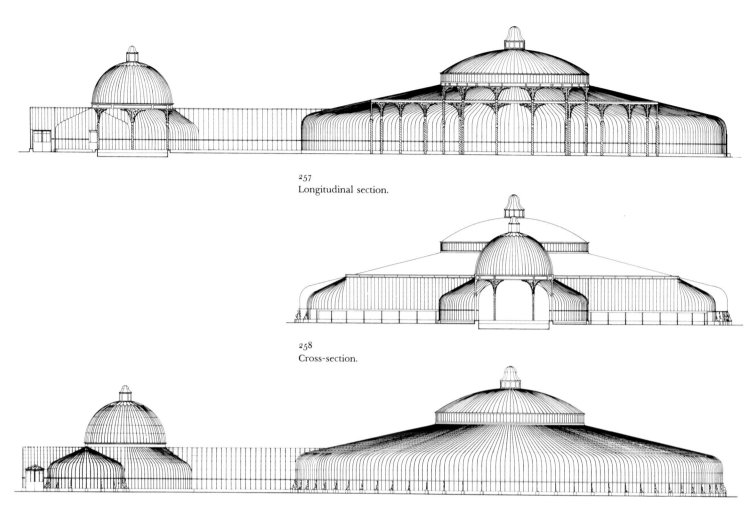

257
Longitudinal section.

258
Cross-section.

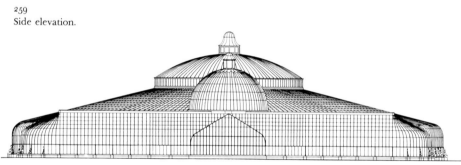

259
Side elevation.

260
Front elevation.

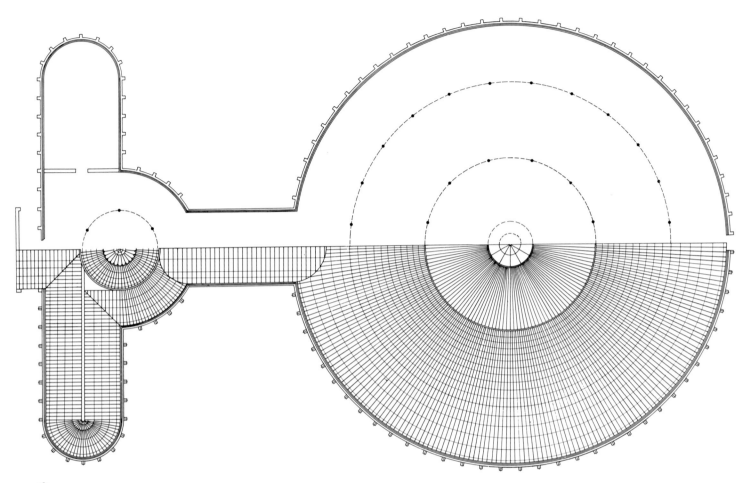

261
Ground-floor plan
and view of roof.

forming an interior of striking beauty. The large Dome is 471 ft. in circumference and is carried on 36 iron pillars, arranged in two circular rows. Following the general design observed elsewhere, the centre of the dome is occupied by a pond 185 ft. in circumference, the uses of which are as novel as they are varied. Underneath the pond is a chamber 14 ft. in diameter, where it is proposed to place an orchestra, whose music will form a melodious mystery to strangers in the coming festivities. The chamber will be so constructed that the sounds of the instruments may be admitted or shut out of the Dome at will, and in this way it is expected that charming diminuendo and crescendo effects will be obtained from the invisible performers. When this artifice is not employed, it is intended to place in the centre of the pond a fairy fountain which will throw up 40 jets of water to a height of 35 ft. while electric lights placed in the roof will be directed upon the rising and falling spray, tinting it with changing hues of gold and silver, and all the colours of the rain-bow. If, however, the requirements of a large audience are superior to all other considerations the mechanical arrangements are such that in an hour the water may be discharged from the pond, which being boarded over will give sitting accommodation for some 800 persons. The large Dome is floored with iron fretwork supplied by Messrs George Smith & Son, and raised on timber sleepers. Underneath are about 3 miles of copper tubing, 3 in. diameter for the purpose of supplying heated air to the building. The conservatory is abundantly supplied with gas, some 600 jets being ready for use after dark in the large Dome. The corridor connecting the two Domes gives entrance to a retiring and a refreshment room. All through the buildings are statues and busts of poets, composers, orators and philosophers. The Art Palace has been erected under the personal superintendence of Mr. Kibble by whose fine taste and large experience in the culture and arrangement of flowers, etc. it has greatly benefited."[75]

The Glasgow crystal palace was opened festively in 1873, and in its first decade was used for art and flower exhibitions, concerts, and mass public entertainments. At ceremonies held in honor of Benjamin Disraeli, in 1873, and William Ewart Gladstone, in 1879, 4,000–5,000 people were present. In 1881 the Royal Botanical Institution, with the support of the City Corporation, acquired the right to purchase the Kibble Palace at a price of £25,000. It was altered to a winter garden by the installation of heating and filled with tropical plants, and thus it reverted to its original purpose.

The glass vault of the large dome is supported on 36 cast-iron columns arranged in two concrete rings. The inner ring has 12 columns, and the outer ring 24. The weight of the roof is carried by two 12-inch-deep ring-shaped ribs, probably made of cast iron, and transmitted down the columns. Richly decorated cast-iron brackets serve as lateral reinforcement. The columns, less then 5 inches in diameter, are decorated with spiral fluting in the Baroque style and have small Corinthian capitals. The smaller dome of the building is supported in a similar way on six columns. The surrounding rings are made of prefabricated parts, which are built as boxes open at the sides and which are bolted to each other and to the columns and brackets. The curvilinear arched ribs of the glass skin lie either immediately on the retaining rings or, in the case of the central part of the dome, on a low tambour. The ribs are made of wrought-iron section, and small angle sections are bolted to them. The distance between the ribs at the bottom is 12 inches. The network of ribs runs across the slope of the roof up to a vertical annulus which rests on a 14-inch-high sandstone ring. The tambour-shaped transition is made via two horizontal rings made of cast iron section and mounted 39 inches apart. The thrust of this reinforcing member, which projects outward as a cornice and which has a decorative zinc gutter, makes possible the ring of ventilating windows that goes all around the building. The ribs converging to the apex of the dome terminate at a lantern ring, which likewise is made from prefabricated sections bolted together. The insertion of the ribs into this ring is a masterpiece of filigree work. The tapering glass panes are held by means of a flower-shaped decorative crown, and only every third rib actually continues into the ring. The glass corridors are built with the same ribs, but without columns; here, in contrast to the ideal Loudon structure, flat iron section is used for additional reinforcement (fig. 134b).

The technical perfection of the structure is demonstrated by the section lines of the parabolically curved surfaces at the intersection of the vaulting of the dome and that of the corridor. The rib of the section line is developed with no detriment to the construction without the constraints of the glass-and-iron structure. The remarkable feature of this filigree structure is that the static properties of the material are exploited to their extreme limits. There is nothing obvious to show that in any deformation of the skin by the force of the wind the glass comes into play as a reinforcing element. The extreme exploitation of the strength of the material is exhibited by the deformation of the dome that has appeared as a rotation of the ribs. This movement, which has involved the rotation of the glass panes in the sashes allowed by the slack in the glazing, has not endangered the structure of the building.

On the conversion of the Kibble Palace into a winter garden, a hot-water heating plant designed by Sir William Hooker (the director of the Kew Gardens) was installed. The boilers were contained in a small building to the south of the main building. The heating pipes leading to the periphery of the building are held on brackets under the boards supporting the plants; those in the center are laid in three rings in the plant beds.

Single glazing is used. The glass panes near the ground are 13 inches wide and 35 inches long and are curved to match the arched transition from the tambour to the roof. They taper upward to the middle of the central dome. Ventilation is possible through the row of windows in the tambour. All the windows can be rotated about the horizontal axis, and this ensures a good flow of air from below. Discharge of air is via louvers in the upper lantern.

The building is extant and well maintained.

Source: archives of Glasgow Botanic Gardens.

References: ZfBW, 1887, vol. 37, parts 1–3, p. 76; Smith 1971; Deutsche Bauzeitung (publ.), *Baukunde des Architekten*, 1902, vol. II, part 5, p. 371, figs. 141–143.

Glasgow Green

People's Palace
Winter Garden (figs. 564, 565)

The winter garden in Glasgow Green Park is part of an exhibition hall, the main building of which is a museum made of stone with a central octagonal dome. The base of this is an elongated rectangle with a semicircular end. Above this base is a high glass barrel vault terminated by a hemidome, which in turn is enclosed by a low ridge roof forming a corridor around the outside. This gently sloping roof rises from a facade on a stone base and is supported on the inside by a row of cast-iron columns, which are reinforced at their tops by braced girders forming a surrounding gangway. Rising above the columns are broad arched rafters which carry the barrel vault. These rafters follow the profile of the roof, changing from a curve at the base to a straight section above. The lower flange of each girder is a continuous arch. A glass vault with an elegant sweep is created by this combination of straight and curved

lines. The interior reminds one of the high and wide spans of the braced girders of railway stations of the period.

This winter garden, built around 1880, is extant and well maintained.

Source: archives of Glasgow Botanic Gardens.

Göttingen

University Botanical Garden
Small Conservatory (fig. 566)

The "kleines Gewächshaus" (small conservatory), built around 1850 by an unknown architect, has three sides made of masonry with a glass lean-to roof above a south-facing glass front, the ridge of which is supported by two extremely slender cast-iron columns. Both purlins in the middle of the sloping glass surface are prestressed by round steel section below. The vertical glass front and the roof are formed by delicate iron sash bars, which hold the glass panes like overlapping scales on a fish. The building is extant.

Grimston Park, Yorkshire

Winter Garden (fig. 567)

The small Grimston Park winter garden (ca. 1830–1840) is part of a castle-like establishment. The space built as an orangery and immediately accessible from the living room has narrow pilasters and is terminated by a glass-roofed architrave. The rectangular room is divided into two parts at the ceiling level by a transverse beam. The larger, square part is covered by a small glass dome built in the Loudon style. The transition from the iron ring of the dome to the square of the architrave at the corners is accomplished by the triangle of the glass spandrel and by trapezoidal glass areas along the architrave. The smaller part is covered by a simple glass hipped roof. The iron sash bars of the cupola and the hipped roof display extremely fine filigree work and constitute a conscious architectural contrast to the stonework. Noteworthy is the use of the unusually slender iron columns below the architraves across the interior. As in the Brighton Pavilion of John Nash (1808), the columns are made in the form of palm trees. The building is extant and well maintained.

Hackney, near London

Loddiges Nursery
Camellia and Palm House (figs. 262–267)
architect: J. C. Loudon
builders: W. and D. Bailey Co.
built ca. 1820
demolished

At Hackney, then on the outskirts of London, the accomplished botanist Conrad Loddiges founded in 1771 a commercially oriented nursery. In the following decade a number of interconnected hothouses were built, with a total length of more than 980 feet. Charles Rohault de Fleury, the builder of the glasshouses in the Jardin des Plantes in Paris, visited the Loddiges establishment in the course of a study tour in 1833 and called special attention to the fact that "its extent is so great that it creates a wonderful impression." At that time, after the demolition of the Bretton Hall palm house, it was the largest glass building for plants in the London area.

The hothouses had a U-shaped plan and partly enclosed an inner yard. Two hothouses below the buildings stood out on account of their size: the warm house for palms and the temperate house for oranges and camellias. Both these structures had vaulted glass roofs.

The palm house, 80 feet long, 69 feet wide, and 33 feet high, was supported on two rows of hollow cast-iron columns (fig. 263, 266). The vaulted roof had a wooden frame.

The other hothouse (fig. 264–267) had a space frame entirely of iron. This was the first large hothouse with a frame made completely of iron, and it proceeded directly from Loudon's experiments with curvilinear roofs at Bayswater from 1817 (fig. 141). Rohault describes the structure as follows:

The building intended for large orange bushes adjoins at the rear to other glasshouses with lean-to glass roofs and is combined with them. It has a rectangular base ending in two quadrants and is 36 m long and 7 m wide. The curved rafters are supported at four points: first by the 1 m high strip footing at the front; secondly by eight iron columns of 8 cm diameter which also support a cast iron purlin of 14 cm depth and 8 cm width; thirdly by eight wrought iron bars of 40 mm diameter, on which rests an iron wall plate of 13 mm depth and 40 mm width; and fourthly and finally by the brick wall at the rear on which stands the only glass wall in the building and which can be opened for ventilation purposes. The curved iron rabbet beams of 40 mm depth and 13 mm width are 16 cm apart. The detailing of this glasshouse deserves no praise in respect of aesthetic beauty. Nevertheless, the overall impression of the same is satisfactory, and it is one of the largest forcing houses which

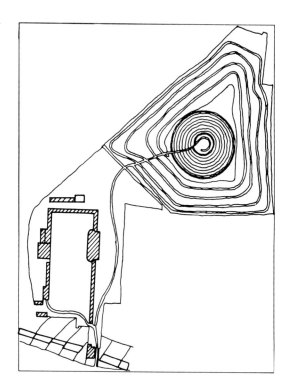

262
Site plan, 1837.

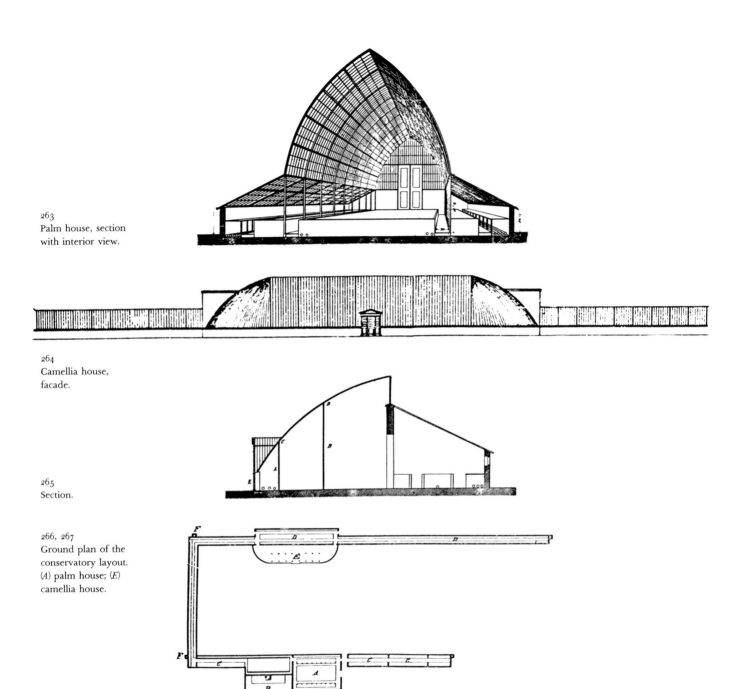

263
Palm house, section
with interior view.

264
Camellia house,
facade.

265
Section.

266, 267
Ground plan of the
conservatory layout.
(A) palm house; (E)
camellia house.

have been made with iron frames. One can criticize the irregularity in the positions of the supporting points, and the very small size of the glass panes—a defect moreover which it shares with all other English forcing houses.[76]

The curvilinear roof structures, made of slender wrought-iron sash bars, were supported by two purlins on two rows of columns, in contrast with the self-supporting shell structures later used by Loudon. The very slender columns were placed about 23 feet apart. The basis for their use must have been the flat curvature of the glass shell and the incapacity of the abutment to resist the outward thrust.

The whole layout was heated by steam generated in a central boiler room. The palm house had an artificial rainmaking device. When the nursery closed in 1854, Joseph Paxton bought up all the exotic plants and replanted them in the Crystal Palace at the Sydenham.

Reference: Allgemeine Deutsche Bauzeitung, 1837, vol. 2, no. 48, pp. 397–400.

Hackney, near London

Glasshouse with Hemidome (figs. 268, 269)

diameter: 39 feet
height: 23 feet
builders: W. and D. Bailey
built: ca. 1820
demolished

Rohault describes in connection with the Hackney buildings a type of glasshouse, built on the Loudon principle, that came into more frequent use in England: "We have illustrated here another glasshouse likewise built by Bailey with curved glass walls, although this is not in Mr. Loddiges' establishment. This glasshouse is very elegant, which can be understood from the drawings provided. According to the statement of Messrs. Bailey it cost 500 pounds sterling. All English glasshouses with curvilinear iron space frames are, with a few exceptions determined by local conditions, built on the same principle."[77]

The Baileys erected a similar building for Lord St. Vincent at Rocketts in Essex. Loudon describes it in *The Green House Companion* (1824) as "a most elegant house on this principle." The basic shape of this building—a quarter-dome—had been proposed in 1815 by George Mackenzie as the ideal shape for a hothouse. Its starting point was the alignment of the glass vault according to the course of the sun. Loudon used this structural form from 1817 on.[78]

References: Gloag 1970, p. 48; *Allgemeine Deutsche Bauzeitung,* 1837, vol. 2, no. 48, pp. 397–400.

268
Facade.

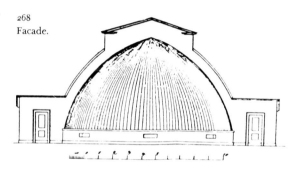

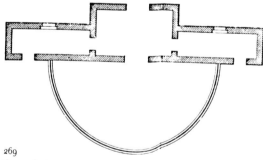

269
Ground plan.

Herrenhausen, near Hannover

Park Herrenhausen
Palm Houses (figs. 270–278, 568–571)

From the series of hothouses erected in the Berggarten of Georg II August, Elector of Hannover during the eighteenth and nineteenth centuries, the two outstanding palm houses by Georg Ludwig Friedrich Laves (1846) and Auhagen (1879) are examples of significant span and structure. The palm house designed by the versatile architect and builder Laves is of historical interest because it brought the development of classical hothouses to perfection. Auhagen's objectively designed building was the tallest hothouse in Europe; it exemplified the new possibilities inherent in the use of rolled-iron section in a space frame.

The background to the origin of these hothouses was the passion for collecting, motivated by royal prestige, which made the Berggarten at the start of the nineteenth century one of the palm centers of Europe.[79]

Laves's palm house was situated in the Berggarten with its axis perpendicular to the large avenue connecting the castle to the mausoleum. Laves prepared two designs for this palm house. The first, not in fact built, shows the main room in the ground plan as a combination of a rectangle and a circle. This arrangement created a kind of central space opening onto two wings. The effect is further strengthened by the roof structure, following the outline of the base, which forms a cone above the circular middle part; this cone is intersected by the longitudinal hipped roof. The east, south, and west sides have vertical glass walls. The rear wall and the corner pillars are of solid masonry. The glazed surfaces lie between wooden columns, which are reinforced on the front by cast-iron half-columns. The main entrance is in the middle of the south front. The side rooms, of solid masonry, are in two stories on the north side. Two anterooms located at the ends of the wings contain stairways to the cellar and the upper stories and give entry to the kitchen and a few side rooms. The round building at the rear contains a three-axis "garden room" opening onto the palm house, which is accessible from the garden via a terrace with a pergola. In the eastern of the two anterooms that provide entry at the side to the garden room, there is a semicircular staircase which leads on the first story to a balcony and an "upper room for looking into the palm house." The living accommodations for the garden staff are on the left in the first story. There are six heating installations in the cellar. All the conduits lie under the soil. The frieze of the

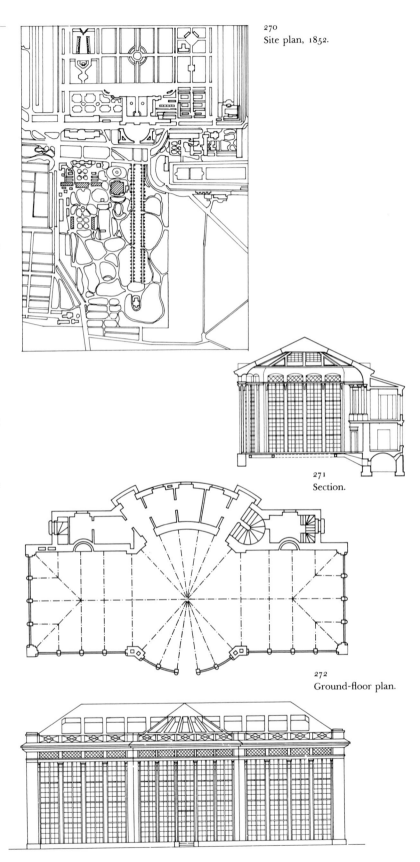

270
Site plan, 1852.

271
Section.

272
Ground-floor plan.

273
Front elevation.

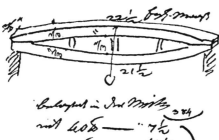

274
Laves's sketch of un-
dertrussed beam.

building is interrupted to obtain light. The main
cornice carries wrought-iron latticework between the
shafts. The roof is covered with metal and has a row
of skylights. The modified design that was actually
used resulted in a shorter building and smaller side
rooms (figs. 271–273). The garden room on the north
side is intended for larger assemblies and is on the
first story; the living accommodations for the garden
staff are located below. The skylights are larger than
in the first design to make fuller use of the distance
between the rafters; hence, the structural principle of
the palm house is noticeable in the roof too.

The load-bearing structural members are of solid
masonry on the north, and there are masonry corner
pillars on the south. In addition, there are slender
wooden columns and there are semicircular cast-iron
columns in the glass facade on the front. The roof
framework is supported on a new invention of the
time. From existing copies of drawings by Auhagen
it emerges that the roof construction was based on
the well-known "Laves beam." There are undertrussed beams in which the compressive forces are
counteracted by special members. The simplest arrangement is that the beam is split lengthwise down
the middle for almost its whole length and the lower
and upper elements are separated by spreaders (fig.
274). This increases the moment of inertia of the
beam considerably; hence, the strength can be
matched to the position of the moment curve. The
chief difficulty is in the clamping together of the
ends of the beam. This serves to take up the thrust
and shear forces. The joint is made by straps and
bolts. In a later version, a beam assembled from two
parts came into use. This allowed the use of a
straight upper beam combined with an undertrussing
element. This type of construction was used not only
for roof trusses but also for bridges.[80]

There are two authentic prototypes of Laves's
building: the Wilhelmshöhe palm house by Johann
Conrad Bromeis, in Kassel (1822), and the Pfaueninsel
palm house by Albert Dietrich Schadow and Karl
Friedrich Schinkel (1829). The intersection of the cir-

cular central structure with the rectangular wings
used at Kassel was taken up again in the ground
plan of the Herrenhausen hothouse, and the spatial
arrangement of the Pfaueninsel hothouse, with an
apse developed in the center, was used in Laves's
hall-type structure.

Because in the matter of art Hannover was under
the influence of Berlin in the first half of the nineteenth century, it is possible that Laves had actual
knowledge of the palm house on the Pfaueninsel. As
the painting by Blechen in the Berlin National Gallery shows, the style of the glass wall appears as if it
had been copied exactly. The Kassel palm house was
in fact a common source for transformations of the
antique orders into a framework of columns acting
as a screen.

The reason for the rebuilding of the palm house
by Auhagen was the amazing growth of the Herrenhausen palm collection and the size the older palms
had reached. At first Auhagen only wanted to increase the Laves house by dismantling the rear part.
Several designs to that end are preserved in the
Cumberland collection of drawings. However, during
the extension project it was decided to create a completely new replacement for the old palm house. Auhagen was commissioned in 1875 by the Royal Building Commission to produce a plan for the building of
a new palm house of "major proportions."

The vast glass-and-iron building that arose in
1879–80 was architecturally not very successful, either
in its interior space or in its exterior. It is reminiscent of factory buildings of the early twentieth century. One can deduce the compromise involved from
the ground plan and the structure of the building,
which must have been arrived at through some consideration of the old palm house, the retention of the
avenue of palm trees, and the disturbance caused by
the change of position of the palm trees during the
construction. If we look at the almost square base,
we see that the towerlike structure is located not at
the point of intersection of the two axes of symmetry but on the north side, nearer the side wall. This
arrangement of the ground plan works so that columns placed in the interior support the asymmetri-
cally placed towerlike structure symmetrically. This
arrangement can be understood only on the assumption that further building was envisaged.

The architect Auhagen described the structure as
follows:

*All iron components with the exception of the cladding of
the shafts, cornices, gutters, and supporting plates of the galleries are made of wrought iron or rolled section. The stanchions consist of braced members, the outer perpendicular
flanges of which are made of four pieces of angle iron in*

275
Ground-floor plan.

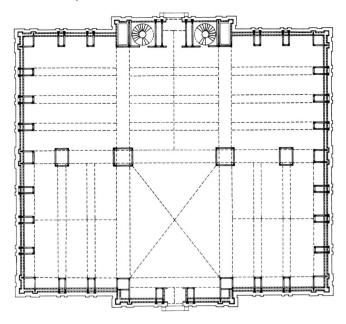

276
Section.

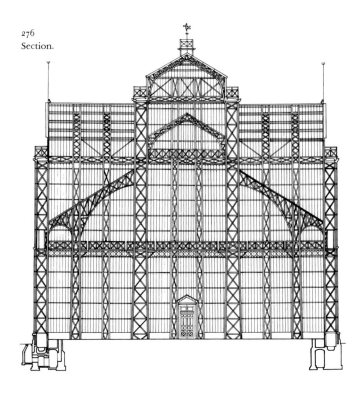

277
Facade.

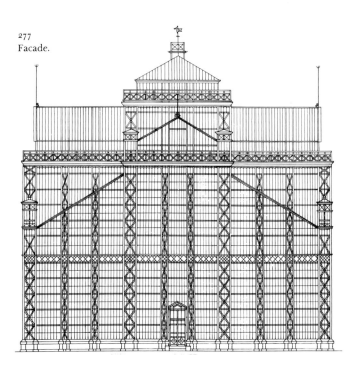

278
Woodcut, 1882.

shading sheets but also for the maintenance of the building. The zinc roof sheds the water into gutters placed behind the main cast-iron cornice, from where it runs down into the interior of the building into the conduit lying below the hot-water pipes, and then into drains, an arrangement which, copied from the palm house at Schöneberg Botanical Garden near Berlin, has proved very satisfactory here as well as there, and which has the advantage that some evaporation of the water is brought about. The rectilinear form chosen throughout for the roof is in contrast to the curved surfaces so often favored in respect of the more solid and more cheaply produced glazing as well as in respect of the use of shading. The rafters are made of strong braced girders in harmony with the stanchions, which at the same time have the job of strongly reinforcing the walls with respect to each other. Rolled-iron bars are incorporated into the walls between the stanchions, and in the roofs between the rafters at average distances apart of 1.6 m, to which the sash bars are riveted for the accommodation of the glazing. Whereas in the wall panels the rebates for the internal glazing are on the inside, in the roofs the glass is fixed in from above and held in by putty. The weight of the iron structure is 510,200 kg, of which 139,600 kg is cast iron. Double glazing is used throughout, except for the interior walls of the staircase. The glass panes are fitted 12 to 15 mm lapping each other in the usual way, on the inside wall of the staircase laid in zinc plated lead sash bars, and on the other inside walls as narrower panes of glass abutting each other.

The building is heated by a low-pressure hot-water system and steam heating, but the latter is chiefly intended only for heating the soil, because the plants are no longer standing in tubs but planted out in the soil. Besides this it serves to provide the necessary degree of humidity in the air. For the ventilation of the building there are provided in the foundation numerous, partly inside, partly outside, adjustable air passages and louvers, as well as in the lantern. These can be opened and closed; the former from the galleries, but the latter from below by means of aligned axle drives operated by chains. The hurricane-force winds of 14–15th. October 1882 proved the strength of the building and passed it by without causing any vibration whatsoever, nor dislodging any glass panes, although it uprooted many of the strongest trees. This proved not only the efficiency of the glazing but also the particularly conscientious execution of the iron space frame. The senior engineer of the company that carried out the work, Eisenwerk Lauchhammer, Herr Rose, deserves special praise for his painstaking work on the detailing, which at times was extremely difficult.[81]

References: Die Gartenzeitung, 1882, vol. 1, pp. 7–147; ZfBW, 1916, vol. 66, parts 1–3, pp. 30–40; Herrenhausen 1666–1966 (1966).

such a way that they simultaneously determine the distance between the outer and the inner glass wall. Because of this distance the sides of the angle iron are only 65 mm, so there remains between the latter one further space of 5 mm only interrupted by the coupling pieces (fish plates), which in combination with the empty space between the flange and the cladding on the stanchion is sufficient to prevent the formation of the troublesome frost on the inner side of the stanchions. All the stanchions, and particularly those of the central building on the north side, are firmly anchored into the foundations, and in addition they obtain important reinforcement through the inner and the roof gangways which surround the building on all sides, in that horizontal girders are incorporated which are capable of withstanding the wind pressure and transmitting it to firm supporting points. A central and two side bridges are incorporated, which can be raised to facilitate the movement of tall trees from one part of the building to another. At the level of the second of the two roof galleries both central stanchions are on the other hand joined by a solid braced gangway in order to obtain a firm longitudinal reinforcement of the building.

The gangway of the roof gallery consists of oak planks with 25 mm wide gaps through which the water runs down on to the zinc roof below. A solid wrought iron balustrade prevents accidents by falling from these galleries, which are very useful not only for the placing and the removal of the

Hluboká nad Vltavou (Frauenberg)

Schwarzenberg Castle
Winter Garden (figs. 279–281, 572–575)

length: 141 feet
width: 33 feet
height: 26 feet

The winter garden at Hluboká, built between 1840 and 1847 by the Viennese architect Franz Beer, is, like its descendant in Lednice (Eisgrub), an expression of feudal prestige. In contrast to the accumulating wealth of the middle class, which was becoming important through manufacturing, the nobility had to demonstrate the wealth of its estates, its traditional base. As at Lednice, here also an estate was rebuilt, at great expense, in the Neo-Gothic style. With the abundant use of cast iron in the overdone mock-Tudor decoration and the erection of a winter garden made of cast iron, wrought iron, and glass, the new industrial building material—iron—was recognized as suitable for prestige buildings. This aesthetic expression had in its background not only the model of the modernized English country mansion but also the awakening interest of the feudal landlords in the development of the iron mines located on their properties.

With the acquisition of the old castle fortresses at Hluboká in 1661 by Johann Adolf I, the Schwarzenberg family had established itself in Bohemia. Around 1839, at the same time as Lednice, Hluboká was rebuilt. The greater part of the castle was demolished. Also demolished were the adjacent household and administrative buildings, which stood in the way of the transformation of Hluboká into a pure prestige building. A riding-school hall was added between 1845 and 1847, and the cast-iron-framed winter garden was built as a decorative link between the castle and the riding school.

The rectangular base of this glasshouse is covered by a ridge roof along its length. The north front is of solid masonry; the south front, which faces the castle yard, is entirely of glass. The entrance projects from its center as a strongly accentuated front feature. A small flight of steps made of wrought iron is likewise covered by a glazed load-bearing structure. The glass ridge roof is supported on ribs forming a frame, with riveted and bolted joints. Braced ironwork stanchions are an integral part of these ribs, widening from below upward, projecting outward into the interior, and shortening the span of the roof truss. The space frame is formed by the combination of the roof truss and the braced stanchions, which are placed about 11 feet apart and which make up a space-forming element. If one considers the relatively small span (about 33 feet) in connection with the construction, the disparity between the terms of the brief and its execution becomes evident. The supports and the ridge elements of the front exterior are richly decorated with Gothic ornamentation and are purely decorative, playing no part in the load-bearing structure.

The interior space and the exterior show complete divergence in their designs. Whereas the front exterior has a prestige function related to the castle architecture, the interior is reminiscent of the techniques used in factory buildings. The copious use of cast iron for the facade of the winter garden is continued in the front of the castle. On its upper east part it is covered with abundant interlaced decorative work, Gothic arched bars, and pillar work, all of which contribute to the formation of continuous cast-iron loggias. The contrast between the heavy masonry work and the filigree cast-iron ornamentation is a shape-forming architectural element. On account of its ability to reproduce even the smallest shapes with extreme precision, the use of cast iron allowed the creation of Gothic elements that could never have been executed in stone.

The building is extant and well maintained.

References: Silva-Taroucca 1910, vol. 4, part 2, pp. 35–45; *Le château de Hluboká* (Prague, 1966).

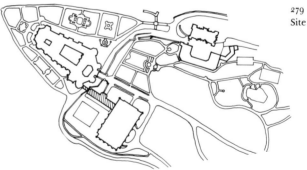

279
Site plan, 1910.

280
Ground-floor plan of Schwarzenberg Castle winter garden.

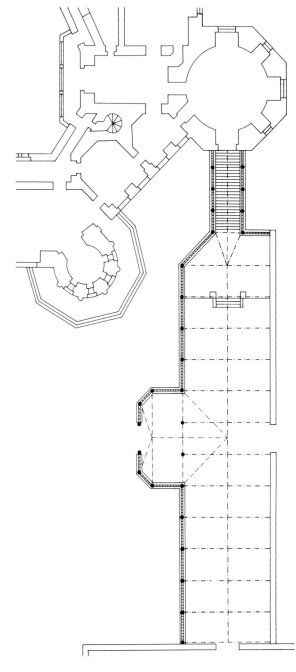

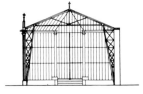

281
Section.

Hove, Sussex

Anthaeum
Winter Garden

The architect of the Surrey Zoological Gardens (1831), the teacher and gardener Henry Phillips, built the Anthaeum in Hove one year later. This glass palace was the largest of its kind.

In 1825 Phillips designed an "oriental" garden in the vicinity of his house in Brighton. In the center of this garden there was a glass hothouse large enough to accommodate a palm garden, a literary institute with a library, a museum, a reading room, and a science school. In 1832 this project was taken up again in the form of the Anthaeum in Hove. The building, which had a circular central structure with a glass dome, was designed to contain tall trees, a fish pond, rock formations, and an amphitheater for 800 people.

The construction was almost complete in July 1833 according to a report by Joseph Paxton, who visited the building site.[82] The height of the dome was 60 feet, the diameter 170 feet. No previous dome structure had reached such a size. Twenty arched cast-iron ribs formed a vault with an elliptical cross-section. The 37-inch-deep ribs narrowed toward the apex of the dome to 24 inches and converged into a retaining ring 7 feet in diameter. Each rib was bolted together from six cast-iron parts. A 12-foot brickwork ring served as the foundation for the space frame. Light cast-iron purlins in the form of a horizontal ring joined the ribs.

During the construction, a wooden supporting frame was erected and bolted to the iron space frame until the whole was finally assembled. The architect supervising the construction, Anson Henry Wilds, severely criticized the lack of diagonal strutting between the ribs. Because no special precautions had been taken with regard to the assembly of the cast-iron members, and an extra installation would have led to considerable additional cost, the firm carrying out the construction declined to incorporate diagonals, probably on the opinion that they would be structurally superfluous. When the temporary frame was removed, the unreinforced space frame suffered deformation under its own weight, and some of the horizontal members buckled. On September 12, 1833, J. C. Loudon visited the site and found the apex of the dome fallen in. The lower half of the iron structure and all the masonry remained usable, and the architect Charles Augustus Busby (a colleague of Wilds) tried to rebuild the Anthaeum; however, this project proved unsuccessful. The collapse of the dome caused Phillips to go blind through shock, and he died a few years later.

References: Hix 1974, p. 114; Chadwick 1961, p. 94.

Innsbruck

Botanical Garden
Palm House (figs. 282, 576, 577)

length: 180 feet
width: 29 1/2 feet
height: 43 feet
built 1905

The palm house in the Innsbruck Botanical Garden, an anonymous design built straightforwardly according to the principles of the new technology, anticipated the technical and aesthetic developments of the following period. Laid out on a rise, the high cubic building with a pyramidal roof—the true palm house—is adjoined by wings with ridge roofs, which are stepped in height and width. The impressive interplay of cubic forms is strengthened by the gentle slope of the glass skin, through which the latticework of the space frame can be clearly seen. The structure is based on a framework which is recognizable through the layout of the sash bars forming the skin. Braced girders in the shape of stanchions and purlins make a rigid space frame that carries a suspended facade in front, which we recognize today as a simple execution of the job. In its formal language the building (which survives) is reminiscent of the cubist architecture of later times.

Source: archives of Innsbruck Botanical Garden.

282
Ground-floor plan of
Innsbruck palm
house.

Karlsruhe

Residenz
Conservatories (figs. 283–289, 578–581)

The conservatories of the Karlsruhe Residenz are less important as individual buildings than as a coherent ensemble in the form of a Romantic architectural prospect. The overall design, integrating many buildings, is the work of Heinrich Hübsch, who had already made a name for himself designing important public buildings in Karlsruhe. Starting from the castle there arose a series of plant houses, a winter garden, a massive gateway building with two towers and a banquet hall, a high palm house with a victoria regia pool and lateral wings, and a house for the gardener with an orangery and a banquet hall attached to it.

Hübsch also had to consider the urban layout of Karlsruhe, which dates from 1715. At that time the Lustschloss of the Margrave Karl Wilhelm was so designed that the castle tower was in the center of the whole layout, which was divided into 32 sectors by radiating lines. Around 1802 the sectors allocated to the city had become so filled in with houses that Friedrich Weinbrenner was given the job of extending the radial plan with new roads and open spaces. In this connection, the Botanical Garden, which had become too small, was reorganized.

The garden was sited on the left side of the castle, as an extension to its wing at the boundary between the park and the city. In 1809 Weinbrenner built an orangery and two plant houses there. In 1853 further extensions were entrusted to Hübsch, who was asked to integrate the new buildings architecturally with the castle. In contrast with Weinbrenner, who in his design for the orangery had followed strict principles of symmetry and subordination of the various parts of the building, Hübsch grouped the complex of buildings artistically, in an irregular sequence, in the

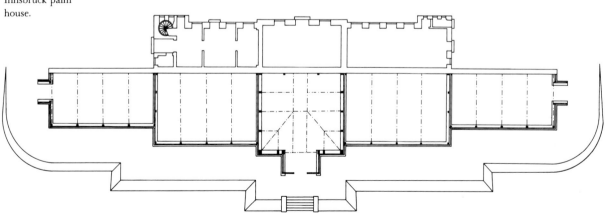

283
Site plan (extract),
ca. 1860.

sense of an architectural prospect of Romantic character derived from the principle of the landscaped garden. His main objective was to create a multiplicity of forms and materials through the alternation of glass and solid buildings and varied spatial forms. Hübsch himself has written about this: "In conformity with its purpose to serve the plant kingdom which we have assembled here in the fullness of all its forms and diversity of color, so that it is in harmony with the layout of the surrounding garden, we do not find the principle of an inflexible symmetry and geometric severity maintained here, but there is in the whole layout some greater degree of freedom adhered to, and variety of form stands out clearly, and there is a consideration of the artistic effect so far as the correct basic architectural principles will allow."[83]

Hübsch's classical orangery, 197 feet long, 49 feet wide, and 29 1/2 feet high, could be used as a banquet hall as well as a plant house. The orangery had as its centerpiece a glass dome, the proportions of which relative to the solid masonry Hübsch took care not to make too large Hübsch described it thus:

The new orangery stands out at the edge of the castle garden on the city side, approximately in a north to south direction. Because the trees that were to be housed here are very numerous and sometimes of considerable height, the building had to be as spacious as possible. But because on account of these two factors, and the fact that the line of the road leading up to its end pavilion for the orangery proper part of the building, there was a distance of only 60 m left; this caused the architect to give the building the considerable width of 15 m and as a result of that the masonry parts could not in fact be less than 9 m high, because they would have appeared much too compressed with the moderately high glass roof. Likewise the end pavilion at the wide Stephanienstrasse required a higher aspect, which it obtained in the form of a glass dome. The same effect is created when the four corners of the lower part of the building are planted with groups of evergreen shrubs, as if growing out of the general greenery; and the architect has also considered that some boxes were to be set out on the balcony, from which ivy plants would not only form hanging festoons but would grow from the ribs of the dome with the intention of enlivening the high upper part of this rotunda. One end of this building now joins on at right angles to the rest of the building as an uninterrupted extension which extends to the castle, with which it is in immediate contact, so that one can gain access from the same, passing through the whole length of the extension as far as the banquet hall at the opposite end. This building has the considerable length of 120 m. One can make a summary of the main individual parts of the unbroken row of buildings from the orangery to the castle as follows. A high pavilion with a passage through it to the castle botanical garden with its English layout stands almost on the axial line between the orangery and the cas-

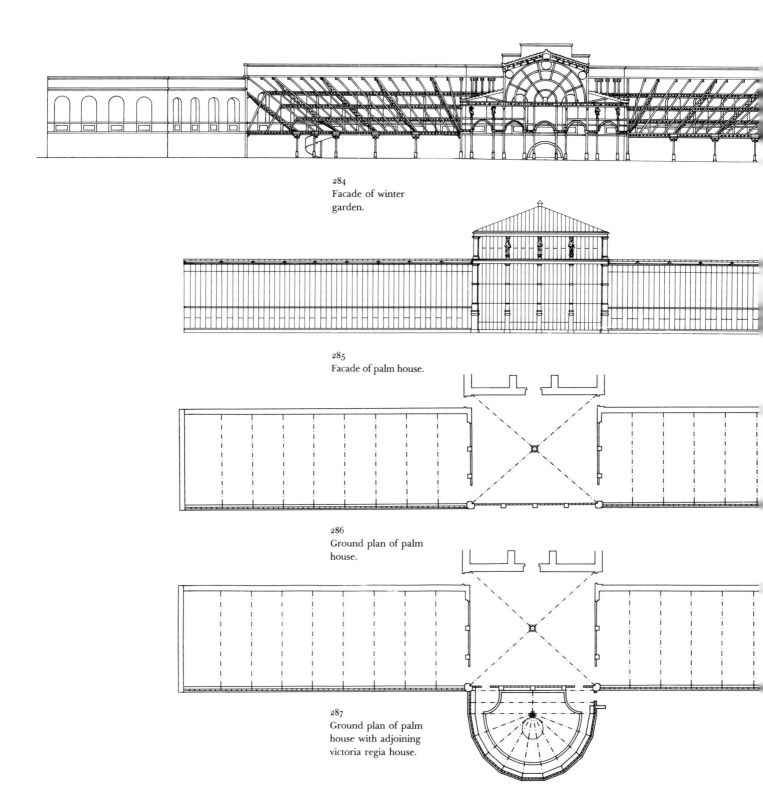

284
Facade of winter
garden.

285
Facade of palm house.

286
Ground plan of palm
house.

287
Ground plan of palm
house with adjoining
victoria regia house.

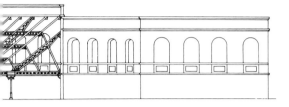

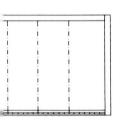

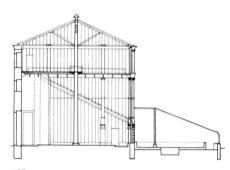

288
Section through central pavilion of palm house.

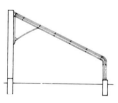

289
Section through wing of palm house.

tle; above the passage there is an assembly room from which one has a view over the city and the surrounding area. . . . One half of the whole layout from the orangery to this pavilion consists of a dwelling for the castle gardener, then there is a high palm house in front of which in a sunken semicircle there is installed a heated pond for victoria regia and other exotic aquatic plants; on either side of this are two temperate houses. The other half of the whole complex has a gallery built in the crescent between the pavilion and the castle, and in front of this closed passageway there is a winter garden which constitutes a particularly important part of the whole group of buildings. We see here groups of southern trees and other plants, which are protected during the winter by glass walls and a glass roof, but which stand out in the open during the summer months of the year after removal of the walls and the roof.[84]

The architectural value of Hübsch's palm house (figs. 285–289, 578–580) lies in contrast between the cubical central pavilion and the gently sloping vaulted glass surfaces of the wings and the victoria regia house. The central pavilion (the palm house proper) has the elegant character of a temple, an impression that is strengthened by the caryatids supporting the roof framework. The framework of the extremely narrow pilasters, the architrave, and the caryatids is made of red sandstone. Only with difficulty will one find another stone building in which the load-bearing masonry work is reduced in such a radical way to a filigree skeleton. The cross-section achieved by this means would likewise be justified in having a cast-iron supporting framework. The architect probably intended to equate the fragility of the glass and the stonework and thus to achieve a Romantic effect. To what extent this architectural target had to be reached at the expense of a logically designed load-bearing structure is shown by the central iron column used, which, while serving also as a ventilating pipe, helps to support the flat pyramidal roof. It must have been included so that the load of the roof would not be supported entirely by the facade front. The central pavilion terminates outward on a solid masonry base wall, which also forms the foundation for the glass roofs of the wings. The framework of the glass roofs was made almost entirely of wood in the original construction. After a few years, the woodwork in all the hothouses was almost completely destroyed by rot and the glass roof had to be renewed. In 1863 the glass roof of the palm house was reconstructed in iron to the design of Joseph Berckmüller. The same was done in 1868–69 to the wings and the victoria regia house, under the supervision of Jakob Friedrich Dyckerhoff. The victoria regia house was later demolished, but the palm house is extant and well maintained.

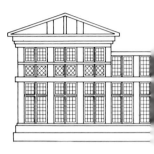

The winter garden (figs. 284, 581) has an arcuate layout and is 394 feet long and 39 feet wide. A masonry base wall with arched openings forms a clearly visible termination to the semicircle and the passageway situated behind it. The base wall also forms the foundation for the iron space frame, consisting of gently sloping braced girders and cast-iron columns. An iron space frame forms the center of the layout, which has the form of a three-story pavilion and which resembles the palm house. The slender cast-iron pilasters and caryatids used here recall the stone ones in the palm house. The whole iron framework serves to support the lean-to glass roof of the semicircle, which is removable in the summer.

Originally designed in wood by Hübsch, and built in 1857, the winter garden owes its present form to J. F. Dyckerhoff, who in 1868–69 replaced the wood with iron and added the central building.

References: Valdenaire 1926; Breymann 1877, p. 91, plate 48.

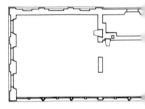

Kassel

Wilhelmshöhe
Great Conservatory (figs. 290–293, 582–584)

length: 269 feet
width: 56 feet
height of central pavilion: 52 1/2 feet (after rebuilding, 62 feet)
architect: Johann Conrad Bromeis
built 1822
rebuilt 1887

The Great Conservatory in Kassel is an architecturally splendid example of a hothouse formulated in the classical style. Conceived as a pavilion structure, with a central dome connected by lower wings to square corner buildings, this hothouse represents a radical design in stone orangery architecture, with its continuously glazed window and roof surfaces. These surfaces form simple three-dimensional spatial forms—cubes, pyramids, cylinders, and hemispheres—which are interrelated by the filigree sash bars. The architect relied on the segmented form, taken from the buildings made of glass panes by Friedrich Ludwig von Sckell in Nymphenburg and those in the Munich Botanical Garden. However, in contrast with those buildings, there is the monotony of arrangement into rows broken only by the supporting structure of the iron columns and stone pilasters, and the architrave projecting slightly beyond the glass surface of the front of the building. The projecting central part, with its glazed hemisphere above, contrasted with the flat glass surface and gave

290
Site plan, 1927.

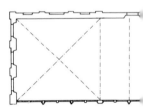

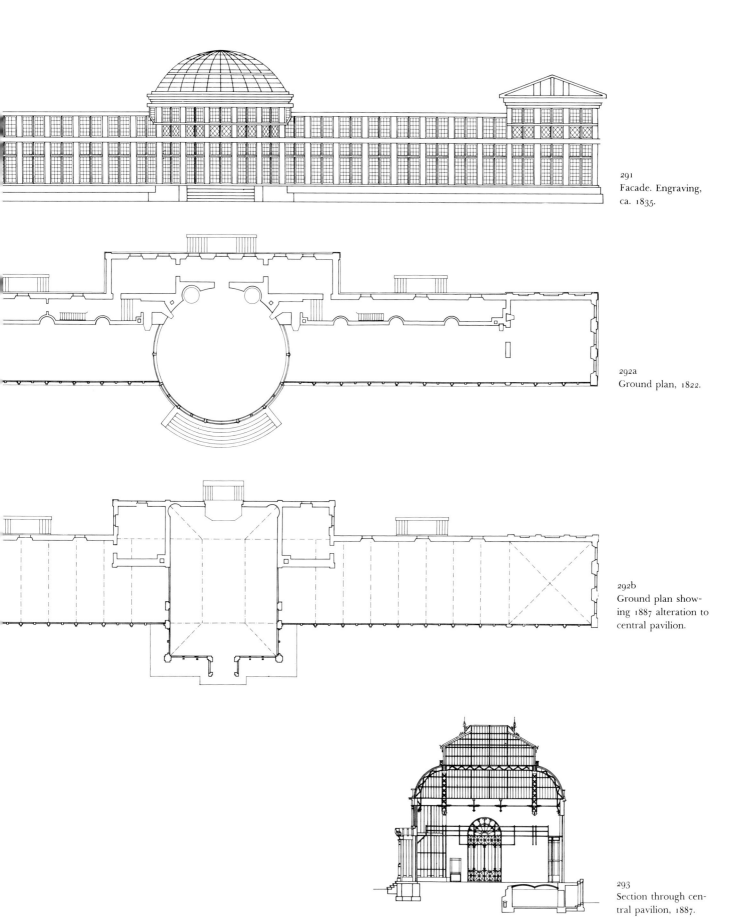

291
Facade. Engraving, ca. 1835.

292a
Ground plan, 1822.

292b
Ground plan showing 1887 alteration to central pavilion.

293
Section through central pavilion, 1887.

the whole building its dominating central feature. This central part was later replaced by a cube-shaped pavilion with stone pilasters and a suspended glass vault.

Following the hothouse types common in Germany, this glasshouse was built in the pavilion style, with plane surfaces and simple three-dimensional basic shapes. The central section, with its flatly curved glass dome, was in striking contrast with this style. This glass vault was the first large structure of its kind in Germany. One may presume that Bromeis, who had previously used cast iron for the Teufelsbrücke, made its whole space frame of iron. J. C. Loudon included a schematic drawing of the front of this hothouse in his *Encyclopaedia of Gardening* (fig. 291), but this does not show the type of construction used for the space frame. The present ground plan shows that the dome was supported in the front by eight cast-iron columns and in the rear by solid masonry (fig. 292a). Masonry forms the whole of the north face, including the adjoining rooms, and at the same time serves as a foundation for the rafters of the glass ridge roof. The high corner pavilions are also bounded at the side by masonry work; this gives way on the front to pilasters, which are terminated by flat pyramidal glass roofs. Rows of cast-iron columns form the basic framework of the building. Half-round cast-iron columns with flat capitals project from the glass surface. Resting on a stone base, they support a continuous architrave, which in the 1822 design also surrounded the central structure. The ridge roofs of the wings were also supported by it. The iron columns in the central pavilion, corresponding to the greater height, are placed one above another in order to reinforce the pyramid roof at the front. The original rafters probably consisted of pre-stressed iron members inserted in harmony with the columns. They were replaced with an iron structure made of rolled section and tie bars during the rebuilding of the central pavilion in 1877. Curved rolled sections were inserted in the spandrels of the vault and the vertical window of the front to stiffen the supporting structure; these were fixed to the middle of the columns by brackets. During the rebuilding of the central pavilion in 1887, the circular dome was replaced by a rectangular piece formed of stone pilasters and architraves and crowned with a glass vault sloping down on all sides (figs. 292b, 293). One could also consider the Edinburgh palm house as the prototype of such a space design. Braced steel girders, following the curvature of the side of the roof, form the ribs. Two ribs extending over the wide part of the pavilion intersect with two longitudinally placed beams, which then run diagonally into the corners of the pavilion. Tie bars at the springing take the outward thrust of the vault. This braced structure supports the weight of the lantern.

Source: city archives, Kassel.

References: Messerschmidt 1927; Loudon 1835, p. 208.

Killikee, near Dublin

Colonel White's Conservatory (fig. 294)

length: ca. 115–130 feet
architect: Richard Turner
built ca. 1845–1850
demolished

This curvilinear conservatory demonstrated Turner's mastery of the glass-and-iron filigree structure. It was an elongated glasshouse with semicircular ends, roofed with a glass vault reaching down to the ground. The space frame was built solely of sash bars, and the fact that every fifth bar was made thicker gave the roof a fine rhythmic form.

As in the wing sections of Turner's hothouses in Belfast and Dublin, the sash bars coming down from the ridge were first straight, then gradually changed to a curve, and were anchored in a low base of cast-iron frames with ventilators rather than windows. The sashes formed a pointed vault, which terminated in hemidomes above the two semicircles of the base. One may assume that the glass vault in the vicinity of the sloping glass surface was supported on the inside by rows of thin tubular columns, as in Belfast and Dublin.

A high glass rotunda in the middle of this long building cut into the glass vault. Vertical glass walls, made in the same way as the wings, formed a cylinder that terminated above in a cast-iron ring. This ring functioned as the base of the steeply sloping glass dome, which itself terminated in a cone. A small lantern for ventilation crowned the apex. The height of the ridge line of the long wings was the

294
Engraving, 1853.

same as that of the retaining ring of the rotunda. It had a row of cast iron palmettes as decoration. This was the only ornamentation of this purely structural building, apart from the small brackets near the base of the rotunda. The intersection of the two curved surfaces—the nave and the high cylinder—brought about a space form of high architectural quality. In McIntosh's 1853 *Book of the Garden* the beauty and elegance of this conservatory were rated appropriately and it was proposed that the adjoining masonry utility rooms on the north side be replaced by a continuation of the glass vault.

Reference: McIntosh 1853, vol. 1, p. 376.

Cologne

Botanical Garden
Flora (figs. 295–299, 585–588)
length: 187 feet
width: 95 feet
height: 66 feet
architects: H. Märtens, Georg Eberlein
built 1864
demolished 1914

The Cologne flora, built in 1864 and combining a palm house with a public recreation center, was the first building of its kind in Germany. With it began a series of flora buildings, the peak of which can be seen in the Frankfurt and Berlin floras. The Jardin d'Hiver in Paris can be considered as the definitive model for this type of building.

Like the other floras, this building was intended to extend the enjoyment of a tropical environment by the addition of entertainment facilities. Characteristic spatial and structural features were combined with the generally accepted layout of intersecting barrel vaults supported by ribs. The intention of accommodating a palm garden and restaurant facilities within a single space turned out to be impractical, however. The layout of the catering facilities, which were situated at the side of the palm garden, demanded masonry work. Thus, the illumination of the greater part of the palm garden could only come through the glass roof. This fusion of two spatial functions had an adverse effect on the plants. In order to eliminate this drawback, there was a functional and spatial separation in the later flora buildings. A competition for the extension of this flora was won by Georg Eberlein, who tried to solve the problem by situating a palm house transversely in relation to the assembly rooms.

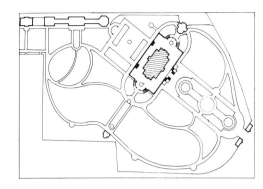

295
Site plan of Cologne
botanical garden, 1862.

That the building created a sensation of the first order is underlined in a report on the opening:

The focus of the festival was the glass palace executed in the grand manner, which will serve both as a winter garden and as a winter recreation center. The gigantic roof is made of iron and covered with glass. . . . Between the flower beds and clumps of shrubs one finds elegant marble tables with seats. Giant candelabra with countless gas jets spread daylight into these beautiful rooms, which remind us of the legend of the Albertus Magnus Winter Garden. . . . Thousands of people gently moved along the pathways filled with the scent of flowers and delighted in the glimpse of the sea of light and its magical effect on the beds of flowers, the bushes, and the murmuring water. That was indeed a magnificent aspect! Amidst it all were the sounds of music and the cheerful talk of the four thousand people who attended the opening ceremony.[85]

The old botanical garden in Cologne, founded in 1801 on the site of the Jesuit College in Maximinenstrasse, had given way to a railway station. In the 1850s it was reestablished in conjunction with the newly founded zoological gardens at the edge of the present-day suburb of Riehl. The success of the company that was formed to operate the zoological gardens and the great interest aroused in the public prompted the wealthy citizens of Cologne in 1862 to create a botanical garden with recreational facilities for summer and winter. Under the chairmanship of Eduard von Oppenheim, who was already involved in the management of the zoo, the Flora AG company was founded to design a new center for social life in connection with the zoo and its restaurant.

The park of the flora was created to the design of the garden architect Peter Joseph Lenné. The layout, corresponding to that of an English garden, included an ornamental promenade. The combination of the botanical garden with a recreation center and a palm garden was said by Lenné to have "from the start . . . a great and fertile future."[86] The flora was

built in 1864, on the basis of designs by the architect
H. Märtens, in the form of a glasshouse "of a colossal magnitude, for which the London Crystal Palace
served as a model."[87]

The building, erected on an elongated rectangular
base, was enclosed by masonry walls on the outside
and by two intersecting semicircular glass-and-iron
barrel vaults. The vaults rested on double columns.
Between the columns and the surrounding masonry
a corridor was created, onto which round arched
windows opened, forming a kind of arcade. The
crossing of the barrel vaults formed a large luminous
space. The barrel vaults were terminated at the outer
ends with richly decorated rosettes made of glass
and iron, as in Paxton's Crystal Palace. The building
stood on a raised base with broad staircases on all
sides. The entrances were axially located, and the internal staircases to the basement and to the galleries
were in the corners of the building. The glass roof
structure consisted of two-hinge arches made of
curved, braced iron girders. These arches sprang
from fan-shaped iron brackets, which transmitted the
forces to the cast-iron double columns. The latter
were held together by a girder that formed a ceiling
cornice, as well as by cast-iron arches at gallery
level, in conjunction with the masonry work. The
vault over the crossing was supported by two braced
arched girders following the diagonal intersection
lines of the glass barrel vaults.

Märtens solved the technically difficult problem of
the crossing of the two vaults in an elegant way.
Four quadruple columns were used instead of double
columns. These formed a kind of bundle of cast-iron
pillars with brackets attached to the top so that the
large arches over the crossing were positioned diagonally. The springing for the construction of the vault
was consciously accentuated as an important functional element. The distribution of the forces could
be judged from the appearance of the girders. In this
respect the transparency of the Cologne flora is comparable to that of the contemporary railway-station
concourses; however, the concourses did not have
the problems involved in the intersection of barrel
vaults because of the longitudinal arrangement of
their platforms.

Source: Stadtmuseum, Cologne.

References: *Illustrierte Zeitung*, 17.9.1864, vol. 43, no. 1107, pp.
196, 197; *Flora und Botanischer Garten Köln*, 1966; *Illustrated
London News*, 17.6.1865, vol. 46, no. 1320, pp. 595, 596.

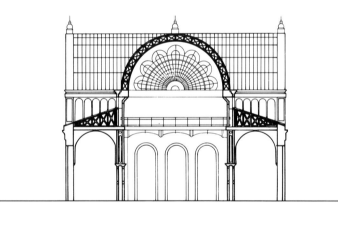

296
Cross-section.

297
Ground-floor plan.

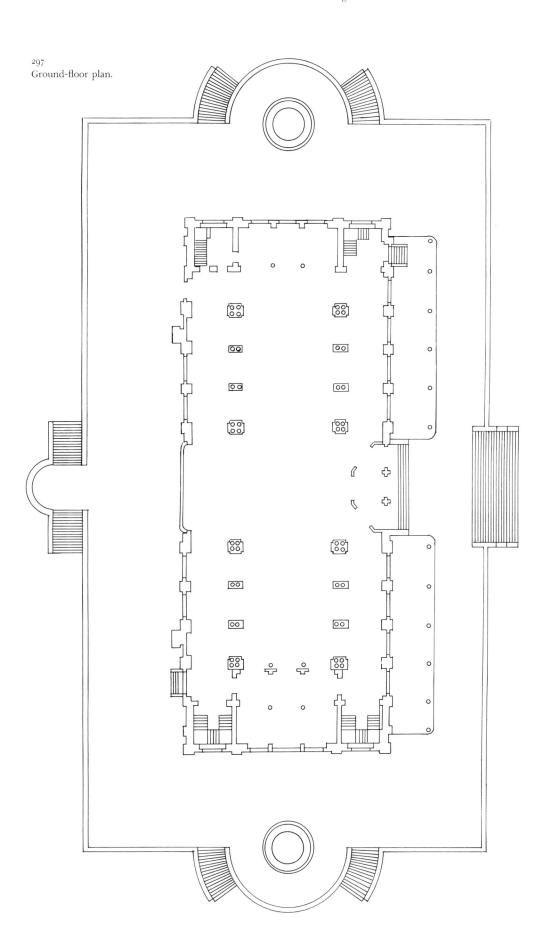

298
Engraving of Co-
logne flora, ca. 1865.

299
Engraving of Co-
logne flora, 1864.

Copenhagen

Botanical Garden
Palm House (figs. 300–304, 589–592)
length: 308 feet
built 1872–1874

The palm house in the Copenhagen Botanical Garden has a spatial affinity with the Baroque summer residence. With its axial construction, its accentuated central pavilion with wings and corner pavilions, its raised position, and its terrace layout in the front, it translates this building type into a glass-and-iron filigree structure. The hothouses at Brussels, Syon House, Berg bei Stuttgart, and Munich were the forerunners of this spatial concept.

The design of this palm house has been customarily attributed to the architect Tyge Rothe, although an 1879 publication mentions the industrialist and art lover Johann Carl Jacobsen as a partner in the work. What part Jacobsen had in the design of the palm house is difficult to determine. It is, however, certain that he was the founder of the palm house. An advocate of glass-and-iron structures, Jacobsen was also capable of designing them. This can be authenticated from the design stages of the Ny Carlsberg Glyptotek. The layout of an individualistic glass-and-iron palm house and winter garden adjoining the residential part of Jacobsen's Carlsberg Brewery also points in that direction. These hothouses were built on the curvilinear principle and were based on English examples. One may assume that the experience Jacobsen gained from his hothouse buildings had an influence on the design of the Copenhagen palm house.

The palm house has a high central pavilion and two wings which terminate in corner pavilions. The

300
Site plan, 1881.

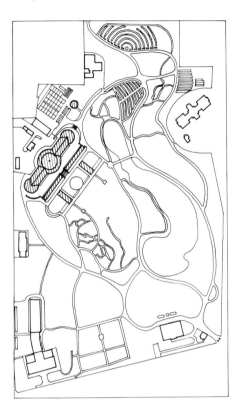

301
Engraving, 1881.

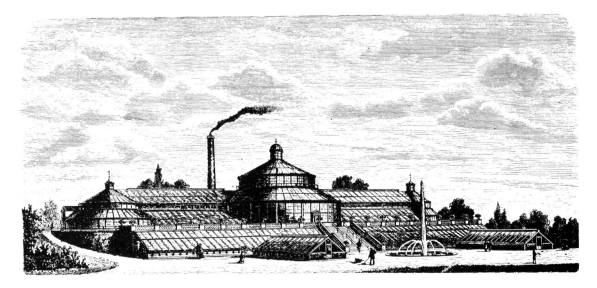

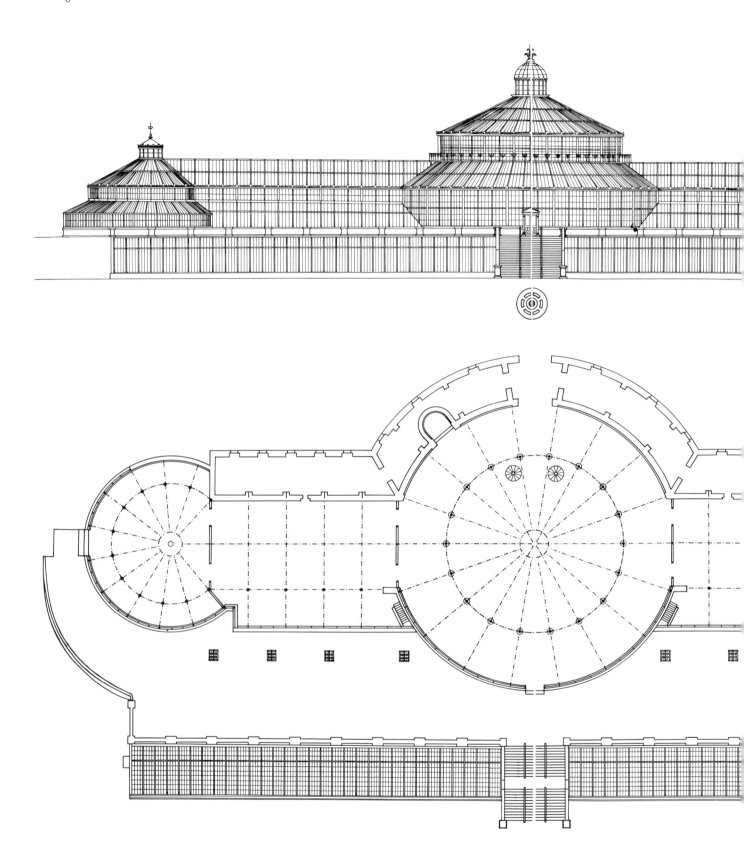

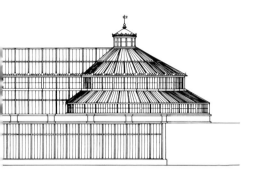

302
Facade.

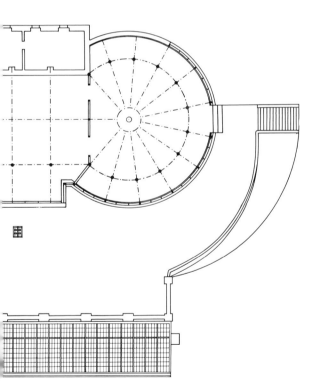

303
Ground-floor plan.

circular central pavilion, 98 feet in diameter, is made up of the simple geometrical forms of a cylinder and a cone. A ring of eighteen cast-iron columns 24 1/2 feet high, joined by cast-iron arches, supports a conical roof which has a small lantern. There is a low gallery at the level of the cast-iron arches, likewise with a lean-to roof. The central pavilion obtains a differentiated spatial form from this double staging of the same basic types of cylinder and cone, and this raises the architectural focal point of the whole building. The glass ridge roofs of the long wings adjoin at the level of the gallery and intersect the conical roof. The wings are also stepped. Their fronts are formed by gently sloping lean-to roofs. The wings terminate in rotundas 61 feet in diameter, which have the same construction as the main central rotunda. Their height is the same as the ridge line of the wings. A solid structure on the north side runs the whole length of the building and contains the workshops. All the roof surfaces have the same angle of slope: 33°. They are supported on rolled-section rafters. The individual sections of the building are separated by glass partitions. The roofs are fitted with ornamental cast-iron gutters. The cast-iron supporting members were designed with special care, particularly the 24 1/2-foot-high columns. They consist of three parts (base, shaft, and Corinthian capital) with attached brackets, and they are clearly bolted together. The glass front on the south side stands on a low stone base, in front of which is a wide terrace with a stairway. Sloping glass surfaces extend the glass ensemble, running up into the parapet of the terrace.[88]

As with most glass buildings on the Continent, the need for double glazing makes the use of plane surfaces for the roof an obvious choice. There is here an attempt to abolish the disadvantages of this plane construction with regard to the illumination of the plants by the use of circular rotundas topped with conical glass roofs. "In a few of these hothouses the roofs are curvilinear and have a curvature which ends in hemidomes which allow the plants to receive the greatest possible amount of light from all sides. But even if in this respect the curvilinear form is preferred, it introduces on the other hand the double inconvenience of requiring very rigid and expensive constructions and of making the fitting as well as the maintenance of the glazing very difficult, particularly when double glazing must be used, as in our climate, so that the difficulties of obtaining sufficient ventilation in the upper part of hothouses put it out of consideration. These factors brought about the use of linear forms. However, in order to retain as far as possible the advantages of the curvilinear structure,

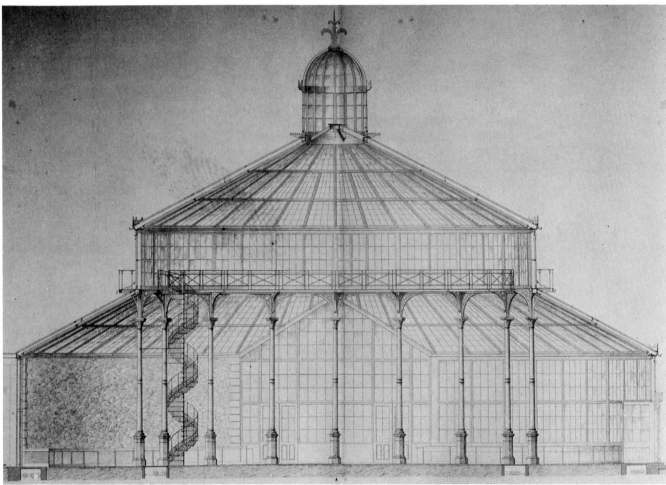

304
Watercolor and pen-
cil drawing, ca. 1872.

305
Section through cen-
tral pavilion. Litho-
graph, 1879.

glasshouses, particularly the most important—the palm house—have been given round shapes with vertical and sloping surfaces and are transfused with light from all directions."[89] The iron structure is glazed not only on the inside surface but on the outside too, where the glass is held by a wooden framework. This double glazing is necessary in the northern climate in order to prevent the formation of condensation drips on the cold inside surfaces, which would damage the palms. This expensive but technically unobjectionable solution to the condensation problem has been applied here. All the glazed areas of the hothouse except the lantern have wooden frameworks. The glass panes are mostly of colorless Belgian glass. The sash bars are made of galvanized iron. The roof glazing has longitudinal sash bars only; the glass panes are held in by lead.

All the hothouses are heated by steam through a system of pipes.[90] It is possible to heat the space between the double glazing to melt snow on the outside, and to prevent the formation of condensation on the inside. The heating plant is in the cellar.

The building is extant and well maintained.

Source: archives of Botanisk Have, Copenhagen.

References: DBZ, 1881, vol. 15, no. 23, pp. 133–135; no. 25, pp. 145, 146; Jacobsen and Rothe 1879.

Copenhagen

Villa Jacobsen, Carlsberg Brewery
Winter Garden

architect: Johann Carl Jacobsen
built 1876

The private winter garden of the Jacobsen family is part of a villa built in the style of classicism on the site of the Carlsberg Brewery, in the immediate vicinity of the production area and the laboratories. The winter garden is adjacent to the mansion and is an integral part of it. The vaulted glass roof of the winter garden rests on a stone archtrave, which in turn is supported on a row of Doric columns. This building terminates at one end in a semicircular

apse. The glass roof is correspondingly vaulted by a hemidome at that end. The space frame consists of longitudinal and transverse purlins and ribs with sash bars lying in them. There is a lantern along the ridge for ventilation. Behind the row of columns is a corridor containing benches and statues.

The building is extant and well maintained.

Source: library archives, Ny Carlsberg Glyptotek, Copenhagen.

Copenhagen

Ny Carlsberg Glyptotek
Winter Garden (figs. 307, 593, 594)

length: 141 feet
architect: Vilhelm Dahlerup
built 1904–1906

A glass-domed winter garden filled with palms dominates the Ny Carlsberg Glyptotek. The 130-foot-high dome, which sits on top of a tambour, is also a major feature in the city's skyline.

The Glyptotek combines an extensive palm garden with an art collection. The promenade leading to the art gallery begins and ends among tropical plants. A fountain and stone seats invite one to linger. The glass dome and the vaulted glass roof of the lower gallery create a well-lit interior. The Glyptotek is the only remaining building of its kind, size, and architectural quality in Europe.

The layout of the Glyptotek (which is near Tivoli Park) originated in 1897 in the plans of the architect Vilhelm Dahlerup. It owes its origin to the Jacobsen family, which in 1888 had announced the gift of its private art collection to the public. Johann Carl Jacobsen had already contributed to the building of the large tropical house in Copenhagen between 1872 and 1874. In 1904 he pressed for the extension of the Glyptotek. This was effected in 1906, likewise under Dahlerup's supervision, in the form of a domed winter garden with surrounding galleries. The antique works of art collected by Jacobsen were moved here and combined with modern works under one roof. It is possible that the idea of creating a winter garden as the centerpiece of the museum came from Jacobsen, who had not only indicated his preference for glass-and-iron palm houses but also had called for the construction of a special winter garden on the site of the Carlsberg Brewery.[91]

The Glyptotek winter garden, surrounded by the masonry work of the art gallery and the assembly rooms, occupies a large rectangular space in which cast-iron columns are arranged on a square ground plan in such a way that one side of the square is ad-

306
Site plan, ca. 1900.

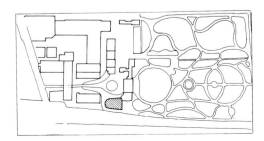

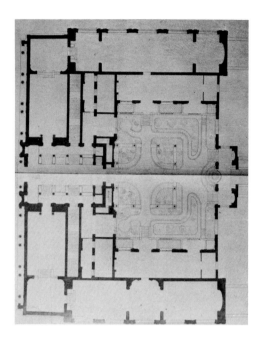

307
Ground-floor plan,
from design, ca. 1905.

jacent to the enclosing wall of the entrance side. The twelve columns, about 62 feet high, are bolted together from three separate parts and support a riveted braced girder, by which means the transition from the dome to the circle is effected by diagonal girders in the corners of the square. There is a horizontal octagonal braced girder on the inside, in which a steel octagonal ring is fitted at the level of the upper flange. The cast-iron framework of the tambour rests on this structure, which contains arch windows and which supports a gallery both inside and outside. The dome, with its lantern, is supported by sixteen cast-iron arches, which are mutually reinforced by a lattice of narrow curved transverse and longitudinal ribs. The joints are strengthened by triangular plates, and this creates the impression of a vault formed by glazed boxes. The flatly arched braced girders of the lower glass roof, attached at the level of the tops of the capitals on the columns, span the gallery formed by the square of columns and the three sides of the enclosing masonry wall. This, interrupted by large openings and two stories, supports the other end of the girder. The art gallery is visually connected with the winter garden on all sides through openings in the two-story-high enclosing wall. The winter garden is laid out centrally in the axis of symmetry of the museum complex and is joined to the main entrance via an assembly hall.

Source: library archives, Ny Carlsberg Glyptotek.

Reference: Poulsen 1974.

Cracow

Palm House
The palm house at Cracow, built in 1872 and now demolished, was a high, box-shaped glass-and-iron building on a square base surrounded by delicately framed facades, which extended between slender iron columns. Pierced iron arches joined the columns together and gave the facades their rhythm. An inner glass vault supported on columns rose above the square iron ridge; this was raised by the addition of a square framework with vertical glass surfaces.

Langport, Somerset

Forcing House (figs. 308–310)
length: 49 feet
width: 16 feet
architect: J. C. Loudon
built 1817
demolished

The Langport forcing house is of historic interest because it was one of the first curvilinear hothouses, having been built in the same year as the experimental buildings at Bayswater. Leaning against a solid brick wall, it served as a peach and grape house. In spite of its small size, it had the characteristic features of Loudon's structures. The curved glass roof was carried only on thin wrought-iron sashes. The building was terminated by quarter-domes, each of which had the typical convergence of the sash bars toward the apex. The ironwork was erected by W. and D. Bailey.

Reference: Loudon 1822.

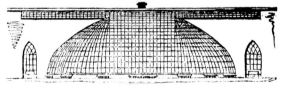

308
Front elevation.

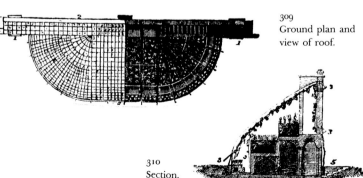

309
Ground plan and view of roof.

310
Section.

Lednice (Eisgrub)

Liechtenstein Castle
Winter Garden (figs. 311–313, 595–598)

length: 302 feet
width: 44 feet
height: 33 feet
built 1843

The winter garden at Liechtenstein Castle is the only extant hothouse on the Continent built on Loudon's principle of curvilinear construction, the basis for which was first published by Loudon in 1817. The fact that in Britain and Ireland there now exist only four large buildings of this kind increases the historical importance of the building at Lednice.

The fact that this winter garden is fully functional today refutes the theory—widespread during the nineteenth century—that this method of construction was unsuited to the Continental climate. The structure is in excellent condition after painstaking restoration work.

The winter garden was erected by the Englishman Devian in conjunction with the rebuilding of the castle in the Romantic style, which was begun in 1843 under the direction of the Viennese architect Winkelmüller. The winter garden is joined to the castle by an anteroom. It is built on ground which rises 10 feet above base level to the north, facing a landscaped park, so that the Winter Garden becomes the termination and focal point of the classically laid out parterre garden. The heating plant and plant workshops are located in a basement.

The space frame of the winter garden, a long barrel vault with a hemispherical end, is built on slender cast-iron columns, 7 inches in diameter at the base, which imitate bamboo stalks and have capitals shaped like leaves. The columns support a lightly-cambered sheet-metal roof shaped like a table with a small pagodalike structure for ventilation, all of this on longitudinal iron beams. The distances between the columns are 12 feet along the axis and 14 feet across it. The half-barrel-vault structure rests on a continuous stone base and abuts onto the longitudinal beams of the table-like structure. The glass vault is carried by curved iron sash bars, as in Loudon's buildings (fig. 312). Double sections are used instead of single sash-bar window section, and they are set 12 feet apart, corresponding to the distance between the columns. The sash bars are spaced 9 inches apart. The surface is glazed with small glass panes lapped like tiles. The panes are very small because, not being curved as in Richard Burton's buildings in Dublin and Belfast, they cannot produce the neces-

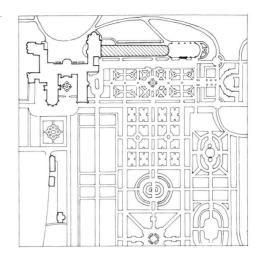

311
Site plan, 1910.

sary curvature themselves. There is no horizontal reinforcement between the sashes. The quarter-sphere end of the winter garden is glazed in the same way. The structure is remarkable because there is no diagonal bracing to reinforce it against wind pressure. The whole building is supported by the masonry of the castle only in one place; otherwise it is detached all around. The wind forces are resisted by the curvilinear glass-and-iron vault.

The enthusiastic remarks made by Loudon about the structural and functional advantages of his invention are corroborated in the Lednice winter garden. In order to accomplish the building of this large vaulted structure, Davien must have had great confidence in the state of development of British and Irish hothouse construction. It is therefore hardly remarkable that we find here constructional and aesthetic quotations from the highest traditions of British hothouse architecture. The model for this combination of slender cast-iron columns with a slightly curved sheet-metal roof and a tabular space frame may have been the hothouse at Wollaton Hall (fig. 468). The high, delicately fabricated entrance gates could be those at Kew. The development of the columns has its model in the kitchen of Nash's Royal Pavilion at Brighton.

References: Silva-Taroucca 1910, vol. 4, part 2, pp. 27–45; Durm and Ende 1893, vol. 6, part 4.

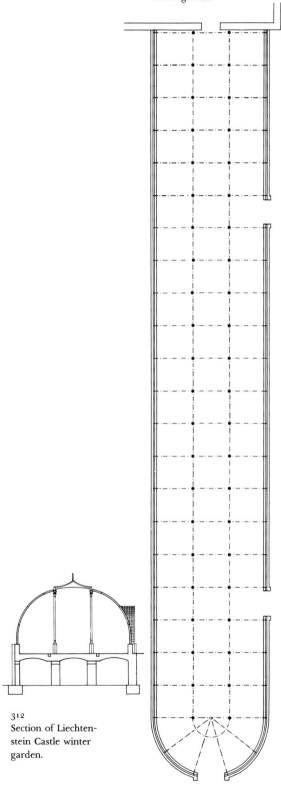

313
Ground plan of
Liechtenstein Castle
winter garden.

312
Section of Liechten-
stein Castle winter
garden.

Leeds

General Hospital
Winter Garden (figs. 314–316)
length: 151 feet
width: 63 feet
height: 60 feet
*architects: Rowland Mawson Ordish and George
Gilbert Scott*
built 1868
demolished

All the buildings of the hospital at Leeds adjoined
the winter garden. Before being converted into a
hospital, these buildings housed the National Exhibition of Works of Art.

The building type used here was the basilica, with
a vaulted nave and low adjacent aisles. The winter
garden, with its extravagant use of cast iron and its
cold decor, was a product of Victorian taste. As was
usual at the time, the iron structure was covered
with crystal ornamentation. The structural ironwork,
executed with great skill in all details of manufacture
and assembly, was evidence of the high standard
reached, belatedly, by British cast-iron technology.

The hall, surrounded by masonry arcades, was
erected as a glass vault above a rectangular base, the
nave of which was supported on two rows of cast-
iron columns. The twelve columns, 31 1/2 feet high
and 24 feet apart, carried a barrel-shaped glass vault,
which sloped down at the ends, and the lean-to
roofs of the aisles. The roofs of the aisles were supported by the enclosing masonry work. The round
columns decorated with capitals continued into a
post with an octagonal cross-section and supported a
cast-iron braced girder which was reinforced by
curved girders. The straight, short rafters of the
aisles were likewise stiffened by girders. The spandrels between these girders and the columns were
filled with cast-iron circles, executed as Gothic ornamentation, which had an additional supporting function. The semicircular arch braced girders running
up to the lantern (which was made like a box and
covered by a flat ridge roof) were set out at intervals
of half the intercolumn distance above the longitudinal braced girders. The lantern served as a longitudinal reinforcing rail between the tops of the
arched girder ribs.

The whole iron structure was made of high-quality
prefabricated parts, assembled at the building site.
The Victorian desire for excessive decoration explains the late use of cast iron for the supporting

314

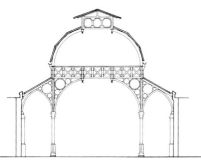

315
Section.

316
Interior view. Engraving, ca. 1870.

structures, which could have been produced more economically in the form of rolled section. The same turning back to a decoratively built structure is found in the Temperate House at Kew (1861), which began the historicism in iron construction of the more important hothouse structures.

Source: archives of Leeds Central Library.

Reference: Walmisley 1950, pp. 29, 30.

Leipzig

Crystal Palace (fig. 317)
architect: Planer
built 1882
demolished

The Leipzig Crystal Palace represents the highest state of development in Germany of the large winter garden combined with an entertainment center. A winter garden 157 feet long and 105 feet wide, surrounded by two-story galleries, comprised restaurants, a café, a theater, a circus, and a hotel. In addition there were workshops, dressing rooms, and skittle alleys in the basement. The whole complex, with overall dimensions of 374 by 177 feet, could accommodate 6,000 people.

The large glass hall is described in the 1885 *Handbuch der Architektur*:

The large concert hall, which doubles as a winter garden, stands immediately adjacent to the parterre room, which one reaches via the covered passage joining both sides of the building. The wide space spanned by a glass roof is surrounded by galleries and assembly rooms. These form a two-story layout and are connected by staircases in the four corners of the oblong base of the main building. The estrade forms a raised walkway several steps above the floor of the hall. The adjoining rooms have a side-by-side layout like a ship's berths. In the transverse axis of the building there is a chamber with an orchestra platform adjoining to the left, and on the right there is a veranda room which is in direct communication with the two-story aquarium and grotto section. There is the spacious stage in the main axis of the hall, opposite the main entrance. Here were performed minor comedies, operettas, ballets, etc. Salon artists of all kinds gave their performances here. The stage is provided with dressing rooms for the performers, connected by staircases, a sunken area, and there is another removable stage behind it.[92]

Reference: Durm and Ende 1885, part 4, iv, pp. 141–143.

317
Ground-floor plan of
Leipzig Crystal
Palace.

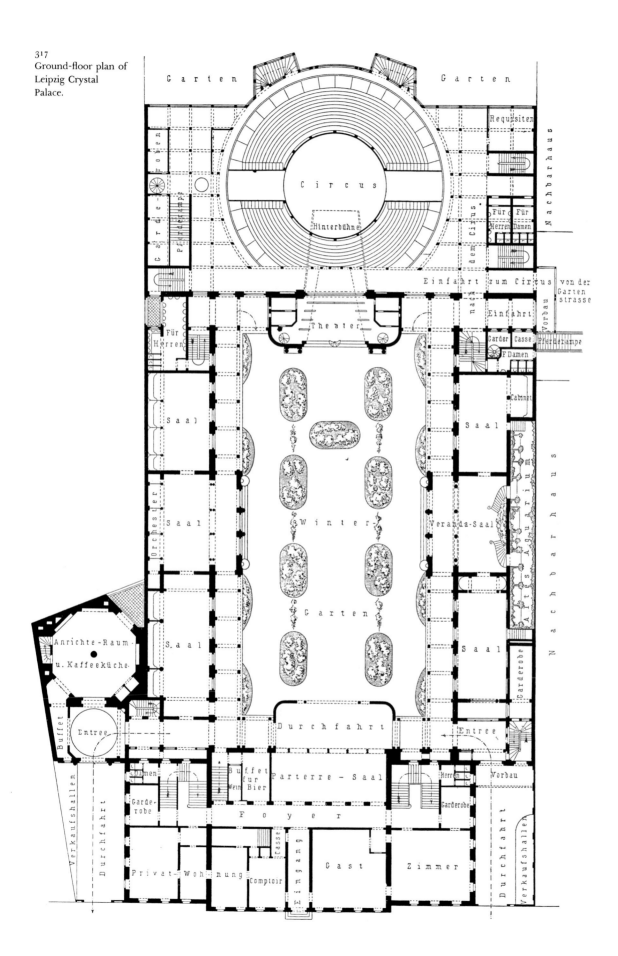

Garten

Garten

Requisiten

Nachbarhaus

Circus

nach dem Circus

Hinterbühne

Garde-roben

Pferderampe

Für Für
Herren Damen

Einfahrt zum Circus von der
Garten
nach
strasse

Vorbau

Für
Herren

Einfahrt

Theater

Garder Casse
F Damen

Pferderampe

Cabinet

Saal

Saal

Orchester

Saal

Veranda-Saal

Artus Aquarium

Nachbarhaus

Winter

Anrichte-Raum
u. Kaffeeküche.

Saal

Garten

Saal

Garderobe

Buffet

Entree

Durchfahrt

Entree

Verkaufshallen

Durchfahrt

Damen

Buffet
für
Wein Bier

Parterre-Saal

Herren

Vorbau

Garde-robe

Foyer

Garderobe

Durchfahrt

Verkaufshallen

Casse

Privat-Wohnung

Comptoir

Eingang

Gast

Zimmer

Leningrad (St. Petersburg)

Palm Houses (figs. 599–602)

The climatic conditions in Russia make special demands on hothouse buildings. For one thing, double glazing or cladding of the iron sashes with wood is needed for the protection of the plants. Added to this is the problem of the weight of snow, which demands stronger members in the space frame.

The Imperial Botanical Garden in St. Petersburg, at the mouth of the River Neva, had an extensive hothouse establishment, built during the reign of Nicholas I (fig. 318). In 1843 the architect Fischer-Uralsky was briefed to design an iron palm house—a single room, 266 feet long, 79 feet wide, and 66 feet high—to replace the old hothouses. The iron frame of this palm house, built between 1845 and 1847, was roofed with curvilinear glass on the English pattern, and the metal sash bars were covered with wood.

Several hothouses built in this tradition followed, among which the extant and well-maintained curvilinear hothouse, built around 1880, was outstanding. In its form and structural execution it has a close affinity with the palm house at Vienna-Schönbrunn. But whereas in Vienna the space frame is outside the glass skin, here it is completely on the inside. The iron sash bars are covered with wood. The interior ribs are anchored in a stone base and are, as in Vienna, curved braced girders. The horizontal members are likewise braced girders.

Besides this curvilinear palm house there is in Leningrad a large palm house on an octagonal base, with tall glass walls, built in 1880. It has a pyramidal roof. Vertical corner columns built as braced stanchions and joined together by a latticework arch support an octagonal annulus, to which the rafters of the roof are attached. With its braced girders forming the space frame, this palm house is reminiscent

of the Herrenhausen tropical house. It is also akin to Russian architecture of the 1920s, which had a preference for latticework girders.

Reference: *Frauendorfer Blätter*, 1850, no. 40, pp. 316–317.

Lille

Palais Rameau (figs. 319, 320)

length: 344 1/2 feet
width: 115 feet
height of dome: 72 feet
architects: Mourcou and Contamine
built 1878

The Palais Rameau in Lille, an exhibition building for plants with an adjacent "Palmarium," reveals an unresolved dispute between historicism and functional development. In the layout of its base and its spatial concepts, it is reminiscent of a three-story church with an apse at one end, a decorative dome, and towers at the main entrance. The solid external walls with large circular arch windows conceal the iron structure of a former palm house, which is only detectable on the outside at the terminating apse. The former roof, once covered with glass, is today boarded over so that light can enter only through the windows in the walls. The metal structure consists of cast-iron columns which support the braced ribs of the roof above the joists. The top flanges of the riveted ribs follow the roof profile; the lower flanges are attached to the frame made by the inscribed arches. The form of the ironwork at the crossing shows the problems associated with the enclosing of space, which are similar to those in the established designs in stone architecture. As in traditional dome construction, an attempt was made to form an octagon above the crossing by means of a pendentive, above which the dome was built. The direct translation of this space frame into glass and iron led to a cumbersome and unnecessarily complicated development that lacks the quality reached in the tropical-house building.

The Palmarium consists of cast-iron window elements forming a stepped cylinder, which is topped by a conical roof. This exterior form creates an internal space with an upper clerestory supported by a row of columns. A lower corridor with a gallery extends the central space.

The Palais Rameau, rebuilt, now serves as a gymnasium.

Sources: Services Techniques, Espaces verts, Mairie de Lille.

References: F. Chon, *Promenades lilloises* (Lille, 1888); Bulletin administratif, 1875, no. 9.

318
Leningrad Botanical Garden, early conservatory layout, ca. 1835.

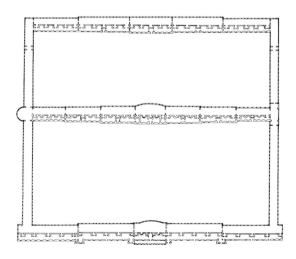

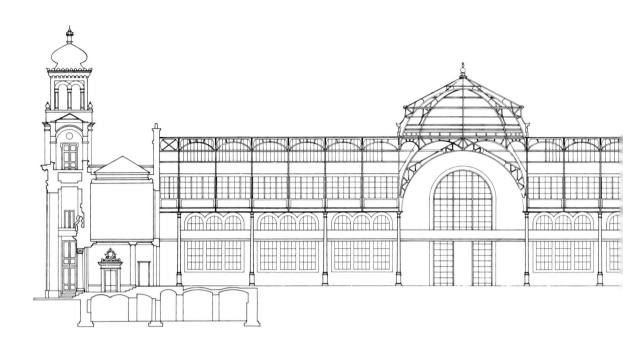

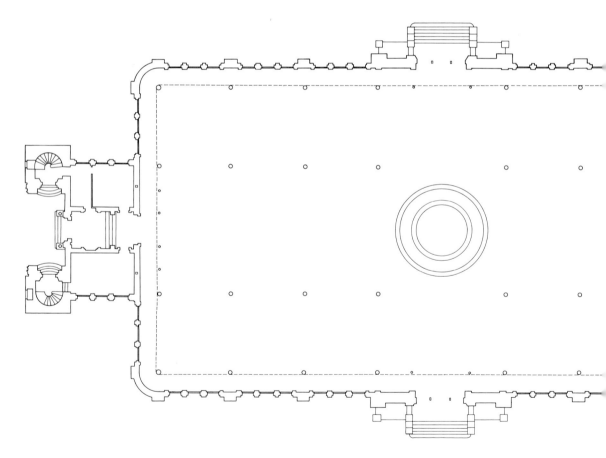

319
Longitudinal section
of Palais Rameau.

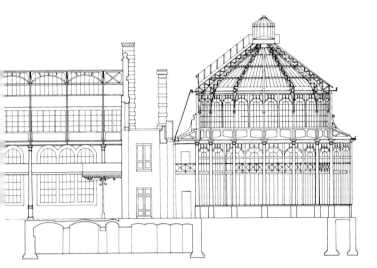

320
Ground-floor plan of
Palais Rameau.

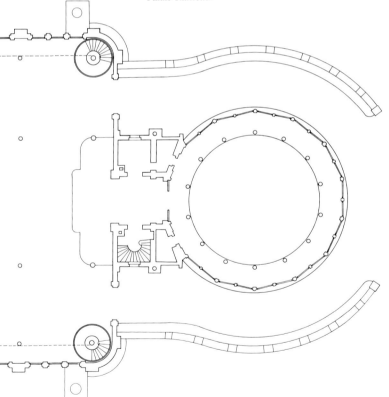

Lisbon, Belém

Palais Burnay
Conservatory (figs. 603, 604)

The conservatory of the Palais Burnay, built around
1910 and still extant, is covered by a glass barrel
vault and is terminated at both ends by delicately
executed rosettes. The artistically curved transition
from the glass barrel vault into the rosette carries
the Jugendstil signature. This impression is further
strengthened by the alternation of colorless and
tinted glass. A stone architrave with four Ionic columns is placed in front of the portal and forms an
attractive contrast between stone and transparent
glass.

Source: Glaeser archive, Museum of Modern Art, New York.

Liverpool

Sefton Park
Palm House (figs. 321–324, 605)

diameter: 105 1/2 feet
height: 74 feet
built 1896

The Sefton Park Palm House is a compact building
erected on an octagonal base with a dome supported
on internal cast-iron columns. Around these is an octagonal ring forming a low gallery with a glass vault
above. The dome is extended upward by a relatively
high lantern. This design gives equal illumination on
all sides—the ideal condition for palms.

The palm house stands on a raised base with red
granite cladding. Eight cast-iron columns about 30
feet in height support the glass vault, which extends
down to ground level. Quadrant-shaped braced girders rest on these columns and terminate in an octagonal lantern ring, likewise built of braced girders,
which for its part supports the lantern. A miniature
cast-iron gallery with round arch window frames
reinforces the dome horizontally. The ribs of the 30-
foot-high ambulatory are like those in the dome.
Rising from ground level, their tops rest directly on
the columns and project inward a little to form seat-
ings for the supports of the inner gallery. The joints
between the cast-iron columns and the lower ribs
are made with very ornamental cast-iron brackets.

One can see from the structure as a whole and
from the detailing that this particularly well-finished
glass-and-iron structure is made of parts produced in
a factory and assembled at the site. From the structural details it is evident that the space frame consists of basic parts that could have been used to

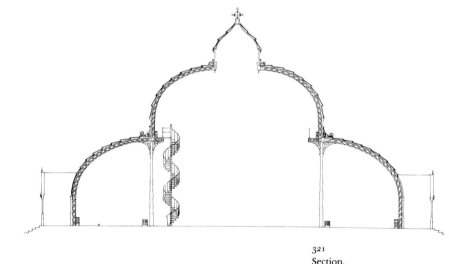

321
Section.

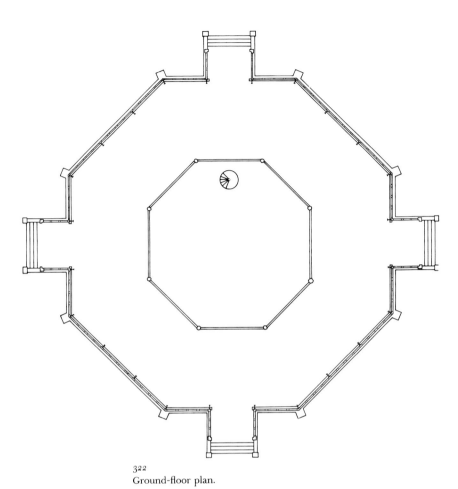

322
Ground-floor plan.

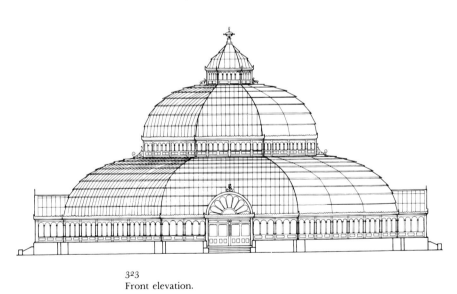

323
Front elevation.

324
Cast-iron column
with bracket.

make other glasshouses in different shapes. The cross-section of the building makes it obvious that by using the same elements one could have built an elongated hall on a rectangular base, similar to Paxton's Great Conservatory at Chatsworth. These facts suggest that we have here a building in the style of the patterns of the Mackenzie and Moncur Company.

Single glazing is used, with the panes lapping each other like roof tiles.

The building is extant and well maintained.

Source: Liverpool City Libraries.

References: Bannister 1950; Hughes 1964, pp. 147–154; Picton 1879; *The British Architect*, 30.7.1886.

London

Syon House
Great Conservatory (figs. 325, 326, 607–612)
length: 282 feet

architect: Charles Fowler

built 1820–1827

The Great Conservatory built in 1827 in the park of Syon House a work from the early days of cast-iron structures. Its completely transparent bell-shaped glass-and-iron dome—the first large structure of its kind—stands out ostentatiously both from the inside and from the outside.

The basic architectural concept of the Conservatory is the Palladian "villa surburbana." (Palladianism has a historical role in British architecture.) A rotunda-capped central building with a temple-style front and with adjoining wings terminating in temple-like pavilions was sited on a generously laid out terrace with broad steps, which comprised a parterre flower garden and underlined the palatial character of the establishment. The facade, built of dressed stone, was designed in the classical manner, with slender pilasters with round arches or straight continuous architraves and with tympana in the center and at the ends. The radically reduced area of stonework and the large window areas create an impression of a glass version of a temple colonnade. The stone base is spanned by a roof which in silhouette corresponds to the Renaissance style, but which is made entirely of glass and iron.

The front of the Great Conservatory faces south, and the wings form a semicircle curving to the south toward the mansion. Whereas the front consists of a row of narrow stone pilasters infilled with large window areas, the north side is of solid masonry up to the central part of the building. The central structure, on a 49-by-49-foot square base, is covered with

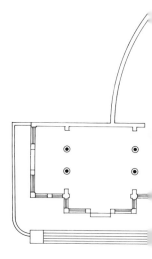

a 59-foot-high glass-and-iron dome. A 33-foot ring of cast-iron columns supports the dome and the tambour via arches set on them and joined together by an iron architrave pierced by circular openings. The high-rising cast-iron ribs that form the vaulting of the dome are held together by three horizontal iron rings and have a cast-iron crown at the apex. The iron rings support the sash bars which converge up to the apex and hold the glass panes, lapped like tiles. The spandrels which fill in the space between the tambour and the lower corners of the stonework are also made of glass and iron, and intersect the sloping glass surface of the temple part. The technical difficulties, plainly apparent, arise from the need to marry the glass roof to the masonry work. The dome space opens onto all sides via an arched beam piercing the architrave and the tympanum and supported on columns and pilasters. This dome is glazed all over on the north and south and assembled from cast-iron ribs. A rosette forms the main entrance to the conservatory. A square hall with circular arched windows and a glazed ridge roof allows access to both sides. Cast-iron ribs 29 1/2 feet long with arched lower flanges and inscribed rings anchored into the external walls carry the weight of the roof (fig. 35). Heretofore, ribs of this design and size had been used only in brick buildings.

The semicircular lower corridors that adjoin this hall have ridge roofs made of smaller rafters. Two of these rafters are supported in the middle by cast-iron columns with brackets (fig. 34). The corridors end in rectangular corner pavilions, which open onto the gardens via glass temple-like fronts.

McIntosh describes and criticizes the Great Conservatory in *The Book of the Garden*:

The detached conservatory at Sion House . . . is elegant in design, and of superior workmanship. It has, however, the fault of being too narrow for its length and height, and also of having the back walls of masonry instead of glass. This splendid structure is in the Italian style, and was designed by Mr. Charles Fowler, an architect of great taste. It is surrounded in front and at the ends by a chaste architectural terrace, and connected at the centre and ends by spacious flights of steps, with an architectural flower-garden, better designed than originally planted. The ground-plan will show the arrangement, which consists of a parallelogram centre, the dome of which is 60 feet high, and glass on all sides, adapted to the culture of stove-trees and large plants. The two wings form each a crescent, terminating in two parallelograms chiefly used for greenhouse plants, oranges, &c. The front elevation consists of stone piers and cast-iron lights: the whole of the roof is composed of the same material, and partly glazed with plate glass. The whole is heated by two steam-boilers placed in a building at a considerable distance and well shut out of sight. Ventilation we have al-

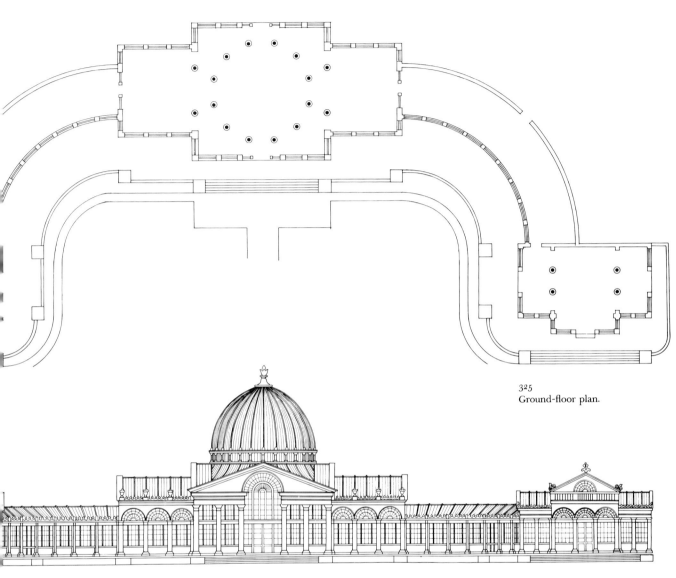

325
Ground-floor plan.

326
Front elevation.

*ways considered as imperfectly effected in this range, and to
this may be attributed in a great degree that want of success
which, for years after its erection, was found to exist—
a result which was experienced in the cultivation of many
plants, not only in this conservatory, but also in others constructed upon similar principles. The crescent wings connecting the centre with the terminating divisions are much too
narrow, which, with the opaque back wall, gives them the
appearance of ordinary greenhouses.*[93]

Christopher Hussey's poem dedicated to the Great
Conservatory expresses the fascination it held for his
contemporaries:

*Her lover's genius form'd
A glittering fane, where rare and alien plants
might safely flourish . . .
High on Ionic shafts he had it tower
A proud rotunda; to its sides conjoin'd
Two broad piazzas in theatric curve,
ending in equal porticos sublime,
Glass roofed the whole, and sidelong to the south
Twixt every fluted column, lightly reared
Its wall pellucid.*[94]

The conservatory is extant and well maintained.

References: McIntosh 1853, vol. 1, p. 368; *Syon Park* (London,
1933).

London

Pantheon Bazaar (fig. 327)

width: 33 feet
height: 23 feet
architect: Sydney Smirke
built 1834
demolished

The London Pantheon Bazaar, an elegant meeting
place in Oxford Street, distinguished itself with its
light, beautifully curved vault, supported on thin iron
sashes without intervening columns and looking like
an inverted boat hull. The roof rested on a cast-iron
framework of square windows and was intersected in
the center by a transverse barrel vault erected above
the entrances. The decoration of the plant-filled bazaar, consisting of fountains, Moorish and classical
ornaments, and sculptures, was created by Charles F.
Bielefield with painstaking care. Fish in small aquariums and tropical birds extended the oriental character of the hall. W. and D. Bailey built the bazaar, to
a design by Sydney Smirke, as a connecting corridor
to Oxford Street and Great Marlborough Street. The
Loudon construction principle is seen in its purest
form here.

Source: J. Troughton collection, London.

327
Pantheon Bazaar, in-
terior view.

328
Glass Menagerie,
general view. Engraving, 1831.

London

Surrey Zoological Garden
Glass Menagerie (figs. 328, 329)

diameter: 105–115 feet

architect: Henry Phillips

built 1830–31

demolished 1856

J. C. Loudon's bell-shaped palm house at Bretton Hall (1827) was enthusiastically considered as a sign of progressive building techniques and architecture. There followed a plethora of glass-and-iron buildings that adhered to Loudon's principle of wide-span domes and vied in size and extent with the glass dome at Bretton Hall. The flatly vaulted dome of the Glass Menagerie erected by Henry Phillips in the Surrey Zoological Garden is an example.

As at Bretton Hall, a ring of cast-iron columns supported the dome, which extended down to a low circular foundation in a flat curve. The space frame of the glass skin was built, as at Bretton Hall, entirely of narrow wrought-iron bars reinforced only by curved glass sheets. The construction principle used here made possible the development of extremely fine filigree work in the space frame.

Edward Cross commissioned Henry Phillips to design the garden and the Glass Menagerie, which was also called the Conservatory. Beasts of prey were the main attraction, particularly the Indian tiger that shared its cage with an English spaniel. The cages, filled with tropical plants, were arranged in a circle within cast-iron columns. Shrubs and trees planted around the perimeter of the dome were another attraction.

After Cross withdrew from his undertaking in 1844 it still carried on until 1855. The menagerie was demolished in 1856 in order to make way for the Royal Surrey Music Hall.

Reference: The Gardener's Magazine, February 1831, vol. 7, part II, p. 693.

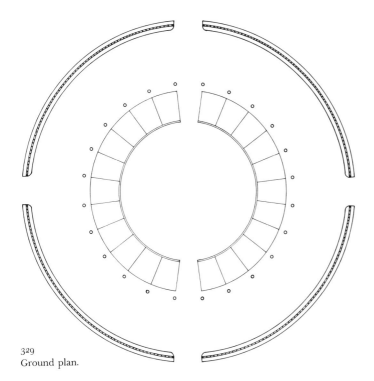

329
Ground plan.

London

Regent's Park

Warm House and Temperate House (fig. 330)

There arose in the 1830s in Regent's Park a complex of detached glass-covered buildings called the Coliseum and serving the public as a winter garden. It comprised an exhibition hall for works of sculpture, imitation waterfalls in an occidental landscape, and an elegantly built forcing house.

Charles Rohault de Fleury, who went on a study tour of Britain in 1833, visited the Coliseum and found two forcing houses particularly interesting. One, a warm house 29½ by 20 feet in area and 23 feet high, was built on a ground plan of two semicircles connected by a rectangular area. The masonry walls were sunk into the ground as far as their tops and supported a glass vault which, as Rohault described it, was "shaped like a dome." The temperate house, 46 by 15 feet in area and 25 feet high, formed a corridor alongside a masonry wall and consisted of two half barrel vaults, one above and to the side of the lower one. A row of columns along the line of intersection between the two vaults carried the weight of the roof. This appears to have been Rohault's model for the curvilinear wings of the Jardin des Plantes.

The architect of these now-demolished buildings is not known.

Winter Garden of Royal Botanical Society (figs. 331–334, 606)

length: 213 feet
width: ca. 100 feet
height: ca. 25 feet
architects: Decimus Burton, Richard Turner
built 1842–1846
demolished 1932

This first large winter garden in England was a remarkable engineering structure. Its pointed arch barrel vault formed a long hall that terminated in apses roofed by domes. Turner's suggestion that a curvilinear ridge roof be used won out over the ridge-and-furrow roof proposed by Burton. All the detailing carried Turner's signature. The delicately assembled sash bars and columns were exploited to the limits of their strength. The structural execution of the iron building is reminiscent of the curved glass roofs in Belfast (1839) and Dublin (1843).

Hix describes this winter garden as follows:

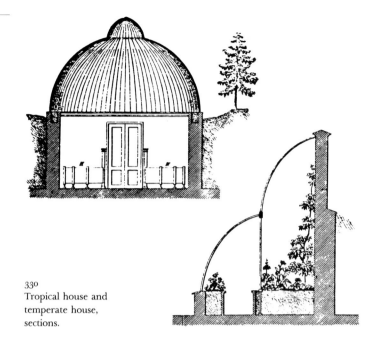

330
Tropical house and temperate house, sections.

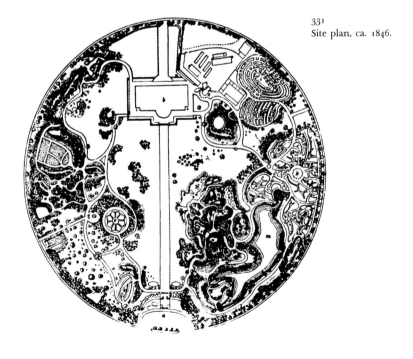

331
Site plan, ca. 1846.

The Botanic Society of London was incorporated by Royal Charter in 1839, and in the following year it acquired the 18-acre "Inner Circle" of Regent's Park previously owned by Jenkin's Nursery. It then commissioned Decimus Burton to design a winter garden. Burton suggested a huge 315 ft by 165 ft wood and glass construction made with five spans of ridge and furrow roofing, the centre span with a curvilinear dome. A model was made, but nothing was done until Burton submitted a revised plan in April 1845, which had an iron ridge and furrow roof. The dome had been removed and a curvilinear apse replaced it in the middle of the front facade. Bids were submitted for the central portion of the large enclosed garden, one from Cubitt and Co. for £5,500, partly made of wood, and the other from Richard Turner which cost less and was made entirely of iron and glass. Thus he outlined in his bid to Burton on 16 April 1845 disproving the latter's advice that wood was cheaper. The Society made some modifications to the design, replacing the end wall with curvilinear lean-tos for strength and appearance. This was acceptable to the cooperative Turner.

Opened to the public on 20 May 1846, the Winter Garden covered an area of 19,000 sq ft and was truly a garden, for the floor was earth, covered with gravel and topped with "pounded" sea-shell. Access into the light and elegant structure was through rows of outward hinged french doors that afforded views in all directions and also provided ventilation. Turner's split pilasters on the wall infilled with red and blue ground glass must have delighted the Victorian visitors. The curvilinear ridge roofs were all supported on 14 ft cast-iron columns that transferred water to the cisterns below. The internal planting arrangement was a departure from the formal style generally followed at that time, for plants were grouped in clumps growing through the white sea-shell and valuable specimens were allowed to stand on their own. Small iron tables were filled with hyacinths and narcissi, and flowers of all description formed what Knight's Cyclopaedia of London (1851) called "a veritable fairy land." To create this climate, temperature was regulated by two Burbidge and Healy ribbed boilers feeding water into nearly a mile of 4-in pipe. Six hot-water pipes ran round the periphery in a 3 ft deep channel and four pipes ran down the middle. The warmed air that rose into shafts placed at intervals throughout the entire area was controlled by iron grilles. The boiler house and chimney were some distance away and the main pipes were led through an outside covered channel. A portion of the glass garden was partitioned off and heated to a higher temperature for the tropical exotics. In addition to the heating pipes, a water-filled tank also went round the wall just below the glass. It was covered over and fitted at intervals with operable grills to control humidity.

Queen Victoria was the first patroness and took great interest in the Garden. Ladies were encouraged to become members and besides lectures and meetings, large flower shows and evening fêtes were held in the summer. In 1871 Turner's Works added an east wing with apse and connecting corridor to the building, then a west wing and apse in 210 to complete the 210 ft symmetrical facade with its three half domes. The original lease came to an end in the late 1920s, and increasing financial difficulties forced the Society to sell its rare plants at auction in September 1931. Despite the efforts of Queen Mary, who was particularly interested in saving the Winter Garden, the Society disbanded in 1932. The grounds were taken over by the Royal Parks Department, but the Winter Garden was eventually demolished.

Today a controversy surrounds the relative contribution of Burton and Turner. The final building had the curvilinear ridge roofs proposed by Turner instead of Burton's ridge and furrow, and an apse instead of a dome to save money. The open pilasters filled with glass, the iron casement window detail and the sliding iron ridge vents were all Turner trademarks. Burton seems to have ended up as the go-between for the society and Turner. J. de C. Sowerby, the Botanic Society's secretary at the time, wrote "this building, constructed of iron, was designed and built by Turner, of Dublin." But, as at Kew, Decimus Burton did influence the overall form of the building, which was based on his early designs.[95]

The principle of construction used in the building of this Winter Garden can be reconstructed from the existing documents. Four glass vaults with flat pointed arch profiles placed in a line formed a continuous space about 215 feet in length. The end vaults were wider and higher than the two between them and formed a kind of curvilinear pleated surface. Slender cast-iron hollow columns 16 feet high carried the Paxton gutters and served to discharge rainwater. The amazing filigree work in the building is obvious in figure 606.

The Loudon principle which Turner took up here depends on the stressing which arises from the curvature of the sash bar section and from the strength obtained from the glass skin itself, which resists the lateral forces. The columns and the arched metal ribs had such a small cross-section that they had little mechanical effect within the space which they supported. That such a light structure could fulfill its function and stand for 90 years proved that a filigree structure of this kind is suitable for permanent use.

References: Hix 1974, pp. 121–123; McIntosh 1853, vol. 1, pp. 368, 369.

332

333
Section, with details
of roof structure and
ventilation.

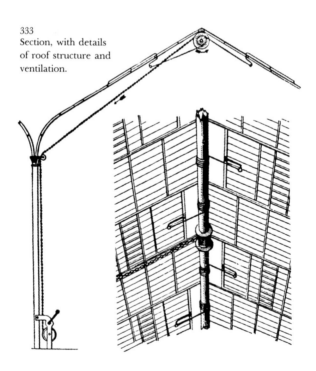

334
View of the illumi-
nated glasshouse.
Colored drawing by
M. M. Runciman,
1876.

London

Kew
Royal Botanic Gardens (figs. 335–346, 613–625)

Conservatories

The Royal Botanic Gardens originated through the amalgamation of two properties owned by the Royal Family in the eighteenth century. King George II and Queen Caroline disposed of their properties Ormond Lodge and Richmond, which stretched along the Thames from Richmond Green to Kew. Around 1759 Augusta, Princess of Wales and mother of the future King George II, founded an 11-acre botanical garden there. During the reign of George III, who ascended to the throne in 1760, the garden achieved fame because of the work of the director, Sir Joseph Banks, and the head gardener, William Aiton. The architectural layout was the work of William Chambers. It comprised among other things an orangery (fig. 623), a pagoda, and ruin architecture. Under George III the garden at Richmond was combined with the one at Kew. Kew Palace was built and the nursery was extended. Little was done about the extension and the maintenance of the gardens, which were in fact seldom used. The public demanded an enquiry, a report was issued, and the gardens were taken over by the state in 1841. Sir William Hooker was appointed to be the first director. Under his leadership, extension and reconstruction were undertaken with the object of opening the gardens to a wider public. In 1845 Hooker investigated the building of the famous Palm House by Turner and Burton. At the same time he founded a herbarium, a library, an agricultural division, and a museum. A further scientific institution, the Jodrell Laboratory, was founded in 1876. The result of these exertions was the influx of an interested public. The number of visitors grew from 9,200 in 1841 to 70,000 in 1847 and 180,000 in 1875. (Visitors to the games and the recreational areas are not included in these numbers.)

The area was increased on the occasion of Queen Victoria's Diamond Jubilee by adding on Queen's Cottage and land in the vicinity of Kew Palace. In 1904 Cambridge College was added and the gardens reached their present extent of about 32 acres.[96]

Kew Gardens in the nineteenth century was considered a large-scale example of the English art of gardening. This is demonstrated by the following description:

The botanical gardens at Kew make a surprising impression on foreigners used to moderate proportions, not only on account of their extent but also because of the grand and picturesque effect of the garden type of layout. This has a particular charm brought about by skillful arrangement of paths, fountains, and buildings, as well as the splendid groups of trees, the wide lawns, and the views thereby created, which are presented in all directions, and with the beautiful and often varied green of the trees in contrast to the hazy tones of the air created magnificent scenes."[97]

Source: archives of Kew Royal Botanic Gardens, London.

References: ZfBW, 1887, vol. 37, parts 1–3, pp. 70–72; *The Builder*, 15.1.1848, vol. 6, no. 258, pp. 29–31; 12.1.1861, vol. 19, no. 936, pp. 23–25; *Die Gartenflora*, 1898, vol. 47, pp. 75, 75; McIntosh 1853, vol. 1, pp. 119–123, 367, 368; Deutsche Bauzeitung (publ.), *Baukunde des Architekten*, 1902, vol. 2, part 5, p. 343.

Architectural Conservatory (figs. 336, 337, 624)
length: 87 feet
width: 44 feet
height: 26 feet
architect: Jeffry Wyatville
built 1836

The Architectural Conservatory, a classical building in the form of a temple, is an example of the application of the design of the traditional masonry orangery to a glasshouse. Masonry shafts, columns, architraves, and tympanums designed in the best Greek tradition conceal the cast-iron space frame of the glass roof (figs. 336, 337). This space frame consists of 40-foot-long cast-iron ribs, the top flanges of which form the sloping roof profile. These ribs increase in depth toward the apex and are pierced by circular holes. Each is supported by two slender cast-iron columns and, at the springing, on the masonry architrave of the side walls. The whole interior receives plenty of light because of the tall glass surfaces of the facades, which reach up as far as the tympana of the ends. This transparency is achieved while retaining the form of the antique temple. This architectural concept is reminiscent of Fowler's Syon House conservatory.[98]

Reference: McIntosh 1853, vol. 1, pp. 119–123, 367, 368.

Palm House (figs. 338–343, 613–619)
length: 362 1/2 feet (center building 134 1/2 feet)
width: 100 feet
height (without dome): 63 feet
architects: Richard Turner, Decimus Burton
builders: Richard Turner, Hammersmith Works
built 1844–1848
restored 1958

The palm house at Kew was described by a contemporary critic as "one of the very finest plant-houses in the world. Its graceful lines and admirable proportions make it as pleasing to the eye as it is possible for a structure of glass and iron to be."[99] Charles

335
Site plan, 1975.

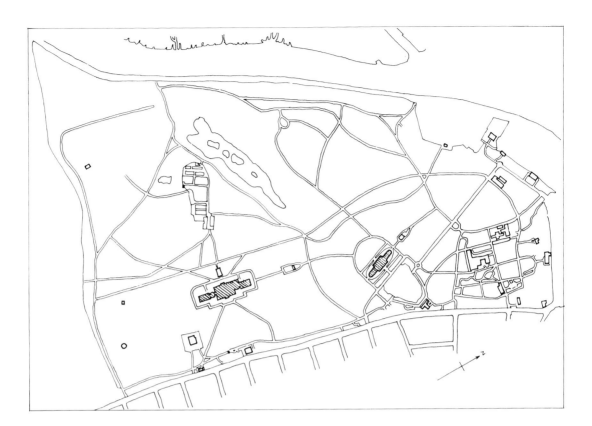

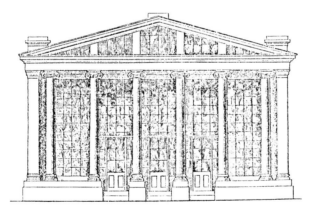

336
Front entrance of
Architectural
Conservatory.

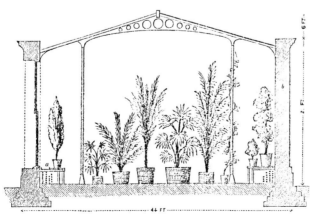

337
Section of Architec-
tural Conservatory.

McIntosh mentions this palm house in *The Book of the Garden* as "the most complete specimen of hothouse architecture that this or any country can boast of." These emphatic statements are not unfounded. The Kew palm house combined the Loudon principle of curvilinear shells with the Paxton design to express a new spatial concept with a high degree of technical quality.

The palm house was strictly limited to pure geometrical forms. The aim was to place the supporting framework as close as possible to the glass skin. A precondition for that was the greatest possible exploitation of filigree structural elements. The space frame recedes from the eye; there remains the appearance of a taut skin that partly reflects and partly transmits the light, thus giving the building a disembodied look. The central part of this palm house has the same form as that of the Great Conservatory at Chatsworth, which is not surprising because Burton had previously worked with Paxton. The cross-section of the central part of the Kew palm house confirms the kinship with the earlier model (fig. 226, 339). As at Chatsworth, the semicircular shell is mounted on two rows of cast-iron columns, to which are attached quadrant-shaped roofs over the aisles. The latter extend down to a masonry base wall. Thus, the building is a very large basilica, but instead of wooden ribs its frame is made entirely of iron. There is a new spatial concept in the three-dimensional intersection of the two wings with the central part, which results in a continuous interior space 360 feet long. The harmonious appearance of the building is the direct result of the use of the

quadrant-shaped shell as the basic space-forming element. The central part and the wings are made from this basic element, which always has the same amount of curvature. This was the prerequisite for the vigorous application of the framework principle, which made it possible to use repeatedly the same structural elements and therefore allowed the prefabrication of glass and iron parts. Curved wrought-iron ribs, placed about 12 feet apart, formed the main support for the vault.

A spatial form different from that at Chatsworth was achieved through the use of quadrant-shaped shells, which intersect at the joint between the wings and the center and at the ends of the building. Plane surfaces were used only for the straight vertical sectors of the vaults and in the small lantern roof, where they were needed for purposes of ventilation.

The Kew palm house is an early example of a spatial concept based on an effective space frame, which on the one hand is determined by the rib separation and on the other hand by the radius of curvature. The space frame here is not just an expedient but is itself a spatial concept in which mass production is applied to each individual structural element. In spite of the consequent limitation of the various types of parts used, diversity in design was still possible.

The main elements of the space frame are 42-foot-long arched girders made of I-section wrought iron, which were assembled from separate parts about 12 feet in length. They are fixed at the side into cast-iron sockets in the concrete wall, above which there are large blocks of granite. In the central part they are mounted on hollow round cast-iron columns,

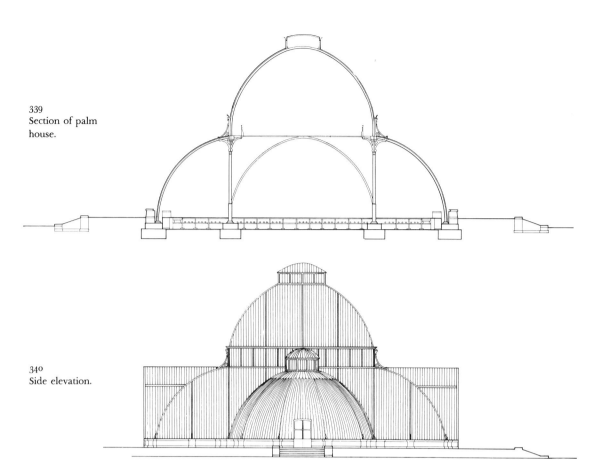

339
Section of palm
house.

340
Side elevation.

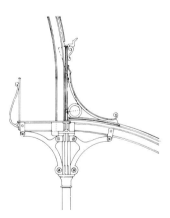

341
Connection between
column and rib,
structural details.

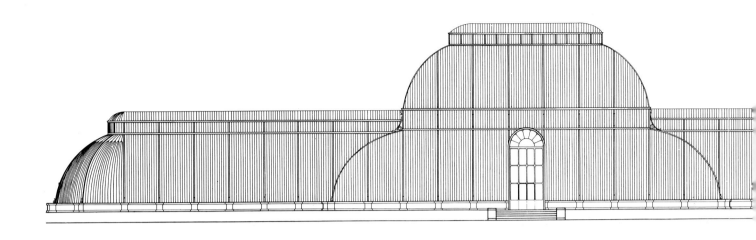

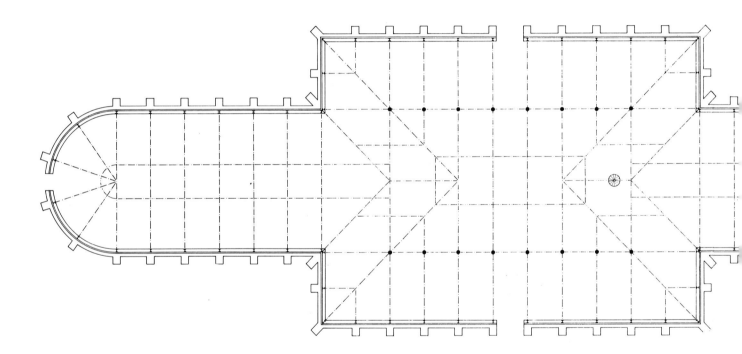

342
Front elevation of
palm house.

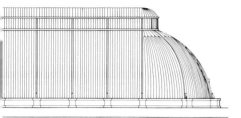

343
Ground-floor plan.

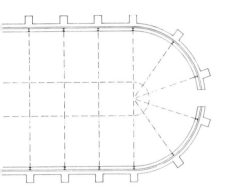

which also carry the ribs of the upper dome structure and the lantern. They form the springing for the gallery supports in the central part, which are reached via two elegantly made winding staircases. A surrounding circular annulus of the same thickness as those forming the ribs joins the columns together. The ribs in the semicircle form continuous beams in the wings. All ribs are joined together by wrought-iron tubes which function as spacers. Tensioning cables 1 1/2 inches in diameter, welded together to make long lengths, are contained in these tubes. They form continuous tie bars running round the whole building. The tension applied to these ties after the building was completed holds the glass vault together in the horizontal plane. Reinforcing ribs, 10 feet apart, take up the outward thrust of the arched profile and act in the manner of purlins.[100]

A new technical principle was applied here: In one cross-section the tensile and compressive forces are dealt with separately in such a way that the tension is resisted by the cable in the core while the compression is supported by the wall of the tube. This principle forms the basis of all prestressed structures of later times. Turner used this construction principle for the first time in the Kew palm house, and he patented it in 1846. This invention does away with an otherwise necessary I beam, and the filigree work is not impaired by heavy members. It became possible to ensure the necessary strength of a large structure like the palm house at Kew with the minimum amount of iron and to bring about a hitherto unattainable lightness in the structure.

In addition to this there are prestressed iron elements along the facade in the middle part of the ribs at the level of the balcony diagonally across the interior, likewise mutually reinforced by iron rods. The top part of the roof of the central part is supported on twenty tubular cast-iron columns, ten on each side of the nave. They conduct the rain collected in the gutters of the upper part of the roof into cisterns which are placed all over the interior of the building. The central columns terminate at the top in wide projecting capitals with a decoration (imitating plants) made from prefabricated cast-iron brackets. The bolts are hidden by small iron rosettes (fig. 341). As is also usual, the decoration is where it is of value for indicating the transmission of forces between the various parts of the structure—for example, at the transition of the upper part of the roof to the surrounding vault of the aisles below, and at the base of the aisle ribs on the stone basement wall. The distribution of forces is made visually clear in the ornamental design of the brackets. There arises an interplay of concave and convex lines along the ribs. It can be demonstrated that none of the ornamentation used here, nor the small cast-iron scrolls, serves as an end in itself, but that it was developed from the structural function of the component concerned. The problem of the thrust of the six ribs in the quadrant-shaped ends of the wings was solved convincingly by means of a shoe; this attests to the builder's command over the use of material.

The two portals at the main entrances in the central part of the palm house are individual elements with vaulted roofs. Their extraordinary height (nearly 30 feet) made it possible to bring large palms into the building. They extend the glass dome of the central part in the same way that the wings do along the axis of the building, and at the same time they enrich the silhouette of the building. The glass fronts of the portals were executed with amazing elegance. The fact that the space frame holding the glass is made of iron section with chamfered edges originates from the best English classical tradition and shows that great attention was paid to the smallest detail.

The Kew palm house was built on a mass of heaped-up soil. "A spacious terrace, with the necessary steps, surrounds the whole, and being somewhat elevated above the ground level, gives the appearance of solidity and breadth of base for the stupendous structure to stand on."[101]

The original hot-water heating plant consisted of two boilers patented by Burbidge, Healy & Co., with about 27,900 feet of heating pipes laid underground. The pipes were laid along the facade beneath 4-foot-square cast-iron gratings. This heating plant ensured an inside temperature of 80°F when the external temperature was 20°F. The boilers were housed in two cellars close to the hothouse. Provided with sufficient storage for fuel, they were connected by a 558-foot tunnel to a coal bunker located adjacent to a road. The coal was supplied and the ashes taken away by a truck pulled along the rails in the tunnel. The concept of a completely transparent building in an open position as a center of attraction would have lost its effect had a masonry structure such as a chimney been erected in its vicinity. Therefore, it was decided to erect the campanile-style chimney at a distance.

The original glazing consisted of curved glass panes, about 39 by 9½ inches. The glass was tinted green with copper oxide to filter some of the heating effect of the sun's rays. This idea (originally proposed, according to McIntosh, by a man named Hunt) was tested for the first time in this building.

The 2-inch-deep sash bars made of T section run from the base to the apex of the vault. The glass panes are lapped like roofing tiles and are held in with putty. This is the same system that Turner used for the curvilinear conservatories in Dublin and Belfast.[102]

The Illustrated London News of September 2, 1848, and August 7, 1852, and The Builder of January 15, 1848, ascribed the design of the Kew palm house to Decimus Burton and the execution of the ironwork to Richard Turner. However, such a division between the designer and the builder is not demonstrable in respect to the pioneering technical achievement in the palm house. The structural development of an engineering work of great compass and high technical quality stipulates a close relationship between the concept and the actual construction. It is no wonder, therefore, that more recent enquiries have cast doubt on the assertion that Burton was author of the design. In the Architectural Review Peter Ferriday ascribes the design to Richard Turner.[103] This surmise strengthens the view of R. Desmond, who has ascertained from the Kew archives that the first design by Decimus Burton (1844) was rejected by the director of the Royal Botanic Gardens, William Hooker, because it had too many columns. Turner, coming from Dublin to London, presented to Hooker and his committee a scale model having a central part with two wings. Turner's design, complete with an estimate of costs, was accepted in principle and recommended for further consideration. Burton and Turner engaged in mutual criticism of each other's work, and then took up a constructive approach to the design. Burton assented to Turner's design of a base plan with a central rectangle and two wings. Burton then incorporated this scheme into a second design, in which he used the approximate cross-section of the Great Conservatory at Chatsworth for the central part of the glasshouse. On the basis of this mutual cooperation, Turner was officially commissioned to build the ironwork. After the spatial form had been decided, the engineering work and the design detailing were essentially left to Turner.

Source: archives of Royal Botanic Gardens, Kew, London.

References: ZfBW, 1887, vol. 37, parts 1–3, pp. 70–72; The Builder, 15.1.1848, vol. 6, no. 258, pp. 29–31; 12.1.1861, vol. 19, no. 936, pp. 23–25; Die Gartenflora, 1898, vol. 47, pp. 75, 76; McIntosh 1853, vol. 1, pp. 119–123.

Temperate House (figs. 344, 345, 620–622)

length: 580 feet
width at center: 138 feet
height at center: 59 feet
architect: Decimus Burton
built 1859–1863
extended 1895–1897

The temperate house at Kew, to the south of the large palm house, is one of the largest glasshouses in Britain. It has exactly double the area of the palm house. It marks a turning away from the transparent, thin-membered curvilinear glasshouse and from Paxton's type of construction.

The large plane surfaces of the hipped glass roof were developed in such a way that one-third of their surface area could be opened. This required a special frame for sliding windows instead of continuous sash bars. The cast-iron ribs and columns that carry the weight of the roof are closely spaced and are executed in a heavier style than was usual for hall buildings glazed along the top, along the ridge. The solid structure of the iron space frame, with the arch-shaped lower flanges of the ribs, and the rows of double columns, outside which there are low aisles, give the middle part of the building the character of a railway-station concourse. Cast-iron webs in the ribs with decorative cut-outs strengthen the impression of the strength of the space frame. The cast-iron ribs were at that time already being considered as mature structural forms. One may assume that the architect had a conservative attitude, pursued a decorative approach, and once more preferred to use cast iron as the material. The external appearance of the building, which has a masonry base wall and a projecting portico made of stone pilasters, also speaks in favor of that assumption. The building obtains its transparency from the glass roof, and the glass and iron material making up the hothouse does not have any appreciable effect. Considering these aspects, one can proceed to say that the architect, who had started out from classical architecture, surrendered himself to this style quite deliberately here and, by way of opposition to the engineering works of Paxton and Turner, wanted to assert himself.

The central part of the temperate house, built in 1861, consists of a rectangular hall supported on two rows of double columns set 12 1/2 feet apart. These double columns surround a space 138 feet long, 62 feet wide, and 59 feet high, which is covered by a ridge roof on trusses without ties. The rafters are made of bolted-together parts, as is usual with cast iron, and have straight top flanges and curved lower ones. The web between them is made of decoratively pierced cast iron (figs. 54, 344). [Classical roof trusses of this kind had previously been used in the Diana-bad in Vienna (1842) and in the Saint-Geneviève Library (1844).] The ribs support a glass roof, which is divided by teak posts. The lower part of the glass roof is attached to the pairs of columns, forming aisles 37 feet wide. The masonry of the basement wall is pierced with arched windows. Two octagonal pavilions with pyramidal roofs and lanterns adjoin the central part. Between 1895 and 1897, rectangular glass wings repeating the basic shape of the central building were added to the pavilions (fig. 345). The contractor for the work of the 1861 part of the building was the renowned structural steelwork firm W. Cubitt and Co.[104]

The building is extant and well maintained.

Source: archives of Royal Botanic Gardens, Kew, London.

References: ZfBW, 1887, vol. 37, parts 1–3, pp. 70–72; *Die Gartenflora*, 1898, vol. 47, pp. 75, 76; Deutsche Bauzeitung (publ.), *Baukunde des Architekten*, 1902, vol. II, part 5, p. 343.

Victoria Regia House (figs. 346, 625)

floor area: 46 by 46 feet
height: 20 feet
architect: Richard Turner
built ca. 1850

The victoria regia house in Kew Gardens is, in spite of its modest size, noteworthy for its iron roof structure. The ridge roof is supported by steel trusses attached to T beams. Forged round steel bars in rings, attached with clips, form the reinforcing elements in these triangular trusses. The space above the large victoria regia pool obtains its bright and airy character from this adventurous execution of the ironwork.

The building is extant and well maintained.

Source: archives, Royal Botanic Gardens, Kew, London.

Reference: Deutsche Bauzeitung (publ.), *Baukunde des Architekten*, 1902, vol. 2, part 5, p. 343.

344
View in hall of central pavilion of Temperate House.
Engraving.

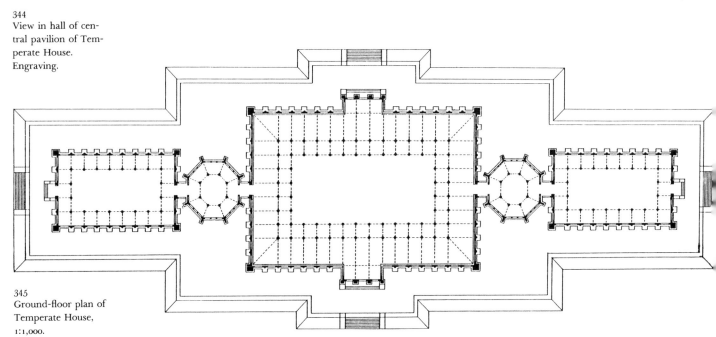

345
Ground-floor plan of Temperate House,
1:1,000.

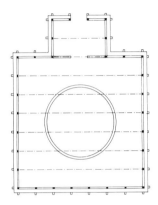

346
Section and ground
plan of victoria regia
house at Kew.

347
Paxton's first sketch
for the Crystal Pal-
ace, 1850

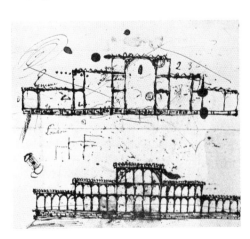

London

Hyde Park
World Exhibition, 1851
Crystal Palace (figs. 349–360, 362, 363, 626, 627, 631, 648)
architect: Joseph Paxton
builder: Fox and Henderson Co.
built 1850–1851

On February 21, 1850, an executive committee created for the purpose of assembling a World Exhibition (with the primary purpose of demonstrating the
quality of British industrial products and opening up
new markets for them) announced an international
competition for the design and construction of a
large exhibition building on a piece of land in Hyde
Park. The building was to cover an area of almost 16
acres at the lowest possible cost, and was to accommodate separately the various divisions of the
exhibition.

Although only one month was allowed for the
preparation of the designs, 233 candidates entered.
Richard Turner of Dublin and Hector Horeau of
Paris received "special mention" for their designs.
Both were engineers experienced in the construction
of glass-and-iron buildings, and each had based his
design on construction principles he had developed
in the building of hothouses and winter gardens.
Turner proposed a single large area, 1,939 feet in
length and 407 feet in width, with semicircular cast-
iron ribs forming three longitudinal bays. These ribs
and two rows of iron columns were to support a
barrel-vault roof with skylights along the aisles. (This
structure reminds one of the cross-section of the
wings of Turner's tropical houses in Dublin.) The
aisles were to be crossed by a transept with a superimposed glass dome. Horeau designed a five-bay
glass-and-iron basilica. The aisles were to have lean-
to roofs, here likewise combined with a transept.

The judges could not make up their minds to accept either of these designs and authorize construction to go ahead. Instead they formed a committee,
which, with the help of Matthew Digby Wyatt,
Charles Heald Wild, and Owen Jones, submitted its
own design. In its basic concept this building was to
be conventional, with an accent on the prestige effect. Conceived partly in masonry, it did not fulfil
the requirements of reuse, rapid construction, and
low price. The estimated cost of the materials alone
was between £120,000 and £150,000—approximately
as much as the total cost of the building later completed by Joseph Paxton.

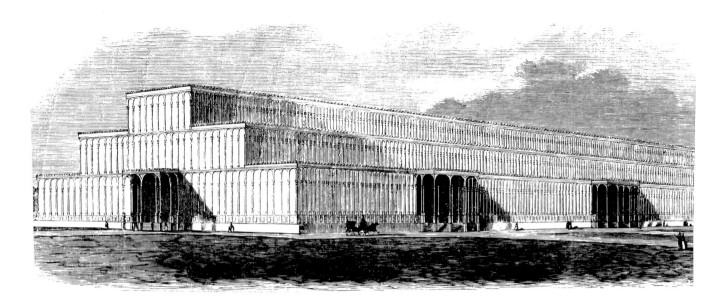

At the invitation of the building committee, with which he had some personal connection, Paxton was asked to provide a design for the exhibition building. On June 11, 1850, during some legal proceedings over the Midland Railway Station in Derby, Paxton sketched his first ideas for the Crystal Palace (fig. 347).

The proposal had to be made within a very short time, before July 10. To this end, Paxton at once entered into partnership with Robert Lucas Chance, a glass manufacturer, and with the firm of Fox and Henderson of Birmingham. Fox and Henderson were specialists in cast-iron and wrought-iron construction. The base plan of the exhibition building had to correspond exactly with that of the committee. The estimate of costs which the firm produced, £150,000, was reduced to £79,800 on the stipulation that after the dismantling of the building the materials were to become the property of the building contractor.

Paxton's design was, as he had previously announced, more cost-effective than the one the committee proposed. It complied with all the requirements of the competition, including the date of the opening of the exhibition (about which there was now some doubt). However, the committee was not willing to abandon its own plan and give the commission to an outsider who was neither an architect nor an engineer.

On July 6, 1850, Paxton published his design in the *Illustrated London News* (fig. 348), with the following comments:

The accompanying design, by Mr Paxton, FLS, of a building for the Exhibition of the Industry of All Nations in 1851, has been considered and planned with a view to its fitness for the objects intended, as well as to its permanent occupation or removal to another site for a winter garden or a vast horticultural structure; and which might, if required, be used for a similar exhibition to that intended in 1851.

A structure where the Industry of All Nations is intended to be exhibited should, it is presumed, present to parties from all nations a building for the exhibition of their arts and manufactures, that, while it afforded ample accommodation and convenience for the purposes intended, would, of itself, be the most singular and peculiar feature of the Exhibition. It is hoped, with all deference to others, that the design in question will prove so. The plan is made to fit the ground proposed for the Exhibition in Hyde Park; and very little alteration would have to be made to the ground-plan already proposed by the Building Committee.

The building is a vast structure, covering a space upwards of twenty-one acres; and, by the addition of longitudinal and cross-galleries, twenty-five per cent more space may be obtained. The whole is supported by cast-iron columns, resting on patent screw piles: externally it shows a base of six feet in height. At each end there is a large portico or entrance veranda; and at each side there are three similar entrances, covered in for the purpose of setting down and taking up company. The longitudinal galleries running the whole length of the building, together with the transverse galleries, will afford ample means for the display of lighter articles of manufacture, and will also give a complete view of the whole of the articles exhibited. The whole being covered in with glass, renders the building light, airy, and suitable. Every facility will be afforded for the transmission on rails from the entrances to the different departments; and proper means will be employed for hoisting the lighter sorts of goods to the galleries; in which, and on the columns, there will be suspension-rods, chains, &c., on which to hang woollen, and linen manufactures, and all other articles requiring to be suspended. Magnifying glasses, worked on swivels, and placed at short distances apart on the galleries, would give additional facilities for commanding a more perfect general view of the entire Exhibition.

348
First design, July 6, 1850. Woodcut.

The extreme simplicity of this structure in all its details will, Mr Paxton considers, make this a far more economical building than that proposed in the Illustrated London News of the 22nd June. One great feature in its erection is, that not a vestige of stone, brick or mortar is necessary. All the roofing and upright sashes would be made by machinery, and fitted together and glazed with great rapidity, most of them being finished previous to being brought to the place, so that little else would be required on the spot than to fit the finished materials together. The whole of the structure is supported on cast-iron columns, and the extensive roof is sustained without the necessity of interior walls: hence the saving internally of interior division-walls for this purpose. If removed after the Exhibition, the materials might be sold far more advantageously than a structure filled in with bricks and mortar, and some of the materials would bring in full half the original outlay.

Complete ventilation has been provided by filling in every third upright compartment with luffer boarding, which would be made to open and shut by machinery: the whole of the basement will be filled in after in the same manner. The current of air may be modified by the use of coarse open canvas, which by being kept wet in hot weather, would render the interior of the building much cooler than the external atmosphere.

In order to subdue the intense light in a building covered with glass, it is proposed to cover all the south side of the upright parts, together with the whole of the roofs outside, with calico or canvas, tacked on the ridge rafters of the latter. This would allow a current of air to pass in the valleys under the calico, which would, if required, with the ventilators, keep the air of the house cooler than the external atmosphere.

To give the roof a light and graceful appearance, it should be on the ridge and furrow principle, and glazed with sheet glass. The ridge and valley rafters will be continued in uninterrupted lines the whole length of the structure, and be supported by cast-iron beams. These beams will have a hollow gutter formed in them to receive the rain water from the wooden valley rafters, which will be thence conveyed through the hollow columns to the drains. These drains will be formed of ample dimensions under the whole of the pathways throughout.

The floors of the pathways to be laid with trellis boards, three-eighths of an inch apart, on sleeper-joists. This kind of flooring is both economical and can always be kept clean, dry, and pleasant to walk upon. The gallery floors to be close-boarded.

After the Exhibition is over, and on the supposition of the structure being removed to another site, should be made carriage-drives and equestrian promenades for winter use while pedestrians would have above two miles of galleries for promenades, and more than two miles of walks on the groundfloor. At the same time plenty of space will be left for plants, &c.

It is important to state that, by the adopting of the proposed design, no timber trees need to be cut down, as the glass would fit up to the boles of the trees, leaving the lower branches under the glass during the Exhibition; but Mr

Paxton does not recommend this course, as, for the sum of £250, he would engage to remove and replace every living tree on the ground, except the large old elms opposite to Prince's Gate.

Only a few years ago, the erection of such a building as the one contemplated would have involved a fearful amount of expense; but the rapid advance made in this country during the last forty years, both in the scientific construction of such buildings and the cheap manufacture of glass, iron, &c., together with the amazing facilities in the preparation of sash-bars and other woodwork render an erection of this description, in point of expense, quite on a level with those constructed of more substantial materials.

No single feature, but the structure as a whole, would form a peculiar novelty in mechanical science; and, when we consider the manner of supporting a vast glass roof covering twenty-one acres on the most secure and scientific principles, and filling in a structure of such magnitude wholly with glass, Mr Paxton ventures to think that such a plan would meet with the almost universal approval of the British public, whilst it would be unrivalled in the world.[105]

This article won public support for Paxton's plans, and they were approved by the committee on July 25, 1850.

The building committee had stipulated the preservation of the large elm trees in Hyde Park, without additional cost, under the roof of the exhibition building. Paxton promised to find a solution: "I went direct with Mr Fox to his office, and while he arranged the ground plan so as to bring the trees into the centre of the Building, I was contriving how they were to be covered. At length I hit upon the plan of covering the Transept with a circular roof similar to that on the great conservatory at Chatsworth, and made a sketch of it, which was copied that night by one of the draughtsmen, in order that I might have it to show to Mr Brunel, whom I had agreed to meet on the ground the next day."[106]

The specifications that the building had to be constructed within an extremely short time, at low cost, with extensive resale of the structural parts after dismantling, led to a construction method which was largely controlled by mass production. "The extraordinary importance of this undertaking lies, apart from the short period for planning and building, particularly in the techniques of the method used, i.e. organization of labour, which is to be compared with modern production line manufacture of machined products."[107] A detailed critical-path analysis of the operations was an unconditional requirement for the coordination of all the work processes involved in the various methods of fabrication of the building components, some on the site, some away from it. The progress of the construction was to be controlled by a plan for the production and assembly of prefabricated parts, according to Paxton's words that the operation should function like a machine. On July 30, access was gained to the building site. Detailed planning began immediately and lasted 4 months. In parallel with that, important structural matters were considered. The first column was set in position on September 26. By the end of January, after 4 months of building, the space frame was standing. The whole structure was complete after 6 months, and the exhibition opened on the appointed day, May 1, 1851.

The construction was carefully reported in the press. On October 12, 1850, *Panorama* reported:

A corridor forms a central avenue, which extends uninterruptedly for 1,848 feet from the east of the building to the western end. The most difficult part of the work is to include within the building the mature elms which are higher than 90 feet. The builders have wisely applied themselves to this problem first. Semicircular ribs, which will cover the trees, are supported on columns which will be set up in groups of three, one above the other. The first tier of columns, which are joined together by light cast iron beams, form squares of 24 feet sides, giving a surface area of 576 square feet. These girders simultaneously support a gallery on both sides of the central nave which takes in the complete length of the building. Below the gallery the squares provide excellent space for the display of decorative ceilings, and we have reason to believe that the Exhibition Committee has made it known that this space is to be kept available for the Exhibition's decorators. Each of these beams is tested by an ingenious hydraulic jack as soon as it is erected into position, and the enormous ribs of 72 feet span have been completed this week and are ready for assembly. There will be 16 units. The footings for the columns will consist of concrete made from Dorking limestone, and the gravel used in the trenches. The base for the columns will be laid above the concrete.

Almost all these footings have been constructed by this week. There are approximately 1,500, and — as one of the most difficult parts of the work — they must be made properly and accurately, in fine and dry weather. More than 500 men are diligently doing the job, and when more of the cast iron parts have arrived the number of workmen will probably increase.

On November 30 this journal carried a further report:

There is no delay on the part of the builders and steady progress can be expected by the onlookers. The promise is being kept, as the Duke of Wellington during his visit last week has declared: What has been accomplished in the last seven weeks shows what can be further accomplished in the remaining months. The western end has been built; both the bottom and the second tier of columns have been put into position. Several thousand feet of the transverse girders and the space frame work for the base have been erected, and the glazing of the roof proceeds apace without a break, al-

though there are some attempts at delay on the part of a few workmen. The attempt by the glaziers to obtain higher wages has been immediately suppressed. The progress of their work has been delayed and it has been decided that they will be paid on a piecework basis. Some of the glaziers, led on by dissatisfied individuals, have been on strike, but because replacements can be quickly found, several of them soon gave in and asked for reinstatement, and it was decided to consider them if more workmen were needed. . . . New methods of production, testing, and assembly tools have been developed and used for the production and assembly of the building elements. Every single rib has been tested on the building site by means of a hydraulic jack. Before this process was used the full loading of the beams has been simulated by a body of soldiers marching in step. The ribs were raised by a crane in the test rig and then taken to a storage depot, from which they are taken and assembled when required. Lifting equipment was developed, the load capacity of which determined the maximum weight of the building elements. No element weighs more than one ton. A steam-powered machine has been specially constructed for making the window sashes. The glazing wagon has been specially made for glazing the roof.[108]

The magnitude of the building operation can be seen from the following quantities and dimensions: 3,300 cast-iron columns, 1,128 pillars for the aisles, 2,224 beams, 550 tons of wrought iron, 3,500 tons of cast iron, 900,000 square feet of glass (weighing 400 tons), 34 miles of drainage parts, 30 miles of gutters, and 202 miles of sash bars.[109] The total space enclosed above the 7,766,150-square-foot base and the 207,350-square-foot gallery came to 33 million cubic feet.

The capital for this project was raised by public subscription and credit from the Bank of England. Before the building could be erected it was necessary for there to exist not only the technical means of production, but also a definite stage in the accumulation of capital so that funds could be raised in the short time that remained. It is of historical interest that, owing to the rationalized method of construction used for the Exhibition Building, the World Exhibition made a profit. In contrast, the Vienna World Exhibition of 1873 closed with a considerable loss.

The London Exhibition Building could accommodate 17,000 exhibitors and over a million exhibition items. There were more than 6 million visitors.[110] The whole of the building was constructed on the basis of a single basic space module. The glass industry determined the size of this. At that time in Britain the industry could supply panes up to 49 inches long and 10 inches wide. The length of the glass — approximately 4 feet — was the unit dimension, which when multiplied by 4 determined the design of the structure. Previously, in the Great Conservatory at Chatsworth, Paxton had taken a pane length of 4 feet for the basic unit in the design. The logical step forward from this was to use the 4-foot module to determine not only the surface area but also the spatial dimensions. This gave a structural frame of 6 × 4 = 24 feet, determining the area as well as the height. This in turn determined the standard distance between the columns, and hence the length of the cast-iron (or wooden) beams. There were four types of beam: standard 24-foot beams, 48-foot beams, and 72-foot beams in the nave or in the aisles (fig. 58).

The whole building was, in its ground plan, a long, narrow rectangle with a nave and a transept in the middle (fig. 349). The overall length from north to south was 1,848 (77 × 24) feet, and the total width was 408 (17 × 24) feet. The open and unpartitioned nave that formed the central part of this total area was 72 (3 × 24) feet wide and was crossed in the middle by an equally wide vault forming the transept. The nave and the aisles were divided vertically into galleries. These galleries, which ran in four parallel lines along the whole length of the building on each side of the nave, were joined by short gangways, which ran around the transept to form a continuous route. They were accessible via eight double stairways.

The building was constructed in three stories, corresponding to the galleries. Ernst Werner has analyzed the modular structure: Except for the 72-foot-long beams at the intersection between the nave and the transept, all the beams were 3 feet deep. The columns on the ground floor measured about 22 feet up to the top flange of the beam. Each of the other two stories had 17-foot columns up to the lower flange of the beams. The height of the stories was 20 feet. All three stories gave a total height of about 62 feet. Counting in the roof structure, the nave was 64 feet high.[111]

The basic element for mass production was determined by the three-dimensional space frame, conceived at first in the abstract. Paxton translated this space-frame design into a minimal number of actual structural parts (building elements and the joints between them) in order to make possible the manufacture of large numbers of a particular item and thus to assembly and reuse.

The footings of the columns were based on gravel and were made of Dorking limestone. The footings projected 4 inches above ground level and were provided with cast-iron base plates for the columns. A tube was incorporated in each base plate through

which the rainwater coming down the column could flow. During October 1850, 500 workmen were occupied in making the 1,500 individual footings.

Like the footings, the cast-iron columns which were bolted one above the other to make up the three stories were standardized by shape and size. The hollow columns all had the same outside diameter, but were made with different wall thicknesses corresponding to the variation in the loads they had to support. In this way it was possible to mass produce the ribs and girders associated with them, and likewise the columns, in standard sizes. The bottom columns, 19 feet long, were bolted to the central column via connecting pieces, which were made in such a way that they simultaneously served as brackets to hold the gallery. Their height was determined by the 3-foot-deep beams between the columns. The connecting piece allowed joints to be made in four directions for all the kinds of beams. At the same time, it was also possible via the bolted joints of the connecting piece to fix the diagonal. This major joint, which could comprise ten individual joints, clearly shows the technical standard which engineering construction had reached by the time this building was erected. It was not only a simple bracket for the beams, but it had cleats and pins for attaching the beams to its whole length and thus was capable of transmitting the forces to the columns. Thus, the building obtained rigidity through the cross-members as well, in a way that would have been impossible with ordinary masonry work. (See figures 77, 84, 360.)

The cast-iron beams used for the gallery were 3 feet deep and 24 feet long. Each was divided into rectangular sectors formed by diagonals and by vertical posts. The cast-iron beams all had the same lengths and depths; only the thickness of the metal was varied to suit the load to be carried. Before being used, the beams were tested by means of a hydraulic press; the lighter ones for the roof were loaded to 9 tons, those for the galleries to 15 tons. The weight of the lighter beam was about 1,100 pounds and that of the stronger one about 1,320 pounds. These beams were used to span a 24-foot space. A total of 2,141 were needed. (See figures 58a, 84, 350, 355.) Having constant depth, the beams were designed to match the distribution of forces; they widened in the middle and narrowed at the ends where they joined the columns. Through this adaptation of the shape to the force distributions and the simultaneous minimizing of the cross-section, designs arose which were able to increase the dominance of the straight line and confer a diversity of shape on the building. The planks of the wooden floor were laid on the gallery beams. The 17-foot-long central

349

350
Construction work,
January 1851.
Woodcut.

351
Covering the tran-
sept, January 1851.
Woodcut.

352
Interior view of
nave, showing struc-
tural details, Febru-
ary 1851. Woodcut.

column was joined by the connecting piece to the
bottom one, and by another similar piece to the top
column of the three. This column, also of the same
length, carried the top bolted joint and the roof girders of the long nave. The undertrussed beams of
the ridge-and-furrow roof were laid transversely on
the braced beams between the columns (fig. 357). A
special longer beam spanned the 72-foot space across
the nave (fig. 58b); it had the standard depth and
could be connected to the joints just like the other
beams. The vertical posts were made of wrought
iron, and the struts of wood.

In the calculation of the load capacity of the roof
beams it was assumed that the roof was covered
with snow to a depth of 1 foot, and that the 24-foot
beams would have to carry 5 1/2 tons, the 48-foot
beams 11 tons, and the 72-foot beams 16 tons. The
roof was horizontal, and it was stepped corresponding to the nave and the aisles. The roof skin was
made on the ridge-and-furrow principle. Wooden
Paxton gutters 24 feet long formed the valley beams.
Placed transverse to the cast-iron beams, they were
undertrussed by an iron bar and two iron posts and
were thus bowed upward, with the usual hogging.
These gutter beams were tilted slightly so that the
rainwater could run away. There were small channels on either side of the gutter beams to remove
the condensation from the inside surface of the glass.

A total of 2,940 of these so-called Paxton gutters
were used; they lay 8 feet apart. The sashes for the
glass were nailed to the sides. These carried the
ridge, which did not need any further support. They
were joined at the ends by bars to the main gutter.
This, likewise made of wood, lay immediately on the
braced beams. Fixing the gutters to the beams increased the strength of the whole space frame. (See
figures 22b, 359, 360.)

Removing the rainwater was quite an important
problem because of the large roof surface. It was,
however, solved through Paxton's experience in the
building of hothouses. As in the victoria regia house
of 1849 and in the 1851 patent (fig. 98), the water
flowed horizontally in two planes, one above the
other, in a system of primary and secondary gutters.
The rainwater and the condensation arrived at the
secondary (Paxton) gutter from the sloping glass surfaces; then the water went across into the primary
gutter system, and from this through the hollow columns into the drainage system.

The 6-foot-deep braced beams at the intersection
of the nave and the transept on the east and west
sides (fig. 58c) were of the kind then used for
bridges. These deep and close-meshed braced beams
were made of wrought iron with cast-iron end
pieces, and were bolted together. They had double
tie bars, a structural innovation that reduced the cost

353
Interior view of
transept, January
1851. Woodcut.

354
Glazing wagon using
Paxton gutters as
rails, December 1850.
Woodcut.

of material while increasing the resistance to buckling. The length of the joint with the connecting piece in the column was doubled, corresponding to the double length of the beam, and normal joints in the other directions were possible for the standard beams. Because these larger beams carried the weight of the barrel vault of the transept, an extra column at each support point was used to transmit the load down. The barrel vault of the transept, with its 72-foot span, was only 2 feet wider than the nave of the Great Conservatory at Chatsworth. It was made of curved Paxton gutters like those at Chatsworth. (See figures 44, 45, 351, 353.) However, individual parts of ribs were no longer assembled on the site. Ready on the ground was a complete unit made of ribs and purlins and diagonal bracing, which only needed to be hoisted into position. This major element of the space frame had a glass surface of about 3,700 square feet.

Like the main load-bearing structure, the sash bars and the Paxton gutters of the roof were exploited to the limits of their strength. The reduction of the width of these gave the whole building its high degree of transparency. The visual lightness of the roof obtained its effect from the density of the structure.

Ridge-and-furrow glazing was used, as at Chatsworth. The glass vault of the transept terminated in rosettes at both ends. The few diagonal members that were necessary to give the rigidity needed by the building were made of round steel section joined together in clamping rings. These clamping rings were provided with a decorative cast-iron cover plate in the form of an eight-rayed crystal. This also reveals the architect's intention to accentuate the structural elements in the building by careful development of their function and to bring them into the view of the observer.

In the facade, the 24-foot separation of the supporting cast-iron columns was divided into three panels by two vertical posts at 8-foot intervals. Cast-iron arches were inserted between the columns, together with spandrels. The glazing was fixed in a single frame between the columns. In its construction this facade was modeled on Paxton's victoria regia house (1849). Wood infilling was used for the ground floor instead of glass. The exterior walls of the open spaces consisted of glass surfaces below the braced beams, which were themselves glazed (fig. 358).

The ventilation of the building was effected in the same way as in Paxton's other glasshouses. In the upper part of each story a row of vents was incorporated in the surrounding wall, along the whole length of the building. The ventilation louvers in the

Testing the Galleries of the Great Exhibition Building.

355
Loading test of cast-
iron braced beams,
March 1851.
Woodcut.

356
Glazing work in the
lower part of the
Crystal Palace, No-
vember 1850.
Woodcut.

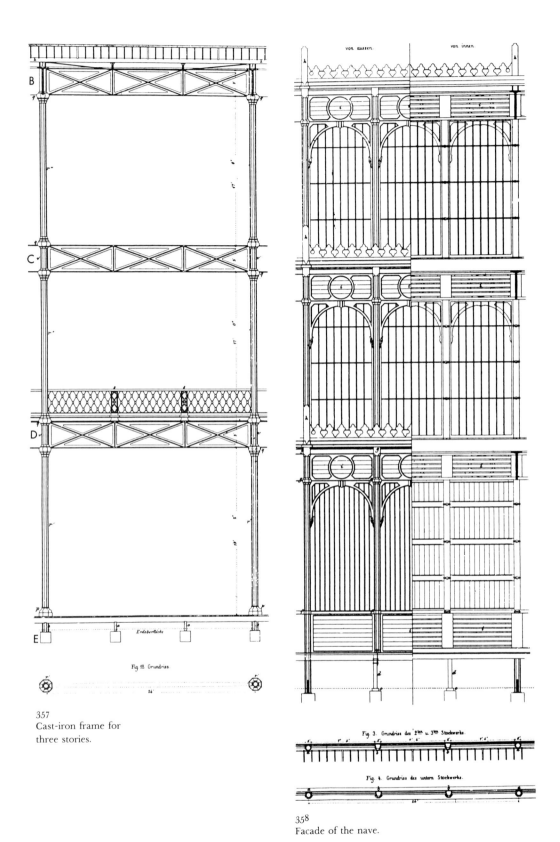

357
Cast-iron frame for
three stories.

358
Facade of the nave.

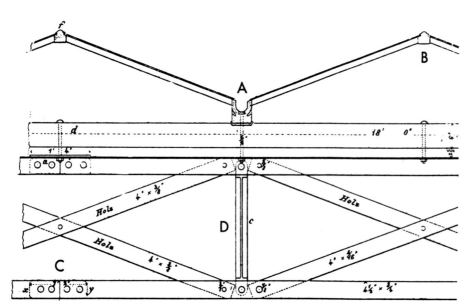

359
Detail of the ridge-and-furrow roof with braced girders of the nave.

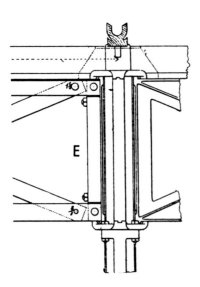

360
Joint between column and girders.

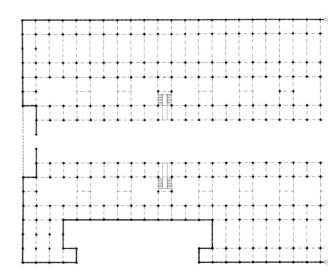

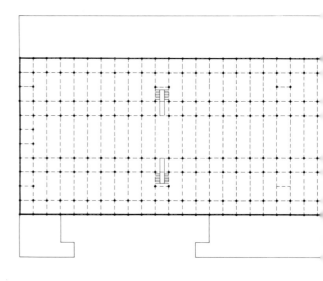

361
Joseph Paxton being
given a slice of the
profits of the 1851
World Exhibition.
Cartoon.

362
Ground-floor plan,
1:1,000.

363
Plan of first story
(gallery), 1:1,000.

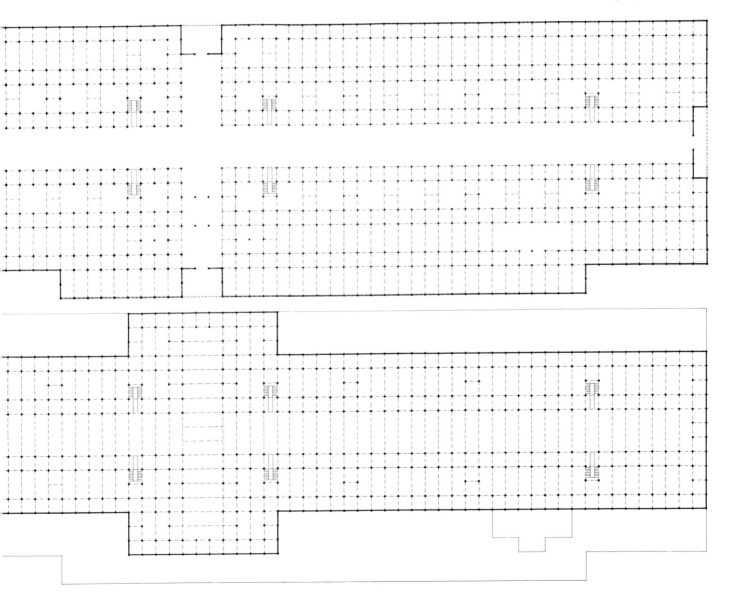

ground floor were located in 4-foot-high balusters. These louvers, made of sheet iron, could be opened or shut to allow control of the air stream. There was also an appreciable surface area in the roof allocated for ventilation. The total surface area of the vents was 41,800 square feet.

The total glass surface of the exhibition building was 900,000 square feet. The panes, made by Chance Brothers of Birmingham, were 49 inches long and 10 inches wide (as noted above) and 1/16 inch thick. The glass had a total weight of 400 tons, which was one third of the year's production of the British glass industry at that time.

As at Chatsworth, a machine devised by Paxton was used to glaze the roof. The ridge rafters of the Paxton gutters served as tracks for the wheels of the glazing wagon. The wagon had a cover so that the glazing could continue in bad weather. There was a box on either side of the wagon to hold the glass. The wagon could accommodate two or three glaziers.

In spite of the high quality of Paxton's solutions to the various problems, defects did appear in the building. These can be explained by the application of the hothouse type of structure to a large exhibition hall. The maximum amount of sunlight was needed for hothouses, but here that was troublesome because of the heating effect. Paxton tried to avoid this by fitting linen sheets at critical points in the roof surfaces. The trees below the transept provided shade there. Water fed from a fountain dampened the linen sheets on hot summer days, for additional cooling. Another problem was damage to the glass: ". . . every rainstorm caused a significant loss through the damage to the exhibited objects, because new leaky parts of the roof kept occurring, often arising from broken panes caused by warping of the long wooden sash bars. In order to guard against this trouble in the best way possible, and using the minimum material, the individual sections of the objects displayed were covered with oilcloth, because of which the overall impression of the whole was of course impaired. However the two main bays were free from this trouble."[112]

The Crystal palace was dismantled in 1852 and rebuilt in Sydenham, where it burned down in 1936. (See the following article.)

Source: archives of J. Russel and Sons, London.

References: Allgemeine Bauzeitung, 1850, vol. 15, pp. 277–285, sheets 362–367; ZfBW, 1852, vol. 2, parts 1, 2, pp. 44 ff.; Schild 1967; Werner 1970; Chadwick 1961; Durm and Ende 1893, 4, part 4; Illustrated London News, 6.7.1850, 9, vol. 17, no. 434; further reports until 28.6.1851, 10, vol. 18, no. 497.

London

Sydenham
Crystal Palace (figs. 628–630)

The Crystal Palace has died in Hyde Park only in order to rise like a phoenix, not from a pile of ashes, but from its pile of columns, girders, and glass roof, to make its appearance again at Sydenham, beautified and embellished. (Die Gartenlaube, 1853, vol. 1)

The principles of objectivity, permanence, and fixed location, which held up to this point, were decisively broken for the first time with the construction of the Crystal Palace at Sydenham. The new rationalization of building methods was made obvious to all by the dismantling of the space frame of the exhibition building in Hyde Park and its reassembly at Sydenham. Early attempts in that direction go back to the development of the hothouse, in which the principles of prefabrication and standardization were applied to the making of building elements which could be put together in different ways in order to adapt to the changing seasons and to the growth of plants.

The Sydenham Crystal Palace, which had a large winter garden at its center, also contained reminders of its predecessor. In the *Handbuch der Architektur* the architect Alfred Messel gives the following description:

The iron and glass as well as the flooring used for the Hyde Park exhibition palace were used again, with the exception of the roof glazing and the space frame of the transept, to erect at Sydenham, within attractive gardens, a large building dedicated to permanent exhibitions of various kinds, the so-called Crystal Palace. The architectural supervision of the construction was once more entrusted to Paxton. The overall layout was again based on a unit dimension of [24 feet], and the total length of the building was [1,608 feet], that is, about [240 feet] less than the length of the Hyde Park building. Wings [574 feet] in length were built on at each end, and at the southern end a [722-foot]-long enclosed passageway led to the railway station. The whole arrangement has a far more striking effect than the Hyde Park Crystal Palace. The long face of the building here is interrupted not only by a central transept but also by north-to-south transepts. The flat roof of the nave of the earlier building has—like both transepts—been given a semicircular vault, but [it is] lower than the vault of the middle transept. The central transept, about [72 feet] in height, and the other two, about [49 feet], thereby project a powerful shadowing effect as seen from the gardens. Basement walls have been built along the length of the front to offset the slope of the ground and serve as powerful anchorages for the whole building. In the interior too, a more favorable effect has been achieved by the vaulting over the nave, by the positioning of columns in pairs at intervals of about [72 feet], and by the more open views in all directions. In order to achieve this last, only one gallery has been built along the exterior wall. A hot-water heating system, including 27 steam boilers, serves to heat the building.

The main attraction of the Sydenham Crystal Palace, occupying the transept and the aisles alongside the nave, was a winter garden containing plants and trees from every climatic zone and rare birds in large cages. Technological, zoological, geographical, and art collections and a permanent market for all kinds of products made it possible for the visitor to have an "edifying and instructive stroll."

The launching of a joint stock company preceded the building of the Sydenham Crystal Palace in 1852. This Crystal Palace Company stated its purpose as "to build a universal temple for the education of the great mass of the people and the improvement of their recreational pleasures." Enjoyment of nature coupled with education was to bring this about. All the shares had been bought within 14 days of the issue of the prospectus. This proves that great profits were expected from the venture. Paxton was appointed director of the winter garden, the park, and the tropical houses.

Source: archives of J. Russel and Sons, London.

References: Durm and Ende, 1885, 4, part IV, p. 472; *Allgemeine Bauzeitung*, 1852, vol. 17, pp. 299–304, sheets 506, 507; *ZfBW*, 1852, vol. 2, parts 1, 2, p. 44 ff., sheets 13, 14.

London

Great Victorian Way (Project) (fig. 364)

architect: Joseph Paxton

The construction of the Crystal Palace in 1851 created the stimulus in the following year for real enthusiasm for building in glass. This was helped by the fall in the price of glass. Among the multitude of projects of that time, one utopian proposal by Paxton, in 1855, is noteworthy. Before the decision to move the Crystal Palace to Sydenham, Paxton considered the possibility of preserving his main work on the spot. He gave as the reason for this preservation of the Exhibition Building the intention to change it into a gigantic winter garden dedicated to the public. The glass cover put over the large Hyde Park elms during the building of the Crystal Palace had already imparted to the building the aspect of a covered landscape. The project for its conversion into a winter garden, published in the 1851 report "What is to become of the Crystal Palace?," was a logical widening of the existing facilities. "In the Winter Park and Garden I propose," Paxton said, "climate would be the principal thing studied, all the

furnishing and fitting up would have special reference to that, so that the pleasures found in it would be of a character which all who visit could share; here would be supplied the climate of Southern Italy, where multitudes might ride, walk or recline amidst groves of fragrant trees, and here they might leisurely examine the works of Nature and Art, regardless of the biting east winds or the drifting snow. . . . In the Winter Park and Garden, the trees and plants might so be arranged as to give great diversity of view and picturesque effect. Spaces might be set apart for equestrian exercise and for carriage drives, but the main body of the building should be arranged with the view of giving great extent and variety for those who promenade on foot. . . . Beautiful creeping plants might be planted against the columns, and trailed along the girders, so as to give shade in summer, while the effect they would produce by festooning in every diversity of form over the building, would give the whole a most enchanting and gorgeous finish. . . . I should recommend the wood boarding round the bottom tier of the Building to be removed and replaced with glass. . . . In summer I should recommend the whole lower glass tier to be entirely removed so as to give, from the park and the houses opposite the Palace, an appearance of continuous park and garden."[113]

Paxton's deep fascination with the idea of a landscaped park transplanted into the city was shown by his project for a gigantic boulevard covered by glass, which was to encircle the center of London, connecting the railway stations and at the same time serving as a circulation route for other traffic. The concept of an endless continuum was to be embodied in a glass-and-iron structure similar to the vaulted transept of the Crystal Palace in size and construction. The cross-section, with constant dimensions of 72 feet in width and 108 feet in height, was to cover a promenade for pedestrians and a highway for wagons and coaches, set in an artificial landscape. Eight railway lines were to be carried in closed galleries parallel to the glass vault on the higher levels. The partly masonry bottom level of the glass vault was to be used for dwellings, offices, entertainment facilities, and hotels. The total length of this gigantic glass ring, which was to cross the River Thames three times by bridges, was to be 10 miles. A larger promenade was proposed in the area of Kensington Gardens.

The project was to be effected in separate phases. The total cost, estimated to be 34 million pounds, was to be raised from private capital according to Paxton's proposals. Although it aroused great public

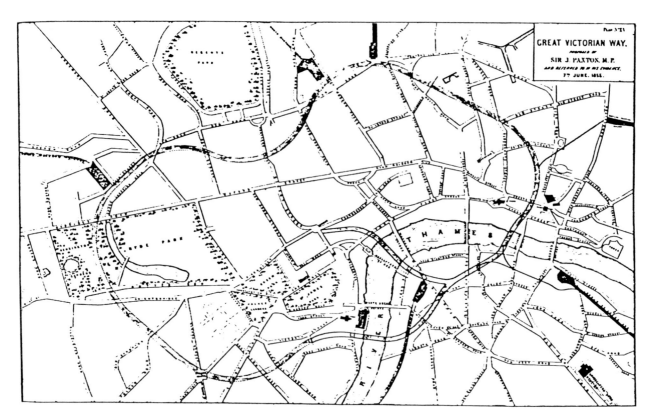

364
Site plan.

interest and was considered by a select committee, the project had to remain a dream. It foundered on lack of profitability and lack of effective interest on the part of the state.

References: McGrath and Frost 1961, pp. 134–138; Chadwick 1961; Geist 1969.

London

Covent Garden
Floral Hall (figs. 365, 632)
length: 279 feet
width: 75 feet
height: 52 feet
height of dome: 91 feet
architect: Edward Middleton Barry
builder: Henry Grissell
built 1857–58

Among the numerous glass-and-iron buildings of the 1850s which took up the structural form of the 1851 Crystal Palace as a model, and therefore put to the test its influence on consequent buildings, the Floral Hall in Covent Garden was one characteristic example. Noteworthy here was the way in which the prototype was taken up (exactly or with modifications) on every possible occasion. The architect transported

the form of the Crystal Palace transept, with its glass barrel vault terminated by large semicircular rosettes, into the immediate vicinity of prestige architectural styles stamped with classicism. Out of the confrontation between the objectivity of an engineering design and the conventional architectural style there arose a building that claimed its aesthetic consummation on the basis of the quality of the construction without any reference to Greek, Roman, or Gothic orders.

After the fire at the Italian Opera House in 1856, Frederick Gye, who had leased the site from the Duke of Bedford, decided upon a reconstruction. The design of the Covent Garden Opera House was entrusted to E. M. Barry, the son of Charles Barry. After the demolition of the Piazza Hotel adjoining the theater, in 1858, Gye commissioned the same architect to design the immediately adjacent Floral Hall on the south side of the theater. It was primarily to serve as a market for flowers, plants, and seeds for the benefit of the Covent Garden Market neighborhood. However, the leaseholder met opposition from the Duke of Bedford. As a result of this, the Floral Hall served as a center for concerts and exhibitions and as a drill hall. After the hall came into the possession of the ninth Duke of Bedford, in 1887, it was altered into a market for imported fruit and therefore returned to its original purpose. An outbreak of fire in 1956 destroyed the glass vault and the dome.

365
Front entrance.
Woodcut.

In the rebuilt Floral Hall, still in existence today, only the surrounding walls and columns of the old structure remain.

In 1859 a correspondent of the *Illustrated London News* described the construction of the Floral Hall in detail:

This large iron structure, which is now nearly completed, has been erected for F. Gye, Esq., the proprietor of the Royal Italian Opera (from the design of Edward M. Barry, Esq., architect) by Mr. Henry Grissell, Regent's-canal Ironworks, London. . . . the building runs parallel with the new Opera House. . . . from the design of the same architect. . . . The floor of the hall forms an excellent example of iron construction. It consists, longitudinally, of 47 cast-iron girders of great strength, with 240 others intersecting them transversely. These are flanged to support hollow tile arches turned between them. The longitudinal girders are 18 inches in depth, and the transverse ones 13 inches.

This ornamental structure has a frontage of 75 feet in Bow Street, forming one of the principal entrances; and the total length of the building is 280 feet. Transversely the building is divided into a nave and two side aisles, the former being 50 feet and the latter 12 feet 6 inches each, giving a clear width of 75 feet. . . . The . . . cast-iron columns . . . support eight wrought-iron semicircular principals, connected with wrought-iron purlins, and filled in with sashbars glazed with bent glass. . . . The height from the floor to the crown of the arch is 52 feet.

A lantern 6 feet wide runs the entire length of the roof. . . . At the south end of the building is a handsome dome, 50 feet in diameter, and its extreme height is 91 feet from the floor of the hall. . . . The structure, when complete, will be a fine specimen of the iron architecture of the nineteenth century.

Reference: *Illustrated London News*, 15.10.1859, 18, vol. 35, no. 998, pp. 370, 371.

London

Muswell Hill
Palace of the People (Project) (figs. 366, 633, 634)

The architect Owen Jones, who had previously worked at the side of Joseph Paxton on the design of the Crystal Palace (particularly on the paintwork and the interior decoration), was the author of the project for the "Palace of the People" (1859). The intention was to build the Palace of the People above a large railway station, which was to connect with the London and North Western, Eastern Counties, Great Western, and Great Northern Railways. The railway was not only to be the medium of transport for the masses of visitors expected, but at the same time was to help create the project by making available the required capital for a joint stock company—"The

Great Northern Palace Company." The intention was to bring in visitors from factory districts all over Great Britain by special trains without any changing of stations. Moreover, the location of the Palace of the People, in Muswell Hill, in North London, was to encourage the inhabitants of the city to visit it. Visitors to London's West End were expected to come here, without having to use the overcrowded London streets. It was estimated that there would be one million visitors a year. The project was to be combined with land speculation—not an unusual matter for nineteenth-century railway companies.

The focal point of the complex was to be a gigantic winter garden, 200 feet in diameter. There was to be a concert hall for 10,000 people adjoining the winter garden, with art galleries, a museum, and places of entertainment accommodated in two elongated aisles (336 by 120 feet) and two 72-foot-wide wings. The winter gardens were to be directly connected to the underground railway by stairways and at the same time were to serve as waiting rooms for the railway passengers.

The Palace of the People project resulted from the enthusiasm arising from the Crystal Palace in Hyde Park and at Sydenham, and was the largest winter garden with a central dome conceived up to that time. Two years later Paxton proposed a similar project for Saint-Cloud, near Paris (fig. 367).

The basic structure was modeled on the space-frame principle used in Paxton's Crystal Palace—cast-iron frames in a multistory building with a ridge-and-furrow roof. The dome of the circular winter garden, encompassed by four viewing towers, was to be made from large arched ribs converging into a clamping ring. Transverse members, also made of braced girders, were to form horizontal rings to join the ribs together. In the sectors thus formed, transverse ties were to be incorporated to make a fine network across the interior of the dome. The crossing point of these ties was to be decorated with star-shaped cast-iron moldings. The apex of the dome was to terminate in a ray-shaped rosette. The surrounding annulus holding the ribs was to rest on a masonry ring with a surrounding gallery, below which were to be archway entrances. The gallery itself was to serve as a kind of "hanging garden," so that the tropical landscape would be on two levels.

References: *Illustrated London News*, 12.2.1859, 18, vol. 34, no. 959, p. 148; 5.3.1859, 18, vol. 34, no. 963, p. 226.

366
Woodcut depicting
projected "Palace of
the People."

367
Joseph Paxton, Crys-
tal Palace, Saint-
Cloud, Paris (project).
Engraving.

London

Muswell Hill
Alexandra Palace (fig. 368)

architect: John Johnston
built 1872–1874

The Alexandra Palace was in its time the largest recreation center in a single building. Served by the
London railway network, it was conceived to provide
diversions and artistic exhibitions for great numbers
of people. The design of the Palace was much like
that of the Palace of the People project, which was
intended for the same site.

The Alexandra Palace, brought into existence by a
joint stock company, had large winter gardens combined with concert halls and theaters, restaurants,
cafés, lecture rooms, and exhibition halls. At its
opening 90,000 visitors were accommodated. The
building stood within a 220-acre park with lakes for
boating and swimming, racetracks with grandstands,
a cycle track, areas for athletics, and a cricket pitch.
In spite of all these offerings, the Alexandra Palace,
which was conceived as a permanent festival hall,
did not fulfil the expectations of the company.
Within a year of its opening it had to be leased out
for exhibition purposes.

In the 1885 *Handbuch der Architektur* the building is
described as "one of the most magnificent undertak-
ings in the world," and continued:

*The Palace . . . comprises a rectangular building complex
[898 feet] long and [425 feet] wide. It has a built up area
of [7.4 acres]. The high five-story central hall rises in the
middle and occupies the whole width of the building transversely from north to south. Two large open courtyards with
fountains and decorative gardens adjoin the central hall on
both sides, along the main axis. Elongated galleries for exhibition purposes adjoin these courtyards on the north side,
and next to these are the concert hall on one side of the
center and the theater on the other side, both approximately
of the same size. Corresponding to these there are on the
south side foyers, coffee rooms, restaurant and banquet rooms
equipped with service rooms, and open colonnaded halls.
There are large conservatories along the longitudinal axis,
communicating with the central hall via the above-mentioned galleries and foyers and closing off the courtyards.
The library, reading rooms, discussion rooms, and lecture
rooms on one side, and the administration rooms on the
other side, are set out in rows and are complete with the
necessary anterooms and side rooms, as well as a covered
subway and the main entrances at the east and west ends
of the establishment on the ground floor. Above the restau-*

368
Ground-floor plan.

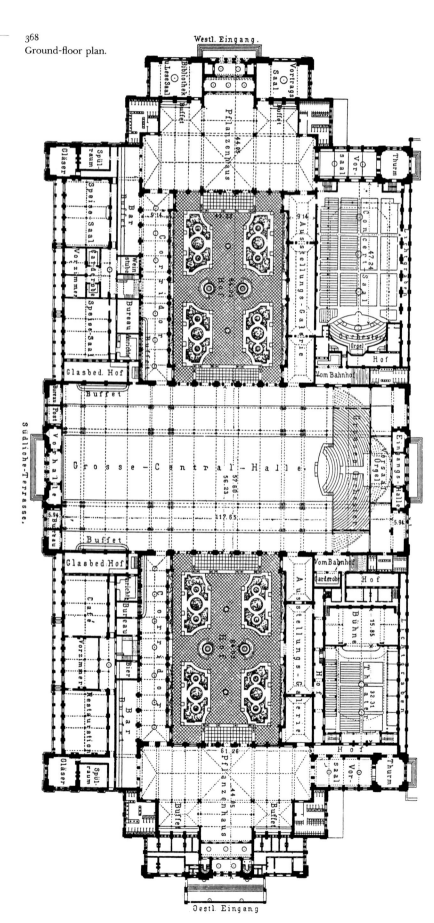

rants of the front there is on the upper story a row of other rooms serving the same purposes; below these in the base-ment there are kitchens and cellars.

The central hall of the rebuilt Alexandra Palace burned down in 1980.

Reference: Durm and Ende 1885, 4, part IV, pp. 143–145.

London

Brompton

Winter Garden (fig. 370)
length: 210 feet
width of middle bay: 46 feet
height: 71 feet
architects: John Arthur Hughes, Captain Fowke
builder: Handyside and Co.
built 1860–61
demolished

The Royal Horticultural Society's Winter Garden in London was laid out on a terrace and is an example of a large conservatory that developed into a basilica-type building with a vertical element like a clerestory below the main vault and above the lower surrounding gallery. The development of this form as the result of recurring spatial motifs made possible a constructional advance which depended on the use of prefabricated parts. This was the basis of the origin of conservatory buildings which, designed independent of the building site, were offered for sale by catalog.

The Brompton winter garden was built in connection with the great Garden Exhibition of 1861, the overall plan of which (fig. 369) was designed by the architect William Andrews Nesfield.

The hipped main vault rose above two rows of cast-iron columns. Delicately made iron sash bars and curved braced girders formed the frame of the roof, which was joined to the columns via a miniature cast-iron gallery. The lower gallery was covered not by a vault but by a lean-to roof. There was a projecting glass roof around the front and the sides.

About 175 tons of cast iron and 70 tons of wrought iron were used in the space frame. From this ratio one can see that cast iron played a major part in the structure of this architecturally pretentious glasshouse. The desired ornamentation could have been executed only in cast iron.

Kiosk (fig. 371)
The widespread use of cast iron in connection with oriental types of ornamentation is shown by the kiosk designed for the British dominions and colo-

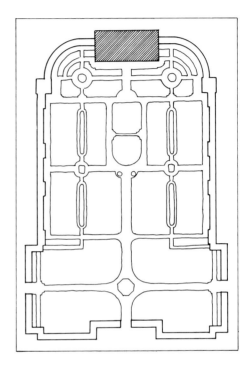

369
Site plan, 1860.

370
Brompton winter
garden.

371
Owen Jones and
Rowland Mawson
Ordish, prefabricated
kiosk for India,
Brompton, 1861, in-
terior view.
Engraving.

nies, particularly India. This was a hall-type building built around 1870 by the architects Owen Jones and Rowland Mawson Ordish. The basilicalike hall, 80 feet long, 40 feet wide, and 42 feet high, was supported only on the cast-iron columns forming the frame of the exterior walls. A network of richly decorated cast-iron ribs supported the clerestory structure, while the ribs continued upward to form a pointed arch vault. The building was designed as a completely prefabricated structure that could be dismantled and reassembled.

Reference: *The Builder*, 19.5.1860, part 18, no. 902, pp. 311, 312.

Lyndhurst (near Tarrytown, N.Y.)

Conservatory
length: 380 feet
width: 95 feet

The elongated conservatory at Lyndhurst was the first glasshouse made completely of iron in the United States, and at the same time the largest there.

In 1838 the well-known architect Jackson Davis was commissioned by General William Paulding to build a conservatory, which shortly afterwards came into the possession of George Merritt. The central pavilion, 80 feet long and 95 feet wide, was covered with a curved glass vault. A projecting entrance like an apse extended this rectangular ground plan. A 100-foot masonry tower with an onion-shaped top made of glass was built on the center axis of the building, behind the central pavilion. Lower wings with curvilinear roofs, adjoining the pavilion, made the whole into a U-shape layout. The glass vault, with its flatly pointed arch, gave the building a Gothic aspect. There were shops, rest rooms, a billiards room, a gymnasium, and a bowling alley in the building. The private conservatory was filled with exotic plants and vines.

The building burned down in 1880 as the result of a chimney fire, shortly after it had been acquired by Jay Gould, the railway magnate. The firm of Lord and Burnham was commissioned to rebuild the conservatory on the old foundation. The tower was removed and the sides of the central pavilion were rebuilt with a hipped roof. The space frame, still in a good state of preservation, consists of curved iron ribs converging to the ridge. They support a low ventilating lantern running along the line of the roof ridge.

Reference: Hix 1974, pp. 95–97.

Lyon

Jardin d'Hiver (figs. 372, 373)

architect: Hector Horeau
built: 1847
demolished

The Jardin d'Hiver was opened in December 1847. In
only 7 months there arose on the left bank of the
River Rhone in the Parc de la Tête d'Or an octago-
nal-base building made of cast iron and glass, the
central hall of which was crowned by a lantern
above a lean-to roof and surrounded by a low
ground-floor gallery. The roof was built of curved
cast-iron trusses with straight top flanges made of
wood and bottom flanges extending almost to floor
level. The reinforcing iron spandrels were infilled
with ornamental open ironwork. The central hall and
the surrounding gallery were built to the same design principle (figs. 38, 372). Flowers, bushes, and
trees filled the center. The high gallery space served
as a promenade, where sweetmeats, birds, and curiosities were sold at small kiosks. On the north side
there were a restaurant and a café with a view of the
Rhone; on the west, separated by a glass wall, was a
rock garden with tropical plants.

Source: Société d'Etude d'Histoire de Lyon, Cours Gambetta.

Reference: Boudon 1972.

Lyon

Parc de la Tête d'Or
Great Conservatory (figs. 374–377, 635, 636)

length: 230 feet
width: 98 feet
height: 69 feet
architect: unknown
built 1877–1880

The Great Conservatory at Lyon comprised five adjacent glasshouses, rising in height from the outer
ones to the central one. All in the Gothic arch style,
with gable ends and pointed baults, they formed an
architectural ensemble in the manner of a row of
houses. In the interior, the three central houses
joined to make a single hall. Each of these three
hothouses had a nave and two aisles.

The deliberate acceptance of the spatial form of
the Gothic cathedral and the translation of it into a
steel-and-glass structure corresponds to the tradition
of eclecticism. The forms brought about by historical
trend in the structural development are designated
as non-progressive. The architectural style was, however, primarily decided by the soaring glass vaults,
which created a magnificent and truly homogeneous

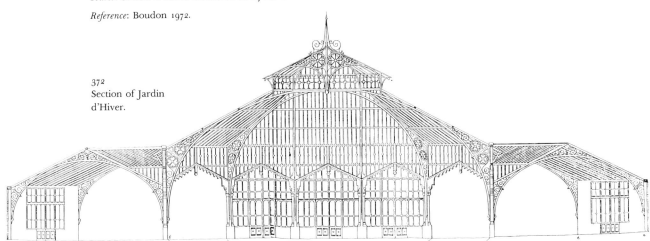

372
Section of Jardin
d'Hiver.

373
Watercolor of Jardin
d'Hiver, 1847.

space. The delicate sash-bar work of the facade and
the repetition of a basic motif, with the skillful effect
of the rise toward the center, gave this building its
original charm.

The building has been ascribed to Joseph-Gustave
Bonnet, but also to Hector Horeau. The naming of
Horeau as a possible designer may go back to the
fact that in 1872 he made a preliminary design for
an "exhibition palace" in the Parc de la Tête d'Or.

The 69-foot-high nave of the central pavilion of
the Great Conservatory rests on two rows of five
slender 29¹/₂-foot cast-iron columns. Each of these is
made in two parts with a capital and a base. They
are joined together by iron arches, which support a
continuous beam, which in turn supports the gallery.
The arches form the only reinforcement in the longitudinal direction of the bays. The load of the
pointed glass vault is carried by the beams, on the
rows of iron columns on each side. The latter are
joined together at the top by an external gallery. In
line with the main columns in the bottom part of the
structure, the roof (made of curved filigree ribs) rests
on the vertical framework of the gallery. The simple
iron ribs, which span 33 feet, are reinforced by
wrought-iron ornamental latticework webs, which
widen from the springing to the apex of the arch.
This makes a two-hinge arch. Attachments looking
like gallows, joined to the vertical frame members,
provide additional lateral reinforcement. Sloping inward to the Gothic vaults, they have the function of
vestigial flying buttresses. The adjacent aisles are
likewise built with vaults, up to the level of the interior gallery, and are carried on columns which are
aligned with the lower part of the main rows of columns. This construction principle is repeated in the
smaller pavilions on either side of the central one,
but with the difference that the nave is not raised.
The outer parts of the complex end in low, flatly
vaulted glass buildings with pointed arch profiles and
hipped octagonal ends.

The central pavilion of the Great Conservatory
was pulled down at the start of the 1970s and replaced by a new building, which does in fact have
the same basic external profile; however, the architectural unity was destroyed by the use of thicker
steel section and polygonal instead of continuously
curved forms. The wings are well maintained.

Sources: Jardin Botanique de la Ville de Lyon, Parc de la
Tête d'Or; Société d'Etude d'Histoire de Lyon, Cours
Gambetta.

Reference: R. Dovin, *Le Jardin Botanique de Lyon* (Lyon, 1970).

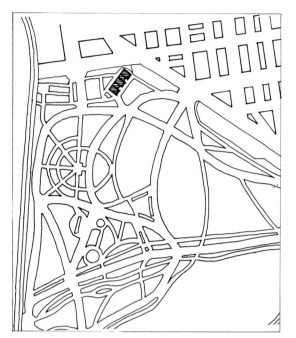

374
Site plan, 1970.

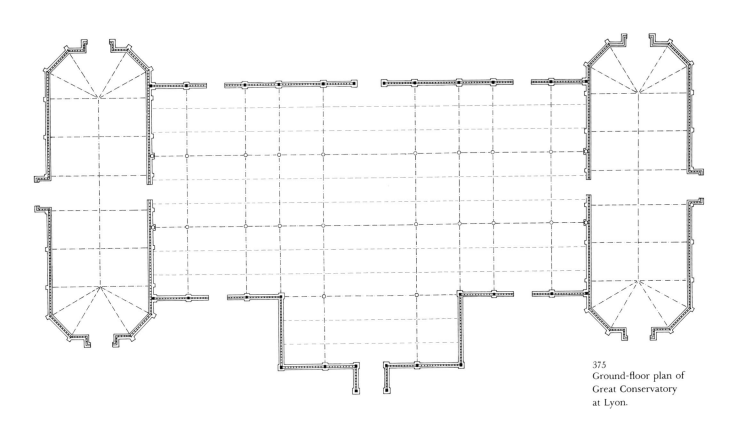

375
Ground-floor plan of
Great Conservatory
at Lyon.

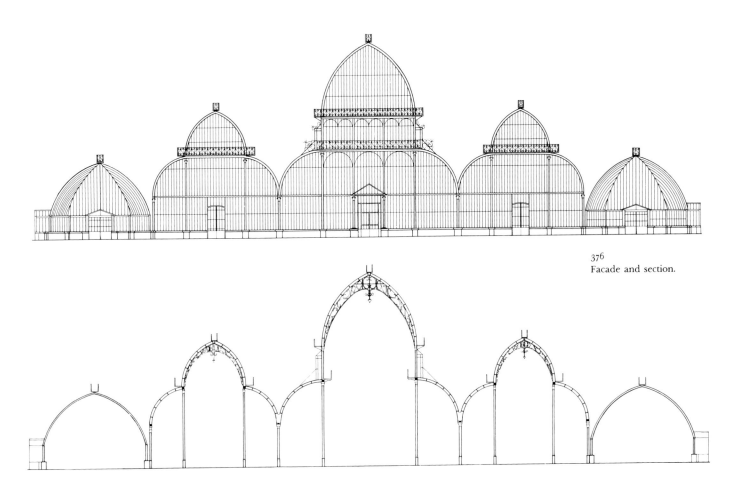

376
Facade and section.

Madrid

Parque del Retiro
Palacio de Cristal (figs. 378, 637)

length: 157 1/2 feet
width: 105 feet (long bay, 52 1/2 feet)
height: 66 feet
architect: Valázquez Bosco
built 1887

Plant houses are an exception in southern lands. This vaulted glass-and-iron building was intended for the exhibition of plants and flowers from the Phillipines. Its facade is reflected in the water of the lake on which it is built, giving the architecture a light, suspended character; this recalls the Palm House at Kew.

The overall appearance of the interior has the character of ecclesiastical architecture, as so often appears in the eclecticism of the nineteenth century. This is seen in the dome above the crossing of the nave and transept, and in the ambulatory. The spatial configuration of the churches of the Middle Ages has been translated into an elegant glass-and-iron building. The space frame is supported on rows of cast-iron columns, which carry on one side the roof of the low ambulatory and on the other side the 39-foot-high main vault. Light metal plate ribs with fish-gill-shape cutouts form depressed arches which span the aisles. A narrow surrounding gallery provides the transition between the two vaults of different heights. A braced beam at the crossing supports the dome, which is capped with a small pyramidal lantern.

Many of the structural details (such as the slender, riveted cast-iron beams in the miniature galleries and the hipped dome of the large palm house) are reminiscent of the two palm houses at Vienna-Schön-

brunn. However, the glasshouse in the Retiro Park is certainly not comparable in architectural effect to the Great Palm House of Sengenschmid, the ironwork of which iterates in smooth lines the distribution of forces, as in bridge building. The Madrid building recalls the English exhibition buildings of the 1850s, but on a smaller scale. The solidly built portico shows a reverence for Palladio.

The building still exists today, but instead of plants there are exhibitions of various objects, particularly works of art.

Reference: Die Bauwelt 71, part 29, 1980, pp. 1258, 1259.

Magdeburg

Friedrich-Wilhelms-Garten
Palm House (fig. 379)

length: (minus wings): 80 1/2 feet
width: 56 feet
height: ca. 46 feet
architects: Stadtbauinspektor Jansen, Stadtbaurat Peters
built 1895–96
destroyed 1945

The Magdeburg hothouses did not have any new design elements in their structural and spatial form. Noteworthy here are the simple cubic forms of the large palm house, which had added-on buildings for various purposes with correspondingly different cross-sections. All were made with large glass facades, split up only by delicate sashes and frameworks.

The gift of the well-known plant collection of the industrialist Gruson to the city of Magdeburg was the reason for the building of these hothouses. To meet the wishes of the benefactor, a part of an older city park was chosen for the site. This area was easily reached from the city and was in the immediate

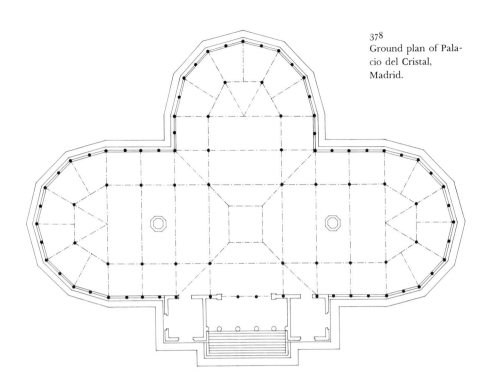

378
Ground plan of Palacio del Cristal, Madrid.

379
Ground-floor plan of Magdeburg palm house.

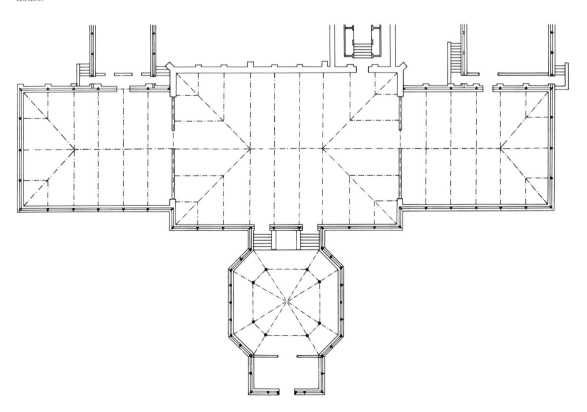

vicinity of a city-owned casino which had a much-visited garden. Some of the components of the old Gruson conservatory were reused to save costs. This circumstance had some control over the rather random appearance of the general layout. The buildings comprised three tropical houses in a row, containing palms, cycads, and ferns. A temperate house built out from this axis served as the entrance. Adjoining this group of glasshouses were several smaller ones on the north side. There was a masonry building on the rear north wall, the cellar of which housed the central heating plant. This building held rooms for the garden staff, machinery, a library, and two apartments for the gardeners.

All the buildings were built on concrete foundations. The low base wall had brick cladding and a granite plinth. The glass-and-iron building stood on this. It was made of delicate cast-iron frameworks and rolled iron section. As with most German hothouses, curved roof surfaces were not used here. The palm, fern, and cycad houses were provided with double glazing and ventilation. The other houses had single glazing. The north wall of the exhibition house was made of masonry, with marble glazing. Fresh air came through simple openings for ventilation and through top-hinged louvers with gear drives at the ridges and gutters. The structural ironwork of the exhibition building in the front came from the Mosenthin Company of Leipzig.

References: ZfBW, 1897, vol. 47, parts 1–3, pp. 31–42, sheets 8–10; Deutsche Bauzeitung (publ.), *Baukunde des Architekten*, 1902, vol. II, part 5, pp. 368–371.

Morel and Louis Martin Berthault. The large conservatory east of the mansion was built about the same time, definitely before 1808. It was one of the earliest hothouses, and had continuous glazing at the front rising from a masonry wall. The front of the building was essentially a large sloping glass roof, changing to vertical glazing at the bottom and at the top, assembled entirely of sash bars (probably made of iron).

Laborde describes the park and conservatory thus:

The gardens at Malmaison are excellent on account of the amount and beauty of the rarest foreign plants. Because this fine collection was built up with persistent care we have here in fact the true botanical garden of France. The soil too was exceptionally favorable for the rapid growth of plants. The tropical house, laid out on a very extensive site, contains the rarest types of plants and is maintained in the same way as the tropical houses at Schönbrunn and Kew. Its form, however, is more graceful. Behind the tropical house there is a room decorated with fine paintings, where one can enjoy the view of plants and enjoy their scent too. It is a pity that this building does not communicate with the house, because then it would serve as an excellent ornament, especially in winter. We note here, once and for all, that the practice of siting tropical houses in the middle of the park instead of combining them with the main buildings greatly reduces their charm, which the same layout would ensure if they were placed in their proper places.

References: Laborde 1808; Bouvier and Maynial 1949.

Malmaison, near Paris

Parc de la Malmaison (figs. 380, 381)

length: 151 feet
width: 20 feet
architect: Jean Thomas Thibault
built: ca. 1803
demolished

The gardens at Malmaison (west of Paris, not far from Versailles) are described in Alexandre de Laborde's *Description des nouveaux Jardins de la France* (1808) not only as a progressive garden in the new style (meaning the English garden) but also as one of the most important botanical gardens in France. The mansion and the park were acquired at the beginning of the nineteenth century for the Empress Josephine. The park was enlarged and reorganized as an English garden in conjunction with the reequipping of the house under the supervision of Jean Marie

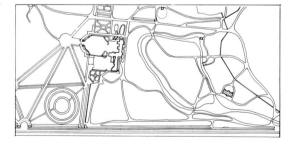

380
Site plan, 1808.

381
Copper engraving of
Malmaison conserva-
tory, 1808.

Meiningen

Ducal Park
Orangery (figs. 382, 383)
length: 69 feet
width: 56 feet
height: 36 feet
architect: unknown
built 1800
demolished

The orangery at Meiningen, part of a romantic garden in the Ducal Park, may be considered an early forerunner of the prefabricated building. A kind of grotto, built of stone and nestling in a wooded hillside, formed the end of the orangery. It also served as a small dwelling for the gardener and contained the underground heating plant. The horseshoe-shaped area of the orangery faced south toward a lake. In summer it appeared as a romantic rock scene; in winter it changed into a building with a sloping glass roof facing south. The parts of the orangery were made in the simplest way and restricted in number so that this annual assembly and dismantling could be easily carried out. One can see in this primitive form of prefabricated house the basic principles of the prefabricated iron-frame glasshouses, which came later: the construction of the space frame from standard components, the careful design of elements and joints suited to the box system, and the provision for reuse of the material without waste. This hothouse had simple spatial organization and could be altered to suit the needs of the season.

Reference: Allgemeines Deutsches Garten-Magazin, 1806, vol. 3, part II.

Munich

Nymphenburg
Royal Gardens
Three Conservatories (figs. 384–389, 638–641)
These three glasshouses, erected around 1800 by Friedrich Ludwig von Sckell, belong to the group of early hothouses on the Continent built on a basis of scientific botany and building technology. Sckell was stimulated by the many classical hothouses built toward the end of the eighteenth century in England, and he further developed these to meet continental requirements. Particularly with his glasshouses at Nymphenburg and in the Old Botanical Garden in Munich, he created a spatial concept that was to have a lasting effect on the development of hothouse building in Germany. Sckell used classical stylistic

382
Summer arrangement of Meiningen orangery. Engraving.

383
Ground plan and section showing winter arrangement of Meiningen orangery. Engraving.

elements in his buildings, such as large continuous surfaces and long lines, symmetrical construction, and limitation of ornament to the simplest characterization of the building components. The hothouse building, with its extensive glass surfaces, offered him the opportunity of systematically pursuing the use of additive elements in the design to give his buildings that repetitive style which is characteristic of classicism, which however is dissolved and negated in a radical way. In this respect Sckell's buildings were forerunners of the functional architecture of the modern industrial era. Apart from the solid parts, which exhibit classical forms, he conceived his Munich buildings in such a way that interchangeable basic parts could be used to form different structures. One can regard his hothouses built in the period 1807–1820 as examples taken from a catalog of types in the sense of Jean Nicolaus Louis Durand.

The importance of Sckell to the development of the hothouse in Germany is comparable to that of J. C. Loudon in Britain. On the Continent, and particularly in Germany, the Loudon type of building was taken up reservedly. The climatic conditions that occur in mainland Europe—snow, ice, hail, and greater cold—figured in the controversy over the use of iron-frame buildings, and in the background stood the retarded state of industrialization.

Sckell favored a large surface, perpendicular glass walls, a lean-to or a ridge roof, and strictly uniform rectangular components. In contrast to Loudon's, the space frames and sashes of Sckell's hothouses were (with one exception) made of wood. As in Joseph Paxton's buildings, these wooden elements were reduced to the structural minimum, particularly where used as sash bars. A later substitution of iron for wood was to be expected, as with Paxton's work. The logical course of such an interpretation is shown in the rebuilding of Sckell's first hothouse with standard iron section by C. Mühlhofer in 1867. One can regard the glass facades of Sckell's Munich hothouses as early prototypes in the evolutionary series that led to the space frames of warehouses, railway stations, and exhibition buildings of the nineteenth century.

After his appointments as the director of garden construction and superintendent of the royal gardens of the Bavarian king, Maximilian Joseph, Sckell obtained in 1803 the commission to design a plan for the gardens of the royal summer residence at Nymphenburg. In 1809 he was commissioned to plan a botanical garden in Munich "of a natural character" and in the geometric style. The series of hothouses already built by Sckell, and regarded as progressive, formed part of the general plan. Sckell did not automatically incorporate these in his English garden.

The sites of the hothouses were geometrically incorporated in the park together with the flower and botanical gardens (fig. 384). "But," he wrote, "because nature does not herself plant such gardens, so these two cannot be combined with their artificial forms, nor with them or their imitations, that is to say with gardens gone wild. Such uniform layouts must therefore stand by themselves—one must come upon them unexpectedly and be surprised by them. Therefore a shrubbery should conceal them."[114]

It was characteristic of Sckell's classicism that he allotted to the hothouse, with its elongated and rhythmically divided glass front, combined with a frame of solid buildings enclosing it, a satisfactory aesthetic formula, in conformity with accepted concepts of style. One example of this is the building in the Old Botanical Garden (figs. 391–393). He wrote that he had "endeavored to give the conservatory an architectural value (because this is so seldom the case with this type of building)," and had "adorned both end portals or entrances with the Doric order in the purest proportions and following the rules of building have provided them with fronts." Sckell found, however, that the vertical glass wall was not only more aesthetically effective than the inclined, but also more functional. "This construction is far more

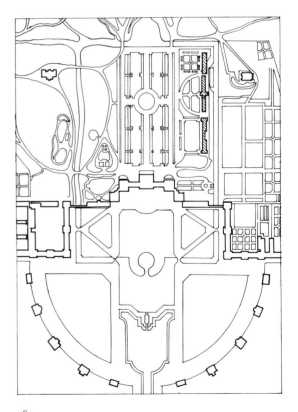

384
Site plan, 1830.

beautiful for conservatories and more durable, and, at least in our climate, to be much preferred to sloping glass surfaces, because we often have frost penetrating 3 to 4 feet into the ground, and much snow and hail. Windows like those in England which are tilted at 65° would be able to protect the plants, both from the cold and from the penetrating water from melting snow, and no more from hail, because there these natural events are not so destructive as in our land. In addition to that, on days when there is much snow or heavy rain, the sloping glass has to be covered with cloths or screens to prevent drops of water falling on the plants, as a result of which the plants have to do without the beneficial effect of light. All of these disadvantages disappear with vertical windows."

Sckell tried to avoid the disadvantageous effect of the hothouse illuminated only via vertical glass panes by a special ceiling design. "Because the plants can do without diffused light much less than they can do without rays direct from the sun, I have tried to increase the illumination by making the ceiling curved, not horizontally but elliptically (abatjour), so that it is able to receive more rays from the sun and to refract these onto the plants. This type of construction has wholly lived up to expectations. The plants live in this well-illuminated hothouse in the most exuberant health, and in the purest air. Hence every plant grows upright because it has no shortage of light; even those most distant from the glass wall do not need to bend down to face the light. The ellipse spreads daylight and brightness everywhere."[115]

Sckell did not use flues for heating, but powerful iron stoves. In 1830 he installed in one of the Nymphenburg conservatories the first hot-water central heating system in Germany.[116]

The introduction of the English garden into Germany, in which Sckell played a major part, was bound up with the acceptance of the classical hothouse in the British style. In 1773 he had undertaken, on the behalf of Prince Carl Theodor, a study tour of England. "He applied his attention with great zeal to scientific botany, and prefabricated herbaria, in the botanical gardens at Kew and Chelsea; he described hothouses and forcing houses and missed no opportunity to widen his knowledge in every branch of the art of gardening."[117] According to Arnold Tschira, the classic hothouses of Richard Bradley (1750) and T. Lightoler (1762) are plainly recognizable as prototypes of Sckell's buildings. These were heated houses with solid corner pavilions.

The three hothouses in the Royal Gardens at Nymphenburg were built as a group in a line perpendicular to that of the castle and facing south.

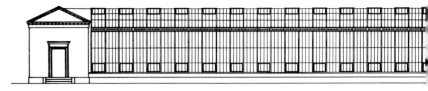

385
Iron hothouse, front
elevation.

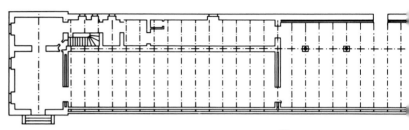

386
Iron hothouse,
ground plan.

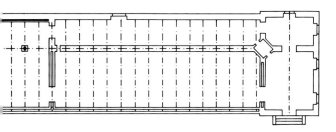

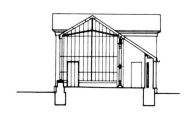

387
Iron hothouse,
section.

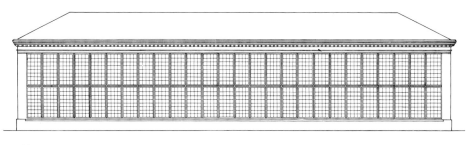

388
Palm house, front
elevation.

389
Palm house, section.

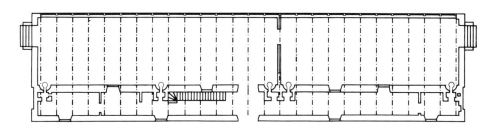

390
Palm house, ground
plan.

The first conservatory at Nymphenburg (figs. 385–387, 638, 640, 641) was built in 1807. According to Tschira it was the only glasshouse built by Sckell of glass and iron exclusively. "The very long unpretentious glasshouse was intended for plants from Japan, China, Dutch East Indies, Australia, East India, South America, and the interior of Africa. The actual plant area was covered with a flat glass roof; its only decoration a cast-iron ornamental frieze at the gutter. The flattish, gabled, corner pavilions accommodated the private rooms of the king at one end, and those of the gardeners at the other end."[118] This conservatory was 262 feet in length.

The second conservatory, which faced west, was built in 1816. Sckell placed the simple pavilion in the center of this one. The two wings obtained their light only via the vertical windows of the wall. The roof vault is quadrant-shaped here.

The third building (figs. 388–390, 639), built in 1820, is a palm house. It adjoins the second conservatory on the west side. Tschira writes: "With its shape, having a high glass south-facing wall, it reverts to a form which can be found here and there in Germany, which we have previously met at the Belvedere glasshouse in Vienna, even if in a more massive form there. It is not beyond the bounds of possibility that Sckell, who did indeed come from employment in Bavaria, knew of a similar design by Johann Peter Ernst Rohrer dated 1741–1745 for a glasshouse in Rastatt and used it as a model."[119] The building has a characteristic large glass facade of noble proportions, a delicately made wooden framework, wooden sashes, and a sloping ridge roof. It is 153 feet long, 38 feet wide, and 39 feet high at the ridge. Well maintained, it is now in use as a café.

Source: Bayerische Verwaltung der staatlichen Schlösser, Gärten und Seen, Schloss Nymphenburg.

References: Sckell 1825; Tschira 1939, pp. 94–96; Pfann 1935, p. 9.

Munich

Old Botanical Garden

Conservatory (figs. 391–393)

length: 459 feet
width at center: 34 feet
architect: F. L. von Sckell
built 1818
demolished ca. 1860

The conservatory in the Old Botanical Garden was the largest of its kind built by Sckell. It was, like its forerunners, kept to simple forms. There was a verti-

cal glass wall, approximately 400 feet long, extending between the two masonry corner pavilions. The central part was accentuated by a hipped roof rising above the line, resting on narrow pillars. By itself, this middle part resembles the Nymphenburg palm house.

The conservatory, combined with residential quarters and storerooms, lay at the northern end of the botanical garden, with its glass front facing south. The gardens were laid out in the form of geometrical segments. Sckell wrote: "Botanical gardens shall be laid out symmetrically and uniformly, because one usually displays plants according to a systematic pattern." According to Sckell, the conservatory was meant to enclose the garden in a well-proportioned way, "but also to ensure a beautiful pictorial and artistic appearance even without considering its strict uniformity."[120]

Source: Bayerische Verwaltung der staatlichen Schlösser, Gärten und Seen, Schloss Nymphenburg.

References: Sckell 1825; Tschira 1939, pp. 94–96; Pfann 1935, p. 9.

Glass Palace (figs. 394–399, 646, 647, 649–651)

length: 787 feet
width: 276 feet
height: 82 feet
architect: August von Voit
builder in charge: Ludwig Werder
construction firm: Cramer-Klett
built 1853–54
burnt down 1931

The Glass Palace, one of the largest glass-and-iron buildings of the nineteenth century in Germany, followed the structural principles developed by Paxton in the Crystal Palace. Its iron columns, visible on the outside, had extensive undecorated areas of glass between them, and the pleated roof stood out in silhouette. Radical in the simplicity of its form and its detail, the building was deemed worthy and up to date by contemporary observers. It was intended to be used as a tropical house after the end of the industrial exhibition for which it was erected; however, its giant size frustrated this intention.

The Glass Palace was built in 1853–54 on the site of the Old Botanical Garden in the center of Munich, near the railway station. In the spring of 1851 King Maximilian II had advertised a competition, but it produced no result. However, two years after the London World Exhibition had set the scene, the intention was translated into reality.

The Botanical Garden had been completely rebuilt around 1850 and was no longer really suitable as a garden. At the same time, this site's central location and its proximity to the railway made it very suitable for a large industrial exhibition. When the old conservatory (by Sckell) was demolished, it was kept in mind that after the exhibition parts of the Glass Palace could serve as a hothouse. A committee was set up which, on the instructions of the state, commissioned the Royal Superintendent of Works, Voit, to design a hall for 6,600 exhibitors. It is indicative of the business arrangements in Bavaria, compared with those in Britain, that a joint stock company was not formed here, but the state became the organizer and the building contractor. The short period allocated for the construction, from the autumn of 1853 to the summer of 1854, meant that a masonry structure did not come into consideration, but only building materials that allowed a high degree of mass production. Roth writes: "On September 29, 1853, . . . Voit concluded a contract with the manufacturer Cramer-Klett of Nuremberg for the construction of the whole building by June 8, 1854. The contract contained a penalty clause for delay; for every day of the first week 100 gulden, but for every day of the following weeks 2,000 gulden as compensation."[121]

A track was built from the railway station to the building site for the transport of the building materials and the exhibited goods. The building was completed in 87 days, with the use of 1,700 tons of iron (compared with the 4,000 tons used in the Crystal Palace in London), 37,000 panes of glass, and 2,000 cubic meters of wood. The cost was about one million gulden. A contemporary report describes the construction process thus:

The magic spell which the glass palace built for the great London Exhibition has created has become so persistent that any other constructions built for similar cases of this kind no longer seem to have the same effect. The Englishman Paxton has become de rigueur for the Munich Exhibition building, and, like the London Crystal Palace in Hyde Park, the Munich Glass Palace rose in light and elegant forms on the site of the former Botanical Garden. The greenery of the plants, and the scented flowers, must make way for the products of human industry. The foundation work was started on October 18 of the previous year, but on February 27 of the next year the first columns of the building were raised and in not much more than 3 months the building was completed, ready for the opening of the exhibition in the middle of June. The rapid construction of such a space and the possibility of its opening on time for the exhibition of the products of industry could only have been achieved by the use of the materials iron, glass, and wood. The forging and fabrication of all the iron parts could be carried out in advance in the renowned foundry of Mr. Cramer-Klett of Nuremberg, and thus the whole Glass Palace was in fact really piled up there and only brought out piece by piece to be assembled at the site. Because dry material alone came into use for this purpose, the objects to be exhibited were exposed to none of the dampness of walls which otherwise occurs in new buildings.

The Exhibition Building was laid out as a rectangle [787 feet] in length and [164 feet] in width, intersected at right angles in the middle by a [276-foot]-long and [164-foot]-wide transept. The nave and transept were divided into three bays, of which the middle one is [79 feet] wide and each of the side bays [39 feet] wide. The side bays are in turn divided by a row of columns on which the surrounding wall rests; the transept itself rises higher than the nave. In this way there has arisen a stepped three-story structure which, combined with the separated arrangement of the transept and the wings projecting on either side of it, gives the building a lively external appearance. The delicate iron structural members, the shining masses of glass, the discontinuous but upward-soaring galleries, and finally the flags flying at the top, all make a contribution to the beauty of this building. The Munich Glass Palace is in every way a building of more pleasing appearance than the one in London; only the type remains the same. The response from the German industrialists and the Austrians has been extraordinary, and so far the objects announced as being exhibited already demand more space than exists.[122]

The Glass Palace was built on a supporting framework of 20-by-20-foot units. The transept was 8 units wide and 40 units long. Inside this frame, cast-iron columns were placed so that they formed three continuous rows around the perimeter of the building. This arrangement allowed the stepping back of the building on all sides, by which means the assembly of the gigantic mass of the building was possible. The interior of the nave and the transept was free of columns, with a clear span of 79 feet. The clear height of this gigantic hall was 66 feet in the nave and 82 feet in the transept. The surrounding row of columns carried a gallery and the stepped roof. The gallery was accessible by stairs in the transept and at the ends of the nave.

As with Paxton's Crystal Palace, the space frame was made of prefabricated columns and ribs. The cast-iron columns had octagonal cross-sections, with four semicircular lesenes, and were hollow inside, like Paxton's, to carry off the rainwater. The columns were provided with bases and capitals. The cross-sections were square where the joints were made with the ribs. The columns had small brackets as springing for the ribs. The joints were made by bolts. The cast-iron girders were diagonally braced, 4 feet deep and spanning 20 feet, like the ones Paxton used. They supported on one side the wooden planks of the gallery and on the other side the stepped-back roof.

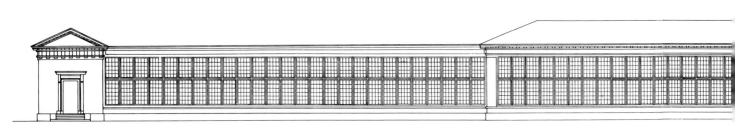

391
Front elevation of
conservatory.

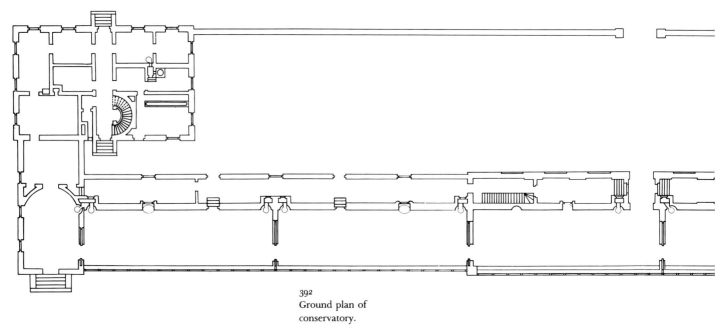

392
Ground plan of
conservatory.

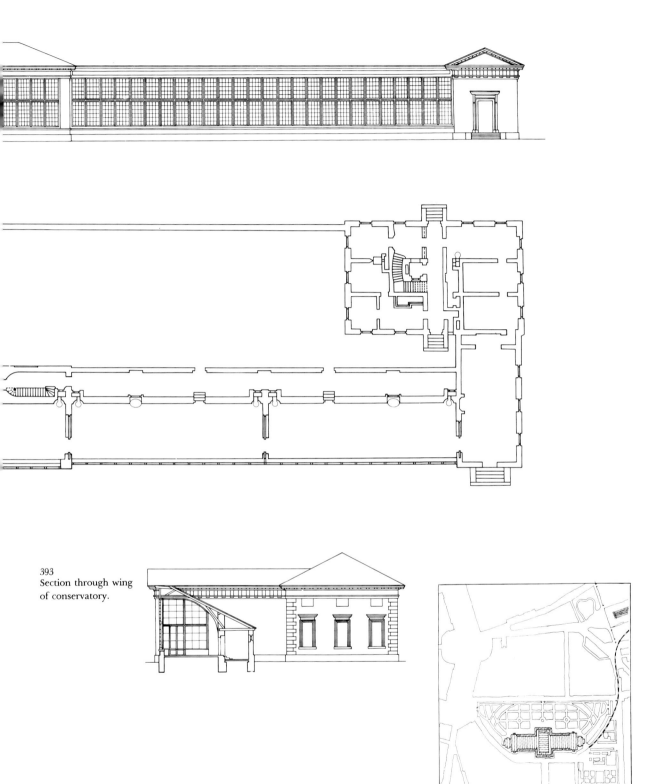

393
Section through wing
of conservatory.

394
Site plan, 1854.

395
Steel engraving of
Glass Palace by Jo-
hann Poppel, 1854.

396
Ground-floor plan of
Glass Palace, 1:1,000.

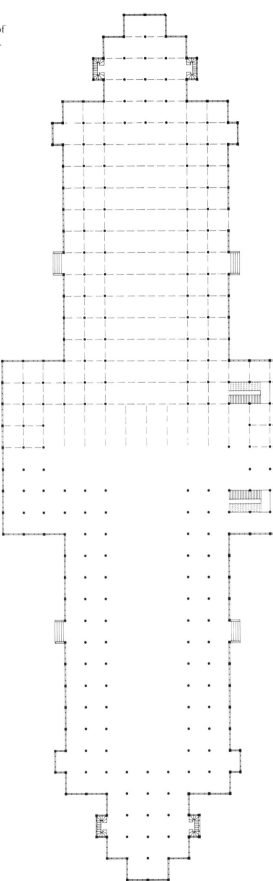

The glass roof was made in the ridge-and-furrow system and was supported on iron sash bars. Rainwater was led from the roof by iron gutters to the columns. These lay directly above the beams, running along them. In contrast to the Crystal Palace, the gutter was not made as a self-supporting load-bearing beam placed transverse to the main beams. Because of the great length of the glass panes chosen, the roof had to be made with closely spaced gutters (Paxton gutters), 8 feet apart, transverse to the direction of the main beams. The spanning of the nave and transept was achieved by using a beam made partly of wood, likewise reinforced by diagonal bracing. Iron tensioning cables, housed in the lower flange, were stressed to provide some hogging for the beam. The framework of columns and joists stood on the stout supporting beams at the intersection of the nave and the transept, and supported the ridge-and-furrow roof on 79-foot beams. The wind forces in this area were resisted by iron diagonal members (figs. 59, 397–399).

Karl Wittek describes the structure as follows:

. . . the members at the awkward places in the structure were made of wrought iron. The braced girders were made partly of cast iron and partly of wrought iron. The upper and lower flanges were constructed of two angle-iron sections and flat iron bar according to the length required in these pieces. Seventeen vertical connecting pieces made of cast iron were bolted in between. Sixteen cross-shaped members were also incorporated, the main struts of which were made of oak; the bracing struts were joined together at the crossing points with bolts. . . .

The resident engineer of the Munich Glass Palace construction, Ludwig Werder of the Cramer-Klett Co. (later MAN), built a special machine for machining the columns. The columns in the Munich Glass Palace are fixed into brick foundations by means of special mountings. They consist of three or four shafts placed one on top of another, and bolted together. . . . greater thicknesses of the cast iron were used than for the London building. In the latter only the gallery beams were made of cast iron; in Munich the connecting beams were of cast iron as well as the gallery beams. In London the wrought-iron main beams were bolted together; in Munich they were riveted. In Munich strengthening of the tie members was undertaken after a few years when the opportunity arose.[123]

The dismantling of the Glass Palace became a matter of discussion in 1912. State Minister Freiherr von Soden-Fraunhofen, who was interested in its preservation, enumerated its uses to date: five industrial exhibitions, 32 art exhibitions, 26 agricultural exhibitions, four arts-and-crafts exhibitions, and an electrical-goods exhibition. In addition, plays were staged and festivals held. The large number and di-

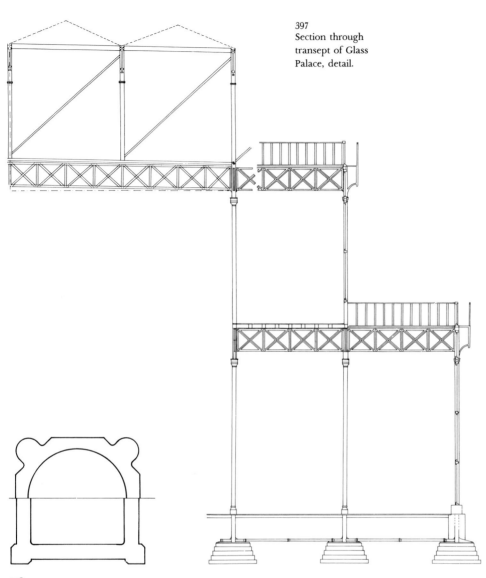

397
Section through
transept of Glass
Palace, detail.

398
Section through col-
umn of Glass Palace.

399
Detail of cast-iron
braced girder of
Glass Palace, show-
ing joint with
column.

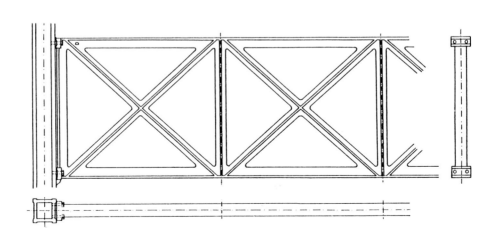

versity of uses put to the test the modern concept of a space that could be used for many purposes. The Glass Palace burned down in 1931 (fig. 651).

Sources: Münchner Stadtmuseum; Stadtarchiv München.

References: Roth 1971; Wittek 1964; *Zeitschrift des Vereins zur Ausbildung der Gewerke*, 1854, vol. 3, parts 1–4, pp. 1–3; Hütsch Volker, *Der Münchner Glaspalast 1854–1931* (Munich, 1980).

Munich

Residenz
Winter Gardens (figs. 400–402, 652–655)

In exoticism, the winter gardens of the Bavarian kings Maximilian II and Ludwig II were not inferior to the other buildings of these kings. To build a winter garden—complete with tropical plants, pagodas, summer houses, lakes with swans, and painted landscape vistas—on top of an existing palace could only be the idea of a visionary.

Numerous designs for winter gardens in the southern and northern parts of the Residenz testify to the intensity with which the combination of a glass-and-iron building and an existing piece of prestige architecture was pursued and an appreciation for the new building material, iron.

If one neglects the external appearance, in which the solid masonry of Renaissance architecture is combined with a glass vault, one can compare figures 652 and 655 with the middle-class prestige architecture of public buildings, such as floras, arcades, and railway stations. However, if one disregards the purpose of this building, it appears that the glasshouse was used as a shell to cover a romantic interior that could be enjoyed only by the king and his court.

Private winter gardens were as a rule joined directly with the living accommodation and set out adjacent to the house. The concept of a winter garden on the roof was a venturesome undertaking and a break with current architectural schemes. With the collaboration of August von Voit there arose two winter gardens which are important both spatially and structurally. The information on these winter gardens is very sparse and controversial. The exact layout of the buildings can be surmised only from plans and photographs of the northern one (fig. 400).

The winter garden in the southern part of the Residenz was built facing the Max-Joseph-Platz, near the entrance to the New Residenz Theater and the State Theater, in 1854. The architects, Franz Jakob Kreuter and August von Voit, had put a series of projects to Maximilian II before one of them was chosen and

put into effect. Communicating with the "Yellow Staircase," the monumental entrance to the apartments of Ludwig II, the winter garden was designed with a length of 203 feet and a width of 108 feet. In order to reduce the great width of the span, the iron structure was executed in the form of a three-bay hall. The central bay, spanning 59 feet and built as a continuous glass roof, was supported on cast-iron columns which were placed in rows 21 feet apart. The lean-to roof was carried by wrought-iron braced rafters. The winter garden sheltered a tropical landscape laid out in the form of an English garden, with a pagoda built at the south end. An open stairway led directly into the anteroom, onto which the Yellow Staircase and the suite of rooms adjoined (fig. 401). This building was demolished in 1900.

The second large winter garden, built between 1867 and 1869, was commissioned by Ludwig II. This glass-roofed three-story structure faced the palace gardens on the north and the Kaiserhof on the south. The architects, August von Voit and Karl von Effner, built on the T-shaped ground plan of the existing masonry building below a 56-foot-wide barrel vault of iron and glass. (fig. 402). This was an extremely bold undertaking. It was not only a matter of transmitting the great weight of the soil and at the same time keeping the moisture within it, but also a matter of transmitting the weight of the vault to the old masonry. The problem was probably solved by inserting beneath the soil some anchors to hold the iron girders together.

Arched braced girders with three degrees of freedom formed the roof trusses of this winter garden. These were fitted on the floor along the external wall, 4½ feet apart. (Arched ribs were quite exceptional at the start of the 1840s; they did not come into common use until the development of the iron bridge.) The upper and lower flanges of the braced girders consisted of rolled U-section iron. (According to Karl Wittek there is a remaining piece of the iron ribs of the 1854 winter garden still in existence in Nuremberg, in the factory premises of Mannesmann AG. From the results of his research, which includes a test of the actual material used, the sections appear to have been made of rolled puddled iron.[124]) The glazing was on the inside and the outside, and was integral with the space frame. The ventilation was via a flat lantern. The structural members of the space frame glittered through the glass skin without standing out too boldly. A continuous glass vault almost 230 feet long provided the space for a magnificent tropical landscape. An illusion of depth was created with the help of murals depicting mountain scenery. From the plans and photographs in the ar-

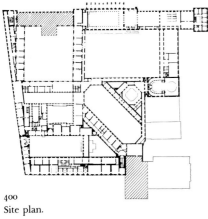

400
Site plan.

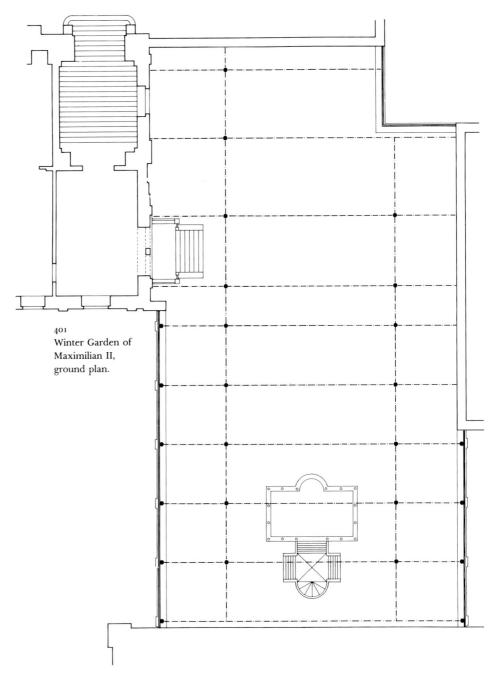

401
Winter Garden of
Maximilian II,
ground plan.

402
Winter Garden of
Ludwig II, ground
plan and section.

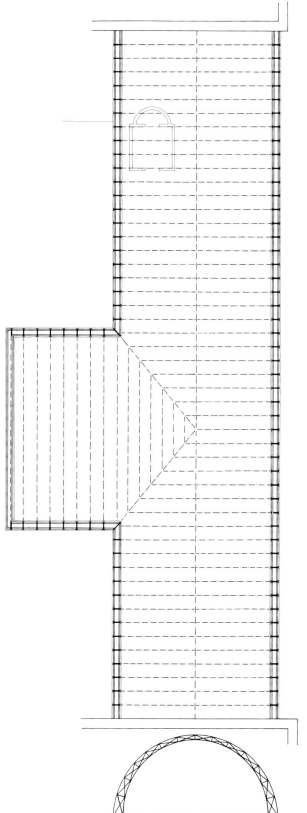

chives it is evident that kiosks, a blue silk marquee, a fisherman's hut, a lake with a waterfall, and swans all heightened the exotic nature of the landscape (fig. 654). This building was demolished in 1887.

Sources: Stadtarchiv München; Bayerische Verwaltung der staatlichen Schlösser, Gärten und Seen, Schloss Nymphenburg; Geheimes Hausarchiv, Munich.

References: Wittek 1964; Ranke 1977.

Munich

Old Botanical Garden, Luisen-/Sophienstrasse
Great Palm House (figs. 403–408, 642–645)
length: 259 feet
greatest width: 49 feet
greatest height: 59 feet
architect: August von Voit
built 1860–1865
demolished

The Great Palm House was, in its technical and architectural execution, one of the most important glasshouses of its time. With its rich decorative fittings made of cast iron, it was one of the most splendid buildings of its kind in Germany. Voit's experience in the field of exhibition buildings, particularly the Munich Glass Palace, is seen here in the structure of the space frame, especially in the design of the braced ribs. The iron space frame was, except in a few places, outside the glass of the facades and the roof.

The original intention was to use the structural parts of the Glass Palace for the building of the Great Palm House. This scheme foundered because of the continued use of the Glass Palace for exhibition purposes and because of the high costs that demolition and reassembly would have involved. This intention highlights the close relationship between conservatory and exhibition buildings—which shared not only the extensive use of mass production but also similar purposes (the display of the contents)—and demonstrates that the exhibition building, which stemmed from the hothouse, fed back to hothouse design the experience gained in the course of its development.

The Great Palm House was built in the northern part of the Old Botanical Garden, near the Glass Palace. The major axis of the palm house was placed parallel to that of the Glass Palace. The front of the glasshouse faced south; its north-facing rear side was protected by the botanical museum, as shown in figures 404–407.

The form and the construction of the two parts of the building, conservatory and museum, were determined by their functions. The architect grasped this well, and combined the two parts into an architectural unity. The contrast between filigree iron structures and solid masonry work, as already practiced in classicism, was used here on the grand scale. The complex was given a solid basement, which was built in the form of a terrace toward the south of the garden. The heating plant, the workshops, and the storerooms were here. In front of the building and toward the garden there were two smaller conservatories and an aquarium aligned at right angles to the Great Palm House and the Glass Palace.

The Great Palm House, which was designed to accommodate treelike tropical plants and palms more than 40 feet high,[125] was built on a square base, which was vaulted over with a 49-foot-diameter dome, without further supporting members. The long roof, hipped at the ends, adjoined the dome. The columns, the cornices, the gallery beams, and the horizontal flanges of the line of girders along the exterior of the front were made of cast iron; all the other metal used in the construction was wrought iron or iron plate. The main ribs of the dome were braced girders, supported in the upper gallery by cast-iron double columns. These braced ribs were some of the earliest examples of two-hinge arches. The railings, too, were built of braced beams. The eastern and western walls of the square were carried in the same way by the railings of the lower gallery. The main ribs of the dome—the arched braced girders—joined at the apex to form a ring-shape lantern.

The braced girders developed as balustrades had the function of load-bearing members, supporting part of the weight of the facade and reinforcing it. We can therefore correctly regard the Great Palm House as an early iron-frame building. The two wings were built outward, with a 32½-foot-wide central structure having a ridge roof, a ridge-shaped pavilion, and a semicircular end structure. All the main ribs of the roofs were made of braced girders, which in the lean-to roof parts were supported on one side by cast-iron I-section stanchions and on the other by cast-iron plates. The lean-to roof sloped downward at an angle of 18° and ran without a break via a 12-inch-radius curve in the vertical wall. This transition was accomplished through the use of curved iron sheet.

Voit described the construction principle as follows:

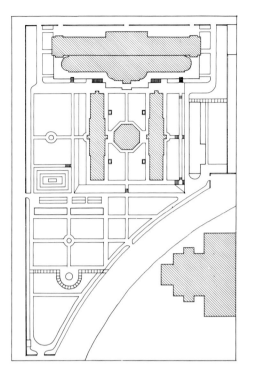

403
Site plan, 1867.

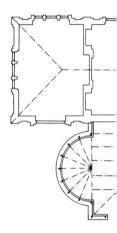

In order to reduce the heat-flow losses caused by the internal and external temperature difference for such good heat conductors as glass and iron, all the external skin has been double-glazed, and indeed in such a way that the structural parts of the outer skin are almost completely separate from those of the inner and are in contact at only a few points. The joints, which are made at every [6 feet] height, have at the same time to create a continuous flat horizontal glass barrier which impedes the circulation of the layer of air between the inner and outer glass skins and therefore helps to equalize the temperatures. There is a [4.8-inch] space between the inside and outside glass skins. With smaller separation the heat escapes too quickly, but with greater separation circulation of the intervening layer of air can occur. Because the dripping of condensation from the inside of the roof is known to be harmful to plants, to prevent this the sheet-metal gutters were laid below the projecting structural members. However, these brought in other disadvantages, and apart from them the iron structures and gutters are obtrusive and do not add to the beauty of the buildings. One therefore thought of avoiding the use of horizontal joints as much as possible, also any vertical drip-point projections from the cooling surfaces, and has transferred all load-bearing iron members to the outer skin. The internal skin is therefore not interrupted by any structural members and is only supported by T-section sash bars. All the glass panes be-

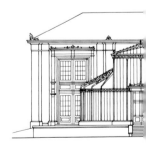

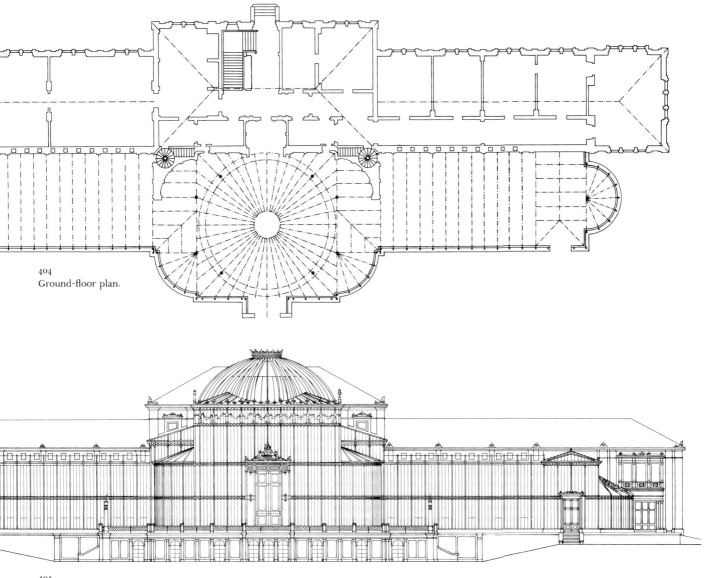

404
Ground-floor plan.

405
Elevation of garden
side.

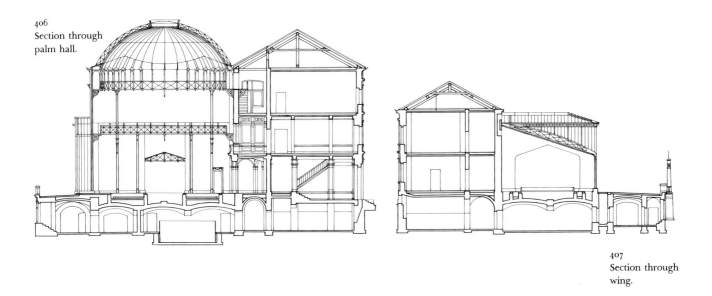

406
Section through
palm hall.

407
Section through
wing.

408
Detail of ornamental
cast-iron work of
palm hall.

tween them are butt-jointed together, not lapped, so as not to hinder the downward flow of drops of condensation. The glass panes of the external skin have been given a downward convex profile and are concave upward, forming a gutter to discharge the water down the middle, and they overlap each other from opposite sides to a depth of [0.6 inch] without the use of putty or other material. Each upper sheet is attached to the one below it by metal glazing clips firmly pressed to the sash bars and to the ridge, with the crevices plugged with linseed-oil putty.[126]

The boilers were accommodated in the basement of the building. The hot-water pipes were laid 2 feet deep in brickwork channels, covered by iron gratings. To bring the cold air descending at the outer walls into the circulation system, there were branching channels leading off the main ones toward the basement wall and discharging hot air there. These too were covered with iron gratings. The entire heating plant was made by Haag of Augsburg. A contemporary observer noted that "the ventilation must be more powerful in the tropical houses than in the temperate houses. To this end the basement wall is pierced every [9 feet, 4 inches] by openings [12 inches] wide and [6 inches] high, which can be closed with cast-iron shutters. In addition, the sliding glass panes in the upper ring of the palm house's dome can be moved by mechanical means. There are also two ventilating louvers in each of the east and west walls at the level of the upper gallery. To renew the air in the tropical and temperate houses there are further openings in the north side masonry wall below the lean-to roof, which communicate by conduits with the outside air and which can be closed from the inside by shutters. A window on rollers on the south wall of the temperate house can be moved in each space between the sash bars; in the tropical house only half of the area has this arrangement."[127]

Sources: Münchner Stadtmuseum; Stadtarchiv München.

Paris

Jardin des Plantes
Conservatories (figs. 409–416, 656–658)
length: 262 feet each (pavilion: 66 feet)
width: 66 feet
height: 49 feet with base
architect: Charles Rohault de Fleury
built 1833

The conservatories in the Jardin des Plantes were among the largest glasshouses of their time. In them were combined the cubic forms used on the Continent and the curvilinear glass roof structures favored in Britain. The contrast of the plane surfaces of the

corner pavilions with the downward-sweeping glass vaults produced a seductive beauty and was praised by the contemporary world.

A natural slope was skillfully used to make terraces. Similarly shaped hothouses, arranged like mirror images, formed the axis of the layout, which was reached via an imposing ramp. The buildings were made up of simple geometric forms. The glass vaults were framed by a stepped glass cube, and at one end were cut into by diagonal steps; at the other end they were terminated by the large corner pavilion. This interplay of cubic forms, brought into prominence by the use of the new materials, corresponds in essence to Le Corbusier's early definition of the architecture of the New Objectivity.

A report dated 1868 describes the Jardin des Plantes as follows:

The Parisian Jardin des Plantes, which embraces on its site the whole range of natural sciences, is one of the most beautiful places for strolling in the whole world and combines the pleasing with the useful. Originally laid out by Guy de la Brosse, the physician to Ludwig XIII, it was greatly extended a hundred years later by the natural-history researcher Buffon. The most important men of science, like Winzlow, Jussieu, Fourcroy, Bernadin de Sainte-Pierre, Cuvier, Geoffroy-Saint-Hilaire, taught at this institute and laid the basis for its worldwide reputation. The zoological division captured the curiosity more, through the lively exchange of views and the life which was dominant there; but the botanical division, and particularly the forcing houses, have an exclusive and powerful attraction. These hothouses are laid out with extraordinary good taste, and combine in a relatively small space such an amount, such a wealth of plants, that one often asks oneself how it was possible to accommodate these giants of the tropical world so skillfully that they do not lack space, light, and air. The tropical-house complex is divided into four parts: the east and the west pavilions, the curvilinear pavilion, with two stories, and the Dutch forcing houses. The east pavilion has a moderate temperature and contains plants from New Zealand, New Holland, and the central plateau of Mexico. In the constant-temperature warm west pavilion the vegetation of the tropical lands unfurls its magical splendor. The plants of the Antilles, Central Africa, and India crowd together here and entwine their magnificent foliage. Beneath all these shadows a bewitching fountain from the chisel of Brion sprays its stream of water, the vapor from which even increases the temperature. Everything prospers, grows, and flowers in this stifling atmosphere. A staircase at the end of the curved forcing house leads to the upper story. There is an elegant group of marble figures at the foot of the steps. The upper story is devoted to the Euphorbiaceae from Central Africa; the cacti, and all the thick-leaved plants. This collection, the most beautiful in Europe, has been brought here from the Cape of Good Hope. There is also the Dutch forcing house, warm, and divided into three rooms, through the middle of which

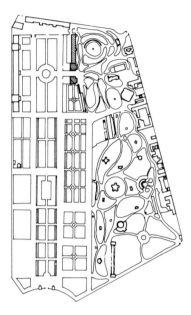

409
Site plan, 1837.

one enters. The middle room contains a large aquarium. The victoria regia, the queen of water plants, unfurls on the water of the pond, magnificent in the splendor of its large round green leaves.[128]

Before the building of these hothouses, Rohault had toured England to learn about the construction and heating of the newest hothouses there. The high technical level of the execution and the use of certain formal elements of English hothouse construction can be attributed to this visit. The exemplary workmanship evident in the prefabrication and the assembly of these conservatories led to many imitations on the Continent, for example in Liège and Ghent. Sigfried Giedion described Rohault's building in his book *Space, Time, and Architecture* as a "prototype of all large forcing houses made of iron." Giedion continued: "In contrast to the English hothouse of that time by Paxton, the strength of this high pavilion depended only on its cast iron columns and beams."[129] In fact there was no other glass-and-iron hothouse of this order of magnitude in existence at that time that was bolted together from prefabricated parts. The prefabrication showed a degree of development, in respect to the design and technology of the cast-iron work and the assembly techniques, that already matched that of Joseph Paxton's post-1850 buildings.

The conservatories consist of two large pavilions flanked by wings with curvilinear roofs. They are glazed on the front and the sides; the back wall is of masonry. Cast-iron columns 36 feet high form the supporting structure of the pavilion. They are placed along the facade and in the interior in the format of a 13-foot-square matrix. Together with the iron ribs of the roof, they constitute an important advance in the development of iron-frame buildings. The columns in the facade, which form the foundation up to the roof-gutter level, are made of at least six separate parts, bolted together one above the other. This division of the columns follows from the assembly method and from considerations of statics. A short column footing was anchored into the masonry base wall with four bolts. Above that stood the shaft, richly decorated on the outside and exposed on the inside as a hollow half-column. (Only the corner columns were made round.) The next element was a stanchion made of U sections bolted together, which served as a reinforcement in that it halved the length of the columns subject to buckling. In this horizontal framework, which ran all around the facade, there were additional half-columns. Above this were short connecting pieces with cast-iron brackets extending outward, which were fitted with a gutter to lead the rainwater to the inside of the column. The final as-

410
View of both pavil-
ions. Woodcut,
ca. 1852.

411
Copper engraving,
1837.

sembly, which carried the roof rib, was a horizontal composite beam made of U-section beams bolted together, to which was bolted a box section which served as a rainwater gutter and a gallery support. This was concealed on the outside by decorative cast-iron fascias. The inside columns, consisting of three parts bolted together, had, in contrast with the outer columns, a cruciform cross-section.

The remarkable feature of the roof structure is that the longitudinal and transverse wrought-iron beams were not assembled as primary and secondary beams, but formed an identical structure in both directions. Because of this, the roof structure was an early form of space frame. Braced girders formed the supporting elements, which followed the profile of the roof, and which were reinforced in the middle by crossed diagonal elements. A ridge lantern rested on this structure and served for ventilation. The roof structure was supported on masonry at the back. The curvilinear wings consisted of two stories, one located to the side of and below the other, and 13-foot-wide galleries were trussed by iron bars below. This construction principle corresponds to the well-known Loudon method of prestressing beams.

According to an 1885 engraving (fig. 657), the right wing was rebuilt in 1854 as a large palm house, glazed on all sides. The exterior shape of 1833 was retained, but the interior division into two terraces was abolished. There arose a continuous interior space with a raised central glass vault and an adjacent surrounding lower glass vault. Therefore, this building (which adjoined the corner pavilion) obtained the spatial form of a basilica. The space frame of the hall consisted of arched braced girders in a filigree construction.

The tropical plants in the left pavilion and its wings, particularly the palms, needed a minimum temperature of 15°C. The right pavilion, intended as a temperate house, required a minimum temperature of 5°C. The main heating system was a steam system; a warm-air system was used as a supplement. Boilers with hot-water pipes and two steam boilers served to generate the heat. The former were installed in the basement behind the left pavilion. The heated air was ducted in through tunnels to the glass fronts and expelled upward at a temperature of 50°C. To prevent the plants from drying out, the hot air was humidified by passing it over a pool of warm water before it entered the hothouse. The two steam boilers were installed in the foundations below the hot-water boilers. The steam was fed through copper pipes in four 4-inch-diameter cast-iron tubes, which had a slight slope so that any condensed water could

413
Ground-floor plan.

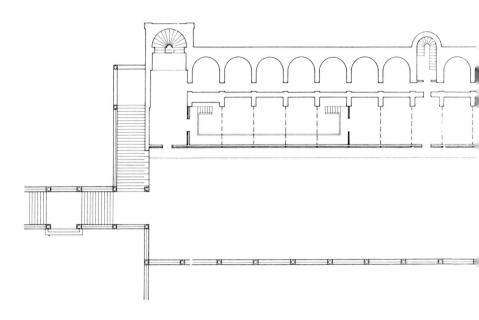

412
Structural details of
pavilion.

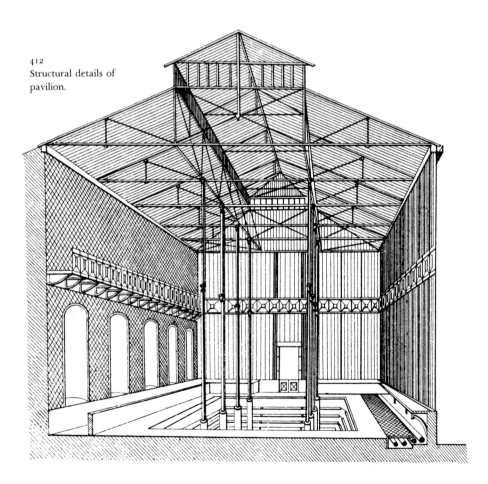

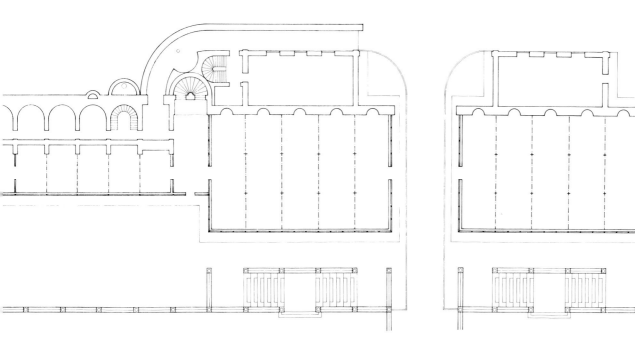

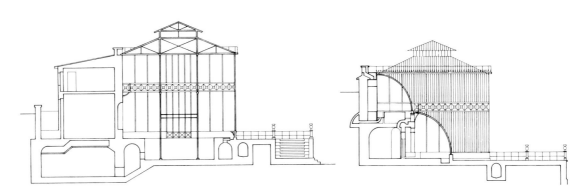

4¹4
Section through pa-
vilion and wing.

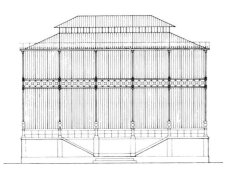

4¹5
Facade of corner
pavilion.

flow back to the boiler. The pipes ran along the facade in a channel covered with cast-iron gratings. A water-spray installation contributed to the environment. Rotatable ventilating flaps driven by a rod in the middle, and opening windows in the glass skin, provided ventilation. The windows in the lantern also had similar actuating shafts, which were operated by chains. The conservatories were single glazed.[130]

A contemporary comment on the Jardin des Plantes follows:

When one has walked through all the pathways of the landscaped garden; when one has seen all the animals in their very varied forms and habitats; when one has breathed in the scent of the plants collected from places all over the world, one has still to visit the glasshouses closed to the public, in which all the flowers and exotic plants are gathered together. These glasshouses are open to a small number of privileged people. It is a true piece of good fortune to be able to enter into these beautiful rooms, where one discovers the sense of unknown richness. There is nothing more beautiful than the interior of these glasshouses. Emerging from the dark avenues of fir trees which broaden out onto "Labyrinth Hill," one suddenly finds oneself in a hot steamy atmosphere, amongst giant vegetation which the tropical sun causes to sprout upward like green rockets from a pregnant soil. The impression created by the contrast is difficult to describe. Having entered, one experiences a deceptive illusion, which also has a further effect when one has resumed the promenade outside. The River Seine, seen from afar, is framed by these palms, these coconut trees, this banana plantation, which grow upward in the glasshouses, and it is difficult not to start dreaming about the Nile or the Ganges. The wealth of vegetation which one had just previously wondered at, the animals which one has seen, create the impression of a new world which suddenly comes to an end.[131]

Some of these buildings are extant in reconstructed condition.

Sources: Bibliothèque Nationale, Paris, Cabinet des Estampes; H. Roger-Viollet Archive, Paris.

References: Rousseau 1837; *Über Land und Meer*, 1868, 10, vol. 20, no. 20, p. 328; *Allgemeine Deutsche Bauzeitung*, 1837, vol. 20, no.33, pp. 271–274; Texier 1852–53; Neumann 1862; Giedion 1976, p. 137.

416
Palm house, Jardin des Plantes, 1854, section.

Paris

Champs-Elysées
Jardin d'Hiver (figs. 417–421, 659–664)
length: 328 feet
width: 131 feet
height: 66 feet
built 1846–1848
demolished ca. 1860

The Jardin d'Hiver evoked amazement, as did the Crystal Palace a year later. An early masterpiece of structural engineering work, it had a pervading influence on the further development of winter gardens, exhibitions, and railway stations.

Gottfried Semper, who visited the Jardin d'Hiver in its opening year, compared its glass vault to the Gothic cathedrals. City functions were held in this winter garden, in a place which the citizens had just previously been using as a promenade and a boulevard. Besides an extensive plant display with fountains and rock formations, this space contained a café, a bakery, billiards rooms, music rooms, flower stalls, bird cages, and a picture gallery.

The task of the builder of the Jardin d'Hiver was to solve the technical problems that arose from the shape of the base. There were no prototypes of such a construction at that time. The railway-station halls of that time, such as Paddington Station in London, had only simple wrought-iron ribs for the space frame. Paxton, who visited the Jardin d'Hiver in its opening year, probably received from it the stimulus to convert the Crystal Palace into a winter garden.

The Cologne Flora, which started the line of development of the German floras, took the Jardin d'Hiver as its model.

The Jardin d'Hiver was situated on the land between Rond Point and Avenue Marboeuf. In front of it stood the first Paris winter garden, built at the beginning of 1846, which the public rejected on account of its layout and which was therefore pulled down only 6 months after its completion. Only 121 feet long, 29 1/2 feet wide, and 18 feet high, this garden was not large enough to serve as a winter promenade and a social meeting place for the Parisians. Hector Horeau had already built a magnificent winter garden made entirely of glass and iron for the citizens of Lyon. Paris, "the metropolis of the nineteenth century," did not wish to be inferior. In spite of the enormous price of land in the Champs-Elysées (the cost of the site came to almost two-thirds of the total cost of the Jardin d'Hiver), the joint stock company formed in 1846 reckoned that the Jardin d'Hiver would be a profitable venture. However, this company went bankrupt in 1848 because of fraudulent speculation. Another company took over the business and continued it. Created out of speculation, the Jardin d'Hiver also fell victim to it; it was demolished in 1860.

The axial layout of the Jardin d'Hiver determined its spatial form. A nave terminating in an apse was brought together with a short transept, likewise having apses at its ends. Thus arose a building roofed by intersecting glass barrel vaults and hemidomes over the apses. The barrel vaults were supported on rows of double columns, which simultaneously carried a gallery around the interior at a height of 33 feet. The masonry, interrupted by numerous round arch windows, did not quite rise to the level of the gallery. It formed the foundation for the sides of the glass roof. The glass vault in the middle part of the nave reached down to the ground.

Gottfried Semper described the impression of space and the function of the building in a critical report dated 1849:

This beautiful establishment can serve as a model and a guiding principle for all similar buildings because its size and the richness of its layout provides experience of the costs involved. . . . The establishment has been erected and controlled by a commercial company to serve as a place of assembly and general entertainment and recreation for the fashionable world. Concerts and sometimes balls are held there every day, and particularly on Sundays and feast days, when as many as 7,000–8,000 people often are present. The company became bankrupt as a result of the February revolution and on account of fraud, and its assets were liquidated by the creditors. . . .

The whole creates a wonderful impression, for although the largest part of the winter garden serves as a concert hall and only a part of it can be used for plants, it is still an imposing sight when one steps out of the leafless and snow-covered Elysian Fields into the midst of this artificial world in its full majesty and luxuriance. The layout of the winter garden is excellent in respect to the tasteful combination of paths through the area in horizontal and vertical directions [and] the ingenious and artistic separation of the groups of plants and the lawns. The structural ironwork is partly concealed by climbing plants, and the diversity and splendor of the latter arouse wonder.

Facing the middle of the large lawn stands a Chilean pine, a wonderful tree, which is [49 feet] hight and which cost 10,000 francs. What distinguishes the winter garden from other treasures of the plant kingdom in particular is its very rich camellia collection. In March 1849 more than 200,000 flowering camellias were on display. The garden is approximately [656 feet] long, [131 feet] wide, and [66 feet] high. Entering through the beautiful vestibule, in which there are cloakrooms and closets, one reaches a long anteroom in which paintings and various decorative objects for gardens are displayed for sale and the most popular newspapers are set out for sale. In this anteroom there are also the steps to the staircase by which one reaches the upper rooms and the gallery, which on great occasions are used as assembly rooms and for banqueting. From this anteroom one enters the garden. One stands on a raised platform, from which fourteen tiers lead down to the orchestra pit in which concerts are held. This platform runs around the garden and is planted with laurels and orange trees, as well as having countless groups of potted plants which surround the symmetrically laid out statues, vases, and fountains. The large fireplaces installed in both apses offer a very pleasant meeting place.

There are various basement rooms adjoining the concert hall, for skittles, billiards, and other games. These rooms are located under the platform of the semicircle to the right of the entrance. Correspondingly below the platform of the left semicircle there are practice rooms for the musicians, dressing rooms for vocalists, etc. The temperature of the winter garden is kept at an average of 12°C. The water in the fountains and springs has the same temperature. The true garden part starts beyond the rooms kept available for concerts and dances, and here is gathered together an assortment of the most beautiful plants from the five continents, planted on open ground. The lawn, which forms a fresh evergreen carpet, joins the tree and plant sections and is traversed by irregular curved footpaths strewn with yellow sand. Aquatic plants, set out in separated ponds here and there, spread their succulent leaves over the still water and the hidden depths. The adjoining paths are also enhanced with flowers on trellises. . . . and in a concealed room stands a birdcage populated with richly and brightly feathered exotic forest dwellers.[132]

417
Site plan, 1849.

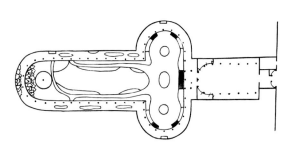

418
Section through
nave.

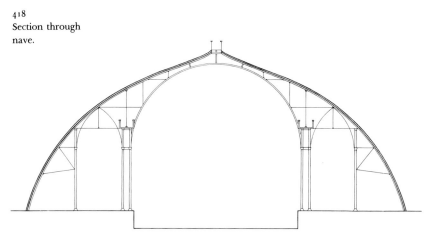

The space frame of the glass roof consisted of wrought-iron ribs, supported on the inside by extraordinarily slender pairs of cast-iron columns joined together. It was supported on the outside by a masonry foundation, well provided with windows, and in the nave by separate columns. The inner pairs of columns were reinforced horizontally by the gallery at a height of 33 feet. The crossing was spanned by two diagonal braced ribs. The supports in the crossing consisted of four columns joined together. If one considers the section of the nave, one is impressed by its lightness and by the way in which it was constructed. One may assume that the structure was conceived as a single braced rib, 131 feet long, extending down to the ground. Its upper flange carried the flatly vaulted glass bell on top, and when the whole was seen in section it was seen as an assemblage of three aisles created by the structural arrangement of the row of columns (figs. 418, 662). Fifty tons of cast iron and 81 tons of wrought iron were used.

The short construction time of 8 months suggests that there was a thoroughly worked out construction plan. The name of the builder is uncertain. John Hix[133] and Sigfried Giedion say it was Hector Horeau. Semper names the engineer Moehly and the architects Meynadier and Charpentier. The engineer Rigolet was named as the builder in an 1860 article in *Architecture pratique*.

The glass panes were fastened together with S-shaped metal glazing clips. The glazing was single, as was the general practice in France. Condensation from the damp atmosphere in the Jardin d'Hiver was so prevalent that gutters had to be hung below the glass to remove the water.[134]

The heating system consisted of two steam boilers of 40 horsepower each and a smaller one of 8 horsepower. There were also two steam engines to oper-

ate the pumps. Only one of these was in use at a given time; the other was kept in reserve in case the first failed. All the pumps had backups as well.

A contemporary critique of the Jardin d'Hiver follows:

The structure of the building is a simple one, but neither in technical nor in artistic aspects could it be called perfect. All the ironwork is painted white, which is highly deleterious to the base columns. A gallery runs all round the winter garden, above the columns, which is used partly to display plants aloft, partly to provide the best means of distributing the artificial rain, finally to carry the candles and other forms of illumination used on great festive occasions. Gas is not used for lighting because it has been found to have a harmful effect on the plants. The illumination is by wax candles. Were the company in a better financial state, it would have by now installed oil lamps or resin gas, which does not harm the plants. Heating is by steam, which is circulated through copper tubes, because the hot-water heating system which was installed initially was not sufficient for this large space. The waterwork system is excellent. It is operated by an 8 horsepower steam engine.

Two fountains stand just by the entrance, and opposite them two more. Then there is a cascade with statues in the most distant part of the rotunda. A waterfall cascades over an artificial mass of rock, and from out of the pond in front of it there rises a 60-foot-high jet of water. All this is operated by a few small machines and gives the whole a fairy-like charm, particularly in the stillness of the twilight where these waterworks bring about a lively sound in the high-vaulted glass dome. The effect of sunshine on the garden is very beautiful, but it seems even better in the moonlight, when the light of the moon is reflected in the rising water, dark shadows are cast on the smooth shimmering lawn, and tender sounds come from the galleries. One believes oneself to be transported to a dreamworld and to be surrounded by fairies and other elemental spirits. In no other places have I heard the music sound so pleasant. The elastic glass vault forms a true resonant body, and the sounds have a force, brightness, and liveliness which could not be achieved in any other way. "The building of the Winter Garden," says the published guide, "is a triumph of private industry. In

419
Ground-floor plan.

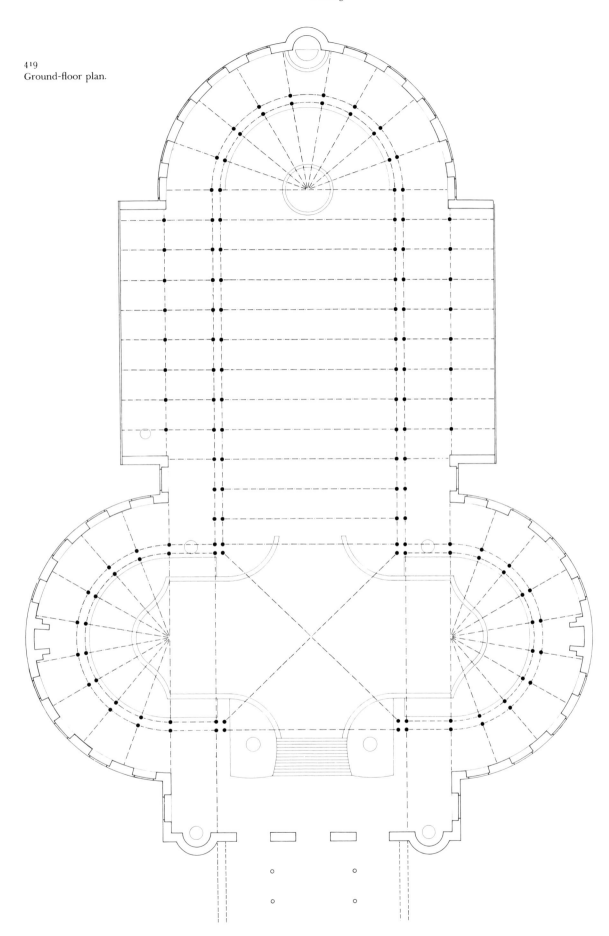

421
Section through nave, showing fountain.

less than three quarters of a year a palace has been raised up, 120 feet wide, 300 feet long, almost 60 feet high, built entirely of glass and iron, a palace, the construction of which demanded a covered surface of 3,000 square feet, in which 100,000 pounds of cast iron and 165,000 pounds of wrought iron were used. This palace has been erected within a period of 8 months, with all its rooms, above and below ground, its numerous appendages, its large buildings, and its shops, apparatus, and machines. The sum spent on the building is modest in comparison with that which the hothouses of the gardens required. . . .

The first winter garden was built in Paris in 1845, but was much smaller. The new winter garden occupied the same site as the old and is located in the large boulevard of the Champs-Elysées. The peristyle, decorated with four beautiful caryatids by Klagmann, forms a receding semicircle. Next to it is a large room, intended for the display of objets d'art; to this adjoins a curved open staircase, by which one descends to the garden. The first view astounds one. The arrangement and the general plan of the building lets itself be best compared with a Gothic church with its nave and transept. The transept part is represented by an elongated oval, which is called figuratively the rotunda, and stands out prominently above the average width of the garden of 120 feet × 30 feet. The garden, moreover, has all the imposing ground dimensions of a cathedral, almost the height as well, and, in order to make the analogy complete, an upper gallery of a truly airy form which runs 30 feet above the ground and which seems to be suspended in midair. The flowers and shrubs on display therein give the appearance of the hanging gardens of Semiramis. The masonry walls with numerous windows extend almost up to the gallery. The roof and the dome are entirely of glass, which is supported on cast-iron beams and braced frameworks. Four vases form some of the most beautiful decoration in the garden . . . ; also very beautiful are the two Renaissance fireplaces. The heating was by two 25 horsepower steam engines, which worked on unnoticed in the basement. The cost of the plants was 300,000 francs. Included in that cost is an Araucaria excelsa; next to this is a most remarkable group of fifteen palms. Combined with the garden are numerous associated outbuildings, a reading room, a coffeehouse, a shop selling fine soaps, a locale for the exhibiting of paintings, a concert hall, several restaurants, [and] other facilities. The original design was by Mr. Meynadier, but the execution of it was by the company, which placed the commission for the building of the winter garden in the hands of the architect Charpentier.[135]

Source: Cabinet des Estampes, Bibliothèque Nationale, Paris.

References: *Zeitschrift für praktische Baukunst*, 1849, vol. 9, pp. 516–526; *Moniteur des Architectes*, 694; 11, vol. 58, pl. 693, 694; Texier 1852–53, pp. 9, 10; *The Gardener's Chronicle*, 14.2.1846, vol. 6, no. 7, p. 102.

Paris

Hall of 1855 World Exhibition (fig. 422)

architects: C. F. Viel, Alexis Barrault, Bridel
built 1855
demolished

The building constructed for the Paris Industrial Exhibition of 1855 had a three-bay layout with a nave 121 feet wide and aisles each spanning 79 feet. After the exhibition, the nave was made into a winter garden adorned by statues and by a winding stream with an arched bridge. The ironwork of the barrel vault consisted of braced ribs made as two-hinge arches. The latticework of the ribs placed close together above two rows of columns created a heavy effect. The ribs rested on downward-pointing cast-iron shoes which had to transmit the roof load. Continuous purlins provided longitudinal reinforcement.

References: Wittek 1964, p. 55; *Illustrated London News*, 9.7.1859, 18, vol. 35, no. 982, p. 28.

Paris

1900 World Exhibition
Garden Hall (figs. 424–426, 667, 668)

length: 277 feet (each pavilion)
width: 111 1/2 feet
height: 66 feet
architect: Charles Albert Gautier
built 1900
demolished

Here is an example of the enhancement of the glasshouse from its status as a simple piece of objective building to that of a prestigious exhibition building. Two glass halls, built as mirror images of each other, were laid out parallel to the bank of the River Seine. Gautier conceived a space between the two halls as an open terrace, from which a wide stairway led down to the Seine. The whole complex had a length of 778 feet.

The shape of the hall, twice as high as it was wide, was determined by the richly decorated ribs, which complemented the oriental aspect of the exterior. The restrained and delicately executed structure did not become—like the other iron-frame buildings of the World Exhibition—a decorative end in itself, but permitted a clear understanding of the spatial concept. In spite of the great expenditure on decoration, this was one of the few late hothouse buildings to do justice to the materials iron and glass.

422
Winter garden of
1855 World Exhibi-
tion. Engraving,
1859.

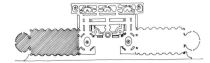

423
Site plan of 1900
World Exhibition.

424
View of Garden Hall
from the Seine.
Engraving.

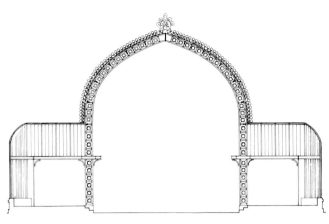

426
Section of Garden
Hall.

425
Ground-floor plan of
Garden Hall.

The 59-foot-wide hall was formed by high ribs running from the ridge down to the ground. Braced girders of rolled steel made up the two-hinge arches. The space frame was held together by narrow 26-foot-long lattice purlins in the longitudinal direction. Additional narrow ribs prevented any outward bulging of these purlins. The sash bars of the glass vault stretched above the main space frame. Semicircular apses with vertical barrel vaults at the sides between the main ribs increased the interior space. This spatial concept corresponded to that of a Baroque church. A glass vault on an elliptical base was attached to the outer end of each wing; these were connected to the main halls by short corridors with pointed arch roofs. Highly decorated iron minarets were attached to the corners of the two halls.

Source: Cabinet des Estampes, Bibliothèque Nationale, Paris.

References: Meyer 1907, p. 123; Durm and Ende 1902, part 1, p. 373; Schild 1967, pp. 164 ff.

Pau

Jardin Public
Winter Garden (figs. 669, 670)
architect: Bertrand
built ca. 1898
demolished

Around the turn of the century, after the series of glass-and-iron hothouses and exhibition buildings had in essence come to an end and new space forms seemed to be exhausted, the architect of the winter garden in Pau tried to create a kind of glass grotto. Among solid buildings in the conservative style of Beaux-Arts architecture he erected on an elliptical base a glass pavilion containing a palmarium, a café, a casino, and a music hall. An elliptical ring of sixteen iron columns supported a glass dome resembling an overturned boat. On the outside it carried a ring-shaped vault, which stood on the iron frame-

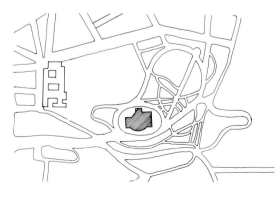

427
Site plan, 1910.

work of the facade and on masonry work. This iron vault formed a gallery around the elliptical central hall. The Expressionistic effect of this glass architecture originated from the intersection of the inner dome and the ring dome. Pointed arch vaults extended between the columns and were anchored into box-shaped capitals. The vertical curved sash bars that formed the load-bearing structure of the vault were robust in comparison with their English forerunners. Glass barrel vaults running down to the capitals gave the glasshouse its exotic grottolike aspect. The Winter Garden had a wide projecting glass roof on the outside, which, together with the elliptical dome rising beyond it, was an allusion to the main building of the Paris World Exhibition.

Reference: McGrath and Frost 1961.

Pavia

Orto Botanico
Conservatory (figs. 428–431, 671, 672)
length: 171 feet
width: 23 feet

The Orto Botanico was one of the oldest and most important botanical gardens in Europe. The Orto dei Semplici, a medicinal-plant garden, was founded in 1556, and in 1763 or 1764 the first professorial chair of "Botanica Generale" was established. To serve the growing needs of science, a glasshouse was built in 1776 by G. Piermarini, mostly of wood. A year later, L. Canonica rebuilt this glasshouse with iron window frames in an attempt to solve the problem of the rapid rotting of wooden sashes in a humid environment. This was the first, hesitant step in the effort to use durable material in constructing the sloping glass surfaces that are so important to the efficient use of sunlight.

The use of stone to make rafters for the sloping plane of the windows brought the need for additional support to reduce the bending moment. Small round stone columns with capitals and bases were used for this purpose.

The conservatory, which comprised two wings and an architecturally accentuated portal, divided the Orto Botanico in two. The large sloping glass surfaces were supported on small brackets at the cornice. The building (now demolished) is noteworthy less for its architecture than for its place in the history of glasshouse development.

Source: archives of Orto Botanico, Pavia.

Reference: Giacomini 1962.

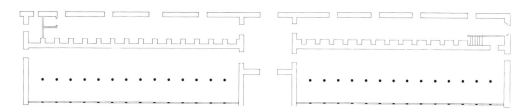

428
Ground plan of
Orto Botanico
conservatory.

429
Section.

430
Front elevation.

431
View from the gar-
dens. Engraving,
ca. 1800.

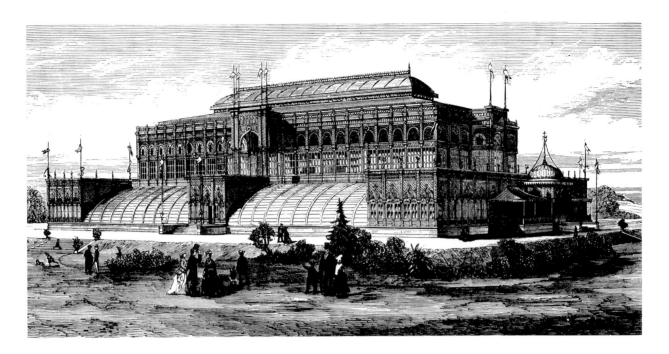

Philadelphia

World Exhibition, 1876
Horticultural Hall (fig. 432)

architects: Hermann J. Schwarzmann, G. R. Pohl

built 1876

demolished

The Horticultural Hall of the 1876 World Exhibition in Philadelphia was an example of the turning away from the practical form of the large glasshouses built between 1850 and 1860. Its engineering features were concealed by a profusion of historicizing ornamentation, which was no longer a method of expressing the structure.

The Horticultural Hall was described as follows in a contemporary report:

The Horticultural Hall is built of iron and glass in the Moorish style of the twelfth century, and in later years it will be one of the most beautiful ornamental buildings in the West Park. The building has a length of [384 feet] and a width of [190 feet], and the height of the apex of the lantern (an elegantly built roof light) is [72 feet]. The conservatory proper is in the middle of the building, and has a length of [231 feet], a width of [80 feet], and a height of [55 feet], above which there is the lantern [170 feet] long, [20 feet] wide, and [14 feet] high. The main structure of the building consists of a decorative arrangement of solid columns which are [10 feet] apart and [20 feet] high. The bases of these columns are marble, the shafts brightly colored moulded bricks, and the capitals richly carved sandstone,

and the arches between are also of brickwork. There is a [5-foot-wide] gangway at a height of [20 feet] along the sides of the inner glasshouse. On the north and south longer sides of the glasshouse and separated from it by a wide passage there are four hothouses, each [100 feet] long and [14 feet] high, with curvilinear glass roofs, which are divided in the center by a [30-foot-wide] richly ornamented vestibule. On the short front there are similar vestibules, and at both sides of these there are large [30-foot-high] rooms which are intended for use as restaurants, reception rooms, and offices. Elegant steps lead from the vestibules to the four external galleries, [100 feet] long and [10 feet] wide, which are supported by the iron ribs of the curvilinear roofs of the hothouses. From these galleries one can reach the ceilings of the above-mentioned rooms on the short sides of the buildings; they form with these a large promenade. . . . There is access to the east and west entrances by steps of blue marble from the terraces.

Reference: *Über Land und Meer*, 1876, 18, vol. 35, no. 20, pp. 400, 402.

432
Woodcut of Horticultural Hall at Philadelphia.

San Francisco

Conservatory (fig. 673)

A high octagonal pavilion with a glass dome forms the core of this cast-iron-frame conservatory, built around 1890. Eight cast-iron columns carry the dome, rising above a tambour with a projecting iron ridge. A glass vault adjoining the tambour is supported on the framework of the vertical lower walls, so that there is a central space in the interior with a surrounding gallery. The lower wings adjoin this on both sides, and likewise have curvilinear roofs. The restrained cast-iron decoration restricts itself to setting off the structural elements. The building is extant.

Sezincote

Indian Villa
Conservatory (fig. 674)

The Indian Villa at Sezincote, designed in 1806 by Samuel P. Cockerell in the "Indian style" for his brother-in-law, had a conservatory attached to it. The building of this conservatory was stimulated and assisted by Humphrey Repton.

A glass corridor adjoining the villa forms an arc, with fan-tracery pointed-arch glass windows, and ends at an octagonal pavilion with minaret lanterns and small, slender corner towers. The sash bars were made of cast iron to a very high standard. The pillars between the windows are on masonry foundations.

In 1817, J. C. Loudon proposed extending the conservatory by the addition of curvilinear glass roofs, with domes on the end pavilions. Loudon's design (fig. 433) suggested the possibility of taking up the Indian style in glass and iron.[136]

The building is extant and well maintained.

Sheffield

Botanical Gardens
Glass Pavilion (figs. 434, 435, 675–679)

The botanical gardens at Sheffield were founded in 1833 on the initiative of a group of eighty citizens who had formed a Botanical and Horticultural Society. A competition was announced for the design of the glasshouse, and Joseph Paxton, who was well known as a specialist in glasshouse construction, was one of the judges. The winner of the second prize, B. B. Taylor, who had proposed a vaulted glass dome, was entrusted with the execution of the building work.

The glass pavilions were built with great care (the masonry work comprised three different kinds of stone) and were filled with an impressive collection of tropical plants for the time. The 1849 inventory lists 240 species of tropical and subtropical plants.

Financial difficulties in 1844 compelled the founding society to sell the gardens to the newly formed Second Sheffield Botanical and Horticultural Society, for £9,000. The Second Society raised the capital needed by selling 1,800 shares for £5 each. Every shareholder obtained a family ticket entitling him and his family to visit the gardens at any time.

From 1844 to 1897 the Society organized great festive occasions for the public on four days every year. A theater and a comic-opera house were built. The gardens were the scene of receptions and banquets, and the Glass Pavilion housed many of these activities.

The Glass Pavilion, with its filigree glass dome built above cast-iron supports, is one of the oldest surviving examples of a technically advanced engineering structure that has as its object the spanning of a wide space by a curvilinear glass roof. The stone foundation corresponds to the traditional type of prestige architecture, and this makes a great contrast

433
J. C. Loudon, curvilinear conservatory, extension to Indian Villa at Sezincote (project, ca. 1817).

434
Site plan, 1930.

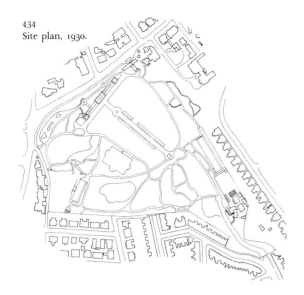

435
Lithograph, 1836.

with the transparent glass dome. The ribwork formed by the extremely slender wrought-iron sash bars following the fall line makes the space frame of the roof unique. We have here before our eyes in a single example the development of Loudon's work and of Turner's Dublin and Belfast buildings. The plastic form of the glass-and-iron structure, which appears as if it had been pushed upward by internal forces, is held together by iron tie rods attached to a surrounding architrave. This is carried by slender cast-iron columns, which, concealed on the outside, are fixed behind the masonry work. The stone pilasters of the facade and the solid walls of the north side, are not directly load bearing but serve only as necessary buttressing. The form of the hipped glass dome on the rectangular base reminds one of the main vault of the Great Conservatory at Chatsworth (built in the same year), which was made with wooden ribs. It was at Sheffield that this form was first technically perfected in an iron structure.

The central pavilion is 52 1/2 feet long, 33 feet wide, and 33 feet high. The aesthetic effect of the glasshouse is increased by the powerful coherence of the high central and corner pavilions and by the low connecting corridors between them. Whereas the pavilions are covered with airy curvilinear roofs, the corridors are covered with simple ridge-and-furrow glass roofs much like that of Paxton's victoria regia house at Chatsworth. By this spatial and structural arrangement one of the most beautiful early glasshouses in Britain was created. Since the demolition of the connecting corridors it can no longer be considered complete, but the remaining part is well maintained. The building is, in its original concept, the living representative of the progressive state of British glasshouse construction around 1836. Here Loudon's theoretical approach to converting the glass skin and its sash bars into a space frame by itself was combined with the rationality of a prefabricated, industrially produced building.

Source: Head Office, Recreation Department, Sheffield.

Reference: A. L. Winning, ed., *The Botanical Gardens, A Brief History* (Sheffield, 1970).

Strasbourg

New Botanical Garden
Great Conservatory (figs. 437–440)

length: 246 feet
width: 43 feet
height: 66 feet
architect: Hermann Eggert
built 1877–1882
demolished at end of century

The Great Conservatory in Strasbourg was a pavilion-type building constructed of simple geometrical forms and with strict objectivity. The narrower purposes of academic teaching and of scientific research were in the main decisive for the layout of the hothouses at Strasbourg. Besides that, an effort was made to present a rich picture of the plant kingdom to the public. The latter was the reason for the building of the Great Conservatory.

The symmetrically laid out Great Conservatory, with its numerous corners, can be regarded as representative of a hothouse type consisting of a central pavilion, two wings, and corner pavilions, and provided with solidly built side rooms. The middle part of the building was a tropical house; the two ends with the corner pavilions served as temperate houses. The building appears, with the simple, straight planes of its facades and roofs, more like a Continental hothouse. According to the report of the architect, Eggert, the simple cubic forms were called for by the intention to simplify the shadowing effect by limiting the number of projecting parts and by the use of plane surfaces for the roofs to keep the operating and maintenance costs low. "The use of

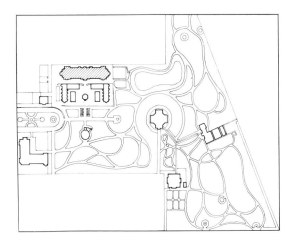

436
Site plan, 1887.

curved roof surfaces has been entirely avoided, because . . . the replacement of curved glass panes entails great difficulty and greater cost [and because] protection from the cold is much easier with plane roofs, especially when solid eaves are used, as in the present instance."[137] Also, the choice of straight roofs allowed the use of rolled iron section and mass-produced glass. The powerful accenting of the subordinate building elements, such as gangways and fireplaces, emphasized the functions of the building as a laboratory and a "plant factory."

Wrought iron (in combination with cast iron in some structural members) was used for the space frame, particularly for the columns supporting the high elements. The 66-foot-high middle pavilion had cast-iron columns arranged in pairs on an octagonal base. The inner ring of columns carried, on braced beams, the tambour, the sloping polygonal roof, and the lantern. The outer ring of columns supported the lower part of the facade and the eaves. Round wrought-iron arches, springing from the capitals of the columns, supported the load of the central structure. Braced girders with curved bottom flanges were used in the corners of the tambour to transmit the load to the columns. The execution of the lower end pavilions was similar. The cast-iron columns were arranged in groups of three in the corners of the square ground plan.

The adjoining wings were covered by an asymmetrical ridge roof. The longer front slope of the roof was supported by the framework of the perpendicular glass wall, the shorter rear slope by the masonry of the adjoining rooms. Round wrought-iron arches contributed to the strength of the space frame here, too. The ridges of the wings and the eaves of the pavilion were provided with catwalks, which were attached on the outside, at the edges of the glazing (fig. 440). These were deliberately included as architectural features.

The architect must have been conscious of the disadvantage of the use of iron members in respect to condensation. In order to avoid drips, the iron sash bars were fitted in iron "seats," which were designed so that the condensation could trickle freely down the sashes.

Single glazing, with semi-transparent glass, was used throughout.

There were two narrow ventilators in the central hall of the tropical house, above the base wall; eight in the roof of the dome; and eight in the vertical wall of the lantern. In the longitudinal direction there were four wide ventilators on each side above the base wall and in the shorter north-facing roof

surface. The cool house had even more ventilation; there were four ventilators in each of the end buildings above the base wall and in the lanterns, and in the long buildings all the squares above the base walls and in the north-facing roof surfaces were left open. In addition, all the roof surfaces of the corner buildings were removable. A net of gangways and ladders was incorporated for the maintenance of the ventilators and the blinds; all parts of the roof were accessible. The heating pipes of the tropical house were set in wide brick-lined channels in the floor and covered with cast-iron gratings; those of the temperate house were exposed above the floor.

Reference: ZfBW, 1888, vol. 38, parts 4–6, pp. 162–211, sheets 30–33.

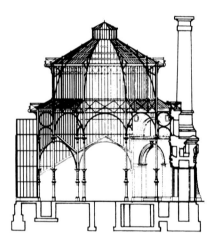

437
Section.

438
Ground-floor plan.

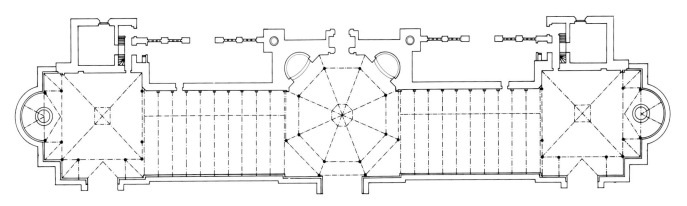

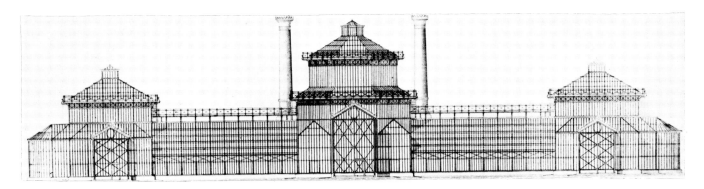

439
Front elevation.

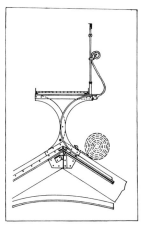

440
Detail of roof ridge
showing catwalk.

Stuttgart-Hohenheim

Hohenheim Park
Iron Conservatory (fig. 442)

The conservatory at Hohenheim, near Stuttgart, was probably the first iron-frame hothouse in Germany, if not the first on the Continent. It was built in 1789, ten years after the construction of the first cast-iron bridge over the River Severn.

The idea of an iron-framed house came to Prince Karl Eugen of Hohenheim after his visit to the establishment at Neuilly in Paris. It arose in connection with the concept of an English garden with Romantic associations. The layout of this garden was designed around 1772, at the time of the building of Hohenheim Castle. In 1776 Karl Eugen chose this castle for his permanent residence, giving up the prestigious "Solitude." The prince had resigned his political position after the collapse of his case in a dispute over an inheritance settlement in the Provincial Diet. His chosen exile in a Romantic-style garden was at the same time an expression of the widespread escapism among the European nobility.

According to the wishes of the prince, a "paradise back-to-nature zone" was to be created at Hohenheim, in which he alone could enjoy, as master of a fictitious colony, the innocent joys of the "Golden Age." There would be nothing here to remind him of the political ferment of the pre-revolution period. A chronicler of the time described the gardens thus: "Among the ruins of old Roman buildings stand decorated rooms, concert chambers, private rooms, baths, grottoes, caves, amusement areas, garden houses, and country huts, which are provided with the necessary domestic equipment and with tools. There is a small garden attached to each household, and a path, a wood, and a field. They are planted out with the various fruits and vegetables of Württemberg, and with many foreign plants and shrubs. Between shady poplars a brook meanders through the whole meadow, over the banks of which project old moss-covered volcanic rocks."[138]

There were few technical reasons for the choice of iron as a material for the conservatory, but there was a desire to use something exotic. With its simple cubic form and its ridge roof, the Iron Conservatory had an affinity with the ruin architecture. Built of a dense network of iron lesenes and sash bars, it reached a height of 49 feet. As the first building with a frame made entirely of iron, it aroused amazement:

A conservatory which was made only of iron bars and glass—it was made and assembled by the people of the Königsbronner Iron Foundry—was a great rarity. . . . The invention had indeed come from England, and the portrayal of an English layout and the trappings belonging thereto appears to have been suggested by the "Pocket Book for Nature and Garden Lovers" of 1796. It comprised three rectangular glass buildings with iron space frames, in which recesses were incorporated which could be heated by underground channels. There were planted out here, as in the winter garden, the most costly and tender plants of the Hohenheim collection.[139]

References: pocket calendar, Natur- und Gartenfreunde, Tübingen, 1796; Nau 1959, pp. 102 ff.

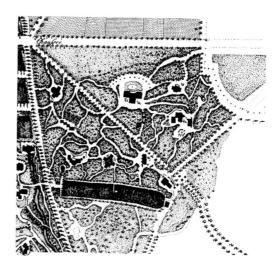

441
Site plan, copper engraving, 1796.

442
General view, 1796.

Stuttgart-Berg

Villa Berg
Conservatory (fig. 443)
architect: Christian Leins
built 1845
demolished

The conservatory at Berg was one of the first wrought-iron structures in Germany. With its two wings made with curvilinear vaults, it reflected the construction principle of Loudon, which until then had been taken up in only a few places outside Britain.

One may assume that the architect, mindful of the hothouses by Rohault in the Jardin des Plantes, had incorporated some of their features. Leins had worked during his professional training with Ludwig von Zanth, the architect of the cast-iron-frame glasshouses of the Wilhelma (1842–1846), and then during his sojourn in Paris in 1837 with Henri Labrouste, the architect of the ironwork of the Bibliothèque Sainte-Geneviève and the Bibliothèque Nationale. Leins put the experience gained in the studio of this teacher and the stimulus to use glass and iron in buildings was put into effect by Leins at Berg.

In an 1852 report the layout is described thus: "From the front . . . one obtains a view similar to that of the pleasure seat at Rosenstein, but on account of the rather higher position it takes in an even greater compass. From the north side one has a view of the Rosenstein Park and the Moorish pleasure gardens of the Wilhelma, to which there is a contribution from the most beautiful vineyards with extensive upland plains in the background. The west side has a lovely view into the valley of the Kessel. . . ."[140]

A square masonry building formed the focal point of the symmetrical layout. On the ground floor was an orangery opening onto a series of arcades, and above that was the summer residence of the crown prince and the princess. The arc-shaped layout of the hothouses (made wholly of iron and glass) adjoined this pavilion on the left and the right. The glass vaults ended at two cylindrical rotundas of different heights. The blunt conical roofs of these rotundas were topped with lanterns. If we consider the design as a whole, then we see here the Palladian version of the "villa suburbana" as a new architectural objective.

The above-mentioned report describes the interior of the conservatory as follows: "If we go to the right from the orangery down a few steps into the conservatory, we then find ourselves in an attractive winter garden containing the most beautiful of temperate house plants. . . . In the adjoining rotunda there is a mass of rock, in front of which a waterfall gushes bubbling out of a gigantic shell. . . . we enter into the other glass vault, in which there is an excellent collection of camellias and azaleas. . . . The rotunda adjacent to this part is equipped for hothouse plants. In the center is a round pond made of Carrara marble, which obtains its water from a spring. . . . On the latticework of the glass wall, magnificent climbing plants ascend to the apex of the dome."

The vaulted glass wings had as forerunners the designs of curvilinear English glasshouses—for example, Loudon's first design for the Birmingham Botanical Horticultural Garden (fig. 190). Turner used similar structural forms in his "Conservatory for a First Class Residence" (fig. 294). The simple geometrical rotundas, built without ornamental work, proclaimed the objectivity that was to characterize the anonymous engineered buildings of later decades; the silo and the gasometer buildings of the nineteenth century were anticipated here. Leins's buildings attained an elegance that was based on the dominance of the structural material and which otherwise was found only in English buildings.

References: Deutches Magazin für Garten- und Blumenkunde,
1852, vol. V, pp. 93–95, 126–128; Wittek 1964, p. 30.

443
General view of Villa
Berg. Lithograph,
1852.

Stuttgart

Wilhelma and Conservatories (figs. 444–448, 680–690)

length: 305 feet
width: 75 1/2 feet
width of corner pavilion: 38 feet
height of corner pavilion: 38 feet
architect: Ludwig von Zanth
builder: Wasseralfingen Iron Foundry
built 1842–1846

This establishment, completed shortly before the 1848 Revolution, is a late example of a feudal estate in the sense of a "villa suburbana." The conservatories, laid out symmetrically with respect to the living accommodations, constitute an important part of the architectural ostentation. The architect, Ludwig von Zanth, described the layout: "This villa, conceived in the style of the Italian royal estates, comprises living accommodation surrounded by hothouses, colonnades, kiosks, belvedere, banquet hall, and domestic quarters, which are combined with the garden layouts, in which flower beds, streams, springs, and tree plantations are laid out in a regular manner and alternate with each other."[141]

In the years 1837–1853 there was created, in a continuous building program at an overall cost of 1.5 million gulden, an establishment stretching from the valley of the River Neckar up to the heights of Rosenstein Park. The eighteen buildings were arranged in such a way that they formed a self-contained system of pathways.

The importance of the glasshouses lies less in their dimensions and their space frames than in the extensive use of cast iron. The precision reached here is without parallel in the history of cast-iron construction in Germany. The intention of bringing about the illusion of "Moorish" architecture produced a building in which the oriental ornamentation had a structural function and, at the same time, performed the interpretation. The rather flat cast-iron space frame covered with glass has bold outlines—clear cubic forms—which give it the aspect of modernistic architecture.

The layout of the Wilhelma was entrusted to von Zanth by King Wilhelm of Württemberg, and was designed and executed by him between 1836 and 1853. The Wilhelma occupied the outermost part of the royal park of Rosenstein, at that time one hour's journey on foot from Stuttgart and located in the vicinity of Cannstatt. Von Zanth described the start of

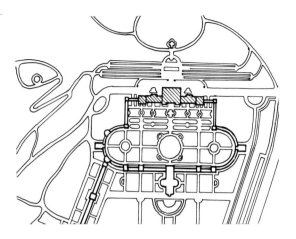

the work in detail in *Wilhelma, Maurische Villa,* an elaborate edition of his plans which he published in 1855:

The first works carried out were delegated to the gardener. He altered the slope of the high ground which contains the Rosenstein country residence at those places where the country road to Ludwigsburg adjoined it. This layout, which was executed independent of any overall plan, later became a source of embarrassment and difficulties. In other respects the site remained unused until 1839, when the king commissioned the building of a small playhouse. It was to be part of the park, without becoming a hindrance to later works on account of its position, but at the same time to be easily accessible to the public. In order to satisfy both requirements it was located at the junction of the two roads to Stuttgart and Ludwigsburg, which bordered the park. The playhouse was started in the spring of 1839 on the basis of my designs, and was opened on May 29, 1840, on the occasion of the king's birthday. It owes its origin to the refusal of His Majesty to consent to the erection of a gaming house, which had been sought for the purpose of procuring numbers of visitors to the mineral springs at Cannstatt. . . . Soon after the completion of the playhouse His Majesty told me of his wish to build a garden house on this part of the estate, intended for the use of the king himself but sufficiently spacious so that the court could assemble there. The order went further than that, as follows: to locate the living accommodation in combination with ornamental conservatories and to bring into use the Moorish style of building for it. Its position was predetermined to some extent, in that the existing terraces and steps were to be taken into consideration and were to be brought into the design of the new layout. Hence arose the need to align the central axis of it with the main axis of my design. There remained only the one question to be answered: Should it be built at the foot of this slope which the terraces occupy, or at the top of it? In the first instance one had to expect very uncertain ground conditions and forfeit the view to the Neckar valley. This choice was consequently not considered. The site on the hill itself offered the most splendid, the most desirable association between the new buildings and the surrounding landscape. There was only one drawback to this outstanding advantage; the con-

servatories could not be adequately protected without some trouble, but it was possible to surmount that. It was decided in consequence to take the middle course, to build the conservatories halfway up the slope. This decision put the living accommodation, with its plant houses, immediately below the existing terraces and approximately [16 feet] higher than the level of the ground at the foot of the slope, which from there toward the road to Stuttgart descended about 33 feet. In this way one obtained a part of the view of the landscape, and onward to the picturesque bends in the River Neckar, and at the same time one obtained the upper part of the hillslope as a protection at the rear of the conservatories.

After these preliminary matters had been decided, and the design as well, they were modified to match the sum of money allocated; the kind's approval was obtained, and in the spring of 1842 the building of the residential accommodation and all the adjacent conservatories began. In the course of the building work, when it was in an advanced state of progress, His Majesty gave me the commission to produce a design for a garden surrounding the whole piece of land, with the special instruction to include a covered walk in the same, from the park entrance as far as the residential area, at the same time joining it onto the large banquet hall. I will not discuss here in more detail the difficulty of bringing the buildings into harmony with the locality, particularly on account of the irregular direction of the major axis in relation to the boundary line by the road from Stuttgart. The residential accommodation and the conservatories were started in the spring of 1842 and were completed in July 1846. They were opened with a festival held in connection with the marriage of His Royal Highness the Crown Prince to Her Imperial Highness the Princess Olga of

Russia. The execution of the colonnaded walks, the open and curved stairways and kiosks, the layout of the terraces and flower beds, the streams and waterways, the arrangement of the lawns and tree plantations, and the banquet hall building all made heavy demands during the following years. The last was opened on October 21, 1851. In the few lines left there remains to be said the last word about this building, the name of which, Wilhelma, is reminiscent of that of its royal founder. The Moorish building forms have not yet in our day been called upon to serve as models for a building work of any importance. This privilege has so far gone to the building methods of the Greeks, the Romans, the Byzantines, and the Italians, and finally to the Gothic arch. With the exception of the so-called mosque in the gardens at Schwetzingen near Mannheim, which can hardly be taken into consideration in this context, to my knowledge no earnest attempt has been made, in Germany at least, to adapt the Moorish building forms, which are suited to the climate and conditions of their homeland, to essentially different latitudes. There were no signposts put out to indicate the correct path to take for the solution of this problem; one had to seek out the correct directions oneself, and to my mind these were only to be found in the basic principles of Greek art, which have proved their full value irrefutably in the most outstanding, the most diverse concepts. They were matters of consideration of the most famous master builders of different times and lands, from which fruitful doctrines developed, the examples of which I had all the more to follow when I made stipulations about the building method, the principles of which when they are peculiar to the same do not emerge from the existing buildings; these have much more the stamp of an unfettered inspiration than more binding and recognized principles. There is also the matter of avoiding the mistakes in these building methods without renouncing the

445
General view. Engraving, 1871–72.

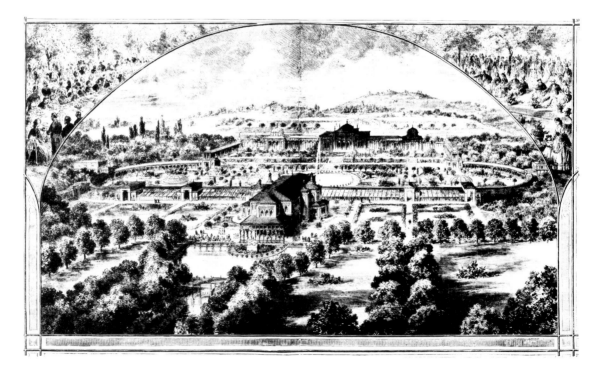

advantages which their often seductive but generally capricious adornments offer. . . . The notion one usually associates with Moorish buildings rests in general on the descriptions which Eastern people weave into their narratives, which do not always correspond with reality. Nevertheless, one establishes claims thereto for something wonderful which it is not possible to satisfy always; however, when this ambitious expectation cannot be fully satisfied, it is not to remain totally ignored. There must, through the characteristic wealth of techniques inherent in this building method, be the means to bring about a powerful effect of fantasy, without grasping that assistance which the intellect, and the tastes being tested, struggle against. To all these important considerations are allied the ever so serious requirements to satisfy all the real needs of each part, and at the same time to give it the form which truly corresponds to the purpose of the Moorish form, and particularly to use the building materials available. These are stone of various colors from nearby quarries; brick for the lower-rank buildings; and cast iron, the strength and possible ornamentation of which are suitable for the arches, domes, kiosks, and columns and roofs of the covered paths. The above remarks illustrate the basic point of view which has influenced the design and execution of the Wilhelma.[142]

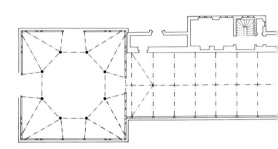

The royal residential apartments and the adjoining conservatories form the core of the Wilhelma. The architect could not carry out his 1842 design until he had (on the king's instructions) reduced the estimated cost from 600,000 to 200,000 gulden. The subsequently ordered installation of a water heating plant raised this sum to 235,000 gulden. The architect was expressly answerable for strict adherence to the estimated cost. Final expenditure on the building came to almost 300,000 gulden. Rumors circulating about the "fairy castle" put the cost even higher. Von Zanth expressed his opinion on that point: "The two Swabians who so confidently stated the cost of the building to me have talked with such loud mouths that I would be happy if only one-sixth of what they said were true. I could then work in comfort and would not have to swallow a mass of ideas which I ought not to entertain, because it is not possible to carry them out with the means at my disposal . . . this could very well delay the building."[143]

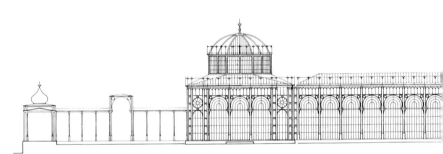

Not only the layout, but the construction of the building too showed that the Wilhelma was a "fairy castle" built for the courtly life. The king himself never lived in it regularly, and only a few chosen people were allowed in to see it. "From the start the king gave the strictest orders that no one should be allowed to enter the Wilhelma without his personal permission."[144] Not until after the death of the king, in 1864, was entrance made slightly easier, and not until 1880 was it opened to everyone in the line of succession.

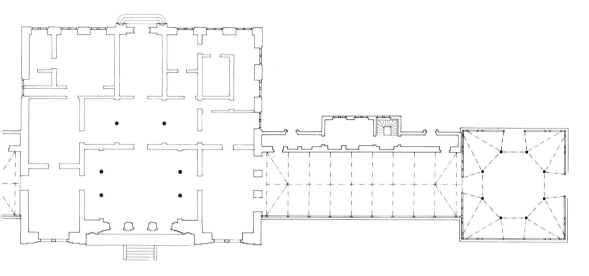

446
Ground-floor plan.

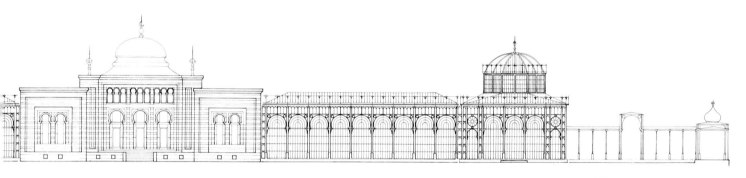

447
Front elevation.

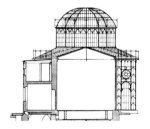

448
Section through
conservatory.

A newspaper correspondent wrote in 1871–72:

Happy to be in contact with the magic of the Swabian soil, the party of people climbed up a gently sloping path to the Wilhelma laid out at the foot of the Rosenstein. Astonishment seized the visitor, caused by the contrast which unexpectedly appeared here before his eyes. A German landscape has just now entranced his sight. Everything reminded him that he stood in the midst of the modern life of culture—but in a few steps he believes himself to be carried off into another world, into the fairy tale world of legends and the Thousand and One Nights. He no longer beheld the Hellenic forms of the Rosenstein, which had just before aroused his wonder . . . , but here are the palaces of oriental nobles, the magical spaces of the Alhambra and the Caliph's Seraglio, which the creator of this wonderful establishment, whose name it bears, has suspended before his eyes. One perceives small, only moderately high buildings capped with golden crowns, ornamental kiosks. . . . Style and fittings, ornamentation, colors, and forms are all derived from Moorish patterns. . . . Now the vast conservatories come into sight, the high vaulted roofs of which make him forget he is not in the open air. A southern vegetation unfurls itself here in the most magnificent fullness and glowing wealth of color, and, enchanted, the eye becomes fixed to the tropical plants with their gigantic leaves; to the slender palms which raise their superb fan-shaped crowns far into the heights. A path decorated with peculiar arabesques leads to a ballroom fitted out with lavish ostentation, and to a hall with pools of water and fountains, from the walls of which Turkish lances and shields, coats of armor, and curved Saracen sabers look down. And now we move on to the open, into the splendid garden which brings together everything that art permits to wring from a northern sky.[145]

The solidly built living rooms form an architectural unity with the adjacent glasshouses. The functional combination of living rooms with a private winter garden has seldom been accomplished on such a grand scale. Via an entrance hall one reaches a spacious inner courtyard, which receives its light from the middle of the ceiling through a crystalline glass roof. Galleries around the courtyard lead to the rooms on the mezzanine level above, to the assembly rooms, and to the upper gallery of the main salon, which is intended for the orchestra. The living rooms and the dining hall, which open onto the conservatories, are situated to the left and right of the assembly rooms. "The residential accommodation is a copy of that which in oriental houses goes by the name divan. . . . Because of the intention to make this room serve as a day room, every consideration has been taken into account in the matter of design features which could bestow on it charm and delight. Large windows present to the eye the garden outside and the valley of the Neckar; on the opposite side the eye is drawn to the anteroom, the walls of which are

covered with pictures which have an exuberant alternation of the most beautiful landscapes of Cairo, Algiers, and Constantinople and reproductions of alluring sketches of life in the Orient. Finally, the adjacent spacious plant houses offer the mellowness and the scent of their blooms, and for the various seasons of the year the most pleasant stay."[146]

The middle pavilion, with its gilded copper dome, contains living quarters. The adjoining wings of the conservatories end in pavilions with glass domes. The rear wall of the room connecting to the end pavilion is made of masonry as a protection against the cold north winds. The part of the conservatory adjacent to the residential area is covered with a low ridge roof, which is supported on simple cast-iron filigree roof trusses, with cast-iron struts and a horizontal tie bar of round steel. The roof is firmly anchored to a continuous cast-iron beam in the front of the building, so that only every other roof truss is supported directly on cast-iron posts in the front. The square corner pavilion has an inner ring of eight cast-iron columns joined together by arches, above which rises the octagonal glass dome with its tambour and gallery. A gently inclined glass roof at the level of the gallery provides the transition from the octagon to the cube. It forms a central space in the interior, with a low gallery, resembling the kind of room found in a small mosque, but completely translated into glass and iron.

The facade consists of assembled cast-iron parts, joined together by frames which are reinforced by semicircular arches, between which there are spandrels consisting of iron rings and horizontal bars. These elements make up the framework on which the whole structure is based. The principle of prefabrication, which first manifested itself on an industrialized basis with cast iron, had a broad controlling effect on the structure of the facade elements. The structural plane, the load-bearing frame, was separated from the plane of the glazing. The latter is fastened onto its own frame, which was fitted into the cast-iron load-bearing frame from the inside. This separation of load-bearing and non-load-bearing structural members simplified in a radical way the joining of glass surfaces and cast-iron elements. Here was created the technical possibility of making a large surface area of glass in the form of the same prefabricated basic elements. The prefabrication of all building components was the basic principle of the construction work, and was pursued to the last detail.

A description of the building procedure used for the building of the Wilhelma documents the new industrial method. The strength of the structure originates from the individual elements, but only when the whole structure is assembled complete in a load-bearing unit. "With the erection of one of the iron-frame conservatories by the Moorish palace it was absolutely necessary for the iron columns and trusses to be joined together without any break, because otherwise there would be a danger that in a strong wind or bad weather during construction the columns with the trusses would have buckled and collapsed. . . ."[147]

The importance of von Zanth's architectural achievement lies not only in his pioneering use of in-dustrialized building methods but also in the aes-thetic effects he obtained from this mode of procedure. The king's order to incorporate the orien-tal or Moorish style was for von Zanth not a hin-drance; on the contrary, this style made it possible to press forward to the extreme limits of filigree structures. Every basic element in all its details was a matter of painstaking work on the design. Von Zanth recognized the possibilities of cast iron to reproduce even the faintest relief in sharp outline, as in the minting of a coin. Thus, he created cast-iron mem-bers which on one hand distinguished themselves by showing in the light the finest outline and on the other hand stood out as distinct silhouettes from the continuous glass surfaces behind them (fig. 681).

The building is still in existence without decay. (The residential part has been rebuilt; the conserva-tories are well maintained.)

Source: plan archive, Staatliches Hochbauamt II, Stuttgart.

References: Gerhard 1936, pp. 70–100; *Über Land und Meer*, 1871–72, 14, vol. 27, no. 10, p. 5; *Deutsches Magazin für Garten- und Blumenkunde*, 1852, vol. 5, pp. 63–64; Zanth 1855.

Stuttgart

Conservatories (figs. 687, 688)
length: ca. 130 feet
width: ca. 79 feet
height: ca. 33 feet
architect: Ludwig von Zanth
built: 1852–53

The layout of these conservatories allowed the build-ing of the covered entranceway to the Wilhelma complex. A three-bay hall built above a rectangular base forms the central part. Three continuous glass ridge roofs, parallel to each other, are supported on rows of cast-iron columns. The horizontal reinforce-ment and the support of the roof guttering was ef-fected by flat cast-iron arch segments, which are pierced with circular openings in the flanges. The

sloping roofs are carried on rolled iron section. The cast-iron braced beam that surrounds the facade (fig. 26b) provides the only ornamentation. The three aisles are identical in structure and dimensions.

The conservatories are extant.

Source: plan archive, Staatliches Hochbauamt II, Stuttgart.

Toronto

Allan Gardens
Conservatory
This conservatory, built around 1900 in the classical style, has an iron dome structure made of lattice-work ribs. The ribs converge into a retaining ring, which supports a small dome above a lantern. The sash bars that provide the lateral reinforcement are incorporated in three-dimensional joints of iron bars with the main ribs. Thus there arises a crystal-like ornamentation, logically derived from the structure, which determines the appearance of the vaulted ceiling.

Tübingen

Old Botanical Garden
Great Conservatory (figs. 449, 450, 691, 692)
length: 208 feet
width: 52 1/2 feet
height: 46 feet

This conservatory, built in 1885–86 near Tübingen University to a design by Building Inspector Albert Koch, replaced a conservatory built in the first half of the century. The design was the outcome of an 1884 journey made by Koch and a colleague to see glasshouses at Heidelberg, Strasbourg, and Freiburg.

The conservatory proper was a glass-and-iron building consisting of a square central structure with a flat hipped roof and symmetrical wings with flat ridge roofs. These were supported on masonry at the rear, while the front rested on the vertical glass wall. The glass-and-iron structure was supported at the corners by masonry buildings sited at right angles to the longitudinal axis. The space frame consisted of rolled-steel stanchions, roof trusses, and purlins. The curved steel sections fastened to every truss empha-sized the rhythm of the structure and formed an aes-thetic counterpoise to the straight lines of the space frame. The catwalks at the eaves of the central build-

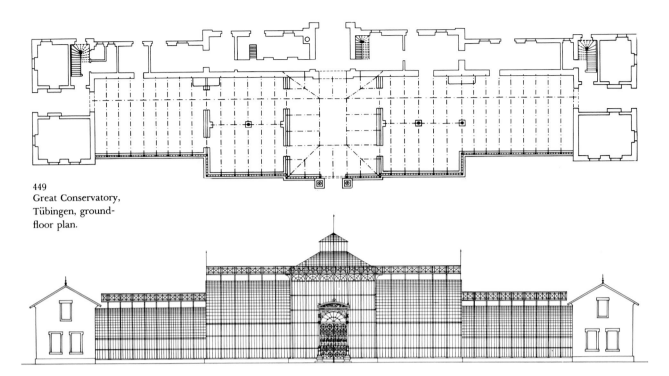

449
Great Conservatory,
Tübingen, ground-
floor plan.

450
Front elevation.

ing and at the ridges of the wings were fitted with railings. Double glazing was used, except in the roof of the central building.

The conservatory was torn down in 1969.

References: E. von Schulz, "Das grosse Gewächshaus im alten botanischen Garten," *Attempto*, 1969, part 33/34, pp. 9–19; *Die Bauwelt*, 6.10.1969, vol. 60, part 40, pp. 1326, 1344–1346.

Warsaw

Lazienski Park
Orangery (figs. 451, 452, 693)

length: 197 feet
width: 43 feet
height: 52 1/2 feet
architect: Krakau
built ca. 1840

This orangery, built in the former Royal Gardens, is a beautiful example of a conservatory in the style of late classicism. Enclosed by masonry on three sides and covered with a sheet-metal roof, it is glazed along its south-facing front. The glass surface and the roof are supported on hollow cast-iron columns, which accommodate the window frames between them (fig. 452). The middle of the building has masonry pillars and a barrel vault. In the plane of the facade there is a 26-foot-diameter rosette of the finest cast-iron work, modeled on an English pattern.

The building is extant and well maintained.

Warsaw

Palm House
built ca. 1890
demolished

This iron-frame palm house had an elongated rectangular base, which was covered by a glass roof with an upturned boat profile. The entrances in the middle were through a short transept, emphasized by the same glass vault. The ribs and the posts in the facade were riveted and were located in the plane of the glass.

Vienna-Hietzing

Duke of Brunswick's Gardens
Conservatory (fig. 453)

length: 197 feet
width: 29 1/2 feet
height: 39 feet
built ca. 1850
demolished?

The Duke of Brunswick's conservatory at Hietzing adjoined a palace and served as a winter garden. With its imposing length, made entirely of iron and glass, it united the formal language of classicism with the Loudon-type curvilinear glass surface. A contemporary writer said of this building:

451
Orangery, Lazienski
Park, Warsaw,
ground plan.

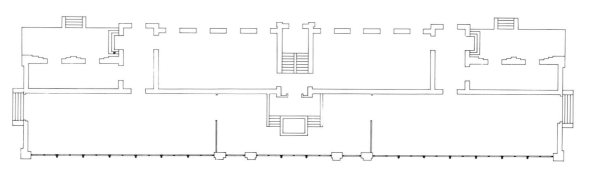

452
Detailed section of
cast-iron column.

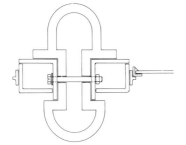

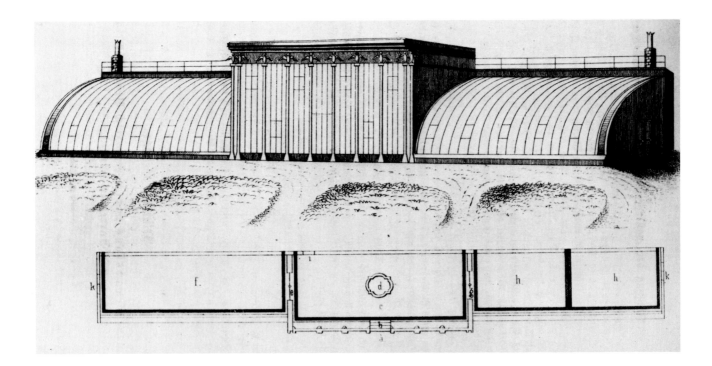

453
General view and
ground plan of con-
servatory at Vienna-
Hietzing. Engraving.

The whole length of it comes to [197 feet] and is divided into three sections, of which the middle one consists of a flower salon with upright windows and a gently sloping roof, together with the half-arch-shaped glass roofs of the two wings which contain temperate- and hot-climate plants. All three sections are backed by a masonry wall. The floor of the interior is sunk [30 inches] below ground level. The middle of the salon includes a marble pool, which holds the water falling from a fountain. The vault is made of [0.2-inch-thick] glass sheets in order to withstand hailstones better. There are windows for ventilation, not only in the front but also in the rear wall, by means of which the interior temperature can be kept at the level required. The masonry work that forms the rear wall is built so that it can perform the necessary functions of shading and protection. Heating is provided via channels which are sunk into the ground; their tops are covered with iron gratings at floor level. Coke is used for fuel, which, with the very efficiently drawing stove, ensures any temperature desired.[148]

There is in Hietzing a small conservatory of similar construction (fig. 700); its relationship to the above-mentioned building is uncertain.

Vienna-Penzing

Mayer Gardens
Forcing Houses (fig. 454)

length: 148 feet
width: 33 feet
height: 23 feet
built 1830–1834
demolished

The two cast-iron forcing houses of the banker Johann Mayer at Penzing exemplify the architectural ostentation favored by the wealthy in the 1830s. These were the middle-class descendants of the nearby conservatories of the Duke of Brunswick. A contemporary description follows.

The banker Johann Mayer, head of the wholesale firm J. H. Stametz and Company, had the two conservatories built over several years in his gardens at Penzing, near the royal pleasure seat at Schönbrunn, and demonstrated his refined taste and his preference for horticultural and ornamental buildings in this, and in many other layouts in his extensive estate. An appropriately motivated attention to the Tudor style was set as the standard for both buildings. The first conservatory was built to the design by the Clerk of Works [Pierro] Nobile, and includes besides the rooms for plants a pavilion at each side, which is joined not only to the latter, but also to the gardens through large doors, and through the two windows at the side there was a view of the flower beds in the gardens. The niches in the far wall are decorated in

454
Front elevation,
ground plan, section,
and detailing of
forcing houses at
Vienna-Penzing.
Engraving.

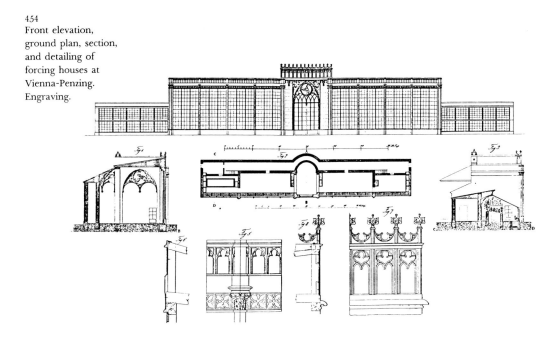

*the same way as the windows, but contain mirrors instead
of transparent glass panes. The columns between each group
of windows are made of cast iron.*

*The second conservatory was built a few years later by
the architect Schedel. There was a stipulation to incorporate
a salon in the middle of the building for the grander social
occasions, the same to be in communication with the conservatory rooms, and moreover to have two smaller forcing
houses for lower plants at both sides. In other respects an
adherence to the Norman style was also important here. All
cornices are made of cast iron, and have been executed very
neatly, and in accordance with the drawings, and under
the supervision of the publisher of the Allgemeine Bauzeitung, at the Royal Salm Ironworks at Blankso in Mähren,
which under the leadership of the meritorious and well
known chemist Dr. Reichenbach made important mechanical
innovations. Heating is by smoke, and the conduits consist of
rectangular flues made of clay bricks. All the ironwork of
the cornice is painted with three coats of light gray oil paint.
The first two coats have had sand added to them; only the
last, moderately thin, has been applied as a pure oil paint.
This type of coloring has lasted very well, and the whole resembles sandstone perfectly.[149]*

The second of the two forcing houses surpassed
the first in size and in variety of ornamentation. A
pylon-type structure with masonry pilasters framing
a large Gothic arch window formed a central pavilion. The two lower wings of the conservatories
proper adjoined it. The glazed framework and the
rows of cast-iron columns terminated at the top in a
Gothic frieze.

Vienna-Schönbrunn

Schönbrunn Park
Conservatories

The park at Schönbrunn (fig. 455) is one of the most
important and well-preserved Baroque gardens in
the French style. The botanical garden, founded in
1753, became one of the best in Europe. In 1860,
after the last large collecting expedition, the plants
filled four glasshouses. None of these buildings exist
today; in the 1881s they were replaced with the
Great Palm House and the Sundial House.

Great Palm House (figs. 456–458, 694–697)
length: 364 feet
width: 92 feet
height: 82 feet
built 1880–1882
architect: Franz von Sengenschmid

The Great Palm House is intended to demonstrate
the possibilities of ironwork in contrast to the traditional building materials masonry and wood. The
flowing lines of the curved girders are only realizable
in steel. The glass surfaces incorporated in the steel
structure produce a form that is determined only by
the play of concave and convex lines, particularly in
the pavilion. Although the glass shell is built of a
combination of vertical and curved surfaces, the traditional separation of wall and roof has been abolished in this building. Rising out of the basement
wall, the glass shell extends without a break up to

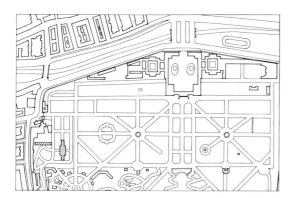

455
Site plan (extract),
1972.

456
Engraving, 1885.

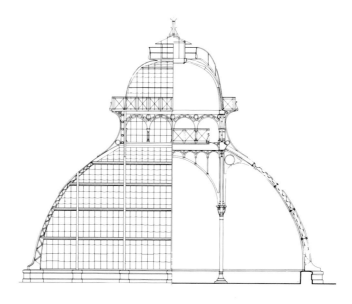

457
Section through cen-
tral pavilion.

the lantern, with no edges. Ironwork on the outside had previously been used at Laeken, in the Munich conservatories by August von Voit, and in the Frankfurt Flora, but nowhere with the results seen here: an iron frame rising from the base and visible on all sides.

The base of the house is axially symmetric. The high central pavilion, 128 feet long and 92 feet wide, is adjoined laterally by two 49-by-56-foot wings, which in turn are bounded by square corner pavilions with 69-foot sides. The roofing is of curved and plane glass surfaces, which extend as a continuous surface from the 39-inch-high base wall to a lantern. The left pavilion serves as a temperate house, the central part as a palm house, and the right pavilion as a tropical house.

The structure is made of wrought iron, apart from the columns of the central part and the domes at the ends. The basic elements of the ironwork are riveted curved lattice ribs, which run into box-section girders in the pavilion structures, which themselves are supported by cast-iron columns. On these is built a vertical cast-iron framework of columns and arches, which likewise transmits the load of the dome above it via box girders. The central dome is made of arched latticework girders, above which there is a lantern. Arch-shaped cast-iron bars, added for reinforcement at the joints of the load-bearing members, strengthen the impression of the seamless transition of the load-bearing members into one another. Curves are the dominant elements in the structure. The arched ribs are held together by braced purlins. A prominent rib effect in the space frame is created by the combination of curved and straight girders, which is reminiscent of the structure of a boat's hull upside down. The principle employed here is that there are curved surfaces in one direction only, which intersect in hipped corners above a rectangular base, so that the difficult and expensive glazing of spherical surfaces is avoided.

The curved braced girders constructed for the intersection line of the curved surfaces are splayed outward diagonally and also emphasize the flow of the lines over the corners. The connecting parts leading to the pavilions are vaulted over with curved ribs which run up to a joint at the ridge. The cast-iron columns and the reinforcing arches are executed more conventionally than the other designs. Formal, not structural considerations led to the development of a kind of miniature Roman gallery made of cast-iron columns, which are combined in a complicated way with the sheet-metal arched girders. The development of these structural members (figs. 457, 696)

was the only compromise made by the architect and the builder with the historicizing taste of the times. The vault of green glass panes fixed on the inside is double glazed and is made in such a way that the rebates for the putty face outward. Numerous ventilation louvers in the glazed shoulders of the roof and in the ridge lantern ensure plentiful and rapid ventilation of the whole glasshouse.

The palm house is heated by steam and hot water. A special heating installation with three tubular boilers with Tenbrink burners was fitted. The steam generated is fed to heating chambers below ground level.

The weight of the whole structure was originally 723 tons, of which 61 tons were wrought iron and 122 tons cast iron for the columns and the cladding. The cost of the ironwork was 220,000 florins; with the heating plant, masonry, foundations, stone, glass, and paint, the total cost was 600,000 florins. The construction was carried out under the supervision of the architect, Sengenschmid, and the court iron builder, Ignaz Grindl. Sigmund Wagner was the structural engineer.

A contemporary description follows:

The summer residence of the imperial court in front of the gates of Vienna, the magnificent, famous Schönbrunn, celebrated through so many historical memories, has obtained a new ornamental feature. The old glasshouses of the botanical gardens, which do not come up to the requirements of beauty, nor to the standard of modern plant growing methods, have vanished, and in their place emerges a palm house laid out in the very greatest of proportions. This imposing building has been designed by the court architect Sengenschmid, who was commissioned by the court to undertake a study tour of all the leading plant-cultivation establishments in Europe in order to learn at first hand about the latest improvements in building techniques and the erection of monumental hothouses, and to create the same in the Schönbrunn temple of flowers.

According to the judgment of the experts, the virtuoso has solved the problems of his difficult task in the most successful way. The view of the gigantic glasshouse is one of considerable effect: it rises in harmonious relationships, with its smooth contours both softly and powerfully at the same time above the green background. When its glass vaults glisten in the sunlight it lights up and sparkles like a fairy castle. By virtue of its size, the Schönbrunn palm house is the greatest of all the European hothouses built to a coherent design. What gives the building its graceful character is the outstanding use of curved swelling lines and the avoidance of the borrowing of forms from stone architecture and wooden buildings so common in iron constructions.

In botanical and technical respects the Schönbrunn palm house ought to stand as the most perfect establishment of its kind, and should provide a home as snug as it is splendid for the plant treasures it is intended to accommodate. But also, stylistic and structural aspects mark it out as an interesting advance in the artistic development of iron buildings, because the past offers no model for the architectural use of this modern building material; buildings either appear in the unartistic forms of the practical but ugly purpose-built structures or put on the deceitful mask of the stone and wood building. "In the Schönbrunn palm house," says the admirable art critic Ilg, "the form of the whole is suited to the material; the curve rules over the contour purely and simply. The straight-line element which supports the central part is strictly limited to the support of the interior. Thereby the effect of similarity between columns has been avoided, so that the form of the bars does not have the proportions of the stone and wood column and preserves the type of style in which the capital appears less as the base which is holding the load and much more as the junction point for the wide-spreading bar elements. Where more slender columns have to be used at the junction of beams, every relationship with the stone pillar arrangement is again avoided. It appears that the pillars have not been made in one piece but poured together like bundles from above, where their capitals are in harmony with the extremely slender leaf forms and remove any impression of the horizontal load supporting work. These highly modified capitals represent the only form of stone architecture used in the whole building; the rest is iron construction throughout. The total effect creates an artistic impression, concerning the cause of which we can give no proper account. It expresses the artistic force of the material by this artistic treatment of its objective, but we do not yet know the root cause of such an impression. Indeed, we stand at the beginning of a new and dark road on foreign soil; but for me it is as if this building, in the way that the rod of the water diviner works, had firmly jerked upwards."[150]

The palm house is extant and well maintained.

Source: plans room, Schönbrunn Castle.

References: *Der Bautechniker*, 1885, vol. 5, no. 22; Kronfeld 1923; *Illustrierte Zeitung* 22.4.1882, vol. 78, no. 2025, pp. 325, 326.

Sundial House (figs. 459, 460, 698, 699)

length: 148 feet
width: 48 feet
height: 51 feet
architect: unknown
built in 1885

The roof structure of the Sundial House is built of arched ribs spanning 48 feet, which are made of braced girders with large areas of sheet metal and horizontally reinforced by latticework purlins. The roof vault of the iron ribs slopes down at the rear. On the north side it stands on a 28-foot-high wall extending up to the gutter; on the other side it stands on latticework stanchions which form the vertical parts of the ribs. A large hall space without internal supports was created by the use of this structural principle.

458
Ground-floor plan of
Great Palm House.

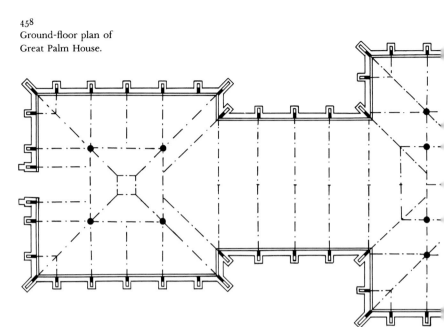

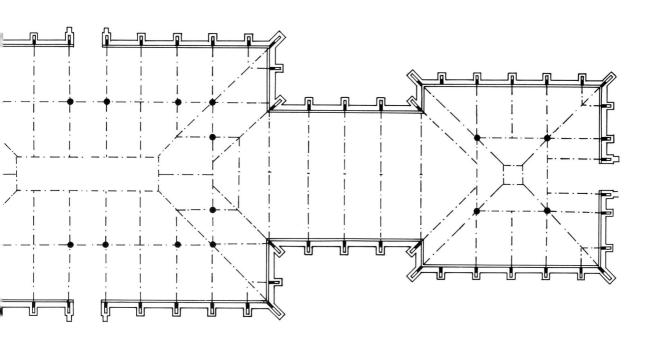

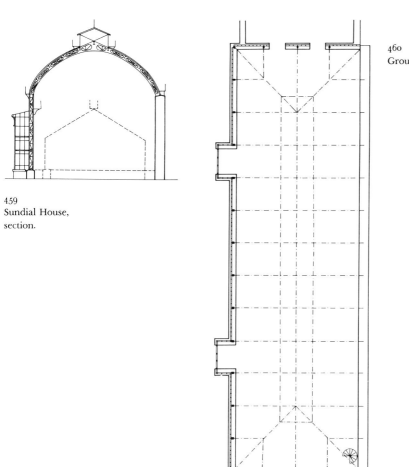

459
Sundial House,
section.

460
Ground-floor plan.

In contrast with the Great Palm House, single glazing was used here. The structural ironwork is outside the glass skin. Light galleries are built along the ridge and at the eaves. Ventilation is obtained through a continuous ridge lantern.

The Sundial House is extant and well maintained.

Source: plans room, Schönbrunn Castle.

Vienna

Burggarten

Old Winter Garden (figs. 461–463)
built 1823–1826
architect: Louis von Remy
demolished 1901

The Old Winter Garden, built in the classical style, had extensive iron structures, particularly in the framework of the vertical windows which formed the walls. The architect made use of a part of the old fortress masonry for the rear wall of the winter garden. The main building was 427 feet long and 43 feet high. The top was flat and completely solid. The middle building obtained its prominence from an arrangement of Corinthian columns. The areas between the columns, and the central and top structures in the wings, were fully glazed up to the attic. Whereas the high banquet hall in the center was covered with a flat roof, the wings were provided with sloping windows and a sun trap.

Around 1900 the architect Friedrich Ohmann was commissioned by the court to produce proposals for a new winter garden on the foundations of the old conservatory. Two-thirds of the winter garden was to serve as a temperate house. Several designs were required, because the director of the royal gardens wanted a curved glass surface facing south and the master of the royal household wanted the inclusion of a garden salon. The plans for the work were approved in 1901, and the Old Winter Garden was demolished and the new building started in 1902.

Source: plans room, Hofgang.

Reference: Tschira 1939.

New Winter Garden (figs. 465, 466, 701, 702)
length: 394 feet
width: 52 1/2 feet
height: 56 feet

Ohmann's conservatory, with its solid corner pavilions, its accented middle pavilion, and the solid layout of its columns and wings, is related to its predecessor. However, in contrast to this, and corre-

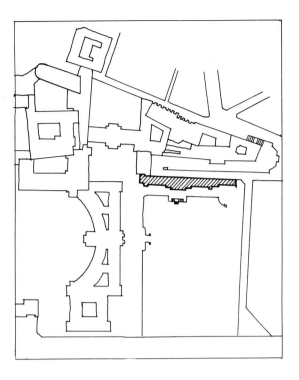

461
Site plan (extract).

sponding to the possibilities presented by iron construction, the area is covered by a barrel vault in the middle and by a half barrel vault over the wings.

Riveted semicircular sheet-metal girders make up the ribs of the iron structure. With the help of thin purlins, they carry the double glazing of the roof (fig. 466). The principle of the glazing was the formation of a continuous glass surface on the inside below the space frame. The effect of dripping condensation is reduced in this way. From the outside, the curved glass surface appears to be stretched between the ribs.

The strongly prominent structure was consciously treated as a shape-creating element. The ranking of the structural elements gives the building a rhythmic appearance, which is taken up and reinforced by the stone architecture of the balustrade and the arrangement of the columns.

The formal language of the New Winter Garden is that of the Viennese Jugendstil, in which the influence of Ohmann's teacher Otto Wagner comes through clearly.

This building is extant and well maintained.

Sources: plans room, Hofburg; personal papers of Hans Pfann.

References: R. Wagner-Rieger, *Wiens Architektur im 19. Jahrhundert* (Vienna, 1970); A. Lhotsky, *Die Baugeschichte der Museen und der Neuen Burg* (Vienna, 1941); Tschira 1939.

462
Old Winter Garden,
interior view. Litho-
graph, ca. 1840.

463
View from the gar-
dens. Lithograph,
ca. 1840.

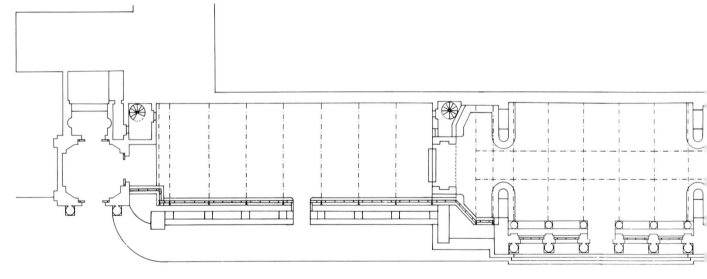

465
Ground-floor plan.

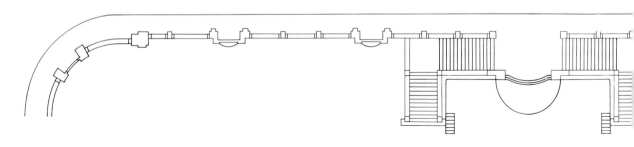

464
New Winter Garden,
earlier design. Draw-
ing, ca. 1900.

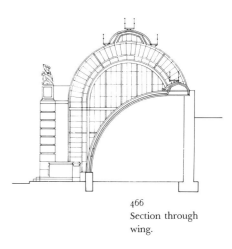

466
Section through
wing.

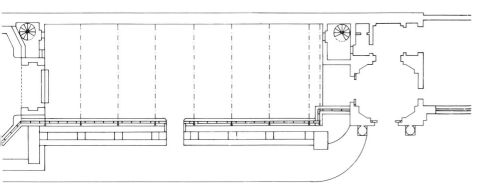

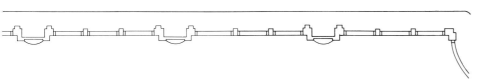

]

Wollaton Hall, Nottinghamshire

Camellia House (figs. 467–469, 703–708)

length: 92 feet
width: 49 feet
height: 21 feet
architect: unknown
builders: Thomas Clark firm, Birmingham
built 1823

The Wollaton Hall camellia house is the earliest prefabricated glasshouse still in existence. The load-
bearing structure determines the pathway system inside. Along the pathways, parallel lines of cast-iron
columns are joined at the top by sheet-iron vaults.
Prism-shaped glass roofs cover the separated areas of
plant beds between the pathways. With this basic
structural concept, it was possible to produce a rigid
space frame that allowed an extremely fine filigree
execution of the columns. The basic structural frame
is closed on the shady side by solid masonry and on
the south side by a completely glazed classical facade
with half-columns and a projecting architrave.

Cast-iron columns and sheet-steel vaults form a
space frame for the glass roof. The springing for the
glass-and-steel vault forms gutters which lead rainwater into the hollow iron columns. The extremely
thin 12-foot-high columns are provided with elegantly shaped bases, capitals, and fluting (figs. 22a,
73, 468, 469).

The irregularly shaped ground plan is controlled
by the crossing axes of the pathways, which are
aligned with the entrances. There are surrounding
pathways along the enclosing walls. This pathway
system, embracing rows of columns and covered
with iron vaults, is glazed over at the intersection
points in the center and at the entrances. The conservatory exploits very effectively the play of light
and shade by the alternation between glass and iron.

*References: The Story of Wollaton Hall, fourth edition (Not-
tingham, 1976); McIntosh 1853, vol. 1, pp. 360 ff.; Neumann
1862, pp. 173–179.*

467
Ground plan.

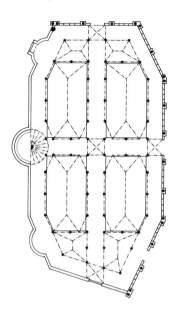

468
Section.

469
Detail of cast-iron
column.

470
Thomas Clark and
C. R. Cockerell, The
Grange, Hampshire,
1825, interior view.
Engraving.

Photographs, Engravings, and Plans

471–477
Charles Lanyon
and Richard
Turner, palm
house, Botanical
Garden, Belfast,
1839–40, 1853.

471
Dome structure of
central pavilion.

472
Central pavilion.

473
View of dome.

474
Gallery around
dome.

475
Wing.

476
Column with scroll-
work in wing.

477
Roof.

478, 479
Schadow, palm
house, Pfaueninsel,
Berlin, 1829–1831.

478
Interior. From a
painting by Karl
Blechen, 1834.

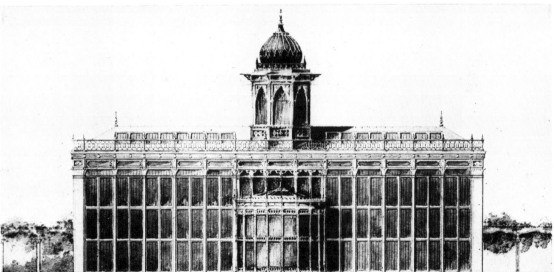

479
(above) General view.
Painting, ca. 1835.
(below) Design, with
tower.

**480, 481
Bouche, Herter,
and Nietz, Great
Palm House, Royal
Botanical Garden,
Berlin-Schöneberg,
1857–1859.**

480
Photograph taken
shortly before demo-
lition, 1910.

481
Interior photograph,
taken shortly before
demolition, 1910.

482
Koerner, hothouses,
Botanical Garden,
Berlin-Dahlem,
1905–1909. View
from southeast.

**483–485
Koerner, Great
Palm House, Bo-
tanical Garden,
Berlin-Dahlem,
1905–1907.**

483
After rebuilding.

484
View inside glass
vault, ca. 1907.

485
Longitudinal section,
with tropical flora,
1910.

486
Behrens, AEG tur-
bine hall, Berlin-
Moabit, 1909. Sup-
port footing.

487
Koerner, Great Palm
House, Botanical
Garden, Berlin-
Dahlem, 1905–1907.
Support footing.

**488–491
Koerner, subtropi-
cal house, Botani-
cal Garden, Berlin-
Dahlem, 1908–09.**

488
Front entrance.

489
Side elevation, detail
of facade.

490
Detail of window.

491
Towers with bridge.

492
Stier and Otzen,
winter garden,
Berlin-Dahlem,
1871–1873. Interior
view, ca. 1880.

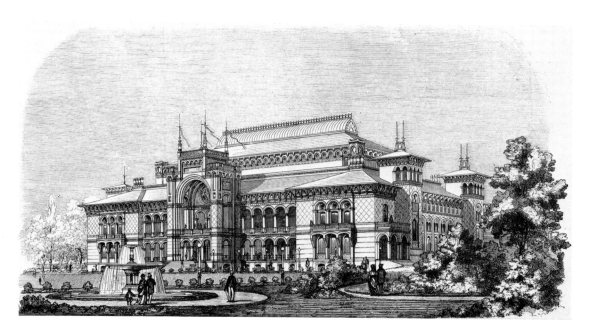

493
Stier and Otzen,
flora, Berlin,
1871–1873. Assembly
hall. Engraving, 1873.

494
Hermann von der
Hude and Julius
Hennicke, Central
Hotel, Berlin,
1880–81. Interior
view of winter gar-
den, ca. 1881.

**495, 496
Conservatories of
Duke Adolf von
Nassau, Biebrich,
1846–1861.**

495
Two-bay exhibition
hall. Lithograph.

496
Three-bay exhibition
hall, 1861.
Lithograph.

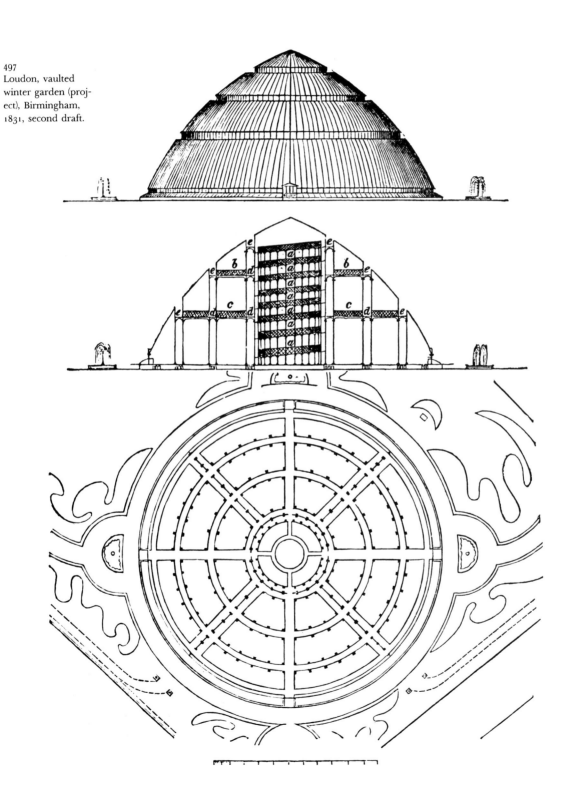

497
Loudon, vaulted
winter garden (proj-
ect), Birmingham,
1831, second draft.

498
Osborn, conservatory, Botanical Gardens, Birmingham, 1869. Detail of corner column.

**499–501
Conservatory, Bo-
tanical Garden,
Breslau, 1861.**

499
Facade of wing with
ridge-and-furrow
roof.

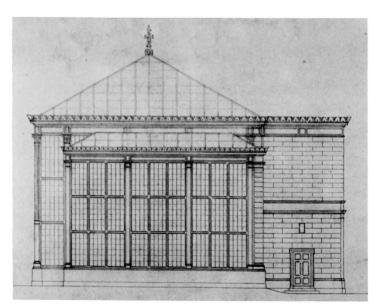

500
Side elevation
(design).

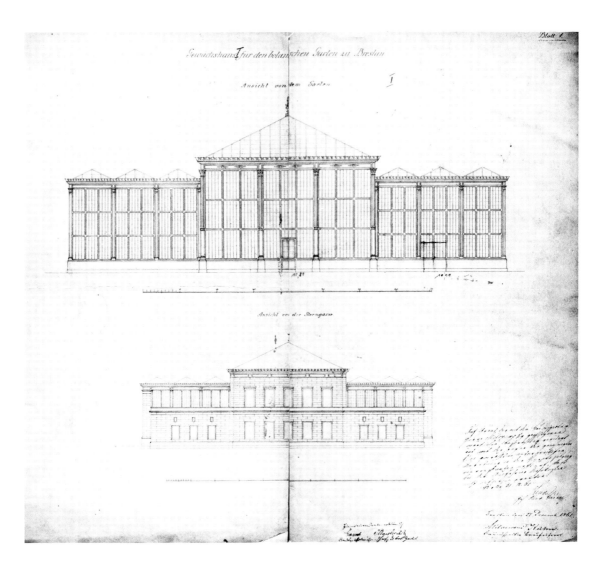

501
Front and rear views
(design).

502, 503
Suys, Gineste, and
Meeus-Wouters,
Great Palm House,
Botanical Garden,
Brussels, 1826–27.

502
View from garden.

503
Rotunda of Palais de
Flore.

504–512, 514–518
**Royal Park, Lae-
ken, Brussels.**

504
Jardin d'Hiver,
1875–76.

505
View inside dome of
Jardin d'Hiver.

506
Springing of roof
truss of Jardin
d'Hiver.

507
Panoramic view of
conservatories. (cen-
ter) Jardin d'Hiver;
(left) Serre du Congo,
1886.

508
Site plan of conserv-
atories. (1) Loggia
and Serre d'Intro-
duction; (2) Serre aux
Palmiers; (3) galerie;
(4) Sacristie; (5) Serre
Chapelle; (6) Pavilion
des Palmiers; (7) gal-
erie; (8) Serre circu-
laire; (9) Serre aux
Azalées; (10) Serre
pour confection des
bouquets; (11) galerie;
(12) Serre de Diane
and Pavillon de Nar-
cisse; (13) galerie; (14)
Ancien Pavillon de
Narcisse; (15) Galerie
souterraine; (16) Es-
calier blanc and Em-
barcadère; (17) Serre
du Congo; (18) An-
nexe aux Palmiers;
(19) Jardin d'Hiver;
(20) Annexe aux
Fougères; (21) Oran-
gerie; (22) Annexe de
l'Orangerie; (23)
Serre du Théâtre;
(24) Serre Salle à
manger; (25) Serre
aux Camélia; (26)
Serre Maquet; (27)
Nouvelle Orangerie;
(28) galerie; (29) Serre
aux Rhododendrons;
(30) Nouvelles Serres
à fleurs; (31) Serres
du Plateau des Pal-
miers; (32) galerie;
(33) Petite Serre aux
Orchidées; (34)
Grande Serre aux
Orchidées; (35) Petite
Serre aux Orchidées;
(36) Forcerie.

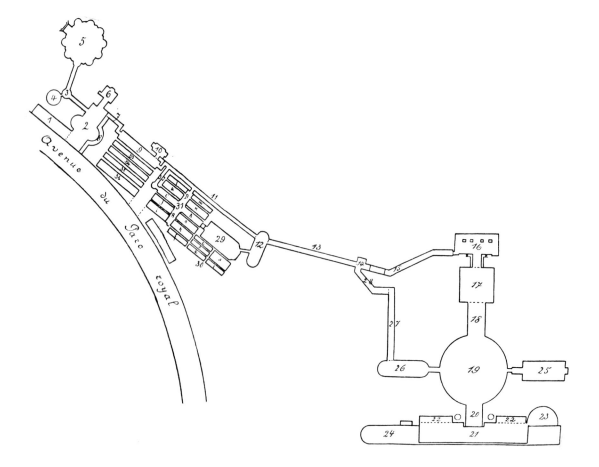

509
Jardin d'Hiver,
1875–76. Engraving,
1876.

510
Serre du Congo,
nave.

511
Serre du Congo.

512
Serre aux Palmiers,
1885.

513
Balat, victoria regia
house, Botanical
Garden, Bouchot,
1859.

514
Balat and Maquet,
Jardin d'Hiver, Lae-
ken, 1875–76, lantern
dome and crown.

515
Serre du Congo.

516
Hall structure, 1885.

517
Hall structure, 1886.

518
Serre Chapelle, 1886.

519–525
D. and E. Bailey,
palm house, Bicton
Gardens, Budleigh
Salterton, Devon,
ca. 1843

519
Front view.

520
Glass vault of side
dome.

521
Glass vault of main
dome.

522
Side view.

523
Side view.

524
View of interior of
side dome, showing
filigree columns.

525
Details of cast-iron
stanchions.

526
Milner, Palm hall,
Pavilion Gardens,
Buxton, 1871.

527–535
Paxton, buildings at Duke of Devonshire's estate, Chatsworth, Derbyshire.

527
Great Conservatory.
Photograph, ca. 1900.

528
Great Conservatory,
views inside nave.

529
Interior of victoria
regia house. Paxton's
daughter is shown
standing on a leaf.
Engraving, 1849.

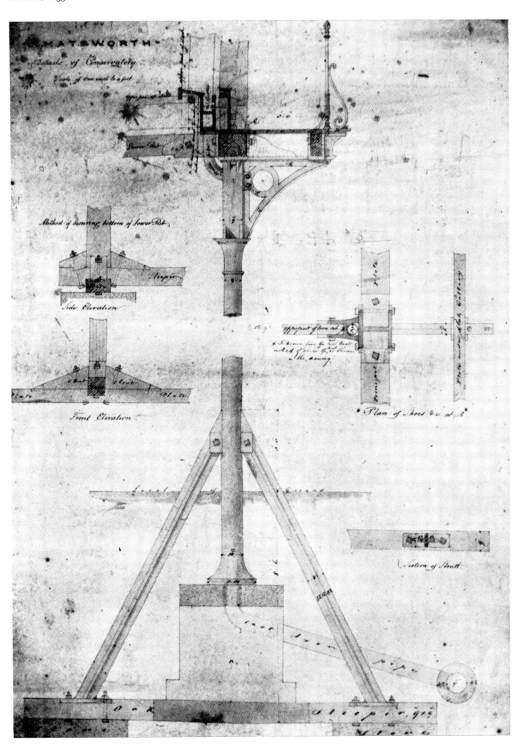

530
Structural drawing of
column, 1835.

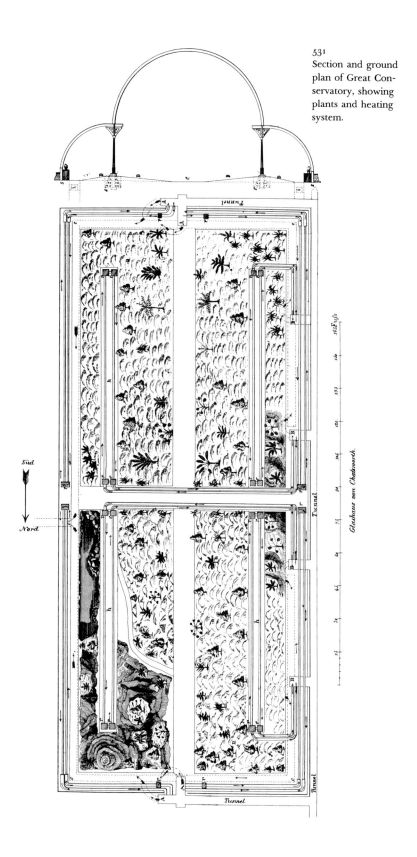

531
Section and ground
plan of Great Con-
servatory, showing
plants and heating
system.

53²
Remains of base wall
of Great Conservatory.

533
Conservative Wall.

535
Interior view of Conservative Wall, with view of orangery.

534
Central pavilion of Conservative Wall.

**536–540
Turner and Clancy,
conservatories, National Botanic Gardens, Glasnevin,
Dublin, 1842–1850.**

536
Central pavilion,
1850.

537
View of glass vault
in central pavilion.

538
Detail of facade of
central pavilion.

539
View inside right
wing, 1842.

540
Small pavilion of left
wing, 1842

541, 542
Paisley, New Palm
House, National
Botanic Gardens,
Glasnevin, Dublin,
1884.

541
Side view.

542
Front view.

543–548
Matthienson, palm
house, Royal Bo-
tanic Gardens,
Edinburgh, 1858.

543
Front view.

544
View inside main
vault.

545
Structural details of
column.

546
View of aisle vault
above gallery.

547
Aerial view of roofs
of old palm house,
1834 (above), and
new palm house,
1858 (below).

548
View of main vault
of palm house.

549

549–553
Roster, palm
house, Orto Botan-
ico, 1874.

55¹

552
View inside nave.

554–556
Kayser, flora, Palm
Garden of City of
Frankfurt,
1869–1871.

554
Panorama, 1870.

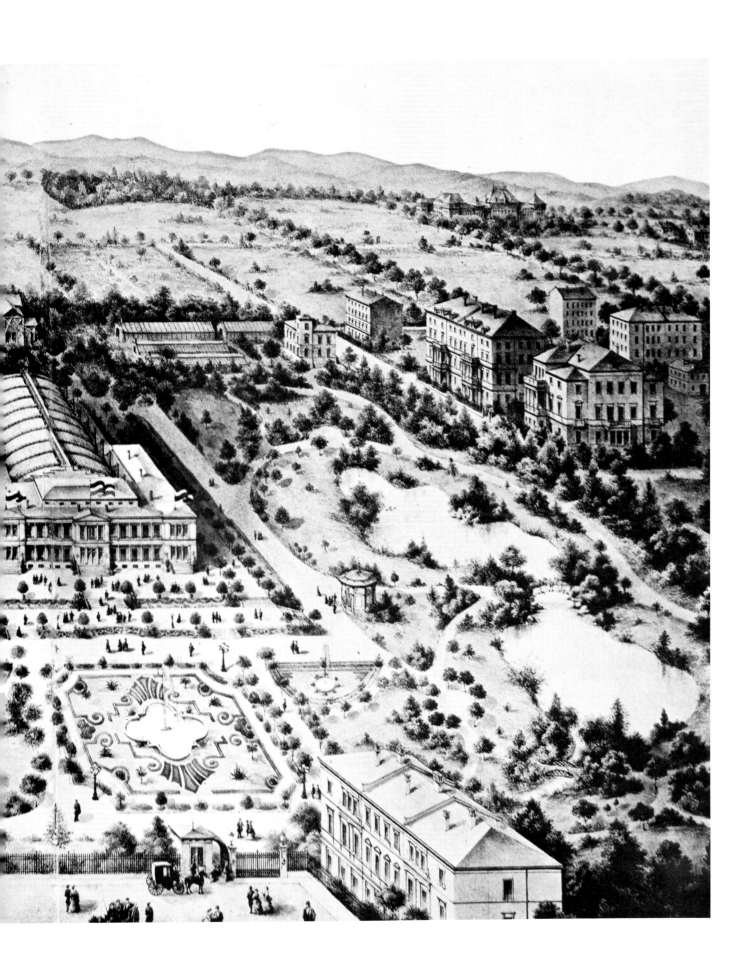

555

556
Interior view. En-
graving, 1870.

557–563
Kibble, Kibble Pal-
ace, Botanic Gar-
dens, Glasgow,
1872.

557

558
View inside gallery
around main dome.

559

560

561

562
Detail of column
with spandrel.

564, 565
People's Palace,
Glasgow Green, ca.
1880.

564
Side view.

565

566
Small Conservatory,
Göttingen University
Botanical Garden.

567
Winter garden,
Grimston Park,
Yorkshire, 1830–1840.

568, 569
Laves, palm house,
Park Herrenhau-
sen, 1846–1849.

568
Lithograph of exte-
rior view.

569
Series of design
drawings.

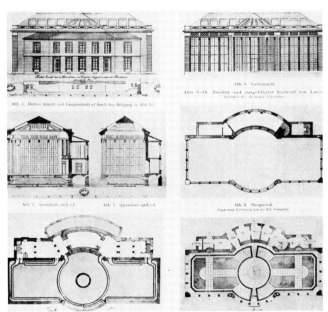

570, 571
**Auhagen, palm
house, Park Her-
renhausen, 1879.**

570
Photograph, 1916.

571
Interior view. Engraving, 1882.

572–575
F. Beer, winter garden, Schwarzenberg Castle, Hluboká nad Vltavou, 1840–1847.

572
Entrance portal.

573

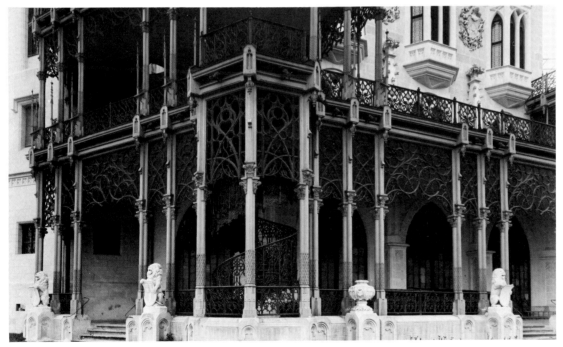

574
Photograph of castle,
showing cast-iron
balustrade.

575
Detail of balustrade.

576, 577
Palm house, Botanical Garden, Innsbruck, 1905.

576

577

578–581
Hübsch, conserva-
tories at Residenz,
Karlsruhe,
1853–1857.

578
Central pavilion of
palm house, 1857.

579
Central pavilion and
wing.

580
Facade of central pa-
vilion, details.

581
Detail of winter garden, showing it partially dismantled for summer.

582–584
Bromeis, Great
Conservatory, Wil-
helmshöhe, Kassel,
1882.

582
Central pavilion.

583

584
Interior view of
wing.

585–588
**Märtens and Eber-
lein, flora, Botan-
ischer Garten Köln-
Riehl (Cologne),
1864.**

585
Site plan by Lenné.
Lithograph, 1862.

586
Lithograph showing
the flora.

587
Photograph, ca. 1880.

588
Photograph of interior of glass vault, ca. 1880.

589–592
Rothe and Jacob-
sen, palm house,
Botanical Garden,
Copenhagen,
1872–1874.

589
View of rotunda.

590

591
Detail of facade of
rotunda.

592
View of interior of
rotunda.

593, 594
Dahlerup, winter
garden, Ny Carls-
berg Glyptotek,
Copenhagen,
1904–1906.

593
View inside dome.

594
Section through the
winter garden (de-
sign), 1897.

595–598
Devien, winter garden, Liechtenstein Castle, Lednice, 1843.

595
View of parterre, with castle in background.

596
Interior view of winter garden.

597
Details of cast-iron
columns.

598

599–602
Palm houses, Bo-
tanical Garden,
Leningrad (i.e., St.
Petersburg),
1880–1900.

599
Vaulted palm house.

600
Octagonal palm
house.

601
Entrance portal to
vaulted palm house.

602
Front view of octag-
onal palm house.

603, 604
Conservatory,
Palais Burnay,
Lisbon, ca. 1910.

603
Front entrance.

604
View of roof.

605
Mackenzie and Mon-
cur, palm house, Sef-
ton Park, Liverpool,
1896. Entrance front.

606
Burton and Turner,
winter garden of
Royal Botanic Soci-
ety, Regent's Park,
London, 1842–1846.
Photograph, ca. 1930.

607–612
Fowler, Great Conservatory, Syon
House, London,
1820–1827.

607

608
Interior view be-
neath dome. (Coping
was a later addition.)

609

610
Roof construction of
wing pavilion.

524

611
Detail of entrance
portal of central
pavilion.

612
Roof construction of
wing.

613–619
**Turner and Bur-
ton, palm house,
Royal Botanic Gar-
dens, Kew, London,
1844–1848.**

614
View of central
pavilion.

615
Detail of roof sup-
ports of central
pavilion.

616
Inside of dome end
of wing.

617
Entrance portal of
central pavilion.

618
Dome end of wing.

619
Engraving depicting
palm house and vic-
toria regia house,
1852.

620–622
Burton, temperate
house, Royal Bo-
tanic Gardens,
Kew, London,
1859–1863.

620
Front entrance of
central pavilion.

621
Roof supports of
central pavilion.

622
Interior view of cen-
tral pavilion.

623
William Chambers,
orangery, Royal Bo-
tanic Gardens, Kew,
London, ca. 1760.

624
Jeffry Wyatville, Architectural Conservatory, Royal Botanic Gardens, Kew, London, 1836. Gable front.

625
Turner, victoria regia
house, Royal Botanic
Gardens, Kew, Lon-
don, 1852. Detail of
roof trusses.

**626, 627
Paxton, Crystal Palace, Hyde Park,
London, 1850–51.**

626
Interior view of
transept.

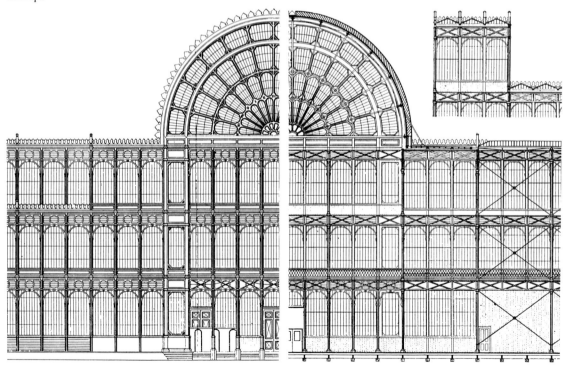

627
Elevation and
section.

628–630
Paxton, Crystal Palace, Sydenham,
1852–1854.

628

629
Glazing work in
progress.

630
Details of supporting
structure.

631
Woodcut (1851) depicting visitors to East Indian Bazaar in Crystal Palace at Hyde Park.

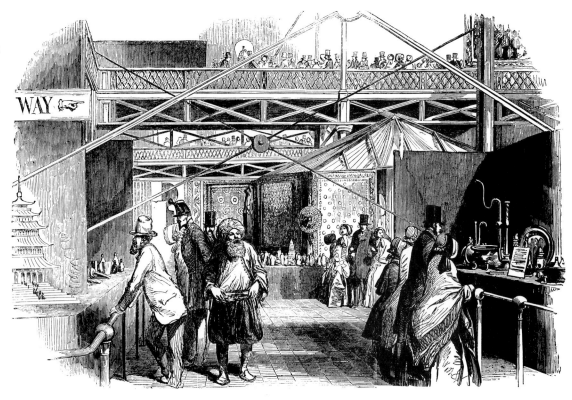

632
Barry, Floral Hall, Covent Garden, London, 1857–58. Woodcut (1859) depicting front entrance.

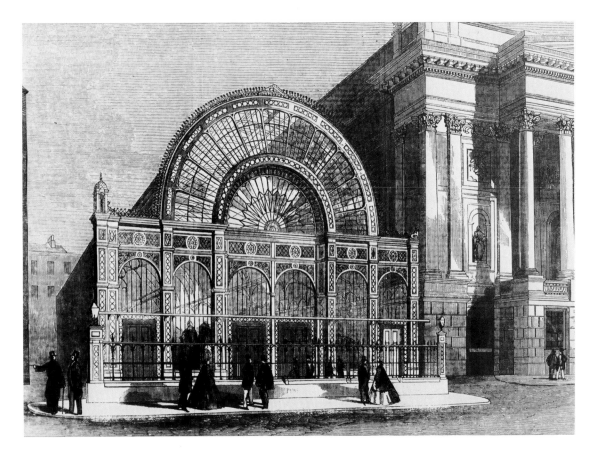

633, 634
Jones, People's Palace (project), Muswell Hill, London, 1859.

633
Woodcut depicting view from park.

634
Woodcut depicting
interior of central
winter garden.

635, 636
Great Conserva-
tory, Parc de la
Tête d'Or, Lyon,
1877–1880.

635
(above) View of cen-
tral pavilion; (below)
general view. Photo-
graphs, ca. 1970.

636
Interior view of ad-
joining palm hall.

637
(below and right)
Bosco, Palacio de
Cristal, Parque del
Retiro, Madrid, 1887.

638–641
F. L. von Sckell,
conservatories,
Royal Castle Gar-
dens, Nymphen-
burg, Munich,
1807–1820.

638
Iron Conservatory,
1807.

639
Palm house, 1820.

640
Iron Conservatory,
roof structure.

641
Iron Conservatory,
details of facade.

**642–645
A. von Voit, Great
Palm House, Old
Botanical Garden,
Munich, 1860–1865.**

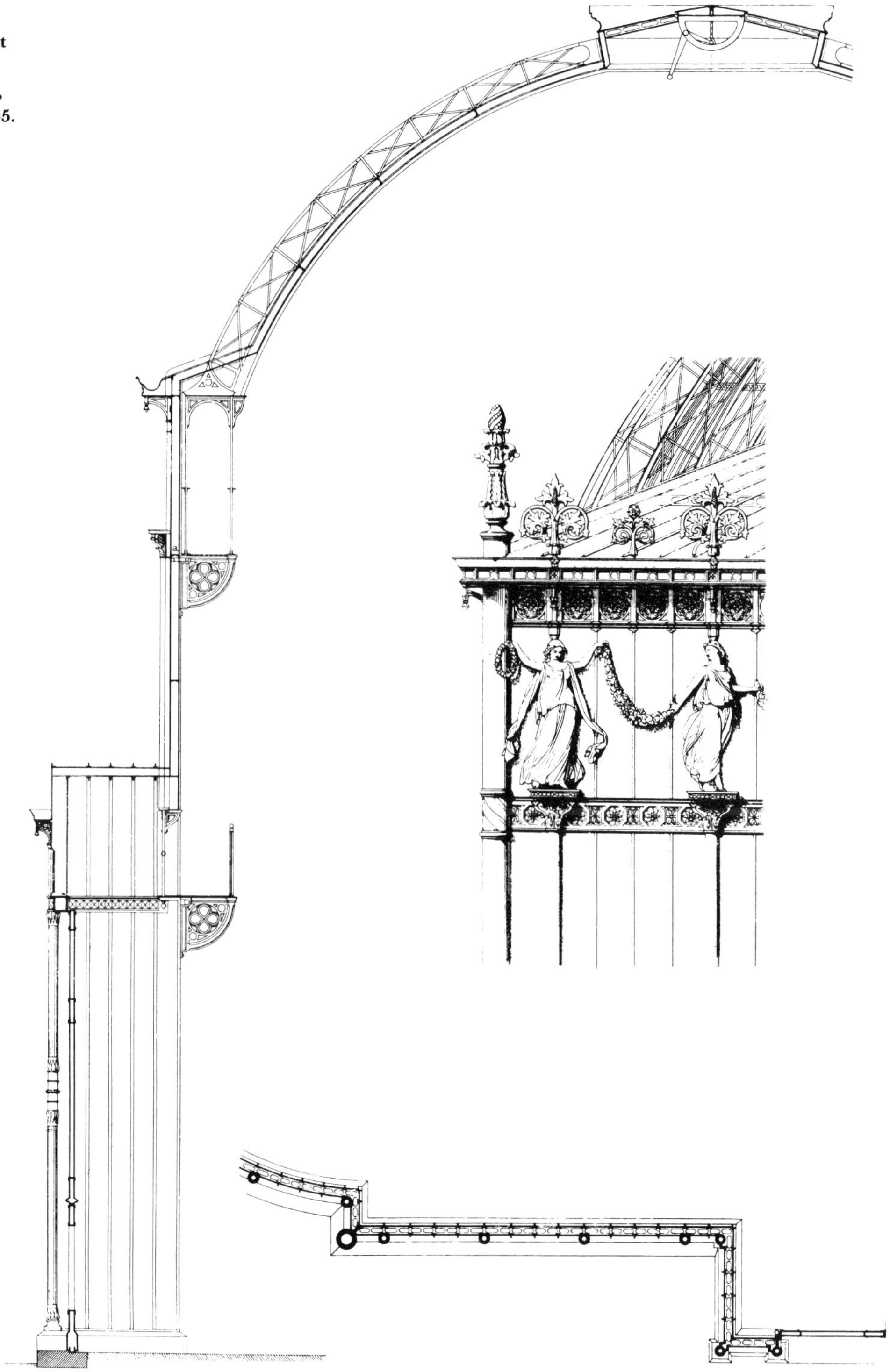

642
Section through
palm hall; horizontal
section along facade;
details of facade.

643
Engraving, ca. 1865.

644
Photograph, ca. 1920.

645
Details of cast-iron portal.

**646, 647, 649–651
A. von Voit, Glass
Palace, Old Botani-
cal Garden, Mun-
ich, 1853–54.**

646
View from transept
in long hall. Engrav-
ing, 1854.

647

648
Paxton, Crystal Pal-
ace, Hyde Park,
London.

649
Interior view of long
hall.

650
Section through long
hall.

651
Remains of iron
structure after 1931
fire.

652–655
A. von Voit, winter
garden of Ludwig
II, Residenz, Mun-
ich, 1867–1869.

652
Watercolor.

653
Watercolor of
ground plan.

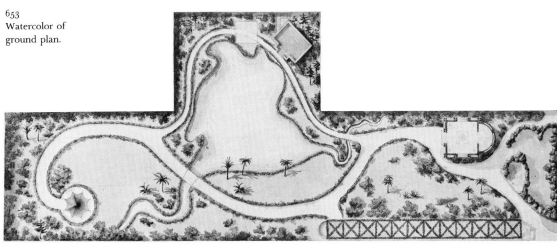

654

655
Design sketches of
glass vault and
ground-plan details
of entrance.

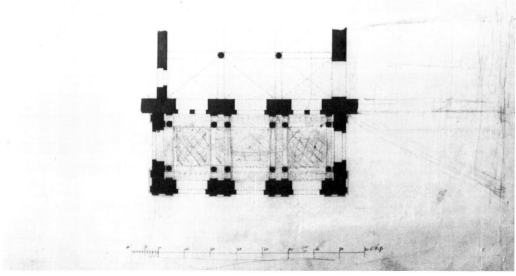

656–658
C. Rohault de Fleury, conservatories, Jardin des Plantes, Paris.

656
Lithograph.

657
Engraving (1885) depicting extension to palm hall.

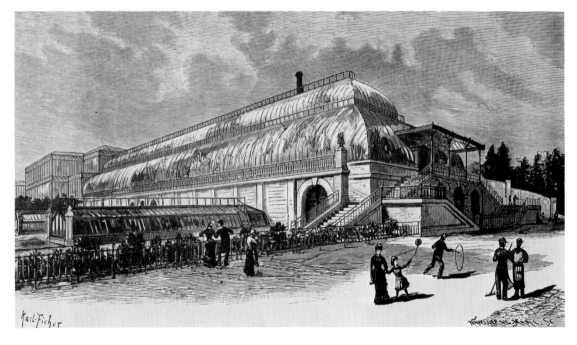

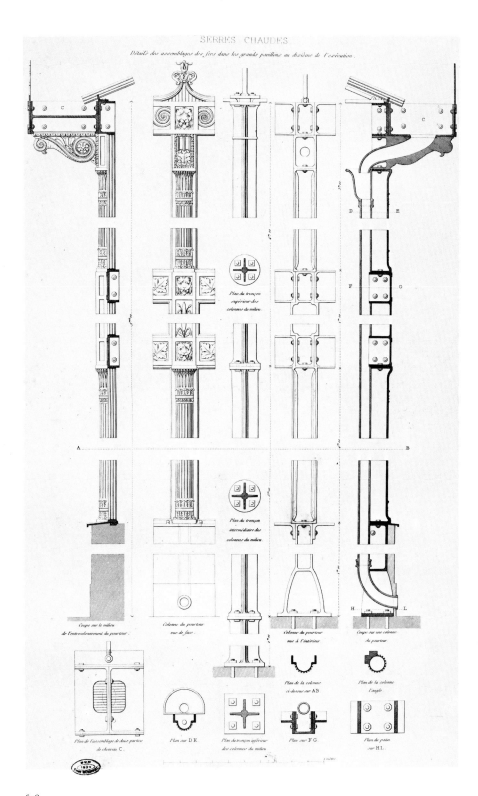

658
Details of construc-
tion of corner
pavilion.

659
Engraving (1852–53)
depicting open-air
concert, Champs-
Elysées.

660, 662–664
H. Meynadier de
Flamalens, Char-
pentier, and Rigo-
let, Jardin d'Hiver,
Champs-Elysées,
1846–1848.

660
Engraving, 1852–53.

661
Share certificate of
Compagnie Emmobi-
lière des Serres des
Champs-Elysées,
1846.

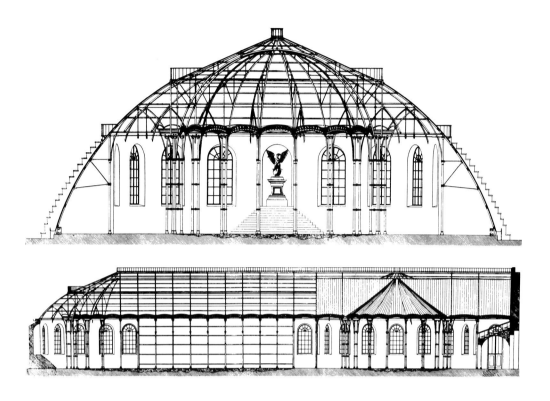

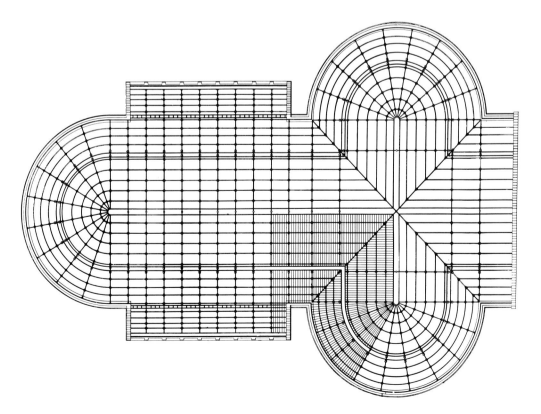

662
Rigolet, structural
drawings.

663
Section showing
fountains (above);
ground plan (below).

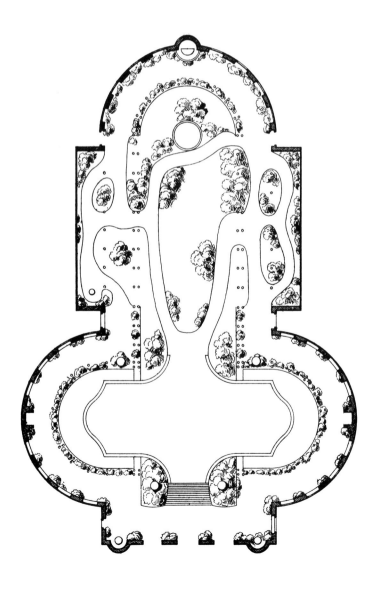

664
Lithograph.

665, 666
Horeau, ideal de-
signs for glass ar-
cades and winter
gardens.

665
Watercolor, 1852.

666
(above) Project for
covering boulevards
of Paris. Watercolor,
1866. (below) Hôtel
de Ville. Pen draw-
ing, 1871.

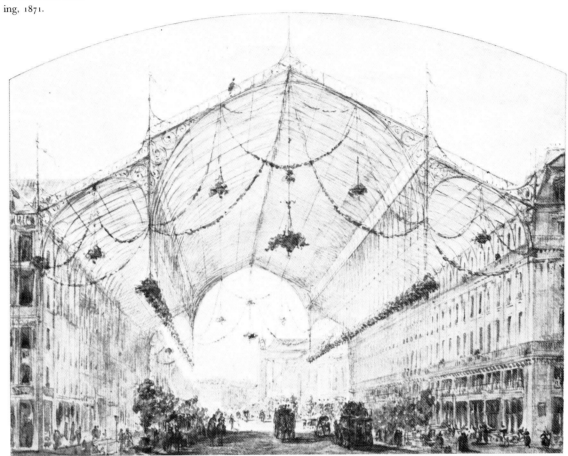

667, 668
Gautier, Garden
Hall, World Exhibi-
tion, Paris, 1900.

667
Front entrance.

668
(above) View from
Seine; (below) inte-
rior view.

669, 670
Bertrand, winter
garden, Jardin Pub-
lic, Pau, 1898.

669
Interior view of
plant hall.

670

671, 672
Piermarini and
Canonica, conserv-
atory, Orto Botan-
ico, Pavia,
1776–1780.

671

673
Central dome, con-
servatory, San Fran-
cisco, ca. 1890.

674
Repton and Cockerell, conservatory, Indian Villa, Sezincote, 1806.

674a
Engraving by J. Martin.

674b

675–679
Taylor, Glass Pavil-
ions, Botanical
Gardens, Sheffield,
1836.

675
View of the three
pavilions.

676
View inside glass
vault of central
pavilion.

677
Side view of central
pavilion.

678
Front view of central
pavilion.

588

679
Sash-bar work in
central pavilion.

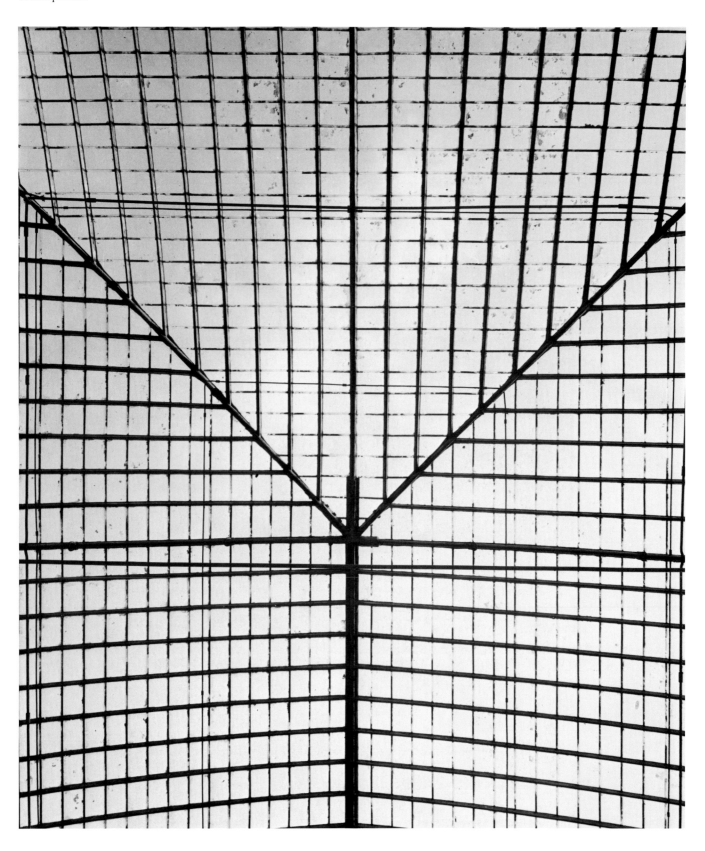

680–690
L. von Zanth, con-
servatories, Wil-
helma, Stuttgart,
1842–1846, 1852–53.

680
Corner pavilion.

681
Details of facade of
corner pavilion.

682
View inside dome.

683
View inside wing.

684
Interior corner of
dome.

685
View of corner pavil-
ion showing
gangway.

686
Facade details and
roof gangway.

687
Palm hall, 1852–53.

688
Palm hall and culti-
vation houses.

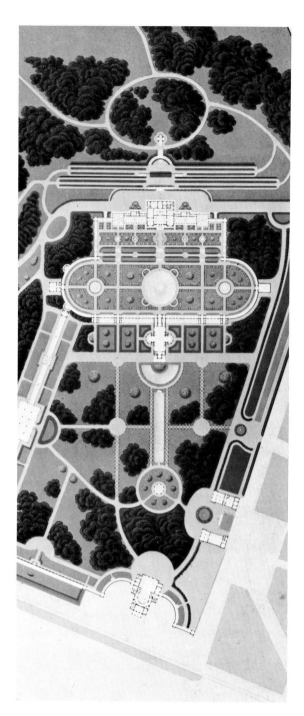

689
Ground plan of cas-
tle gardens. Litho-
graph, 1855.

690
Panorama. Litho-
graph, 1855.

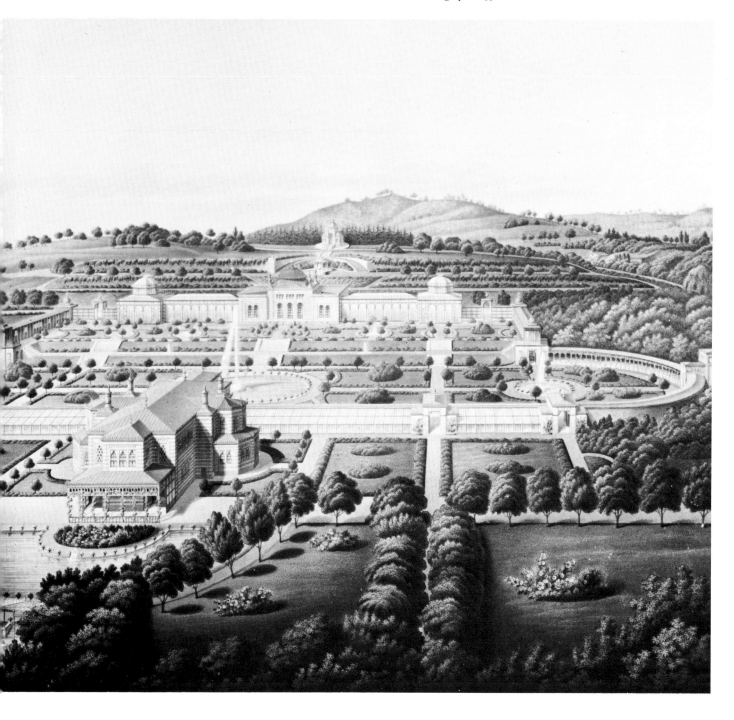

691, 692
Koch, Great Con-
servatory, Old Bo-
tanical Garden,
Tübingen, 1885–86.

691

692
Design in watercolor.

693
Orangery, Lazienski
Park, Warsaw,
ca. 1840. Central
part.

694–697
F. von Sengen-
schmid, Great Palm
House, Park Schön-
brunn, Vienna-
Schönbrunn,
1880–1882.

694

695
Central pavilion.

696
Interior view of central pavilion.

697
Interior view of central pavilion.

**698, 699
Sundial House,
Park Schönbrunn,
Vienna-Schön-
brunn, 1885.**

698
Front.

700
Small Conservatory,
Vienna-Hietzing,
ca. 1850.

701, 702
Ohmann, New
Winter Garden,
Burggarten,
Vienna, 1902.

702
Central pavilion.

703–708
Clark, camellia
house, Wollaton
Hall, 1823.

703

704
Details of facade.

705

706
Roofscape.

708
Column.

707
Roofscape.

References for the Text

1. Meyer 1907, p. 58

2. Ibid., pp. 55 ff.

3. See also Giedion 1928, 1976; Gloag and Bridgwater 1948; Henning-Schefeld and Schmidt-Thomsen 1972; Benevolo 1978; Pevsner 1976; Hitchcock 1958; Roisecco 1972.

4. Meyer 1907, p. 55.

5. Giedion 1976, p. 454.

6. Wilde 1977, vol. 1, pp. 393–427.

7. Giedion 1976, p. 455.

8. Häberlin 1855, p. 107.

9. Hartog 1962, p. 39.

10. Hegemann 1976, p. 207.

11. Quoted in ibid., p. 262.

12. Quoted in ibid., p. 264.

13. Baumeister 1876, pp. 184 ff.

14. Quoted in Réau 1954, p. 31

15. Frégier 1840, vol. 2, pp. 51 ff.

16. Réau 1954, p. 33. By the time of the Commune and the Directoire, the "Commission des Artistes" had thoroughly considered the rigorous urbanization proposals for Paris, which however remained a paper exercise. Not until such proposals became realizable on an extensive scale in the context of boulevards was there any action; this was stimulated by the land speculation of the joint stock companies involved.

17. Haussmann, *Mémoires*, 1890–1893, vol. 3, p. 530.

18. Ibid., p. 173.

19. Texier 1852–53, p. 183 (description of the conservatories in the Jardin des Plantes, Paris).

20. Dickens 1838, *Oliver Twist*.

21. Fourier 1966, p. 174.

22. Ibid., p. 11.

23. *Encyclopaedia of Gardening* (London, 1822). German translation (Weimar, 1923–24) quoted in Tschira 1939, p. 99.

24. Posener 1968, p. 21.

25. Ibid., pp. 22 ff.

26. Quoted in ibid., p. 26.

27. Semper 1849, p. 524.

28. *The Builder*, 15.12.1855, vol. 13., no. 671, pp. 603, 604.

29. Posener 1968, p. 35.

30. Howard 1907, quoted in Posener 1968, pp. 57,58.

31. Ibid., p. 62.

32. Hegemann 1976, p. 214.

33. Behne 1973, pp. 67 ff.

34. Id.

35. Id.

36. Scheerbart 1971, p. 27.

37. Ibid., p. 65.

38. Sternberger 1974, pp. 156 ff.

39. Gurlitt 1888, pp. 166–173.

40. Lucae 1869, pp. 294–306.

41. Title of the book by Giedion, 1929.

42. Le Corbusier 1963, p. 25.

43. Ibid., p. 173.

44. Ibid., pp. 99 ff.

45. Ibid., p. 86.

46. Mendelsohn 1924, p. 211.

47. Le Corbusier 1963, pp. 15, 179.

48. Ibid., p. 102.

49. Ibid., p. 207.

50. Cf. Giedion 1929, p. 26.

51. Realis, pp. 60 ff.

52. Sckell 1825, p. 1.

53. Ibid., p. 4.

54. Loudon 1817.

55. Loudon 1818, pp. 1 ff.

56. Sckell 1825, pp. 181 ff.

57. Ibid., p. 181.

58. Neumann 1862, p. 180.

59. Chadwick 1961, pp. 72 ff.

60. Semper 1849, pp. 522–524.

61. Pett 1966, p. 62.

62. *Über Land und Meer*, 1871–72, 14, vol. 27, no. 10, pp. 5,6.

63. Neumann 1862, p. 171.

64. Ibid., pp. 175, 176.

65. Chadwick 1961, pp. 104 ff.

66. *Gardener's Magazine*, 1839, vol. 15, p. 450.

67. *Gartenzeitung*, 1882, vol. 1, p. 80.

68. Ranke 1977, pp. 143, 144.

69. *Über Land und Meer*, 1869, 11, vol. 22., no. 32, p. 522.

70. Fontane 1969, pp. 72, 73.

71. *DBZ*, 1872, vol. 6, no. 1, p. 29 (Schinkel Festival).

72. Quoted in Fischer 1970, p. 104.

73. Schoser 1969, p. 14.

74. McGrath and Frost 1961, pp. 134 ff.

75. *Allgemeine Bauzeitung*, 1852, vol. 17, p. 299.

76. *Illustrated London News*, 1859.

77. *Jardins en France*, 1977, p. 18.

78. Quoted in ibid. p. 49.

79. Dietrich 1860, pp. 143 ff.

80. Sachs 1875, p. 6.

81. Ibid., p. 10.

82. Humboldt 1845, vol. 1, p. 55.

83. Eichler 1881, vol. 1, pp. 34 ff.

84. *ZfBW*, 1867, vol. 17, parts 7–10, pp. 315 ff.

85. Tschira 1939, p. 11.

86. Pfann 1935, p. 5.

87. Tschira 1939, p. 89.

88. Pfann 1935, p. 4.

89. Tschira, 1939, p. 97.

90. Ibid., p. 98.

91. Pfann 1939, p. 3.

92. Bouché 1886, p. 15.

93. Chadwick 1961, pp. 70 ff.

94. Loudon 1817, p. 74.

95. Jordan 1913, p. 31.

96. Quoted in Tschira 1939, p. 66.

97. Bucher 1971, pp. 51 ff.

98. Scheerbart 1971, pp. 42, 43.

99. McGrath and Frost 1961, p. 41.

100. Ibid., pp. 41 ff.

101. Fischer 1970, p. 27.

102. Ibid., pp. 27 ff.

103. McGrath and Frost 1961, p. 44.

104. Fischer 1970, p. 80.

105. Meyer 1907, p. 55.

106. McIntosh 1853, vol. 1, pp. 119–123.

107. McGrath and Frost 1961, p. 45.

108. Chadwick 1961, p. 97.

109. McIntosh 1853, vol. 1, pp. 108 ff., 134 ff.

110. Pfann 1935, p. 3.

111. *Deutsches Magazin für Garten- und Blumenkunde*, 1872, vol. 25, p. 194; Seemann 1856, p. 11.

112. Dietrich 1860, pp. 605, 606.

113. Ibid., pp. 683, 684.

114. Troll 1926, p. 47.

115. *Deutsches Magazin für Garten- und Blumenkunde*, 1872, vol. 25, p. 196.

116. Gulf Stream region excluded.

117. *Deutsches Magazin für Garten- und Blumenkunde*, 1872, vol. 25, p. 197.

118. Ibid., p. 198.

119. Ibid., pp. 194 ff.

120. *Die Gartenflora*, 1876, vol. 25, p. 111.

121. *Deutsches Magazin für Garten- und Blumenkunde*, 1872, vol. 25, p. 291.

122. Seemann 1856, p. 23.

123. Kazvini 1872, p. 231.

124. *Deutsches Magazin für Garten- und Blumenkunde*, 1872, vol. 25, p. 288.

125. Matthew 21:8; John 12:12, 13.

126. *Deutsches Magazin für Garten- und Blumenkunde*, 1872, vol. 25, pp. 227, 228.

127. Ibid., vol. 25, p. 198; Humboldt 1849, vol. 1.

128. Seemann 1854, pp. 42 ff.

129. Kronfeld 1923, p. 29.

130. Ibid., p. 68.

131. *Herrenhausen 1666–1966*, p. 27.

132. Humboldt 1845, vol. 1, p. 97.

133. Bouché 1886, p. 213.

134. Neumann 1862, p. 182.

135. According to Seneca's account "naturalium quaestionum," the Romans probably knew about water heating equipment for their baths, but they did not use the method of recirculating the water to the boiler.

136. Neumann 1862, p. 189.

137. Id.

138. Ibid., p. 192.

139. Id.

140. Ibid., p. 250.

141. Ibid., p. 251.

142. Ibid., p. 250.

143. Meissner 1821.

144. Pfann 1935, p. 7.

145. Bouché 1886, pp. 28 ff.

146. Durm and Ende 1893, part 4, VI, 4, p. 403.

147. Dietrich 1860, pp. 369 ff.; Bouché 1886, pp. 28 ff.

148. Tschira 1939, p. 100.

149. Quoted in Ibid., p. 99.

150. Jordan 1913, p. 31.

151. C.I. and W.I. signify cast iron and wrought iron.

152. Marx 1970, vol. 1, p. 376.

153. Ibid., p. 372.

154. Ashton 1951, pp. 87 ff.

155. Marx 1970, pp. 379 ff.

156. Id.

157. Ibid., pp. 381, 382.

158. Kuczynski 1964, vol. 22, pp. 84 ff.

159. Cf. Johannsen 1925, pp. 122 ff.

160. Marx 1970, vol. 1, pp. 382, 383.

161. Johannsen 1925, pp. 130 ff.

162. Marx 1970, vol. 1, p. 384.

163. Cf. Beck 1879, vol. 3, pp. 503 ff., 1069 ff., 546 ff.; Johannsen 1925, pp. 110 ff.; Marx 1970, pp. 300 ff.; Werner 1975, p. 36.

164. Beck 1879, vol. 3, pp. 246 ff., 518, 580 ff.

165. Cf. Marx 1970, pp. 382 ff.; Werner 1975, p. 38; Johannsen 1925, pp. 131 ff.; Beck 1879, vol. 3, p. 755.

166. Cf. Beck 1879, vol. 3, pp. 756 ff.; vol. 4, pp. 295 ff.; Mertens 1977, p. 33; Voigt 1965, pp. 255 ff., 367 ff.; Johannsen 1925, pp. 130 ff.; Wiedenfeld 1938, p. 45; Werner 1975, p. 43; Hennig-Schefold and Schmidt-Thomsen 1972, p. 14.

167. Beck 1879, vol. 4, p. 285.

168. Voigt 1965, pp. 362 ff.

169. Ibid., pp. 225 ff.

170. Marx 1970, p. 383.

171. Mertens 1977, p. 33.

172. Voigt 1965, pp. 225 ff.

173. Beck 1879, vol. 3, pp. 756 ff.

174. Ibid., p. 761.

175. Beck 1879, vol. 4, pp. 295 ff.

176. Johannsen 1925, pp. 130 ff.; Voigt 1965, pp. 367 ff.

177. Johannsen 1925, p. 131.

178. Wiedenfeld 1938, p. 45.

179. Hennig-Schefold and Schmidt-Thomsen, 1972, p. 14.

180. Werner 1975, p. 43; quoted in Schadendorf 1965, p. 64.

181. Mertens 1977, pp. 39, 40.

182. Ibid., p. 31.

183. Cf. Ashton 1951, pp. 13 ff.; Beck 1879, vol. 1, pp. 963 ff.; Gloag and Bridgwater 1948, pp. 3 ff.; Johannsen 1925, p. 75; Mertens 1977, p. 27; Werner 1975, pp. 12 ff., 20.

184. Ashton 1951, pp. 24 ff.; Beck 1879, vol. 3, pp. 6, 161 ff., 376 ff., 615, 757 ff., 1064; vol. 4, p. 92; Johannsen 1925, pp. 97, 106, 123–126; Schild 1967, p. 10.

185. Piwowarsky 1958, pp. 4, 5.

186. Cf. Beck 1879, vol. 4, pp. 102, 107, 155, 161, 764, 864 ff.; vol. 5, p. 1376; Johannsen 1925, pp. 98, 134, 138, 146 ff.; Mertens 1977, p. 46; Giedion 1976, p. 135; Scheerer 1848, vol. 1, pp. 406–527.

187. Kuczynski 1964–65, vol. 23, p. 33; vol. 24, p. 87.

188. Weyrauch on the increase in bridge spans in the nineteenth century, in *ZfBW*, 1901, vol. 51, parts 7–9, pp. 465 ff.

189. Meyer 1907, p. 43.

190. Ibid., pp. 29 ff.

191. Straub 1949, pp. 71 ff.; Werner 1975, p. 49.

192. Meyer 1907, p. 37.

193. Straub 1949, pp. 152 ff.

194. Beck 1879, vol. 3, p. 63.

195. Giedion 1976, pp. 157 ff.

196. Brunet 1809.

197. Benevolo 1978, vol. 1, p. 21; Rondelet 1812–1817.

198. Meyer 1907, p. 40.

199. Werner 1975, p. 50.

200. Hamilton 1941, pp. 139 ff.

201. Gatz and Hart 1966, p. 9.

202. Beck 1879, vol. 4, p. 208.

203. Ibid., pp. 208 ff.

204. Ibid., p. 212.

205. Wittek 1964, p. 7.

206. Gloag and Bridgwater 1948, p. 193; Wittek 1964, p. 9.

207. Straub 1949, pp. 217 ff.

208. Wittek 1964, p. 11.

209. Ibid., p. 18.

210. Werner 1974, p. 164.

211. Meyer 1907, p. 47.

212. Werner 1974, pp. 276 ff.

213. Breymann 1890, vol. 3, p. 5.

214. Ibid., p. 1.

215. *Allgemeine Bauzeitung*, 1862, vol. 27, pp. 239, 240, atlas sheets 510–514.

216. *Illustrated London News*, 1.3.1851, 10, vol. 18, no. 472, p. 176.

217. Mäurer 1865, p. 108.

218. Foerster 1903, p. 75.

219. Wittek 1964, p. 18.

220. Meyer 1907, p. 160.

221. Baumeister 1866, pp. 85 ff.

222. Id.

223. Pfann 1935, p. 3.

224. Brandt 1876, pp. 34 ff.

225. Wittek 1964, p. 10; Benevolo 1978, vol. 1, p. 48.

226. Fairbairn 1859, p. 7.

227. Gloag and Bridgwater 1948, p. 192.

228. Beck 1879, vol. 3, p. 761; vol. 4, p. 295.

229. Gloag and Bridgwater 1948, p. 193.

230. Durm and Ende 1896, 3, vol. 3, part 1, p. 63.

231. Ibid., p. 61.

232. McIntosh 1853, vol. 1, pp. 546 ff.

233. Brandt 1876, pp. 386 ff.

234. McIntosh 1853, vol. 1, pp. 382 ff.

235. Höltje and Weber 1964.

236. Meyer 1907, p. 18.

237. Ibid., p. 20.

238. Wittek 1964, p. 13.

239. Stroud 1962, pp. 116, 131.

240. McIntosh 1853, vol. 1, pp. 366 ff.

241. Ibid., p. 365.

242. Werner 1973, p. 256.

243. *Die Bauwelt*, 24.11.1969, vo. 60, part 47, pp. 1677–1681.

244. Werner 1973, p. 256.

245. Pevsner 1976, p. 242.

246. Curl 1973, p. 25.

247. Wittek 1964, pp. 13, 94.

248. Loudon 1817, p. 74.

249. McGrath and Frost 1961, p. 119.

250. *Allgemeine Bauzeitung*, 1849, vol. 14, pp. 108–110, atlas sheets 253–255.

251. Ibid., 1852, vol. 17, pp. 139–142, atlas sheets 469–475.

252. Chadwick 1961, pp. 73–103.

253. McIntosh 1853, vol. 1, p. 374.

254. Ibid., p. 122.

255. Mäurer 1865, p. 107.

256. Heinzerling 1878, vol. 2, p. 1.

257. Wittek 1964, p. 6.

258. Walmisley 1950, pp. 29, 30.

259. Wittek 1964, p. 28.

260. *Allgemeine Bauzeitung*, 1863, vol. 28, p. 115, atlas sheet 568.

261. Wittek 1964, p. 29.

262. Brandt, 1876, pp. 427 ff.

263. Id.

264. Schoser 1971, pp. 1–4.

265. *ZfBW*, 1887, vol. 37, parts 1–3, pp. 70–72, atlas sheet 18.

266. Wittek 1964, pp. 40 ff.

267. Loudon 1817, p. 74.

268. Ibid., p. 75.

269. Id.

270. Chadwick 1961, pp. 98, 99.

271. Werner 1970, p. 35.

272. *Allgemeine Bauzeitung*, 1850, vol. 15, pp. 277–285, notice sheet 341, atlas sheets 362–367.

273. Chadwick 1961, pp. 107 ff.

274. Werner 1970, pp. 38 ff.

275. *Allgemeine Bauzeitung*, 1850, vol. 15, pp. 277–285, notice sheet 341, atlas sheets 362–367.

276. Wittek 1964, p. 15.

277. Bouché 1886, plates XXIII, XXIV.

278. Wittek, p. 50.

279. Giedion 1976, p. 174.

280. *Zeitschrift für praktische Baukunst*, 1849, vol. 9, pp. 515–526, plate 54.

281. *Allgemeine Bauzeitung*, 1852, vol. 17, pp. 299–304, atlas sheets 506, 507.

282. Walmisley 1950, p. 21.

283. *Illustrierte Zeitung*, 17.9.1864, vol. 43, no. 1107, p. 197.

284. Breymann 1854, vol. 3.

285. McIntosh 1853, vol. 1, pp. 363 ff.

286. Ibid., pp. 368 ff.

287. Chadwick 1961, p. 94.

288. McIntosh 1853, vol. 1, pp. 376 ff.

289. McCracken 1971, p. 27.

290. Chadwick 1961, pp. 157, 158.

291. Gayle and Gillon 1974, p. viii.

292. Ibid., p. 16.

293. Breymann 1890, vol. 3, p. 80.

294. Bannister 1950, pp. 231 ff.

295. Meyer 1907, p. 160.

296. Giedion 1976, p. 140.

297. McIntosh 1853, pp. 361, 362.

298. Chadwick 1961, pp. 77–80.

299. McIntosh 1853, vol. 1, p. 120.

300. Brandt 1876, p. 285.

301. Scharowsky 1895, p. 41.

302. McIntosh 1853, vol. 1, p. 368.

303. Sturges 1970; Gayle and Gillon 1974, p. x.

304. *Allgemeine Bauzeitung*, 1837, vol. 2, no. 33, pp. 271–274.

305. Chadwick 1961, pp. 70 ff.

306. Curl 1973, p. 26.

307. Gloag and Bridgwater 1948, p. 192.

308. Skempton 1956, pp. 1029 ff.

309. Gayle and Gillon 1974, p. v.

310. Sturges 1970, plate XVI.

311. Loudon 1832.

312. Werner 1970, p. 20.

313. Gloag and Bridgwater 1948, pp. 201 ff.

314. Werner 1970, p. 30.

315. Ibid., pp. 35, 49.

316. Mertens 1970, p. 40.

317. McGrath and Frost 1961, pp. 134–138.

318. *Allgemeine Bauzeitung*, 1852, vol. 17, pp. 299–304, atlas sheets 506, 507; Geist 1969, p. 216.

319. Wittek 1964, p. 15.

320. Roth 1971, p. 2

321. *ZfBW*, 1867, vol. 17, parts 7–10, pp. 315–324; atlas sheets 34–39.

322. Wittek 1964, p. 17.

323. Bouché 1886, plates XXII–XXIV.

324. Chadwick 1966, p. 146.

325. *Illustrated London News*, 15.10.1859, 18, vol. 35, no. 998, pp. 370, 371.

326. Ibid., 5.3.1859, 18, vol. 34, no. 963, pp. 224–226.

327. Gloag and Bridgwater 1948, p. 249; Roisecco 1972, vol. 1, pp. 460 ff.

328. Brandt 1876, pp. 404–407.

329. Tschira 1939, p. 14.

330. *Allgemeines Teutsches Gartenmagazin*, 1806, 3, vol. 2, part 1, pp. 3–5, plates 2, 3.

331. Nau 1959, pp. 102 ff.

332. Thiollet 1832, p. 24.

333. Gloag 1970, pp. 47 ff.

334. Loudon 1817.

335. Hix 1974, p. 105.

336. Chadwick 1961, p. 75.

337. McIntosh 1853, vol. 1, p. 371.

338. *Gardener's Chronicle*, 31.8.1850, vol. 10, no. 35, pp. 548, 549.

339. Bannister 1950, pp. 231–246.

340. *Allgemeine Bauzeitung*, 1850, vol. 15, p. 448.

341. Ibid., 1852, vol. 17, p. 222, atlas sheet 488.

342. Gloag and Bridgwater 1948, p. 250.

343. *Gardener's Chronicle*, 8.8.1868, vol. 28, no. 32, p. 858.

344. Gloag and Bridgwater 1948, p. 250.

345. Messenger 1880, p. 6.

346. McIntosh 1853, vol. 1, p. 109.

347. Gloag and Bridgwater 1948, p. 201.

348. Wittek 1964, p. 21.

349. Beck 1879, p. 205.

350. Ibid., p. 266.

351. Loudon 1818, p. 2.

352. Gloag and Bridgwater 1948, p. 45.

353. Mäurer 1865, p. 35; Beck 1879, vol. 3, p. 631.

354. Heinzerling 1876, vol. 1, p. 1.

355. Beck 1879, vol. 4, p. 266.

356. Mäurer 1865, p. 33.

357. Ibid., p. 107.

358. Ibid., p. 103.

359. Fairbairn 1859, p. 62.

360. Mäurer 1865, p. 105.

361. Wittek 1964, p. 33.

362. Ibid., p. 30.

363. Hübsch 1825, p. 19.

364. McIntosh 1853, vol. 1, pp. 382, 383.

365. Ibid., p. 384.

366. Heinzerling 1878, vol. 2, pp. 1, 25.

367. Wittek 1964, p. 50.

368. *Zeitschrift für praktische Baukunst*, 1849, vol. 9, pp. 515–526, plate 54.

369. Heinzerling 1878, vol. 2, p. 2.

370. *Illustrierte Zeitung*, 17.9.1864, vol. 43, no. 1107, p. 197.

371. Heinzerling 1878, vol. 2, p. 2.

372. *Der Bautechniker*, 1885, vol. 5, no. 22, p. 152.

373. *Deutsche Bauzeitung*, 1902, vol. 2, part 5, p. 373.

374. Wittek 1964, p. 64, 65.

375. *DBZ*, 1873, vol. 7, no. 32, pp. 121 121, 125; no. 40, pp. 149–151; no. 44, pp. 163–166; no. 46, pp. 171, 172; no. 64, pp. 258, 259, 269, 270.

376. *ZfBW*, 1909, vol. 59, parts 4–6, pp. 202–222, fig. 20, atlas sheets 25–30.

377. Ibid., 1916, vol. 66, parts 1–3, pp. 30–40.

378. Ibid., 1887, vol. 37, parts 1–3, pp. 70–72, atlas sheets 14, 15.

379. Hix 1974, pp. 146, 147.

380. Meyer 1907, pp. 131–133; *Deutsche Bauzeitung*, 1902, vol. 2, part 5, p. 361.

381. Quentin 1964, pp. 152–155.

382. *ZfBW* 1866, vol. 16, parts 1–3, pp. 7–34, atlas sheets 10–14.

383. Id.

384. Ibid., 1888, vol. 38, parts 1–3, pp. 43–82, atlas sheet 18.

385. For 1, 2 7–9, see Siegel 1960, p. 241; for 3 see Wittek 1964, pp. 67, 121; for 6 see Breymann 1890, vol. 3, p. 251.

386. Dischinger 1928.

387. Loudon 1833, p. 7.

388. Ibid., p. 24.

389. Hix 1974, p. 111.

390. Ibid., p. 112.

391. Id.

392. Ibid., p. 26.

393. Loudon 1822, p. 357.

394. McIntosh 1853, vol. 1, p. 542.

395. Durm and Ende 1894, 3, vol. 2, part 5, pp. 298 ff.

396. Mäurer 1865, p. 224.

397. Breymann 1890, vol. 3, pp. 187, 188.

398. Gloag 1970, p. 45.

399. *Allgemeine Bauzeitung*, 1837, vol. 2, no. 48, pp. 395 ff.; no. 49, pp. 403 ff.

400. McIntosh 1853, vol. 1, p. 547.

401. Ibid., p. 364.

402. *Deutsches Magazin für Garten- und Blumenkunde*, 1866, vol. 19, p. 214.

403. *Allgemeine Bauzeitung*, 1837, vol. 2, no. 48, pp. 395 ff.; no. 49, pp. 403 ff.

404. Loudon 1833, p. 24.

405. Loudon 1818, p. 5.

406. Ibid., p. 4.

407. *The Builder*, 23.12.1843, vol. 1, no. 46, p. 552.

408. Mertens 1977, p. 1.

409. Ibid., p. 2.

410. Josch 1942; Piwowarsky 1958; Brandt 1876, p. 98.

References for the Catalog

1. McIntosh 1853.
2. Pett 1966, p. 2.
3. Eichler 1881, vol. 1, pp. 34 ff.
4. *Architektenverein zu Berlin*, 1896, vol. II, pp. 252–256.
5. Bouché 1886, p. 15.
6. Ibid., pp. 15, 120.
7. Martius 1965, pp. 262 ff.
8. Neumeyer 1973, pp. 15–19.
9. *Die Gartenflora*, 1894, vol. 43, p. 4.
10. Neumeyer 1973, p. 17.
11. *DBZ*, 1873, vol. 7, no. 32, p. 121.
12. Ibid., p. 122.
13. *DBZ*, 1873, vol. 7, no. 44, p. 164.
14. Ibid., no. 64, p. 259.
15. Ibid., p. 269.
16. Id.
17. Id.
18. *DBZ*, 1873, vol. 7, no. 32, p. 121.
19. *Über Land und Meer*, 1871, 13, vol. 26, no. 48, p. 14.
20. *ZfBW*, 1869, vol. 19, parts 8–10, pp. 432–435.
21. *ZfBW*, 1881, vol. 21, parts 1–3, p. 176, atlas sheets 38–42.
22. Id.
23. Ibid., p. 181.
24. Hix 1974, p. 164.
25. *ZfBW* 1909, vol. 59, parts 4–6, pp. 202–222, atlas sheets 25–30.
26. Koerner 1910, p. 15.
27. *Deutsches Magazin für Garten- und Blumenkunde*, 1861, vol. 14, pp. 84–91.
28. Loudon 1835, pp. 336, 337.
29. Loudon 1832, vol. 8, pp. 407–432.
30. McIntosh 1853, vol. 1, pp. 363, 364.
31. Id.
32. Balis and Witte 1970, p. 9.
33. Ibid., p. 11.
34. Ibid., p. 15.
35. Borncrêpe 1920, p. 185.
36. Id.
37. Meyer 1907, pp. 131–133.
38. Borncrêpe 1920, p. 177.
39. James 1973, pp. 3–9.
40. Hix 1974, pp. 25–27.
41. Loudon 1818, p. 1.
42. Fintelmann 1882, vol. 1, pp. 31–83.
43. Chadwick 1961, pp. 72–103.
44. Ibid., p. 74.
45. Ibid., pp. 75, 76.
46. Ibid., p. 76.
47. Report of the Commissioners, 1852, pp. 304, 312.
48. Chadwick 1961, p. 98.
49. Loudon 1839, vol. 15, pp. 450 ff.
50. McGrath and Frost 1961, p. 128.
51. Chadwick 1961, p. 94.
52. Ibid., p. 96.
53. Ibid., p. 95.
54. Quoted in ibid., p. 97.
55. Fintelmann 1882, vol. 1, pp. 31–83.
56. Chadwick 1961, p. 78.
57. Ibid., p. 102.
58. Ibid., p. 103.
59. McGrath and Frost 1961, p. 119.
60. McCracken 1971. p. 42.
61. *Illustrated London News*, 18.3.1865, 24, vol. 46, no. 1306, pp. 258, 262.
62. Walmisley 1950, pp. 21, 22.
63. *Gardener's Chronicle*, 23.5.1874, vol. 34, no. 21, p. 662.
64. Ibid., 1.12.1855, vol. 15, no. 48, pp. 790, 791.
65. Siebert 1908, pp. 96 ff.
66. Ibid., p. 97.
67. Ibid., p. 99.
68. *Über Land und Meer*, 1870, 12, vol. 24, no. 41, pp. 6–12.
69. Meyer 1907, p. 173.
70. *Die Gartenflora*, 1872, vol. 21, p. 116.
71. Ibid., p. 115.
72. Siebert 1908, p. 96.
73. *Möller's Deutsche Gärtner-Zeitung*, 2.6.1906, vol. 21, no. 22, pp. 257 ff.
74. Quoted in Smith 1971, pp. 15, 16.
75. Ibid., pp. 19–21.
76. *Allgemeine Bauzeitung*, 1837, vol. 2, no. 48, pp. 395 ff.
77. Ibid., p. 400.
78. Ibid., p. 398.
79. Meyer 1966, pp. 23–28.
80. Höltje and Weber 1964.
81. *Die Gartenzeitung*, 1882, vol. 1, pp. 53–55.
82. Chadwick 1961, p. 94.
83. Valdenaire 1926, p. 67.
84. "Karlsruhe im Jahre 1870," in *Baugeschichtliche und ingenieurwissenschaftliche Mitteilungen*, 1872, p. 66, 67.
85. *Illustrierte Zeitung*, 17.9.1864, vol. 43, no. 1107, p. 197.
86. Id.

87. Id.

88. Jacobsen and Rothe 1879, p. 5.

89. *DBZ*, 1881, vol. 15, no. 23, p. 133.

90. Jacobsen and Rothe 1879, p. 5.

91. Poulsen 1974, pp. 10 ff.

92. Durm and Ende 1885, 4, part 4, p. 142.

93. McIntosh 1853, vol. 1, p. 368.

94. McGrath and Frost 1961, p. 119.

95. Hix 1974, pp. 121, 122.

96. Plaistow 1970, pp. 1, 2.

97. *ZfBW*, 1887, vol. 37, parts 1–3, p. 70.

98. McIntosh 1853, vol. 1, p. 367.

99. McCracken 1971, p. 42.

100. *The Builder*, 15.1.1848, vol. 6, no. 258, pp. 29–31.

101. McIntosh 1853, vol. 1, p. 119.

102. Ibid., pp. 119–123.

103. *Architectural Review*, 1957, vol. 21, no. 721, pp. 127, 128.

104. *ZfBW*, 1887, vol. 37, parts 1–3, pp. 70–72.

105. Chadwick 1961, pp. 107 ff.; *Illustrated London News*, 6.7.1850, 9, vol. 17, no. 434, p. 13.

106. Chadwick 1961, p. 111.

107. Schild 1967, p. 53.

108. *Allgemeine Bauzeitung*, 1850, vol. 15, pp. 277 ff.; *Illustrated London News*, 1.3.1851, 10, vol. 18, no. 472, p. 176.

109. Gloag and Bridgwater 1948, p. 201.

110. Durm and Ende 1893, 4, VI, part 4, p. 481, 482.

111. Werner 1974, pp. 26–29.

112. *ZfBW*, 1852, vol. 2, parts 1, 2, p. 44.

113. McGrath and Frost 1961, pp. 134 ff.

114. Sckell 1825, pp. 181 ff.

115. Ibid., pp. 182, 183.

116. Tschira 1939, p. 85.

117. Sckell 1825, p. ix.

118. Tschira 1939, p. 95.

119. Id.

120. Sckell 1825, p. 180.

121. Roth 1971, p. 18.

122. *Die Gartenlaube*, 1859, vol. 6, p. 158.

123. Wittek 1964, pp. 15, 43.

124. Ibid., p. 112.

125. *ZfBW*, 1867, vol. 17, parts 7–10, p. 316.

126. Ibid., pp. 317, 318.

127. Ibid., p. 318.

128. *Über Land und Meer*, 1868, 10, vol. 20, no. 20, p. 328.

129. Giedion 1976, p. 137.

130. *Allgemeine Bauzeitung*, 1837, vol. 2, no. 33, pp. 271 ff.

131. Texier 1852–53, p. 183.

132. *Zeitschrift für praktische Baukunst*, 1849, vol. 9, pp. 516, 517.

133. Hix 1974, p. 118.

134. *Zeitschrift für praktische Baukunst*, 1849, vol. 9, p. 520.

135. Ibid., pp. 521–524.

136. Hix 1974, p. 84.

137. *ZfBW*, 1888, vol. 38, parts 4–6, p. 202, atlas sheets 30–33.

138. Nau 1959, p. 102.

139. Id.

140. *Deutsches Magazin für Garten- und Blumenkunde*, 1852, vol. 5, pp. 93 ff.

141. Zanth 1855, p. 1.

142. Ibid., pp. 11 ff.

143. Gerhard 1936, p. 86.

144. Id.

145. *Über Land und Meer*, 1871–72, 14, vol. 27, no. 10, pp. 5, 6.

146. Zanth 1855, pp. viii–xx.

147. Gerhard 1936, p. 83.

148. *Deutsches Magazin für Garten- und Blumenkunde*, 1859, vol. 12, pp. 113, 114.

149. *Allgemeine Bauzeitung*, 1837, vol. 2, no. 44, pp. 395 ff.

150. *Illustrierte Zeitung*, 22.4.1882, vol. 78, no. 2025, pp. 325, 326.

Bibliography

Anderson, A. 1764. *An Historical and Chronical Deduction of the Origin of Commerce, from the Earliest Account to the Present Time, Containing a History of the Great Commercial Interests of the British Empire.* Vol. III. London.

Architektenverein zu Berlin. *Berlin und seine Bauten.* Two parts. Berlin, 1877 and 1896. Vols. I–III published in conjunction with Vereinigung der Berliner Architekten; 1972, parts I–XI.

Ashton, T. S. 1951. *Iron and Steel in the Industrial Revolution,* second edition. Manchester.

Bannister, T. 1950. "The First Iron-Framed Buildings." *Architectural Review,* vol. 107, no. 637, pp. 231 ff.

Baumeister, R. 1866. *Architektonische Formenlehre für Ingenieure.* Stuttgart.

Baumeister, R. 1876. *Stadterweiterungen in technischer, baupolizeilicher und wirtschaftlicher Beziehung.* Berlin.

Balis, J., and E. Witte. 1970. *Histoire des Jardins Botaniques de Bruxelles 1870–1970.* Brussels.

Beck, L. 1879. *Die Geschichte des Eisens.* Four vols. Brunswick.

Behne, A. 1919. *Wiederkehr der Kunst.* Berlin.

Benevolo, L. 1978. *Geschichte der Architektur des 19. und 20. Jahrhunderts.* Two vols. Munich.

Blunt, W. 1973. *The Dream King Ludwig II of Bavaria.* London.

Bouché, C. D. and J. Bouché. 1886. *Bau und Einrichtung von Gewächshäusern.* Bonn.

Bouvier, R., and E. Maynial. 1946. *Der Botaniker von Malmaison.* Berlin.

Borncrêpe, H. 1920. *Les serres de Laeken.* Brussels.

Börsch-Supan, E. 1967. *Garten-, Landschafts- und Paradiesmotive im Innenraum.* Berlin.

Boudon, F. 1972. *Hector Horeau. 1801–1872.* Exhibition catalogue, Musée des Arts Décoratifs, Paris.

Brandt, E. 1876. *Lehrbuch der Eisenkonstruktionen mit besonderer Anwendung für den Hochbau.* Berlin.

Breuer, K. 1923. Die Pfaueninsel. Dissertation. Berlin.

Breymann, G. A. 1849–1854. *Bauconstruktionslehre.* Four vols. Stuttgart.

Brunet. 1809. *Dimensions des fers qui doivent former la coupole de la Halle aux Blés.* Paris.

Buchanan, R. A. 1972. *Industrial Archaeology in Britain.* Harmondsworth.

Bucher, L. 1971. "Kulturhistorische Skizzen aus der Industrie-Austellung aller Völker." *Kat. Die verborgene Vernunft. Funktionale Gestaltung im 19. Jahrhundert,* Neue Sammlung, Munich, Jan.–March.

Carus, C. G. 1955. *Neun Briefe über Landschaftsmalerei geschrieben in den Jahren 1815 bis 1824.* Dresden.

Chadwick, G. F. 1961. *The Works of Sir Joseph Paxton.* London.

Chadwick, G. F. 1966. *The Park and the Town.* London.

Curl, J. S. 1973. *Victorian Architecture, its Practical Aspects.* Newton Abbot.

Deutsche Bauzeitung und Deutscher Baukalender. *Baukunde des Architekten.* Two vols. Berlin.

Dickens, C. 1838. *Oliver Twist.* London.

Dietrich, L. F. (ed.) 1860. *Encyclopädie der gesamten niederen und höheren Gartenkunst.* Leipzig.

Dischinger, F. 1928. *Schalen und Rippenkuppeln.* Berlin.

Douin, R. 1954. *Le Jardin Botanique de la ville de Lyon.* Lyon.

Downie, A. "Kibble Palace Centenary." *Glasgow Herald,* 16.6.1973.

Drexler, A. (ed.). 1977. *The Architecture of the Ecole des Beaux-Arts.* London.

Durm, J., and H. Ende (eds.) *Handbuch der Architektur.*

Eichler, A. W. (ed.). *Jahrbuch des Königlichen botanischen Gartens und des botanischen Museums zu Berlin.*

Engels, F. 1973. *Anti-Dühring.* Herrn Dührings Umwälzung der Wissenschaft (Engels Studienausgabe), Hamburg. Vol. 2.

Engels, F. 1891. *Die Entwicklung des Sozialismus von der Utopie zur Wissenschaft.* Berlin.

Fairbairn, W. 1854. *On the Application of Cast and Wrought Iron to Building Purposes.* London.

Fintelmann, H. 1882. "Mein Besuch in Chatsworth." *Gartenzeitung.* vol. 1. pp. 31–35, 76–83.

Fischer, W. 1970. *Geborgenheit und Freiheit. Vom Bauen in Glas.* Krefeld.

Foerster, M. 1902. *Eisenkonstruktion der Ingenieurshochbauten.* Leipzig.

Fontane, T. 1969. *L'Adultera.* Munich.

Fourier, C. 1808. *Théorie des quatre Mouvements.*

Frégier. 1840. *Des classes dangereuses de la population dans les grandes villes.* Two vols. Paris.

Gatz, K., and F. Hart. 1966. *Stahlkonstruktionen im Hochbau.* Munich.

Gayle, M., and E. von Gillon. 1974. *Cast-Iron Architecture in New York.* New York.

Geist, J. F. 1969. *Passagen. Ein Bautypus des 19. Jahrhunderts.* Munich. English edition: *Arcades.* Cambridge Mass., 1983.

Gerhard, O. 1936. *Stuttgarts Kleinod.* Stuttgart.

Giacomini, V. 1959. *Orto Botanico.* Pavia.

Giacomini, V. 1962. *All Origini dell' Orto Botanico nell' Università di Pavia.* Pavia.

Giedion, S. 1928. *Bauen in Frankreich.* Leipzig and Berlin.

Giedion, S. 1929. *Befreites Wohnen.* Zurich and Leipzig.

Giedion, S. 1971. *Space, Time and Architecture.* Cambridge, Mass.

Goecke, T. (ed.) 1897–1904. *Baukunde des Architekten.* Two parts, four vols. Berlin.

Gloag, J., and D. Bridgwater. 1948. *A History of Cast-Iron Architecture.* London.

Gloag, J. 1970. *Mr. Loudon's England.* Newcastle.

Gottgetreu, R. 1880–1890. *Lehrbuch der Hochbau-Konstruktionen.* Three vols. Berlin.

Gurlitt, C. 1888. *Im Bürgerhause.* Dresden.

Häberlin, K. L. 1973. *Die Bauten des neunzehnten Jahrhunderts im park von Sanssouci. Eine Sammlung von 14 zeitgenössischen Aquarellen von V. Arnim et al. und einem Parkplan von Kohles nebst einer Beschreibung von C.L. Häberlin, gen. Belani aus dem Jahre 1855.* Potsdam-Sanssouci.

Hamilton, S. B. 1941. "Use of Cast-Iron in Buildings." *Transactions of the Newcomen Society,* vol. 21, pp. 139-155.

Hartog, R. 1962. *Stadterweiterung im 19. Jahrhundert.* Stuttgart.

Haussmann, G.-E. 1890-1893. *Mémoires.* Four vols. Paris.

Hegemann, W. 1930. *Das steinerne Berlin.* Berlin.

Heinzerling, F. 1878 and 1889. *Der Eisenhochbau der Gegenwart.* Vols. 2 and 3. Aachen and Leipzig.

Hennig-Schefold, M., and H. Schmidt-Thomsen. 1972. *Transparenz und Masse. Passagen und Hallen aus Eisen und Glas 1800-1880.* Cologne.

Hinz, G. 1937. *Peter Joseph Lenné.* Berlin.

Hitchcock, H.-R. 1958. *Architecture, Nineteenth and Twentieth Centuries.* Harmondsworth.

Hix, J. 1974. *The Glass House.* London; Cambridge, Mass.

Höltje, G., and H. Weber. 1964. *Georg Friedrich Laves.* Hannover.

Hoffmann, W. 1971. *Ideengeschichte der sozialen Bewegung.* Berlin.

Howard, E. 1946. *Garden Cities of To-morrow.* London.

Hübsch, H. 1825. *Entwurf zu einem Theater mit eiserner Dachrüstung.* Heidelberg.

Hughes, Q. 1964. *Seaport, Architecture and Townscape in Liverpool.* London.

Humboldt, A. von. 1808. *Ansichten der Natur mit wissenschaftlichen Erläuterungen.* Two vols. Stuttgart and Tübingen.

Humboldt, A. von. 1845-1858. *Kosmos. Entwurf einer physischen Weltbeschreibung.* Four vols. Stuttgart and Tübingen.

Jacobsen, J. C., and T. Rothe. 1879. *Description des serres du jardin botanique de l'université de Copenhagen.* Copenhagen.

James, N. D. G. (ed.) 1973. *Bicton Gardens.* Norwich.

Johannsen, O. 1924. *Geschichte des Eisens.* Düsseldorf.

Jordan, H. 1913. *Die künstlerische Gestaltung von Eisenkonstruktionen.* Two vols. Berlin.

Josch, K. 1942. *Gusseisen als Baustoff.* Stuttgart.

Kazvini. 1872. "Merkwürdigkeiten der Welt und Wunder der Schöpfung." *Deutsches Magazin für Garten- und Blumenkunde,* vol. 25.

Koerner, A. 1910. *Die Bauten des Königlichen Botanischen Gartens in Dahlem.* Berlin.

Kronfeld, E. M. 1823. *Park und Garten von Schönbrunn.* Vienna.

Kuczynski, J. 1964-65. *Die Geschichte der Lage der Arbeiter und des Kapitalismus.* Vols. 22-24. Berlin.

Laborde, A. de. 1808. *Description des nouveaux jardins de la France.* Paris.

Le Corbusier. 1922. *Vers une Architecture.* Paris.

Lopatto, A. E. 1951. *V. G. Schuhov.* Moscow.

Loudon, J. C. 1817. *Remarks on the Construction of Hothouses.* London.

Loudon, J. C. 1818. *Sketches of Curvilinear Hothouses.* London.

Loudon, J. C. 1822. *Encyclopaedia of Gardening.* London.

Loudon, J. C. 1832. "Birmingham Botanical Horticultural Garden." *Gardener's Magazine,* August 1832, vol. 8, pp. 407-432.

Loudon, J. C. 1732 "Recollections of a Tour made in May 1829." *Gardener's Magazine,* August 1832, vol. 8, pp. 407-432.

Loudon, J. C. 1833. *Encyclopaedia of Cottage, Farm and Villa Architecture.* London.

Lucae, R. 1869. "Über die Macht des Raumes in der Baukunst." *ZfBW,* vol. 19, parts 4-7, pp. 294-306.

Mäurer, E. 1865. *Formen der Walzkunst.* Stuttgart.

Martius, L. 1965. "Die Villa Borsig in Berlin-Moabit." *Der Bär von Berlin,* vol. 14, pp. 262 ff.

Marx, K. 1970. *Capital.* Three vols. London.

McCracken, E. 1971. *The Palmhouse and Botanic Garden, Belfast.* Belfast.

McGrath, R., and A. C. Frost. 1961. *Glass in Architecture and Decoration.* London.

McIntosh, C. 1853. *The Book of the Garden.* Two vols. Edinburgh.

Meissner, P. T. 1821. *Die Heizung mit erwärmter Luft.* Vienna. Abstracts: *Allgemeines Teutsches Gartenmagazin,* 1822, 14, vol. 6, part 1, pp. 3-7; *Allgemeine Bauzeitung,* 1838, vol. 3, suppl., pp. 99 ff.

Mendelsohn, E. 1923. "Die internationale Übereinstimmung des neuen Baugedankens oder Dynamik und Funktion." *Architectura,* vol. 28, 1924.

Mertens, G. 1977. *Eisen und Eisenkonstruktionen.* Duisburg.

Messenger & Company. 1880. *Constructions on the Patent System of Messenger and Comp.* Loughborough.

Messerschmidt, H. 1927. *Wilhelmshöhe.* Münster.

Meyer, A. G. 1907. *Eisenbauten, ihre Geschichte und Ästhetik.* Esslingen.

Meyer, H. K. 1966. "Zur Geschichte des Berggartens." In *Herrenhausen 1666-1966.*

Nau, S. 1959. *Die Gärten von Hohenheim.* Stuttgart.

Neumann, M. 1842. *Grundsätze und Erfahrungen über die Anlegung, Erhaltung und Pflege von Glashäusern aller Art* (translated from the French by Freiherr von Biedenfeld; ed. J. Hartwig). Weimar.

Neumeyer, F. 1973. Die Entwicklung bürgerlicher Wohnformen an Beispielen des 19. und 20. Jahrhunderts. Dipl.-Arbeit. Berlin.

Pett, E. 1966. "Die Pfaueninsel." *Berlinische Reminiszenzen,* vol. 12. Berlin.

Pevsner, N. 1971. *Architektur und Design. Von der Romantik zur Sachlichkeit.* Munich. English edition: *Studies in Art, Architecture and Design.* London, 1968.

Pevsner, N. 1976. *A History of Building Types.* London.

Pfann, H. 1935. *Das Gewächshaus in alter und neuer Zeit, seine Beziehung zur Technik und Architektur und zum Garten.* Vienna.

Picton, J. A. 1879. "The Progress of Iron and Steel as Constructional Materials." *Journal of the Iron and Steel Institute*, no. 11.

Piwowarsky, E. 1942. *Hochwertiges Gusseisen*. Berlin.

Plaistow, S. 1970. *Kew. The Royal Botanic Gardens*. London.

Poensgen, G. 1950. *Die Pfaueninsel*. Berlin.

Polonceau, C. 1840. *Revue générale de l'architecture et des travaux publics*, vol. 1.

Posener, J. 1964. "Anfänge des Funktionalismus." *Bauwelt-Fundamente*, no. 11.

Posener, J. 1968. "Ebenezer Howard. Gartenstädte von morgen. Das Buch und seine Geschichte." *Bauwelt-Fundamente*. no. 21.

Poulsen, V. 1974. *Ny Carlsberg Glyptotek*. Copenhagen.

Ramme, W. 1939. *Über die geschichtliche Entwicklung der Statik in ihren Beziehungen zum Bauwesen*. Dissertation, Brunswick.

Ranke, W. 1977. *Joseph Albert—Hofphotograph der bayerischen Könige*. Munich.

Rapp, G. H. 1798. "Beschreibung des Gartens in Hohenheim." *Taschenbuch für Natur- und Gartenfreunde*, vol. 4, pp. 135 ff.

Rave, P. O. (ed.) 1961. *Die Bauwerke und Kunstdenkmäler von Berlin*. Berlin.

Realis. 1846. *Das K.K. Lustschloss Schönbrunn*. Vienna.

Réau, L. 1954. *L'œuvre du Baron Haussmann*. Paris.

Ring, M. 1883–84. *Die deutsche Kaiserstadt Berlin*. Berlin.

Roisecco, G. 1972–73. *L'architettura del ferro*. Two vols. Rome.

Rondelet, J. B. 1812–1817. *Traité théorique et pratique de l'art de bâtir*. Five vols. Paris.

Roth, E. 1971. *Der Glaspalast in München*. Munich.

Rousseau, L. 1837. *Promenades au Jardin des Plantes*. Paris.

Sachs, J. 1875. *Geschichte der Botanik*. Munich.

Schadendorf, W. 1965. *Der Jahrhundert der Eisenbahn*. Munich.

Schaedlich, C. 1966. *Das Eisen in der Architektur des 19. Jahrhunderts. Beitrag zur Geschichte eines neuen Baustoffs*. Manuscript. Habil-Schrift Weimar.

Scharowsky, C. 1895. *Musterbuch für Eisenkonstruktionen*. Third edition. Leipzig.

Scheerbart, P. 1914. *Glasarchitektur*. Berlin. English edition: *Glass Architecture*. London, 1972.

Scheerer, T. 1848. *Lehrbuch der Metallurgie*, vol. 1. Brunswick.

Schild, E. 1967. "Zwischen Glaspalast und Palais des Illusions." *Bauwelt-Fundamente*, no. 20.

Schoser, G. 1971. "Die Biebricher Wintergärten." *Der Palmengarten der Stadt Frankfurt am Main*, vol. 34, part 1, pp. 1–4.

Schoser, G. (ed.) 1969. *Palmengarten Frankfurt a. M.* Frankfurt.

Sckell, F. L. von. 1825. *Beiträge zur bildenden Gartenkunst*. Munich.

Seemann, B. 1856. *Popular History of the Palms and their Allies*. London.

Semper, G. 1849. "Der Wintergarten zu Paris." *Zeitschrift für praktische Baukunst*, vol. 9, pp. 516–526.

Siegel, C. 1960. *Strukturformen der modernen Architektur*. Munich.

Sievers, A. 1908. "Der Palmengarten der Stadt Frankfurt am Main." In *Festzeitung für das 11. Deutsche Turnerfest zu Frankfurt am Main*.

Sievers, J. 1942–1955. *Bauten für die preussischen Prinzen*. Three vols. Berlin.

Silva-Taroucca, Graf. E., ed. 1910. *Die Gartenanlagen Österreich-Ungarns*, vol. 4, part 2. Vienna.

Skempton, A. W. 1956. *The Origin of Iron Beams*. Florence.

Smith, G. T. 1971. *Kibble Palace*. Dissertation, Glasgow.

Sperlich, M., and M. Seiler. 1979. "Schloss und Park Glienicke." *Zehlendorfer Chronik*, part 2.

Sternberger, D. 1974. *Panorama oder Ansichten vom 19. Jahrhundert*. Frankfurt and Berlin.

Straub, H. 1949. *Die Geschichte der Bauingenieurkunst. Ein Überblick von der Antike bis zur Neuzeit*. Basle.

Stroud, D. 1962. *Humphrey Repton*. London.

Sturges, D. W. 1970. *The Origins of Cast-Iron Architecture in America*. New York.

Svedenstjorna, E. 1803. *Reise durch einen Theil von England und Schottland in den Jahren 1802/1803*. Marburg.

Taube, F. 1774. *Schilderung der Englischen Manufakturen*. Vienna.

Texier, E. 1852–53. *Tableaux de Paris*. Paris.

Thiollet, F. 1832. *Serrurerie et Fonte de Fer*. Paris.

Timler, F. K., and B. Zepernick. 1978. "Der Berliner Botanische Garten." *Berliner Forum*, part 7.

Troll, W. 1926. *Goethes morphologische Schriften*. Jena.

Tschira, A. 1939. *Orangerien und Gewächshäuser, ihre geschichtliche Entwicklung in Deutschland*. Berlin.

Valdenaire, A. 1926. *Heinrich Hübsch*. Karlsruhe.

Vierendeel, A. 1900. *La construction architecturale en fer, fonte et acier*. Louvain.

Voigt, F. 1965. *Der Verkehr*. Berlin.

Wachsmann, K. 1959. *Wendepunkt im Bauen*. Wiesbaden.

Walmisley, A. T. 1950. *Iron Roofs*. London.

Werner, E. 1970. *Der Kristallpalast zu London 1851*. Düsseldorf.

Werner, E. 1973. "Die Giesshalle der Sayner Hütte." *Zeitschrift für Industriebau*, vol. 19, no. 6, pp. 256 ff.

Werner, E. 1974. *Die ersten eisernen Brücken (1777–1859)*. Dissertation, Munich.

Werner, E. 1975. *Übersicht über die Grundlagen zur Entwicklung der ersten eisernen Tragkonstruktionen*. Duisburg.

Wiedenfeld, K. 1938. *Die Eisenbahn im Wirtschaftsleben*. Berlin.

Wilde, O. 1977. *Werke in zwei Bänden*. Munich.

Wittek, K. H. 1964. *Die Entwicklung des Stahlhochbaues*. Düsseldorf.

Zanth, L. von. 1855. *Die Wilhelma, maurische Villa*. Leipzig.

Journals and Exhibition Catalogs

Allgemeine Deutsche Bauzeitung, ed. C. F. L. Förster and successors (with atlas, literature, and gazette), 1837, vol. 2, nos. 32–34, 44, 45, 48, 49; 1838, vol. 3, Literature and Gazette, pp. 99 ff.; 1849, vol. 14, atlas sheets 253–255; 1850, vol. 15, atlas sheets 362–367; 1852, vol. 17, atlas sheets 469–475, 488, 506, 507; 1862, vol. 27, atlas sheets 510–514; 1863, vol. 28, atlas sheet 568; 1873, vol. 38.

Allgemeines Teutsches Garten-Magazin oder gemeinnützige Beiträge für alle Teile des praktischen Gartenwesens, ed. F. J. Bertuch and J. von Sickler, 1804–1811, vols. 1–8; continued 1815–1824, vols. 9–18; 1806, vol. 3, II, part I; plates 2, 3; 1822, vol. 14, VI, part I; 1823, vol. 15, VII, parts I, V.

The Architectural Review for the Artist and Craftman, a magazine of architecture and the arts of design, ed. H. de C. Hastings et al.; April 1950, vol. C VII, no. 637; February 1957, vol. CXXI, no. 721.

Der Bautechniker, Centralorgan für österreichische Bauwesen, ed. Klasen and Röttinger, 1885, vol. 5, no. 22.

Die Bauwelt, Zentralorgan des gesamten Baumarktes, 6.10.1969, vol. 60, part 40; 24.11.1969, vol. 60, part 47.

The Builder, an illustrated weekly magazine, ed. G. Godwin et al.; vols. LXVI–XCII, ed. H. Heathcote; 23.12.1843, vol. I, no. 46; 15.1.1848, vol. VI, no., 258; 21.10.1848, vol. VI, no. 298; 15.12.1855, vol. XIII, no. 671; 19.5.1860, vol. XVIII, no. 902; 12.1.1861, vol. XIX, no. 936; 20.7.1861, vol. XIX, no. 963; 31.1.1863, vol. XXI, no. 1043; 13.6.1863, vol. XXI, no. 1062.

Deutsche Bauzeitung (DBZ), published in association with the Architektenverein, Berlin (later the Verband Deutscher Architekten und Ingenieur-Vereine, Berlin), 1869, vol. 3, no. 23; 1872, vol. 6, no. 1; 1873, vol. 7, nos. 32,40,44,68; 1876, vol. 10, no. 87; 1881, vol. 15, nos. 23, 25.

Deutsches Magazin für Garten- und Blumenkunde, Zeitschrift für Garten- und Blumenfreunde und Gärtner, ed. W. Neubert, 1852, vol. 5; 1859, vol. 12; 1861, vol. 14; 1866, vol. 19; 1872, vol. 25.

The Gardener's Chronicle and Agricultural Gazette, a weekly illustrated journal of horticulture and allied subjects, ed. Lindley et al. 14.2.1846, vol. 6, no. 7; 31.8.1850, vol. 10, no. 35; 1.12.1855, vol. 15, no. 48; 8.8. 1868, vol. 28, no. 32; 23.5.1874, vol. 34, no. 21; 11.11.1876, vol. 36, no. 150; 20.1.1877, vol. 37, no. ?; 18.10.1882, vol. 42, no. ?.

The Gardener's Magazine and Register of Rural and Domestic Improvements, ed. J. C. Loudon et al. (from 1826); August 1832, vol. VIII; July 1839, vol. XV; August 1839, vol. XV; January 1843, vol. XIX.

Die Gartenflora, allgemeine Monatsschrift für deutsche, russische (vols. 7–33) und schweizerische Garten- und Blumenkunde, ed. E. Regel et al. (from 1898: organ of Verein zur Beförderung des Gartenbaues in den preussischen Staaten, ed. L. Wittmack), 1872, vol. 21: 1876, vol. 25; 1894, vol. 43; 1898, vol. 47.

Die Gartenlaube, illustriertes Familienblatt, ed. F. Stolle and A. Dietzmann, 1859, vol. 6.

Die Gartenzeitung, Monatsschrift für Gärtner und Gartenfreunde, organ of Verein zur Beförderung des Gartenbaues in den kgl. preussischen Staaten, ed. L. Wittmack, 1882, vol. 1.

Herrenhausen 1666–1966, Katalog der Jubiläumsausstellung in Hannover, Orangerie Herrenhausen 19.6.–28.8.1966.

The Illustrated London News, 6.7.1850, 9, vol. XVII, no. 434; 16.11.1850, 9, vol. XVII, no. 455; 7.12.1850, 9, vol. XVII, no. 450; 4.1.1851, 10, vol. XVIII, no. 463; 11.1.1851, 10, vol. XVIII, no. 466; 25.1.1851, 10, vol. XVIII, no. 466; 1.2.1851, 10, vol. XVIII, no. 467; 1.3.1851, 10, vol. XVIII, no. 472; 3.5.1851, 10, vol. XVIII, no. 481; 14.6.1851, 10, vol. XVIII, no. 493; 28.6.1851, 10, vol. XVIII, no. 497; 12.2.1859, 18, vol. XXXIV, no. 959; 5.3.1859, 18, vol. XXXIV, no. 963; 9.7.1859, 18, vol. XXXV, no. 982; 15.10.1859, 18, vol. XXXV, no. 998; 18.3.1865, 24, vol. XLVI, no. 1306; 17.6.1865, 24, vol. XLVII, no. 1320.

Illustrierte Zeitung, wöchentliche Nachrichten über alle Ereignisse, Zustände und Persönlichkeiten der Gegenwart, 17.9.1864, vol. XLIII, no. 1107; 22.4.1882, vol. LXXVIII, no. 2025.

Jardins en France 1760–1820. Pays d'illusion. Terre d'expériences. Catalog of exhibition at Hotel de Sully, Paris, 1977.

Möller's Deutsche Gärtner-Zeitung, 2.6.1906, vol. 21, no. 22.

Moniteur des Architectes, Revue de l'art ancien et moderne, 1860, 11, vol. LVIII, plates 693, 694.

Panorama, 12.10.1850; 30.11.1850; 1.1.1851.

Report of the Commissioners appointed to enquire into the Cost and Applicability of the Exhibition Building in the Hyde Park, London 1851–52, Cmnd. 1453, pp. 304–312.

Revue genérale de l'architecture et des travaux publics. Journal des architectes, des ingenieurs, des archéologues [et al.], ed. C. Daly, 1840, vol. 1; 1841, vol. 2; 1870–71, vol. 28.

Taschenbuch für Natur- und Gartenfreunde, ed. G. H. Rapp, Tübingen, 1795–1799; 1798, vol. IV.

Über Land und Meer, allgemeine illustrierte Zeitung, ed. F. W. Hackländer, 1868, 10, vol. XX, no. 20; 1869, 11, vol. XXII, no. 32; 1870, 12, vol. XXIV, no. 41; 1871, 13, vol. XXVI, no. 48; 1871–72, 14, vol. XXVII, no. 10; 1876, 18, vol. XXXV, no. 20.

Zeitschrift für Bauwesen (ZfBW), published by Königliche Technische Bau-Deputation and Architekten Verein, Berlin, ed. G. Erbkam et al. Vols. 37–70 published by Ministerium der öffentlichen Arbeiten, Berlin; vols. 70 ff. published by Preussisches Finanzministerium. 1852, vol. 2, parts 1,2, atlas sheets 13–14; 1863, vol. 13, parts 4–6, atlas sheets 25, 26; 1866, vol. 16, parts 1–3, atlas sheets 10–14; 1867, vol. 17, parts 7–10, atlas sheets 34–39; 1869, vol. 19, parts 4–10; 1881, vol. 21, parts 1–3, atlas sheets 38–42; 1887, vol. 37, parts 1–3, atlas sheets 14–15, 18, 30–33; 1888, vol. 38, parts 1–3, atlas sheet 18; parts 4–6, atlas sheets 30–33; 1901, vol. 51, parts 7–9; 1909, vol. 59, parts 4–6, atlas sheets 25–30; 1916, vol. 66, parts 1–3, atlas sheets 8, 9.

Zeitschrift für praktische Baukunst, Monatsschrift zur Verbreitung gemeinnütziger Kenntnisse im Gebiete des gesamten Bauwesens, ed. J. A. Romberg, 1849, vol. 9, plate 54.

Zeitschrift des Vereins zur Ausbildung der Gewerke, published by Kunstgewerbeverein München, 1853, vol. 3, part 4, sheets 1–3; 1854, vol. 4, part 1, sheets 1–3.

Zentralblatt für Industriebau, 1973, vol. 19, no. 6.

Zentralblatt der Bauverwaltung, published by Ministerium der öffentlichen Arbeiten, Berlin; vols. 40 ff. published by Preussisches Finanzministerium, ed. O. Sarrazin and H. Eggert. 1882, vol. 2; 1883, vol. 3.

Sources of Illustrations

1. Werner Hofmann, *Des irdische Paradies* (Munich, 1974), p. 242.

2. Ibid., p. 176.

3. McIntosh 1853, vol. 1, fig. 12.

4. Gloag 1970, p. 75.

5. Posener 1968, pp. 57, 61.

6. Neumann 1862, plate XXXXIII, fig. 176, 177.

7. (a) Austrian National Library, Vienna; (b) Hix 1974, fig. 117; (c) Tschira 1939, p. 100, fig. 79.

8. Neumann 1862, plate XX, fig. 82.

9. *Über Land und Meer*, 1869, 11, vol. 22, no. 32, p. 525.

10. Seeman 1856, p. 1.

11. Library, Botanical Garden, Berlin-Dahlem.

12. *Allgemeines Teutsches Garten-Magazin*, 1823, vol. 17, plate 14; 1822, vol. 17, plate 1.

13. *Gartenflora*, 1876, vol. 25, plate 860.

14. (a) McIntosh 1853, vol. 1; (b) ibid.

15. (a) Bouché 1886, fig. 35; (b) Hix 1974, p. 36.

16,17. Drawings by Kohlmaier and Sartory (hereafter listed as K. and S.).

18. Cabinet des Estampes, Bibliothèque Royale Albert I, Brussels.

19. Beck 1879, vol. 3, p. 761.

20. Wittek 1964, pp. 7, 93.

21. (a) Drawing by K. and S.; (b) McIntosh 1853, vol. 1, p. 123.

22. (a) Drawing by K. and S.; (b) Chadwick 1961, p. 91.

23. Bouché 1886, plates XXII–XXIV.

24. Brandt 1876, p. 289.

25. Chadwick 1961, p. 91.

26. Drawing by K. and S., after photographs.

27. Meyer 1907, p. 2.

28. Wittek 1964, p. 13.

29. *Zentralblatt für Industriebau*, 1973, vol. 19, no. 6, p. 255.

30. Wittek 1964, pp. 13, 95.

31. *Allgemeine Deutsche Bauzeitung*, 1862, vol. 27, atlas sheet 510.

32. Stroud 1962, p. 116.

33–35. Drawings by K. and S., after photographs.

36. McIntosh 1853, vol. 1, p. 367.

37. Ibid., p. 365.

38. Boudon 1972, p. 43.

39. Ibid., p. 47.

40. Gayle and Gillon 1974, p. vii.

41. Drawing by K. and S., after Loudon 1817, plate 10.

42. Reconstruction by K. and S.

43. *Allgemeine Deutsche Bauzeitung*, 1849, vol. 14, atlas sheet 253.

44. Chadwick 1961, p. 86.

45. *Allgemeine Deutsche Bauzeitung*, 1850, vol. 15, atlas sheet 367.

46. McIntosh 1853, vol. 1, p. 120.

47. Ibid., p. 375.

48. Drawing by K. and S., after original plan in archives of Royal Botanic Gardens, Edinburgh.

49. Central Library, Leeds.

50. Drawing by K. and S., after plan in archives of Staatliches Hochbauamt II, Stuttgart.

51. Drawing by K. and S.

52. Bildarchiv der Landeshauptstadt Wiesbaden.

53–55. Drawings by K. and S.

56. Loudon 1817, plate IX.

57. Reconstruction by K. and S.

58. *Allgemeine Deutsche Bauzeitung*, 1850, vol. 15, atlas sheet 366.

59. Drawing by K. and S., after original plans in Stadtmuseum, Munich.

60. Bouché 1886, plates XXIII, XXIV.

61. Brandt 1876, p. 407.

62. Drawing by K. and S. from *Zeitschrift für praktische Baukunst*, 1849, vol. 9, plate 54.

63. Meyer 1907, p. 62.

64. Walmisley 1950, p. 21.

65. Wittek 1964, p. 121.

66,67. McIntosh 1853, vol. 1, figs. 21, 22.

68. Hix 1974, p. 155.

69. Beck 1879, vol. 3, p. 375.

70. Giedion 1976, p. 143.

71. Drawing by K. and S., from photograph.

72. Cabinet des Estampes, Bibliothèque Nationale, Paris.

73. Drawing by K. and S., after McIntosh 1853, vol. 1, p. 120.

74. (a) Gloag and Bridgwater 1948, p. 256; (b) drawing by K. and S.

75. Chadwick 1961, p. 87.

76. McIntosh 1853, vol. 1, p. 120.

77. Wachsmann 1959, p. 17.

78. (a) Brandt 1876, p. 285; (b) Scharowsky, 1895, p. 50.

79,80. Drawings by K. and S.

81. Cabinet des Estampes, Bibliothèque Nationale, Paris.

82. Gayle and Gillon 1974, p. xi.

83. Wittek 1964, p. 8.

84. *Allgemeine Deutsche Bauzeitung*, 1850, vol. 15, atlas sheet 365.

85. Drawing by K. and S., after original plans in Stadtmuseum, Munich.

86. *ZfBW*, 1867, vol. 17, parts 7–10, atlas sheet 37.

87. Drawing by K. and S., after Bouché 1886, plates XXII, XXIII.

88. Bouché 1886, plates XXII, XXIV.

89. Drawing by K. and S., after original plan in archives of Botanical Garden, Breslau.

90. Durm and Ende 1893, part 4, VI, 4, p. 421.

91. *Illustrated London News*, 12.2.1859, 18, vol. 34, no. 959, p. 103.

92. (a) Tschira 1939, p. 14; (b) ibid., p. 69; (c) *Allgemeines Teutsches Garten-Magazin*, 1806, 3, vol. 2, part 1, plates 2,3.

93. Tschira 1939, p. 76.

94. Nau 1959, p. 103.

95,96. Chadwick p. 82.

97. McIntosh 1853, vol. 1, p. 371.

98. Chadwick 1961, p. 91.

99. *Gardener's Chronicle*, 31.8.1850, vol. 10, no. 35, p. 549.

100. Chadwick 1961, p. 184.

101. Schild 1967, p. 47.

102. *Gardener's Chronicle*, 8.8.1868, vol. 28, no. 32, p. 858.

103. Messenger & Co. 1880, plate 13.

104. *Allgemeine Deutsche Bauzeitung*, 1873, vol. 38, p. 103.

105. Wittek 1964, p. 57.

106. Ibid., p. 101.

107. Drawing by K. and S., after original plan in Bayerische Verwaltung der staatlichen Schlösser, Gärten und Seen, Schloss Nymphenburg, Munich.

108. Wittek 1964, p. 105.

109,110. McIntosh 1853, vol. 1, pp. 383, 384.

111. Wittek 1964, p. 54.

112. Drawing by K. and S., after plans in Schloss Schönbrunn, Vienna.

113. Drawing by K. and S., after *Deutsche Bauzeitung* (publ.) 1902, vol. 2, part 5, fig. 146.

114. Drawing by K. and S., after *DBZ*, 1873, vol. 7, no. 64, p. 258.

115. Drawing by K. and S., after Koerner 1910, p. 26, fig. 11.

116. Drawing by K. and S., after *Die Gartenzeitung*, 1882, vol. 1, fig. 19.

117. Gloag 1970, p. 48.

118. Wittek 1964, p. 121.

119. Ibid., p. 122.

120. *Illustrated London News*, 5.3.1859, 18, vol. 34, no. 963, pp. 224, 225.

121. Drawing by K. and S., after Architektenverein zu Berlin (publ.) 1896, vol. 2, p. 254.

122. Drawing by K. and S., after Meyer 1907, pp. 131, 132.

123. Wittek 1964, p. 122.

124–126. Loudon 1817, plates IV, V.

127. Hix 1974, p. 85.

128. *Gardener's Magazine*, August 1832, vol. 8, p. 420.

129. Ibid., p. 422.

130. Hix 1974, p. 112.

131. *Allgemeine Deutsche Bauzeitung*, 1837, vol. 2, no. 33, fig. 3; Rousseau 1834, p. 433.

132. (a) Gloag 1970, p. 45; (b,c) McIntosh 1853, vol. 1, p. 547.

133. *Allgemeine Deutsche Bauzeitung*, 1837, vol. 2, no. 49, p. 403.

134. (a) Sperlich and Seiler 1979, p. 27; (b) drawing by K. and S., from measurements.

135. Gloag 1970, p. 1.

136. *Illustrated London News*, 3.5.1851, 10, vol. 18, no. 481, p. 343.

137. Loudon 1818, figs. 1–11.

138. Ibid., figs. 12–19.

139. Ibid., figs. 20–36.

140. Ibid., figs. 37–42.

141. Gloag 1970, p. 46.

142. Drawing by K. and S., after site plan: Frazer's Guide, 1851, in McCracken 1971, pp. 30, 31.

143. McCracken 1971, pp. 35.

144. Ulster Museum, Belfast.

145–147. Building reproductions by K. and S.

148. Landesbildstelle, Berlin.

149. Drawing by K. and S., after design drawings by G. Schadow, in archives of Staatlicher Schlösser und Gärten Verwaltung, Schloss Charlottenburg, Berlin.

150. Drawing by Hans Junnecke, after photograph in archives of Staatliche Schlösser und Gärten Verwaltung, Schloss Charlottenburg, Berlin.

151. Sievers 1954, pp. 167–171.

152. Drawing by K. and S., after site plan in Architektenverein zu Berlin (publ.) 1896, vol. 2, p. 252.

153. Bouché 1886, p. 15.

154,155. Drawing by K. and S., after plates XXII, XXIII.

156. Drawing by K. and S., after plate XXIV.

157,158. Drawings by K. and S., after Architektenverein zu Berlin (publ.) 1896, vol. 2, pp. 254, 255.

159. Neumann 1862, fig. 175.

160. Ring 1883–84, p. 114.

161. Drawing by K. and S., after site plan in Architektenverein zu Berlin (publ.) 1896, vol. 1, p. 551, fig. 673.

162. Archiv des Landes Berlin.

163. Drawing by K. and S., after *DBZ*, 1873, vol. 7, no. 32, p. 125.

164. Architektenverein zu Berlin (publ.) 1887, part 1, section 1, p. 344.

165. Drawing by K. and S., after *DBZ*, 1873, vol. 7, no. 40, p. 149.

166. Drawing by K. and S., after ibid., no. 64, p. 259.

167. *Über Land und Meer*, 1871, 13, vol. 26, no. 48, p. 8.

168. *DBZ*, 1873, vol. 7, no. 64, p. 259.

169. Drawing by K. and S., after city plan of Berlin, 1900.

170. *DBZ*, 1869, vol. 3, no. 20, p. 232.

171,172. Drawings by K. and S., after ibid.

173. Ibid., p. 233.

174. Ring 1883-84, p. 106.

175. Drawing by K. and S., after *ZfBW*, 1881, vol. 21, part 1, p. 176.

176. Ibid., Atlas sheet 42.

177. Drawing by K. and S., after ibid., atlas sheet 39.

178. Drawing by K. and S., after ibid., atlas sheet 42.

179. Drawing by K. and S., after ibid., atlas sheet 42.

180. Ring 1883-84, p. 125.

181. Drawing by K. and S., after 1964 guidebook to Botanical Garden, Berlin-Dahlem, p. 1.

182. Drawing by K. and S., after Koerner 1910, figs. 47, 48.

183. Drawing by K. and S., after ibid., fig. 11.

184. Drawing by K. and S., after ibid., fig. 7.

185. Drawing by K. and S., after ibid., fig. 1.

186. Drawing by K. and S., after ibid., figs. 29, 31.

187. Drawing by K. and S., after ibid., figs. 30-33.

188,189. Bildarchiv der Landeshauptstadt Wiesbaden.

190. *Gardener's Magazine*, August 1832, vol. 8, pp. 414, 415, 420, 422.

191. *Illustrated London News*, 28.6.1851, vol. 17, no. 497, p. 622.

192. Drawing by K. and S., after 1930 city plan in Central Library, Bournemouth.

193. *Gardener's Chronicle*, 20.1.1877, vol. 37, no. 160, p. 77.

194-196. Drawings by K. and S., after design drawings in Central Library, Bournemouth.

197. Drawing by K. and S., after site plan in 1870 guidebook to Botanical Garden, Breslau.

198. Reproduction of building by K. and S.

199. Drawing by K. and S., after 1860 design drawings in archives of Breslau Botanical Garden.

200-202. Neumann 1862, figs. 76-78, plate XIX.

203. Loudon 1833, fig. 1732.

204. Drawing by K. and S., after 1885 city plan in archives of city of Brussels.

205. Cabinet des Estampes, Bibliothèque Royale Albert I, Brussels.

206,207. Drawings by K. and S., after Neumann 1862, fig. 71.

208. Cabinet des Estampes, Bibliothèque Royale Albert I, Brussels.

209. Drawing by K. and S., after site plan in archives of city of Brussels.

210,211. Meyer 1907, pp. 131-133.

212. Drawing by K. and S., after Meyer 1907, p. 131.

213. Drawing by K. and S., after *Deutsche Bauzeitung* (publ.) 1902, vol. 2, part 5, fig. 128.

214. *Gardener's Chronicle*, 11.11.1876, vol. 36, no. 150, p. 7.

215. Drawing by K. and S., after site plan in James 1973, p. 1.

216-218. Reproductions of buildings by K. and S.

219. Drawing by K. and S., after site plan, Department of Technical Services, Town Hall, Buxton.

220. Chadwick 1966, p. 146.

221. Chadwick 1961, p. 83.

222. Drawing by K. and S., after ibid., p. 34.

223. Ibid., p. 82.

224. *Deutsche Bauzeitung* (publ.) 1902, vol. 2, part 5, p. 356.

225. Reproduction by K. and S., after Neumann 1862, fig. 136, plate XXXIII.

226. Drawing by K. and S., after Chadwick 1961, p. 86.

227-229. Drawings by K. and S., after *Gardener's Chronicle*, 31.8.1850, vol. 10, no. 35, pp. 548, 549.

230,231. Ibid., p. 549.

232. Chadwick 1961, p. 91.

233. Hix 1974, p. 117.

234. McGrath and Frost 1961, p. 118.

235. Drawing by K. and S., after site plan in *A Short Guide to the Gardens* (Dublin, 1975), p. 1.

236-238. Reproductions of buildings by K. and S.

239. Gloag and Bridgwater 1948, p. 254.

240. *Illustrated London News*, 18.3.1865, 24, vol. 46, no. 1306, p. 258.

241. Drawing by K. and S., after 1890 site plan in library of Royal Botanic Gardens, Edinburgh.

242-245. Drawings by K. and S., after original plan dated ca. 1857 (ibid).

246. McIntosh 1853, vol. 1, p. 791.

247. Reproduction of building by K. and S.

248. *Gardener's Chronicle*, 23.5.1874, vol. 34, no. 21, p. 669.

249. Drawing by K. and S., after site plan in Siebert 1908, p. 13.

250,251. Meyer 1907, pp. 173, 174.

252,253. Drawings by K. and S., after Siebert 1908, p. 74.

254. Schoser 1974, p. 77.

255. Drawing by K. and S., after 1970 site plan in archives of Botanic Garden, Glasgow.

256. *The Baillie*, November, 1873.

257–261. Drawings by K. and S., after reproductions in Smith 1971, pp. 90, 91.

262–269. *Allgemeine Deutsche Bauzeitung*, 1837, vol. 2, no. 48, plate CLXXIII.

270. Drawing by K. and S., after 1852 site plan in Meyer 1966, p. 142.

271–273. Drawings by K. and S., after *ZfBW*, 1916, vol. 66, parts 1–3, sheet 9, figs. 5–9.

274. Höltje 1964, p. 208.

275–277. Drawings by K. and S., after *DBZ*, 1876, vol. 10, no. 87, figs. 3, 4, 17.

278. *Gartenzeitung*, 1882, vol. 1, fig. 2.

279. Drawing by K. and S., after site plan in Silva-Taroucca 1910, p. 47.

280. Drawing by K. and S., after ibid.

281. Reproduction of building by K. and S.

282. Drawing by K. and S., after original plan in archives of Botanical Garden, Innsbruck.

283. K. and S. Archives, Berlin.

284–289. Drawings by K. and S., after plans of a building reproduction (dated 1939) in archives of Botanical Garden, Karlsruhe.

290. Drawing by K. and S., after site plan in Messerschmidt 1927, p. 37.

291. Drawing by K. and S., after Loudon 1835, p. 208.

292,293. Drawings by K. and S., after plans for conservatory at Wilhelmshöhe (sheets 2–4), Stadtbauamt, Kassel.

294. McIntosh 1853, vol. 1, fig. 20.

295. Drawing by K. and S., after 1862 site plan.

296,297. Drawings by K. and S., after *Deutsche Bauzeitung* (publ.) 1902, vol. 2, part 5, p. 375, fig. 150.

298. *Illustrated London News*, 17.6.1865, 24, vol. 47, no. 1320, p. 596.

299. *Illustrierte Zeitung*, 17.9.1864, vol. 43, no. 1107, pp. 196, 197.

300. Drawing by K. and S., after site plan in *DBZ*, 1881, vol. 15, no. 23, p. 133.

301. Ibid.

302,303. Drawings by K. and S., after *DBZ*, 1881, vol. 15, no. 25, pp. 145 ff.

304. Watercolor and pencil drawing, ca. 1872, archives of Botanisk Have, Copenhagen.

305. Jacobsen and Rothe 1879, plates I–XII.

306. Drawing by K. and S., after site plan (ca. 1900) in library of Ny Carlsberg Glyptotek, Copenhagen.

307. Ground plan, 1905. Ibid.

308–310. Hix 1974, p. 23.

311. Drawing by K. and S., after site plan in Silva-Taroucca 1910, p. 27.

312,313. Reproductions of buildings by K. and S.

314. Walmisley 1950, fig. 22.

315. Drawing by K. and S., after ibid., plate 30.

316. Gloag and Bridgwater 1948, p. 255, fig. 309.

317. Durm and Ende 1885, 4, part 4, p. 141.

318. Loudon 1835, p. 244.

319,320. Drawings by K. and S., after plans: Mairie de Lille, Services Techniques, Espaces verts.

321–324. Drawings by K. and S., after plans in Liverpool City Libraries.

325,326. Drawings by K. and S., after McIntosh 1853, vol. 1, fig. 16.

327. J. Troughton collection, London.

328. *Gardener's Magazine*, February 1831, vol. 7, p. 693.

329. Drawing by K. and S., after plan in ibid.

330. *Allgemeine Deutsche Bauzeitung*, 1837, no. 49, sheet CLXXV, figs. 1–5.

331–334. Hix 1974, pp. 121–123.

335. Site plan by K. and S., after 1975 guide to Botanical Gardens at Kew, p. 49.

336,337. McIntosh 1853, vol. 1, p. 367, figs. 506, 507.

338. *Builder*, 15.1.1848, vol. 6, no. 258, p. 31.

339–343. Drawings by K. and S., after ibid., pp. 29–31.

344. Ibid., 12.1.1861, vol. 19, no. 936, pp. 23, 24.

345. Ibid., p. 25.

346. Drawing by K. and S., after Durm and Ende 1893, 4, part 4, 4, p. 426, figs. 503–505.

347. Chadwick 1961, p. 92.

348. *Illustrated London News*, 6.7.1850, 9, vol. 17, no. 434, p. 13.

349. Ibid., 1.2.1851, 10, vol. 18, no. 467, p. 72.

350. Ibid., 4.1.1851, 10, vol. 18, no. 463, p. 8.

351. Ibid., 11.1.1851, 10, vol. 18, no. 464, p. 17.

352. Ibid., 1.2.1851, 10, vol. 18, no. 467, p. 72.

353. Ibid., 25.1.1851, 10, vol. 18, no. 466, p. 57.

354. Ibid., 7.12.1850, 9, vol. 17, no. 458, p. 432.

355. Ibid., 1.3.1851, 10, vol. 18, no. 472, p. 176.

356. Ibid., 16.11.1850, 9, vol. 17, no. 455, p. 396.

357. *Allgemeine Deutsche Bauzeitung*, 1850, vol. 15, atlas sheet 365, figs. 11, 12.

358. Ibid., figs. 2–4.

359,360. Ibid., atlas sheet 366, fig. 1.

361. Chadwick 1961, p. 33.

362,363. Drawings by K. and S., after *Allgemeine Deutsche Bauzeitung*, 1850, vol. 15, atlas sheets 363, 364.

364. County Council Library, London.

365. *Illustrated London News*, 15.10.1859, 18, vol. 35, no. 998, p. 371.

366. Ibid., 5.3.1859, 18, vol. 34, no. 963, p. 225.

367. Chadwick 1961, p. 183.

368. Durm and Ende 1885, 4, part 4, p. 144, fig. 154.

369. Drawing by K. and S., after site plan in *Builder*, 19.5.1860, vol. 18, no. 902, p. 312.

370. Gloag and Bridgwater 1948, p. 250, fig. 305.

371. Hix 1974, p. 107.

372,373. Boudon 1972, pp. 13, 44, 55.

374. Drawing by K. and S., after 1970 site plan in archives of Jardin Botanique de la ville de Lyon, Parc de la Tête d'Or.

375,376. Drawings by K. and S., after plans (ibid).

377. Archives of Jardin Botanique de la ville de Lyon, Parc de la Tête d'Or.

378. Drawing by K. and S., after *Bauwelt*, 1980, vol. 71, part 29, p. 1255.

379. Drawing by K. and S., after Deutsche Bauzeitung (publ.) 1902, vol. 2, part 5, p. 368, fig. 137.

380. Drawing by K. and S., after Laborde 1808, plate 1.

381. Ibid., plate 6.

382,383. *Allgemeines Deutsche Garten-Magazin*, 1806, 3, vol. 2, part 1, plates 2,3.

384. Drawing by K. and S., after site plan (ca. 1830) in Stadtarchiv, Munich.

385-390. Drawings by K. and S., after plans in archives of Bayerische Verwaltung der Staatlichen Schlösser, Gärten und Seen, Nymphenburg Castle, Munich.

391-393. Drawings by K. and S., after Sckell 1825, p. 182.

394. Drawing by K. and S., after *Zeitschrift des Vereins zur Ausbildung der Gewerke*, 1854, vol. 3, part 4, sheet 2.

395. Stadtmuseum, Munich.

396. Drawing by K. and S., after *Zeitschrift des Vereins zur Ausbildung der Gewerke*, 1854, vol. 3, part 4, sheets 1,3.

397-399. Drawings by K. and S., after 1852 construction plans in Stadtmuseum, Munich.

400-402. Drawings by K. and S., after plans in Geheimes Hausarchiv, Munich.

403. Drawing by K. and S., after site plan in *ZfBW*, 1867, vol. 17, parts 7-10, sheet M.

404-407. Drawings by K. and S., after *ZfBW*, 1867, sheets 35-37.

408. Ibid., sheet 37.

409. Drawing by K. and S., after site plan in Rousseau 1837, p. 1.

410. Texier 1852-53, p. 183.

411. Rousseau 1837, p. 433.

412. Neumann 1862, plate IX, fig. 40.

413-415. Drawings by K. and S., after *Allgemeine Deutsche Bauzeitung*, 1837, vol. 2, no. 33, pp. 271-274, sheet CXLVI, figs. 1-6.

416. Musée National d'Histoire Naturelle, Paris.

417-419. Drawings by K. and S., after *Zeitschrift für praktische Baukunst*, 1849, vol. 9, plate 54.

420. Cabinet des Estampes, Bibliothèque Nationale, Paris.

421. *Zeitschrift für praktische Baukunst*, 1849, vol. 9, plate 54.

422. *Illustrated London News*, 9.7.1859, 18, vol. 35, no. 982, p. 29.

423. Drawing by K. and S., after site plan in *Deutsche Bauzeitung* (publ.) 1902, vol. 2, part 5, p. 372.

424. Meyer 1907, p. 123.

425,426. Drawings by K. and S., after plans in *Deutsche Bauzeitung* (publ.) 1902, vol. 2, part 5, p. 373, plate IX.

427. Drawing by K. and S., after site plan (ca. 1910) in archives of H. Roger-Viollet, Paris.

428-430. Drawings by K. and S., after plans in archives of Orto Botanico, Pavia.

431. Giacomini 1959, p. 85, fig. 25.

432. *Über Land und Meer*, 1876, 18, vol. 35, no. 20, p. 400.

433. Hix 1974, p. 85.

434. Drawing by K. and S., after site plan in head office of Sheffield Recreation Department.

435. Ibid.

436. Drawing by K. and S., after site plan in *ZfBW*, 1887, vol. 37, parts 10-12, atlas sheet 67.

437-440. Drawings by K. and S., after ibid., 1888, vol. 38, parts 4-6, atlas sheets 30-33.

441. Nau 1967, p. 13.

442. Ibid., p. 103.

443. *Deutsches Magazin für Garten und Blumenkunde*, 1852, vol. 5, p. 160.

444. Drawing by K. and S., after site plan in Zanth 1855, plate 1.

445. *Über Land und Meer*, 1871-72, 14, vol. 27, no. 10, pp. 8-9.

446-448. Drawings by K. and S., after plans in archives of Staatliches Hochbauamt II, Stuttgart.

449,450. Drawings by K. and S., after *Attempto*, 1969, parts 33-34, p. 10.

451,452. Reproductions of buildings by K. and S.

453. *Deutsches Magazin für Garten und Blumenkunde*, 1859, vol. 12, p. 113.

454. *Allgemeine Deutsche Bauzeitung*, 1838, vol. 3, no. 44, p. 399, sheets CCXL, CCXLI.

455. Drawing by K. and S., after 1972 city plan of Vienna.

456. Bayerische Verwaltung der staatlichen Schlösser, Gärten und Seen, Nymphenburg Castle, Munich.

457-460. Drawings by K. and S., after plans in Nymphenburg Castle, Vienna.

461. Drawing by K. and S., after 1972 city plan of Vienna.

462,463. Tschira 1939, pp. 106, 107.

464. Hofburg, Vienna.

465,466. Drawings by K. and S., after plans in Hofburg, Vienna.

467,468. Reproductions of buildings by K. and S.

469. McIntosh 1853, vol. 1, p. 361.

470. Meyer 1907, p. 57.

471-477. K. and S. archives, Berlin.

478,479. Staatliche Schlösser und Gärten Verwaltung, Charlottenburg Castle, Berlin.

480, 481. Library of Botanical Garden, Berlin-Dahlem.

482,483. K. and S. archives, Berlin.

484,485. Koerner 1910, pp. 13, 14.

486-491. K. and S. archives, Berlin.

492. Staatliche Schlösser und Gärten Verwaltung, Charlottenburg Castle, Berlin.

493. *DBZ*, 1873, vol. 7, no. 32, p. 126.

494. Staatliche Schlösser und Gärten Verwaltung, Charlottenburg Castle, Berlin.

495,496. Archiv der Landeshauptstadt, Wiesbaden.

497. *Gardener's Magazine*, August 1832, vol. 8, pp. 420-422.

498,499. K. and S. archives, Berlin.

500,501. Archives of Botanical Garden, Breslau.

502-507. K. and S. archives, Berlin.

508. Borncrêpe 1920, p. 194.

509. *Gardener's Chronicle*, 11.11.1876, vol. 36, no. 150, p. 6.

510-517. K. and S. archives, Berlin.

518. Archives, City of Brussels.

519-526. K. and S. archives, Berlin.

527. Chadwick 1961, p. 84.

528. Ibid., p. 85.

529. *Illustrated London News*, 17.11.1849, 8, vol. 16.

530. Reproduction drawing from ibid., p. 87.

531. Neumann 1862, plate XXXIII, figs. 136, 137.

532-546. K. and S. archives, Berlin.

547. Library of Royal Botanic Gardens, Edinburgh.

548-553. K. and S. archives, Berlin.

554. Schoser 1969, pp. 106, 107, fig. 79.

555. K. and S. archives, Berlin.

556. *Über Land und Meer*, 1870, 12, 24, no. 41, p. 9.

557-567. K. and S. archives, Berlin.

568. City archives, Hannover.

569. *ZfBW*, 1916, vol. 66, parts 1-3, figs. 5-9.

570. Ibid., fig. 25.

571. *Gartenzeitung*, 1882, vol. 1, fig. 34.

572-584. K. and S. archives, Berlin.

585-588. Graphics collection, Kölnisches Stadtmuseum.

589-593. K. and S. archives, Berlin.

594. Library, Ny Carlsberg Glyptotek, Copenhagen.

595-602. K. and S. archives, Berlin.

603,604. Glaeser archives, Museum of Modern Art, New York.

605. K. and S. archives, Berlin.

606. Archives of H. Roger-Viollet, Paris.

607-618. K. and S. archives, Berlin.

619. Royal Botanic Gardens, Kew.

620-625. K. and S. archives, Berlin.

626,627. Chadwick 1961, pp. 132, 133.

628-630. Archives of J. Russel and Sons, London.

631. *Illustrated London News*, 14.6.1851, 10, vol. 18, no. 493, p. 563.

632. Ibid., 15.10.1859, 18, vol. 25, no. 998, p. 371.

633. Ibid., 12.2.1859, 18, vol. 34, no. 959, p. 103.

634. Ibid., 5.3.1859, 18, vol. 34, no. 963, pp. 224, 225.

635,636. K. and S. archives, Berlin.

637. Manfred Schonlau, Berlin.

638-641. K. and S. archives, Berlin.

642. *ZfBW*, 1867, vol. 17, parts 7-10, atlas sheet 37.

643,644. City archives, Munich.

645. *ZfBW*, 1867, vol. 17, parts 7-10, atlas sheet 38.

646-649. City archives, Munich.

650. *Zeitschrift des Vereins zur Ausbildung der Gewerke*, 1854, vol. 4, part 1, sheet 3.

651. City archives, Munich.

652. Geheimes Hausarchiv, Munich.

653. Bayerische Verwaltung der staatlichen Schlösser, Gärten und Seen, Nymphenburg Castle.

654. City archives, Munich. Photograph by J. Albert.

655. Geheimes Hausarchiv, Munich.

656-658. Archives of H. Roger-Viollet, Paris.

659,660. Texier 1852-53, p. 10.

661. Cabinet des Estampes, Bibliothèque Nationale, Paris.

662. *Moniteur des Architectes*, 1860, vol. 11, plates 693, 694.

663. *Zeitschrift für praktische Baukunst*, 1849, vol. 9, plate 54.

664. Cabinet des Estampes, Bibliothèque Nationale, Paris.

665,666. Boudon 1972, pp. 55, 95, 131.

667. *Deutsche Bauzeitung* (publ.) 1902, vol. 2, part 5, chap. 4, fig. 146.

668-670. Archives of H. Roger-Voillet, Paris.

671,672. K. and S. archives, Berlin.

673. Glaeser archives, Museum of Modern Art, New York.

674. (a) Hix 1974, p. 86; (b) K. and S. archives, Berlin.

675-688. K. and S. archives, Berlin.

689,690. Zanth 1855, plates II, III.

691. K. and S. archives, Berlin.

692. *Attempto*, 1969, parts 33, 34, p. 10.

693-708. K. and S. archives, Berlin.

Name Index

Adanson, Michel, 48
Aiton, William, 141
Albrecht, Prince of Prussia, 31
Alphand, Jean, 8
Alphonso XII, King of Spain, 33
Althans, Carl Ludwig, 83, 84
Anderson, James, 55
Arkwright, Edmund, 67
Arminius, 7, 10
Atkinson, William, 53

Bacon, Anthony, 53
Badger, Daniel, 114
Bage, Charles, 105
Bailey, D. and E. (formerly W. and D.) Co., 62, 72, 87, 88,
    111, 119, 132, 135, 141
Balat, Alphonse, 4, 32-33, 61, 64, 127, 128
Banks, Sir Joseph, 141
Banks, Robert, 73, 114
Barrault, Alexis, 63, 95
Barry, Charles, 73, 114
Barry, Edward Middleton, 63, 109
Bauhin, Casper, 40
Baumeister, Reinhard, 10, 11, 78
Bauschinger, Johann, 99
Beaumont, Elie de, 119
Beck, Ludwig, 69, 119
Behne, Adolf, 21
Behrens, Peter, 124
Bélanger, François-Joseph, 72, 96, 97
Bellhouse, E. T., & Co., 115
Bernoulli, Johann, 72
Berzelius, Jöns Jakob, 71
Bessemer, Sir Henry, 71, 114, 149
Birkinshaw, John, 68, 69, 79, 120
Block, Ernst, 14
Böckmann, Wilhelm, 36
Boerhaave, Hermann, 48
Bogardus, James, 104, 114, 118
Bonaparte, Princess Mathilde de, 25, 33, 34
Bonnemain, M. 53
Bonpland, Aimé, 51
Bontemps, Georges, 47
Boos, Franz, 51
Borsig, August, 36, 51
Bouché, Carl David, 5, 63, 81, 94, 95, 108, 109
Boulton, Matthew, 68, 79, 82, 83, 99, 105, 107
Bradley, Richard, 58
Bramah, Joseph, 68, 73
Brandt, E., 102, 103
Brecht, Bertolt, 61
Brehm, Alfred Edmund, 39
Breuer, Marcel, 24
Bromeis, Johann Conrad, 62, 97
Brown, Lancelot, 41
Brunet, P., 72, 96, 97
Brunfels, Otto, 40
Burne, William, 63, 84, 85
Burton, Decimus, 59, 62, 63, 82, 83, 88, 89, 92, 95, 102, 103,
    116

Caesalpinus, Andreas, 40
Candolle, Auguste Pyrame de, 41
Carstensen, G. J. B., 63, 85, 86, 98
Caus, Salomon de, 111, 112
Chadwick, George F., 5
Chambers, William, 40, 41
Chance, Robert Lucas, 47
Charbannes, Marquis de, 53
Chibon, M., 120
Clark, Thomas, 57, 62, 80, 81, 100-102, 113, 118
Clark and Hope Co., 113
Coalbrookdale Co., 101
Cockerell, Charles, 31, 32, 58
Cockerell, Samuel Pepys, 26, 62
Cort, B., 69
Cort, Henry, 68, 71, 79, 120
Coulomb, Charles Augustin de, 72
Cramer-Klett Co., 107
Cremona, Luigi, 73
Cugnot, N. J., 69
Culmann, Carl, 73, 90, 121, 122
Cuvier, Baron George, 41, 77

Dahlerup, Vilhelm, 38, 64
Darby, Abraham II, 68-70
Darby, Abraham III, 83
Darwin, Charles, 41, 50
Darwin, Erasmus, 67
David, Carl, 5
Decamps, Alexandre Gabriel, 8
Deer, F., 62
Delacroix, Eugène, 8
Deleuze, M., 120
Delorme, Philibert, 122
Derby, Earl of, 53
Devonshire, Duke of, 32
Dickens, Charles, 12, 106
Dischinger, Franz, 130
Dohna-Poninsky, Countess, 7, 10
Doré, Gustave, 12
Duleau, A. J. C., 73
Duvoir, Léon and René Co., 53

Eberlein, Georg, 60, 64, 96, 124
Effner, Karl von, 33
Eggert, Hermann, 64
Eiffel, Gustave, 124
Element, J., 68
Ende, Hermann, 36
Endlicher, Stephan, 41
Etzel, Karl von, 83, 85
Euler, Leonhard, 72
Eytelweins, A., 73

Faccio de Douiller, Nicolas, 48
Fairbairn, Thomas, 79
Fairbairn, Sir William, 73, 80, 120
Flachat, Eugène, 120
Fontane, Theodor, 36
Ford, Henry, 16
Fourier, Charles, 12, 15, 16
Fowke, C., 63
Fowler, Charles, 58, 62, 75, 82, 84, 97, 100, 117

Fowler, Thomas, 53
Fox and Henderson Co., 93
Frederick I, King of Prussia, 51
Frederick II, King of Prussia, 51
Frederick William III, King of Prussia, 31
Frost, A. C., 5
Fuller, W. Buckminster, 129
Fulton, Robert, 69

Galilei, Alessandro, 58
Gauguin, Paul, 20
Gautier, Charles Albert, 64, 124, 125
George IV, King of England, 57
Giedion, Siegfried, 9
Gildermeister, Charles, 63, 85, 86, 98
Gilly, David, 10
Gilly, Friedrich, 9
Goethe, Johann Wolfgang von, 41, 49, 77
Gould, Jay, 36
Gray and Ormson Co., 63
Greiner, H., 125
Greiner, O., 124, 125
Gurlitt, Cornelius, 22
Gye, Frederick, 18

Handyside, Andrew, 63
Haussman, Baron Georges-Eugène, 7, 8, 11, 12, 18
Hay, John, 53
Hegemann, Werner, 10, 19
Hennicke, Julius, 38, 64
Herter, Gustav, 63, 81, 94, 95, 108, 109
Hesse, Ludwig Ferdinand, 90
Hessing, Friedrich von, 38
Hire, Phillippe de la, 72
Hittorf, Jakob Ignaz, 121
Hix, John, 5, 132
Hobrecht, James, 7, 10
Hodgkinson, Eaton, 73
Hood, Charles, 53
Hooke, Robert, 72
Hooker, J. D., 51
Hope, Henry, 113
Horeau, Hector, 4, 58, 62, 74, 85, 86, 117
Howard, Sir Ebenezer, 18–20
Howe, J. L., 73, 92, 93, 95, 118, 122, 123
Hübsch, Heinrich, 121
Hude, Hermann von der, 38, 64
Hughes, John Arthur, 63
Humboldt, Alexander von, 31, 41, 50–52, 77
Hunt, R., 47
Huntsmann, Benjamin, 68

Jacobsen, Johann Carl, 38, 64
Jacquin, Nicolaus Joseph, 25, 51
Jessop, William, 69, 79
Johnson, John, 64
Jones, Alfred G., 63, 97
Jones, Inigo, 31
Jones, Owen, 39, 109, 110, 127
Jones and Clark Co., 113
Jordan, Hermann, 5, 59
Josef I, Emperor, 25
Jussieu, Antoine Laurent de, 41
Jussieu, Bernard de, 41

Kayser, Friedrich, 60, 64
Keller, Jean, 38
Kent, William, 40
Kewley, James, 143, 144
Kibble, John, 38, 64, 134, 135
Knight, Thomas A., 47–49, 54, 55, 58, 111, 141, 142
Koch, A., 64
Koerner, Alfred, 61, 64, 124, 125

Labrouste, Henri, 29, 83, 87
Lanyon, Charles, 63, 98
Laves, George Ludwig Friedrich, 80, 82, 120, 121
Le Corbusier, 21, 23, 24, 45
Leibniz, Gottfried Wilhelm, 72
Leins, Christian, 121
Lenk, Elisabeth, 15
Lenné, Peter Joseph, 10
Leopold II, King of Belgium, 31, 32
Lillie, James, 79
Linden, Jean Jules, 51
Lindley, John, 41
Linné, Carl von (Linnaeus), 40, 41, 48, 49
Loddiges, Carl, 53–55, 111, 130
Long, J. Stefan, 73, 92, 93, 95, 118, 122, 123
Loudon, John Claudius, 4, 5, 15–17, 21, 26, 27, 37, 45, 47, 48, 53–55, 57–59, 62, 72, 74, 82, 87, 88, 92, 93, 95–97, 100, 102, 105, 106, 111, 113, 117–119, 126, 129–137, 139–148
Louis XIV, King of France, 11
Lucae, Richard, 22
Ludwig II, King of Bavaria, 27, 33, 64, 75, 123, 125
Ludwig Ferdinand, Prince of Bohemia, 33
Luer, W., 64

McGrath, Raymond, 5
McIntosh, Charles Rennie, 5, 15, 47–49, 80, 84, 89, 97, 100, 117, 121–122, 135, 136
Mackenzie, Sir George, 47, 48, 55, 58, 87, 111, 126, 130, 136, 141, 142
Mackenzie and Moncour Co., 64
Magnis, Count, 55
MAN Co. (formerly Cramer-Klett Co.), 107
Maquet, Henri, 64, 128
Maria de la Paz, 33
Maria Theresa, Empress, 51
Mariotte, Edmé, 72
Märtens, H., 60, 64, 96, 124
Martin, Emile, 87, 88
Martin, Thomas, 71
Marx, Karl, 67
Matthienson, R., 63, 91
Maudsley, Henry, 68
Maximilian II, King of Bavaria, 27, 33, 60, 63, 75
May, Ernst, 24
Meissner, Paul Traugott, 55
Mertens, G., 70
Messenger & Co., 116
Meyer, Alfred Gotthold, 5, 99
Meynadier de Flamalens, H., 63, 96
Michel, Eugen, 5
Milner, Edward, 63, 90, 92, 109
Moller, Georg, 126
Mosely, William, 18

Napoléon I, Emperor of France, 9
Napoléon III, Emperor of France, 11
Nash, John, 26, 51, 99, 100
Nasmyth, James, 69
Nassau, Duke Adolf of, 31, 33, 91
Navier, Louis M. H., 72, 73, 120
Nehou, Louis Lucas de, 46
Neilson, James B., 71
Neumann, M., 5, 27, 28, 32, 53, 54, 63, 110
Newcastle, Duke of, 113
Newcombe, Thomas, 68
Newton, Sir Isaac, 72
Nicholas I, Czar of Russia, 32

Ordish, Rowland Mawson, 63, 75, 89, 91, 96, 97, 110, 117
Otto, Frei, 129
Otzen, Johannes, 125
Owen, Robert, 16

Parnell, J., 120
Paulding, William, 36
Paxton, Sir Joseph, 1, 3, 4, 16, 18, 28, 32, 38, 39, 45, 47–49, 58, 59, 61–63, 72, 74, 78, 80, 81, 83, 88, 89, 93, 95, 96, 98, 102, 103, 105–109, 113–118, 121, 123, 140
Payne, John D., 68, 82
Perkin, A. M., 53
Persius, Ludwig, 135
Pfann, Hans, 5
Phillips, Henry, 38, 62, 74, 97, 117, 132, 133
Piscator, Erwin, 24
Platt, Sir Hugh, 53
Polonceau, Camille, 73, 90, 91, 123
Pückler-Muskau, Hermann Furst, 9
Purnell, John, 68

Ranke, Winfried, 33
Ravenné family, 36
Réaumur, René-Antoine de, 70, 73
Rennie, John, 73
Repton, Humphrey, 26, 31, 57, 58, 62, 82, 84, 89
Reynolds, Richard, 69, 73, 79
Rigolet, M., 63, 95, 96, 123
Rilke, Rainer Maria, 8
Rohault de Fleury, Charles, 4, 58, 62, 63, 75, 100, 101, 104, 117, 121, 133, 135, 136
Rohault de Fleury, Hubert, 75
Rondelet, Jean-Baptiste, 72, 73, 78
Rosebery, Lord, 7
Roster, Giacomo, 64
Rothe, Tyge, 64

Saint-Hilaire, Etienne Geoffrey, 41
Salt, Titus, 16
Savery, Thomas, 68
Scharoun, Hans, 21
Scharowsky, C., 102, 103
Scheerbart, Paul, 21, 45, 61
Schinkel, Karl Friedrich, 9, 10, 26, 31, 90, 111
Schwedler, Johann Wilhelm, 74, 95, 124, 128, 129
Sckell, Friedrich Ludwig von, 25, 27, 62, 121
Scott, George Gilbert, 91
Semper, Gottfried, 18, 28, 29, 31, 37
Sengenschmid, Franz von, 60, 61, 64, 124, 125

Shaw, Norman, 18
Siemens, C. W. von, 71, 149
Siemens, F. von, 71, 149
Smeaton, John, 68
Smirke, Sydney, 132
Soufflot, Jacques-Germain, 72, 73
Steckhoven, Adrian von, 51
Stephenson, George, 69
Sternberger, Dolf, 22
Stevens, L., 120
Stevenson, Robert, 120
Stevin, Simon, 72
Stier, Hubert, 60, 64, 124, 125
Strack, Heinrich, 36, 62
Strutt, William, 105
Suys, Tieleman Franciscus, 58, 62
Svendenborg, Emmanuel, 73

Tanger Foundry, 80
Taut, Bruno, 21
Taut, Max, 21
Taylor, B. B., 23, 132
Telford, Thomas, 73
Texier, Edmond, 11, 12
Theophilus Presbyter, 46
Theophrastus, 40
Thiollet, François, 111
Thomas, Sidney Gilchrist, 149
Tredgold, Thomas, 53, 73, 79
Trevithick, Richard, 69
Triewald, Martin, 53
Tschira, Arnold, 5
Turner, Joseph Mallord William, 8
Turner, Richard, 4, 59, 62, 63, 74, 80, 88, 89, 97–100, 102–104, 109, 117, 118, 122, 123, 132, 134

Veugny, M. G., 90, 121
Victoria, Queen of England, 32, 37, 113
Viel, C. F., 63, 95
Viéta, François, 72
Voit, August von, 4, 27, 33, 42, 63, 64, 75, 94, 95, 107, 108, 117, 123, 125
Voltaire, 40

Wallich, Georg Charles, 51
Wallis, Gustav, 50
Watt, James, 67, 79, 82, 83, 99, 105, 107, 117
Wendland, Herman L., 51
Werner, Ernst, 94
Wiegmann, R., 73, 90, 121
Wilde, Oscar, 7, 8
Wilkinson, Isaac, 70
Wilkinson, John, 68–70, 83
William of Orange, Prince, 51
Winckler, E., 74, 124
Wittek, K. H., 78
Wyatt, John, 67
Wyatville, Sir Jeffry, 63, 84, 85

Young, Thomas, 73

Zanth, Ludwig von, 32, 62, 83, 90, 91, 104
Zorés, Charles F., 78, 80, 89, 120

Index of Place Names

Publisher's note: This is an index to the main text of the book. The catalog, which begins on page 151, is arranged alphabetically by place names and thus requires no index. For a complete list of the buildings and designs included in the catalog, and their locations, see pages 153–155.

Alicante: Palm groves, 51
Altdorf: Botanical garden, 43
Augsburg: Kurtheater Göggingen, 38

Balmoral Castle: Iron dance hall, 115
Basle: Market hall, 129
Bedford Park, 18
Belfast
    Botanical garden, 42, 98, 99
    Palm house, 47, 63, 74, 100, 104, 127, 132
Berlin, 9, 10
    Borsig factory, 36
    Central Hotel, 38, 64
    "Decoration and surrounding highway for the city of," 10
    Friedrich Memorial, 9
    New Museum, 99
    Ostbahnhof, 124
    Palm house (Pfaueninsel), 31, 64, 65
    Prince Albert's palace, 31
    Schickler sugar factory, 90
    Tiergarten, 9
    Unter den Linden, 9, 38–39, 64
    Unterspree Bridge, 124
    Villa Ravené winter garden, 36
    Winter gardens, 31, 36–38, 60, 64, 125
Berlin-Charlottenburg
    Flora, 124, 126
    Gärtnerhaus, 10
Berlin-Dahlem
    Botanical gardens, 21, 135
    Great palm house, 61, 63, 81, 124, 125
    Subtropical house, 64
Berlin-Moabit
    Borsig Gardens, 36, 62
    Turbine hall, 124
Berlin-Schöneberg
    Great Palm House, 94, 95, 108, 109
    Old botanical garden, 41, 42, 44
    Victoria regia house, 127
Biebrich am Rhein
    Conservatories, 31, 33, 91
    Exhibition hall, 62, 92
Birmingham: Botanical gardens, 16, 97, 105, 106, 118, 131, 133
Bochum, 124
Bologna: Botanical garden, 40
Bonn: Old palm house, 63, 109, 110
Boston: Factory buildings, 104
Bradford, 16
Breslau: Botanical garden, 63, 109, 110
Bretton Hall, Yorkshire, 59, 60, 62, 65, 72, 74, 97, 100, 111, 130–132, 136
Brighton: Royal pavilion, 51, 100
Brussels
    Botanical garden: Great Conservatory, 58, 62
    Laeken: Royal Park, 32–33, 61, 64–65, 75, 127–128

Buckingham Palace: Architectural conservatory, 84, 85
Budleigh Salterton, Devon, Bicton Gardens: Palm house, 62, 65, 101, 104, 129, 132
Buxton: Pavilion gardens, 63, 90, 92, 109

Capesthorne Hall, Cheshire: Davenport Conservatory, 62, 93
Chartres: Cathedral, 87, 88
Chatsworth, Derbyshire
    Glasshouses, 3, 58, 102, 117, 118, 131
    Great conservatory, 28, 32, 38, 47, 59, 62, 65, 74, 85, 87–89, 103, 123
    Old orangery, 113–114
    Victoria regia house, 58, 62, 74, 114, 115, 118
Chester: River Dee bridge, 119
Chiswick Gardens, 62, 87, 88, 132
Clumber Park, Nottinghamshire: Forcing house, 113
Coalbrookdale, 69, 70, 82–84, 101
Cologne: Flora, 38, 60, 64, 96, 110, 124
Constantinople: Steam-powered mill, 114
Copenhagen
    Botanical garden, 42
    Glasshouses, 61, 135
    Jacobsen Winter Garden, 36
    Large palm house, 36, 64
    Ny Carlsberg Glyptotek, 36, 38, 64

Darmstadt: Herrengarten, 9
Deepdene Castle (Yorkshire): Swinton Park winter garden, 113, 114
Derby: North Midlands Trijunct Railway Station, 15, 48
Dresden: Frauenkirche, 129
Dublin
    Botanical garden, 42
    Broadstone Station, 74
    Colonel White's conservatory, 62, 74, 98
    Glasnevin: National botanical gardens, 59, 65, 87–89, 99, 102–104
    Phoenix Park vinery, 74
    Royal Canal bridge, 92
    Winter gardens, 60, 63, 95–97, 124
    Winter Palace, 75, 110

Edinburgh
    Gas works, 90
    Royal Botanical Garden, 40, 42, 60, 63, 89, 91
Eisgrub. *See* Lednice
Elche: Palm groves, 51
Enville Hall (Staffordshire): Conservatory, 59, 63

Florence: Botanical garden, 42, 64, 116
Frankfurt am Main, 38, 60, 64
Frauenberg. *See* Hluboká nad Vltavou

Glasgow
    Kibble Palace, 38, 60, 64, 129, 130, 134, 136–137
    Winter gardens, 64
Gravesend, Kent: New Market, 75
Grimston Park, Yorkshire: Winter garden, 100

Hampshire: The Grange, 31, 32, 57, 62, 100, 113, 117
Hampton Court, 40
Hardwick Hall, 45

Heidelberg: Orangery, 111, 112
Herrenhausen, 9, 51, 61, 65
    Auhagen palm house, 64, 126
        Berggarten, 51
        Laves palm house, 120, 121
Hluboká nad Vltavou, 62, 111, 137
Hove, Sussex: Atheneum, 62, 74, 87, 97

India, 116
Innsbruck, 61, 64

Jena: Zeiss Planetarium, 129

Kassel: Wilhelmshöhe, Great conservatory, 62, 97
Kew
    Architectural conservatory, 84, 85
    Orangery, 59, 63
    Palm house, 41, 47, 51, 59–61, 63, 74, 88–89, 102, 103, 118,
        126
    Royal Botanical Gardens, 40, 41, 65, 99, 120, 131
    Temperate house, 60, 63, 82, 83, 91, 92, 95
Killikee: Colonel White's conservatory, 62, 74, 98
Kreuzberg Memorial, 111

Laeken: Royal Park, 32, 33, 61, 64, 65, 75, 127, 128
Langport, Somerset: Forcing house, 65, 111
Lednice: Liechtenstein Castle winter garden, 65, 100, 131,
    132
Leeds: General Hospital winter garden, 38, 63, 75, 89, 91,
    110
Leipzig: Flora, 110
Leningrad. See St. Petersburg
Leyden: Botanical garden, 40, 43
Liverpool, 53
    Lime Street Station, 74, 89, 120, 123
    Market hall, 90
    Palm house, 64, 128
    Sefton Park, 128
London
    Alexandra Palace (Muswell Hill), 64, 110
    Architectural conservatory (Kew), 84, 85
    Aviary, 74
    Bayswater House, 27, 58, 62, 72, 111, 135, 137, 148
    Brompton winter gardens, 63, 116
    Camellia house (Hackney), 100
    Carlton House, 57, 62, 82, 84, 99, 100, 117
    Coliseum, 59, 62, 65
    Covent Garden, 18, 63, 75, 109
    Crystal Palace (Hyde Park), 1, 3, 16, 18, 32, 39, 45, 47,
        59–61, 63, 70, 74, 77, 78, 89, 92–94, 102, 103, 105–107,
        109, 110, 114, 118, 119, 121, 123
    Crystal Palace (Sydenham), 39, 63, 74, 96, 107, 123
    "Crystal Way," 18
    "Exhibition Palace," 58, 74, 85, 86
    Glasshouse of Sir Henry Bessemer, 114
    "Great Victorian Way," 18, 39, 74, 107
    Hungerford Market, 75
    Joiner Street bridge, 119
    Kensington Royal Kitchen Garden, 141
    King William Street, 18
    Loddiges Nursery (Hackney), 53–55, 111, 130
    Orangery (Kew), 59, 63

Paddington Station, 69
Palace of the People (Muswell Hill), 39, 109, 110, 127
Palm house (Kew), 41, 47, 51, 59–61, 63, 74, 88, 89, 102,
    103, 118, 126
Pantheon Bazaar, 132
Regent's Park, 7, 37, 74, 102, 134
Royal Albert Bridge (Chelsea), 75
Royal Horticultural Society, 63, 116
Surrey Zoological Garden, 38, 132, 133
Syon House, 41, 58, 62, 75, 82, 84, 97, 100, 102, 104, 118
Temperate house (Kew), 60, 63, 82, 83, 89, 91, 92, 95
Lyon
    Botanical garden, 42
    Market hall, 78, 83, 85, 89, 119
    Winter garden, 58, 62, 65, 85, 86

Mainz: Cathedral, 126
Manchester: Spinning mill, 79, 81–83, 99, 107
Mannheim: Garden exhibition, 129
Meiningen: Orangery, Ducal Park, 111, 112
Milan: Cathedral, 9
Milford: Warehouse, 105, 118
Munich
    English garden, 9
    Glass Palace, 60, 63, 65, 75, 78, 94, 95, 107, 108
    Great palm house, 63, 75, 108, 123
    Iron conservatory (Nymphenburg), 62, 65, 121
    Winter garden of Ludwig II, 33, 64, 75, 123, 125
    Winter garden of Maximilian II, 60, 63, 75

Newcastle upon Tyne, 53, 68
New Lanark, 16
New York
    Crystal Palace, 63, 85, 86, 95, 98, 110
    Factory buildings, 104, 105, 114, 118
Nottingham: Wollaton Hall, 57, 62, 65, 80, 81, 100, 101, 113,
    117, 118, 131

Oxford: Botanical garden, 40

Padua: Botanical garden, 40
Paris, 9–11
    Boulevards, 11, 12
    Champs-Elysees, 37, 74, 121
    Chateau des Fleurs, 74
    Crystal Palace (Saint-Cloud), 39, 98
    Eiffel Tower, 124
    Exhibition Hall for Garden Science, 124
    Halle aux Blés, 72, 96, 97, 129
    Halles Centrales, 74
    Jardin d'Hiver, 7, 16, 28, 29, 37, 58–60, 63, 74, 95, 96, 100,
        118, 123, 124, 127
    Jardin des Plantes, 40, 58–60, 62–65, 75, 100, 101, 104, 105,
        118, 121, 132, 133
    Marché de la Madelaine, 90, 121
    Palais de l'Industrie, 63, 95, 110
    Palais National, 18
    "Panorama," 121
    Passage du Saumon, 75
    Quai d'Orsay, 53
    Sainte-Geneviève library, 29, 83, 85, 87
    Slaughterhouse, 120
    Winter garden of Princess Mathilde de Bonaparte, 33, 34, 36

World Exhibition (1855), 71, 95, 114, 116, 123
World Exhibition (1867), 120
World Exhibition (1900), 125
World Exhibition (1956), 129
Pisa: Botanical garden, 40, 43
Poissy: Villa Savoie, 23
Porto: Douro bridge, 124
Potsdam
    Pfaueninsel, 52
    Sanssouci: Chinese Teahouse, 51

Réunion Island: Market hall, 90
Rome: St. Peter's, 129

St. Johann: Locomotive shed, 128
St. Louis: Factory buildings, 104
St. Petersburg
    Botanical garden, 42
    Orangery, 25
    Palm house, 61, 64
Salerno: Botanical garden, 40
Salford: Cotton mill, 105
Saltaire, 16, 18
Sayn: Foundry hall, 83, 84
Schwöbber: Glasshouse, 112
Sezincote, Gloucestershire: Indian Villa, 27, 31, 32, 58, 62, 80,
    131
Sheffield: Botanical garden, 42, 132
Shrewsbury: Flax spinning mill, 105
Strasbourg: Great conservatory, 61, 64
Strassnitz: Hothouses, 55
Sturge: Hothouses, 54
Stuttgart: Wilhelma
    Conservatories, 62, 80, 82, 83, 90, 91, 100, 104
    Moorish Villa, 32
Stuttgart-Berg: Villa Berg, 31, 32, 121
Stuttgart-Hohenheim: Iron conservatory, 57, 62, 111, 112

Tarrytown: Lyndhurst, 36
Tübingen: Old botanical garden, Great conservatory, 61, 64

Venice: Botanical garden, 40
Versailles: Orangery, 25
Vienna
    Botanical garden, 42
    Dianabad, 83, 85
    Imperial castle gardens, 51
    Lower Belvedere, 111, 112
    Palm house, 116
    Sugar refinery, 55
Vienna-Schönbrunn, 65
    Botanical garden, 51
    Great palm house, 60, 61, 64, 124, 125
    Orangery, 25, 30, 111, 112

Weimar: Castle, 55
Wiesbaden: Castle, 126
Windsor: Frogmore forcing houses, 113
Woburn Abbey, 80
Wroclaw. See Breslau